OXFORD MEDICAL PUBLICATIONS

Imposing Aid: Emergency Assistance to Refugees

Imposing Aid

Emergency Assistance to Refugees

B. E. HARRELL-BOND

OXFORD   NEW YORK   NAIROBI
OXFORD UNIVERSITY PRESS
1986

Oxford University Press, Walton Street, Oxford OX2 6DP

Oxford New York Toronto
Delhi Bombay Calcutta Madras Karachi
Kuala Lumpur Singapore Hong Kong Tokyo
Nairobi Dar es Salaam Cape Town
Melbourne Auckland

and associated companies in
Beirut Berlin Ibadan Nicosia

Oxford is a trade mark of Oxford University Press

Published in the United States
by Oxford University Press, New York

British Library Cataloguing in Publication Data

Harrell-Bond, B.E.
Imposing aid: emergency assistance to refugees.
—— (Oxford medical publications)
I. Title
362.8'7   HV640.4.G7
ISBN 0-19-261543-2

Computer typeset by SB Datagraphics, Colchester, England

Printed and bound in
Great Britain by Biddles Ltd,
Guildford and King's Lynn

To Andrew Chernocke Pearse

Human existence cannot be silent, nor can it be nourished by false words, but only by true words, with which men transform it. Once named, the world in turn reappears to the namers as a problem and requires of them a new naming. Men are not built in silence, but in word, in work, in action-reflection.

Paulo Freire, *Pedagogy of the Oppressed*, (trans. by Myra Bergman), Ramos, New York, Herder and Herder, 1970:70

The risk involved in sociological work is that it will service ideologies far removed from the particulars of human purposes or else be received as an art to service the vague humanitarian aesthetics of its consumers, its lay readers and middle-class students. In the first case, the ideological reception of sociological work hardly begins to fathom the depths of human injury and comes far too soon to conclusions regarding the tissue of human connections and the viruses of relation, contract, and organization. In the second, the aesthetic perception of sociological work is disembodied from the intersensory and ancestral connections of mankind, whose infinitude defies dissection into science or art to such an extent that any observation risks obscenity and distortion. Moreover, the very aesthetic sensibility for which such risks might be undertaken has an awesome public ability to absorb injustice, beauty, rage, horror, and wild frivolity.

John O'Neill, *Making Sense Together: An Introduction to Wild Sociology*, Heinemann, London, 1975.

Foreword

ROBERT CHAMBERS

The intractable problem of millions of refugees, displaced persons, and victims of famine in rural Africa will not go away. The famines of Ethiopia, Sudan, Chad, and other countries in 1984 and 1985 have attracted attention as sudden emergencies, but underlying them are long-term trends. Even on an optimistic view, the future prospects in Sub-Saharan Africa are appalling. Over the past two decades, the numbers of political refugees have grown from hundreds of thousands to millions. To these are now added millions who move *en masse* in distress because of loss of livelihood and starvation. Population in Sub-Saharan Africa is projected to grow by 3.0 per cent per annum for the next two decades, with a doubling time of some 24 years. The rural populations, after allowing for large-scale rural to urban migration, may rise by at least 50 per cent during the same period. On top of this, environmental degradation is widespread, with soil erosion, deforestation, and desertification. For ten of millions of rural people, economic decline, political instability, and ethnic tensions promise a worse future. Even if the rainfall failures of the early 1980s prove exceptional, the next two decades will probably see more, not fewer, crises, involving more, not fewer, people in the terrible decision to leave their homes and flee, destitute and desperate, from fighting, persecution, and famine, in search of safety, shelter, and food. At the same time, deeper indebtedness and the poverty of African Governments, less land for agricultural settlement, and fewer work opportunities in downwardly spiralling economies, will make it harder to host and help refugees, and harder for refugees to help themselves.

Despite the scale and awfulness of these forced mass migrations, there has been little systematic study of rural refugees and rural refugee relief work in Africa or indeed elsewhere. Until recently, refugee studies itself has not been recognized as a subject. Most books and papers on refugees and refugee programmes have had urban and elite biases to the neglect of those—in Africa the vast majority—who are rural, less well-educated, and poorer. Until recently, rural refugees have rarely been the starting point or central concern of research: they have usually been noticed and mentioned only in passing and not as the primary focus. In consequence, debates on policy questions like the relative merits of organized agricultural settlements and self-settlement have not been well-informed. It has been easy to think of rural refugees as an undifferentiated, uneducated mass. The points of view of refugees themselves have not been well-represented. Nor have the attitudes, behaviour and problems of those who work in humanitarian and government agencies been examined. On the positive side, able efforts have been made to consolidate and communicate professional knowledge, for example in the journal *Disasters* and in the excellent UNHCR *Handbook for emergencies*. But the fact remains that at a time when unprecedented numbers of desperate people have been migrating, struggling to survive in or out of camps, and dying, we who are not desperate or dying have still been negligently ignorant of what is really going on.

Just how ignorant we have been is exposed in this book. To my knowledge there has been no previous study like it. Conrad Reining, also in the south Sudan, was the first social anthropologist to see colonial officials as part of his field and write them up in his classic, *The Zande scheme*. With *Imposing aid*, Barbara Harrell-Bond has given us a successor from the same region but with differences. The period is post-colonial, the occasion the crisis of massive influxes of refugees from Uganda. The people in the field are the refugees, their Sudanese hosts, and the staff of voluntary, humanitarian, and Government agencies. The book is timely and immediately relevant. In a more leisurely tradition, Reining took ten years from fieldwork to publication; but in keeping with the scale, importance, and urgency of the issues, Harrell-Bond, with assistance from Oxford University Press, has taken a matter of months. The main fieldwork, as researcher and participant–observer helping in the administration of official programmes, was conducted in 1982–3; and several chapters also draw in the experiences and findings of a team of committed researchers from Oxford who spent two months in the area in 1984.

There is much here that will be seen as new. Many readers will, like me, be surprised and shocked at how much we have been wrong and how much we have to learn. Those concerned with food supplies, nutrition, health, planning and implementation in emergencies, and management and administration of refugee and other relief programmes, will find much to ponder. Perhaps more important, though, are the changes of perception which are opened up. Refugees speak and show the vivid awfulness of their experience, the brutality, terror, and desolation. Stereotypes dissolve under the impact of examples. Rural refugees in Africa, so easily thought of as statistics, are revealed as intelligent, articulate, and different individuals. Like other human beings, only more so than most others, they suffer, struggle to survive, need their self-respect, and have to mourn their dead. Convenient myths that somehow rural Africans are different—less sensitive, less individual, less vulnerable to trauma than others—cannot survive this book.

No one will feel comfortable with this book. Much of it disquiets, not least the difficulties, conflicts, and shortcomings of voluntary, national, and international agencies. Evenhandedly, Dr Harrell-Bond spares neither herself nor others in recounting what happened, what was said, what done and what not done. In a fine tradition of social anthropology, she has not only observed others, but also herself, and reported on her own fallible human reactions and behaviour as well as those of others. In doing this, she sets a standard of introspection and honesty for others to follow, and shows us at first hand, from within, some of the personal stresses and dilemmas of those who work in mass refugee situations, and the courage and commitment needed to deal with them. She takes us intimately into the relations of refugees, hosts, and voluntary and official organizations, laying bare realities which have to be faced in order to learn how to do better.

The danger is, though, that strong reactions will distract readers from learning and from pondering and acting on the many positive lessons of the book. One such reaction could be to blame organizations or individuals. An antidote is to ask how one would have behaved oneself in similar conditions, under similar stress. Another reaction is defensive. Some who work in voluntary, humanitarian, or government organizations may feel threatened by the critical self-examination which the book invites. Some may even be tempted to search the text for error to justify rejecting the larger lessons; but if they do so, they, and future refugees, will be the losers. And yet another reaction could be the most damaging: to condemn aid and urge its termination. Negative academics will find here plenty of grist to their mills. They will not lack bad incidents to feed destructive cynicism. They will find plenty to quote selectively to argue that it would be better to do nothing. But before reaching such conclusions, they should reflect: on the terrible suffering of so many; on how difficult it is for those who try to mitigate that suffering: and on how much worse things would be if nothing were done. Moreover, Dr Harrell-Bond is clear on this point. The sane and humane thing to do is not to stop aid, but to augment and improve it. Honest examination of reality, however unpalatable, is a necessary painful means to that end. The challenge of this book is to recognize, embrace, and correct error. The message is not to do less, but to do better.

Let me commend this book to all concerned. They are many: refugees, who speak through these pages with such eloquence and who may come to understand more about humanitarian agencies; academics, activists, and journalists concerned with mass deprivation and migration; and especially those involved in humanitarian work, whether in headquarters or the field, and whether in foreign or national voluntary agencies, host Government departments, bilateral aid agencies, or international organizations like UNHCR, UNICEF, WFP, FAO, or WHO. They in their turn may come to understand better both refugees and themselves, and to see themselves the other way round, in the refugees' eye view.

Imposing aid applies most directly to refugees and rural Africa but its value and relevance is wider, touching the behaviour and attitudes of the development and social welfare professions and their clients generally, on the organization of relief, and on the survival strategies of those who endure extreme deprivation. For all those concerned with refugees and others who migrate in distress, this is more than essential reading; it is essential learning. To the new professionalism which refugees deserve from those, not themselves refugees, who work with and for them, this book is a major contribution.

Preface

Refugees are one of the most serious problems of our time. Daily the numbers escalate. No one really knows how many people have been uprooted but one may be very sure the problem in Africa is not going away. Chambers (1985a) predicts that between now and the year 2004, another twelve to fifty million 'mass distress migrants' in Africa will require assistance, their movements caused by war, civil disturbance, persecution, food shortage, and famine. Meanwhile, relief budgets climb and humanitarian agencies proliferate.

William Shawcross's *Quality of Mercy* is one of the rare opportunities for the public to examine the work of some of those humanitarian organizations that the world has created in an attempt to bind its self-inflicted wounds. But the problems Shawcross depicts are general; they have been around for forty years. Inside the agencies it is well-known that the same mistakes have been repeated over and over again. Howard Adelman, director of the Refugee Documentation Project, York University, Ontario, in his study of the United Nations Relief and Works Association (UNRWA), has found a similar pattern of outside intervention which left behind as many problems as the humanitarians set out to solve. UNRWA was instigated both to help preserve the peace and to provide a short-term relief and works programme while refugees were either repatriated or integrated into the economic life of the local communities. Thirty-five years later UNRWA continues to exist with over 17,000 employees. In only nine of those thirty-five years can some form of peace be said to have existed in the Middle East.

Why is there no tradition of independent, critical research in the field of refugee assistance analogous to that for development studies? It is assumed that the impact of development projects will be evaluated, but humanitarian programmes have never been subjected to the same scrutiny. As one observer put it, 'Refugee organisations are becoming more and more an almost impregnable system, protected by the strong shell of their mandate to dispense what is regarded as "charity"'. (Alternative Viewpoints 1984.) Many readers, including refugees, may react to the contents of this book much as did one of my assistants in the field, Lali Ferdinand Vuciri, an interrupted secondary school student.

My findings in this research were things I had never known before. The research in itself has been a revelation to me. Although I am refugee myself, I came to learn much more about the refugees than I had known before. But the people who were experiencing such fates were refugees like myself and they came from the same country as me.

Hopefully, one result of reading this book will be to stimulate others to say as he said, '...from my findings, I have developed certain ideas for the research....and I imagine if I had the time, I would develop a research on my own and do it in an original way from my own conception.'

Given the body of literature which evaluates the impact of aid, few practitioners in the development field (who think about such matters) still retain unquestioned confidence that their interventions are always beneficial to the recipients. Nevertheless, development projects are expected to have measurable, usually visible, and hopefully, positive outcomes. Refugees are, by contrast, viewed as a temporary phenomenon, and money given for their assistance falls under emergency relief – a budget line on a par with an interstellar black hole. From the funders' point of view, concern for accountability is limited to establishing the financial credentials of the agencies through whom aid is channelled, and ensuring that it reaches those for whom it is intended. The importance of evaluating the impact of relief programmes is not widely appreciated.

Recruitment to development work does not lay great stress upon the personal motivation of staff. '... for donor and recipient alike aid policy is shaped by self-interest; enlightened self-interest, no doubt, but self-interest all the same. For aid is about trade, about making friends, and influencing people, about investment now for dividends...Moral issues may be bandied about, but only bandied.' (Bell 1984.)

Humanitarian work, on the other hand, is thought to be selfless, motivated by compassion, and by its very definition suggests *good* work. Most voluntary agencies place as great an emphasis upon the motivations of their employees as upon their technical expertise. Some sacrifice certain material comforts to work overseas. This, together with the relative insecurity of the profession (and in some cases, the low salaries received), may reinforce the notion that work under a humanitarian banner is above question. And, as relief is a gift, it is not expected that any (most especially the recipients) should examine the quality, or quantity, of what is given.

The research reported in this book is a first attempt to make an independent study of an emergency assistance programme. For it I selected the emergency assistance programme in the Yei River District, southern Sudan as the location for the study. I began by observing the role of the interveners – both expatriate and host government staff – and the nature of their interventions in response to an influx of refugees from Uganda.

There are a number of types of interventions involved in the assistance programme for refugees. There are the two types of international aid agencies: the United Nations High Commissioner for Refugees (UNHCR), and non-governmental (NGOs) or international voluntary agencies. In southern Sudan, there were also two indigenous voluntary agencies providing assistance and at one time an abortive attempt was made by refugees to organize their own humanitarian group. The Sudan government established the office of the Commissioner for Refugees (COMREF) under the Ministry of Interior to administer refugee programmes in the country. This office appointed project managers in refugee-affected areas; one was assigned to Yei, responsible to the general project manager for the south.

I observed other types of outsiders who have an impact on refugee assistance programmes. Various foreign delegations occasionally visit. For example, when Ambassador Douglas, an advisor to President Reagan, visited Yei River District, he saw wheelbarrows being used to transport the very ill to the clinic in one settlement. Afterwards UNHCR was under pressure to supply the district with an ambulance.

Journalists also play a very important role. International power politics influence the extent and the manner in which an emergency is covered. One of the effects of media publicity is to attract more international agencies as well as more financial aid to an area, but another is the way journalists contribute to the stereotyping of refugees as helpless. However, both host governments and international agencies are wary of the press. Depending on the situation and their vested interests at a particular time, they may concoct ways of keeping journalists out, or of limiting their access to information. Alternatively they may actively encourage and facilitate press coverage of an incident. Very few journalists reached the remote area where this study was conducted.

Researchers themselves intervene; this study included a team of refugees which actively participated in evaluating the assistance programme, wrote reports, addressed agency meetings, and discussed findings with government administrators and refugee communities. The effectiveness of assistance needs to be continually assessed. Hopefully, involving refugees in monitoring projects would encourage greater flexibility in the responses of everyone to both delivering and receiving aid.

Refugees began entering southern Sudan from Uganda in 1979, and by March 1982 the influx had reached emergency proportions. This situation persisted throughout most of the fieldwork, which was carried out during two six-month periods in 1982-3. The numbers of refugees living in assisted settlements escalated from 9000 in March 1982 to 47,311 at the end of September. By September 1983, when this study was completed, the UNHCR office count of assisted refugees in settlement was 95,000.

After the first six months of observing the emergency programme from the perspective of the agency, government, and other outside interventions, a team and I conducted a survey of a random sample of all assisted refugees. Data describing 10,675 individuals, members of 2017 households, were collected in 22 settlements and 3 transit camps. There were also those refugees who had remained self-settled in the district, outside the relief system. At the time their numbers were greater than those under the aid 'umbrella'. Interviews were administered to 3814 of these households in several localities. The study also included the local population and its relationship to the aid programme and to the refugees. In the course of conducting interviews, members of the team recorded verbatim responses: 75 exercise books were filled. Over 200 children's drawings of 'refugee life' were collected and about 100 hours of refugee voices were recorded in the course of my own interviews. Specialized studies of markets and schools were conducted both in settlements and in the areas where unassisted refugees were living within the Sudanese community. A lawyer on the team examined the way disputes within the settlements were handled and studied the courts throughout the district. His research was continued for a further nine months after I left the Sudan.

Fortuitously, another team, funded by the Overseas Development Administration (ODA), was conducting a survey of Yei River District, preparing an overall development plan for the area. Originally this plan was to have been designed without taking account of the refugee population. When it was discovered that refugees outnumbered the locals by a ratio of at least 2:1, it became clear that they could no longer be ignored. Our two teams were able to collaborate in the field to some extent, and the refugees' and my own knowledge of Yei River District and its people was greatly increased by the information collected by the ODA team. Both studies were fortunate in having recourse to the official census data for the district collected in both 1981 and 1983.

The aim of the research, so far as possible, was to describe the actual living situation of the refugees, the impact of various assistance groups, their interconnections, and their impact on each other. From this it is hoped that the assistance programme may be assessed within the context of the people's own efforts to organize and develop their communities. The overwhelming focus of this study is on the economic impact of the programme, but as it had other social and psychological consequences as well, these must be included in its assessment.

The aim of the assistance programme was to help refugees become economically independent. Aid programmes acknowledge that there are categories of people, referred to as 'vulnerable groups', who will never be able to support themselves. Definitions of vulnerability usually only include orphans, widows, the socially or physically handicapped, and sometimes women-headed households. In this study the definition of vulnerability is widened and is related to the overall objective of the assistance programme: that refugees should become self-sufficient through agriculture. Refugees who are unable to achieve this goal, for whatever reason, are considered vulnerable.

The assistance programme laid great stress on equity: everyone had a right to the same amount of food rations and material aid. Observations in 1982-3 suggested that many households were unlikely ever to be capable of supporting themselves through agriculture. By treating all refugees as equal the programme had the unintended consequence of exacerbating economic differences, with the most vulnerable groups growing ever more dependent and impoverished. This trend was confirmed by following up vulnerable households in one settlement in 1984.

In 1984 a multi-disciplinary team of seven Oxford students spent two months in Yei River District to conduct further research. Four settlements and their surrounding Sudanese communities were included in their studies, in addition to a mixed population of unassisted refugees and locals living near Panyume. Studies were made of household economies and these data were linked to the development of trade, markets, and the taxation system of the district. The situation of vulnerable families was surveyed and a mental health scale was administered to a sample of adults. A nutrition survey was also undertaken and case histories of the families of malnourished children were collected. Bilharzia and intestinal worm surveys were made. Work was done with a library and a self-help senior secondary school which opened in September 1984. Both the library and school are'integrated' projects, i.e. they involve both Sudanese and refugees. I refer to the team's findings at several points throughout the book.

This book is organized into two parts. The introductory chapter surveys some of the assumptions behind the present approach to assisting refugees, my own assumptions which led me to undertake this study, and discusses the methods which were applied. Chapter One describes the characteristics of the Ugandan influx into southern Sudan from 1979. Chapters Two and Three look at the operational effects of the assumptions about how best to help refugees, by first describing the way the settlements were organized and the programme was administered, and then examine some demographic features of the refugee population. Part Two of the book looks at the results of the delivery of such services as protection, food, medicine, education and employment. I go on to consider the question of the vulnerable categories and the psychological problems of refugees. Finally on the basis of some evidence, I consider the possible long-term impact of the refugees and the aid programme on the district. This book draws heavily on case material. Individual statements have been selected to illustrate general problems which were observed or revealed by the statistical data collected.

This case study of the emergency assistance programme in Yei River District has a significance far beyond the specific refugee and host communities living there. The location of the research, southern Sudan, was directed by the objectives of the study - to examine an international humanitarian response to an emergency refugee influx. While the findings cannot always be generalized to every emergency, they do raise profound questions concerning the role of relief, its link with development, the role of voluntary agencies and international organizations, and the impact of outside interventions and funds on the capacity of host governments to manage their own affairs. While a study of emergency assistance to refugees, the book argues that the very concept, refugee, may be an artificial category maintained more for the convenience of donors than for the people involved.

'Time for solutions' was the slogan of the Second International Conference on Assistance to Refugees in Africa (ICARA II) held in Geneva in July 1984. This conference has been described as representing a 'milestone', even a 'turning point', in the search for the ever elusive 'durable solutions' for refugees in Africa. While recognizing that aid programmes have failed dismally to bring refugees off relief rolls and onto the path of economic independence, and to help them 'integrate' into the social and economic fabric of their host community, ICARA II still aimed to convince 'donors' that even *more* outside intervention is required. 'Additionality' was the term which was invented to describe the amounts of money required, over and above development budgets, to support projects which would aid refugee-affected areas and 'integrate' refugees and their hosts. Without doubt additional funds *are* urgently required. The question is who will be determining how they will be spent?

Implicitly, and at times explicitly, ICARA II also marked the growing disfavour into which the large and bureaucratic UN agencies have fallen and a growing preference for NGOs to carry out projects. One government, Britain, pledged *all* of its 5m Sterling 'additional' funds to be spent on projects designed and executed by its own voluntary agencies.

Although the aim of ICARA II was to find funds to support projects which would strengthen the infrastructure of refugee-affected areas in host countries, rehabilitation programmes for returnees were also included in the submissions put to 'donors' (i.e. governments which support the budget of UNHCR). Although most refugees would no doubt argue that there have been no significant changes in the political situations which led to their flight which would allow them to return home in safety, rehabilitation programmes have been mounted in both Ethiopia and Uganda. There is reason to be concerned that the assumption that aid determines the movements of people may have the greater weight in decisions as to which ICARA II projects will receive funding, thereby cancelling the main thrust of the new approach to develop refugee-affected areas. Certainly the mood among donors favours the return home of refugees from these two countries.

So despite the enthusiasm of the humanitarian community for the results of ICARA II, there is little evidence to suggest it actually does mark a change in the basic philosophy of how refugees are best assisted. There has still been no research which would indicate how aid might actually facilitate such goals as 'integration' of refugees and their hosts. Even the term, 'integration', has yet to be defined. According to at least one observer, ICARA II was

...a great disappointment. This opinion, I admit, is not shared by representatives of many other non-governmental organisations who were present....I found the format and the presentations dull and, at times, insulting....There was no dialogue or give-

and- take; speeches had all been prepared well in advance without any reference to what had been previously said....There were no surprises...

I was further disappointed at the colonialism evident in Geneva. That colonialism, the wealthy whites of World One being benign to their darker brothers (very few sisters) of the Third World, was quite transparent. It was compounded by those representatives of African countries who have been co-opted by the life style of the West. I find it more and more difficult to believe that decisions concerning refugees can be made in palaces and Mercedes. Worst of all, the refugees of Africa were not represented!! (Moan 1984.)

Are the same mistakes which have been made over the last forty years about to be repeated, this time on an even grander scale?

Oxford   B.E.H.-B.
May 1985

Acknowledgements

I met Andrew Pearse only a year before he died and then on only two occasions, but the inspiration for my work since that time has been drawn largely from those encounters. The first time he was addressing Oxford students at a meeting on 'development'. He challenged his audience to think how they could put the skills they were acquiring at University to the service of the poor, how research was one way to empower the powerless. I never had the opportunity to thank him, but he spared one long afternoon with me when he was already in pain from the illness which claimed him.

It was quite by chance that Ugandan refugees became the case study for this book. In order to examine the proposition, that it was the organization and delivery of emergency assistance which accounted for many of the problems observed later on, I needed to study an emergency influx. If the experiences of these refugees living in southern Sudan teach us any lessons on how funds and other resources might be better used, then all refugees will join me in thanking them for co-operating, usually very willingly. Very few held any illusions that this research was going to relieve their personal sufferings.

I also want to thank the Saharawi refugees, living in tents near Tindouf, Algeria, for first demonstrating that it is possible to use the experiences in exile to transform a society as long as those who assist them do not remove from them the authority to do so. I thank Malcolm Harper, then working at OXFAM, for stimulating my thinking along these lines.

I first began to learn about the special problems of refugees in 1956–7 when I was working for the Church Federation, Los Angeles, resettling Hungarians. I thank Bela in particular. His long and bitter sufferings in the US taught me that being removed, without choice, from home and family can never be fully compensated.

Anyone who has lived in the Sudan will appreciate how impossible it is to properly express one's gratitude for the warmth and hospitality they offer. Where else can one not be surprised to hear a taxi driver respond. 'Whatever you wish', to the question, 'How much?'. It is not by chance that the Sudan has such a liberal, open-door policy towards those who flood across its borders. It is a way of life in the Sudan. I thank them as a people and a individuals for the continued kindness they proffer everyone. I cannot begin to name all who helped me with this research, but they include the staff of the Office of the Commissioner for Refugees in Khartoum, Gedaref, Port Sudan, en Showak, Juba, and Yei. They opened their files, provided transport, housed, fed, and once even clothed me and, most important, taught me a great deal from the perspective of the hosts. Karen Abu Zayd, in addition to all of the other help she gave, took time to criticize earlier drafts of some chapters.

The Overseas Development Administration funded my fellowship at Queen Elizabeth House. The Wenner Gren Foundation and the Universities Field Staff International also contributed to the costs of the fieldwork. A Fellowship from the Institute for the World Study of Politics funded some of the costs of writing. I thank them all. I also thank Mr. Jan Heidler and the United Nations High Commissioner for Refugees. Mr. Heidler arranged a UN travel document and guaranteed access to the field. It would have been difficult if not impossible to have conducted this research without such support and access to data. I am also grateful to those others within UNHCR, both in the Sudan and in Geneva, who appreciated the importance of an independent evaluation of their assistance programme.

I was more than fortunate to find Mr. Sjoerd van Schooneveld as the programme officer organizing the emergency assistance programme I wanted to study. I believe there are many who share my view that it was one of the best field operations. I think, however, that he would agree with me that it could not have been done so well had it not been for Nehemiah Iyega, the project manager, and Monique.

My most immediate intellectual debts, after Andrew Pearse, are to Robert Chambers and Ahmed Karadawi. Before them, of course, was a long line of anthropologists who belong to what is perhaps the most humanistic of all disciplines. Some may argue the history of anthropology is one of complicity with imperialism, but today the problems facing populations which are suddenly forced to cohabit an area against their will cry out for the skills of, and the information that can be generated by, anthropologists. Any attempts to assist such communities without applying the anthropological approach are unnecessarily handicapped. One hopes that more anthropologists will see their relevance to such crisis situations as arise as a result of forced migration. There is an urgent need to provide local communities with information about each other's cultures as well as to inform the agency personnel who are working among them.

So many people helped in the collection of data used in this book that the only reason my name appears as author is that I must bear the final responsibility for the interpretation. Many 'stranded' students, young people whose education had been interrupted by the war, helped at different times. The team of assistants include Atima Ayoub, Adile Sakia Bornfree, Aluma Brahan, Tom Andima Dradria, Gabriel Dramundria, Agalla Emanuel, Lali Ferdinand, Onzima George, Data Charles Male, Johnson Oryema, Philip Ramaga, Atali Restito, Bua Guido, John Twagirayesu, and Aluma Ponziano. The names of others appear throughout the book, but I especially thank John Issa. The Oxford University students, whose work is cited, went to southern Sudan in 1984 to follow up on my research. I learned a great deal from them and the discussions we have had played a part in the development of this book.

Many people read through parts of the manuscript and gave advice, but I especially thank Dr. Julie Marcus and Belinda Allan. I have received guidance in the analysis of the statistical data from Paul Griffiths, but most of the work was done by David Brunswick who deserves special mention, not only for working long hours, but for taking a serious interest in what we were learning from the data. Professor Howard Adelman was enormously helpful in suggesting how to organize the book. Rita Giwa, not only typed and re-typed drafts, but, as she has done for all of my writing over the past ten years, suggested improvements in both style and content. So many others helped with typing final drafts. I thank Greta Ilott, Fiona Frank, Jane Higgens and Maggie Corson. I thank my husband, Dr. Samuel Nwafor Okeke, and all the other members of our household for their love and forebearance. Completing the research and writing required the abandonment of my domestic duties, as well as long absences from Oxford. I am grateful to Oxford University Press who, recognizing the timeliness of this book, have produced it in record time.

I thank those within the House who first suggested the idea of establishing a programme of refugee studies at Queen Elizabeth House which has grown out of the ODA fellowship. Many members of the House have given support, but especially Shirley Ardener, Dr. Helen Callaway, and Dr. Frances Stewart. There is no doubt, however, that the person who has given the greatest support to me in this research as well as to the development of the Refugee Studies Programme, has been Arthur Hazlewood, the Warden of Queen Elizabeth House.

Contents

MAP 1 : THE SUDAN AND ITS NEIGHBOURS

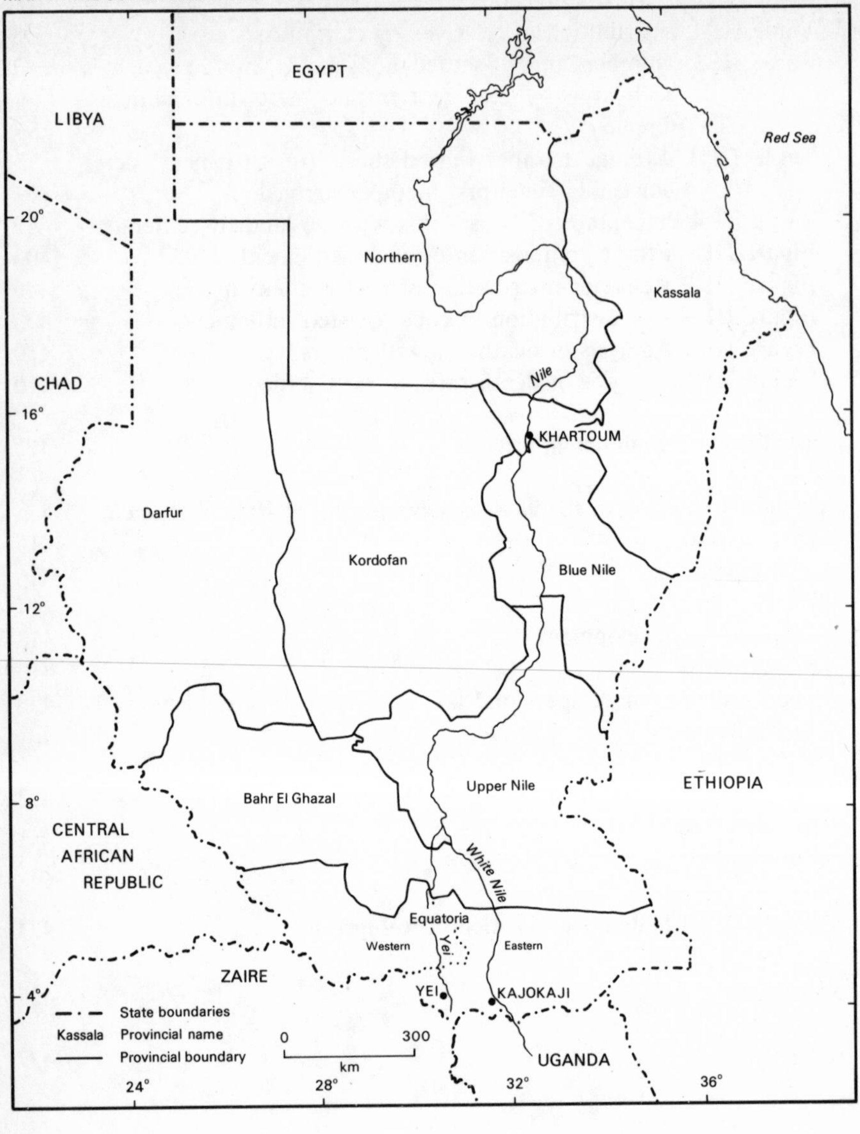

EGYPT

LIBYA

Red Sea

20°

Northern

Kassala

CHAD

16°

Darfur

Nile

KHARTOUM

Kordofan

12°

Blue Nile

8°

Bahr El Ghazal

Upper Nile

ETHIOPIA

CENTRAL
AFRICAN
REPUBLIC

White Nile

Equatoria

Western   Yei   Eastern

ZAIRE

4°

YEI   KAJOKAJI

State boundaries
Kassala   Provincial name
Provincial boundary

0   300
km

UGANDA

24°   28°   32°   36°

MAP 2: LOCATION OF REFUGEE·SETTLEMENTS

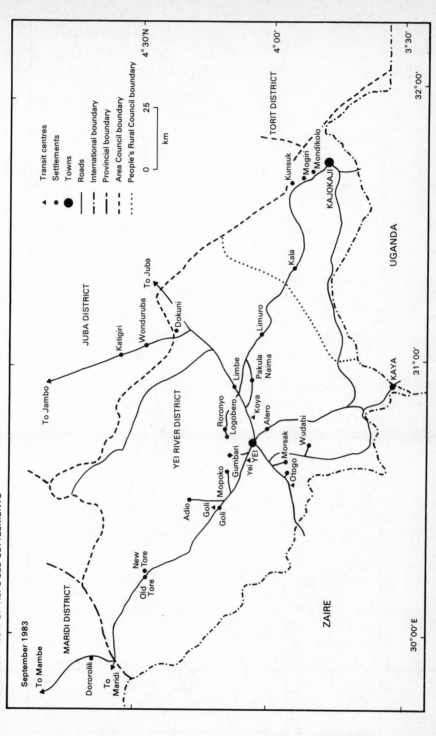

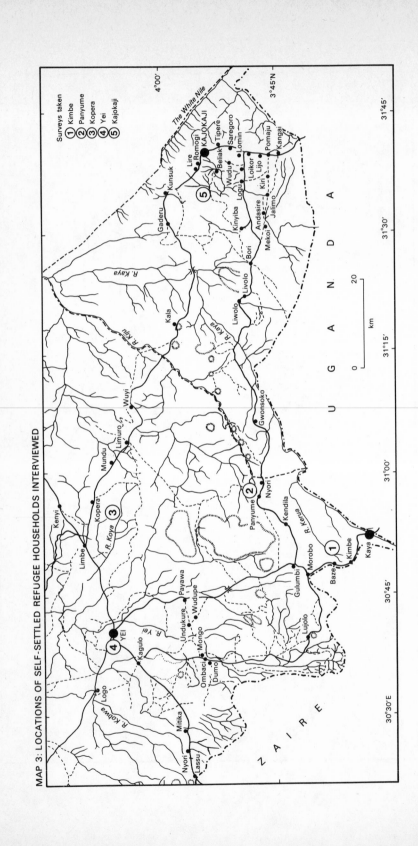

MAP 3: LOCATIONS OF SELF-SETTLED REFUGEE HOUSEHOLDS INTERVIEWED

Surveys taken
① Kimbe
② Panyume
③ Kopera
④ Yei
⑤ Kajokaji

Introduction

Durable solutions

The political crises in Africa which have led to the growing exodus of people from their homes have become increasingly intractable. According to the United Nations High Commissioner for Refugees (UNHCR), the UN office responsible for protecting and assisting refugees, at the beginning of the last decade there were less than one million African refugees. Depending on who is counting, the number is up to five million.(Greenfield 1984.) This alarming escalation of numbers began in earnest in 1978. The drought, particularly severe in Ethiopia since 1982, which has also severely affected other parts of the continent, has added yet another dimension to the problem of mass exodus.

UNHCR publications often commend Africans' traditional hospitality towards refugees. Many African officials are cynical about such praise. They believe it has simply excused neglect of the problem they face. Most host countries are confronted with unparalleled economic crises on the domestic front and can ill afford the luxury of hospitality. They complain that although Africa hosts half of the world's refugees, the allocation of UNHCR's budget has never reflected this reality. (Rwelamira 1983.)

From the point of view of UNHCR there are basically only three 'durable' solutions available for African refugees: voluntary repatriation back to their home country; resettlement in another country; or integration into the host society mainly by establishing them in agricultural settlements in their first country of asylum with the aim that refugees should become economically independent in the shortest possible time. There is little promise that any other African host is prepared to follow the precedent set by Tanzania which granted citizenship to a large segment of its refugee population. (Ayok Chol 1983a.)

Resettlement in a third country as a durable solution for African refugees, in terms of the numbers affected, is insignificant. Even if they were to be accepted, there are very few refugees who, unless guaranteed employment, would opt to be relocated in yet another poor African country, and the mood of industrialized countries towards receiving African refugees from this continent is highly restrictive.

The close of the period of anti-colonial wars saw UNHCR achieve a considerable success in repatriating refugees back to their countries of origin. After Algeria, refugees were returned to Guinea-Bisseau, Mozambique, Angola and Zimbabwe. But at the very time refugees were being repatriated back to Uganda following the overthrow of Idi Amin in 1979, many thousands more were spilling out over its borders. Except for the refugees from Namibia and South Africa, civil war continues to be the major cause of exodus for the growing numbers of refugees on this continent. Programmes for the rehabilitation of returnees have been funded for Ethiopia and Uganda; they have been severely criticized. (Crisp 1984; 1984*a*.) At present, repatriation under circumstances of strict voluntarism involves only a small number.

This book is concerned with the third of these 'durable' solutions to the refugee problem in Africa: settlement in the host country. In particular it examines an emergency programme mounted in response to an influx of refugees from Uganda into southern Sudan.

Accepting that most African refugees are likely to remain in their country of asylum for a protracted period of time, the objective of the aid programme is to help refugees become integrated and economically self-sufficient. The term 'self-sufficiency' has not been clearly defined, but for the donors of aid and international agencies which distribute it, it has implied the point when refugees have reached a state which permits the withdrawal of aid. For refugees to become economically independent, it is necessary that they be incorporated into the economic system of the locality in which they have settled. Thus assisting refugees represents a special case of a long-term development problem.

Social engineering

There is keen awareness of the failures of the settlement policy, but generally it is assumed that the fault lies not with the aid programme, but with the refugees themselves. Initially, my own research was based on a modification of the widely held hypothesis that refugees are to blame for the failures of the aid programme and for their continued economic dependence. The rural settlement policy itself was not questioned: at the outset I assumed that such a programme provided an ideal basis for taking positive advantage of the potential for social transformation which some believe displaced communities represent. Nor did I initially question the notion that refugees become negatively dependent as had been reported to me by experienced workers in the field. The stereotyped view that refugees everywhere are excessively and unreasonably demanding is too widely accepted for one not to be tempted to believe that it has some basis in fact.

I did, however, suspect that a major reason for this psychological dependency might lie in the manner in which relief is given and the supplicatory role which the refugee is forced to assume in the initial period of an emergency.

Establishing a rural settlement involves social engineering. My reading of the literature produced by agencies responsible for the policy suggested that the full implications of this reality had escaped attention. Although refugee assistance is concentrated on establishing rural agricultural settlements, few individuals employed by international agencies to administer their programmes have either relevant training or any experience in rural development. This fact has imporant implications for the implementation of aid programmes.

I began this research with the assumption that if, throughout an emergency, allowance was made for the maximum participation of refugees in the organization and administration of their new communities, many of the problems associated with dependency could be mitigated. Participation has become a buzz word in discussions of rural development. Having conducted field work in West Africa since 1967, and having wearied of learning about failed development projects, I began to look for some success stories. Between 1979 and 1981 I visited three communities in Senegal where peasants had organized themselves for 'development'. Although each was affected in different ways, outside political forces - both national and international - were threatening their success. Ironically, often 'aid' was the tool used to de-stabilize the solidarity of these communities. (Adams 1979.)

Then I was invited by OXFAM to write an up-date report on the Sahrawi refugees in Algeria. (Harrell-Bond 1981.) Algeria has permitted the Sahrawi complete autonomy in the areas where they have settled; there are no outsiders living or working in their camps. The success of this community in mobilizing its own resources to cope with its problems despite its dependence on capital inputs from outside the camps, suggested that perhaps the 'dependency syndrome' observed among refugees elsewhere was the result of the way in which aid is managed by humanitarian agencies.

The methodology which was adopted for this research was inspired not only by my experience, but by Andrew Pearse, to whom this book is dedicated. In a seminal paper (Pearse and Stiefel 1979) it was pointed out that what is really needed is research into anti-participatory *ideologies*. 'Although there are endless examples of directly repressive measures and acts against popular participation, it is the anti-participatory character of ideologies that provide the most persistent control as they mould attitudes and expectations of one group in relation to the others.' (ibid.) The attitudes of humanitarian aid workers towards refugees (and towards their African hosts) are a case in point.

This book is not only, in these authors' words, a 'critique of discriminatory ideologies', it is an attempt to show how expensive, ineffective, and wasteful are anti-participatory structures. Aid which is imposed from outside not only usurps the roles of the host, suppresses the creative energy of the refugee who could have been helped to help himself, but provokes responses which are hostile and unproductive for all concerned. (Fanon 1964;1967.)[1]

[1] Dependent people cannot usually afford to express their true feelings towards their beneficiaries, nor are the latter accustomed to listening to their views. The majority of the participants at the International Symposium, 'Assistance to Refugees: Alternative Viewpoints' (Harrell-Bond and Karadawi 1984), held in Oxford were either representatives of African host governments or refugees from the continent. One journalist took me aside the first day asking what was going on. He had never been at a meeting where people were so angry. Aid officials were also apparently shocked at the fury being directed towards them. But after three days of 'catharsis', participants were working together to produce the resolutions and recommendations which appear in Appendix I.

Participation is about empowering the poor to take control of their own lives, about being able to involve themselves effectively in decision-making. At a minimum this requires providing the means to acquire access to information and providing opportunities for people to examine both the external forces which oppress them as well as their own values and beliefs which condition their responses. Only then can the poor begin to devise strategies to combat the forces which oppress them.

Our research plan tried to allow refugees to participate both in analysing their situation and in conveying their views about the aid programme. In each settlement I attempted to explain to refugees how aid is organized, who is involved, and what are their rights and duties in relation to the assistance programme. At the end of the survey my team and I reported to settlers what we had learned about their community. Some evidence of the results of this approach may be seen in Appendix V, 'A Report to the Inter-agency Meeting at Kala Settlement', which was written and presented by our research team.

Originally I had intended to restrict the study to those refugees within the aid system - that is, to the rural settlement programme. Although unassisted or self-settled refugees are known to be in the majority in most host countries in Africa, and are thought by some to be the more vulnerable (Chambers 1979), the initial decision to ignore them in this research project was related to the objectives of using the data to advise on the policy of agencies and donors.

UNHCR directs most material and human resources towards the settlement programme. Thus, I believed improving present approaches to be a high priority for all concerned with the impact of aid. Moreover, the scale of an investigation by one researcher must necessarily be limited. Focusing on the settlement programme appeared to be the most cost-effective approach. Although I knew that only a fraction of refugees in the Sudan were recipients of aid, I believed that all refugees *should* have access to an assistance programme. The narrowness of my view is demonstrated by the fact that in the list of those who I believed might find the research useful (UNHCR, voluntary agencies, and donor governments), I had not even included host governments! Perhaps one reason I left them out of the list was that I also believed there is a difference between how government officials and humanitarian agency field staff view the poor. Chambers observed that there are only a handful of researchers who have access to and understanding of the rich and detailed system of knowledge of the poor, but these do not influence development while government organizations and staff who are engaged in development are ignorant of and *conditioned to despise that knowledge.* (1983:84, emphasis added.) I believed that, by contrast, humanitarians would be eager to close this information gap and that participatory anthropological research ought to be the best means to do this. Therefore the main objective of the study was to assess the quality of the delivery of that aid in the settlements.

In short I began this research with many of the same assumptions held by the humanitarian community concerning the best approach to refugee assistance. In particular, I assumed that more aid was needed from outside the country. Although questioning the approach of outsiders, I did not question the need for them to supplement the work of the host government. I believed that humanitarians were honest people of good will. I shared the assumption that aid should be distributed equally among refugees, and that the assistance programme should insist on economic democracy. While having studied and written about the politics of development aid, I too believed humanitarian assistance was a *different* case.

It was the discovery that there are refugees who do not accept the view that rural settlements are the best solution for them, and that most of them have actively rejected aid - in some cases to the point of starvation - that first directed my attention to the self-settled refugees. I learned that refugees are not passive recipients of relief dispensed by assistance programmes that are designed in offices far from the borders they cross. Rather, refugees are an active and dynamic factor in the outcome of all interventions. I concluded it was necessary to widen the scope of the study.

There is an urgent need for independent research into the effectiveness of aid programmes. 'In-house' studies of refugee programmes do not question the basic assumptions which lie behind their own policies. Although I shared many of the assumptions of the humanitarian workers, the advantage I had was that as an anthropologist, I was trained to use field research to question them. Moreover, some early experiences during my field-work precipitated the process of questioning the assumptions with which I had arrived in the Sudan.

I had not sought permission from the Sudan government to conduct research before I arrived. Originally it had been agreed that I would spend only a short time in this country to become familiar with UNHCR's manner of working, and then move on to Somalia for fieldwork. UNHCR had issued me with an official UN travel certificate and had guaranteed me access to the field. A friend at the Ford Foundation in Khartoum arranged my entry visa. Although more or less formally there on UNHCR business, I nevertheless on arrival went first to the office of the Commissioner for Refugees (COMREF).[2] I was already acquainted with the outgoing commissioner. Discussions with the staff, particularly with the assistant commissioner for refugees, Ahmed Karadawi, helped to put into a wider perspective a great deal of what had already begun to puzzle me in my reading of the documents and in interviews with humanitarian officials in London and Geneva.

I then travelled with the new commissioner on a tour of settlements in the east. At each camp, the refugee committee was called and, after

[2] Most outsiders assume UNHCR has complete authority over refugees, and tend to ignore government offices. Local officials resent this and it probably accounts for the difficulties some have in getting those documents which UNHCR cannot issue.

introductions, they proceeded to list their complaints and demands. On one occasion when the delegation was too exhausted to continue, I went alone with a Sudanese official to another settlement. I was chatting with a few refugees about changes in family law practices now that they were living in the Sudan. The official asked the settlement committee to join us, and they proceeded to list the deficiencies of the programme. Irritated with this break in an interesting conversation, I asked why they were telling me all this: I had nothing to do with the aid programme. I went on to tell them about the 'good' Sahrawi refugees whom I found extremely reluctant to complain. The committee members retorted angrily, informing me that they did not like their *role* any more than I did, but what else (other than recite their woes), were they supposed to do when a European visited their camp?

Outsiders carry their own expectations of refugees' behaviour into such dramaturgical events, so it is not surprising that refugees play the role expected of them. As one Ugandan explained to me, even the very term 'refugee' is imbued with meaning, assigning a particular role to individuals who decide (or are forced) to accept assistance.

... our people believe that to be a refugee is to be taken care of by UNHCR. But people on the border, they don't think they are refugees. After crossing the Ugandan/Sudan border, they believe that since they are still self-supporting, they are not refugees. When they see you pack to come to the settlement, they say 'so you have accepted to be a refugees'. They use the 's' on the word 'refugee' even if you are a single person, without knowing the connotation, even when they are actually refugees in the Sudan!

The perceptions of their role held both by refugees and by outsiders, impose serious methodological problems on the researchers. It would be only logical if refugees withheld information in an interview which might jeopardize their material existence. Disparities between empirical data collected in the interviews compared with that available from the agencies had to be constantly examined for their implications. For example, when UNHCR was sure that every refugee had been issued a blanket, and we found 13 people using only one, it was necessary to look further than simply dismissing the respondents as dishonest. These were the sorts of discrepancies which alerted us to the need for a much broader approach. Our investigations into the causes of such small discrepancies also began to indicate that there were alternatives to the official explanations of the situation. We began to see that from the refugees' point of view, the 'aid umbrella' looked very different; in this case it offered very little protection from the elements. Later in our research, we came to see the importance of the missing blankets more clearly and to understand how one large family could come to own only a single blanket. We found that even blankets played an unexpected role in both the economic and the cultural life of refugees, a role that will be described in detail later in the book.

Integration

Although the objective of assistance to refugees is said to be their integration into the host community, the term 'integration' has not been satisfactorily defined. For the aid community, those refugees who are not assisted, have not only settled 'spontaneously', but have also achieved *'spontaneous integration'*, and are thus not in need of assistance. Their success is attributed to the belief that as colonial boundaries intersected established communities, people who fled acoss a border are welcomed by their kith and kin with whom they share common origins, language and culture. These are important but not sufficient conditions for integration. The most important one is the availability of resources. There has been little research to test such assumptions, but both Chambers (1979) and Hansen (1979) demonstrate that few of such self-settled refugees have achieved economic independence and the burden they impose on already scarce resources mitigates against their security.

A very simple definition of integration would be of a situation in which host and refugee communities are able to co-exist, sharing the same resources - both economic and social - with no greater mutual conflict than that which exists within the host community. Such a definition will not stand up to detailed analysis. For a start, the level of conflict may well have increased *within* the host country as a result of pressure of greater numbers. Moreover, co-existence does not necessarily imply equality of access to resources and even the absence of measurable conflict would not necessarily preclude the exploitation of one group, or segments of it, by another. For example, some highly skilled Ugandans got employment by pretending to be Sudanese, but lacking nationality certificates, they were kept on a very low salary and enjoyed none of the normal protection accorded employees.

Despite such reservations, there may be some advantages in adhering to this simple definition. The present lack of agreement on the meaning of the term 'integration' and its general association with 'assimilation' and 'permanence', have created a resistance on the part of both host countries and refugees to any policy which appears to be promoting the absorption of the refugee community into the country of asylum. The fact that is overlooked in these debates is that only a *minority* of African refugees are presently objects of aid programmes. Most are surviving by dint of their capacity to co-exist with locals under extremely difficult conditions.

The data from southern Sudan lends support to the view that were assistance programmes to be directed towards resolving the economic and social deprivations which result from dramatic demographic changes without distinguishing the recipients, then economic, and perhaps even some social 'integration' (and thus the protection of the refugees) could be better achieved. As we shall see, the perception of those refugees under the aid 'umbrella' as privileged led to resentment and an escalation of tension between them and their hosts. Moreover, such an approach would ensure from the outset that aid budgets would have a lasting impact on the host's economy rather than disappearing into the 'black hole' of relief.

Why settlements?

There are several arguments for the policy of concentrating assistance to refugees in Africa on the creation of planned agricultural settlements.

To attract money, refugees must be *visible*. It is difficult to count the numbers of self-settled refugees, and even if they could be identified, the policies of most refugee agencies are too inflexible to allow them to devise a programme which would assist a target population which is 'mixed up' with the local community. Given the nature of international aid, host governments have found it impossible to convince donor governments to spend monies earmarked for refugee assistance expanding the economic and social infrastructure which would cope with such dramatic demographic changes.[3]

Distinguishing between victims of mass distress migrations has always been for the convenience of donors, since the immediate *physical* needs of those who flee across international boundaries are the same as for the internally displaced. In the Sudan this has been thrown into sharp relief by the Sudanese drought victims who have moved from the north and the west in search of food. A separate *ad hoc* committee was set up to deal with their needs and among other donors, the European Economic Communty (EEC) sent a team to devise a long term solution for these involuntary migrants. The plan for Kordafan and Darfur, at least at its earliest stage of formulation (March 1985), was to place them in settlements. However, the leader of the EEC team of experts was very concerned. He knew that there were some 200,000 famine victims congregated in feeding centres in Darfur and Kordafan, but he also knew the numbers of starving were much greater. Once he had his settlements laid out, his problem was going to be how to *find* the others.[4]

Another argument for moving refugees into settlements is the need for security. The most serious protection needs are found among those who have settled themselves around borders and are at risk of attack by the armies of

---

[3] In Tanzania a formula has been worked out. If a village has 200 refugee families, some assistance towards supporting the infrastructure of that community is provided. (Dr Benson Nindi, personal communication.)

[4] I asked why he *wanted* to find them. After all, their invisibility meant that they were part of some indigenous social unit and why did he not simply help everyone who was needy *wherever* they were? I also pointed out another danger: Ethiopia is already criticized for its movements of peasants to settlements in the south. How would he avoid forcing Sudanese into his settlements? Once so much money had been invested, both the EEC *and* the government would have a vested interest in peopling them.

their country of origin. If a host government properly secures its borders against such attacks, it risks military confrontation. As will be discussed in Chapters One and Four, incursions by the Ugandan government's army (UNLA) into the Sudan was the major cause of insecurity for refugees. Sudan's desire to maintain good diplomatic relations with Uganda led them to turn a blind eye on most occasions, even though many Sudanese were also among the victims of these attacks.

The possibility that refugees may use their country of asylum as a base for guerilla warfare is the major argument for insisting that refugees are moved away from borders. The OAU Convention specifies that refugees should be located at a 'reasonable' distance from borders, but this distance has been variously interpreted. There are differences of opinion as to whether the settlement policy encourages political organizations among refugees to flourish or whether it serves to neutralize this threat through their total de-politicalization.

There is also a general impression that the presence of a refugee population in a host country gives rise to a higher rate of crime. Given the extreme poverty of both guests and hosts, and the competition which arises over the use of increasingly scarce resources, it would not be surprising if this could be demonstrated. The policies of some host governments suggest they may believe that the control of refugees, law and order, is facilitated by keeping them in settlements. (Ayok 1983.) In Sudan, for example, over the years there have been periodic roundups and removals of refugees from Khartoum to settlements. At the time such expulsions appear to have been an attempt to reduce the number of unemployed and destitute from the streets of the city. However, the round-up which took place before the OAU meeting was clearly for political reasons. Urban refugees are the more politically articulate and those in Khartoum could well have embarrassed their host government by demonstrations.

Humanitarian agencies assume that refugees always require relief and that material assistance must come from outside the host country. Moreover, there is a general assumption that left to their own devices, refugees would remain perpetually dependent on relief; outsiders are therefore needed to get the refugees to be self-supporting. The best means of doing this, it is assumed, is to put them into planned settlements in which they can be managed. The importance placed on this mode of assisting refugees is demonstrated by the high proportion of the UNHCR budget for Africa which is spent on settlements. In 1982 it was 58 per cent. (Rwelamira 1983.)

There are three stages to the settlement programme. First refugees are given relief aid and transported to camps, to inhabit houses built for them or which they are expected to build for themselves. During the second stage they are provided with land, tools, and seeds, and primary education is organized. During this period refugees are expected to be motivated to work and to get on their own feet quickly, by being told that there will be a gradual reduction in their food rations after the first harvest. In the third stage, aid is withdrawn, on the grounds that refugees should by then be 'self-sufficient' and 'integrated' into the local community.

Among the international agencies, there is a general assumption that as most African refugees are from rural areas, they are therefore experienced farmers. This is also the rationale for the policy of concentrating outside assistance, wherever possible, on the establishment of planned agricultural settlements. However, policy makers appreciate the need for the diversification of settlement economies and great effort and finance have been invested in repeated skills inventories and surveys aimed to identify viable income generating projects (e.g. ILO 1982). However, efforts to provide refugees with an alternative or supplementary means of earning a living have achieved very uneven and unsatisfactory results.

Given the aim that settlements should bring refugees to a state of self-sufficiency through agriculture, the results have often been disappointing. In fact, seldom has it been possible to withdraw aid. Moreover, when aid has been withdrawn, the refugees' standard of living has sometimes fallen, necessitating the resumption of a relief programme. According to Clark and Stein (1984:6) only thirteen out of 86 settlements in Africa have ever achieved 'durable self-sufficiency'.

The responsibility for the failure of the settlement policy has been laid at the feet of the refugees themselves. Representatives of the international humanitarian community usually arrive on the scene of an emergency influx of refugees some time after it has begun. The refugees they encounter are often in extremely poor physical condition. It is necessary to provide food, shelter, water, and medical services, and to concentrate effort on saving lives. During this period it is believed that refugees adopt attitudes and behaviour which impede their progress towards self-sufficiency. These negative responses - usually referred to as the 'dependency syndrome' - are thought to develop when refugees are the objects of relief.

The prevalent theory suggests that by the time it is possible to consider longer-term solutions, dependent behaviour has already become entrenched. Among relief organizations, a kind of working hypothesis has developed: the more you give, the more dependent people become. In order to counteract this attitude, various forms of external pressure have been placed on refugees in settlements with a view to encouraging them to take on more responsibility for themselves. Such 'pressures' range from paying 'incentives' to refugees who have built their own houses or sanitary facilities, to the threatened or actual withdrawal of food rations.

Helpless refugees

One assumption which is shared by both host governments and the international humanitarian agencies is that refugees constitute a problem, a burden, rather than an economic opportunity. Outsiders view African refugees as *helpless*; as needing outsiders to plan for them and to take care of them. This assumption is the cornerstone of nearly all appeals for funds. Agencies vary in the degree of dignity with which they transmit images of refugees, but *all* rely on a public which will respond to media portrayal of extreme human suffering and starvation. Observing a collection of UNHCR posters, Martin Barber, Director of the British Refugee Council, commented on the persistent 'psychological reaction to refugees as people for whom "we must do something"'. The posters depicted all the refugees in attitudes of submission or helplessness. 'They were waiting for something to happen. They were holding out their hands. The photographer was standing up and they were sitting down.' While some agencies are becoming quite concerned about the public becoming rapidly satiated with the 'starving child appeal' and funds drying up, the nature of the contemporary refugee problem suggests that this form of marketing of refugees will continue.

The packaging of refugees has altered dramatically since the post-Second World War days. Following the war the 'free world' found itself encumbered with a refugee population of an estimated nine million. One document which proposed how they should be assisted welcomed their flight as confirmation of the tyranny of the East, to neglect them would endanger liberal democracy. So, it argued, in the struggle to maintain democratic life in the face of the more 'disciplined solidarity and far-reaching plans of the Kremlin', there was 'no choice but to secure decent conditions of life for the millions of expellees, or face the full consequences of their hostility and its deadly exploitation by the Kremlin.'[5]

In this document appeals for assisting these refugees were based not only on immediate political self-interest, the protection of democracy from communism, but on the unique potential for economic growth and the opportunity for 'population integration' afforded by the uprooted.

Congested Europe and under-populated and underdeveloped overseas democracies - both would benefit. The general lines of co-operation would be fittingly inspired by the principles distinguishing the European Recovery Programme: self-help, mutual help, and American backing where advisable. Indeed, this would be, in terms of human beings, a complement to the economic reciprocal aid of OECD. ... the West would consciously stand for an integration of democratic co-operation in the population field. If the West begins to accomplish this further miracle, it will strengthen hope and confidence among free citizens, and will create them among the vast ranks of the Dispossessed and Desperate - the Refugees.

[5] The terminology and quotations in this and the following paragraph are taken from a document entitled, 'Proposal for a new era of emigration', from the files of Clark M. Clifford, Papers of Harry S. Truman, The Harry S. Truman Library. I am grateful to Robert Rice III who supplied this and other material concerning this period. Some of this discussion appears in Harrell-Bond (1985).

These post-war refugees in Europe were both anti-communist and white. The latter was important, as it was believed that once the receiving countries (Australia, New Zealand, North and South America) were fully convinced of the potential of refugees to fuel their economies (and, in the case of the United States, to provide the 2.5 million civilian labour force required by defence related industries), the 'reception countries overseas will clamour for white population.' Racial bias is further demonstrated in the expression of regret that 'the Union of South Africa with its dangerously small white population is actually calling a halt to immigration'.

Today, however, most refugees are not white. They originate from, and are hosted by some of the poorest countries in the world. Even if the racial factor does not bias immigration policy, those countries which opened their doors in the 1950s today suffer relatively depressed economies and high unemployment rates. And there are fewer cases where it is possible to give clear-cut explanations for refugee flows in terms of the 'communist threat'. Furthermore, in some cases, refugee organizations are avowedly 'socialist' and, in the view of donor governments, represent a political danger. What else is left besides human misery and helplessness upon which to base appeals for funds?

The image of the helpless refugee, desperately in need, reinforces the view that outsiders are needed to help them. At the international symposium, Assistance to Refugees: Alternative Viewpoints held in Oxford, March 1984 (Harrell-Bond and Karadawi 1984), one refugee related her experience with an aid worker.

She said, 'You cannot be a refugee.' But I told her, 'I am one.' It is because I can speak English. [This] changes the images of a refugee from ... the starving children of the posters, to real people who used to manage their own affairs and then became displaced. This image ... is so world-wide that I decided not to get angry ... The fact that our status has changed does not mean that our abilities have gone down.

Employment practices reflect the imagery of helplessness. In southern Sudan the medical programme was, up to December 1984, run by a European nurse. The refugee medical doctor, who earlier had single-handedly organized a medical programme for the civilians trapped inside Uganda, was allowed only limited responsibility. Two of his Ugandan colleagues who applied to work in the programme were told that their services were not required. Both were employed elsewhere in Africa, one with the World Health Organization. Among the refugees in the south is a former principal of an agricultural college. He was unemployed but the agencies drafted in a number of inexperienced and less-qualified personnel from the US and Europe to *run* the agricultural programme *for* refugees. The advertisement for one position of agricultural advisor illustrates the point. The advertisement asked for applicants who would be able to *teach* Ugandan farmers how to grow sorghum, sweet potatoes, and cassava, whereas the most serious problem the refugees faced was lack of hoes and seeds.

Unable to recruit from overseas in time, one agency in the south did employ a professional agriculturalist from within the refugee community as its agricultural co-ordinator. Although holding a degree from Makerere University and formerly responsible for an entire district in Uganda, he was not treated like a professional. He was not entrusted with information concerning the limits of the budget - vital information required for planning. For the first year he was not provided with a typewriter or typist. He was supplied with a motorbike, an extremely dangerous mode of travel; only expatriates were allowed access to this agency's landrovers.

The role of host governments

As well as assumptions about the helplessness of refugees, within the humanitarian community there is also the implicit assumption that host government institutions are too weak, and that their personnel are insufficiently trained to manage a refugee assistance programme. It follows from this assumption that outside managers are essential. It also follows from this assumption that host governments lack the ability to contribute to the aid programmes developed by outside agencies for refugees. Unlike the development field where today projects must be negotiated between governments and the foreign 'experts', refugee agencies who devise assistance programmes expect the host government to approve their plans without question.

The assumption that host governments lack the capacity to cope with refugee management underlies the funding policies of donor governments and UNHCR. But there is another, contradictory, view that also influences the judgements of many field workers: this is that host governments are *not* weak or incompetent. On the contrary, they are seen to be *remarkably efficient*, their main business being to oppress and exploit the poor within their own societies. Thus, for two quite different and mutually exclusive reasons, humanitarians come to view themselves as the best advocates for refugees. (Karadawi 1982.)

Whether viewed as incompetent or sinister, government bureaucracy is perceived as an obstacle to the free exercise of charity. For many outside 'experts', contacts with local officials are limited to those instances when a signature is required on a document or when some crisis arises which forces them to turn to local officials for help. As a result, relations between agency staff and host government officials are characterized by mutual distrust, defensiveness, and antagonism. As Karadawi (1982) observed, the relationship between the aid-giving community and the aid-receiving government is 'like an alliance between two parties who agree on goals but eye each other with suspicion'. In the resulting cloud of distrust, 'Their constitituencies are forgotten; the local host and refugees' perception of asylum are hardly taken notice of or involved in decision making.' (ibid.)

The system for channelling relief funds supports views that outsiders hold of themselves and of their host government. Very few donor governments will agree to give money unilaterally to a host government. Most funds are directed through UNHCR or NGOs. As normally UNHCR is not an implementing agency, it is the practice for it to contract a voluntary agency to carry out specific projects for which UNHCR supplies the funds. Government offices which are established to take responsibility for refugees are themselves sometimes funded through the UNHCR budget. In the case of the Sudan, many Sudanese are employed in the office of the Commissioner for Refugees (COMREF). They now receive higher salaries than they would in another government office, their wages being 'topped up' through UNHCR support. Thus programmes are designed and implemented in terms of the adage, 'He who pays the piper, calls the tune.'

There is another, usually unspoken, assumption that African officials are essentially corruptable, and this assumption influences agency employment practices. During an emergency, whatever their background, almost any white face which arrives on the scene has the chance of a job. One expatriate, for example, who had no appropriate training, was responsible at times even for recruiting medical staff. Since the employing agency did not consult with the Ugandans, who could have scrutinized and evaluated qualifications, many errors were made.

The assumption of local corruption leads also to inordinate attention being given to the question of the accountability for government spending. In Sudan, officials from COMREF believe that sometimes visits are made to their private homes to see if there is any evidence that they have been pocketing assistance funds.[6] It is worth noting that no system has yet been devised to ensure that either consultants or agency staff are themselves accountable for the *impact* of the programmes they design, be it to their own constituencies, to their host governments or to the refugees they purport to assist.[7]

In the development field, not only are projects negotiated between governments, but foreign 'experts' are usually required to work *with* their

[6] Not all share the assumption that white people are 'naturally' honest. According to one driver, they are less likely to steal because of their high visibility in Africa. One night in Yei after a settlement foreman had been found guilty of selling used clothing, I asked the driver how he would protect the store. He said, 'Give the key to a white man. He can't sell anything in the market.'

[7] This is also true of academics who act as consultants in development work. Being employed as a consultant brings status among one's peers (and usually extra income). But, unlike the reviews of publications which may affect one's career, reports written for development projects are not subjected to similar professional judgement. Normally they are 'classified' and usually unsigned.

local counterparts - usually in the latter's office. Moreover, whether or not they exercise it, governments have the right to inspect the credentials of development experts before they arrive. In contrast, relief agencies are not subject to such standards and there are, unfortunately, too few examples where consultative relations have been established with local officials. There is a tendency to avoid any control over dispensing charity and, wherever possible, to 'evade any responsibility to a government bureaucracy. In Sudan, when there was an attempt by COMREF to have a say - to mitigate competition between agencies, to redress the imbalance between wasteful duplication of services in some areas to the neglect of others, or to require some standards of competency of agency personnel - the office was likely to be accused of being "militaristic" '. (Karadawi 1982.)

Who pays the most?

There is another prevalent misconception about who is bearing the greater financial burden for refugee support. International humanitarians are usually convinced that outside aid covers the greater portion of the costs, but if one ever assessed the value of the land refugees used, one would be likely to find it far exceeds outside donations. Furthermore, *most* refugees are not assisted and the hosts are sharing their already fragile social services with them.[8] Host government officials in Africa are caught between their genuine concern for the refugees and their wish to honour international agreements to provide asylum, and the increasingly hostile grassroots response from their own impoverished people in refugee-affected areas.

In March 1984 the then Sudanese Minister of Interior described the deteriorating relations between local people and refugees in eastern Sudan.

A week ago I was in Gedaref and Kassala ... Three years ago I asked people, 'Do you want the refugees with us here?' ... the opinion was divided. Now when I went, the number [of refugees] had grown tremendously in towns, in conditions of very limited resources. One of the officials ... said to me that if I convene a meeting ... the answer would now be very negative. I try to bring this to your attention and the world's attention, that we are racing against time. We in Africa depend largely on our biggest asset, which is the hospitality of our people ... there is a limit to this. If we can't come forward with something tangible, it is very difficult to stop the resentment of the people, which is the real bank on which we are counting.

The need for funds to maintain levels of assistance for the needy within their borders and the manner in which refugee programmes are funded has

---

[8] A first and very interesting attempt has been made to document the hidden costs to the Sudan of hosting refugees. (Osman and Kurssany 1984.)

encouraged host governments to try to attract funds with the threat to close their borders and/or force existing populations of refugees out.[9]

Instead of recognizing that host countries make the largest contribution to refugee support and are the least able to do so, the humanitarian community implicitly assumes and they (as well as governments which produce refugees) often explicitly express the view that host governments are mercenaries, capitalizing on their refugee guests. As one agency worker put it: 'Let's face it. Sudan can't close her border to refugees ... If she did, she will be shutting out millions of dollars of foreign aid. That is the real name of the game.' (Karadawi 1982.) Disputes over 'the real name of the game' have serious implications for the design and implementation of aid programmes. The near total breakdown in relations between the government and the international agency community in Somalia had its origin in a similar assumption about motivations. Failing to recognize that most of its refugees did not live in assisted settlements, some described the Somali government's attempt to use food aid for its expanded population, in which refugees were indistinguishable from locals, as 'diversion' and 'corruption'. (Mark Malloch-Brown, Alternative Viewpoints 1984.) Journalists are not infrequently fed such allegations by political attachés from the country of origin of refugees. It is easier to repeat such stories than leave the comfortable city and conduct serious investigative journalism.

Humanitarianism and politics

Humanitarian organizations have assumed the role of the 'conscience of the world'. Working as they do in some of the poorest outreaches of the globe, they bring the problems of the suffering to national and international attention.

There has been a proliferation of humanitarian agencies since the Second World War, especially over the last two decades. A vast system of patronage has developed within the humanitarian community. (Lissner 1977.) Some of the larger NGOs have promoted the development of smaller, more specialized agencies which they fund through their own budgets. In Africa, indigenous church-based organizations and NGOs are dependent for nearly all their funds on larger international consortiums.

Appeals for refugee assistance after the Second World War were overtly political. When, however, the office of the U.N. High Commissioner for Refugees was established, its work was defined as being entirely *non-political*. Nevertheless, political considerations continued to be important in determining the response to a refugee crisis. In 1956-7, when Hungarians fled

[9] The example of Thailand is often cited by Sudanese officials. *The Guardian* 24 December 1984 reports a recent example of the use of this threat. Here the Sudanese commissioner has added his weight to the argument that international humanitarians should find a way to get food behind the battle lines in Tigréy and Eritrea to prevent a greater influx.

into Western Europe, although responsibility for organizing and funding the relief operation fell to a great extent upon churches and voluntary agencies, the policies of the cold war still influenced their reception and support.

The need to depoliticize refugee assistance may perhaps be the reason why governments originally turned to churches and voluntary agencies whose raison d'être is humanitarianism. The general assumption of their political neutrality has, no doubt, served to reduce tensions between neighbouring states who have sent or received refugees. This may even be the reason why some donor governments have resisted extending their mandate to include development projects for refugees. This could imply political commitment to the exiled groups by donors who wished to maintain the myth that humanitarianism could be separated from politics.

The constituencies of churches and secular NGOs can be a force for political dissent within most liberal democracies and at times they have lobbied against the foreign policy of their home governments. (Lissner 1977.) But the freedom of church groups and voluntary agencies to oppose US policy abroad has been directly challenged by recent developments in Washington. The US government has threatened to withdraw the tax-exempt status of organizations that engage in political advocacy. (Nichols 1984.) In Britain, voluntary agencies are constrained by the Charity Commissioners' declaration 'that the elimination of social, economic, political or other injustices' is outside the permitted scope of 'legal charitable endeavour'.[10] (Diplomats from refugee-producing countries have been known to write to charities which support refugees from Eritrea or Tigréy, etc., reminding them of the provisions of the Charity Act). In fact, since the passing of the US Mutual Defence Assistance Control Act in 1951, and the discussions of the Nathan Report in Britain the following year, both the US and British governments have taken the view that the proper role of state-assisted humanitarian agencies is to be complementary to their foreign policy. (Lissner 1977:97-119)

Threats and warnings are only one way in which humanitarian agencies are persuaded to toe foreign policy lines. The growing dependence on government funding has had an even greater effect on discouraging dissent and neutralizing a potential adversary relationship into one of partnership. (Kline 1984.) It is extremely difficult, if not impossible, for a humanitarian agency that receives substantial amounts of government money to act as an advocate for an oppressed group whose interests contradict those of either donors or hosts.

Political considerations are the hinterland to policy concerning aid to refugees. The danger of the assumption that it is possible to separate politics from humanitarianism is that it prevents an examination of the effects of local, national, and international politics on refugee policy. Ironically, refugees are always more secure if their host has openly antagonistic relations

[10] See an interview with Michael Harris, *The Guardian*, 5 October, 1984.

with their country of origin. The 1983 agreement to exchange refugees between Uganda, Kenya, and Tanzania, following the revival of warm relationships between the former members of the East African Community, is just one graphic example. Despite the diplomatic rhetoric about humanitarian assistance to refugees not constituting an unfriendly political act, refugees are nearly always the pawns in relations between states.

It is an open secret that Afghan refugees are allowed, some say even supplied with, arms, while still under the 'aid umbrella'. Over the years, the offices of the Eritrean independence movements have been closed or allowed to operate freely, depending on the prevailing political climate between the Ethiopian and the Sudan governments. The relationship between organizations claiming to speak for the Oromo and the Somali government is more complex. (Greenfield 1980.) By very definition, refugees represent the eye of many a political storm.

Liberal democracies tolerate political diversity and NGOs often illustrate this diversity by the places they select to work in and the people they choose to assist. Refugee communities are themselves factionalized. The first groups of refugees entering Sudan after World War Two from the Ethiopian side included landowners and religious leaders closely associated with the former regime of the emperor. Two British-based agencies have managed to confine their assistance to these conservative groups. The history of refugees in the area is a long one.

Some agencies take pride that their political neutrality is demonstrated by the fact that they are able to work on *both* sides of a border. In truth, within such agencies there are very hot debates as to whether it is right to give legitimacy to whichever regime is thought to be the more oppressive.

There was a sharp divergence of views between agencies over the repatriation programme for refugees from Djibouti back to Ethiopia. (Harrell-Bond 1985.) More recently, some international agencies have come in for attack from others for assisting those who have been relocated from the drought and war-stricken Tigréy to Asosa in the south of Ethiopia. The numbers who have escaped into the Sudan support the allegation that the resettlement is not altogether voluntary.

The push/pull factor

Underlying all such explicit and implicit assumptions concerning the role of humanitarian agencies in assistance programmes for refugees in Africa is the fundamental belief that material aid in and of itself has the power to move populations. Aid, it is believed, can attract people from point a to point b and back again to point a. (Sadruddin Aga Khan 1981.) Humanitarians thus face a dilemma. To prevent mass starvation, aid is obviously needed. Yet to provide assistance risks the danger that yet more people will be attracted across borders. A delicate balance must be struck. Aid should thus be evenly distributed on a per capita basis and assistance should not be so generous that refugees seem better off than their hosts. In practice, the measure of this level seems to be that of the very poorest members of the host society. Too much assistance - and refugees will be encouraged to settle down in the host country. Too little assistance - and the humanitarian community gets a bad name. When repatriation is deemed to be in the political interest of either the country of origin, the host, or the donor governments (who wish to decrease or terminate financial obligations), aid is gradually reduced or cut off and inducements are handed out on the other side of the border. On arrival on 15 July 1984 in Arua, some returnees were issued with a blanket, a panga, a plastic bucket, a basin and a mug. In Djibouti, although refugees were also given 'economic incentives' to return, very few were willing to move. One agency worker thought that the reluctance of so many to repatriate may have been because 'those who returned to Ethiopia had high expectations of the services that would be provided for them ... any resulting feeling of disappointment could be filtering back to those still remaining in Djibouti'. (Lock 1984.)

The control of this powerful tool of manipulation has been delegated by donor governments to humanitarian agencies. The questions asked by agencies are: how much, what kind of aid, where, who, and when. What is never questioned is *who* should make these decisions. The result of the failure to ask this question leads to misallocation of scarce resources, misapplication of aid. If aid were to come from inside the host country, or if management responsibilities were shared with hosts and refugees, the monopoly held by outsiders would be broken.

The power struggle between those who give aid and those who receive it is not unlike that portrayed in the book, *One Flew Over the Cuckoo's Nest*. (Kesey 1973.) Sheldon Gellar describes this as the 'Ratched-McMurphy model'; with agencies which control development funds taking Nurse Ratched's role.

Nurse Ratched, who runs a ward in a mental hospital with an iron hand ... has the right to define the inmates' problems, and to assign prescriptions to resolve them. Thus she defines sanity ... [and] insanity ... and tells the inmates what they have to do to overcome their unfortunate state. She has the resources and power to coax and coerce her charges to accept her recommendations and methods ... Nurse Ratched sets the agenda, controls the discussion, and resists any questioning of her approach. (Gellar 1983.)

Those who talk back, like the martyr McMurphy, are likely to incur the wrath of Nurse Ratched, who feels obliged to domesticate or destroy him in order to re-establish her unquestioned authority and regain control of the ward.

Standing as they do at this epicentre of political and economic power, like Nurse Ratched, the daily experiences of agency personnel in the field continually confirm and reinforce their views, of themselves, of the helplessness of refugees, of the incapacity of local institutions and officials, and of the function of the distribution of aid.

Their isolation and alienation from the local reality shields them from evidence which would contradict their assumptions. (Chambers 1983.) If it is difficult to lure Welsh coalminers with economic incentives to leave their villages for employment in other parts of Britain, how much less likely is it that the meagre rations of World Food Programme, plastic dinnerware, a hoe and a panga[11] would have caused hundreds and thousands of Africans to flee their ancestral homelands and to seek refuge in the Sudan.[12] Like so many other assumptions which remain unexamined, the assumption that refugees are in some sense created by the bounty of aid programmes proves to be an illusion. Taken alone, any one of the assumptions that I have mentioned may not be particularly serious. But taken together, they add up to a view of the refugee world which is distorted.

What we are discussing are assumptions which are never (or rarely) explicitly articulated, but which may be seen to be parts of a collective view of refugees and the role of humanitarian organizations in assisting them. Not every person involved in humanitarian work shares these assumptions and many will hotly deny being guilty of believing in any of which have been described. The problem is that *all* outsiders are part of a society which believes that ours is the most highly evolved, that our values are superior, and that our technical knowledge is the most efficient.[13] Even those who are the most liberal and open to different ways of behaving are, under the stress of a refugee situation, likely to fall back on such assumptions.

I noted earlier in the chapter, in the discussion of social engineering (page 2), that the failures of the settlement policy are evident and are widely known, but the cause of the failure is considered to lie with the refugees themselves. However my early experiences in the field forced me to look elsewhere for the cause of failure.

One reason why it is so difficult for policy makers to see that the problem may lie elsewhere than with the refugees, is that their assumptions about the nature of the people and the dynamics of the society in which they are working are quite wrong. One is always limited in what one can see by one's beliefs. Since I am arguing that the participation approach is the best way of learning, it is important to consider the methods I used in more detail.

[11] A panga or machete is a broad heavy knife used in agriculture.

[12] Representatives of the Relief Society of Tigréy told me that during the recent exodus from the famine, many Tigréyans had to be persuaded to go to the Sudan.

[13] I recently discussed the problems of our implicit racist values with a group of university students about to embark on voluntary humanitarian work in the (so-called) third world. I was arguing in favour of allowing people to set their own priorities and against field-workers deciding in advance what is best for those they assist. 'But,' one young woman interjected, 'even when you give a bicycle to a child, you first teach him how to use it.' Everyone, including the young woman, sat in silence as I quietly reminded them we were not talking about children.

Methods of this research

Appendix II contains a description of how the study was presented to the refugees, their responses to the research, and the questionnaires used. Other details of methods applied and problems encountered are described at relevant points throughout the book. Briefly, the research was participatory, action-oriented, and consultative. It went beyond participant observation or applied research, where typically the researcher analyses a current programme and advises the planners. Instead, the study involved members of the community concerned in determining the type of data needed and how it could be obtained. I employed a team of researchers and together we were consciously acting as agents of social change by reporting our findings to the refugees and discussing the implications with them. The report relies heavily on case material and individual statements which illustrate general problems.

Refugees were encouraged to help to assess the assistance programme (and themselves) in a number of ways. For example, early in the study I wrote and circulated an essay on some of the current explanations of why programmes fail to bring refugees to a level of economic independence. I asked refugees to reply to these 'charges'. I sponsored an essay contest with some suggested titles aimed at stimulating more reflection on these issues. In each settlement, after concluding the survey, my team and I had a discussion with refugees about what we had learned. The approach was to drop pretences and recognize that *all* research is influenced by personal values, and to attempt to make these explicit at every step, including project formulation, data collection, and the interpretation of results. (Oakley 1981; Laslett and Rapoport 1975.)

The advantage of the participatory method of research is the range of experiences it affords of the dynamic of relationships and interconnections between locals and outsiders. Because of the extreme shortage of staff in Yei in 1982, I was asked to assist the UNHCR programme officer in a wide range of activities. These included helping to select sites for settlements. This task put me in contact with local hosts who sometimes welcomed the refugees, and sometimes expressed resentment towards them. I conducted a census of one settlement for UNHCR and was responsible at times for distributing food. This, and the many other meetings in settlements which I attended (alone or with the programme officer), exposed me to the refugees' perceptions of their experience of asylum, their attitudes towards each other, the locals, and towards the aid programme. For example, I watched a dramatic reversal in the attitudes of refugees when they were moved to a settlement from a self-settled area. I had met them earlier when they depended entirely on themselves, and was able to observe at first hand the behaviour change from independence to dependency.

Living in one settlement in 1982 I was able to get a glimpse of relationships between refugees and the NGOs. Refugees had been told to organize co-operatives which would then be supplied with inputs for income-generation. It was not enough to organize the people who had particular skills; refugees were required to design a project which demonstrated its economic viability. A group of tailors and I tried (unsuccessfully) to assess the market for clothing among the settlers (most of whom had no money), the capital costs, the running costs (labour, raw materials, and transport), and to predict the profit margin, in order to satisfy the NGO of their 'worthiness' for investment.

It was while living in this settlement that I first discovered that some refugees believed that I was a spy. The Ugandan refugees were always suspicious of new faces, believing (probably correctly at times) that the Ugandan government regularly sent spies among them. Prior to my arrival in the Sudan, a Swedish nurse, employed by the Sudan Council of Churches (SCC), had visited opposition forces at Midigo, inside Uganda. The SCC dismissed her upon her return to Juba, and she left the country. When, coincidentally, shortly after her visit, the Uganda National Liberation Army (UNLA) overran the guerrilla base, some refugees were convinced she had passed information to the UNLA, thus accounting for the attack and for suffering the failure of her 'promise' to get medicines to the thousands of civilians who were trapped in this area. Throughout my research, I frequently met refugees who were present at the meeting at Midigo, Uganda, and who were convinced I was the nurse they had met there. The fear that the research was a guise to supply the 'Obote' government with information, always had to be faced in the settlements, but in the self-settled areas suspicions were even greater. Members of the team of assistants were similarly distrusted. After the research was over, the suspicions of some were exacerbated by the false reports of Sudanese, formerly part of the 'Amin' regime, who were drivers for the UNHCR repatriation mission in late September. An economist on my team, a Rwandese, was said to have been seen in a military uniform at a roadblock in Uganda. In fact, he was in my company in Juba at the time.

The UNHCR compound was always filled with people with individual problems. I interviewed them for the programme officer and this led me to appreciate the fallacy of the policy of equity. Not all refugees have the same needs. There was no budget for these individual cases and over the weeks I found I had given out fantastic amounts of my own money; eventually I had to adopt the policy of not carrying any money when dealing with such cases. For example, one day a refugee hobbled to the office and lay on a hard bench outside the door, groaning in agony. One hand clutched his belly, the other held out a note from the hospital doctor which informed the office that the patient required emergency surgery for a hernia, but there was no fuel to sterilize the instruments. Could the UNHCR kindly supply the refugee with money to go to the market to buy charcoal and kerosene? Having no relatives around, presumably the refugee was expected to have staggered to the market and then back to the hospital before he collapsed on the table for his surgery. I paid and the Sudanese project manager, present with a vehicle, transported him. The man survived, but again had to return to ask me for money for the special diet the doctor prescribed.

In another instance I arranged for the burial of a child who died outside the office. This threw me into contact with the local Protestant clergyman who, early in the morning, still in his pyjamas, responded to my appeal to organize the digging of the grave without cost. (The UNHCR had apparently no budget to cover such expenditures.) Refugees in the hospital were dependent on relatives to feed them. Not only were there no facilities for families to live at the hospital, but food rations were only distributed in the settlements. I met with the Catholic priests who agreed to distribute food to refugees stranded in Yei. When violence broke out among refugees, twice in 1982 involving murders, I travelled with the commissioner of the police who, having no fuel, was dependent on an UNHCR vehicle to move to the scene of the crime.

In order to be able to estimate the numbers of refugees likely to enter Sudan and needing assistance, I spent time along the border interviewing refugees, Sudanese soldiers and, at times, those who were on leave from fighting against government forces inside Uganda. Opposition fighters were based inside Uganda, but many had their families either self-settled or in the assisted settlements. In 1982 they followed a rota system which allowed men to come into the Sudan to cultivate for a few weeks. From them I was introduced to the complexities of the Ugandan civil war and was led to explore the various factions within the refugee community. Later, most of them abandoned the battle, to live as refugees themselves.

Visits to Kenya and these walks along the border which separated the Sudan, Zaire, Uganda, alerted me to the important commercial links between the three neighbouring states. Coffee originating in Uganda was brought into Sudan via a private road built by a Zairois businessman which passed through the Kaya military base. The advantage to traders was the lower amounts of 'duty' collected by the military compared to those charged by the official customs post at Baze, a few miles north.

At the UNHCR office there was a dearth of information at all levels and collecting it for the programme officer fitted my research requirements as well. For example, when refugees began hurling accusations of sorcery at one another accompanied by violence and killings, it was necessary to find out the Sudanese legislation concerning this matter.

In 1983, I accompanied a repatriation mission into Arua, Uganda, and was able to investigate the conditions of Ugandans in rural areas near this city. There it was also possible to interview individuals who had repatriated on foot, without the assistance of UNHCR, and to seek their opinion on the wisdom of a general return of refugees to Uganda.

I attended meetings that UNHCR organized to co-ordinate the aid programme and I was able to observe what Chambers (1983:29) has described as the 'Gulfs of incomprehension, even hostility and dislike, [which] exist between disciplines, professions and departments, and between headquarters and the field.' I observed at first hand what he has also noted, that such attitudes separate foreigners and nationals, 'with their distinct life style, access and resources'. And I *experienced* the results of the 'less clear-cut but more general and enduring cleavage. This is the divide among rural development outsiders, between those who analyse and those who act, between academics and practitioners' which Chambers (1983:29) also pointed out.

The research had adopted a participatory model which aimed to encompass all the actors who were part of the assistance programme - at the official level where UNHCR, NGOs, and Sudan officials interacted and at the grassroots level where religious, ethnic and social groups interacted - and to understand the interactions and interconnections between the various groups. But as the research progressed, an important gap in the range of participants became apparent - local Sudanese had not been included from the outset. When I recognized this problem, I began inviting local chiefs and their people to meet refugees and to discuss their common problems, but it was too late to apply this generally. An impediment to involving Sudanese in such discussions, which had developed by 1983, was a growing hostility among local people towards refugees in settlements. Refugees were seen to be recipients of international aid in which local people had no share. This hostility manifested itself in an increase in security problems for refugees, and I regret that I did not use my research as a possible means of encouraging greater dialogue between refugees and their hosts. The question of tensions between hosts and refugees, and between outsiders and their hosts at all levels, will be taken up at several points throughout this book. It is fundamental to the recommendation that assistance to refugee-affected areas should be determined on the basis of demographic changes and perceived needs, rather than focusing on one group within a community which is itself already impoverished. To continue this kind of selective approach to aiding the poor only creates ill-feelings. As one Sudanese official put it, 'Everything UNHCR does for refugees has the effect of putting us against each other.' So closely was I identified with the aid programme that I, too, was accused - at least by two Sudanese - of 'causing trouble between refugees and the locals.'

Recognizing the acute need for some statistical data to evaluate the programme, when I returned in 1983 I employed a team of assistants. Their involvement in the research extended the participatory method of data collection; through them I was able to glimpse yet another dimension of refugee relationships at both official and grassroots levels.

Learning from the poor

Anthropology has been under-valued and under-utilized. The power of its methods to produce data to illuminate contemporary issues, however, speaks for itself. As Robert Chambers observed: 'We have moved a long way in the research approach from participant observation to participant organization. Purists may throw up their hands in horror and point to the danger of distortion and propaganda. But in the next decade those outsiders who have the courage and vision for such reversals, and who communicate their experience widely to others, will be at one cutting edge of rural research' (1983:73.)

The problem is *how* to communicate what I learned and how to represent fairly so many perspectives. In a situation which involved so many conflicting parties and interests I risk offending the feelings of *many* individuals who saw themselves as doing good. I have great sympathy for them because, as I reveal in Chapter Two, I also thought along the same lines. But the stakes are too high: the other half *is dying*. Over the next two decades greater amounts of assistance than ever before are going to be required from the rich countries to help the poor in Africa. More and more humanitarian aid workers are going to be propelled into the field to help the victims of natural and man-made disasters. In the interests of those upon whom this aid will either be imposed or bestowed, my reporting must be honest; after all my greatest accountability must be to them. If refugees are not to be placed in double jeopardy, if they are not to become victims of aid as well as victims of disasters, our moral complacency must be punctured. None of them can afford the luxury of our vain posturing. At the same time, and however serious were my efforts to explore a social process from the insiders' point of view, I was always a spectator and as such I was limited by my own categories of thought in what I could see. The picture can never be totally complete. I was, and I remain, an outsider. Chambers also reminds us all that there is 'no complete escape from the way outsiders project their ideologies and values into analysis and prescriptions, but he recommends two antidotes.

... first, repeatedly to enquire and reflect upon what poor people themselves want; and second, to return again and again to examples of the unacceptable, and to analyse these, rather than theoretical abstractions. A continuous enterprise of seeking to learn from the rural poor and of exercising imagination in seeing what to do is one way of setting directions and correcting course. Without this, outsiders' interventions are all too easily propelled by paternalism in directions which leave people worse off ... than they were before (Chambers 1983:146.)

Whether or not in the long run, the assistance programme in Yei River District has left people worse off or not is impossible to judge, but no-one could argue that it was not paternalistic.

It must be noted that the UNHCR *Handbook* (1982-3) argues for an awareness of the need to involve and consult refugees in planning, and against a rigid policy of assistance. It recommends sensitivity to the traditions, customs, and even to the tastes of the refugees. It sets standards for the quality and delivery of food and medical services which cannot be faulted. Why were these standards not upheld?

Nearly everyone involved in refugee assistance is too painfully aware of its shortcomings: aid is always too late, it is always insufficient to meet the need, and over and over the same mistakes are made. Yet programmes continue to be mounted which are based on the assumptions that led to failure in the past. These are that aid must come from outside, and that outsiders must manage it; that host governments lack organizational capacity, and refugees are too helpless to take responsibility for themselves. Why do these assumptions persist despite all the contrary evidence?

It should be recalled that refugees are assisted by people who regard their task first and foremost as humanitarian. Humanitarian assistance is governed by compassion and compassion has its own mode of reasoning. It is the confusion between feeling and thought which causes distortions. Technical assistance which is the aim of development programmes can be evaluated, but compassion is a moral virtue which cannot be measured. It is the moral loading of humanitarian assistance which denies the need for review and which prevents scrutiny. It is not simply that compassion overshadows logic and fact, although it often appears to do so, but rather that the assumptions that lie behind compassion are often based upon false premises. Western notions of compassion tend to be inherently ethnocentric, paternalistic, and non-professional. Many humanitarian aid programmes fail for precisely these reasons; because the logic of compassion is believed to be morally right, it is the *reality* which must be wrong and which must be bent to conform to a compassionate template. Discussion of aid programmes conducted under the banner of humanitarianism concentrates therefore not on reasons for failures, but on competing claims to moral rectitude. The struggle for moral supremacy can be fierce indeed.

Given the unspoken view of their mission, humanitarians ask individuals and governments, out of charity, to give funds to allow them to bind up wounds, comfort the weak, save lives. Compassion expects everyone to agree on the method. Since they are guided by a moral virtue, compassion, any obstacle in the path of carrying out humanitarian objectives must be *immoral*. And, since the objective is to do good, it is inconceivable that recipients will fail to be grateful.[14]

[14] At the Oxford symposium participants were served a 'simulated' lunch. That is, they were given the opportunity to taste the ingredients in the World Food Programme's food basket for refugees - beans, rice, oil, and milk. While eating this food, one refugee explained to his companion at the table that they were eating not one meal, but a whole day's ration at one time and, moreover, as he noted, refugees in settlements seldom see all four items at any one time. The response? 'If you refugees do not appreciate what we are doing for you, we should quit.'

Outsiders, as Chambers has observed, need imagination to envisage the real and ramifying effects of their actions, they need to think about the causal chain which flows from them. He notes that social science researchers could help by tracing through 'such centre-outwards linkages in the human detail of case studies'. (1983:197). I believe, with Chambers (1983), that the most valid method of presenting such research is through the case study method. This book aims to provide at least a partial description of the personal details of the links in the process of imposing aid. Scholars who read through the following account of the emergency assistance programme for refugees in southern Sudan will see the relevance of theories which have been developed in several related fields. This is particularly the case for studies of involuntary migration and my intellectual debt to a great number of studies which are not cited in this descriptive account will be obvious. Some of these are discussed in Hansen and Oliver-Smith (1982). There is also a body of literature on resettlement schemes resulting from the construction of dams, following natural disasters, and those imposed as part of agricultural schemes. The basic lesson which emerges from all these scholarly studies is that while human societies everywhere are able to adapt, and that migration and resettlement may be one method, the *imposition* of these solutions, denying as it does fundamental human rights, create more problems than they solve.

PART 1

1
Patterns of flight

Introduction

While the problems of Uganda have their roots deep in history, the immediate cause of the influx of refugees into the Sudan and other surrounding countries was the overthrow of the government of Idi Amin in 1979. Amin had himself taken power from President Obote through a military *coup* in 1971. Throughout the Amin period Obote lived in exile in Tanzania. President Nyerere had allowed his country to be the centre of efforts to organize opposition groups.

In retaliation for this provocation, Amin ordered his troops to undertake what has been described by the officer responsible for co-ordinating it from Kampala as 'Amin's war of adventure'. Ugandan forces entered Tanzania. This attack was repelled, but only after loss of life and property. It gave a long awaited opportunity. In 1979 Nyerere directed the invasion of Uganda by the Tanzania Peoples' Defense Force (TPDF) and the Ugandan National Liberation Front. The ultimate objective was the overthrow of Amin's regime and the restoration of the legal government of Milton Obote. Nyerere is against the military in politics: that was his justification. Plans for a provisional government made in exile put Yusuf Lule as President. His rule lasted only 68 days. Godfrey Binaisa took up the office, but the military intervened just a few months before the elections in December 1980.

The *wakombozi*, the local term for the Tanzanian soldiers, occupied the country up to the period just before the elections, replaced by the Ugandan National Liberation Army (UNLA).

The newly-formed UNLA excluded all former members of the Ugandan military, even those who had been recruited and trained under British rule. Former Ugandan soldiers were disarmed, issued with surrender certificates and advised to go back to farming. Although comprising members of most ethnic groups, the UNLA is dominated by the Acholi and Lango, groups which suffered most under Amin and which had demonstrated an abiding loyalty to Obote. Following the withdrawal of the TPDF, a war of revenge was undertaken by the UNLA, particularly affecting the north-west Nile and Madi districts, the area and people most closely associated with the government of Idi Amin. In response, opposition groups became active in various parts of the country. Since 1981 the history of Uganda has been one of continual bloodshed and violence. Although organized opposition has been reduced in terms of the numbers of active groups, fighting still continued in different parts of the country. 1983-4 saw some disintegration of Obote's support. There were refugees from most parts of Uganda living in all the neighbouring countries and even further afield. The numbers of refugees from Amin's regime were but a handful by comparison. Whereas formerly there were less than 2000 registered refugees in Sudan, in 1984 there were at least 300,000.

The first influx

Although most living in exile in Yei River District reported that they were forced out of their homes in 1979, the majority moved only short distances and returned home once the government had fallen. Among those who came with the intention of remaining, few accepted assistance.

That Sudan, Zaire, and Kenya would receive refugees from Uganda was highly predictable long before anyone crossed borders in mid-1979. Tanzania had made no secret of the fact that it intended to 'liberate' Uganda by overthrowing the Amin regime. Given the degree of international support for this action, success seemed probable. Within Uganda there was also support for the liberation forces, and many were involved in planning the military strategy for the overthrow of Amin. Nevertheless, it took roughly seven months for the Tanzanians to reach Kampala. The President, Idi Amin, did not leave the capital until 11 April, and on 13 April 1979 he was still broadcasting from Soroti.

Despite all the rumours that the liberation army intended to eliminate all the Madi, Alur, Lugbara, and Kakwa because of the association of their home area (the West Nile) with Amin, most Ugandans attempted to remain within the country. The exodus from Uganda into the Sudan and Zaire in 1979 was highly selective, consisting mainly of people who had particular reasons for believing that their lives were in danger.

Upon news of the invasion, such people began leaving Uganda. Of those who came to the Sudan, some took up residence along the border, negotiating access to land with local chiefs. Others found accommodation (or built it) in the border towns of Kaya and Baze, customs posts on the Uganda and Zaire borders. Many settled down in Yei and Juba, others managed to make their way to Khartoum or left the country.

They came in private cars, lorries, buses, and some even escaped by helicopter. They moved with tractors, cattle, and those who had the means made several trips back and forth to bring their property out of Uganda. Others arrived without possessions or transport. The Sudan authorities took the first initiative by arranging provisional accommodation for them in classrooms, free during the school holidays. People were living in temporary shelter in Kaya, Yei, Kajo-Kaji, and Juba. Food was provided by local authorities from their limited resources and by the National Relief Committee. According to the UNHCR office records in Juba, by the end of

May 1979, the numbers of refugees 'having crossed the border and in need of help was estimated to range between 20,000 and 25,000 and more keep pouring in'. (Greenfield 1979; 1979a). But it was not until early June that appeals for external assistance were finally forwarded from Juba to the UNHCR office in Khartoum. The Sudan Council of Churches (SCC), Juba, later reported that 40,000 people entered the Sudan in 1979.[1]

The Kakwa

Language and occupational background influenced the decisions that the different groups of refugees took in their struggle to survive in exile. The community which fled first, and which was perhaps most able to obtain access to farmland and to integrate in the Sudan, was the Kakwa. Their close identification with Idi Amin, a Kakwa-speaker (said to have been born in Zaire), may be the reason that more Kakwa came in 1979 than in any subsequent year (42 per cent of the self-settled Kakwa refugee households interviewed). Their language is understood by Kakwa-speakers in the Sudan as well as in Zaire. The attitude of local officials may be one measure of their successful integration. When I came to conduct interviews in two areas where the Kakwa refugees had settled, local police - fearing that UNHCR, with whom I was identified, would encourage their removal from the area - denied any refugees were living there. In one of these areas, where now every inch of land was farmed, refugees found only six Sudanese households when they arrived in 1979. Among those Kakwa interviewed in self-settled areas, just over half reported having formerly been dependent on agriculture in Uganda. Their acceptance by the local Kakwa community is demonstrated by the fact that only 1.9 per cent of the settlement population is Kakwa, compared with 28 per cent of the self-settled households interviewed. It is interesting, moreover, to examine the occupational background of those Kakwa who *did* opt for the settlement: only 16.4 per cent had farmed for their living in Uganda, 58.7 per cent were dependents with no means of earning an income, and 11.9 per cent were students whose studies were interrupted during the war. Although only one member of each household was interviewed among the self-settled, in 1983, only 5.8 per cent of those interviewed had been students just prior to 1979 and 8.9 per cent were dependents. The Kakwa resistance against moving to settlements is demonstrated by the fact

---

[1] As this study is based on data collected in Yei River District which lies on the west bank of the Nile in Eastern Equatoria, it does not include those who settled on the east bank or went directly to Juba or elsewhere. Refugees settled on the east bank from 1979 with the major influx in 1980-1. By 1983 there were 70,000 refugees there living in assisted settlements and agency workers have the impression that most of these are Madi. Those who are familiar with the area believe there are as many or more refugees living outside settlements, a pattern similar to that found in Yei River District.

that among the people interviewed, only 6 had registered in a settlement in 1980, 3 in 1981, 73 in 1982 and 119 in 1983.

The Nubi

Another group of refugees who fled Uganda in the early period of the influx into the Sudan are the so-called Nubi people. Their association with Amin may account for their early departure from Uganda. Over half the Nubi community included in this research had entered the Sudan in 1979. By the end of 1980, 93.2 per cent of those Nubi living in assisted settlements were already living in exile. (Among the self-settled Nubi households interviewed, 81.8 per cent also reported that they had crossed the border within this period.)

The Nubi are said to be descendants of Emin Pasha's troops and thus originally 'Sudanese'. (With the fall of Gordon in Khartoum, Emin Pasha, together with his army, was driven out of the Sudan in the 1870s.) The term Nubi has been widened to include those - mainly Lugbara - who have married a Nubi. As a community, the Nubi are Muslims (as are thousands of Lugbara). (Middleton 1965.)

Having earned their living through petty trade and hawking, many benefited from the expulsion of the Asians during Amin's rule; it is said that Amin allowed some of the Nubi simply to take over their vacated businesses. Most of these people entered the Sudan through Kaya. The Arabic dialect which they speak has a limited correspondence with the *lingua franca* ('Juba Arabic') and it facilitated their resumption of trade. Many moved away from the border to Juba or settled down in Kaya and Yei.

Late 1979 also marked the beginning of the assistance programme. The first agricultural settlement, Tore (now called 'Old Tore' because of the establishment of another settlement directly adjacent), was opened and government officials transported these people from Kaya to Yei and then the long distance to Tore. Refugees report they had no choice but to join the lorries. Given the economic background of the Nubi, the unsuitability of this approach to their assistance could have been foreseen.

By 1983 Nubis made up only one per cent of all the settlement population and appeared in the sample of interviews in only four settlements. Altogether 103 Nubis were interviewed and 60 of these were still living in Old Tore. Only 20 of these had been gainfully employed in Uganda; the remainder were students or other dependents, with a high proportion of elderly widows. Of those who had worked in Uganda, only six were men, and only one of these had been a farmer. The self-settled Nubi households had similar occupational backgrounds and were unsuited to agriculture as a way of earning a living. Of those interviewed only eight of the adults had any previous experience in agriculture or fishing.

The Nubi response to the settlement programme demonstrates the aptness of a comment made by one refugee from Limbe settlement: 'To be a refugee, you have to learn to lie.' By 1982, the population of Tore had become notorious for its ability to subvert relief aid. Without adequate staff to monitor the programme, the settlement committee was providing the UNHCR office with the 'statistics'. Relief food was being supplied for a population of over 2,000, while the actual numbers were certainly less than half. With the surplus, some of the settlers were reconstructing their lives around their normal occupation of petty trade and hawking. Scarcely any of the first settlers had planted a seed since their arrival. In 1982 it was concluded that people in Old Tore had been there long enough to have reached self-sufficiency; food rations were cut drastically. By 1983 the residents were receiving *no* rations. Only 17 of those interviewed, or 14.5 per cent of the population of Old Tore, had been there from 1979. All the others, transported and settled at such enormous cost, had simply disappeared. Most of those who remained behind were the very elderly, the sick and the disabled, or the very young. These are the particularly vulnerable categories of people about which I shall have much more to say later. Among the original settlers was an elderly man, who, being completely alone and unable to fend for himself, was forced to beg each day's meal from either the local Sudanese or from settlers who could afford to share some food with him.

The military

Members of the Uganda military also entered with the first influx in 1979. Most officers who entered the Sudan (many also went to Zaire) took up residence in Juba. The formation of the Uganda National Rescue Front in 1979, under the temporary leadership of Moses Ali, was conducted with at least the informal permission of the Juba government and the security forces. Those who accepted assistance at that time are likely to have concealed their identity, as did most in the course of this research. Less than one per cent of the sample of assisted refugees indicated that the military was their former occupation, and among the self-settled none were so identified. The tendency was for former Ugandan soldiers to claim to have been 'only cultivators' - which accounts for the relatively literate population of farmers. The overall average number of years of schooling reported by those giving farming as their occupation in Uganda was 1.52 years. But, among the men in this group, 20.2 per cent reported having spent three or more years in school. Moreover, 8.6 per cent of those with more than ten years in school said they were 'only cultivators' in Uganda.

The Sudan, particularly the south, lacks technically trained personnel in almost all fields and the arrival of qualified Ugandans was rightly seen by the Sudanese authorities as an opportunity for the southern economy. A considerable number of educated Ugandans got employment. While the Sudan Asylum Act 1974 allows for the employment of refugees who have acquired a work permit, there was general ignorance among the locals and the agencies of the existence of this legislation. Instead, most refugees who have jobs acquired their Sudanese nationality certificates by irregular means. Early on, some officials in Juba were encouraging this absorption of refugees into the workforce. Later - as tensions between locals and Ugandans increased - refugees were forced to hide their real identity to get employment. Employed Ugandans began to fear that their lack of knowledge of the Arabic *lingua franca* might be discovered. Most Ugandans who obtained employment other than that provided by agencies had to lie about their nationality. This had serious repercussions on their relationships with their compatriots. In some cases when Ugandans lost their jobs, it was necessary to resume 'refugee' identity to obtain assistance or employment with agencies. When copies of the law were finally distributed in Yei River District, tensions between the communities were too high to implement it. For example, most of the professional staff of the National Tobacco Company (NTC) were 'ex-Ugandans', but in 1983 when NTC attempted to employ a Ugandan mechanic, the Sudanese employees threatened to go on strike.

Sudanese returnees

The first group entering the Sudan in 1979 also included Sudanese who had sought refuge in Uganda during the Sudan's civil war, and who had not returned home after 1972. By 1981 the Sudan government estimated that it had received some 60,000 of its nationals from Uganda. According to their local connections, occupational background, and wealth, they settled down in various parts of the region. For example, a few kilometres outside of Kajo-Kaji, towards the Uganda border, is a market area where all the shops are owned by newly-returned Sudanese. At least a few returnees were peasant farmers and those interviewed near Panyume claimed to have returned to family land. Others returned with sufficient funds to establish larger businesses; the hotel in Yei was built by a man who returned in 1979. Up until 1983 he owned the only means of public transport between Yei and Juba, using buses formerly owned by private bus companies in Uganda. Later another bus company operated in the district, owned by a refugee who escaped in 1982 from Mbale, Uganda. Formerly he operated within Uganda and between Kampala and Nairobi. He managed to move with his buses into the Sudan.

Within Equatoria the return of many Sudanese professionals had an important impact upon Sudan's political developments. They supported Nemeiry's 1983 abrogation of the 1972 Addis agreement which dissolved the southern regional government and instituted a policy of decentralization. The change allowed some of them to take up vacancies in the civil service on the departure of those who were forced to return to their own home areas. Their influence accounts in part for the lack of enthusiasm in Equatoria in 1983-5 for joining the rebellion against the Khartoum government. (Malwal 1985.)

Although it is generally assumed that those Sudanese who returned in 1979 and after, did so with sufficient education or capital to re-establish themselves, this was not always the case. At the beginning, when there was no assistance programme, both Sudanese and Ugandans relied mainly on their own resources to survive. Later however, as the trickle of Sudanese continued, the programme discriminated in favour of Ugandans, or more accurately - non-Sudanese. In 1982 a wave of refugees included a Sudanese woman whose Ugandan husband had just been killed. She and her children were in a miserable condition, but when asked for blankets for this family, UNHCR said she did not qualify even for such limited assistance - the family was a Sudanese problem!

Similarly, a Sudanese returnee with his Kenyan wife and ten children lived in absolute poverty in Yei from 1979. Even after he died in 1982, there was considerable confusion as to whether his widow could be assisted through the refugee aid programme. When she had first presented herself to the UNHCR office in Yei for help, she claimed that her husband had died one year previously and that she was alone with ten children. Was she a refugee? The UNHCR office could not decide. Anyway, there was no budget for 'urban refugees' as the programme was restricted to helping refugees who agreed to go to settlements. She would not agree to go to a settlement because it meant withdrawing her children from school in Yei. She was employed as a domestic servant. Five days later she came to work totally distraught, saying that her child had died. A UNHCR consultant drove her home to find her *husband* lying dead on the floor of the house, his body not yet cold.

After his burial (paid for by personal contributions of the staff) had been arranged, one suggestion was that the only solution was to contact the Kenyan embassy in Khartoum, asking them to assume responsibility. But even if this had been done, the husband's Sudanese family would not have agreed to parting with their deceased relative's children. Later the woman lost her job because of alleged theft.

Among the returnees were a number of the more notorious henchmen of Idi Amin, Sudanese who had been specially recruited to serve the regime. One of the less well-known facts about the Amin regime is the role played by foreigners from Kenya, Zaire, and the Sudan in carrying out some of the worst atrocities. Lacking any personal links with the local people which might have restrained them from excessive violence, they were ideally suited to protect Amin's position. As one Ugandan explained,

Amin recruited people who had nothing by way of military training and he uplifted them from virtually nobody to very high ranks in the army, specifically to keep a watch on his staff college trained officers whom he feared would overthrow him, like Brigadier Taban Lopayi [a Sudanese], a former houseboy. Some of these people couldn't even hold a map the right way up.

Taban now lives near Yei. His living room is decorated with photographs which record major events in Amin's career.

Such individuals, and many other Sudanese who enjoyed the higher standard of living in Uganda, would like to return there. Some have given support to two opposition groups which were fighting against the Ugandan government troops. Such solidarity with the Ugandans who opposed Amin's overthrow (or were fighting to overthrow Obote) doubtless facilitated the reception of many who arrived in the first wave of refugees in 1979.

The problem of the mixed loyalties of the returnees and their association with Ugandans directly linked with Amin is highly complicated. For example, the connection with the Sudanese security and other top government officials in the Sudan of one notorious figure, Juma Oris, facilitated the formation in 1979 of the Uganda National Rescue Front. This ex-minister in Amin's government grew up in Nimule, the Sudanese border town on the east bank of the Nile. He had built a house in Juba which he rented to the British Council representative. When in 1981 the refugees wanted to form a humanitarian group he introduced them to the Minister of Interior in Khartoum. Later, when he discovered they planned to exclude all the ex-military, particularly anyone associated with Amin, he allegedly persuaded the Security to arrest John Yebuga, one of the leaders. Unaware of Oris's background (he was said to be wanted to answer a charge of murder in Uganda), he gave evidence to UNHCR of Yebuga's 'political' activities. Fortunately due to Amnesty's interventions, the latter was released from prison after a year.[2]

While some of the Amin supporters brought sufficient wealth (Ugandans would describe it as 'loot') to set up businesses, others found their way into the employment of aid agencies. Some have even managed to get jobs within refugee administration, others were drivers. Ironically, mostly through ignorance, they have been legitimized by such employment; their presence was a source of confusion, and in some cases, a threat to the security of refugees. Others have been reduced to poverty. One such returnee, formerly a governor of a region, now sells *sambosa* (beans, rice or meat fried in pastry), to the UNHCR staff in Juba. This food was first introduced to Uganda by Indians.

---

[2] It was surprising that anyone would rely on Oris for confirmation that John Yebuga fell outside the ambit of their protection role because he had engaged in 'political' activities. Oris might be assumed to have had good reasons for wanting to be sure that the prisoner was not released. Oris had been recruiting Ugandan refugees on the grounds that they would be going to Saudi Arabia to train and would return to overthrow Obote. In fact, he was recruiting for the Sudan government who had agreed to send soldiers to fight in Iraq. Yebuga discovered this plot and warned refugees not to sign up. It was only after these details were published in *Africa Confidential* (2 November, 1983) and Amnesty presented the case to Nemeiry on the occasion of a visit to Washington, that Yebuga was released.

The liberation

Since most Ugandans welcomed the overthrow of Amin, they did not think of seeking asylum outside their home country. But from 1979 onwards people have found themselves forced out of their homes, buffeted about by a power struggle which had little meaning for them. They moved in response to immediate physical danger and to the need for food. These movements back and forth amidst the ferment of the anarchical power struggles of Uganda have since 1979, taken a shocking toll of human life; the consequences for Ugandan society are immeasurable.

It took nearly two months from the fall of Kampala in April 1979 for the liberation army to reach Koboko. The northern part of Uganda west of the Nile was not occupied until June. When the war began, people moved out of their compounds and into the bush. Those who were near the Zaire or Sudan border crossed it. Heads down, everybody waited.

But already any semblance of normal society had been severely disrupted by the march northwards and the subsequent occupation of the area. John Avruida describes this.

The liberators moved north to Koboko. Here they found nearly no living soul, for this was the place for more destruction. But the people were aware of this beforehand and had fled. In the course of moving to Koboko via a small county on the West Nile called Maracha, they left no hut, granary, chicken hut unburned. All food crops from the fields were either slashed or uprooted.

Once the occupying army was in control, people began moving back to their homesteads. While conditions could hardly be described as peaceful, the people had hopes that they would soon be left to resume their normal lives. Relationships with the Tanzanians are described by Ariartre Simon:

... the Tanzanian Army, who were said to have come to liberate Ugandans, made life hard for the citizens. They looted us proper. They snatched our watches, radios, television sets, bicycles, clothes, motorcars, lorries, machinery in factories ... We did not care ... after all, they would leave the country ... Good enough, they didn't kill.

But there were many cases of indiscriminate killing. Already the failure of President Lule to control the troops was taken by many west Nilers as evidence that they were to become the scapegoats for the crimes of Amin. This fear led many people to give up employment in other parts of the country and return home. As one informant explained, 'My first disturbance was from the Tanzanians in 1979. That year I was working in the Uganda Spinning Mill at Lira. From there I ran home to Moyo District. By then they didn't do anything bad to me.'

Still another reported:

I was first disturbed in 1979. We ran to Sudan but found it hard to stay because of lack of food. When I learnt that the Tanzanians were OK, I returned home with my family in November 1979. I went to Kampala to see my belongings which I left because of the war. I was working with the Ministry of Defence as a clerk. I found all my property looted. In December, I came back home.

But a war of attrition against the people of the area with which Amin was identified had already begun. Again, in Simon's words:

While the Tanzanians were busy looting, the Luo group was busy killing. ... These immoral activities became encouraged when a military spokesman ordered the disarmament of what they called 'Idi Amin's soldiers' in July 1979. Many returned their guns to the new government and went to fill in surrender forms. They expected to be returned to the army because they were trained for Uganda's national army. What happened in those days was very sad. Many soldiers who went to fill in the surrender forms at their various army headquarters in their respective districts never returned to their homes. A good many never reached the prison yards. Their whereabouts are not known up to now. All soldiers became 'Amin's soldiers'. This is ironic. It is the irony of soldiers being owned by people. The soldiers couldn't be Amin's - after all, they had served the British *and* Obote.

Although there is evidence that a good proportion of the men in uniform surrendered their weapons and received the surrender certificates, it must have been a galling experience for them to be told to 'go and dig'. Moreover, they continued to be harassed even though they held a surrender form. According to Avrudia, 'Their lives were not secure, so many fled to the Sudan or Zaire. ... Many civilians were mistaken to be soldiers and these either faced death or endless imprisonment in Luzira.' This period marked the forcible repatriation of refugees encamped inside Kenya. They included civilians as well as military and they were all returned to Uganda by the Kenyan government. 'Some of these faced death, others were miserably tortured and their whereabouts remain unknown.' Still, after Binaisa took over the presidency, there was considerable determination to resume normal life and to rebuild the country. In 1979 in the West Nile alone there had been some 8000 students enrolled in senior secondary schools or other post-primary educational institutions. One of these students who returned to his books, Joago Aligo Brani, relates his experience which reflects the general appreciation West Nilers feel towards Binaisa. During his short rule he at least voiced the need to reconcile the disparate groups in the country.

By 1979 I was in Senior Four. We were interrupted by the liberation ... on 11 April 1979 we had our first term holidays as well. It was the time when Kampala was captured by the liberators. We in the extreme north had very little to worry about. There was the rumour that the liberators were coming to kill all the Madi, Alur, Lugbara, and the Kakwa, but nothing of that happened. In order to protect or secure our lives, some - mostly Kakwas - that year took off into the surrounding countries, namely Zaire and Sudan. During Binaisa's regime things were rather cool [calm]. Trucks were moving freely. But our college (Koboko S.S.) was thoroughly looted by the natives, the Ugandan soldiers and the liberators. So during Binaisa's regime there was reconstruction at the college... After the reconstruction we, the Senior Fours ...

and the Senior Six ... were called ... for our final exams. Results were out. I was taken to Mvara Secondary School ... to study biology, chemistry, and geography.

The relative calm of the period under Binaisa began to break in April 1980, when the Tanzanian occupying forces were gradually replaced by the newly-recruited Uganda National Liberation Army (UNLA) led by officers who had defected to Tanzania and elsewhere during Amin's rule. The further deterioration of conditions was marked by the late May military takeover of Binaisa's government. People relate how they had been warned by the Tanzanians that things would not go well for them after their departure. The bitter reality was soon to become apparent. It was the disturbances of this period which most affected the Moyo districts, the Madi's homeland. Among those living in settlements, 17.8 per cent of the Madi entered the Sudan in 1979 and 56.6 per cent in 1980.

In response to the rise in the number of atrocities against civilians, resistance groups developed spontaneously in many parts of the west Nile, and these culminated in the 'invasion' of Arua by opposition forces in October 1980.

Joago reports his experience at this time:

... the guerrilla war of 7 October interrupted my education. It got me when I was still in Arua. So I had to foot from Arua to our home which is 60 miles for two days. And I arrived home at night when people had gone for sleep. Parents were very happy and excited when they saw me. They thought I was by then killed. After the guerrilla war we stayed in Uganda hiding ourselves in the bush until the time we were forced out by the threat of Obote's army. In July 1982 we then pushed into the Sudan and lost plenty of our property. I also had four orphans with whom I escaped, and they are still with me.

Following this invasion, and before the 1980 elections, between 25 October and 2 November 1980, the government organized a fact-finding tour of Nebbi, Arua and Moyo districts. At Gulu, the five-man team was informed that 'things in West Nile were very bad. Many people have left their homes... Currently there are daily ambushes between [i.e. alongside] Moyo-Yumbe-Koboko road... There is a great deal of misbehaviour by soldiers who are doing excessive looting.[3]

The indiscipline of the UNLA soldiers was exacerbated by their living conditions which were described in this report as 'appalling'. Among the atrocities which the UNLA soldiers had committed was the killing of six people at a mission at Ediofe, 'including one nun'. The general deterioration of relations between civilians and the UNLA which had occurred before the invasion are described in the report.

---

[3] This quotation and the following are taken from Report to the Military Commission by the Team on a Fact-Finding Tour of the Three War-Affected Districts of Nebbi, Arua and Moyo from the 25 October to the 22 November 1980.

The senior army officers in the District were always drunk, involved in *magendo* [smuggling], had lacked command, harassed civilians, and in one or two places, it is alleged that they murdered some people. They also associated freely with Amin's henchmen residing in Zaire and Uganda, giving chance for the men to know exactly their behaviour. In one instance, a County Chief from Koboko who came to report that Amin's men were going to invade, was arrested by Captain Olong and later this chief was killed.

The invading guerilla forces were described as having met with no resistance and having taken Arua with 'virtually nothing, apart from small firearms (pistols, hand grenades, rifles, pangas, spears, and bows and arrows)'. Their motives, according to the team, were:

1. Destabilization of the Uganda Government and disruption of the general elections.
2. Revenge for the humiliation suffered in the 1979-80 war and revenge for mistreatment of their relations by the UNLA.
3. Looting.
4. Military adventurism (craziness).

The team learned how, following the invasion, and 'out of anger', the UNLA had carried out a campaign of revenge against the people which resulted in the wholesale destruction of factories, government buildings, and missions and the burning of houses in which 'many people died'. The result: 'Now civilians run away when they see any soldier in uniform.'

Sophie Abdullah, a Ugandan nurse, living and working in Pakula settlement in the Sudan, was working in Arua hospital at that time.

The army came in very suddenly on 9 October. They began by shooting into the air and then killed a student. Almost all the girls in the hostel were raped. They pillaged and looted. I left with one bag containing a few clothes and my toothbrush. I was one of the lucky ones to manage to escape into Zaire by car. There I joined my seven brothers and my father who had fled to Zaire the previous year. At first we hid in the bush, never knowing when the army would raid. We slept under trees. I am afraid of snakes.

The official report continues: 'There is nobody to be seen along the Madi-Okollo-Arua route. There are less than 1,000 people in Arua staying at the missions... Bishop Tarantino said that he has been reliably informed that 200,000 to 300,000 people have taken refuge in Zaire.' In this section of the report a significant point is underlined: '*We were prevented from visiting Koboko and Yumbe towns. We have learnt that there are no people in these towns.*'

As the team travelled through the area, they saw one scene of horror after another. In Moyo they found that 'The soldiers had been left uncontrolled. They have killed, looted and damaged property at will. They have occupied all the government and commercial buildings in Moyo. They harass those who have taken refuge in Moyo Mission.'

Registrations for voting in the December elections were undertaken and many students living in exile had been involved in this process. Although most of the people were hiding in the bush, great effort was made to find and register them. Some registrars even crossed into Zaire to register Ugandans who had sought safety there. Alleged verbal attacks and threats against the people of the West Nile on Obote's part in his pre-election campaign, did not improve the situation . When he came to Koboko there was an attempt to kill him and he only narrowly escaped. By voting time, 12 December, the UNLA was on the rampage throughout the area, undoubtedly facilitating the 'unopposed' return of Obote's UPC candidates.

One refugee who finally registered for settlement in 1983 describes his family's experiences during that time.

When the war was at its maximum in 1980, we started running from Arua through the bush. When I came to Lodonga, we started collecting cows and goats and other small food stuff for the journey to Sudan. In Keri, two of my brothers (Safi and Kasim) were shot dead. They were assigned the duty of caring for the goats during the escape. When they got killed by the UNLA the goats got lost as well. I was in charge of the cattle. I came to Keyi and then to Cakulia. There my mother decided to go [back] to Lodonga to get cassava. She was shot dead by the UNLA at Rube, near the Kochi River. My father, Fodimola, was also a victim. My mother was called Sura. When my parents were shot, I, with my four brothers, crossed the Kaya River and came and settled in Uniga [Sudan]. We stayed there for one year. We got word that our brothers Brani and Swadiki, were shot at Lodonga Trading Centre by the UNLA.

Still living on the border inside Sudan, he explains what finally led to their decision to come to a settlement.

When our 55 cows were used for purchasing food, we had no other alternative but to come to an assisted settlement. I am fed up of packing people in one tent. I feel I am suffocating, especially when it is hot. East or west, home is better, but I am not going to Uganda if the civil war goes on. I sold our sewing machine to send Habibu to school and to give us at least a day or so to use the balance to release us from the daily casual labour. To start petty trade is difficult for I have no bike to move from place to place.[4]

After the elections, with the Uganda Peoples' Congress (UPC) declared the victor, violence escalated throughout Uganda, but especially in the north-western region. Ariatre Simon describes the attack on Augurua Market, just one of many such incidents which prompted the emergence of more organized resistance throughout the area:

This small market is located by the bank of the river Anyau in Terrego County, 18 miles from Arua town. I was an eye-witness of these happenings. At about 5:00 p.m. East African standard time, when the market was at its highest capacity with about 2000 people in the market square it was surrounded by ... Obote's wicked soldiers. All of a sudden, there was a flow of bullets over the crowd from the western side of the market. These soldiers were led by the UPC youth. What a tragedy! Women threw

[4] This is just one example of a family which came with sufficient property to maintain economic independence. Even marginal assistance might have allowed them to avoid the total economic collapse which brought them to the relief programme.

away babies they nourished, fishmongers, blacksmiths, beer-sellers and many other categories of sellers and buyers sped for their lives. Money, goods, bicycles, and the abandoned babies were left to their misery. Alas! The river had flooded - those who took the river direction jumped into the river no matter whether they knew how to swim or not. Very few of them were saved. A horrible sight it was, hundreds floating drowned. ... One brother ... was shot dead on the spot with more than one hundred of the group. Those corpses remained there, unburied, for weeks ...

Despite the wholesale slaughter of civilians by UNLA (usually in revenge after an attack by one of the bands of opposition groups who, from the time of the elections, were attempting to 'liberate' the West Nile), most civilians *still did not leave the country*. Families would move a few kilometres away from their compounds and build a shelter, only to be disturbed again and forced to rebuild. Some refugees report having built as many as eight shelters or more inside Uganda before crossing the border.

I started suffering in the year 1980 when the UNLA took over the government. I ran to Iwanga with my family. There I stayed two years. In 1982, the army reached Iwanga. That was in February 1982. They started to kill our people and collect our properties such as cattle, bicycles, clothes. ... I moved up to Lodonga which is in Aringa County. There my father was shot.

An informant living at the Koya transit centre during September 1983, Mr Alahayi Korubuga, who did not enter the Sudan until 1983, describes his movements:

In 1979 I was in Kampala and left all my property, including my own tractor. We used a taxi from Kampala to our village in Aringa. I stayed for one month at home. During the second month, the Tanzanian soldiers arrived, stationed at Midigo ... my elder brother was shot by the Kombozi [Tanzanian soldiers] who brought a truck to collect our things. Fifty cows, one landrover, one generator, and one pick-up (Peugeot) were all looted. They continued coming to our home so often. Oseni, my brother, was arrested by them. Up to now he is in Luzira prison. After one week, Ismail, a brother of mine, was shot by the Tanzanian forces in 1979. All the incidents which occurred scared us. We came to Puree, on the Uganda-Sudan border. We stayed in Puree for two years. When the UNLA came, they forced us out. Seima and Bako ... were killed in one spot at Puree in 1983. We came to Mangalotore [inside Sudan] and we stayed for two months. Problems like food, medicine and education were beyond our tolerance. In June we started for an assisted settlement.

The determination of the UNLA to avenge past sufferings for which the people of the West Nile were held responsible was made explicit through inscriptions on walls and trees; for example, 'The Lugbara killed our people, now it must be our turn to kill them.' Civilians took to sleeping away from their homesteads and returning during the morning hours to tend their farms. Markets functioned only in the morning hours.

... in the afternoon one would only meet soldiers in the streets. During this time, the safest person was a concubine, the only neighbour [friend] of the Acholi or Langi. The death toll went very high so that everyone nearly forgot Amin's lawlessness. Death statistics reminded one of Obote's [supposed] statement that Arua or West Nile shall not be spared, but must be turned into a modern national park.[5]

All vestiges of order began breaking down. As people started spending more time hiding in the bush, agriculture was neglected. With property unguarded, civilians joined the soldiers in looting. James Appe (1983) describes the situation:

The state of confusion proved to be beneficial to many people in many ways. Ben, for example, had gathered around himself a group of youths. They made it a point to eat at least three chickens every day in the dead of night. The poor birds were abandoned and the boys went and gathered these and ate them. ... Little children were now being turned into gangs of dangerous people. Some went and ambushed their own brothers en route and looted them. Human conscience was again being destroyed in them.

Amid the chaos, people were rapidly abandoning other social values, as evident in another incident this author relates. Hiding in the bush with his family, he walked, 'just a few smokes away', to visit his friend Ben, who had just erected a rough shelter for himself and his mother. When Appe arrived, Ben was eating a piece of pumpkin that his mother had rescued from their homestead some distance away. They talked about where next they would hide.

... Ben's mother entered the small cleared place where we sat. She greeted me, but her voice sounded distant. She quickly covered up the cooked pumpkin in the cooking pot, grunted and sat down, looking away from us. I knew her thoughts and I was angry. I looked at Ben. He looked down, and I knew he was angry or ashamed at his mother's action. ... Here was Ben's mother, a woman who could call, and who indeed did call me her 'son' on many occasions, suddenly transformed into something quite different. Ben's mother was kind and loving. She had always asked me to stay for every meal I found her preparing. But now she had to cover up the cooked pumpkin for the same person she had so adored. I did not blame her. The forces of nature and the activities of men could thus change charity into hatred and love into war. ... Ben's mother had previously had commitment to a larger community and lived and shared things with them. Now, when her life was threatened, she had as her community only herself and Ben, her son. Next, when we have to run and hide, when gunshots scatter us, she will only have herself to think about - not even Ben. (ibid.)

Early 1981 had seen the spontaneous emergence of fighting all over the area. Peasants joined ex-soldiers attempting to protect people and property from the undisciplined guns of the UNLA and others. Initially impressive successes were scored against the government troops in many parts of the West Nile. Although there was no overall organization to this fighting,

[5] Every Ugandan refugee believes Obote uttered this threat while still in exile in Tanzania. Ironically, the Ugandan government in its submissions presented for funds to the ICARA II conference in Geneva, July, 1984, included a comment to the effect that now that peace had returned to Uganda, the northwest Nile was ripe for tourism.

throughout most of 1981 the region was more or less under local control. A skeletal civilian administrative structure began functioning and some military assistance was coming from outside the country.

While indiscipline characterized the conduct of almost all who carried a gun, the anti-government fighters were, on the whole, better trained than Obote's troops. Many of the anti-government troops were career soldiers whose recruitment pre-dated Amin's rise to power, and they were skilled guerrilla fighters. People who had been displaced by the trouble following the withdrawal of the Tanzanian troops gradually began returning to their homes.

Most of the anti-government fighting was organized under the Uganda National Rescue Front (UNRF). Moses Ali, a Minister of Finance under Amin, was temporarily designated as its leader. He was believed to have funds in Europe and, being Muslim, also had connections in Libya. He had also satisfied those fighting in the bush that he had no desire to bring back an Amin government.[6]

The initial success against Obote's forces encouraged some of Amin's officers who were living (comfortably) in Zaire and the Sudan to return to Uganda. One was Colonel Elly Hassan, who had been living in Zaire and he arrived on the scene after the taking of Arua. Announcing that he had direct contact with Amin, who would supply arms, he demanded recognition as the highest ranking officer. He called his movement the Ugandan Army (UA) and designated Koboko as the central command headquarters. According to refugees who were present, his men commandeered transport to haul television sets and other valuables out of the country, even neglecting to secure the heavy arms and ammunition which had been captured at the Arua barracks. Introducing further division into the loosely organized anti-government forces, Hassan is said to have announced that Koboko would belong only to Kakwa-speakers. Instead of fighting, however, again according to men involved in the fighting at the time, Hassan's men began smuggling coffee out of Uganda to Zaire and the Sudan, and became notorious for their atrocities against the civilian population.

Eventually UNRF coalesced and managed to push the UA out of Uganda, but with heavy losses. This internal fighting weakened the anti-government forces, however, and allowed UNLA gradually to take control. In Arua, some degree of normality had returned by July 1982 and some refugees were returning to the district from Zaire. The military positions in mid-July 1982, are shown on the sketch map (Figure 1:1). Although the UNLA had penetrated the entire area they were tied down to the towns.

Elly Hassan settled down as a refugee near the border town of Kaya in the Sudan. It is said that his 60 or so men concentrated on coffee-smuggling

---

[6] See my unsigned report of an interview with Moses Ali, 'Uganda: UNRF awakens from its slumber', *Africa Now*, August 1984.

activities with the complicity of locals on both sides of the Zaire-Sudan border. Reports that these guerrillas set up roadblocks and looted civilians who tried to pass into Zaire were so frequently brought to the attention of UNHCR that is was difficult not to believe they had basis in fact. They even circulated in the town of Kaya, collecting taxes from refugees on Sudan's territory! Such lack of discipline among the guerrillas led more people to opt for the settlements.

Within Uganda the main victims of violence were civilians. UNLA soldiers, unable to confront the guerrillas in the bush, challenged every civilian who moved outside his homestead or village. Those captured were forced to reveal the whereabouts of others. At one point, many of the captured civilians - including women - were dressed in UNLA uniforms and their commander reported that, after a long battle in March 1982 they found - to their horror - that they had killed their own people.

Dr Umar, the only medical doctor working inside the guerrilla-controlled area, wrote a report on conditions inside Uganda. His report is a graphic description of the inordinate sufferings of the people who remained. After enumerating the population still trapped there and describing the appalling health conditions, he notes,

Death is so common it is no longer a bereavement. Life has lost its meaning. The dead are not even given their due respect. Many are unburied, especially those who perish from the barrel [of a gun]. Those who get buried are wrapped in banana leaves, for burial cloth has become a treasure hard to come by.

By 1982 the UNRF had no other source of arms other than that which they could capture. Internal factionalism increased. As one man who had commanded anti-UNLA fighters near Obongi explained at an interview in Nairobi, any officer who had money or cigarettes could bribe the men of another officer to turn against him.

The soldiers of UNLA had problems of a similar nature. First, it was nearly impossible for the government in Kampala to supply the troops in north-west Uganda, and the guerrillas were frequently successful attacking convoys carrying food and arms. Standing by the UNHCR reception office at the Kaya border in 1982, one could watch UNLA soldiers digging cassava, and there were incidents when these men sold their arms to Sudanese in exchange for food. A number of UNLA men defected to UNRF. Secondly, ethnic and religious tensions sometimes led to violence in the barracks and contributed to the general lack of discipline. A report on September 8, 1982 informed the UNHCR office of a battle which took place inside the barracks at Oraba, the border post just inside Uganda and within site of the UNHCR centre for receiving refugees. 'A lot of guns were shot in the barracks that night but the end result is not known.'

In September, the UNRF held a meeting inside Uganda in an attempt to improve their fighting force. Officers who were 'causing confusion' were discredited and Moses Ali's leadership was repudiated. Efforts were made to contact Major C. Mondo, another officer with a long career in the military who had earned the respect of the troops. It was hoped that Mondo, a Christian, would agree to take command of UNRF forces. He refused. In November, at another meeting in Chei, Arua District, the UNRF approved a civilian political wing. Given the lack of new supplies of ammunition, the efforts to change the character of the UNRF organization were futile.

In October 1982 military information filtered into the Sudan that the UNLA planned to strengthen its forces stationed in the north-west Nile. It was reliably reported to UNHCR that 80,000 civilians were still trapped inside Uganda and were at risk once the dry season allowed the UNLA to

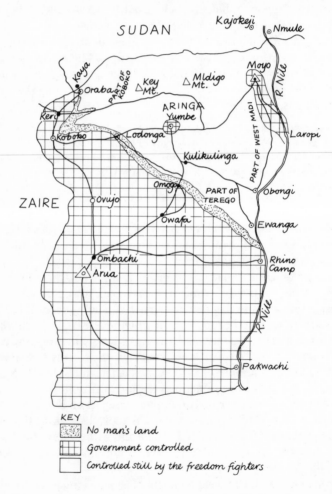

Fig. 1.1. Sketch map of the military positions in the north-west Nile, July 1982

burn the grass and expose their hiding places. In December when the Obote government made its big push northward towards the Sudan border, it met with little resistance and thousands more refugees fled into the Sudan.

Obote's 'Christmas exercise' was described as 'particularly brutal'; 14,000 new refugees entered the country in December and after 4 January the rate of entry increased dramatically. With no food available (to say nothing of blankets, tents, or medicines), OXFAM found the *weekly* ration in one settlement was one kilogram of unground dura (sorghum) and half a cup of fish powder. While children under five need a very minimum of 1000 Kcal for survival, they were receiving only 533 Kcal.

The situation is 'fluid'

Throughout 1981 there had been no peace for the civilians. The fortunes of opposing armies changed from day to day, and civilians moved in response. While some moved into UNHCR settlements, most waited on the border or hid in the bush in Uganda, attempting to keep within reach of food supplies. By the beginning of 1982, thousands of refugee families had established compounds along the entire length of the border. Because there were few Sudanese living there, they were able to get land. Staying on the border not only allowed the refugees to maintain their independence, they were also able to keep in touch with events inside Uganda. Many fighters kept their families in the relative safety of this area. Farming was extensive on both sides of the border at those points where the resistance was still in control. The lack of cohesion and order among anti-Obote forces, together with the general chaos and frequent guerrilla attacks on civilians, gradually led to a loss of confidence in the UNRF. Mounting shortages of food affected soldiers from both sides, as well as the civilians who kept risking their lives by returning to Uganda for food. Civilians were required to pay a modest 'tax' to guerrilla leaders or the local administrators whom they had appointed. In return, a permit was issued which guaranteed safe movement in and out of Uganda. Civilians apprehended by anti-Obote fighters, if without such a permit, were suspected of being UNLA collaborators. While they could be released, usually a relative had to pay several head of cattle; in the absence of such resources some captured civilians were killed. While almost every ethnic group indigenous to Uganda is represented in the refugee population of Yei River District, the majority come from those groups whose homes were in the West Nile and Moyo Districts: Madi, Lugbara, Kakwa, and the Nubi. The ethnic composition of the groups interviewed is shown in Table 1:1. The numbers who entered each year reflect the rise and fall of hostilities.

That many Ugandans fled first to Zaire has been noted. Although UNHCR had mounted an assistance programme there and had set up agricultural settlements away from the border, most refugees did not settle in them. Zaireois soldiers are not noted for their discipline and conditions were

TABLE 1.1: The ethnic composition of refugees in settlements and of households of self-settled interviewed.*

Where living in 1983	Lugbara %	Madi %	Kakwa %	Nubi %	Others Combined %	Number households
In settlements	75.0	20.5	1.9	1.0	1.6	10,588
Self-settled	60.4	7.9	28.0	2.1	1.6	3,747

*The totals in this and all other tables in this book do not always reflect the total number interviewed. This discrepancy is due to errors or to the fact that one or other question was not answered.

TABLE 1.2: Number of households entering the Sudan by year

Year	Assisted settlement %	Self-settled %
1979	11.5	22.2
1980	21.8	9.2
1981	13.0	9.3
1982	41.2	40.0
1983	12.5	19.3
No. of households	2,017	3,777

compounded by the fact that, at various times, their complicity with the Ugandan government permitted UNLA soldiers to enter Zaireois territory and attack refugees who were living there. The head of a family which was waiting for settlement at the Otogo transit centre in 1983 relates their experience:

We were first disturbed in the year 1979. We escaped to Zaire. As conditions improved afterwards, we returned to Uganda. During the 1980 disturbances, we ran back to Zaire. The Zairean soldiers became so aggressive we decided to come to Sudan. We settled around Kaya where we have stayed three years.

Refugees tried to remain near the border so that they could slip back into Uganda for food. But security conditions deteriorated in Zaire. In April

TABLE 1.3: 'What is your mother tongue?' by 'When did you
settle here' (self-settled)

Year	Kakwa %	Nubi %	Lugbara %	Madi %	Others %	Combined Total (households)
1979	41.9	57.1	13.2	7.1	32.0	22.2
1980	10.9	24.7	6.1	21.1	13.6	9.2
1981	10.2	13.0	6.5	24.1	15.2	9.3
1982	26.8	1.3	48.9	33.1	30.4	40.0
1983	10.2	3.9	25.3	14.6	8.8	19.3
No.	1,043	77	2,238	294	125	3,777

TABLE 1.4: 'Mother tongue' by 'year first entered the Sudan'
(assisted)

Year	Kakwa %	Nubi %	Lugbara %	Madi %	Others %	Combined Total (households)
1979	29.4	57.3	8.9	17.8	23.4	11.5
1980	12.4	35.9	12.7	56.6	23.0	21.8
1981	4.5	0	13.2	15.6	7.0	13.0
1982	28.9	6.8	52.1	6.5	36.3	41.2
1983	24.9	0	13.1	3.5	10.2	12.5
No.	201	103	7,943	2,172	256	10,675

1983, soldiers gave self-settled refugees 'notice to quit'; that is, they had a
choice of returning to Uganda or entering the Sudan. In June 1983 10,000
refugees registered for settlements at the reception centres along the border.
Some came directly from Uganda, many were forced out of the self-settled
areas by drought, but most entered from Zaire. Table 1.5 gives the numbers
of assisted refugees in Sudan who first fled to Zaire by the year first disturbed
in Uganda. The table shows a dramatic reduction in that flight direction;
interviews and statements such as the following provide the reason for the
change in numbers who first went to Zaire.

TABLE 1.5: 'Did you first run to Zaire?' by
year first disturbed in Uganda (assisted)

	Year first disturbed in Uganda				
	1979	1980	1981	1982	1983
	%	%	%	%	%
yes	15.54	14.21	7.74	1.33	0
no	84.46	85.79	92.26	98.67	100
Number of households	1,409	359	155	75	5

I was first disturbed in 1979 and we ran to Zaire. We stayed there for four years until April 1983. I decided to seek for further asylum in the Sudan. I left Zaire due to the mistreatment and inhuman behaviour of the Zairean army. Every household item, ranging from a needle up to the human being is very much wanted - dead or alive.

It reveals how the behaviour of the soldiers increasingly discouraged Ugandans from seeking asylum there.

After Old Tore had been opened in 1979, it was not necessary to open another settlement, Kala, until October 1980. Two other settlements were established at about the same time, all three in response to the influx following escalating violence in the Moyo districts of Uganda. When a Ugandan leprosy inspector entered the Sudan with about fifty of his patients, they were settled just across the road from a Sudanese leprosy colony, Mogiri, a few miles inland from Kajo-Kaji. The early influx had also brought thousands of cattle. As, further inland, their cattle would be threatened by tsetse fly, local officials arranged for the owners to settle eleven kilometres from Kajo-Kaji. Even before entering the Sudan, many of the cattle had already been lost to raiding UNLA and guerrilla fighters who looted civilians in flight. Other cattle owners remained on the border with their cows, living on this resource until all were either consumed or sold. Two per cent of the sample of settlements reported bringing cattle - most of these were living in Mondikolo. These people reported having had 3,900 cattle on their arrival, but by 1983 only 520 head were left. Although some cattle were sold or consumed, disease accounted for the loss of 73 per cent. Of those households who arrived with cattle, only 140 households still had *any* cows at the time of the interviews and of these only 2.4 per cent could report a net increase in their herds. The failure to provide veterinary services to save these thousands of cattle has meant an incalculable loss to the local economy. Some cattle owners still living outside settlements, aware of the lack of a veterinary service, resisted moving to settlements on this account alone.

After Tore, Mogiri, Mondikolo and Kala settlements, it was not necessary to open another settlement until July 1981, when Limbe settlement, located on the Yei-Juba road, was established. Of the present population of these five communities, only 31.7 per cent now living there registered in the first year they were opened. This suggests that not only have most of the original settlers in Old Tore abandoned their new homes, but many others have also found alternatives to living in the assisted settlements established for them.

Why did you wait so long?

Early in 1982, when the influx of Ugandans reached 'emergency' proportions, three reception centres were set up along the border. Later in May a fourth, at Nyori, was established, simply because one day the programme officer and I found hundreds of people sitting under a thatched roof (a local church) quietly starving to death. The condition of the Ugandans who came to these reception centres from May through to August was appalling. Still believing that settlement was the better solution for all refugees, I could not fathom the logic of people allowing themselves to die when relief was thought to be available.[7] I could not repress the question 'Why did you wait so long?' as I watched the hundreds of people - not only children but also adults - swollen with kwashiorkor or other nutrition-related diseases, crawl off the lorries. Hundreds were too far gone to be saved by food or medicine, as is confirmed by the death rates collected in the 1983 survey. But resistance to accepting the 'UNHCR umbrella' is clearly demonstrated by the pattern of registration for settlement. Only 20.1 per cent of all those entering the country from 1979 to September 1983 immediately sought (or accepted) assistance on arrival. Table 1.6 demonstrates this preference for remaining independent. And, according to the statements of the 9.4 per cent who registered in 1979 - that the decision to go to a settlement was imposed on them - less than one-fifth of all refugees living in assisted settlements, actually wished to be there.

All other refugees attempted to remain self-settled but conditions along the border made this increasingly difficult. First, there was the shortage of land. Those who entered the Sudan after 1981 found it difficult to acquire agricultural land and later, by 1982, many of them were too weak to undertake farming. There were also great shortages of seeds and tools. And, despite the growth in the number of people living in these border areas, there had not been corresponding growth in medical provision.

---

[7] In actual fact, relief was *not* available; why, is another story. We gave a Ugandan catechist £S50 ($US38: The official rate then was £S 1.31 = $US1.00.) He kept most of this group alive by buying cassava. Two weeks later he sent word he had run out of money. There was still no food in UNHCR's stores; more money was sent.

TABLE 1.6: 'Where did you go next upon entering the Sudan?'
(assisted)

| | Year entered the Sudan | | | | |
| | 1979 | 1980 | 1981 | 1982 | 1983 |
Destination	%	%	%	%	%
Registered in this settlement	9.4	6.0	11.5	23.8	52.5
Remained self-settled	90.6	94.0	88.5	76.2	47.5
Number of households	224	433	262	820	238

People in the assisted settlements were asked how many years they had lived on their own, independent of the aid programme. Table 1.7 shows the number of years self-settled by the year of their entering the Sudan. (Some of these had counted their time in Zaire before entering the Sudan.) These data support the argument that increasing pressures, including economic decline, have gradually forced formerly unassisted refugees finally to move to a settlement.

TABLE 1.7: Number of years self-settled by
year of first entry into the Sudan (assisted)

| | Year entered the Sudan | | | | |
| No. of years* | 1979 | 1980 | 1981 | 1982 | 1983 |
self-settled	%	%	%	%	%
0 or less than a year	27.7	26.2	29.3	**83.2**	**96.0**
1	9.5	22.6	**41.8**	14.0	2.4
2	11.7	**41.7**	24.7	2.3	0.8
3	**40.3**	9.3	4.2	0.2	0.4
4	10.8	0.2	0	0.1	0.4
Number of households	231	439	263	831	253

* Some were reporting the number of years self-settled in Zaire

TABLE 1.8: 'Why did you come to the settlement?' by year of arrival in settlement of first member of household (assisted)

Reason	Year of arrival in settlement					
	1979 %	1980 %	1981 %	1982 %	1983 %	Total %
Lack of food, medicine, education	57.1	18.0	26.4	21.7	29.4	25.6
Malnutrition, illness, death	14.3	21.3	25.5	34.4	32.7	32.6
Heard settlement better	0	9.8	7.3	4.6	4.2	4.7
Harassed/pushed/no choice	28.6	37.7	31.8	29.1	23.4	26.8
Money ran out	0	6.6	0	3.2	4.2	3.6
No-one to help	0	6.6	5.5	6.1	4.9	5.5
Wanted to join family	0	0	1.8	0.5	1.0	0.8
Employment	0	0	1.8	0.5	0.2	0.4
Number of households	7	61	110	884	955	2,017

Refugees living in assisted settlements were asked why they had opted to come, and those living as self-settled were similarly questioned as to why, especially given the obvious suffering of many, they did not go.

Although when asked why they had come to a settlement informants would give one answer or another, the main reasons, the lack of medical facilities and education, affected everyone in the self-settled areas. The shortage of land in 1982-3 meant that latecomers were under the greatest economic stress. The difficulties of survival in the self-settled areas which host so many refugees and yet have received no assistance, are demonstrated by the movements of these people. Note the steady increase in the percentages by year of refugees who have had to leave one self-settled area for another. 'If conditions are so difficult, why don't you register for an assisted settlement?' Table 1.10 gives the replies of informants to this question.

Unassisted refugees were asked what were their main problems 'here'. Interviewers recorded several answers, but presuming the most salient to be the most important, only the first answer was coded. Table 1.11 shows their responses by their answers to the question, 'Why not register for an assisted settlement?' According to informants who answered the question, their most serious problem was access to food, and then medicine; 65.7 reported having no access to a dispensary or even a dressing station. But, interestingly, tools

Table 1.9: 'When did you settle here?' and 'Where did you settle before?' (self-settled)

| | Year settled 'here' | | | | |
Where settled before	1979 %	1980 %	1981 %	1982 %	1983 %
Assisted settlement	0.1	0.3	0.6	0.1	0.3
Other self-settled area	9.4	18.1	27.8	22.2	37.6
Zaire	15.4	31.6	31.8	21.1	12.9
Other place in Uganda	5.7	7.5	2.6	7.5	10.3
First place settled on entry into the Sudan	69.3	42.5	37.2	49.0	51.9
Number of households	838	348	352	1,510	729

TABLE 1.10: 'Why not register for an assisted settlement?' and 'When did you settle here?' (self-settled)

| | Year settled 'here' | | | | |
Reason	1979 %	1980 %	1981 %	1982 %	1983 %
Plan to go soon	3.1	4.0	6.6	8.7	8.2
O.K. here	73.6	78.7	74.6	71.2	63.3
Fear settlements	23.2	17.3	18.4	19.7	26.5
Lack of transport	0.2	0	0.4	0.4	2.0
Number of households	647	277	272	1,200	558

ranked as the next most serious problem. That the need for cash and education were mentioned by an equal number of the respondents suggests that although 74.5 per cent said the children did not go to school, it is likely

Table 1.11: 'What are your main problems here? and 'Why not register for assisted settlement?' (unassisted)

What are your main problems here?	Why not register for assisted settlement?					No.	%
	No reply	Plan to go soon	OK here	Fear of them	Lack of transport		
Food	39.8	53.2	36.2	38.5	72.1	1,467	38.5
Medicine	17.3	10.8	20.8	19.6	5.6	733	19.2
Tools	9.6	9.4	16.0	14.1	11.1	530	13.9
Getting money	7.1	1.5	5.4	3.8	-	200	5.2
Education	3.9	3.9	4.4	10.0	-	197	5.2
Clothing	4.6	4.9	4.9	4.7	5.6	182	4.8
Land	4.7	3.9	3.6	4.5	5.6	153	4.0
Water	0.4	2.0	1.1	0.3	-	32	0.8
Essential commodity	0.6	1.0	0.3	-	-	14	0.4
No problems	0.2	-	0.4	0.2	-	12	0.3
No relatives	-	-	-	0.2	-	2	0.1
Seeds	-	-	0.1	-	-	3	0.1
Home management	-	-	0.1	0.2	-	3	0.1
Security	-	-	0.1	-	-	1	0.0
No reply	11.8	9.4	6.6	3.9	-	285	7.4
Total	100	100	100	100	100		100
Number	831	203	2,123	639	18	3,814	100
% of total	21.8	5.3	55.7	16.8	0.4		100

that many of those who were determined that their children should be educated, had already sent them to a settlement. Of those self-settled children who were attending school, 76.7 per cent were going to government schools, 22.2 per cent were attending schools (or *madaris*) built by refugees, and 1.1 per cent were in schools outside Sudan (probably in Zaire or Uganda).

Insecurity

All refugees who remained self-settled were vulnerable to the conditions of insecurity. Among those who first went to Zaire, 17.0 per cent said they had come to a settlement because of 'harassment', while 28.5 per cent of those who moved directly to the Sudan report harassment as their reason for registering for settlement. This is not to suggest that the Sudanese were even less hospitable to refugees than were the Zaireois. A number of forces were responsible for the buffeting of the self-settled refugees. Early on, those who did not come with sufficient money or property to disappear into the local community camped in abandoned buildings. Officials responsible for the refugee programme at the time, keenly aware of the constraints of international aid, were periodically imposing the settlement policy on those refugees who could be located.[8]

Other factors that influenced the reception of refugees by locals will be discussed when considering the problems of protection and integration in more detail. But certainly, as the Kakwa example demonstrates, a shared language and ethnic background *was* important, and in the case of many Lugbara from Aringa County, occupation was also a major cause of their victimization by locals. By 1983, for example, the notion that 'all Aringas are thieves' was widely accepted. The Lugbara had come late and most men were traders by occupation. It is likely that this stereotype grew more out of their ability to drive a hard bargain than to an actual rise in the number of crimes they committed.

Official 'policy' also changed from time to time with personnel changes in the government office in Yei. On one occasion in 1982, for example, the 'A' Commissioner went on tour of the Kajo-Kaji region. Infuriated by the behaviour of *one* refugee who, among other things, had signed a letter as 'ADC (assistant district commissioner) Kampala', a position he had held under Amin, the Commissioner called meetings of the chiefs and local people throughout the densely populated border area and ordered that *all* refugees be given notice to quit. The method then chosen by some locals to evict refugees was to loot their crops and other property. Many self-settled refugees forced out at this time went to Kansuk, the nearest new settlement at the time of this expulsion. They had, as a group, the longest experience of being self-settled.

The major source of insecurity, however, was *not* the Sudanese but incursions by the UNLA into the Sudan where they killed refugees (*and* Sudanese), burned houses, and looted property. These incursions happened less frequently while the UNRF held most of the area south of the border, but from September 1982 there were regular UNLA forays into the Sudan. These

---

[8] One woman described how she got to Tore settlement. Living nearby with her small children, she had gone to the market at Kaya. Armed police forced her on to the lorry leaving for the settlement. Months later she found her children.

have continued throughout 1984. Even had the Sudan had the political will, the few soldiers stationed along this border would have been insufficient to repel such attacks. My data include details of dozens of incursions, but the following account is typical of what caused many refugees to give up their compounds in self-settled areas.

On 2.11.83 the army crossed into Nambiri village in the Sudan (Ojiga area) in pursuit of the so-called guerrillas. However there were no casualties because all the refugees self-settled there ran away inland. On 2.12.83 the army also crossed into Kangai and Pure villages in the Kajo-Kaji area, to cut off the self-settled refugees into Uganda. In the incident, six people were killed and twenty-three abducted, together with seven Sudanese later released from Arua when they produced tickets [tax receipts]. On 18.12.83 there was heavy fighting between Lissa and Keri at the borders.

It may be that differences in the experiences of death and violence account for the decisions of some households to give up independence and go to the settlements. There was considerable debate among refugees as to whether death rates are higher in settlements or among unassisted refugees. We asked both groups of people to list those who had died in their households from the time they were first disturbed by the war in Uganda in 1979 until they 'settled here'. People were then asked to list those whom they had buried 'here'. For the assisted, 'here' meant the settlement and for the unassisted their present compound. Great care was taken to insist that family members named each person who had died and gave the cause of their death - malnutrition, shot by guerrillas or the UNLA, 'natural causes', etc. (The data were coded as a total of deaths and did not distinguish the causes.)

Analysis of the responses suggests that the death rate in settlements is *lower* than among the unassisted. The average household size in settlements was 5.29 and the overall average deaths per household since arrival was 0.41. The average household size among the unassisted refugees was 7.15, with an overall average of 0.90 deaths per household since settling at the place interviewed. To put it another way: one in every fourteen persons died in the assisted settlements, while one in nine died among the unassisted.

However, the question concerning the number of deaths since the war began in April 1979 and *before* arriving 'here', revealed a staggering contrast between the two groups. Unassisted refugees reported an overall average loss of 1.80 family members per household, while assisted refugees reported an average number of 5.70 family members per household who had died during their flight from Uganda or in Sudan or Zaire. While the recorded data did not distinguish where these people had died, verbatim accounts suggest that many were killed in the Sudan as a result of incursions by the UNLA. The following are typical statements.

The household comprised an old woman living with her son and his three children. He was the spokesman.

We came to Sudan in January 1983 and settled at Kala on the border. That month there was an army incursion which we saw with our own eyes. The UNLA soldiers came to the house and found my two brothers and they were killed on the spot. Their names are Amin Gorobe and Hasin Yakobo. Their two wives and six children were then captured. [Informant lists all their names] ... I returned and buried my two brothers. The rest of the family are still missing.

In the course of this interview, which included details of the death of another daughter in the settlement, the old woman's son said that the family would 'hang themselves' rather than return to Uganda. He went on to say 'I used to be a UPC member. If there was no safety for me, who was safe?'

Another household head in the same settlement, Wonduruba, reported the names of his wife and sister-in-law who were shot together in 1982 by the UNLA '*askari*' (soldiers) inside the Sudan. Yet another 'family' of seven boys (the eldest being 22 years old) reported a similar incident inside the Sudan near Kajo-Kaji. This self-settled family comprised their parents, three sisters, and a 'step-mother and step-father' (i.e. his uncle and aunt). In March 1982, about fifty UNLA soldiers came to the house at six in the morning. Luckily the boys were outside and heard someone inside the house shouting a warning to them. They hid, and saw their step-parents being shot in front of the house, their parents and sisters being marched away at gunpoint, the family's animals (which included 82 cows, 20 goats, 60 sheep, and 48 chickens) being collected by the soldiers, and the house set alight. The boys now live in Wonduruba, a settlement opened in March 1983.

An interviewer recorded the following case in Morsak settlement.

This couple stayed inside Uganda until 1982. Between 1979 and 1982 they say they have built shelters or houses, together with other members of their family, a total of 25 times. During this time, four women in the family were ambushed while collecting water from a stream. Government troops caught them and demanded to know the names of any local members of 'Amin's army'. The women were unable to give any names and were killed. A small boy escaped to relate the story to the others hiding in the bush. In April, this couple, together with their parents, moved into the Sudan. They lived in a separate hut from their father. In April 1983, a group of huts were surrounded by government troops [UNLA], including their father's hut. Eighteen people were killed, including him, the father. This event, compounded by the drought in the area, was enough to convince them that the border area was not safe. They moved to Otogo transit and then on to Morsak on 29 June 1983. Two days later their mother died. Their brother has two wives on the border and has returned to visit them. He has not returned. This young couple are now on their own with their baby which was born in the Ugandan bush. The child is seriously malnourished. The boy has two other brothers who escaped to Zaire and they have no word from them. Their seven goats and twelve chickens were taken by the *Askari*.

The vulnerability of this young couple was emphasized in the remarks of the interviewer. 'It is worth remembering that this young couple are still only aged 19 and 17. Back in Uganda they were dependent on the boy's father, who even allowed him [though married] to go to school.'

The fluidity of the security situation for the self-settled refugees is illustrated by the alarming turn of events in September 1983, and afterwards. With the north-west corner of Uganda cleared of most of its human population, the UNLA stationed at Moyo initiated friendly contacts with the military and civil servants stationed at Kajo-Kaji. Officially the border was closed. Whisky began pouring into the market inside Sudan in exchange for food which was unavailable in that part of Uganda. The military even held a football match in Kajo-Kaji. A delegation of UPC officials entered the Sudan and went as far as Mondikolo and Mogiri settlement. One was said to have carried a handgun. They walked into the settlements and informed people they would be returning with lorries to transport them home.

One local chief reported the matter, sending messages as far as Khartoum, and he angrily confronted the UNHCR officer in Yei, pointing out that if UNHCR refused to protect the refugees in his area, it should then send lorries and remove them to settlements far away. Later in 1984 the local Sudanese officials were persuaded to allow Ugandan intelligence to spend several weeks inside the country. Satisfied that there were no guerrilla bases, they still believed self-settled refugees were supplying the opposition with food. The Ugandan government insisted that Sudan move all the self-settled refugees away from the border.

While earlier UNHCR had contended that altogether there were only 20,000 self-settled refugees in Yei River District, they suddenly became aware of the scale of the proposed operation. The Commissioner for Refugees office was informed in no uncertain terms that UNHCR could not cope with what they now realized would involve moving up to 40,000 people from this sub-district alone. Nevertheless, for those evicted, six new settlements were opened in Mundri District, far away from the border. In June some 10,000 refugees were still waiting in transit camps near Yei. UNHCR had no food to distribute, they were living on the food they had grown and carried with them. As one refugee wrote, 'It is indeed a sorrowful sight.'

As a strategy to prevent the Sudanese from continuing any further forced movement of these self-settled refugees near Kajo-Kaji, UNHCR refused to provide them with any assistance. Nevertheless, the population of refugees at the Mondikolo transit camp rose from 980 in October 1984 to 13,000. Even these people were, it was reported, being 'deliberately under-supplied with food so as to discourage any more coming'. The rise in the numbers of people forced to seek UNHCR assistance in October was the response to yet another UNLA incursion into the Sudan at Kajo-Kaji with '40 refugees abducted'.

At Kaya the situation flared up in November. On 21 November 1984, UNHCR found 'The situation at the border ... very fluid *indeed* with many families in a state of pandemonium.' Once again it had all begun as it had at Kajo-Kaji, with members of the UNLA making overtures to the military commander stationed at Kaya. Already deeply embroiled in commercial affairs with members of the military from both Uganda and Zaire, this commander visited Arua. On 15 November there was an UNLA incursion at Araba Miju, killing three refugees and abducting four others 'who were carried [away] with looted property.' The next day another such incursion left a refugee, Mr Ajuga, dead and his wife abducted, a three week old infant abandoned.

Officially these incidents were blamed on refugees and the Sudanese proceeded to arrest and detain large numbers of Ugandans. These arrests were highly selective, involving only the Lugbara speakers. Several deaths were reported and Saidi Abiriga, a retired Ugandan major and his seventeen year old daughter were both shot in cold blood inside their house near Poki. As was reported, 'There is every indication there was collaboration with the Ugandan army at Oraba, because after he was shot dead, the body was collected and shown to Ugandan army officers who were called from their side [of the border] before it was released for burial.' Two lorry loads of refugees were rounded up from Bazi on 20 November 1984 and 'dispatched to Goli transit'. UNHCR decided however that no food would be issued as hopefully 'they are "vagabonds" who will disappear after a few days to their respective places'. As one observer wrote, 'Each had to make his own way out.'

But now faced with the threat of the forcible removal of up to 50,000 refugees residing in this small triangle (about 25 by 32 kilometres) between the Zaire and Uganda borders, the UNHCR office had 'a) No tents; b) Transport difficulties; c) Not enough food. [There is] food in the store for less than 600 persons for one month, and there is no possibility that WFP [World Food Programme] would send any food in the near future'. UNHCR's message to the Sudanese authorities was that it 'would not be prepared to receive any refugees at this time. Therefore, no lorries should be sent to the border. Should they decide to do so, then nothing much in the way of assistance will be forthcoming from the UNHCR.' At an internal meeting of staff, the head of Yei UNHCR office commented, 'The situation is so bad that it warrants reporting, but since the persons affected are self-settled refugees they are outside UNHCR's protection, not much can be done'.[9]

The self-settled refugees had turned what had been virtually unpopulated bush in one of Yei River District's most fertile areas into highly productive agricultural land. There were, no doubt, many reasons why, since 1979, the Sudan government did not take a tougher line with Uganda concerning these incursions or did not bolster its military capacity to protect the border. But the removal of the self-settled refugees represents a regrettable and unnecessary loss of food production for the Sudan, to say nothing of the additional suffering which such uprootings cause. Most important in terms of

[9] This apparent 'evolution' in UNHCR's interpretation of the limits of its responsibility for protection of refugees is discussed in Crisp 1984 and Harrell-Bond 1985.

the role of UNHCR in protecting refugees, there is no evidence to suggest that the order to carry out these atrocities came from Khartoum. Quite to the contrary, the evidence suggests that it has been the actions of undisciplined individuals, in conspiracy with the UNLA. Some have benefited from the illegal trade which followed from the displacement of much of the Ugandan economy across the border to Zaire. Had the activities of the soldiers at Kaya been reported earlier, they might well have been disciplined. Whether or not the UNHCR office in Yei informed its superiors in Khartoum is not known, but in mid-December 1984, UNHCR Geneva still had not the slightest inkling of any disturbances in southern Sudan affecting refugees. Just before Christmas 1984, word was received that a military clash had occurred at Obongi, a market town inside Uganda, and that once again large numbers of refugees had fled into Sudan at Kajo-Kaji. Indeed, in mid-1985, the situation remained very fluid.

2
Managing emergency relief

'Aid arrives'

Refugees in Africa are being hosted by some of the poorest nations in the world. Their administrative bureaucracy already suffers serious shortages of staff, poor communication, lack of transport, even basic office equipment. But even if poverty did not impose these conditions on the capacity of a host government to respond, normally *no* government bureaucracies, even in industrialized countries, are organized to cope with such contingencies as an influx of refugees, any more than they are ready to respond to the aftermath of a flood, famine, or earthquake. The idea of setting up special offices with staff trained to deal with disasters is very recent. When confronted with a disaster, natural or man-made, most governments rely on *ad-hoc* arrangements.[1] In some cases responsibility for refugees is simply assigned to one or another ministry. Refugees in Hong Kong are administered by the prisons department. Often the military and the police play a leading role.

Governments vary in their determination to control assistance programmes. Ethiopia, for example, has established the Relief and Rehabilitation Commission (RRC) and given it responsibility for all relief programmes. It has institutionalized nearly all aspects of relief management to the extent that it has duplicated many of the functions of other ministries. International humanitarian agencies in Ethiopia have had little choice but to work within RRC's guidelines. But many host countries in Africa have adopted a *laissez faire* approach, handing over responsibility for policy and implementation to UNHCR and/or to an international voluntary agency. Apparently one of the prices of receiving outside aid is the presence of aid personnel to represent the interests of those who fund UNHCR and these include both the donor governments and NGOs (non-governmental organizations). As one African refugee put it, 'Why is it that every US dollar comes with twenty Americans attached to it?' (Alternative Viewpoints 1984.) Presumably, the same question applies to European currency!

UNHCR was established primarily to protect the human rights of refugees and it serves as the channel for multilateral donations. Its funds come from

---

[1] Following the most recent earthquake at Asmara, Algerians organized their response through the Red Crescent and the army. They said they had managed to prevent looting and to co-ordinate international assistance. Involving a *disarmed* military in humanitarian work might also improve relationships between soldiers and civilians. Certainly armies include such skilled professionals as engineers, doctors, logistics experts, etc. who are needed in emergencies.

governments, foundations, or individuals. The growing crisis of mass exodus in Africa and elsewhere has prompted the development of an ever-increasing number of international humanitarian organizations which also get involved in refugee assistance. According to its policy, UNHCR does not itself implement assistance programmes; this work is done by these 'partner', non-governmental, organizations.

Many NGOs rely heavily, if not entirely, on funds from UNHCR for their overseas operations. Such heavy reliance on funding through UNHCR has led to enormous competition among NGOs for contracts. Unfortunately in some cases winning a contract may depend more on its home government's influence with UNHCR, than on the NGO's competence to do the work in the field. (Harrell-Bond 1985.) Yet over and over UNHCR has had to bear criticism for its inability to assess the capacity of an NGO to fulfil its contract.

Once a host country concedes that it requires outside financial help to support a refugee population, if one is not already there, UNHCR establishes an office. The scale of the emergency and the amount of publicity the emergency receives influence the number of NGOs which converge on the scene. For example, in February 1985, the hotels of Khartoum were bursting with delegations which had come to 'assess the situation', but despite the critical need for water in many parts of the country, and despite the attention the emergency had received over the preceding four months, not one additional drilling rig had by then arrived.

There is a very great tendency for outsiders to mistake the poverty of a country for incompetence and a lack of capacity to organize a relief operation. The apparent lack of efficient administrative services - often equated with small offices and run-down equipment - is viewed as a lacuna which humanitarian organizations must step forward to fill. Since they are the conduit for outside funding, many agencies would be surprised if their right also to make policy regarding refugee matters in a host country was questioned. There is an implicit assumption that their wide international experience is a sufficient credential to get on with the work, whatever the local nuances.

However, UNHCR and international non-governmental organizations (NGOs) do not usually get involved in assisting refugees until sometime after an influx of refugees has begun and the host government decides to request assistance or, as in Thailand, is encouraged to do so by UNHCR. (Shawcross 1984.) A situation which justifies outside intervention is usually determined in terms of overwhelming numbers, although the UNHCR *Handbook* (1983:2) defines an emergency as 'any situation in which the life or well-being of refugees will be threatened unless immediate and appropriate action is taken, and which demands an extraordinary response and exceptional measures.'

There is some evidence to suggest that the experiences in the first few

weeks of asylum greatly influence, if not determine, how individuals will
cope with the long term psychological effects of the trauma of exile. (Baker
1984.) In 1979 when Ugandans first arrived in Yei River district, UNHCR
had only two staff members resident in Juba. Direct management of the
limited amount of outside assistance available was organized by Sudanese.
Up to 1982, most Ugandan refugees in the Yei River District were mainly
dependent on their hosts, the Sudanese. Many recall with gratitude the Sudan
Council of Churches (SCC) and Sudanaid, two indigenous NGOs who were
on the spot to help them; but more important was the compassion of most
local people who welcomed, fed them, and often said, 'Here, you can build
your house. You can cultivate this plot of land.' It would be useful to have
more detail concerning the manner in which the local bureaucracy reacted to
the influx, but this is not available. In the self-settled areas, however, we can
glimpse how the local community began to adapt to the social and economic
transformation promised by the arrival of the thousands of Ugandans. Once
the international agencies arrived on the scene, outsiders, no doubt quite
unintentionally, took over the role of hosts. This transformation was to have
serious consequences for the refugees.

The field management of an emergency programme for assisting a new
influx of refugees which imposes a policy of settlement, involves a range of
complicated duties, almost all of which must be organized at the same time.
To list only a few, duties include setting-up reception centres along the
border; ensuring that food and medical services are both available in them
and in the transit camps for refugees who are waiting to go to a settlement;
organizing the daily runs of lorries to the border to collect refugees; counting
and registering refugees at reception points and elsewhere; gathering
information on the size of the population to be anticipated; co-ordinating the
delivery of food and the health, agricultural, and educational services;
finding sites for settlements; surveying the land for agriculture; determining
how water will be supplied; often even organizing the construction of access
roads and bridges; overseeing the maintenance of vehicles and obtaining fuel
supplies; transporting people and supplies to settlements; recruiting and
overseeing staff; organizing accounting systems; planning new budgets and
programmes; reporting; receiving delegations from settlements, from
government, and from abroad (including journalists); supervising the
settlements; dealing with outbreaks of violence among refugees (or between
them and the local people); starting up schools; and attending to individual
refugees whose needs fall outside the scope of the standardized programme.

All these activities depend on an efficient procurement service which is
under the control of personnel who are familiar with the particular demands
of the local environment. For example, local road conditions, and the
availability of spares and services, should determine which vehicles are
ordered; food should be in keeping with customary habits; people should
know how to use the tools which are ordered, etc. It is remarkable that

outsiders have presumed to undertake such responsibility without consulting local expertise. Too few humanitarian aid agencies make sufficient attempt to liase with local officials or with the refugees themselves.

Humanitarians and 'institutional destruction'

Relief programmes are, by definition, temporary. In theory, agencies involved in relief programmes should work in close partnership with the local administration. An emergency and the arrival of trained professionals with experience in managing the logistics of relief should be the opportunity for the host government to strengthen its capacity to manage its own programme after the humanitarians leave. On paper at least the Sudan had evolved a formula which might have achieved these objectives, but there is evidence to suggest that the process of introducing aid from outside has had the effect of weakening the very structures which the Sudan had been developing over several years to manage refugee assistance.

Eliot Morss (1984) suggests that the most important difference between development assistance in the 1970s and earlier decades was not the emphasis on the rural poor...but instead the 'institutional destruction' effects of 'donor and project proliferation'. He describes how foreign donors are contributing to the breakdown of institutions in Africa and suggests that remedial actions are urgently required. Taking Malawi, Lesotho and Zambia as examples, he describes this process of institutional destruction as resulting from the burdens of the expanding numbers of projects and donors, each having its own goals, each having its own requirements for project preparation, with each mission expecting 'to meet with senior government officials'. The result of these and the other demands which he outlines contributes to the reduction of the capacity of the government 'to run its own affairs and to establish its own policies'. This process of institutional destruction, as far as COMREF is concerned, began in earnest from 1980.

The presence of expatriate 'experts' may have a negative effect upon work attitudes. There has been no special training to qualify anyone to manage refugee assistance, yet there are extreme status differences which are marked by salaries. It is not uncommon for expatriates to have even fewer appropriate qualifications for their job than their Sudanese counterparts, but expatriates receive wages which allow them a standard of living far above even what most could afford at home. Even to employ the nomenclature, 'expatriate' or 'expert' rather than the more accurate term, 'migrant worker', emphasizes the superior status outsiders expect to be accorded.[2]

---

[2] I wish I could give credit to the person in a meeting in London who asked the question, 'Why is it that when non-white foreigners work in the UK, they are "migrant workers", but when the British get jobs in Africa they are "experts"?' Morss (1984) talks about 'expatriate technician intensive' projects and observes that 'with world-wide unemployment rates as high as they are, any attempt to "bring the boys home" will meet resistance in donor nations.'

There are also status differences *within* the humanitarian community which affect working relationships; they too are not based upon training, ability, or experience, but follow the salaries which different agencies pay. Many UNHCR officials expect to be recognized as international diplomats. While displaying the UN flag in some circumstances may be useful, it also symbolizes the role they assume *vis-à-vis* other humanitarians.

Morss points out that one of the most 'unfortunate' results, from the standpoint of the recipient, is that 'The expatriates, knowing their salaries are ultimately being paid by donors, become answerable to donors rather than to the government of the developing country.' If economic factors determine the direction of accountability in development projects, how much more will they influence attitudes of humanitarians? Governments usually *want* to fund development projects, but most are very reluctant to support relief agencies' budgets.

For those who might argue against *any* international humanitarian involvement, and there are those who do, there is at least one question which has to be addressed. If African host governments *do* require outside funding for assisting refugees, how will they attract it? Humanitarians represent the consciences of the rich countries of the world. They go to a situation, see the problems, and return to lobby for aid. One solution might be to give recognition to more refugee organizations who could do their own publicity and fund- raising. As we shall see, Sudan has taken an important step in this direction.[3]

The issues raised by the problems the Commissioner for Refugees faced in trying to maintain control over the refugee programme and continuing to develop its own expertise and policy are more complex than might be implied by the brief account which follows. These matters are larger than particular personalities. It is very clear that a different approach to assisting governments which host refugees must be found. What is needed at this point, as Morss also notes, is to begin to 'get major donors talking about the problem'. Outsiders will point to the incompetence and inefficiency of the Commissioner's office which made it necessary for them to take over. After a new Commissioner, appointed in 1982, the staff was expanded, new offices were acquired, and salaries improved, etc. But as Morss puts it, 'You do not really learn how to do it until you have the power to make your own decisions.' New offices, higher salaries aside, COMREF's power to direct policy has been steadily eroded since 1980.

---

[3] The issue of refugee participation and the recognition of refugee-based organizations is an enormously complex one. The debate which took place during the international symposium, Alternative Viewpoints 1984, concerning the relationship of Namibians who are not members of SWAPO to an aid programme which is channelled through SWAPO highlights only *one*.

Some background

In 1967 the Sudan government opened the office of the Commission for Refugees (COMREF), to liase with the police and security as well as with the other ministries which were concerned with a sudden expansion of population in different areas. Most importantly, the Commission was to be the implementing body for all assistance channelled into the country either unilaterally, earmarked for refugees, or multilaterally, through UNHCR. The provincial offices which COMREF established were directly responsible to the central office in Khartoum. Some agencies, including indigenous voluntary agencies, worked with COMREF, providing various kinds of expertise, supplies and funds.

While its work proceeded on an *ad hoc* basis without a separate budget or institutionalized guidelines, it made genuine contributions to policy development. The enactment of the 1974 Asylum Act (even with its limitations)[4] testifies to the success of COMREF in lobbying its government to uphold international conventions concerning the rights of refugees.

Throughout the 1970s with the numbers of refugees growing, Sudan found it increasingly difficult to cope with the financial burden. According to some sources, considerably less than half the refugees in Africa receive assistance (Clark and Stein 1984), but clearly in the Sudan (and elsewhere, Somalia and Kenya, for example), the proportion of unassisted refugees has always been much higher than this. In 1979 the aid programme funded through UNHCR served only 60,000 out of a total population of 441,000 refugees. (In Sudan there has never been a serious quarrel over numbers.) Up to 1980 Sudan received very little outside funding. (Al-Bashir 1978; Karadawi 1977.)

The relative neglect of the refugee problem in the Sudan by international donors had very clear advantages. It meant that the Sudan had time to gain a considerable level of proficiency in administering assistance and to develop its own policy.[5] It was only after 1980 that the humanitarian community began to take a serious interest in the refugee problem in the Sudan. Significant increases in funding began in 1981 and the number of voluntary agencies has been increasing ever since. However, as some Sudanese would describe it, the 'battle for sovereignty' began to be lost in 1979 when Sudan joined in the demand for more funds for African refugees.

---

[4] Sudan entertained a reservation on refugees' right to freedom of movement, allowing the minister to make restrictive rules, but none have ever been formally imposed.

[5] Even the shortage of funds had *some* advantages. Probably only the most needy were being assisted. Recall *most* refugees have never been recipients of *any* aid. If funds had been available and dispensed in terms of local priorities, it is likely they would have been spent on infrastructural development, not on creating artificial settlement communities. On the other hand one must observe that few governments have a good record of responding to the needs of people at the grassroots.

At the May 1979 Pan African Conference on the 'Situation of Refugees in Africa', host countries insisted that the rhetoric of burden-sharing be translated into action. Host countries criticized the international aid agencies for absolving themselves of responsibility through the convenient belief that African refugees were being supported by their kith and kin.

At that time and until 1982, only three professional staff were manning the Khartoum office of COMREF, and there were project management officers in the areas where refugees were congregated. A counselling section had been established in Khartoum which dealt with some of the problems of individual refugees. Up to 1980, UNHCR had a *very* small presence in the Sudan and there were only a handful of international voluntary agencies.

Although none of the staff of COMREF had special training for managing refugee programmes, as its offices expanded throughout the 1970s, recruitment was mainly through secondment from local government staff. The Commissioner himself was a senior civil servant in local government. The men he selected for work in eastern Sudan were among the most experienced. On the whole COMREF's professional staff comprised highly trained local government officials who shared a sense of commitment to the special problems of refugees; their experience of the administration of nationals allowed them to keep the problems of refugees squarely within the wider perspective of the society as a whole.

The Sudan government supported the office of COMREF and COMREF was responsible for implementing its own programme. The accounts of COMREF were audited by the Sudanese Auditor-General and also by UNHCR's own auditing system, but budgetary control of projects was maintained by COMREF. This provided an element of control and the possibility of imposing financial accountability. As it was the policy of COMREF that the Sudanese should implement refugee assistance programmes, it called upon voluntary organizations, including indigenous ones, to act as its partners where it saw a need. Before an outside agency was granted permission to operate in the Sudan, it had to be established that it had the required expertise and, usually, that it had funds. However the numbers of refugees continued to increase and the services in refugee-affected areas were collapsing. The Commissioner began to make plans to strengthen the monitoring capacity of his office and to find ways and means to attract more outside support.

The 1980 Refugee Fund Bill

While it should be unnecessary to explain that governments are made up of factions representing different interest groups, and that politicians (and civil servants) are constantly playing one off against the other in their struggle for power and access to resources, humanitarian agencies do not apparently appreciate the struggle which COMREF faced in dealing with the different ministries which made up *the government*. Although under-staffed and poorly equipped, the main problem for COMREF was not lack of management skills, but lack of power *within* that complex structure. Its authority over refugee programmes was often bypassed. For example, the Sudanese Ministry of Foreign Affairs would sometimes negotiate directly not only with embassies, the OAU, the permanent mission in Geneva, but even with the executive council of UNHCR.

At the symposium (Alternative Viewpoints 1984), the ex-Commissioner recalled the struggle in which his office had been involved, 'battles with the security [forces] to protect refugees from expulsion, battles with government circles to secure more land for refugees, battles with Finance to exempt goods from customs duties, battles with the Ministry of Commerce to secure an adequate share of imported foodstuffs.' Instead of recognizing the positive role outside organizations could play in strengthening the hand of COMREF in these 'battles', the humanitarians only added another dimension to the problem and took, as we shall see, quick advantage of any weakness of the office in its relations with the government. As he put it in his address to the symposium, on top of all these battles were the 'never-ending battles with UNHCR [which were] unnecessary and... irrelevant... I think those battles could have ended.'

In 1979, when Nemeiry made the first of many moves towards the devolution of power to the regions, he reorganized the ministries. The Ministry of Interior was dissolved and some of its different functions attached to regional governments. In the process, COMREF remained in limbo for six months, after which it was temporarily attached to the newly-organized Ministry. Its uncertain status during this time affected its ability to carry out its mandate and to encourage the enforcement of Sudanese law concerning refugees' rights. Most significantly, it weakened its position *vis-á-vis* the international aid community which descended on the Sudan after 1981.

In 1980 the Refugee Fund Bill (1980) was drafted with the purpose of strengthening the office of COMREF. COMREF was to become a semi-autonomous body having four departments, all under an umbrella organization, a national council of aid for refugees. All ministries whose work was affected by refugees should be represented on it and it should have sufficient power to carry out its work. Thus rather than establishing parallel structures for refugee agriculture, refugee health, etc., thereby weakening those ministries by drawing expertise away from them, the programme would work towards integrating refugee assistance by embedding it in the ministries whose work was directly related to the aid programme.

The legislation required, among other things, the pooling of all funds, both those obtained internationally and those from the local budget for refugees. It allowed COMREF to recruit its own staff without reference to other ministries. The Bill gave the council the degree of freedom necessary to negotiate with other ministries directly, for example, with the Treasury over exchange rates on funds given for refugee assistance, and charges on the import of relief items.[6] It would also allow direct negotiation with regional offices over land allocations for settlements and in times of financial difficulties, it would be able to appeal directly to international donors for support. The Refugee Fund Bill (1980) was passed in 1981. COMREF remained under the Ministry of Internal Affairs with the Minister, not the Commissioner, made chairman of the Fund.

Among other significant changes there was also a plan to encourage the development of indigenous voluntary agencies under a national council and to stimulate them to improve their capacity to work with COMREF as implementing partners. There were some thirty such organizations in the Sudan and they included refugee-based agencies as well. It was the policy of COMREF to encourage these latter groups to take on more responsibility for their own communities. They had already proven their superior capacity for implementing projects. COMREF began lobbying to convince the government to recognize these groups so they could enjoy duty-free import privileges. By 1985, three of them, the Relief Society of Tigréy, the Eritrean Red Cross/Crescent Society, and Ethiopian Aid, were given this recognition.

The 1980 Conference

For good or for ill, other African host countries in Africa owe a great deal to the initiative of the former Commissioner for Refugees in the Sudan. Having watched the numbers of refugees building up, but the monies available not increasing proportionately,[7] he decided, as he put it, to 'bring the problem out into the open...It's an international problem, not just a problem for Sudan alone.' (Alternative Viewpoints 1984.) Aiming to secure more funding to develop the infrastructure in refugee-affected areas, the Commissioner announced in December 1979 that the Sudan would organize its own international conference and invite donor governments and international agencies to see for themselves the problems his country was facing. A series of projects was drawn up which would be used to attract funds. The conference was held in June 1980. (Documentation for the June Conference Khartoum 1980.)

International agencies and in particular, UNHCR, did not welcome the idea of this conference. Obviously unilateral aid to a host government which implements its own programmes is the more economical way to assist refugees. If donors were to be convinced of the efficiency of Sudan's approach to assistance, it would then be difficult for international agencies to

---

[6] All materials imported for refugee assistance were duty free, but at one point Nemeiry attempted to impose a 5 per cent defence tax on all items imported into the country.

[7] With nearly half a million refugees, the Sudan still received less than $3 million through UNHCR.

convince governments to fund their own bureaucracies. What if other African governments followed this precedent? It is not unusual for international agencies to protect their turf by arguing against direct aid to poor countries.[8]

UNHCR put its own policy concerning the 1980 conference on paper and the memorandum was circulated to guide the representatives on how to lobby governments. It argued that Sudan was asking for unrealistic amounts of money for unnecessary projects, and that donors should be advised that UNHCR had *already* made its own calculations and adequate projections for increasing aid over the coming three years from its own budget. Rumours also began circulating that the Sudan government was about to launch a campaign to raise revenue by capitalizing on refugees. The UNHCR document arguing against the conference project fell into the hands of the COMREF Commissioner who immediately flew to Geneva and was able to use it to force an unwilling UNHCR to give public support to the conference. After this visit, an inter-agency mission was sent to the Sudan, and, as he reported 'at the same time, we noticed that UNHCR began to look more favourably [on] our requests. Within the same year their contribution rose from less than 3 million to 11 million.' The Commissioner remembered that 'by the end of the year, it rose to $30.4 million.' (Alternative Viewpoints 1984). Recalling this unhappy period, the ex-Commissioner asked why could the donors not ask themselves, 'Why is Sudan launching this campaign? Is UNHCR not helping Sudan enough or what?, [Instead] rumours [went] round that Sudan wanted to boost its own economy. I must tell you that if you are given one billion dollars, it is nothing. It is better not to have refugees, than to [have] to launch such a campaign.' (Alternative Viewpoints 1984.)

Again, it depends on one's viewpoint as to whether or not the conference was a success. It did not raise the funds required to implement the proposed projects, but it drew international attention to Sudan's refugee crisis. Formerly, at any one time there were perhaps five international refugee agencies in the country; by 1982 there were more than thirty operating in the Sudan.

In the meantime, other influences and events were bearing down upon the office of the Commissioner for Refugees. Only a few of the details of the machinations of the various actors involved are available, but those which are known begin to give a glimpse of how the process of imposing aid can unwittingly combine with internal power struggles and serve to weaken local administrative structures.

The US government had entered into agreements to expand its military presence in the Sudan. It had begun its resettlement programme to take

---

[8] In 1981/2 Finland was dissuaded from giving tractors to the Sudan for refugee projects. The argument in this case, among other unpleasant inferences about COMREF's ability to manage projects, was that it was better to import standardized equipment and the major refugee project using tractors in the Sudan was relying on British products.

carefully selected Ethiopian refugees to the US,[9] and the Embassy began to take a greater interest in refugee affairs. The Commissioner began to seek money to implement the Refugee Fund Bill. USAID, apparently appreciating the need for the offices of COMREF to expand, offered to inject funds. If the staff was to be increased, other premises were needed. There was a plan to build offices. Office equipment, for example typewriters, was urgently needed (and still is), and there were not even enough filing cabinets. The office had only two vehicles at its disposal, one donated by a German agency and the other supplied by the government. The Commissioner was using his own car at this time for office work. In order to motivate his staff and at the same time to avoid imbalances between his office and other ministries, a scheme of indirect benefits, including health insurance, was devised. But when additional funds to support the office were available, they came from UNHCR's budget.

A new minister was appointed by Nemeiry and he ordered an immediate auditing of all accounts. It is quite usual for an administrator in the 'third world' to take steps to ensure that he *starts* with a clean sheet - it is vital when later he has to defend himself. (Rumours that COMREF handled large sums from abroad affected its relations within the government, as well as fueling the suspicions of outsiders.) COMREF's accounts were not only in order, but they were found to be holding a credit balance - a precaution taken by the Commissioner in anticipation of an emergency influx. The government decided *it* should be the beneficiary of any interest on these savings, and demanded that the funds be deposited in the accounts of the Ministry of Finance.[10]

During this same period another incident contributed to the air of growing distrust between the agencies and COMREF. Food, unilaterally donated by Saudi Arabia, en route to refugees in southern Sudan was diverted. Even before the Commissioner's office was alerted, the scandal appeared in the British press. The project manager was suspended, but the allegations against him have never been settled in court.

Tensions between the Commissioner and his Minister became known and agency representatives took quick advantage of this weak link. They began to bypass the Commissioner, dealing directly with the Minister. The manipulation of the tensions between the Minister and the Commissioner may have been responsible for the latter's replacement in 1982 by a member of the diplomatic corps who, having spent his career abroad, had no previous

---

[9] The resettlement scheme is an example of how outsiders organize programmes for refugees with little or no reference to the host government. The secret 'operation Moses'is certainly another. (Parfait 1985).Quite apart from the Israel, US, and Ethiopian governments' involvement, the removal of so many thousands of Falasha to Israel was not done without the knowledge of some individuals within the Sudan government and the co-operation of the security, but COMREF discovered 'operation Moses' only through leaked information.

[10] Not surprisingly, given the Sudan government's overall deficit budget, COMREF had difficulty reclaiming these funds when it was necessary to draw against them.

administrative experience in the Sudan. The new Commissioner, along with all the other new staff appointed, had to learn the work of the office almost from scratch.

Despite the legislation which called for the pooling of all funds earmarked for refugee assistance and despite the authority given to the 'umbrella' council established under the Refugee Fund Bill, at this time UNHCR assumed responsibility for monetary control. It opened an account with the foreign-owned Citibank, rather than with Sudan's National Bank.[11]

Under this arrangement, projects implemented by voluntary agencies received funds directly from UNHCR. Instead of being directly under the control of the Commissioner's office, the practice of the tripartite agreement - drawn up between COMREF, UNHCR, and an agency - was established. Understandably, agencies began to regard themselves as answerable to UNHCR, not to COMREF. In March 1985, the Deputy Commissioner complained that there were now agencies working in the Sudan which, as far as he knew, had never even visited his office to introduce themselves.[12]

Under the newly appointed Commissioner, as noted, the offices of COMREF expanded and were re-located in more spacious quarters near the university. The counselling centre, a programme being phased out, was moved to the former offices of UNHCR, while the latter took offices on the upper floors of a new high rise office block. Since 1982 UNHCR has supplemented the budget of the office of the Commissioner and by 1985, with an annual 'topping-up' budget from UNHCR (reportedly £S300,000), the Commissioner could afford to organize an efficient office, to pay his senior staff a higher salary, and to supply the office with a few vehicles. The number of staff has increased, individuals having been seconded from other ministries with no previous experience in refugee affairs. As with expatriate agency personnel, there was no opportunity for them to receive specialized training before assuming responsibility and by 1985 too little time to judge whether experience is the best teacher.

Apparently the US government did not think it was. They convinced the Commissioner to invite another US agency to assess the need for training and to organize in-service courses for COMREF staff. Its representative, who

[11] The complications of exchange rates which are imposed on different sources of money which come from abroad is yet another grey area. If hard currency were deposited in a Sudanese bank, UNHCR would receive it in Khartoum in Sudanese currency. It would not, among other things, benefit from fluctuations in rates and UNHCR would be unable to repatriate surpluses. Why there might be surpluses left over from projects which had been designed, costed, and approved is a subject for research in itself. I was told by the UNHCR officer in charge of education that in one year $50,000 intended for the higher education of refugees in the Sudan had been repatriated because the office was unable to find candidates or places for them to study.

[12] It is a common practice for outsiders to prepare a letter and simply ask either the Commissioner or his Deputy to sign. Both of these men, and the Minister, were rushed off their feet meeting the myriads of journalists, politicians, agency representatives and other delegations visiting the country. There was little time for them to exchange information.

also has no experience in refugee affairs (although the agency claims expertise in imparting management skills), interviewed COMREF staff to ascertain the gaps in skills which needed to be filled. The deputy commissioner appreciated the efforts of the agency's representative, but, as he put it to me, unfortunately his staff were not giving their co-operation. *Imposing aid is never likely to serve Africa's interests.* An African colleague wrote a description of this process in his office in another country. He was asked to prepare a two year plan for training the staff of an office which comprised 706 members.

Our workshop ... was organized by some ... ex-colonials who are still active in this part of the world. Their main objective in discussing such issues was to prepare the way for studies to be conducted by British firms and to formulate projects to be implemented by British contractors. There was a lot of dispute and clashes ... At the end they ... won because they are backed from some people high above!! They were also able to recruit some of their third rate experts, boyscouts like those of ...

Yei River District

The emergency programme, which is the subject of this study was implemented in Yei River District (YRD). With two exceptions, all the settlements included in the survey were located in this district which includes the Kajo-Kaji sub-district. Dororolili and Katigiri settlements lie just over the borders in Maridi and Juba districts. In 1984, following the eviction of the self-settled refugees from Kajo-Kaji, six more settlements were opened in Maridi district.

YRD is bound on three sides by the Nile river and the Uganda/Zaire borders as shown in Map 1. Though poorly maintained, all-weather roads link the district with Juba and connect Yei with the border towns of Kaya, Baze, and Kajo-Kaji. There are only a few feeder roads and during the rainy season these are treacherous or impassable. For domestic water the population relies mainly on surface water or temporary wells. Water-borne diseases are the most important cause of ill health and their incidence is highest during the peak period of agricultural labour activities (Dickie 1983.) Limited primary health care service is available throughout the district. Mandari, a hospital in name only, was located at Kajo-Kaji, and Yei had a hospital with one hundred beds. Education is provided on a 'self-help' basis, i.e. once a community builds a school, the government is committed to provide teachers. Secondary schools were located in Yei, Kajo-Kaji, and Loka and provided places for only a few hundred.

The indigenous population is made up of some eight different ethnic communities deriving from three language groups. The proximity of the borders and experiences of exile of many as a result of the Sudan civil war had produced a quite cosmopolitan though poor indigenous population.[13] Many of the local people have lived in Zaire or Uganda (Dickie 1983). Most of those who have been to school received their education while in exile in Uganda. There has been a considerable migration to Juba and even further afield for employment.[14]

In 1982-3 there was a settled population of perhaps a few hundred northern Sudanese in Yei and Kaya who supply most of the imported goods for sale in the area and purchase cash crops including honey and coffee from the farmers. Most, if not all, of these northerners moved out of Kajo-Kaji after local people banded together and refused to buy from their shops. This solidarity was achieved after the return of southern Sudanese who were in business in Uganda up to 1979. Having very few of their own, the population of the district depended on purchasing cattle from the Dinka who intermittently pass through the district. Their 'visits' became more frequent in 1984, whether in response to the greater demand in the district, or from the pressure of war and drought elsewhere in the south. (McGregor in Wilson *et al* 1985.)

Despite the fact that colonial boundaries divided political and social units, there is not much evidence to suggest that ethnicity or a common history was a major factor in the reception of most refugees from Uganda. There has been some intermarriage between the Kuku of the Sudan with the Madi of Uganda. These two groups live near the Nile on either side of the border. The Kakwa were a minority group in Uganda and because in Uganda they lived adjacent to the Lugbara, many claimed the two groups were related. But the languages they speak are not mutually intelligible. There are Kakwa in the Sudan, and the few Kakwa-speaking Ugandans who were found in settlements bear witness to the fact that is was easier for this group to establish themselves among local Kakwa-speakers.[15] But for the majority of Ugandans language barriers had to be overcome.

Before the 1979 influx of refugees, the population of Yei River District was probably no more than 100,000. This calculation is based on a 1981 study, and the 1983 census, together with the survey data collected in 1982-3. In 1981, the Social Monitoring Study put the total population of the district at 149,824. The ODA team conducting the study for the development plan for the district estimated the population of Sudanese at the time of the 1983 census at 150,000, but they did not have any basis for knowing how many refugees had

---

[13] See Betts' study of the returnee programmes. He quotes a UNDP consultant who noted that 'Paradoxically, while the flimsy structures of modernization in the southern provinces have been shattered, the attitude of the people in all walks of life has changed beyond recognition.' (1974:134.)

[14] Interviews conducted in Panyume found that among 36 households, relatives were working in northern Sudan and Kenya, and one was studying in Egypt. (Wilson *et al*. 1985.)

[15] Language, although extremely important, is only one factor which makes integration more or less difficult for refugees. Refugees 'integrate' as individuals or households, and many factors influence their reception.

already entered Sudan before the 1981 Social Monitoring Study. From the survey of the settlements and interviews of the unassisted refugees it is known that *at least* 43,901 Ugandans were already living in the district by the end of 1980. The 1983 official government census put the population of the district at 355,688, suggesting there could be as many as 250,000 refugees in Yei River District alone.

The difficulty of estimating the total population of such an area at any one time is demonstrated by the fact that *after* the 1983 census, conducted in March, thousands more Ugandans registered for settlement and many of these were new arrivals from Zaire and Uganda. And, as described earlier, at least 18,000 people were disturbed in the Kajo-Kaji area in 1984 and transferred to the Maridi district. In 1983-4 some refugees repatriated back to Uganda, but in December 1984, there was another influx into the Kajo-Kaji area.

To the untutored outsider's eye, Yei River District appeared to raise no major obstacles to imposing a uniform settlement policy. But while it is an area of relatively high potential compared to the rest of southern Sudan, there is in fact great variety within the district in terms of rainfall patterns and the fertility of the soil. Six 'zones' have been distinguished in terms of their potential for agriculture. They range from two with the highest rainfall and the best soils, to three which have the least potential for production, the zones suffering infertile, overcultivated, or thin gravelly soils. While land as such was not in short supply before the arrival of the Ugandan refugees, already some areas - Kajo-Kaji and around Yei - were feeling the pinch from population pressure. Elsewhere large areas of unused land were restricted from use by the lack of water or contamination by tsetse fly as well as the absence of roads to reach them.

During the 1930s, the British colonial administration forced the entire population of the district to move to the roadsides in order to facilitate control and to protect the people from sleeping sickness. The effect of this policy was to cause the Sudanese to rely on the less desirable soils for cultivation. Even though the rule of roadside habitation was relaxed in the 1940s, the pattern of settlement in YRD still reflects this earlier disruption. Today, aside from the main towns of Yei and Kajo-Kaji and a few large villages along the roads, people live in scattered homesteads. The earlier pattern of shifting cultivation has been modified as a result of the location of certain amenities such as schools and markets, the intensification of agriculture, and the increasing importance of perennial crops such as coffee.

YRD rarely suffers extreme food shortages, but food is in shortest supply during the months of June and July. People depend heavily on foraging for wild plants during this period which also coincides with the period of peak demand for agricultural labour. The staple crops which are grown, in order of their importance, are cassava, sorghum, finger millet, and maize. Sweet potatoes are produced all over the district and groundnuts, sesame, cowpeas, pigeon peas, and beans are grown as relish crops. Other vegetables and fruits, (paw paw, citrus, mango, and banana), are seasonally available in different parts of the district. Poultry are kept and goats are found in many parts of YRD. For the Sudanese, cattle are unimportant, their herds having long ago been wiped out by disease and raiding. Rice and tea are grown in the wetter parts of the district. Coffee, tabacco, and the sale of food crops are the main source of cash. As Dickie (1983) states, the farming system in YRD is a combination of hunting, gathering, subsistence agriculture and cash cropping. Practices such as intercropping and staggered planting, and the wide range of crop varieties grown, emphasize the importance of risk minimization, and combine with hunting and gathering to ensure 'a continual supply of food for the family throughout the year'. The most limiting factor on agricultural production (at least before the arrival of the Ugandans) was the supply of labour. Low population density, the low level of technology employed (mechanization is limited to a few grinding mills), the effects of debilitating diseases, and inadequate diets combine at the busiest time of the farming year. Farming depends mainly on household labour, with women largely responsible for weeding and harvesting. These duties conflict with their domestic responsibilities; it is overwork leading to the *neglect* of children, rather than poverty, which probably accounts for the limited degree of malnourishment observed among the Sudanese during this period (Dickie 1983.)

The main off-farm activities of the Sudanese are beer-making, hunting, fishing, gathering honey, and making tools. Although cash crops are increasingly important, there are no doubt several reasons why it was found that the main priority of most farmers was the satisfaction of their subsistence requirements. (ibid). The lack of storage facilities means that farmers must sell their excess at harvest time when prices are lowest. Transport to market is another major constraint.[16] Only a few have managed to combine forces and get their surplus to the Juba market where prices are higher. Prices at the farm gate are set by the northern traders. Perhaps just as important as these constraints on production for cash is the fact that before the arrival of the Ugandans, there were very few markets where one could buy manufactured goods and other commodities which were not locally produced.

In general, the availability of cash does not seem to be the main limiting

[16] It is not only the lack of vehicles. There is no regular supply of fuel in the area. Agencies like UNHCR, ACROSS, NCA, the German Forestry Team (GFT) and the ODA-funded Project Development Unit (PDU) get fuel overland from Mombasa. Whatever fuel is supplied to government offices comes up the Nile from Khartoum by barge. In practice this means that usually in Yei only agencies have fuel available. Others have to rely on black market sources which are exceedingly expensive. During the time I was there it cost £S50 per jerry can. (Given the complexities of exchange rates in the Sudan, the only way to compare this price is by pointing out the £S100 per month was regarded as a proper salary for a university graduate in a ministry).

factor on the expansion of the economy. When the Catholic Centre opened a kindergarten in Yei town, for example, Father Peter received 1000 applications even though the fee was £S40 per annum. Since the school's capacity was only 150, he accepted only one child from each family. Refugees from Otogo who worked as wage labourers for locals reported that farmers near their settlement kept their cash in their houses and sometimes had as much as £S800 stashed in a mattress. Economists rarely have good information on the 'informal' economy. The proximity of the district to the borders meant that YRD was a centre for smuggling gold, diamonds, coffee, and tea. At least one refugee got involved in the gold traffic.

The Programme in the South

As with every refugee emergency, southern Sudan presented some unique circumstances. UNHCR had a branch office in Juba. International voluntary agencies had been entrenched in the south since the end of the 1972 civil war. (Betts 1974.) UNHCR had been involved in the reception of the returnees at that time and a number of organizations had made long-term commitments to the rehabilitation of the south. Attitudes among most aid personnel towards the potential of southerners to take responsibility for their own economy and development programmes were summed up in an article in the *Los Angeles Times* (Powers 1983) in which southern Sudan was denounced as a sinkhole for foreign aid. (Harrell-Bond 1983:19.) COMREF established a general project manager's office in Juba to administer the refugee programme. Unfortunately many of the attitudes held by the expatriate community towards southerners were shared by some northern officials as well. In 1980, when the project manager was alleged to have been responsible for the diversion of a shipment of food for refugees and suspended, he was not immediately replaced. The battle for sovereignty was then between the Juba government and Khartoum. The regional government in the south insisted on the right to name the replacement and disputes over which candidate Khartoum would approve, together with the rescheduling of the 1981 elections in Juba to 1982, further delayed an appointment in the south.

At first COMREF sent its deputy commissioner to run the office. Three voluntary agencies had already been asked to incorporate refugee assistance into their already established aid programmes in Eastern Equatoria and to serve as UNHCR's implementing partners. These were the Norwegian Church Aid, funded mainly by the Norwegian government, and working on the east bank of the Nile; the Africa Committee for Rehabilitation of Southern Sudan (ACROSS), whose funds come from an international consortium of Christian organizations and which already had a small programme in the south; and the Sudan Council of Churches (SCC), an indigenous organization with its head office in Khartoum, which is dependent on funds from an international religious consortium. SCC had had a record of a good standard of work among refugees in eastern Sudan; in the south it had been among the first to respond to the emergency in 1979. It set up the only health service for refugees in the camps opened in 1979-81.[17] Another agency, the German Medical Team, was responsible for the health programme in Yei River District. Headed by a Catholic theologian, an ex-priest, it received its funds from the German government, Caritas, and possibly other sources. Later, the GMT became UNHCR's implementing partner for refugee health in Yei River District.

The influence of the then deputy commissioner's attitude of scepticism towards the southerners' capacity to run their own programmes, compliment-ed those of the staff of the voluntary agencies and head of the UNHCR office in Juba. The incident involving corruption encouraged the expatriate community to take over complete control of the programme. The assistant general project manager, who had survived the scandal of the food diversion, was made acting general project manager, but his fully staffed office played almost no role at all in the planning and implementation of the programme up to 1983.

In addition to the acting general project manager, two project managers were employed to work on the east and west bank programmes. The project manager for the east bank was stationed in Torit. All through 1982 the project manager for the west bank was largely prevented from working in Yei River District. His vehicle, donated by UNHCR, was in a state of disrepair. His efforts to move to Yei were also obstructed by bureaucratic wrangling, and the lack of finances. Again, while a highly experienced and skilful administrator, he made almost no contribution to decision-making during the height of the emergency in 1982. By the time he was able to move to Yei (the central headquarters for the district), too much of his time was spent solving problems and patching up misunderstandings between the UNHCR office and local officials, many of which could have been avoided had Sudanese been allowed to assume major responsibility for the programme from the outset.[18]

UNHCR expanded its branch office at Juba, employed two programme officers to work on the east and west banks of the Nile, entered formal

[17] SCC was also praised for its efficiency and speedy response in 1972 when Sudanese were returning home. (Betts 1974.)

[18] Of course this oversimplifies the problem. In 1983 and once the project management office did begin to assume more responsibility, the office in Yei suffered from the appointment of a number of unsuitable personnel. There is a general lack of professionals in the south and no special training for managing refugee programmes so this is not surprising. However, the most immediate problem for the project manager in Yei was that he had no voice in the selection of many who were sent to work under him. While criticizing outsiders for usurping the role of the host in managing refugee programmes, I do not suggest that the Sudanese could assume management without enormous problems. But they will never begin to tackle them under present approaches to assistance.

contracts with the voluntary agencies, and proceeded, in contradiction of its own policy, to implement the emergency programme once the numbers began to escalate in 1982.

Management of aid in Yei River District

Because the outsiders assumed most responsibility for the day-to-day running of the assistance programme, and because they did not delegate, throughout the 1982-3 emergency, the relief operation in Yei River district was always undermanned. International agency field-workers continually underestimate the abilities of local people, both Sudanese and Ugandan. This is an example of the way in which the logic of compassion is pursued to the point where it helps to create the problems it attempts to solve. Often interpretations of compassion seem to define those in need as helpless, and then work in ways which makes sure that they are useless. The 1982 relief operation is a case in point.

In 1982, the entire programme was supervised by one UNHCR officer who was stationed in Juba. Juba is located some 220 kilometres from Yei (the central headquarters for the district) and the nearest border point where refugees crossed into the Sudan was another 105 kilometres away. Temporary assistance was provided during 1982 by short-term consultants. Only one of them had previous experience in management. The failure to make immediate provision for the technical skills and logistical support required to manage resources effectively on location not only led to great waste, but adversely affected the attitudes of refugees and local Sudanese officials.

When I first arrived in 1982 the programme was being managed from a room in a hotel. Later, two offices were rented - in anticipation of official approval from Geneva - but there were no funds to pay the Sudanese landlord who became increasingly impatient to collect the rent.

There are many ways in which an assistance programme can either contribute to the development of an area, or increase inequalities and resentment. The local council had offered UNHCR land, pointing out that one year's rent would pay the costs of building; later, the offices could be handed over to the town. As the emergency continued both UNHCR and the NGOs required more and more office space, but constrained by policies which plan only for the short term, they continued to rent newly-built office blocks. Two businessmen, not indigenous to the area, profited enormously from the emergency programme as builders and property owners. A local builder could not bid for any of the contracts because he lacked a lorry.

With no budget, the field office was dependent on the programme officer's small portable typewriter; it lacked tables, chairs, filing cabinets and stationery - not to mention the staff to type reports or to deal with individual cases. Maintenance of vehicles depended entirely on the few tools which one refugee had carried with him. Six months from the onset of the emergency in 1982, OXFAM helped out by supplying the Yei office with a set of hand tools for car maintenance. Spare parts were stored in Juba. No vehicle was equipped to repair tyres on the road and even the need to carry more than one spare tyre had not been anticipated. Bad road conditions aside, new vehicles were literally destroyed through bad management, as unsupervised drivers failed to check fluids, and on occasion even drove them into the river to 'wash' the motors! By October 1982 there were only three lorries sufficiently roadworthy to transport refugees and supplies.

The prevailing idea that UNHCR staff should conduct their work from offices rather than in the field, meant that the programme officer was expected to be behind his desk in Juba most of the time. This created serious problems in managing resources and staff in Yei and led to unnecessary difficulties. For days at a time, a storeman in Yei was responsible for directing the transport of refugees and supplies between borders and settlements, and had to handle the large sums of money necessary to keep the programme functioning. Later, when it was discovered he had succumbed to temptation and that fuel was being sold and material aid similarly 'diverted', it was difficult to dismiss him. UNHCR feared he would sue, as had another employee (a driver) when he had been dismissed without following the rules. In the rush of the emergency, few employees in Yei had proper contracts of service.

In mid-1982 the head of the UNHCR Juba office was transferred, and the office was being run by a temporary consultant. With both the representative and his deputy away in Geneva, the programme officer took the opportunity to move to the location of the emergency, despite the fact that authorization had not yet come from Geneva for an office in Yei.

Few expatriate agency staff have previous management experience themselves and lack knowledge of local rules and regulations. Yet usually work is undertaken as if nothing might be learned from consultation or benefit from team work. Up to this time contacts with local officials in Yei had been largely limited to those instances when a signature was required, or some crisis had arisen which required their intervention. The excuse given for bypassing local bureaucracy is the need for the speedy delivery of relief. Local officials have long experience of expatriates who, in their view, flout their authority and ignore their greater knowledge of local conditions. It is not surprising then, that instead of co-operation, expatriate personnel often meet with passive or even active resistance.

Some Sudanese government officials were so angry they reacted in irrational or petty ways. For example, late in 1982, OXFAM sent an emergency medical team to Yei. The programme officer was accused of having failed to observe some minute detail of protocol and the local government official threatened to have the team arrested unless brought promptly to his office for introductions.

In another case a site for a settlement was selected under bizarre conditions, and without proper consultation with the local government offices. (Harrell-Bond 1982: Pt.II.) Later, a politician demanded that this entire settlement be moved, claiming that refugees were living astride his (unplanted) coffee plantation. No one, not even the Yei Commissioner, agreed that this man had any right to the land, nor were they prepared to follow his directive to move the refugees. But the lack of proper documentation in the files of his office made it difficult to defend the decision not to remove the refugees.

Commenting on this discussion of the anger of Sudanese towards field-workers for their failure to observe rules, Howard Adelman suggests that 'The real dilemma is that all networks - bureaucratic, entrepreneurial, political - depend on degrees of trust and not primarily on the rules of the game, though there might be rules.' He asks, 'Does the introduction of strangers into a situation stimulate distrust? Who should the strangers trust? Who can trust the stranger? So it is not just knowledge, or following common rules; there is an *affective dimension* which is ignored by too many scholars.'[19]

And this affective dimension may also be ignored by too many field-workers! Outsiders continually underestimate the latent anger of many Africans. This understandable response has its roots in colonial experience. Simply paying more respect to officials will not resolve it, but outsiders could adopt behaviour which did not exacerbate the problem. Most whom I observed appeared unwilling to bend their life style in order to command the trust of local people. They maintained their 'distance' - even during leisure times - in a society which places great emphasis upon personal relationships. Given the implicit assumption which many carried into the field, that few Africans are trustworthy, it must have been extremely difficult for these outsiders to place their confidence in any official.

The programme officer did attempt to set things right. He began by calling a meeting of agencies working in the district (clandestine because this had been forbidden by the head of the Juba office), and later he held a meeting which included representatives of the local government. His willingness to be 'entrepreneurial' in contrast to rule bound behaviour - particularly when the rules were so arbitrary, laid down by distant authorities, and not reflecting local customs - was the key to any improvement in relations between UNHCR and the Sudanese, and largely accounts for its degree of success.

The division of duties

In 1982 the UNHCR plan devised for the settlements in Yei River District was to follow a 'sectoral' approach. That is, one agency was to be contracted to carry out a specialized task in all settlements. The approach was aimed to

[19] Personal communication.

ensure a standard assistance programme for all refugees in all settlements, to maximize the efficient use of the limited technical expertise available, or, as the programme officer put it, 'to spread the poverty evenly.'

ACROSS was contracted to organize the agricultural programme in all of the new settlements and to undertake the building programme. There was a budget for income-generating activities in each settlement and ACROSS was encouraged to take this work on board as well. As ACROSS was unable to recruit a suitable expatriate, this budget was not implemented.[20] Negotiations were going on with GMT with the aim that it should incorporate the health needs of the refugees into its overall scheme for Yei River District. SCC had organized clinics in the first settlements set up before 1982 and it was continuing to supply medicines and to maintain feeding programmes for the malnourished in Limbe and Tore. The programme officer initiated the first inter-agency meetings in Yei, but there were problems of agency competition from the outset.

In addition to the health programme, GMT wanted the contract for agriculture and building.[21] Having lost out to ACROSS, it employed agriculturalists to serve as advisers to women's 'nutrition' clubs which it organized in the settlements. Discovering that ACROSS had begun to build a clinic in one settlement, the head of GMT rushed around and got someone to begin the foundations for another in the same settlement. He then wrote to the UNHCR office in Khartoum to complain about ACROSS's wasteful duplication and competition.[22] SCC's role in medical services (other than always being willing to provide drugs from its own stores) was gradually eliminated. In 1983, however, as the numbers of refugees in planned settlements increased, the sectorial approach was defeated by the arrival of yet another agency with more powerful outside contacts.

[20] I was told that in the south 70 per cent of the 1981 UNHCR budget had not been 'implemented', the money returned to Geneva. In Geneva the Sudan desk officer had earlier commented to me to the effect that while Sudan was always asking for more money, it never 'implemented'. I was curious. How could a poor country which needed funds not spend them? In eastern Sudan I made a few inquiries and found that in many cases projects could not be started in time because the expert's feasibility study had come up with inaccurate figures, or the funds arrived too late to spend within the budget year. Or, as in this case, the agency was not competent to carry out the work and refused to employ local staff to do it. Among the Ugandans there were several trained and experienced community development workers. But even when this agency bowed to pressure from the UNHCR programme officer to employ more refugees in responsible positions, factors other than training and experience were the basis for recruitment. Some agencies insist their staff meet for Bible reading and prayers. Others will not employ someone who uses alcohol or tobacco.

[21] It also forwarded a proposal for funding a reforestation project directly to the German government, bypassing UNHCR Khartoum. Unfortunately this move was defeated by the head of German Forestry Team (GFT) in Yei. He complained that if GMT got the money, it would rely on GFT to do the work and would not pay them properly. If anyone was to get the contract, it should be GFT.

[22] ACROSS, being a small agency with very little international clout, decided to back out of the conflict.

In the Sudan this agency was called the Southern Sudan Rehabilitation Assistance Project (SSRAP). Its money came from the US Agency for International Development through an Episcopal church organization. In April 1982 SSRAP representatives had visited COMREF in Khartoum proposing to get involved in assisting refugees and Sudanese on the east bank of the Nile in the south. Its budget for the proposed programme was US$3.4 million. COMREF declined the offer.[23] In July a representative of SSRAP together with a local clergyman visited the UNHCR office in Juba. At this visit they proposed to work on the west bank, in Yei River District. Informing them of the sectoral policy, the programme officer advised that the best use of their resources would be to supplement the supplies of hoes, seeds, medicines, clothing, blankets, and even food which were never available in sufficient quantity for all the settlements. SSRAP was unwilling to work in this manner. Agencies require visibility.

In December, 1982 the newly-appointed head of the Juba UNHCR office radioed Yei to ask 'Who are these people?' SSRAP had arrived unannounced, bag and baggage, ready to work. When informed that the contracts had been all given out, SSRAP pointed out that its equipment was in transit from the US to the Sudan and its staff already in Khartoum. Later on the actions of the US embassy representative, who accompanied the head of SSRAP to Juba to help him get established, led UNHCR staff to wonder just who *was* in charge of the new agency.[24]

Pressure to incorporate another agency resulted in the scrapping of the sectoral policy in favour of handing over 'bits of territory' to different agencies. Responsibility for different settlements was given to Sudanaid, a Catholic indigenous agency, ACROSS, and SSRAP. Later on Sudanaid lost its contract, due, it was said, to incompetence, and was replaced by the Gesellschast sür Technische Zusammenarbeit (GTZ). Four settlements in the Kajo-Kaji sub-district were placed under COMREF's general project manager with a new project manager and staff appointed. This arrangement meant that in theory each agency must employ all the expertise required to administer all aspects of its settlement programme - agriculture, education, community development, income generation. Only the health services continued to fall under one agency, GMT. During 1982 its medical services had been given additional temporary support by an OXFAM emergency team; GMT also invited German Caritas to send medical staff for a few weeks, and later on, Médecins sans Frontières began sending teams. In 1984 SSRAP appointed an environmental health specialist, but with the rise of

[23] The reasons, as they were explained, were that the proposal was 'just more of the same'. That is, SSRAP planned to use an inordinate number of expatriates and most of its purchases would be made in the US. Once in the field, however, SSRAP did employ refugees and Sudanese and it learned the hard way that US garden hoes were not appropriate for the local soils.

[24] In a letter to the programme officer, the head at Juba questioned whether or not the local representative of SSRAP would be taking his orders from the US Embassy or from UNHCR.

hostilities in southern Sudan the GMT staff was evacuated. OXFAM withdrew from the health programme and sent a team to concentrate on shallow well protection.

In the scramble for contracts in 1983, SCC, according to the UNHCR correspondence, was actually forgotten. When SCC objected vociferously to UNHCR's playing favourites with the international agencies, to the neglect of Sudan's indigenous organizations, it was appeased by a contract to provide a special programme for the orphans and handicapped.

Refugee participation

During 1982 considerable effort was made to involve refugees in the administration of the programme. Agencies employed them and ACROSS's agricultural programme was entirely in the hands of a Ugandan agricultural officer and a team of qualified refugees. Similarly nearly all of the medical workers in settlements were Ugandan. Office personnel were similarly recruited from among the refugee community. The different agencies did not follow a standard salary policy and when the programme officer attempted to impose such a rule in order to reduce inter-agency competition for qualified staff, he was defeated by a directive to the contrary from UNHCR. More seriously, the agencies and UNHCR did not follow *local* salary guidelines. At one time a refugee typist was being paid a higher salary than was being paid to senior staff in COMREF. The creation of such imbalances was unnecessary and only heightened tensions between employed refugees and local officials.

As each settlement was opened in 1982, UNHCR employed a foreman who, together with an elected committee, was responsible for administering the settlement. Most of the foremen were Ugandans. These foremen were largely selected by the UNHCR programme officer on the basis of 'intuition', rather than on any particular formal qualifications. One had had management experience in a factory in Uganda, another had been a social worker and a teacher, another a primary school principal, some had been drivers, others were ex-airforce. Some proved exceptionally competent for their difficult task, others were dismal failures.[25]

Regular monthly meetings of the foremen and the committee chairmen were held in Yei; and to encourage the sharing of experiences, visits were made to different settlements. Occasionally Sudanese government officials were invited to attend these meetings as were agency staff. These meetings aimed to allow for an exchange of ideas as well as giving refugees a chance to present the problems of their settlements. Although they had no formal role

[25] One, the ex-factory manager, took off with several thousand Sudanese pounds, returning to Uganda. He even greeted his compatriots in the Sudan over Radio Uganda. Later, however, when he lost his job, he wrote an apology to the programme officer, wondering if he could resume his job if he returned.

in determining policy, the programme officer consulted privately with many refugees. He made the UNHCR office files available to them, as well as encouraging them to study the emergency handbooks which described policy. Later he persuaded his superiors to allow a refugee to be employed as UNHCR's agricultural co-ordinator. Again, it was his open-file, free-dissemination-of-information policy which encouraged the degree of trust which was established between the UNHCR office, local officials, and the refugees. The agencies did not happily follow his example. Even those professionally trained refugees who were employed to organize agriculture or income generating projects were not privy to such basic information as the limits of the budget.

In 1983 policy was changed. COMREF had finally appointed a general project manager in Juba and UNHCR began the process of 'handing over' the programme to Sudanese management. Sudanese were recruited to work as settlement officers replacing most of the Ugandan foremen. Most of these settlement officers were recruited from among the unemployed; only those few attracted away from the Ministry of Co-operatives and Community Development by the higher salaries had anything approximating appropriate training for the job of managing settlements. Most were young secondary school leavers. Preparation for their work was limited to a few days of orientation organized by UNHCR. Their task was made almost impossible by the fact that, owing to impassable roads from Kenya the World Food Programme supplies were abruptly interrupted between mid-July to the end of October 1983. Refugees - resenting the 'takeover' by the Sudanese - were convinced that the food shortages were caused by government corruption. In one settlement they threatened their officer with pangas. Many of the younger men were too frightened to remain in the settlements they had been employed to manage.

Becoming 'refugees'

There are several stages in the implementation of an emergency assistance programme. The decision to accept help from outsiders and move into a settlement is normally taken by the refugee himself. It is rare for host governments forcibly to move refugees to a settlement and, mindful of the interests of the donors, UNHCR does not normally go looking for refugees to assist. Usually a reception centre is established at a point of entry on the border when an influx has reached such a proportion that people are found congregated there. In March 1982, this happened at Kaya. Later on, three other reception centres had to be opened at other points along the border - Kajo-Kaji, Livolo, and Nyori. People who entered were directed to the local chief who took note of their presence in his area. Once the border area was saturated, some chiefs advised people to go to reception centres. At times, however, local chiefs objected when self-settled refugees decided finally to register for settlement. At Nyori, for example, some refugees were actually arrested to prevent their departure. As will be suggested in Chapter Eight, there were advantages to hosting refugees in self-settled areas.

Throughout 1982-3 the reception centres were normally manned by refugees. They registered the names of the household head, assigned them to tents, and distributed rations on a daily or weekly basis. Most of the time blankets were in such short supply that those issued at the reception centres were withdrawn as refugees were loaded onto lorries bound for settlements. This practice certainly must have contributed to the spread of scabies and probably other diseases. As the numbers escalated and new sites could not be found quickly enough, refugees were deposited in hastily organized transit camps further inland.

It was in everyone's interest to move refugees out of reception centres as quickly as possible. Clean water was not available and it was not possible to cope with the sanitary requirements of hundreds of people concentrated in a small area. Medical services were non-existent and many people were seriously ill. For only brief intervals feeding programmes were set up for the severely malnourished. Large concentrations of refugees on a border invite security problems. At Kaya refugees were in sight of UNLA soldiers stationed at Oraba. The river marking the border was the source of water which both shared. Sudanese military were posted at Kajo-Kaji and Kaya. At places like Nyori and Livolo there was absolutely no protection. On one occasion in 1982, just half an hour after the programme officer and I had left Livolo, a Ugandan light aircraft circled the reception centre, photographing the refugees huddled below.

The most important and overriding reason for rushing refugees through the reception process and into settlements was the belief that the longer people remain idle, in a state of suspension, unable to do anything for themselves, the greater their tendency towards apathy. But the stories of the events which led up to the point when refugees decided to accept assistance give lie to the argument that African refugees are 'pulled' across borders by 'handouts' and for this reason must be coerced into taking responsibility for themselves.

As was shown in Table 1.8, only a fraction of those who first entered the Sudan before 1982 immediately registered to go to a settlement. Those who came in 1982-3 were those who had exhausted all possibilities of remaining in Uganda. They arrived to find not only no place to settle along the border, but many were in a physical or psychological condition which rendered them almost incapable of taking care of themselves.

Anzelo Boga described his nine-day journey to Sudan which began on 27 December 1982. He went straight to the reception centre at Panyume because, the 'Children were too sick such that if I delayed most of them should have died. But still one died here in the [Goli] transit.' From 1979 he, together with about 30 related families, had moved to a remote place to avoid the 'misconduct of the UNLA'. Eventually 'half' of them joined the UPC for 'cover'. But one brother was captured and 'properly tortured - had his ears cut down.' Held at a military camp at Omogo, he witnessed the slaughter of 'an estimated 70' women and children. 'By luck the brother of ours - who had his ears cut - escaped and came to inform us about the horrible scene. We thought twice and decided to come to the Sudan.' But their exodus was delayed. They met 'bush fighters' who welcomed them, provided them some food and protected them for another long period. Further fighting pushed the group northwards towards Sudan.

On the way we met the soldiers again. We had a few of our property, 45 head of cattle. Our brother who had his ears cut was so powerless, he could not run fast enough because of the tortures he had received. He was recaptured and shot. Immediately we threw down our luggage and ran without anything. We had to carry the small children on our backs. On our way bombs followed us, many were victims as some of the bombs exploded either in front, behind, or sideways. Victims were left and we proceeded. Nobody almost cared for the other. Children were lost and in critical conditions, women even threw their children away so that they could escape.

Those people who registered for settlement at a reception centre after having been self-settled for a period of time, did so only because there was no land, or because they had reached the end of their tether. One woman who had seen her father killed by the UNLA and, on 26 December 1982, two other relatives burnt in a house at Odravu, decribes what was the final straw which broke her determination to remain independent.

On arrival at the border my daughter died - malnutrition. I came alone to the Sudan. Caring for my children defeated me. The only way I survived was to go out early in the morning and work for other people in order to get money or food. It happened that one day as my daily routine, I went out to look for the day's bread. I left the children inside. At about 4:00 p.m. when I returned, I found that one of my children was just lying on the floor dead. It was May [1983]. I decided to come straight to the camp.

While refugees are able to retain their independence from the aid system, they are keenly aware that it is the host government which has provided asylum and that it is the local people and their officials who have made room for them. Although refugees must earn their food through hard labour (this piece work for local farmers is called *leja-leja*), he *is* earning it. More important, on entering the Sudan, one of the first necessities was for a refugee to acquire a local Sudanese patron. This might be an individual peasant household, or the chief, or even the local representative of the Sudan Socialist Union (SSU - the only recognized political party in Sudan at that time). When refugees become embroiled in disputes, and there are many, they are dependent upon their patron, and their wits, to cope within that local power structure.

It should not be surprising that once refugees move under the aid umbrella their perceptions and behaviour change. Numerous signals remind them that they are now being cared for by others. They are registered for assistance in a centre above which the UNHCR flag is flying. The sources of the food that they now eat are clearly marked on bags and tins. Even the colour of the vehicles in which they are transported inform them just who is now in charge of their salvation. They are told where to sleep, and with almost no advance notice, are ordered into a lorry and on a journey which may take many hours, taken to an unknown destination. They ride in the back of an open lorry which may include cows, goats, and chickens as well as up to 100 people. Even if they have clothes (and many adults were reduced to leaves to cover their nakedness), the last vestiges of dignity are threatened by the experiences of the travel from the border.[26] No water is provided on the way, and if one of them becomes ill, they are powerless to stop the lorry. They know not when or where they will eat again. Little wonder that refugees begin to refer to UNHCR as 'their mother and father'. But there is more in the symbolism than might have been construed by outsiders. Unlike a client's relationship with his patron, in the African context parents assume overwhelming authority: usually no decision is taken without consultation and approval. As UNHCR 'children', refugees have little choice but to completely surrender autonomy and freedom of action.

His view of his host, and his host's perceptions of the refugees, are also radically altered by the interventions of outsiders. As long as supplies last, and whether or not he needs all these items, each refugee household is kitted out with a cooking pot, brightly coloured plastic buckets and bowls (essentially useless, because they quickly break), cheap blankets, and rations. Much of the time the cereal supplied was rice, not a staple food for either Sudanese or Ugandans but one to which prestige is attached. In both countries rice is expensive and only eaten on special occasions. Powdered milk was also supplied, a commodity which before few would have afforded. All this material assistance comes from the outsider, and appears in stark

---

[26] Under such conditions it was obviously impossible to transport refugees in a more comfortable manner. But one can only appreciate the horrors of this trip by experiencing it. There were other hazards besides the conditions inside the lorry. On one occasion at a road block police ordered all the refugees off the lorry and forced them to squat on the ground in the dark for inspection. Finally my team was allowed to stand up, while the police and I surveyed the 'human weigh bill', as we called it. A woman was arbitrarily picked out of the list for questioning. Her husband was with her, a guerilla fighter who had been summoned to assist her to get to a settlement. Among the many other matters which were investigated the 'children' were hauled for inspection under light from kerosene lantern. The policeman decided the couple were not the real parents because of differences in the colour of their skin. I quickly suggested the word orphan, and my assistant translated. The police threatened to keep the family behind, but I said I could not leave without them and was prepared to sleep in the station, or outside on the ground with the refugees (who were still squatting outside). The refugees said that had I not been there, their properties would have been inspected and someone would have had to pay before being allowed to continue the journey. We argued about this, my impression being that it was my assistant Charles Male's command of 'Juba Arabic', which was more powerful than my white skin or stubbornness. I believe that in the long run refugees are more secure if their patron is a national. But if my assistants were correct, then perhaps an outsider should ride in the back of each lorry transporting refugees.

contrast with the little offerings the impoverished host had been able to afford before the humanitarians came. Settlements were located in areas far distant from the border among Sudanese who only saw refugees *after* they were under the aid umbrella. They saw lorries groaning with these supplies moving towards the settlements. Little wonder that relationships became convoluted.

Many of the refugees appeared quickly to forget who *were* their hosts. One settlement put up painted signs announcing to all passersby that this was a 'UNHCR settlement'. At Kala a fight broke out after a Sudanese had knocked a child down while riding too fast through the settlement. When the police intervened, it was alleged that refugees denounced their authority; Kala was *under* UNHCR. When supplies ran short in settlements, refugees were convinced the Sudanese officials were diverting goods. Coming from a country which, by comparison with southern Sudan was wealthy and developed, Ugandans already felt superior to the local people. Now with Geneva as their patron, no longer clients of the poorer Sudanese, many Ugandans deserved the reputation they gained for arrogance as, usually over drinks, some even dared to express feelings of contempt. Refugees annoyed Sudanese officials when at public meetings they sang songs praising Geneva or the programme officer, 'Shoodie', as they called him. More than one settlement had a 'Geneva Jazz Band'.[27]

Once in a settlement all the problems arising between himself and the local population with which formerly the refugee had had to cope on his own were now expected, at least by some, to be mediated by expatriates (the parents). In the African context this would be a reasonable assumption. If one runs into trouble which ends up in a court case, no individual goes to court alone. He is accompanied by his relatives, most especially the elders, who must in the final analysis take ultimate responsibility for the consequences of his behaviour. (Harrell-Bond and Rijnsdorp 1975, and 1977; Harrell-Bond 1975*a*; 1975*b*; 1977; Harrell-Bond, *et al.* 1977:202-42.) At the same time refugees recognized and manipulated the power struggles which developed between agencies and government officials.

For some expatriates, the power to make arbitrary and discretionary decisions concerning the dispersal of funds and material aid among their clients was an irresistible temptation. For example, when there was no budget for the milk required by an infant whose mother had none (and lacking it, many starved to death at their mothers' dry breasts), a request

[27] The practice of refugees praising UNHCR through song and dance became a subject of memos of complaint from the government offices! Later, when enthusiasm for UNHCR lessened, the songs grew quiet, but the character of 'Shoodie' remained for the refugees an anchor of consistency and fairness. I believe many Sudanese shared their appreciation for him. When military instability threatened the south, refugees reported to me that although the UN circulated secret evacuation instructions to the expatriate staff, 'Shoodie' had said that if they were driven out of YRD, he might evacuate his family, but he would not leave; he would share their fate.

from Goli settlement for money to buy batteries to run a disco appeared fairly bizarre. Knowing that the programme officer was likely to turn them down flatly, a group of young people went to a temporary UNHCR consultant who approved it. Such inconsistencies in approach produced anxiety and insecurity among refugees and increased the tendency for some to use deceit and manipulation to attain their objectives.

In fact the entire programme became dominated by the distribution of material aid. All relationships centred around its distribution, protecting it from theft or other 'irregularities' and most especially with getting it. Since the organization of the distribution is controlled by outsiders, it is hardly surprising that relationships between agency personnel and refugees are distorted. How can the 'hand' that feeds you tell you to feed yourself? One refugee whom I asked to read through letters from settlements in the files wrote the following note to the UNHCR office.

Arising from my study of the many letters from settlements to the UNHCR, I feel convinced that people from the camps expect and demand more than is within the limits of such organizations. Many of the demands are unreasonable and even ridiculous... Why do the settled refugees have this tendency? The answer seems to be that refugees consider themselves as sick people admitted to hospitals, too weak to get up (and in fact give up trying to get up). They consider themselves like children who need and must be given constant nagging even to stop their own tears. This may be so, but there must be a limit!

Although only a minority of refugees adopted such manners, they were the most visible and managed to create an atmosphere which encouraged the authoritarian response of the outsiders and contributed to the deterioration of relations between refugees and their hosts. Later, however, when supplies failed to come to the settlements and refugees had time to survey their situation more carefully, some of their early enthusiasm for 'Geneva' began to wear thin.

The 'planning' of settlements

Separating relief programmes from the ongoing administration of the development plans and administrative structure of a host government has enormous implications for the future of an area which is suddenly inundated with refugees. Although both hosts and agencies assume refugees to be a temporary phenomenon, experience in Africa proves this to be unrealistic. The international aid community is unprepared to maintain refugees on relief assistance for a protracted period of time. Thus refugees must become economically independent. This requires 'planning', but when the planning of refugee settlements is done in isolation by outsiders who lack the benefit of even such basic information as what are the ecological, economic, and social constraints of an area, the results are bound to be problematic.

A short bicycle ride away from the UNHCR compound in Yei was the establishment of the Project Development Unit. Funded by the British government, PDU was the Ministry of Agriculture and Natural Resources presence in the district. Over the years an enormous amount of information concerning Yei River District had been collected and a number of agricultural specialists, both Sudanese and British, were in residence there. Yet sites for settlements were selected and a uniform agricultural programme was devised and implemented with *no* reference to this reservoir of knowledge.

There was a certain logic behind settling leprosy sufferers at Mogiri and cattle owners at Mondikolo. Mogiri was directly adjacent to a Sudanese leprosy colony and further inland from Mondikolo cattle were threatened by tsetse fly. I do not know the reasons behind the selection of Tore and Limbe, but Kala was obviously chosen as a place for a settlement because no one else lived there. Several years earlier, because of the poor rainfall and infertile soil the Sudanese had abandoned it as a suitable place for habitation. During 1982-3 decisions about where to situate settlements were based on a combination of factors. *None* of these took into consideration the enormous ecological variety of Yei River District.

A first consideration was to find an uninhabited area large enough to lay out a settlement for 3000 people. Although outside of the main towns in Yei River District there was no other village of such a size; this number was thought to constitute a community large enough to be 'economically viable' and small enough to control. Assuming an average family size of five, it was estimated that in order to meet subsistence needs, each would require 10 feddans (10.5 acres). Thus, in addition to the space required for the settlement itself, each would require 25.5 square kilometres of empty, cultivatable land surrounding it. (Land 1981.) One of the conditions of accepting UNHCR's assistance was the Sudan government's commitment to provide land for refugees. Since formally the central government had control over all unused land, once a site was found, it was the duty of the local officials to hand it over to UNHCR. This overlooked the fact that contemporary land law was imposed upon local communities and that probably some group or individual claims 'traditional' rights over every inch of the African continent. Officials could and did override these customary claims, but sooner or later nearly every refugee was to meet the 'real' owner of his land. In relation to the central government a local peasant is nearly as powerless as the refugees. Faced with the usurping of their rights, should it be surprising to find that many Sudanese reacted?

It is not unusual for Africans to hand over rights to unused land to strangers but only after certain ceremonial procedures are observed. At a minimum the stranger must establish a personal relationship with the owner. This may be initiated by presenting the owner with a gift - some food, a goat, or possibly a token amount of money. And this relationship must be maintained by the client - you must be a friend of the owner of your land. Self-settled refugees had no choice but to follow these prescriptions and given the extreme poverty of refugees, many Sudanese waived the obligation to exchange material substance, at least until the refugee had produced a crop. The advantage of this system is that it permits the refugees limited, but specific rights within his new community.

In the early period of the emergency in 1982 UNHCR staff scanned maps of the area. Once they had identified an open place, they expected the 'A' commissioner, the local official responsible for taking this decision on behalf of central government, to approve it. UNHCR was not concerned with his administrative relationships with local chiefs and people. The Yei UNHCR office became acquainted with the local institution of chieftaincy only through bitter experience. (Harrell-Bond 1982, Pt. II.) Later, however, when chiefs began to hear that there were possible benefits of having a settlement in their area since the services - schools, clinics, and wells (not to mention roads and bridges which might get built) - were to be shared with their people, some came forward with offers of land.

Through trial and error, the programme officer learned that it was not only vital for him to have the government's approval of a site, but that it was equally important to meet with chiefs, elders, and as many local people as possible. As a result, the site for Otogo settlement was selected under more sensible conditions. (ibid.) Several times the programme officer and I met with members of this community. We hacked our way through high grass to inspect fresh water springs reported to be there. As a group, agency representatives, a Sudanese education offical, and refugees visited the site. We arrived at the close of Sunday services and frankly discussed with the congregation the possible implications for this minute community of receiving 3000 strangers. As Kakwa speakers, they were reminded that the newcomers were mainly Lugbara and Madi (but ethnic differences as such were never a significant variable). With the sub-chief's son, our delegation trekked several kilometres into the bush and sat down at the place the settlement office would be built. The refugees in the group began to raise the most relevant questions concerning agriculture.[28] We called on the one household situated within the area selected for the refugees, to check out whether they were prepared either to move or to accept so many close new neighbours.

Back at the church, the programme officer asked if the building (a roof only) and the school could be used as a temporary shelter to accommodate the

---

[28] From the refugees we learned for the first time that there is a season in the agricultural cycle when goats are 'released', that is they are allowed to graze freely. Sudanese did not practice agriculture all year round as the Ugandans were accustomed to doing. These goats had ravaged dry season crops planted in river valleys which were avoided by Sudanese, but readily exploited by the refugees whenever possible. The importance of such questions and a host of other issues which they brought up would only be known to local farmers. (Chambers 1983.)

first arrivals until more tents could be found and while a road was being dug to the site. The people were reluctant; they had just dug two new latrines which were insufficient for large numbers. The programme officer promised to pay for more to be dug and to give employment to locals to make the road. Later, as refugees began arriving in the lorries, the ancient, tottering sub-chief used to make the great physical effort to visit. When we had difficulties with certain drunken characters who insisted on looking on as the refugees struggled, sick and nearly naked, out of the lorries, the old chief exerted his authority to remove these nuisances.

A Ugandan, a former social worker, teacher, and preacher, was brought from Mopoko to serve as foreman, to meet and to indoctrinate the refugees on the objectives of the settlement: to become self-sufficient as quickly as possible. At a meeting two months after Mopoko had opened, he stood up to complain about the lack of hoes. As he explained, he had only come to a settlement because his hoe had worn out. Just after crossing the border Father Felix, a Catholic priest from Yei, had given him one. This hoe had allowed himself and his family to survive for a year. On the basis of his 'ode to the hoe', I suggested he might be a suitable person to spur refugees towards economic independence.[29] Very early in the life of Otogo, a group of refugees formed a Red Cross Society. One of their first activities was to build a house for a local handicapped Sudanese.

But we still made at least one serious mistake in relation to local sensitivities. Otogo, the name *we* selected for the settlement, was the name of the beautiful mountain which rose up out of this plain directly behind the site. Later we discovered the place already had a name! Complaints from the chief, the 'A' commissioner, and the education officer began to arrive on the programme officer's desk. Despite all, Otogo has been retained as its name.

Settlements not only needed enough space for agriculture, it was also vital that there was a supply of surface water as UNHCR had no well-digging equipment. In 1982 UNHCR relied on an American who had set up a local business. However, his equipment was inadequate to bore deeply enough and when the rains stopped, his wells dried up. Later, to help out in this crisis, Norwegian Church Aid sent a drilling rig. Adequate equipment did not arrive until 1983. Long squabbles between UNHCR and the Juba government further delayed the programme. An official tried to get control over the rig, insisting that the demands of his own people for clean water in his own region should have priority. Finally, in mid-1983 UNHCR sent a consultant to oversee well-digging and pump repair for the district, but the

---

[29] The programme officer and I often argued about this foreman, he maintaining the latter was *too authoritarian*. Jokes like 'it takes one to know one' aside, no doubt these refugee communities did require a heavy hand at times, but the question was *who* was exercising authority and what was its basis. The creative energy which was released, particularly in the first months at Otogo, found sweet potatoes growing on every inch of vacant land within the settlement and many houses built in record time.

results of this inordinate delay showed up in the disease patterns in settlements. (Wright in Wilson *et al*. 1985.)

The lay-out of the settlements

Despite the UNHCR *Handbook*'s admonitions against establishing camps and its recommendations that a site should reflect a 'decentralized, small community approach, preserving past social arrangements as far as possible' (1983:57), settlements were laid out on a grid pattern. Surveyors were employed to measure out household plots in blocks of 25 plots. Later, when land problems with the locals began to arise, the plot size was increased to a 50 metre square. Each block was to accommodate 24 families, with one plot, number 13, to be preserved for communal purposes. An area in the centre of the settlement was allocated for the 'office' and stores, and spaces were set aside for religious buildings, the school, the clinic, and for the 'commercial' sector.

Households were assigned to plots as they came off the lorries. In Morsak this policy of 'first come, first served', found a severely crippled young man inhabiting a plot at the furthest end of the settlement. He had to cross over a small stream on a log bridge to get to the office for his rations, or to the clinic when he became seriously ill.

In the transfer of people from reception centres at the border to settlements, no effort was made either to promote, or to discourage settlement according to ethnicity. In the hopes that they would find medical services and feeding programmes established at the new site, foremen at reception centres usually sent the most seriously ill and malnourished first; sometimes these services were available, more often not. As a result, the first blocks of a new settlement were usually peopled by the most vulnerable. This appeared to be the only systematic influence on what was otherwise a random distribution. But, as was shown in Chapter One, certain groups moved together from Uganda and this meant that certain settlements were predominantly of one or another linguistic group.

Normally refugees themselves determined the composition of their households. One of the 'problems' which UNHCR tried to control were the 'floaters', people who attempted to register in a different settlement from the one to which they were first assigned. It was presumed their motive was to re-register in a new place to cash in on another distribution of buckets, blankets, tools, etc. In retrospect much of this movement may have been an attempt to find lost relatives; in 1984 a woman reported having been separated from her family since 1982, simply because the lorry in which she travelled to Roronyo settlement was full. Months later she discovered where the rest of her household had been settled. Still, two years later they had not been able to join each other in either settlement.

Once a self-settled household took the decision to move to a settlement it was common to send one able-bodied person ahead, (usually a young man) to examine the situation and prepare for the others. After he had built a house, the family was collected. During most of 1982, the programme officer accommodated family reunions by allowing people to travel back to the border in UNHCR lorries. This was obviously essential since only they could locate their relatives in the bush. Anxious lest Sudan should be seen to be harbouring Uganda's opposition, officials accused UNHCR of transporting guerrillas back and forth to the border to fight. But there never was a base in the Sudan and this was the period in which most of those who had been involved in opposing the UNLA became disillusioned and had withdrawn from active duty. To continue to facilitate family reunions the programme officer obtained permission to send just two individuals from each settlement to trek through the border area with a list of the relatives that the others wanted to join them. To some extent this method was effective, but in 1984 some still complained that their relatives had not been located.

On arrival at a settlement refugees were expected to begin construction immediately. So long as UNHCR's stock was sufficient, and regardless of the size of the family, each plot was supplied with one tent. A plot was 'complete' when it had a *tukul* (a mud house), a kitchen (a roof to protect the fire), a latrine, a drying table for storing cooking utensils between meals, and a rubbish dump. Refugees were told *where* on the plot to locate their house and their latrine. 'Incentives' (i.e. money) were promised to those who finished constructing all of these items.

Administration of the settlements

Earlier in 1982, while two temporary consultants were in charge of opening settlements, they arbitrarily selected leaders to be responsible (with the foreman) for the distribution of food rations in each block. This system of administration proved unworkable with accusations of corruption and mismanagement coming from every quarter. As a result the programme officer *imposed* democracy. He required each block to elect a leader, as soon as all of its 24 households had arrived. Of course, at first most people did not even know each other, but at least there was the sense that the block leader was answerable to them. The problem was that these first positions were temporary, and no date was set for new elections. With no 'constitutional' arrangements, settlers were simply expected to follow directives issued from the UNHCR office in response to each new problem which arose. The system, as it evolved, provided for holding annual elections in each settlement. Each block was to have a leader, an assistant, a secretary, and representatives to serve on the productivity, health, dispute and education committees. Following the pattern I had observed among the Saharawi in Algeria I must admit to having had a hand in this arrangement (Harrell-Bond 1981.)

At first the programme officer insisted that all block leaders speak English. Together they formed the settlement committee and out of their number they were to elect a settlement chairman, vice- chairman, and secretary. (Since refugees were not allowed to handle the budget for a settlement, there was no need for a treasurer.) Guidelines for elections were circulated - filled with advice on how to choose candidates with such qualities as willingness to serve their community with commitment and equity and, most important, without financial or material reward. The administrative structure was designed to provide a direct channel of communication with each refugee family. Records (household census forms) were to be kept by the foreman and block leaders were expected to keep records of all distributions of aid in their blocks. The store and all files were to be open to all refugees during specified office hours for their examination to ensure an equitable distribution. Forms were drawn up for registering births and deaths, but, as was found in 1983, no records of health, mortality, or birth were properly maintained. It was believed that this numbered plot and block system, by providing each refugee with an 'address', would encourage them to identify with their community. Block leaders were expected to encourage a sense of mutual responsibility among households on their blocks, for example, by building houses for the many unable to do so for themselves. Imposing our values, to counter what we believed was the tendency of refugees to reject their social responsibilities, *as we saw them*, was an uphill struggle.[30]

Paid employees in each settlement included, in addition to the foreman, a storeman, surveyors (until the settlement was filled up), and watchmen to protect the store from theft. Except for the foreman, these salaried staff were phased out once the settlement was full. Refugees were expected to take over work on a volunteer basis. Settlements also had paid medical workers, teachers, and agricultural staff appointed by the agencies responsible for these programmes. In a few settlements SCC had appointed (and paid) social workers, but lacked funds to extend these services. During 1982 other settlements relied on volunteer social workers. Later community development workers were appointed and paid.

The budget for each settlement included a sum to pay primary teachers. There was also money to pay people to make the roads and pathways within the settlements and I have already mentioned the incentives promised to all who completed the construction work in their plots. Salaries and other payments were in clear contradiction to the philosophy of self-help. And there were great differences in the policies of different agencies. For example, at Limbe, social workers employed by SCC were trying to get a community centre built by voluntary labour. Someone came along and told

[30] Once I visited a block where a woman had just delivered and the placenta had not separated. She was severely haemorrhaging. The father of the infant was roaring drunk. No one had called the medical assistant. I stormed about the block, looking for someone who would respond to my moralizing. No one did and after I left, she died, untreated.

them it was a waste of time since soon ACROSS would be building a permanent building and would *pay them* to do it. As UNHCR had set itself up as a source of money, it is not surprising that refugees demanded to be paid for *all* work, such as off-loading their own food, assisting in the supplementary feeding of their own children, and once even for digging the programme officer's vehicle out of the mud.

Building schools *for* the refugees also contravened Sudan's policy. As noted, local people must first build a school before the government pays teachers. Many Sudanese students were taught by 'volunteers', some earning as little as £S5 per month, with the pupils spending much of their time cultivating for the teacher. In contrast, settlement teachers were each being paid £S50 per month.

On arrival in YRD in 1982 the first settlement I visited was Limbe. While the UNHCR programme officer was inside a hut paying the primary teachers, I waited outside talking with the volunteer teachers who had started an intermediate school. These volunteers explained that they believed it was also important to provide older children with education, but that it was not UNHCR's policy to support other than primary schools. We discussed the problem of salaries. Before UNHCR had begun to pay teachers, refugees had begun schools themselves and had taught the children under the trees. The moment that salaries became available, the volunteer teachers often found themselves pushed out of their work. There was no system of vetting qualifications and so it was easy to convince the UNHCR staff that so-and-so had no certificate to teach. With the UNHCR budget insufficient to employ enough teachers for all primary-aged children, there was severe competition for all salaried positions; nepotism, not merit, was too often the basis for getting a job as a teacher. (Later the Sudan government took responsibility for vetting qualifications and the situation improved.)

Other problems resulted from the creation of a group of relatively 'fat cats' among a community with no money. One refugee described the problem:

... salaries in the camps has brought a great evil... the teachers themselves are developing a kind of superiority over the rest of the community. That they have money has caused them to misbehave. I remember before Kala was first given a regular supply of food. The teachers had food and they felt good although the other people in their community were desperately looking for food or other means to survive (mainly by working for local Sudanese). There was an occasion when UNHCR brought some food to the camp to share. Though other refugees were not employed and had no means to get regular money, a few had a little... one teacher came and wanted to buy the whole sack of cassava because he had enough money. He knew the food supply was to be kept in stock, but he had money so he wanted the whole sack so that his own family would not starve. He forgot that others who came with their little money wanted their own share. The consequence was the refugees standing around started to challenge that teacher. It was almost to the point of fighting and it might have been bad. If people who were sensible hadn't taken the initiative, he was going to be beaten. Another teacher spent his salary on drink. The wife came and complained that he spent most of his time teaching and when money came, he mismanaged it ... It should have been used on the field.

Volunteer teachers themselves recognized the long-term danger of dependence on UNHCR funds.

... we should all do the work voluntarily. In fact this should apply to all sectors of our social development and health centres. Because, in the long run ... if the UNHCR will not [be here] to pay and we don't get a penny to pay these people, where shall we be? Who will take up the work? Who will pay the teachers? ... It will also apply to the medical system. Now he is being paid, but when UNHCR will not be able to pay these men, we are going to have to pay ... Are we going to allow this sort of way, this system. No. To me I am thinking that it would be good for all the settlements to cut down this sort of payment so that all the work is done voluntarily. I would say that aid should not be given directly as payments to individuals, but as in the case of teachers, to the education committee so that it can give each teacher £S10 or £S20 a month. Then the money will last longer and by then we should be fully self-sufficient and be able to pay them from our own pocket.

The discussion went on to consider the need for the community to organize itself, to farm for the teachers who could not grow their own food while teaching. An example was given of a laboratory technician who was sacked 'because of his professional career in the past' (he had been a guerrilla fighter).

... this guy could look in a microscope to see the worms inside you. The medical assistant, who has no time to see that [and who was usually untrained] could then prescribe the right drug for you. This man was just sitting there, but because he was now not paid a salary, he did not make the tests. He didn't refuse, he was stopped by the government or something .... The community came together and said 'What shall we do for this man?' They agreed to pay him an extra amount of their food rations if he sat in the lab. The community tried to do something, and the last time I was in Kala, he was helping to see what the parasites were.

Another refugee spoke:

Well, again, taking reference to our mother country, Uganda, I remember I have learned one very good lesson from those who are fighting in the bush ... They were not paid either in money or in cattle. However, in cases of emergency, they demanded something. I am sure that if that method was used in the camps, it would be very good. The bush operation in Uganda was on a voluntary basis and it worked perfectly.

As a result of hearing of such discussions, the programme officer decided to introduce a new policy in new settlements. He informed teachers of the budget for education, and placed the responsibility for it in the hands of a school management committee. He suggested that they employ enough teachers for the numbers of children, retaining 20 per cent to buy supplies of paper, pens and other equipment which was always in short supply. Teachers were, he recommended, to be paid an 'incentive', enough for them to employ men to dig their fields, and not salaries. In a paper for the 1982 Khartoum conference (Harrell-Bond *et al.* 1982), we reported on this experiment.

Despite the emphasis it placed on education policy falling in line with that of the Sudan government, and the warning of the salary bill Sudan would inherit when the assistance programme was withdrawn, it was the Sudanese acting project manager who most objected and it was eventually defeated.

Keeping refugees in line

In the efforts to forge these haphazard collections of people into a 'community', the foreman (later the Sudanese settlement officer) had the most demanding role. A first and most important activity was to get the refugees busy building a secure store to keep the food and other items not yet distributed under lock and key. He was expected to meet new arrivals, register them, assign them a plot, issue them with their emergency kit of supplies, supervise food distribution and the work of all of the employed staff. He was expected to hold regular meetings with the committee and with the whole population and, as UNHCR's representative on the spot, to report directly to the programme officer. The programme officer also expected the foreman to monitor the work of the agencies which included the building programme to erect the school, clinic, office, and a permanent store which eventually got under way.

A very demanding monthly reporting system was introduced. It was to include: population figures for each block broken down by sex and age groups; a list of new arrivals in the settlement and where they came from; details of refugees who had 'definitely' departed from the settlement, why they had left and where they were going; the numbers of births, deaths, and their causes. Foremen were also to report on the quantity of food distributed to each block, with a breakdown of different food items; the amount of food and other items in the store on the first and fifteenth of the month; how many tools and other household items had been distributed during the month to each block; a list of all food items received including donations from the organizations; and irregularities which had been observed during the distribution.

Foremen were also to keep attendance sheets for the teachers and the staff employed by the agencies. It was recommended that the foreman insist that these time sheets were signed by the employees. In addition, the foreman was required to ensure that services were opened on time and kept open to schedule. He was also to provide a report on the number of patients treated by the health services, a breakdown of the diseases diagnosed, kinds of medicines distributed, numbers of patients referred, the reasons for referral and where they had been referred; details of any visits of GMT monitoring staff, the main problems the medical staff were facing; and the foreman's overall impression of how well the medical services were functioning.

The agricultural advisor was instructed to keep a journal of his activities and the foreman's monthly report was to include information on the following: acres under cultivation, number of crops grown, description of crop, condition of livestock and poultry, marketing possibilities in and outside the settlements; the main problems faced; and the time of any visits of monitoring staff. Again the foreman was expected to give his overall impressions of how the agricultural services were functioning.

Similar reporting was expected on the work of the community development and social welfare programmes in the settlements. From the social worker's journal the foreman should report on the progress of integrated projects (i.e. involving local people); describe the situation of the handicapped, orphans, widows, and old people with statistics on these groups; details of visits of monitoring staff with dates; and to give a general overall impression of how well these services were functioning. Teachers were also to submit their reports to the foreman to be forwarded to UNHCR and the project management office, as was the school management committee, which had to account for expenditures.

The monthly report was also to include information concerning security: the number of crimes observed and their nature; what steps had been taken in each case; lists of all those imprisoned (including the starting date of detention, accusation, court hearings, judgement and the name of the presiding official). Under this heading, security, the foreman was asked to give a general evaluation of the relationships between the settlers and the local people, the number and nature of meetings between himself and/or the settlement chairman with local officials.

The foreman was also expected to report on the progress of the construction programme: the number of finished pit latrines per block, the number of finished staff houses and other temporary buildings such as the store, workshops, etc., and the progress towards constructing the permanent buildings.

Finally, our exhausted foreman was asked to list any changes in personnel among block leaders or committees and how many meetings were held and what was discussed. And, if he had any particular problems, he was to describe them as well, including any other miscellaneous information he regarded as urgent. Unfortunately, even if foremen had been capable or had the time to complete the gathering of all of this infomation each month, there was another obstacle. The medical workers who had been employed by GMT did not feel responsible to the settlement administration and often refused outright to give information to the foreman. However, there was an attempt to follow the format for reporting and as a result as far as statistics on population were concerned the survey confirmed that UNHCR had fairly accurate records.

The best laid plans of mice and men

Having seen the programme from the perspective of the interveners in 1982,

I also got an opportunity to live for a few weeks in a settlement. Things had gone badly at Goli. The settlement had opened in May 1982 and by September it had a reported population of 5000. The administration had been left in the hands of the settlement committee, as the foreman (a Sudanese) had been regularly called away to help start up new settlements. No election had ever been held (the UNHCR consultants had simply appointed block leaders), and reports (sometimes daily) indicated that much of the material aid was being distributed 'irregularly'. In fact the first week it opened 14 refugees had been detained for breaking into the store. Finally the foreman was returned to his post and was instructed to hold *democratic* elections. Almost immediately, reports came that there was more serious trouble. The programme officer and I made a visit to Goli.

It emerged that despite the fact the guidelines for elections had been laid down, and that there were no special rewards of office other than those which arise from serving others, a bitter struggle over position had developed. Political campaigning had gone on in the mosque (Muslims were in the minority). The authority of the foreman had been insufficient to maintain the principles of democracy.

The programme officer simply cancelled these elections and ordered a complete recount of the settlement. He then instructed me to stay and supervise the census and conduct new elections, block by block. I wrote my report to the programme officer in the form of a letter from Goli, and it is included as an addendum to this chapter.

Addendum

Despite some of the confessed 'paternalism', the following letter perhaps illustrates the belief that the objectives of the programme could be achieved through our interventions. Living at the receiving end of the programme at least had the effect of helping me to begin to question most assumptions concerning how best to assist refugees.

25 September 1982

Dear Sjoerd,

Raphael [the foreman] and I will try to report on our findings here, but I am writing now as he is finishing the re-registration. I will just give you my impressions in a disorganized manner. You may share any of this at the foreman's meeting. Some of it may be so self-evident that it is trivial.

Refugees are suffering acutely from the consequences of the total disruption of 'normal' life. Families have been broken, all the norms of social interaction have been challenged by war, flight, hunger and disease. Survival has become the supreme motive for all actions. The social/psychological consequences are far-reaching. Their correction, in my view - and I know you agree - begins with a very tight administrative system and leaders who manifest sufficient strictness and discipline in their own behaviour to give a beginning sense of security and stability. The role of the foreman in all of this is absolutely crucial. All the problems here in Goli were exacerbated by his absence. Individuals' sense of identity and belonging have been destroyed so that all the sources of identification (religion, ethnicity, family) are at war with one another. None is strong enough to overcome the other because of the distrust of all.

People's confidence in the military has been shattered by the behaviour of government troops and guerrillas. The turmoil in Uganda has meant that every level of social organization from the family to religion to government has been injected with betrayal. *People trust no one.* For example, you may not know it, but one refugee took an exploratory trip to Arua and came back to Goli after deciding it was not safe enough to remain permanently. He had left his family behind. Now, everyone thinks he is a spy for Obote. At nearly every meeting, someone brings up the matter that they are sure that they are being watched by others loyal to the UPC. The fact that trading still goes on from inside Uganda is further fuel for their over-ripe imaginations. Lots of the single men are ex-fighters. For those still loyal to the resistence, these men are traitors for leaving the bush war. For others, the presence of these ex-fighters is a cause of resentment since, as we both know, some guerrillas were no angels as far as the civilians were concerned. The only way to assist them is to provide leaders who represent stability, absolute honesty, and openness - all coupled with strictness and order. How do we do this in the mess we found in Goli (probably typical of every settlement started before Otogo)? Well, I can only report on what has occurred and time will judge the effects.

We began, as you instructed, by cancelling the elections and starting all over from block to block. In each block, all members were asked to be present. They were informed that allocation of food rations was to be based on their physical presence at the count. About four or five people helped (including those who came to the student workshop).[31] Registration forms were held by me, each plot was called, one household at a time. We learned as we went along. Children were required to say their own names out loud when old enough, or not deaf. (There are a lot of deaf children in Goli). At first, when someone was reported sick, one of the team went to check on the number of 'bodies' in the house. By the time we got to block 12, so many claimed illness as an excuse for absentees we thought there was a bloody epidemic! When we asked the medical worker to check on this, we discovered that people were pretending to be sick to inflate numbers!! Too

[31] As an experiment, I had asked each settlement to send two young people to a three day workshop where we had intensively discussed the programme, its objectives, their problems, and how they could work as 'activists' to get their communities more united. That is where I first met some of my team.

late, we demanded all appear in person unless 'dying'! (Even these were checked and they had to respond with their own name.)

Raphael and I suggest the following rule: registration books should *only* be kept by the foreman. No other persons should be allowed to *see* them. Why? Because we found heads of households could remember the *numbers* they had registered on arrival, but they forgot the names (because the composition of their household has changed for one reason or another - legitimate or otherwise). We found many new arrivals had not been registered and many people had 'floated' out. People, particularly children are 'borrowed' from other households to inflate the numbers up to the number recorded on arrival. (Names must be written down accurately and people should be asked to give the correct name on the form to get the food distribution count).[32] We gradually learned to be ruthlessly strict. Co-operation with the census and elections was imposed with the threat of food withdrawal for October.[!]

At the beginning, people thought the exercise was a joke. We retained a very strict and then, even *more* strict manner, always explaining why accuracy was necessary. We explained that World Food Programme (WFP) checked our records; one reason why they don't get enough food is that WFP *assumed* that *all* refugees cheat. But all refugees *don't* cheat, and the *honest suffer*. People who are honest but keep quiet while others cheat are equally culpable.

Raphael became an expert at recognizing faces and those which appeared a second time in the census were publicly humiliated. We kept asking them why they, or their leaders, allowed one person to jeopardize the food supply of all. In some blocks, the leaders were so patently corrupt that we did not permit them to stand for election. [Democracy?]

Voters (all over 16) were counted and advice was given on the kind of leader required for the block. Plot 13 was used for all this activity (although it had *never* been used before as a communal plot). We sat in the sun, amidst shit and rubble and - in some cases - vegetables, but kept reminding them of the purpose of plot 13! We suggest the rule be made that all meetings, all food distribution, must take place in the commmunal plot and that no block leader be allowed to hold any meetings in his own compound. If this were strictly followed, most of the suspicions of mismanagement, favouritism etc. would disappear.

Before the block census I always made a little introductory speech and told how the households would be called, one by one. People were asked to stand up in a line. I asked the children to instruct their elders what a line was and

---

[32] In retrospect, this emphasis on correct names was ludicrous. Ugandans, (at least those from the north-west Nile) naming practices defeated my anthopological skills; I could find no pattern. People receive *many* names at birth and more later on. The majority of names are given when after three days, the mother first presents the newborn to the community. Little children are sent to see the baby and they eat a traditional meal of beans. They dance and sing, and announce the name their parents have instructed them to give the child. One may use any of these names in any order and one may or may not use one's father's name.

also pointed out to them that plot 13 was supposed to be their place to play, but the grown-ups were too lazy to clear it. I made another joke with the children, pointing out how they must take responsibility for calling out their own name as many of their parents had apparently forgotten them (reference to the common practice of borrowing kids to fill up the numbers)! This produced considerable sheepish laughter. I tried to encourage the people in a block - where it did not already exist - to feel like a group and, throughout the census and elections, this *was* encouraged (negatively) as they usually were a group 'under attack'!

It is remarkable how some families have reared self-confident children, and then there are others whose poor little kids did not know what lie to tell regarding their name and age. And this variation did not 'correlate' with the existence of a 'normal' family - some of the 'child-headed' families were the most in order. Each time a line was disorderly, or a name not correct, we made sure that everyone in the block was aware of it. We used shame a lot....

We were enormously encouraged when we found two blocks where everything was in perfect order. Although both suffered the full range of social problems - widows, orphans, the handicapped, etc. - the feeling among them was familial and friendly. All the houses for the vulnerable groups had been completed by the other block members. There was a sense of pride and order and, perhaps one could say (although strange under these conditions), a sense of contentment. A great deal depends on the block leader to bring about such co-operation in these early months of a settlement and, obviously, getting the right person is a matter of chance.

As you will see, our final count is considerably fewer than had been reported - by 500! There are probably 500 others counted who do not belong here. These were ostensibly at 'Tore hospital', 'Mopoko' visiting the 'ill' or in Yei or Kaya, and were struck off on the first round. Re-registration will allow the genuine cases time to reappear and many empty plots and houses have been identified (13). While in the programme we have endeavoured to give refugees the maximum amount of freedom of movement, I wonder if perhaps we've erred. We found families of tiny children with the adults supposedly 'in Kaya'. Mothers also often completely absent themselves, having deserted their kids apparently for another man elsewhere. I don't think it is any favour to encourage this kind of irresponsibility. The system of writing passes for travel means work for the foreman, but until some order is reconstituted it is wise (I think) to provide enough restraints to check this incredible floating around and the abandoning of families of young children. If people are genuinely referred elsewhere for medical care, a record should be kept in the office - some kind of 'in and out' check list - so that people start learning that they are important enough to be accounted for in their settlement. There is an entrenched African tradition of sending children here and there for duties such as to care for elders and the like. This doesn't need to be a problem; such exchanges could be genuinely made, but *somebody* should know about it.

Many block leaders were completely unacquainted with the other 23 families and were apparently surprised by their absence. They have not been impressed before with the seriousness and importance of their role. They fail to report new arrivals, departures, etc.

In each block, the assistant leader was elected separately from the leader. Committees were also elected: productivity, health and education. At least two persons were in each, but there were sometimes three who were voted in to serve. The education committee was elected with the idea that the members would teach *literacy to the blocks*. I will say more about this later, but there was a bloody social revolution going on in Goli between those who could speak (and read and write) English and those who could not. This decision of mine to emphasize literacy was taken 'on the spot' and we will see how it works.

All the first election problems centred around the 'educated' and 'illiterate' factions, which usually also correlated with Christian and Muslim factions. There was one famous meeting they won't stop talking about, where *only English* was spoken. At first I made a big mistake and accused the educated of being elitist and causing divisions. (But I felt damned guilty, because we always expect to conduct our meetings with block leaders in English, and wasn't it a requirement to be a block leader at one point?) Then I discovered there were a lot of so-called illiterates who were crooks and that some of the most concerned people, like the headmaster and the leaders of the two good blocks, were trying to clean things up. Raphael admits he also misjudged things. Because he also does not have much formal education, he found himself also siding with the supposed 'underdogs'.

I must say even cynical me was quite exhilarated when the 'illiterates' began demanding that the UNHCR kick everyone who could speak English out of the settlement and was very amused when one teacher told me he was scared to come out of his house after all the trouble. But *nothing*, tell the radical chics of this world, is ever that simple! That's why I decided that if literacy was a factor, they should bridge the gap by *teaching* it. And, later, when the real situation was more clear, I asked why they didn't teach conversational English. Teachers complain about no equipment, but you don't *need* books for that! Oh yes, new proposed rule: *all* meetings must be translated into *all* languages spoken. It's very sad how little information must have filtered through. I met an old woman who had never *heard* of a tracing service; she knows exactly where on the border her husband is. At the women's meeting today she said, 'You get a backache if you stay a long time without a man'.

Here is what I did. I asked, in each block, how many could *not* read and write. People were often embarrassed about responding, but I pushed them (since I knew how angry everyone was *vis-á-vis* the English speakers). I then went on to point out how Uganda has a famous university, many secondary schools, etc. 'How is it so many did not even learn to read and write?

Something must be wrong in Uganda.' They laughed. I also pointed out how most of the older people had paid the school fees to educate young people and how *everybody* had paid taxes to build the schools. I said out loud what they know all too well, that the educated refer to them as 'illiterates' and it 'ain't a nice word' ... especially since the only difference between them and the educated was that they had no opportunity to go to school. Then I asked how would they like to learn to read and write? The response was impressive and very moving. The range of ages of those who have no formal education is very wide. I explained how literacy teaching could be begun without money and without books and pencils and demonstrated how the letters could be learned using a stick in the dirt. (I am no expert in this field, I hope I won't be hauled over the coals for setting up totally unrealistic expectations.) But, I was saved a bit when I met the new education committees. One of the refugees had two copies of a functional literacy book for teachers and one woman, who doesn't speak a word of English, has taught functional literacy in Lugbara. When the committees met with the teachers yesterday, they decided first to run a course on how to teach literacy. I wish I were around to watch what is going to happen but now the enthusiasm is beautiful to behold. I gave them money for exercise books and pens. I've promised Goli a 'literacy award'. Since I didn't know what to do about rules for winning, I have left that to the headmaster. I suggested that I buy them a radio, but once again, my lack of awareness of their *real* needs was exposed. They suggested that a bicycle would be much better, pointing to all their vegetables which are not getting to market because of lack of transport.[33]

The health committees met with Peter Otuma [the agency-employed Ugandan nurse]. I didn't attend the meeting because my presence slowed everything down, with them translating everything for me. But I have the minutes of the meeting and attach them.[34]

Back to re-registration - we have decided to be absolutely firm about numbers after we finish, because already - within hours of completing it - people are starting to turn up with stories about why they were not there. Block leaders will be advised during the next month to keep a list of names themselves for a check against this moving in and out. It should be noted for other settlements that go through this process, that when we re-registered, all the block leaders came along to learn about problems and to look out for 'floaters' from within the settlement. We wished we'd had them come on the first round. It *is* necessary to make two rounds, as although many blocks

[33] I made the same rash promise in Limbe and a year later one old man who had persevered to learn to read and write a few words claimed his radio! In Goli, and not surprisingly, the whole thing fell apart and so I was spared paying up.

[34] The minutes of this meeting would be worth reproducing, but I left the only copy in the Yei UNHCR office. What they revealed was the value of facilitating (something outsiders *can* do) the meeting of the untrained health committees with the nurse. They asked him for information on all kinds of health problems and in particular about the problem of 'poisoning' and were obviously open to his advice.

initially claimed as many as 50 'new arrivals', on the second go, these numbers were radically reduced.

As long as this terrible dependence on food aid continues, it seems important to maintain this authoritarian and strict approach. One little lapse and the numbers of the dishonest increase. In one block a child appeared for at least the third time. He actually belonged in block 1. I took a stick and whacked him myself! I asked the people why I should come all the way from England to correct their children; none of them had come to help me correct mine! (I would have liked to have given the woman who was claiming the child as hers just to get the pathetic little food ration a good whack too, but the flimsy stick broke on the kid!) Later, back in block 1, where the child lived, I scolded his father and his two wives for parental negligence and advised the father to discipline the child himself. Another boy was repeatedly showing up in family queues. I lost track of faces, but luckily for Raphael and me and the team, we could remember the eccentric-looking used clothes they wear! Repeatedly the message was given - disorder and indiscipline are the problems you ran from. Why did you bring them all here? Cheating on food or in elections in Goli is no different from the crimes you accuse Obote's government of committing.

But, even with all this striving towards accuracy, we continued to make mistakes. For example, in the re-registration, we let the block leaders help the team fill out the forms. In the end we found some missing and duplicates with different numbers for particular plots. So, following this to its logical conclusion, block leaders are not to be depended upon either. No system of control imposed on refugees without their prior understanding and agreement is ever going to work. They *must* have their own leaders, but I kept looking for them in Goli, and there were all too few who were willing to be responsible.[35]

Block leaders are also in desperate need of instruction on record-keeping. All our naive efforts to make sure there were records and that they were open for all to see is subverted by lack of paper, pens, shelves, chairs, etc., etc. I cannot keep *my* notebook clean in this situation: how can they be expected to keep records? I keep thinking of the money it costs UNHCR to charter a plane. It's $6000 isn't it? Wouldn't one trip pay for stationery supplies for all the settlements?

But one encouraging sign that not all our efforts are wasted. Someone has just turned up to report on a family of six who have a plot in Goli and also one in Mopoko! The head of the family was smart enough to be here for registration, but, oops, he missed food distribution today because it wasn't announced in time. The block leader wants to know what will be done with the food rations (for six people)!

---

[35] See Turton and Turton (1984) for an excellent account of how Africans (this time in Ethiopia) assume responsibility for themselves in situations of extreme crisis and re-adaptation when they are left alone to do it.

On food distribution - I witnessed it today, and I must say I was horrified. No information has ever been available to the public on amounts due to them. We posted the contents of the WFP 'food basket' in English and Lugbara. Great interest was shown! Today, there was not enough oil for the settlement, according to the ration, and it came in two forms - solid and liquid - and in litres and pounds! I was amazed at the mathematical dexterity of the block leaders as they tried to figure out the ration. (But in Raphael's absence, they had simply been dividing the amounts according to the numbers of blocks. This despite the rather significant difference in block populations. No wonder the interest in inflating numbers in the smaller blocks to 'look equal'.)

How do *you* divide up pounds and litres of solids and liquids? I had no calculator but I defy anyone to manage this properly without one, or a scale, or containers to carry the stuff away. In the end something went wrong and when the exhausting process had been completed, 48 tins were left over. One suggested this be left for 'visitors': the next meeting of the students was mentioned as an example of such a need. The rule that all food is to be distributed on an equal basis to all settlers was apparently ignored. I said a firm '*No*' to this suggestion, pointing out that students' meetings have nothing to do with cripples, widows, etc. But then, would you believe it, the need for oil to cure the poisoned was mentioned [to be explained later]...

Our naiveté in believing that the information put in the settlements would be disseminated is wonderful! Few had heard of Bulletin No. 1 except for the rules about poisoning accusations. I asked people to come to a lot of meetings. After completing elections, we had a second general meeting and during it I learned a lot more about the confusion of the first election. Rules had not been followed at all. In many blocks, no voting had taken place and a system of sending five representatives from each to vote for the chairman, vice-chairman and secretary was dreamed up. People who were not block leaders were running for office despite your clear instructions. The fight over these positions was so intense that peace was severely threatened. As I said earlier, the antagonisms focused on the 'educated class', and the use of English. One fight which took place in our presence was triggered by an ex-block leader using English to 'humiliate' another who didn't speak it. (These two fellows were assigned work on the fence for the office compound as a punishment, but so far they refuse to accept it. Raphael said that he was withholding their food ration, but of course, they will just eat their wives' or kids' food!) The 'uneducated' were tough enough to frighten the 'educated'. Once I thought I knew what was going on, I called a meeting of 'elders' and invited the 'educated class' to listen. They must have learned a lot from the rage and anger of the elders, that is, the 'uneducated'. It was impressive how the elders and the other uneducated have tried to assert their equality in the situation where, as they put it, 'all are now refugees'. However, because *we* work in English, the majority remain at a disadvantage. They are incredibly suspicious and believe that 'they' (those whom we speak to) bribe us with English! They say that their problems are not heard because they can't speak it. Raphael and I have reacted to this controversy by always using *interpreters*. We have challenged the students' debating society to debate in Lugbara and to use this activity to increase solidarity and debate issues which affect all of them.

Later

The mystery still remains as to why the positions of chairman, etc. were so important as to cause fighting. But the hostility was so intense, even after all those meetings we held and after the elections of the block leaders, that we decided to temporarily suspend the election of a settlement chairman and institute a 'rotating' chairman, with one person from each block taking responsibility to help Raphael in the 'office' compound one day of the month. Since Goli has 30 blocks, it might work. This will also allow tempers to cool and Raphael will get to know the block leaders better. Of course, I have told them this is *my* solution for the moment and that *you* will finally decide. When I announced this idea, the community was absolutely overjoyed because they knew the old guard was doing its best to get itself back in office. Honestly!!

The 'office' (is it the close proximity to the store which still has no lockable door?) has incredible mystique. We are thinking of ways to reduce this. Raphael has had a shelter erected in the centre which, when a mud bench is completed, will seat 27. A game table is being built by the new fellow who has leprosy and is temporarily living in the office compound with us. I promised to send games and people - particularly the elders - will be encouraged to use this as a small social centre, so more people will be around seeing what is going on in the 'office'.

Our first 'collective' and unchaired meeting under the new system was when the ACROSS agency people came to explain the building programme. It was a great improvement on earlier meetings. Since there was no person who was *the* chairman, there was a minimum of 'thank you's' and deference to 'important' personages, and people almost began simply to talk to each other. It will be interesting to see how things proceed following this experiment. I will meet with the block leaders again and allow the 'chairman for the day' to preside and see how it goes. Moreover, if a chairman is a block leader (as the system intended), he has enough work in his own block, and doesn't have the time to be at the office every day anyway.

Now another issue has cropped up - settling cases in the settlement. The two people who fought, as I mentioned, have refused to perform the work punishment Raphael assigned. And there is the case of a man, drunk, estranged from his wife, who beat up another woman in the process of trying to reclaim 'his' possessions (his wife had left him and taken everything

UNHCR had doled out to a relative's compound). This case involved the two couples and the two block-leaders. I heard the accusations and listened to the husband and then told them to go off and let the elders settle it. Can you imagine their decision? First they imposed a £S2 charge for hearing the case (which they pocketed). Then they said that the block leader had to pay £S10 for 'failing to control the husband in his block'. (I think that's quite funny and perhaps not such a bad idea, given all the drunken parties I hear each night!) Then they said the husband had to pay £S25 for compensation to the woman he beat up. They gave him one month to do this. I asked where the hell the husband and the block leader would come up with these amounts. They had an answer. They would *sell* two bicycles which had been *borrowed* from other people not involved in the case at all, but which had somehow been used in moving from block to block in the fracas! Oh yes, they would give half of the £S10 to the woman, topping up the £S25 to £S30, and they would pocket the other £S5 for hearing the case. I blew up. I told them that I had never heard anything so ridiculous. First of all, how could they hock someone else's property to pay this fine? One arrogant so-and-so gave me a lecture on Ugandan law and pointed out the he was an expert. I retorted that they were now under Sudan law, and the only reason I had suggested they talk about this case themselves was to avoid having to fall under the Sudan chief's court down the road, risking the detention of one or more of them, and causing more trouble. They should be able to learn to keep peace in the settlement, but obviously they were not up to the challenge. I immediately returned the borrowed bikes to their relieved owners! Up to that point, I didn't even know they were borrowed, and the owners had (significantly) been too afraid to inform me. Obviously the settlements need an explicit rule that cases which require some punishment may not be heard in the settlement and that no one may impose fines and pocket money for hearing cases. If they can't just do it quietly, that is, settle disputes by talking them out, then the foreman better turn the culprits over immediately to the chief and his police. Settlements are *not* states within a state. This is the Sudan!

It appears that little effort has been exerted by the block leaders to explain anything. The information regarding rules for forming co-operatives is *not* available in Goli. Nor is the amount of the development budget known, or what is required to apply for money. During the ACROSS visit, the social workers were asked all kinds of questions which exposed their lack of understanding of what is required, but no information has ever been given to them as to what they have to do to start an 'economically viable' project. Refugees are not able to do market research to document projected income or costs - both capital and running costs - or to find the sources and costs of raw materials, etc. etc. which is what ACROSS was demanding. It is completely ludicrous to expect inexperienced (or even experienced) people who have no access to transport to do more than they have already done, that is, create societies around existing skills. More serious, and I think you will have to talk with their director about this, ACROSS worries about whether capital investment in the settlements will encourage the 'flight' of viable businesses away from the settlement to Yei![36] This argument is very weak. None of the co-operatives will make the members rich enough to abandon agriculture. It would be difficult anyway for refugees to get licences to operate in Yei or land for their buildings. I fear that all the delays and lack of support for establishing co-ops will end up discouraging the good initiatives already taken, and the money, as usual, will not be spent.

The medical staff here were honestly not aware that they should report to the foreman. They thought that one of the three copies of their monthly reports went to the UNHCR office. There continue to be problems: the need for shoes for lepers, spectacles for people. One man was informed by the agency doctor that *when* an oculist came to Juba, he would be sent to have his eyes tested. Then I discover another such case who has *already been to Juba*, and had his eye tested, and returned today with his new reading glasses from Khartoum. He was, I believe, referred from UNHCR Yei to Juba, not passing through GMT.

No one in Goli knew about the professional register [the book I had installed in each settlement for registering employable professionals]. The paper we wrote on that has not been disseminated. There is no system for communicating with the population and from my observations, very few who could have the will to do so. The 'class alienation' which has caused so much friction in Goli is largely the cause and it seems there is little concern among the educated to change this - although one begins to see some glimmers of hope here and there.

The teachers had not explained their salary position to the community until our general meeting. There was great interest and the obvious 'sacrifice' the teachers are making was greatly appreciated. I never before saw such enthusiasm in Goli. The headmaster made an eloquent speech and one thing he pointed out is of great relevance to the overall policy. He said that because children have been out of school for three years, they have great difficulties disciplining them at first. All the social chaos one sees among adults is demonstrated in the school. Perhaps one should think again about all the delays in implementing educational facilities. Perhaps schools are one familiar institution which brings *order* and which would greatly assist the community in restructuring itself - particularly since there are more than enough trained teachers. (They don't need buildings, but they *do* need equipment.)

---

[36] The settlements were established on the false premise that a community of 3,000+ would be a viable economic unit, supplying sufficient demand for its own products. But, as McGregor discovered, all the district's demand for carpentry products was being filled in Yei by 20 Sudanese who could not expand unless they could get products to Juba. Carpenters in settlements were dependent on the agencies to purchase their products (McGregor in Wilson *et al.* 1985.) In Goli alone there were 13 highly skilled carpenters at the time.

Goli needs a market, including a butcher. People are well-informed about dietary deficiencies and want to supplement their diet with food at the moment only available in Yei. There seems to be a bit of money for some at least - lots of people have managed to sell vegetables, despite having no transport. Raphael has approached the chief and he is agreeable to the idea of a market.

There is no system for providing materials to late arrivals. Sometimes this is because the foreman has not been informed of their arrival. But genuine cases exist. One woman and her children have only one bucket, they never got a hoe or a blanket. Many families have only one blanket for three people (although I realize this is better than in lots of settlements). How people manage in this cold with one blanket for three I cannot imagine. I sleep on the ground as they do, but I have a mat and two blankets under me and three on top. I sleep in my clothes and keep my cardigan on. Most of *them* don't even have clothes enough to cover their bodies. Do you know that worms come up from under the ground in the night and bite? And that this settlement is infested by rats? (The health worker or sanitarian, whatever he is called, gave a great lecture to the general meeting on why they had rats. I had been urging them to get on with building granaries, but he reminded them that it was their own dirty habits which attracted the rats. He pointed out the reasons for each household having a rubbish pit, and the need to clear all empty spaces - which in their present overgrown condition attract the beasts.) But, back to the distribution of materials to those newcomers who never received theirs. I don't know how it can be done without mismanagement by block leaders. Unless, of course, the foreman goes into every house and checks, which would be impossible. I'm afraid that the only fair system would be to have some kind of household ration card given out at the border with destination and any allocation there indicated. The present system is impossible. And, it is made *totally* impossible when there are not enough materials for distribution. Surely there is no excuse (if, as you say, money is not the problem) for not having a minimum kit for every household and in sufficient quantity. It is impossible to maintain equality when items - such as the recent supply of cornflour - comes. How can Raphael distribute 30 50-kilogram bags of cornflour to 4000 people? It's crazy.

And there is another matter. Payment for houses. The health worker has done a good job encouraging everyone to get his house finished, and the latrine, bathing shelter, drying table, kitchen, rubbish pit, etc. finished. Some people have done all these things and now, understandably, wonder why payment is withheld. As one ex-soldier pointed out, if a person who has completed his compound is paid immediately, it will encourage the rest to hurry. They, quite naturally, wonder why this money (which was supposed to be an 'incentive' *for* hurrying) is not paid after so many months.

Goli has the usual problems about getting agricultural land. There is plenty of uncultivated land, but despite all the agreements, the locals resist allowing them to start digging. There is great interest in cash crops, including tobacco *and* forestry. Imagine, one refugee pointed out that since they could never be sure they would ever be able to return to Uganda, they should start planting trees! He gave me a lecture on deforestation problems which refugees were causing and told me that they should be planting citrus to help their diets. He explained how in a couple of years they would already start benefiting. A lot of vital energy and enthusiasm is being wasted because of lack of attention to these matters. [In fairness, Akuti the agricultural worker, had approached the National Tobacco Corporation about growing tobacco.]

Regarding your outline for the foreman's report: in short, my first reaction was that it is too complicated. While foremen can be trained to code age groups, even the wear and tear on the pages of the registration books is going to be a problem. More serious is the complete absurdity of ages recorded. Our census revealed great inaccuracies. Whoever filled in the forms in the first place was not careful. To base much planning on them is clearly useless. I don't want to discourage thorough reporting, but we are asking untrained personnel to do what trained people would find excessive and *they* would have desks, files, lights to work at night, etc. See what comes of it, but I fear it may just overwhelm the majority of our foremen.

As far as record-keeping is concerned, births and deaths are not being properly recorded, but Goli had no foreman. No foreman equals no order in a settlement. But, the biggest problem of all is the lack of paper and proper facilities for people to work. Committees don't even have paper. I have been doling out my money for exercise books and pens because obviously they can't function properly without them.

I could say a lot more about what I have observed here, but the kerosene is about to run out. When my lantern leaves with me, there will be only *one* light left in the entire settlement. It is very dark at night in Goli, but despite that people have tried to organize some social events. Last night we went to watch the young people dancing in pitch darkness. I keep getting visits from delegations from the Muslims, the Catholics and whatever other religion happens to be here. I finally got all of them to meet together to talk about their problems and they are very conscious of the dangerous divisions which have been fostered by successive regimes in Uganda.

They are planning a farewell 'day' for me next Sunday. The most destructive part of my activities here is the sense that they believe that they *needed* someone to come from outside to straighten up their mess. Where *are* the leaders? How *can* we escape this role which is, after all, if you analyse my relationship with them, extremely authoritarian and even fascist?! It raises lots of questions about the role of coercion and who should practise it among a group of people whose society has totally broken down. Have you ever read Turnbull's study of the *Ik*? I see a lot of unfortunate parallels. I will close for now. See you soon and thank Monique for sending the chocolate. I ate it all in one go, hiding in my tent so no one would see me and burying the wrappers the next morning. Sometimes I do not believe that I am in the midst of such a scene of contradictions and hypocrisy. In three days I must have blown £S20 on sugar and tea because I cannot meet with people and drink it in front of them. Oh yes, we preach against drinking - and we should - but I am now trying the local brew every night with Raphael, James and the storeman. It's quite good - tastes a bit like vodka - and I make sure the storeman buys it from a Sudanese, so that I don't encourage the refugee women to start brewing as their main 'income generating' activity. That Buganda woman who tried to kill herself by eating glass last summer has been cooking for us. I pay her. Since I eat the rice and beans with chicken, I cannot understand why the refugees complain about the diet - smile!

Yours,

P.S Oh yes, I should also report that I am leaving £S30 with Raphael to pay the husband who beat up that woman for building a 'reading room' in the office compound. I have promised to send games for the games room and books for the reading room. Then he can pay the compensation to the injured party - I could not bear the trouble which would result if something wasn't done, and it *did* encourage the wife to return to her husband! ['For better or for worse.']

Note:

It should perhaps be mentioned that in the fullness of time it transpired that, along with most reports from settlements, the programme officer never had time to read this letter.

3

Deployed like chessmen

Introduction

As was shown in Chapter One, most refugees attempted to survive without the benefit of the assistance programme. The vast majority of those who were allowed to take decisions themselves, only registered for a settlement under conditions of extreme duress. In 1983 about three-quarters of those interviewed who had settled in the border areas during the first three years of the exodus still maintained that they were 'OK here' (see Table 1:10, page 56). The breakdown of security along the border, and the inadequacies of medical services were the main reasons that people were finally forced to move. The main attraction of the settlements was the availability of clinics and primary schools there. Refugees who arrived during the first three years did instigate the building of many self-help primary schools in the border areas, but the lack of any financial assistance, even for books and stationery, together with occasional government interference,[1] made it impossible to provide enough places for the thousands of children who had been attending school in Uganda.

Other factors from 1982 onwards influenced the movement of people into settlements. The two most immediate obstacles facing refugees after 1982 were the lack of land on which to establish their own farms and reduced opportunities for casual labour in exchange for food. The drought which struck some parts of the district in April/May, 1983, forced large numbers of self-settled refugees to register (at least temporarily) at the Panyume and Kimbe reception centres.[2] Throughout the entire period, but particularly from mid-July 1982, incursions into the Sudan by the Ugandan army influenced some of those who survived these attacks to move to the security of the settlements. But when Sudanese military personnel and certain local

[1] Sudan's educational policy for the south requires parents to build a school before the government assumes responsibility for staffing it. Most of the refugee teachers who were employed in schools recognized by government were paid as 'volunteers' (i.e. £S5 per month). When, together with locals, refugees began to build schools, the government was unable to afford to recognize them in this way. In the Kajo-Kaji area we discovered only one such unofficial school still operating. Any refugee children who were being educated in the sub-district had to attend the Sudanese schools. In a very small area near Kaya there were 12 such unofficial schools. In one of these nearly 500 children, including Sudanese are enrolled. The educational authorities have tried to close these schools, but since the Sudanese also benefit, local pressure kept them open.

[2] For security reasons the reception centres first established at Kaya and Nyori had to be moved inland to these locations. The reception centres at Kajo-Kaji and Livolo were closed and Mondikolo became the reception point for this area.

officials colluded with the UNLA in 1983, and again, at Kaya, in late 1984, large numbers of refugee households were again disturbed.

In 1983 those refugees who were subject to attacks by the UNLA (and those who were uprooted following the Sudan government's decision to succumb to Uganda's demands that they be removed from the borders) at least had the option of moving to a settlement. But in late 1984 when the problem arose along the Zaire/Uganda border at Kaya, UNHCR had by then determined not to extend its programme by opening new settlements, and refugees were left without this option.[3]

Could much of the disruption which families suffered in their country of asylum have been avoided? The evidence suggests that it could. The composition of settlement populations and those who remained self-settled on the border and the economic relations which were established between them, suggest that an assistance policy prepared to respond to need on the basis of demographic changes might have avoided a great deal of the disruption families suffered. Medical and educational services could have been provided. When land ran short, information could have been circulated concerning the whereabouts of other uncultivated areas. Even transport to new places of settlement could have been arranged. But the most important impediment faced by refugees in their efforts to maintain economic independence outside the planned settlements was their lack of security. As one refugee put it, 'People could have survived well on the borders if, and only if ... the Uganda government [had not been allowed] to violate international law and to come in to harass refugees in another country, another sovereign country ... Somebody who has crossed the border and taken asylum somewhere should be safe. But here to be safe is to be safe in inverted commas. It's unfortunate.'

The deployment

As one UNHCR consultant also discovered, 'the refugee population is not divided up into two separate groups of settled and self-settled' people (Day-Thompson 1984.) The reality of the situation became apparent to him when he was responsible for moving the thousands of refugees who had been living in the Otogo and Kaya transit camps - some for up to twelve months and more. He came to the conclusion that the refugee population did not comprise one group of 'broken men accepting charity' with the other, the unassisted, constituting 'those brave individualists maintaining their

[3] In early 1984 when COMREF officials visited the area demanding that the self-settled be moved from Kajo-Kaji to settlements, UNHCR pointed out the millions of dollars required to accommodate so many self-settled refugees. The donors, they said, would be unwilling to come forward with these amounts. Although six new settlements were opened in Maridi District for the thousands who were uprooted during the following months, UNHCR gradually reduced their assistance to any who registered at the Mondikolo reception centre. This policy was aimed at stopping the local officials from disturbing yet more households.

freedom in the face of adversity'. Instead he found that the refugee community is deployed 'like a set of chess-men across the board'.

...because of the infinitely flexible shape of the families making up the refugee population, added to the almost total mobility which is possible [in Yei River District] ... a large part of the refugee caseload (to use a hateful term) switches constantly but especially at harvest and planting times, between camp/settlement and border. It is necessary to leave some family members in the camp/settlement to claim food rations for the whole family, etc., as well as to maintain their right to the allotted plot. Equally it is necessary to have others at the border at all times to tend the growing crops and to maintain a right to the ground and *tukuls* [huts]. It is a perfectly reasonable and understandable system (ibid).

Believing that refugees simply represent a 'normal cross-section human community, [sic] probably reflecting much of what it was before it had to go into exile', he appreciates their strategies as confirming their capacity to use their 'wits and muscle' to survive in a 'pretty difficult world.'

Refugees, at least some of them, *are* highly mobile; 45.6 per cent of the self-settled interviewed still lived in the same place as they did on first entering Sudan. Those who remained close enough to the border were able, so long as the opposition remained in control of the area, to slip back into Uganda for food. Up to mid-1982, through binoculars one could see women cultivating on the Uganda side of the Kaya river even though the UNLA was stationed only a few miles away at Oraba. Others were able to slip in and out of Uganda to trade. For example, during 1982-3 all of the fish sold in Yei came from Uganda. Fishmongers travelled through protected corridors from the Kochi and the Nile rivers to the Sudan. They carried receipts proving they had paid the guerillas a tax for this service. Later, when the UNLA made the last push through the north, the fish trade had to be re-routed through Zaire and the supplies in the market declined. Throughout 1982 the town of Moyo was sealed off, with several hundred people living in the mission under guard by the UNLA, but during 1983 trading began between Kajo-Kaji and Moyo. Some refugees - particularly women - were able to take advantage of the markets established to serve both sides of the border. A considerable volume of trade also occurs between the Zaire border and Yei. (McGregor in Wilson *et al.* 1985.)

The refugee chess-board in Eastern Equatoria encompasses not only the settlements, the border areas, and Yei town, but also areas across the Zaire border, Juba - 160 kilometres in the other direction - and distant parts of the Sudan. It also includes Uganda and other African countries. We asked the assisted refugees about the location of their 'relatives' and found that, in addition to relatives deployed in Africa, 180, or 8.9 per cent of the sample, reported having relatives living somewhere outside the African continent.

In addition to these movements and those back and forth into Uganda for trading purposes or to get food, and quite aside from the official repatriation programme mounted by UNHCR, whenever there was a rumour that life

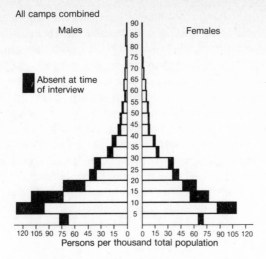

Fig 3.1. Age distribution of all assisted refugees

was secure enough to do so, many people attempt to return to their homes in Uganda. Refugees in settlements were asked whether members of their household had recently returned to Uganda. They were not asked the reasons for such returns or whether or not they were thought to have returned to stay. The location of relatives according to responses to questions posed to refugees in settlements is shown in Table 3.1.

Unfortunately, however, one cannot assume with Day-Thompson (1984) that the dispersal of relatives is always the result of strategic planning for survival or that 'relatives' make up a mutual support group. Ugandans distinguish between kinsmen who would normally live in the same compound, the household, and those who are more distantly related by blood and marriage. Norms of reciprocal obligations only obtain between members of the 'household'. Unfortunately only one of the questions posed to assisted

TABLE 3.1: Location of relatives (assisted)

'Do you have relatives'	'Yes' responses (%)
Outside settlements?	74.6
In Zaire?	43.8
In other settlements?	88.3
Recently returned to Uganda?	17.3

settlers about the location of their kinsmen made this distinction. The response to it shows that while people include members of their household when asked about kinsmen, the numbers upon whom they might reasonably expect to depend is far smaller than these answers imply. Although 43.8 per cent of the households in settlements had *relatives* living in Zaire, only 19.4 per cent had members of their intimate family circle living there. The unassisted refugee households interviewed were only asked one question about the location of kinsmen. They were asked whether any members of their *household* were living in settlements and 31.1 per cent responded 'yes'.

Although more people simply walk home or 'repatriate themselves' than those who join official repatriation missions, the movement of these people is related to their reasons for flight. Those households which reported having relatives who recently returned to Uganda were analysed in terms of the year they first entered Sudan and by the year the first member of the household

TABLE 3.2: Relatives returned to Uganda by year
first entered the Sudan (assisted)

Relatives returned to Uganda	Year first entered the Sudan				
	1979	1980	1981	1982	1983
Yes	11.8	11.1	14.1	25.9	12.8
No	88.2	88.9	85.9	74.1	87.2
No. of households	229	423	256	802	243

TABLE 3.3: Relatives returned to Uganda by year
first household member arrived in settlement (assisted)

Relatives returned to Uganda	Year first household member arrived in settlement (assisted)				
	1979	1980	1981	1982	1983
Yes	0	5.2	17.4	23.7	13.5
No	100.0	94.8	82.6	76.3	86.5
No. of households	7	58	109	853	926

came to the settlement. The results are shown in Tables 3.2 and 3.3. These data demonstrate the relative stability, or determined tenacity, of those who both entered the Sudan and came to settlements during the first two years, compared with those who entered later on. None of those who arrived in 1979 reported having relatives who recently returned to Uganda whereas 23.7 per cent of those who arrived in 1982 report at least someone among their kinsmen having gone back to Uganda. These data support the earlier discussion of the causes of exodus for most of the civilians now in the Sudan; there, I suggested that the most important factor in the exodus was the existence of UNLA. It is the undisciplined soldiery of the UNLA rather than opposition to the present government which has led most people to flee Uganda and it is UNLA's continued vendetta against the civilians which keeps them in exile. Had the transitional government in Uganda not foundered and perhaps had the army been integrated on the lines taken after Zimbabwe's independence, or even had the elections been seen to be free and fair, most of the civilians now living in exile would never have fled.

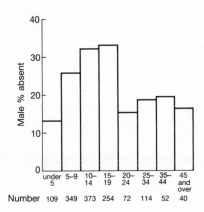

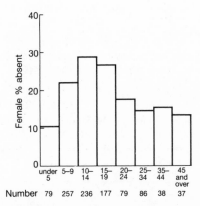

Fig 3.2. Percentage absent in each age group by sex

Absentees: unreliability or mobility?

The survey indicates quite clearly that the demographic characteristics of refugee populations vary dramatically. General statements can therefore be misleading. Again, one cannot assume, with Day-Thompson (1984), that *all* refugees have the same capacity or opportunity to manipulate the advantages of the 'aid system'. All statistical data collected in a social survey must be treated with great caution, but this is particularly the case when studying a refugee population. The analysis of the statistical data included some checks on the internal consistency of informants' responses and some of these will be discussed throughout the book. A reassuring, though very limited, check on the reliability of the data was made by the Oxford team in 1984. They based a more intensive study on the survey sample of households which included individuals who were 'vulnerable'. They found only seven cases where a year later the same people were not at the same location. However, there was some disparity between the survey data and the estimates of the total population of assisted refugees as made by the UNHCR office. This is not surprising given the difficulties of accounting for numbers under the conditions of an emergency programme and the obvious incentive for refugees to inflate their numbers in order to receive more rations.

In addition to this survey, there were three other sources of population estimates. First, in each settlement the settlement officer was expected to keep a register with the names of family members, and his block leaders also had their lists for food distribution. Second, the UNHCR offices kept an estimate of the total population of settlements and transit camps. This estimate was based on the settlement officer's register and on information on numbers of people who were moved by lorry from borders to transit camps or settlements. Third, the World Food Programme also had a population figure for each settlement, but this estimate was 'negotiated' between UNHCR and WFP to determine the food rations for a settlement. My survey results suggest that of those three sources, the Yei UNHCR office figure was usually the more reliable.

According to the UNHCR office, the total population of assisted refugees at the time the survey was completed was 95,050. Assuming that our sample was representative, the survey found a total population of 106,750 - a surplus of 11,700 (12 per cent). In the notes on methods I describe the efforts we made to ensure that all members of the household were present for the interview. Despite such precautions, one had to recognize that, given the general lack of food, it would be only logical for refugees to attempt to inflate their numbers.[4] Certainly agencies assumed refugees always exaggerated their numbers. We therefore scrutinized those who were absent from the interview

---

[4] One must stress again, as is detailed in the notes on methods, we were asking people to stay home from work in their fields, from labouring to earn food when there were no rations, and from clinics when they were ill, etc.

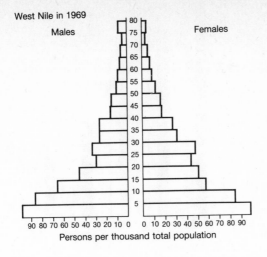

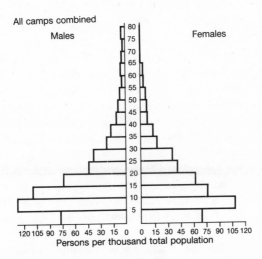

Fig 3.3. Age distribution of settlement population compared with 1969 Census of the West Nile

because it seemed the obvious place to look to find the evidence for such deliberate inflation. However, when examining the distribution of age groups for the total population compared with the distribution of those who were absent in each age group (as shown in Figure 3.3), it seems very unlikely that in such a large sample informants could have invented an absent population to correspond so perfectly with the age distribution of those who were present for the interview. Moreover, there was no correlation between the degree of correspondence of survey results with UNHCR's population

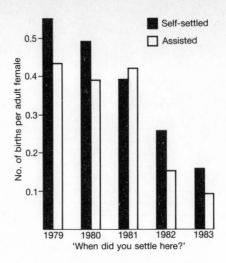

Fig 3.4. Number of births per adult female since settling 'here' (17 years and over)

estimates and the numbers absent from the interviews. While one can draw no firm conclusions from the analysis of the absentees, it does reveal the enormous social dislocation which has occurred.

Among those absent were 922 children, (or 39.2 per cent of absentees), who were said to be enrolled in school. In all age groups more men than women were absent, but the differences are not significant. Figure 3.2 shows the numbers and percentage of each age group for both men and women who were absent from the interview. One might suspect that at least some of the men over 15 years were engaged in fighting inside Uganda, but it cannot be assumed all were: on numerous occasions, men who were absent from the interview visited us in our tents in the evening, explaining where they had been.

The population of the transit camps was notoriously unstable, with people moving in and out during the long months of waiting for a settlement. If one accepts UNHCR estimates as reliable, the data from the survey of Goli, Otogo, and Kaya transit camps account for 7,371 of these extra numbers recorded by the survey leaving only 4,329 'extra' to account for. The total population for Otogo transit camp alone was 54 per cent higher than UNHCR estimates. Many people who were in transit camps were unwilling recipients of aid, people who had been forced out of the self-settled areas by the drought. Once the rains resumed, many people returned to their self-settled compounds. Movement in and out of settlements was further encouraged after mid-July when, in the absence of full standard rations, extra rations of edible fat and other items such as blankets were given to refugees so that they could sell these to buy staple foods.

Two transit camps were close to Yei and I met one refugee whose family was in Kaya who considered himself to be part of this camp's population, although he preferred to remain in Yei, unassisted, until a settlement opened. Given the tendency for the self-settled to send some members of their households - usually the more vulnerable - to settlements, informants in transit camps may have included some of their self-settled relatives as 'absent' members of the household. Informants at Otogo transit reported 225 absentees: 61 of these were aged between 10 and 15; 47 men and 49 women aged 15 and older were also absent.

Table 3.4 compares the survey data with UNHCR's population estimate and shows the number and percentage of differences between it and the survey results. It also includes the percentage absent from interview and the average family size for each. The survey found 8 settlements with a *smaller* total population than that estimated by UNHCR. In 14 settlements the variation (whether higher or lower) between the sample results and UNHCR's estimate was between 0.4 and 11 per cent. There were 5 settlements which had only recently opened - Wonduruba, Dororolili, Dukuni, Adio, and Katigiri. It may be that the progress towards filling Adio and Dororolili had not been regularly recorded in the Yei office, accounting for the higher population according to the survey.

According to our survey, Mondikolo population is greater than UNHCR's estimate by 317 people. This difference is partly explained by the fact that there were a number of people who were ostensibly living in a transit camp, but who, for several months, had been removed from the assistance list. They had moved into the Sudan in early 1983 and, as some had cattle, at first they had been told they could remain at Mondikolo, a settlement established for herdsmen. Later the policy changed and they were asked to move on to another transit camp further inland, in preparation for moving to a settlement when one became available, but they refused even though by this time *all* their cattle were gone. After warning them several times that unless they agreed to move their food rations would be cut off, the programme officer finally took this action. In Mondikolo, I found more than 100 of these people still living in tents or under hastily constructed shelters, most of whom were in an appalling state of health.[5]

[5] The refusal of these people to move to another location where they would receive food, medical and other assistance cannot be explained in terms of mere 'stubborness'. I called an emergency meeting of the heads of these households. Pointing out that murder and suicide are forbidden by all religions, I suggested they were committing both 'sins' by remaining where they and their children would certainly all starve to death. Very few were still strong enough to do piecework for the locals. One family agreed they would leave for a transit camp with the next transport. Another family was willing to move, but the two daughters, their children, and their mother had to wait until their father died. He lay, in their tent, a living skeleton, too weak to be moved. Some eight months earlier he had been diagnosed as suffering from internal parasites but no medication was ever administered. The remaining families were adamant; they would die in Mondikolo. UNHCR had broken its promise that they could remain there; they now refused to accept any other arrangement.

Table 3.4: A comparison of survey and UNHCR population estimates, average household size, and percentage absent at time of interview

Name of settlement	Population according to survey	Population according to UNHCR	Over UNHCR estimate No.	Over UNHCR estimate %	Under UNHCR estimate No.	Under UNHCR estimate %	Absent at time of interview %	Average size of household %
Adio	1,270	1,000	270	27.0	-	-	5.50	3.63
Dororolili	3,520	2,800	720	25.7	-	-	3.98	4.89
Dukuni	2,600	2,476	124	5.0	-	-	13.46	3.66
Goli	5,340	4,792	548	11.4	-	-	23.03	7.42
Gumbari	5,800	5,556	244	4.4	-	-	13.79	8.06
Kala	4,170	4,308	-	-	138	3.2	20.14	4.48
Katigiri	1,030	975	55	5.6	-	-	0.00	2.86
Kunsuk	5,040	5,069	-	-	29	0.6	25.55	6.90
Limbe	3,470	3,359	111	3.3	-	-	24.53	4.28

Limuru	3,590	3,823	-	-	233	6.1	16.38	4.49
Logobero	4,260	3,858	402	10.4	-	-	33.84	4.95
Mogiri	800	808	-	-	8	1.0	26.25	6.15
Mondikolo	1,620	1,303	317	24.3	-	-	25.31	4.38
Mopoko	6,510	5,497	1,013	18.4	-	-	33.85	7.94
Morsak	2,660	2,500	160	6.4	-	-	19.92	4.03
Otogo	4,360	4,344	16	0.4	-	-	31.21	5.19
Pakula	5,340	5,460	-	-	120	2.2	31.14	7.03
Roronyo	3,420	3,930	-	-	510	13.0	26.23	4.22
Tore (New)	3,260	3,780	-	-	520	13.8	9.14	4.53
Tore (Old)	1,170	651	519	79.7	-	-	16.24	6.50
Wonduruba	2,780	3,015	-	-	235	7.8	13.67	3.86
Wudabi	7,240	5,617	1,623	28.9	-	-	40.88	8.83
Transits:								
Goli	4,170	3,788	382	10.1	-	-	7.19	3.90
Koya	11,870	8,900	2,970	33.4	-	-	22.35	4.84
Otogo	11,460	7,441	4,019	54.0	-	-	19.63	5.43

New and Old Tore are adjacent. The UNHCR population estimates for the combined population of these settlements was 4,431; the survey found a combined population of 4,430. However, these two settlements were separately surveyed. While the Old Tore count came to 519 more than UNHCR believed were living there, there were 520 less people than expected living in New Tore!

Wudabi settlement, according to the survey, had 1,623 more residents than UNHCR believed to be there. Wudabi is only 6 kilometres from the Zaire border and about 40 kilometres by foot from the Ugandan border. Just over a range of high hills to the south is an area where many self-settled refugees live - a half day's walk away. Inside Zaire there is a large 'international' market which attracts refugees engaged in petty trade. It might be assumed that some self-settled refugees, perhaps even including some from the Zaire side of the border, had unofficially moved into this settlement, but they would have had to compete for the rations which were based on UNHCR and WFP lower estimates. It was this settlement in which violence erupted when the supply of food was interrupted. The settlers took up pangas against their settlement officer and accused the local Sudanese officials of having diverted food. Throughout 1983, Wudabi was a difficult settlement to manage.

Wudabi had other attractions besides rations and its accessibility to the Zaire border. It was near a tea plantation which employed a large number of workers, and refugees - mainly children aged 12 and upwards - could be seen congregated at the roadside every morning awaiting transport to work. Just before dark, streams of weary children returned to pick their way across the log bridge over the Yei River and walk home to the settlement. Of those absent from the interviews in Wudabi, 49.3 per cent were between 10 and 19 years of age; 39.9 per cent were below the age of 10. Doubtless some of these children were attending schools, held at that time under the trees.

Even while recognizing that refugees send a disproportionate number of children to the settlements because there are schools available, (see Figure 3.1) and that there is a bias in favour of educating boys, there are still problems in interpreting the data concerning children in the 5 to 9 age group. In 1969, according to the West Nile census, there were 171 children per 1,000 in this age group: 86 boys and 85 girls. According to our survey, there were 236 children per 1,000 in this age group: 127 boys and 109 girls.

Were all the absent children in this age group attending school at the time of the interview? Ugandans put a high premium on educating their children. Early in the interview informants were asked how many children in the households were 'able' to go to school. According to the sample, the total was 36,440. They were then asked how many were actually going to school. The total number reportedly in school was 19,950. As only primary schools (and four intermediate schools) were available for children in settlements, we assumed informants were defining 'able to go to school' in terms of the numbers of 5 to 14 year olds in the household. But later on in the interview, when questions were addressed to each individual, the results show there were 24,200 of the 44,960 children between 5 and 14 years of age who said they were attending school, or 4,250 more children than the number earlier reported as being in school. About half of these were 5 to 9 year olds, and 11,530 were said to be enrolled in school. Of these, 3,210 were absent at the time of the interview.

It is difficult to invent the description of an individual required by the interview. These children were born before the civil war began. Their numbers do not therefore reflect either the effects of malnutrition or the hardships of flight on the fertility of their mothers, although both these factors affect children in the under 5 age group who are much more vulnerable to malnutrition and disease. But one might assume that some children in the 5 to 9 age group would also succumb to the perils of flight. A separate examination of even the poor records of deaths available in the settlements showed that large numbers of this age group had indeed died. The nutritional survey carried out in 1984 revealed a very high rate of severe malnourishment among children 5 to 9 years of age (Wilson *et al.* 1985)

The question of whether absenteeism of this age group reflected unreliability or mobility cannot be finally answered from these data. It is even possible that in some cases the numbers of children in the 5 to 9 age group were inflated by descriptions of dead children. However, one must remember that while the survey of unassisted households did not discriminate comparable age groups, there were only about half as many children in the 6 to 16 age group living in unassisted households.

The deployment of households

It may not be assumed that even members of a household form an interdependent support group. As is true everywhere, the norms of family responsibility as well as the actual behaviour of individual members of the so-called extended family within Ugandan society vary according to the closeness of the relationships as well as by the idiosyncracies of individuals.

In this study household types were categorized according to the characteristics of the persons registered as the head of the plot in the settlement. 'Normal' families included those where both a husband and a wife were present, and those married women whose polygamous husbands were living in the same settlement. The heads of other household groups in settlements not constituting 'normal' families in these terms were distinguished by age, sex or marital status. These data are compared with responses about the location of their relatives and shown in Table 3.5.

In the case of the unassisted refugees, data describing type of household in these terms were collected for only 598 cases. In Table 3.6 I have distinguished only the 'normal' families from those headed by single men and women, separating the 18 cases which were headed by young people 16 years

TABLE 3.5: Location of kinsmen by type of family (assisted)*

Locations		'Normal' %	Male under 21 %	Female under 21 %	Adult female %	Adult male %	Widow post-1979 %	Widow pre-1979 %	Combined totals %	No.
Relatives outside settlement in Sudan	Yes	78.3	77.7	73.5	72.3	76.3	61.0	58.2	75.7	1,505
	No	21.7	22.3	26.5	27.7	23.7	39.0	41.8	24.3	483
Household members in Zaire	Yes	24.0	16.5	17.4	16.2	18.6	15.0	10.2	20.5	392
	No	76.0	83.5	82.6	83.8	81.4	85.0	89.8	79.5	1,517
Relatives in Zaire	Yes	50.2	45.5	27.7	31.6	41.8	40.8	30.6	45.1	884
	No	49.8	54.5	72.3	68.4	58.2	59.2	69.4	54.9	1,075

Relatives in other settlements	Yes	90.3	89.3	89.8	87.7	87.5	82.1	82.1	88.8 1,782
	No	9.7	10.7	10.2	12.3	12.5	17.9	17.9	11.2 224
Relatives recently returned to Uganda	Yes	17.6	20.0	22.9	16.3	19.3	11.5	14.3	17.7 349
	No	82.4	80.0	77.1	83.7	80.7	88.5	85.7	82.3 1,620
No. of this type of household		1,071	253	50	181	289	106	67	2,017
% of all households		53.1	12.5	2.5	9.0	14.3	5.3	3.3	100

* The percentages are based on those who answered the question 'yes' or 'no'.

TABLE 3.6 Type of household by size of household (self settled)

Type of household	'Normal'	Male under 16	Female under 16	Single male	Single female	Totals
%	73.9	2.8	0.2	15.6	7.5	100%
Number	442	17	1	93	45	598
Average size of households	7.1	6.1	8	5.3	4.1	Overall average size 7.15

or younger. The other families included men and women who were divorced, separated, widowed, and ten were very elderly widows or widowers. This table also gives the average size of the different types of households.

In settlements, 54 per cent of the households constituted 'normal' families (as I defined them), while among the self-settled interviewed where such information is available, in 73.9 per cent of the households both spouses were present.

In terms of the deployment of kinsmen of the refugees in settlements, these data show that households headed by women generally have fewer relatives elsewhere. This pattern of family dispersal among the self-settled refugees is shown in Table 3:7. More 'normal' families had relatives in settlements than the others. This highly differentiated deployment of households and kinsmen had significant implications for the success of the programme as will be shown in Chapter Six when vulnerable groups are discussed.

There are other discreet variations in dispersal patterns which suggest how difficult it is to generalize about refugees' behaviour. Large differences were found *between* camps. More people living in New Tore, Otogo Transit, Katigiri, Adio, Gumbari, and Wudabi have close relatives in Zaire than do people in other settlements: the percentages by camps ranged from 0 per cent to 61.8 per cent. Replies to other questions about the deployment of relatives revealed similar differences between camps. These are shown in Appendix III, Table III.1, page 398. For example, no one in Mogiri had a relative who had returned to Uganda, while 40.3 per cent of the sample of Goli indicated that one or more relatives had recently returned there.

These differences between the behaviour of people in different settlements can partly be explained in terms of the distances between the camp and the border, or between the camp and the area within Uganda from which people have originally moved. (For example, those who came from lower Terego or

TABLE 3.7: 'Are members of household now in assisted settlements?' by type of family (self-settled)*

Household members now in assisted settlements	Head of household		
	Single male %	Single female %	'Normal' family %
Yes	44.2	46.5	39.6
No	55.8	53.5	60.4
No. of households	110	46	442

* Note that data describing the sex or marital status of household head were collected
in only a small number of interviews of the self-settled.

Maracha, i.e. further away, were less widely 'deployed' than those who came
from Aringa County, just across Sudan's border.)

The deployment of ethnic groups

Ethnicity is also a factor which is related to the dispersal of relatives. Of the
1,027 Kakwa households interviewed in self-settled areas, only 13.8 per cent
had close relatives in a settlement, and only 18.2 per cent of the Nubi had sent
a relative to a settlement. It will be recalled that these two groups entered the
Sudan more or less *en masse* during the first two years of the crisis and had the
advantage of a shared language in mixing with the locals. Many also spoke
Swahili, a language some Sudanese acquired while in exile in Uganda.

It is interesting to compare this ethnic variable with the reasons the
assisted refugees gave for coming to the settlements. Almost half the Nubi
reported that before coming to a settlement they had been harassed or had
run out of money, and 42.3 per cent of the (very few) Kakwa in settlements
gave such reasons for moving to a settlement. Only 10.4 per cent of the
Kakwa had come because they 'heard the settlements were better'. It has
already been noted that when asked why they did not go to a settlement, most
of the unassisted refugees said that they were 'OK here', but apparently the
Nubi, with 94.5 per cent giving this response, were the *most* 'OK'. Perhaps
this reflects their relative success in trading in the self-settled areas.

Almost all of Uganda's ethnic groups were represented in the refugee
population of the district, but the vast majority were Lugbara-speakers. The

ethnic composition of the settlements and of the households of the unassisted refugees interviewed are shown in Table 1.1, page 50, Chapter One. The interviews of the self-settled were conducted in five different areas. The ethnic composition of these households by area and by year of settling at the place interviewed, are shown in Appendix III, Table III.2, page 399. The overall number of Kakwa and Madi appears to be about the same, but by 1983, the majority of the Madi were living in settlements while most of the Kakwa had managed to remain independent. Most of the Madi entering the Sudan went to live on the east bank of the Nile.

It is very likely that the numbers of Nubi are grossly under-represented in these data. Given their predisposition towards trading as a means of livelihood, most Nubi would have been found in centres of market activity and our interviews were mainly conducted in remote rural areas. The pattern of Nubi settlement shows up in the few (170) interviews conducted in Yei town where about one-third of those included were Nubi.

The group of people who have been combined under the category 'others' comprise 9 different ethnic communities from Uganda. (Among the self-settled refugees there were 14 different ethnic groups represented as 'others'.) Although their numbers were small, constituting only 2.4 per cent of the total settlement population, they had a disproportionate impact on social relations. There were, according to the sample, 0.5 per cent or 540 Baganda living in settlements. Coming as they did from a relatively privileged class in Uganda, as a group they had more difficulty adjusting to life in the agricultural settlements.[6] Some of these were women, spouses of members of the Ugandan military. Most were ex-airforce trained as pilots, radar, and radio operators. Some were students who were driven out by the war. A few of the more highly educated men were employed in settlement administration. One, a relative of the Kabaka, the King of Buganda, was first employed as a settlement foreman, and later became head of the Red Cross family tracing service. One young single Muganda living at Wudabi was rapidly sinking into serious depression. He knew his family was in Kenya, but had no way of joining them. Among the self-settled refugees 14 Luganda-speaking householders were interviewed, 35.7 per cent of whom lived alone.

Within the refugee community there were individuals who came from areas associated with Obote's own ethnic group. One woman said she was Obote's 'sister' and reported that he had even attended her marriage to a wealthy Nubi merchant. Despite her family connections and his having formerly supported the UPC, the two of them now live quietly in

---

[6] The relationship of the Baganda to the other ethnic communities in Uganda is not just a matter of educational or financial position. There are many poor, uneducated Baganda. Like the Creole of Sierra Leone, whatever their economic and social status within their own community, the Baganda consider themselves superior to most other communities. (Harrell-Bond *et al.* 1977.) These attitudes began to break down during Amin's rule when some West Nilers began to gain prominence. Like the Creoles, politics affected their relationships and some inter-marriage began to take place between them and the Baganda. (Harrell-Bond 1975)

Wonduruba. On the other hand, many such individuals were suspected by the others as being spies for the present government. There were a number of defections from the UNLA and on occasion these individuals were beaten by their fellow refugees or had to be removed from the settlements to safeguard their lives.

Lugbara and Madi comprised 94.8 per cent of the settlement populations. The ethnic composition of each settlement and the three transit camps is presented in Figure III.1 in Appendix III, pages 404–5. Most settlements were predominantly Madi or Lugbara, but in six settlements one or other of these two groups represented a significant minority. In Old Tore over 50 per cent of the population was made up of 'others'; with Lugbara and Madi combined representing the minority. Even where the population was overwhelmingly of one group or the other, the fact of their shared language did not necessarily promote harmonious relations. The Lugbara were particularly a divided group. They originate from different parts of the West Nile, they have a history of strong clan divisions, and are further factionalized by religion. For example, in Goli settlement, where nearly everyone speaks Lugbara, the population was divided rather evenly on religious grounds. (See Figure III.2, Appendix III, pages 406–7.)

Where are the bells?

The arrival of so many thousands of Ugandan refugees into the district has introduced a new mix of religious affiliations which is likely to have long term political effects on the community as a whole. Religion also has some immediate consequences for the adaptation of the Ugandans and local people to one another. Table 3.8 shows the religious affiliation of the assisted and self-settled refugees.

The most important outside religious influence on the indigenous population of Yei River District was that of Protestant missionaries. This is not the case for all of southern Sudan. Most of the Muslims in the district are traders who originate in the north, and only a few of the locals have converted to Islam. During Sudan's civil war, many of the Sudanese who fled the country were educated and converted in Catholic institutions in Uganda and Zaire, some children were even sent to Rome for study.

Following the return of the Sudanese from Uganda, a Catholic centre was established in Yei, and its cathedral is the largest building in the town. With the funds from his congregation, earnings from a pineapple farm, and some outside support, Father Peter Dada, the priest in charge of this centre, has opened a non-sectarian kindergarten with an enrolment of 150 children. At Lutaya, just a few kilometres outside Yei, another cathedral has been constructed. He and two other priests serve the district. All three were refugees and educated in Zaire or Uganda.

Religion has long been an important variable in the politics of Uganda.

TABLE 3.8: The religious affiliation of refugees
ASSISTED

| Religion | MOTHER TONGUE | | | | |
	Kakwa %	Nubi %	Lugbara %	Madi %	Others %
Catholic	22.9	2.9	35.5	95.5	2.9
Muslim	60.7	95.1	60.6	3.3	95.1
Protestant	16.4	2.0	3.9	1.2	2.0
	100	100	100	100	100
No. of individuals	201	102	7,895	2,150	102

SELF SETTLED

| Religion | MOTHER TONGUE | | | | |
	Kakwa %	Nubi %	Lugbara %	Madi %	Others %
Catholic	43.1	5.9	34.2	88.6	31.7
Muslim	40.6	94.1	60.0	7.5	50.8
Protestant	16.3	0	5.8	3.9	17.5
	100	100	100	100	100
No. of households	877	17	1,610	281	63

Obote himself is a Protestant and his opposition, the Democratic party, is identified mainly with the Catholic religion. During Amin's rule, although representing only a minority of Uganda's population as a whole, the Muslim community gained great prominence. The northern part of the west Nile, the area where most of the refugees lived, was one part of Uganda where Islam had taken root.

For at least some refugees, religion sustained them through the perils of their existence in exile (de Waal in Wilson *et al.* 1985.) And for one at least, the church symbolized everything which meant Uganda. One night by the light of my kerosene lantern, I listened to refugees talk about their experiences. One desperately homesick man began to weep. 'Where are the bells?' he asked. Poetically, he went on to describe his longing to hear the chiming of the bells which the priests had brought (from Italy, he said), and installed in the missions in Uganda.

Just under half of the refugees in Yei River District are followers of Islam. Conversion to Islam during Amin's rule was often a strategic decision. The Catholic priest in Yei took pleasure in pointing out certain prominent Ugandans, now Muslim, whose time of baptism as a Catholic he could remember. One of these, for example, was the ex-vice president, Mustapha Idrissi. On the other hand, it should be remembered that conversion to Catholicism was often a requirement for entrance into a Catholic mission school.

The arrival of so many thousands of Ugandan Catholics has given a new impetus to the Sudanese congregations. The influx included numbers of trained catechists and dozens of chapels have been built in the settlements and throughout the areas where the self-settled refugees live. Regular monthly meetings of religious leaders are held in Yei at the Catholic Centre. Long before I began this research these priests had acquired an intimate knowledge of the conditions along the borders and had compiled lists of the heads of many of the unassisted households.

The growth of his congregation prompted Father Peter to undertake an expanded building programme at the Yei Centre: a residence for the Ugandan nuns who teach at the kindergarten, and rest houses for visitors. Plans were underway to build a primary school for the children who graduate from the kindergarten. The carpentry shop on the site employs refugees. A seminary has also been opened at Tore which includes both refugees and Sudanese in its student body. Sudanaid, an indigenous voluntary agency, has appointed a community development worker to start income-generating projects in rural areas where self-settled refugees live.

In 1983 Father Peter responded to an initiative which came from refugees to build a senior secondary school. He allocated land for the school which was to be built by refugees and Sudanese working together. (Myers in Wilson *et al.* 1985.) This self-help project met with many problems, the foremost being to find a source of food for the students who came from the settlements to build the school. Members of the congregation brought cassava and cobs of corn to the church services to feed the young people building the Lutaya school. Another problem was the cynicism of the agency workers concerning the capabilities of the refugees to help themselves. Some viewed the project as 'elitist'; one asking the students what they would do when the school was completed, build a university? It was very difficult to mobilize workers from the settlements. Communication within settlements was almost non-existent so few even heard of the project until a Catholic lay worker and a member of my team made a special round of settlements to inform them. Nevertheless, in just 14 months Lutaya school opened, with an enrolment of 180 students.[7]

---

[7] The students built the school with only a few days of professional help, they fired 50,000 bricks, and even taught themselves enough carpentry to produce desks. Oxford students, members of the Third World First Society, supplied cash, about £3,000. The agencies, particularly UNHCR, helped by giving cement and roofing materials. The Sudan project management office provided transport for building materials from settlements.

Already in 1982, Father Peter was encouraging his congregation to adopt the traditional music associated with the Ugandans of the west Nile. This *adungu* music is played on hand-made wooden string instruments called by the same name, which range in size to produce a range of tones from base to treble. The choirs and instrumentalists include only children and young people. He brought musicians from one settlement to live at the Centre to teach their art to the Sudanese. He arranged to have a hymn book printed for distribution in the chapels throughout the district. He installed a number of young Ugandan children in his household and paid their school fees so that they could attend local schools in Yei.[8]

The Jesuit Refugee Service (JRS), which has an office in Nairobi, sent a priest to Yei. He was employed locally by the UNHCR office as its education officer. The priest also took an active role in supporting the activities of the Catholic community. He played a crucial role in the building of Lutaya secondary school. It was his connection with the agencies which encouraged some of them to give material assistance to the self-help school project. Although he left the district in late 1984, the JRS sent another priest who took up pastoral duties in the Kajo-Kaji sub-district.

Although the number of Protestants among the Ugandan refugees were far fewer, the local Protestant church also responded to the arrival of refugees. By 1982 they were already including religious leaders from the settlements in the training sessions and Bible classes held in Yei. The Yei Protestant church became more closely linked with the assistance programme with the arrival of the US-based agency, SSRAP. One reason for this was that the agency's policy was to employ Sudanese and these were mainly recruited through the Protestant church.

Although very few of the indigenous people practise Islam, there were mosques at Kaya and Yei where both northern Sudanese and southerners prayed together. In keeping with Islam's tradition of charity, these followers of the prophet were active in assisting individual refugees. Mosques were built in the self-settled areas and in the settlements. Moreover, in most settlements where there was a significant number, Muslims started a *madrasa* (Koranic school). In some settlements the children attended the *madrasa* every day; in others, the class schedule deferred to that of the primary schools which were built and supported by the assistance programme.

Despite their numerical superiority in some of the settlements (Dokuni, Morsak, Katigiri, Gumbari, and Wudabi), Muslims generally felt disadvan-

---

[8]One of these children, a small girl of about nine years of age, had been living on the border with her relatives. Father Peter found her directing a choir of *adungu* singers. Her education had been interrupted for three years. Struck by her intelligence, he asked permission of her relatives to educate her. This remarkable little girl could speak Kakwa, Madi, Lugbara, Juba Arabic, English, and some Swahili. Walking along with a consultant for UNHCR, Susan Goodwillie and me, she asked us whether we lived on the same continent or on different ones.

taged. As in most ex-British colonies, many Ugandans tended to despise Muslim education and although some children go to the recognized schools after receiving their basic religious education, they suffer the disadvantage of having started their English studies much later than others. In eastern Sudan the Islamic African Relief Agency has given some assistance to refugees and some projects are funded through donations from Arab states. There was no such organized programme of assistance through a Muslim agency in the south, where all of UNHCR's partner agencies were 'western' and most were linked with Christian religious organizations. It is understandable that although aid reached the settlements through agencies and programmes which ostensibly did not take account of religious differences, Muslims perceived the programmes as being biased in favour of the Christians. Perhaps it was because of this that when medicines were supplied to Otogo through a Muslim group, the leaders of the local mosque insisted that they were only to be distributed to their members.

Northern Sudanese Muslims who live in the south are generally alienated from the local community because of their dominance of the economy. (McGregor in Wilson *et al.* 1985.) Although they attend prayers with the indigenous Muslims, when the mosque at Otogo settlement held a formal opening, a number of Muslims from Yei attended, but northerners did not join them.

The Sudan government has maintained friendly relations with Obote's Uganda, but sympathy among local officials for the Muslim members of Amin's government who fled to the Sudan had some immediate political consequences. For example, as was discussed in Chapter One, Juma Oris, Amin's Minister of Foreign Affairs, was able to establish strong relations with the state's security forces and with a former Minister of Interior in Khartoum. The imposition of Sharia law (September 1983) occurred too late in my research to observe its effect upon relations between northerners and local Muslims, either refugees or indigenous people, but it is unlikely to have created any greater solidarity among them. Very few Sudanese in any part of the country supported this effort by Nemeiry to consolidate his power.[9] Moreover, Nemeiry's government felt ambivalent about the Ugandan refugees because among the returnees were Sudanese members of the *Anyanya* movement who had fought in the civil war and had not returned home after the 1972 Addis agreement.[10]

[9] A few Muslims, ex-Ugandan soldiers, interviewed near Panyume did express the hope for more assistance to them in the new climate. They asked a member of the Oxford team to carry a letter to Juba and Khartoum requesting assistance for their mosque and expressing a wish for copies of the Koran. (Pankhurst in Wilson *et al.* 1985.)

[10] Charles Meynell, the editor of *Africa Confidential*, contributed to keeping alive the fears of the Sudan government. With no evidence which I could find to substantiate it, he repeatedly made the claim that some Ugandans have links with the *Anyanya*, and some of the *Anyanya* soldiers are now fighting against the central government. See *Africa Now*, November 1983 and *Africa Confidential*, Vol. 24, November 1984.

All Ugandan refugees, whether Muslim or not, suffer the effects of the control which the northern Sudanese merchant class holds over the local economy. In 1984, for example, hoping to fetch the higher prices paid there, a refugee co-operative at Limbe managed to get sacks of potatoes to the Juba market. The northern Sudanese merchants offered to buy the potatoes at a low price but would not permit them to be sold on the open market. After several days, with the potatoes spoiling, the refugees were forced to capitulate. (McGregor in Wilson *et al*. 1985.) Northern Sudanese traders have maintained businesses in Uganda and facilitate the illegal coffee trade into Sudan. That these interests override any religious solidarity based on shared religion was graphically demonstrated in December 1982. Some northern Sudanese traders were murdered inside Uganda and merchants in Kaya blamed the Ugandan guerillas for their deaths. They razed the town wounding both refugees and indigenous Sudanese as well, and at least one of the latter died. Given their numerical superiority, it is a wonder the Ugandans did not react. Although arrests and charges were made, the cases against the traders have never been dealt with by the court.

Some other characteristics of the refugee population

Refugees living in planned settlements are expected to become self-sufficient through agriculture. The plan drawn up was based upon the assumption of an average family size of five persons, which would include three children, two of whom are of primary age. (Land 1981.) The overall average size of households in settlements was 5.29, but they ranged in size from one-person households to one which appeared in the sample at Wudabi in which 26 persons were living in one plot. The average size of households also varied greatly between settlements with the newer ones having the smaller average size (e.g. Katigiri: 2.86, and see Table 3.4). This reflects the practice of the refugees, to first send only a few members of their household to a settlement, sometimes only one person, to build the house; or, as was also very common, to send either the very ill or the children on their own. The plan (Land 1981) for self-sufficiency also assumed that each household would have three persons who were able to cultivate. Table 3.8 shows the numbers of different sized households in the settlement population and the numbers that were reported to be 'able to cultivate'.

The households of the unassisted refugees were larger: on average 7.15 persons. Their households also ranged in size from one person to those having sixteen or more. Unlike the large families in the settlements who were confined to a plot of either 25 metres or 50 metres square, unassisted refugees were able to build enough houses to accommodate their families and some of those which I observed counted several scattered huts as their 'household'. Table 3.10 shows the number and range of household sizes which were interviewed.

The average age of the settlement population was sixteen years. As is discussed in the notes on methods in Appendix II, information concerning the unassisted refugees only distinguish three broad age and sex groups. Table 3.11 compares these with the same breakdown for the settlements.

The population data describing refugees demonstrate the high mortality rates of the youngest children, the lowered fertility of refugee women, and the selective dispersal of different age and sex groups between settlements and the areas where the unassisted are living. As noted, data collected from the unassisted households recorded the numbers of children aged five and under, and then only distinguished adolescents and adults.[11] Among the assisted refugees there were 198 per 1,000 children of five years and under; among the unassisted, the rate was 271 per 1,000. Figure 3.3 shows the age and sex distribution of the total population of the settlements according to standard age group divisions and compares these with the 1969 census of the West Nile.[12]

The number of children under five years of age in the settlements is 150 per 1,000, while in Uganda in 1969 there were 197 per 1,000. For non-statisticians this comparison may appear to indicate that infant mortality ratios have not drastically deteriorated. However, it should be remembered that the overall distribution of age groups per thousand is affected by fewer people in the age groups over 30 years of age among the refugees as compared with the population of the West Nile. Restricting examination to just those under the age of 30, it is found that the 0-4 year olds in settlements comprise 173 per 1,000, while in Uganda in 1969, the comparable figure was 266 per 1,000.

It is interesting to observe that the ratio of men to women in the settlements is higher than it was in the West Nile at the time of the 1969 census. Since colonial times, opportunities for employment in other parts of Uganda had drawn men from this area; women were responsible for maintaining the family left behind. In Uganda, 55.7 per cent of the age group between 15 and 44 were women, while in 1983 in settlements they represented only 48 per cent of the population in this age group. Among the self-settled the percentage of women 17 years and over is 54.3. If those women aged 15 and 16 could be separated from the data and included with the others, probably the percentage of women among the population of the unassisted refugees would be found to be about the same or even greater than that of the West Nile in 1969.

[11] Although the analysis of the distribution of age groups discusses them as though one could have absolute confidence in their accuracy, there are difficulties in collecting such data especially where a large proportion of the population is not literate. Interviewers were experienced in using the method of asking the elderly informants to recall important historical events as a way of judging their age. With the children such methods were inapplicable, but there were few families which did not include one or more educated individuals.

[12] Most of the refugees originate from that area. These are the latest population data available as no census was conducted during Amin's rule and the results of the 1980 Census are not yet available. Moreover, given the disturbances which affected this area from 1979, even if available, the results are likely to be highly unreliable.

TABLE 3.9: 'Number normally in household' by percentage of household 'able to cultivate' (assisted)

					Number in household				
	1	2	3	4	5	6	7	8	9
Average no. able to cultivate per household	0.97	1.43	1.81	2.23	2.54	3.00	3.42	4.02	4.49
% of household able to cultivate	95.80	69.70	60.40	55.40	52.00	50.00	48.10	50.20	49.90
No. of households this size	169	189	199	288	292	280	196	156	88
% of all households	8.40	9.40	9.90	14.30	14.50	13.90	9.70	7.70	4.40

												Totals

	10	11	12	13	14	15	16	18	26	Totals
Number in household										
Average no. able to cultivate per household	4.65	5.03	6.38	5.69	4.25	6.00	7.50	12.00	14.00	5,551
% of households able to cultivate	46.50	45.70	53.10	43.80	30.40	40.00	46.90	66.70	53.80	52%
No. of households this size	78	31	16	13	12	5	2	1	2	2,017
% of all households	3.90	1.50	0.08	0.06	0.06	0.02	0.01	0.00	0.01	98%

TABLE 3.10: Number of people in households (unassisted)

Number of persons	1	2-3	4-8	9-15	16 and over	Totals
Number of household	191	675	1,835	875	238	3,814
% of households	5.0	17.7	48.1	22.9	6.2	100%

TABLE 3.11: A comparison of age and sex groups of assisted and self-settled refugees

| | Unassisted | | | | Assisted | | | |
	Male	Female	%	Number	Male	Female	%	Number
Age group								
0-5	14.1	13.1	27.2	7,417	10.2	9.5	19.8	2,109
6-16	13.3	11.9	25.2	6,874	24.8	18.7	43.5	4,643
16+	21.8	25.8	47.6	12,990	18.4	18.3	36.7	3,922
Totals	49.2	50.8	100	27,281	53.4	46.6	100	10,674

It has already been suggested in Chapter One that occupational background influenced men in arriving at the decision to accept assistance in a settlement. The only systematic information collected by UNHCR was whether a family came from an 'urban' or 'rural' background. Although it was true that 80.1 per cent of the assisted refugees did originate from rural areas, it was a mistake to have assumed that most of these had made their living through farming.

When refugees were asked their occupation in Uganda, only 20.1 per cent reported they had earned their living through agriculture and of these 61.4 per cent were women! And, as far as the men were concerned, this 20.1 per cent may constitute an over estimate since, as has already been noted, many ex-soldiers disguised their former occupation by claiming to have been farmers. This is further confirmed by the fact that nine 'farmers' spoke Russian, Korean, or French. The other Russian-speakers claimed to have made their living in Uganda as labourers, brewers of local beer, or as drivers; four said they had been students. Seventeen others who spoke Korean,

Russian, or French failed to answer the question concerning their previous occupation. And, among those claiming to have been 'only cultivators' in Uganda, 16.8 per cent spoke English. In contrast to the adult men in the settlements, 57.6 per cent of the unassisted refugees said that in Uganda they had been cultivators or herdsmen. Had these men really been farmers, more of them might have been using their skills in the self-settled areas.

That a main attraction of the settlements was the availability of school is dramatically portrayed by the distribution of the children, both by age and by sex. As is shown in Table 3.11 there was 7.4 per cent more children between the ages of 0-5 in the households of the unassisted than there were in the settlements, but the ratio of sexes was not significantly different. On the other hand, there were 18.3 per cent more children in the age group 6-16 living in the settlements and more of these were boys. In Figure 3.3 this male bias in the population of children is further demonstrated for each age group between 5 and 19 years of age.

Any study which concentrates on overall statistical comparisons between two different groups of refugees, between the assisted and the unassisted, has one major flaw. This is that it fails to describe the enormous variation *between* the settlement populations. Figure III.3, Appendix III, shows the detail and the extent of this variation. These are the populations the aid programme aims to help, the human resources which aid programmes attempt to develop. The extreme differences which exist between the settlements will inevitably confound any policy which is imposed uniformly upon all of them.

Fertility

The collection of comprehensive fertility data was beyond the scope of this study. However, the number of infants 'born here' was recorded for both the assisted and unassisted refugees (Table 3.12). As the numbers of adult women (that is, all those 17 years or older) are known, it is possible to make some crude comparisons of the relative fertility of both communities. According to the survey sample, a total of 2,810 births had occurred in the settlements. Among the 3,814 self-settled households interviewed, 2,343 children had been born since 'settling here'. The overall average of births of unassisted households was 0.61 while among the assisted refugees it was only 0.14 births per household. The households of the unassisted or self-settled refugees included an overall average of 1.8 adult women per household: among the assisted, 0.97. As noted earlier, in 53 per cent of the households of the assisted refugees, both husband and wife were present in the settlement and while comparative data for the unassisted is available for 598 households, 73.9 per cent constituted such 'normal' households.

Figure 3.4 compares the number of births per adult woman for both assisted and unassisted by the year of her settling 'here'. These data suggest that with the exception of those settling 'here' in 1981, the fertility of women

TABLE 3.12: Average number of births by women
aged 16-49 by year of settling 'here' (assisted)

Year settled 'here'	Average number of births
1979	0.60
1980	0.46
1981	0.42
1982	0.15
1983	0.09

in settlements appears to be lower than among the unassisted. Moreover, fertility among the unassisted refugee women has remained fairly constant over the years while birth rates appear to have been much more irregular in the settlements.

According to the sample, the total number of adult women in settlements was 19,550 and among the unassisted, 7,054. As data gathered from the unassisted refugees did not distinguish the ages of women over 17 it is not possible to make comparisons of the fertility of women of child-bearing age. Among the assisted refugees, however, 14 per cent of the women were 45 years or older. Presuming that women over the age of 50 have entered menopause, the average number of births for women as compared with the year of settling 'here' are shown in Table 3.12.

Fertility rates are related to nutritional standards. As will be shown later when discussing the delivery of food aid, the unassisted refugees appear to have a slightly more healthy diet than those living in settlements who are primarily dependent upon the irregular supply of rations from the World Food Programme and their own earnings from casual labour. The data also suggest that more of the 'normal' families remain outside settlements. All of the evidence points to the general view that those who are least able to care for themselves opt for living in settlements. The fact that segments of families are sent to the settlements may also have a further disruptive effect upon conjugal behaviour.

It would not be surprising to find that the stress of life in exile also affects normal family life. Extra-marital and pre-marital relations result in considerable social upheaval. In Uganda, pre-marital sex was traditionally avoided by early marriage. Marriages require the full agreement of the relatives of both spouses and the payment of 'dowry', (the term introduced during British rule to describe the transfer of wealth from the husband's family to that of the wife). 'Elopement' was also institutionalized in Uganda; by consummating a relationship, a young couple could present their relatives with a *fait accompli*. Elopements cause disputes, but usually the woman's family is forced to accept a lower amount of dowry. Strong social norms against extra-marital sexual relations lead to some uncertainty concerning the actual marital status of some of the co-habiting couples we interviewed. For example, when asked if, since coming to Sudan, anyone from the household had married, only 6.3 per cent said yes. But, when a more open-ended question was posed concerning how such marriages had been made 'acceptable' to the relatives, 7.6 per cent of the households gave account of their difficulties in getting relatives to agree to a union under the conditions of refugee life. According to the survey sample, only 70 of the marriages had been regularized through dowry payment; of the others, 610 husbands had made a token gift to their wife's parents, and 290 had not paid anything, but the wife's parents had accepted the financial constraints of the husband. In 330 cases the couple had eloped and the matter had not been settled. Their insecurity would have increased if they knew that in 230 other cases the wife's family had already reclaimed their daughter!

There was a general and understandable tendency for refugees to exploit every possible source of revenue to its absolute limit. Data are not available on the amounts of dowry paid in Uganda, and no doubt the realities of refugee life in the Sudan have forced many families to accept much lower amounts. But there is some evidence that families would prefer their daughters to marry Sudanese who can pay 'large' dowries.

Adultery disputes, according to some Ugandans, were not so common in Uganda as they are today in the Sudan. It is now not only very difficult to control the sexual behaviour of women, but the very conditions of exile may make their extra-marital sex life advantageous to the household (see page 328, Chapter Seven). Women move freely throughout the district, and back and forth between Zaire and the Sudan. Following the informal opening of the border between Kajo-Kaji and Moyo in 1983, women also moved in that direction to trade. They are more successful in appealing to lorry drivers to allow them to travel without payment - at least in cash. It would appear that most of the 'undisputed' cases of prostitution occur between Ugandan women and Sudanese men - as refugees can rarely afford to pay for such services.

Husbands may be fully aware of their wives' extra-marital affairs, but since women may earn soap or sugar for the family, they cannot afford to object. Moreover, refugees are always the weakest party in a dispute, and it must be very unusual for a refugee to take a Sudanese to court on any charge.[13] But, if both parties to an extra-marital sexual relationship are Ugandans, husbands do not show the same tolerance and are likely to use any evidence of a wife's unfaithfulness for monetary gain. Adultery cases are heard in a number of fora. Among the self-settled, women are charged in

---

[13] In only a few of the cases collected from trial courts was the plaintiff a refugee.

Sudanese courts; in settlements they may be heard by the refugee dispute committee, by the settlement officer, or by the local court. Charges awarded may go as high as £S100. Payment forces the guilty to sell their property, and in some cases, settlement officers have withheld rations, and sold them to pay the husband.

The fact that in theory rations were distributed on a per capita basis also had an effect on the stability of marriages. Women often taunted their husbands that they no longer had any authority over them now that 'Shoodie' was feeding them! (This was the name the refugees called the UNHCR programme officer.)

Other features of life in settlements are said to be not conducive to normal conjugal relations. Often, when informants were asked whether children had been born since the household came to the settlement, the response would include an aggressive remark on the conditions in which people had to sleep, which provided no privacy. Informants were adamant that Ugandans would never consider having sexual relations in the same room in which children over seven or eight years old were sleeping. Although many of the self-settled compounds had more than one hut and a kitchen, refugees in settlements rarely had more than one. Altogether, 92.8 per cent of the households had access to only one sleeping shelter; 43.5 per cent were still living in one tent (regardless of the numbers in the family); and only 7 per cent of households had two huts or more to accommodate members. But 15.3 per cent had built kitchens and sometimes these also doubled as sleeping quarters.

When available, UNHCR distributed one tent to each plot in the settlements. Refugees were urged to build their houses quickly so the tents could be re-issued to the new arrivals. The desire for some privacy may explain why refugees were so reluctant to give up their temporary tents long after they had finished building a house. It was often necessary to employ coercion. On one occasion at least, the programme officer took an armed policeman with him and they resorted to pulling up the tent pegs.

A normal human community?

Given the wide differences in the demographic characteristics of refugee populations such as household size, age, sex, ethnic and religious affiliation both within settlements and in the self-settled areas - one may not assume, with Day-Thompson (1984), that *all* refugees have more or less the same capacity to manipulate the advantages of the 'aid system'. There are also great variations in education and occupation within these communities. Perhaps more importantly, there is some evidence to suggest that the experience of exile and the availability of the aid programme have combined to erode normative social behaviour, in particular, the respect for reciprocal family obligations which were observed prior to exodus. Since individual reactions to life in exile vary almost infinitely, it is difficult to predict where the intervention of aid will be most required. Giving assistance on a per capita basis does not seem the most useful approach.

As noted earlier, in 1982 I circulated an essay to refugees in settlements which raised questions about the causes of the so-called 'dependency syndrome'. Some refugees replied, also in essay form. As one wrote, 'I have a few points to mention':

We all know that refugees and most of the aid-agents are foreigners of two different categories. The aid-agent leaves his country peacefully ... the refugee leaves his country because of dangerous situations there. It should therefore not be doubted [that is, questioned] why a person who was once a prosperous, rich, happy and responsible man ... loses his [sense of] responsibility in his refugee life ... each one settles to prepare for an independent ... future life... This preparation, coupled with the sorrows of the fact that he once had enough and plenty for his family leave the refugee too busy and sorrowful. He ... thinks very little about any assistance to be rendered to the sick, handicapped, or disabled fellow refugees ...

On the other hand, we have mental disorders. Not all refugees have been soldiers. The refugees who have not [experienced war before] will not come out in their right senses ... where he was surrounded by gunshots with different threatening sounds. These disturbances make somebody lose his sense of thinking to do things in the right way.

... refugees are just like passengers who are caught up in a car accident; whether or not they are seriously injured, the passengers will not be in their right senses just immediately after an accident. So is the refugee, yet deeply worried about why he was forced to leave his country and property, he is not in his right senses in the early stages of refugee life.

Another refugee, Raphael Aar Onzima, wrote an essay which was particularly concerned about the breakdown of social norms. He compares the traditional values of the Lugbara, which he refers to as 'our-ism'. He defines 'our-ism' as follows:

I am because you are. You are because I am, and since you are, and I am, therefore, we are. So 'our-ism' seemed to have been the philosophy or code of thought that guarded, guided, geared and directed [us] before the pre-exile times.

'Our-ism' ... in this case [is a] philosophy which acknowledges nothing as mine or yours or his or hers, but as *ours*, though basically, primarily, and authentically, ownership *does* fall effectively on one particular individual. However, this should not be confused, but rather differentiated from Marxism... among Lugbara, in those good pre-exile days, [things] were done on communal and a voluntary basis, but for an individual.

Once war struck, however,

... the war itself became a society with its own culture of looting, egoism, lack of respect for human life and self- development ... within the short period, a situation of acculturation was inevitable, the Lugbara borrowing more of the war's culture.

The situation of acculturation all began [when] the natural instinct of self protection became irresistably stronger than that of society preservation [which became] remarkably weaker. And the immediate response was for each one to have his or her own secret life in one's own cocoon... Darwin's theory of survival for the fittest became operational... If I can get something to eat [rather] than to feed my children, I still have chance to live...

The problem for the refugees is that like chess-men, some pieces have greater defences against adversity than others. Day-Thompson's stereotyped view of the African family as 'infinitely flexible', and therefore able to deploy its members in strategic places to take fullest advantage of whatever resources are available has some basis in fact. It does not, however, take into sufficient account the extent to which sickness, loss of property, and death have left segments of families lacking the 'pieces to deploy'. In addition, local and very specific economic and political factors limit the options open to each household and family. To view family structures as 'infinitely flexible' is to ignore the existence of a point at which flexibility leads to rupture. It is argued that the rupture of family structures results not only from flight and dispossession, but also from the encounter of the refugee with the institutional structures of humanitarian aid programmes. Where kin groups are no longer able to enforce social norms, many refugees have used the aid system as an excuse for abandoning social responsibility. This is the point of rupture, and aid policies which assume that families are flexing rather than breaking, will continue to underestimate the pressures facing individuals.

PART 2

4

The search for security

Introduction

'Once an individual, a human being, becomes a refugee, it is as though he has become a member of another race, some other sub-human group. You talk of rights of refugees as though human rights did not exist which are broader and more important. We have forgotten that the ultimate recipient of any progress ... is supposed to be the individual, the human being ... One individual's protection is as important as making a camp for ten thousand people.' (Zia Rizvi, Alternative Viewpoints 1984).[1]

The UN High Commissioner's Office was established for the primary function of providing protection to refugees. Although protection officers are often attached to sub-offices, all UNHCR staff are advised to familiarize themselves with the key international instruments which set out the High Commissioner's functions and responsibilities. (*Handbook for Emergencies 1982*).[2]

Because the protection responsibilities of the High Commissioner have been placed on him by the UN General Assembly, he is not therefore dependent upon a request by the host government. 'These activities reflect UNHCR's universally recognized right of initiative in exercising its protection responsibilities as an entirely non-political humanitarian and social body.' (*ibid*. :8). The *Handbooks* go on to advise field-workers on policy and practical action. (1982:8-14; 1983:206-12). It is emphasized that at times refugees may require protection even before their status has been determined and noted that the aim 'is to secure treatment in accordance with universally

[1] I am reminded of an incident involving a refugee whose life had been threatened because other refugees thought he was a spy for Obote's Uganda government. The refugee was a Rwandan. I attempted to present him to one UNHCR officer, but the officer refused to talk with the refugee, saying 'It would take me at least three hours to determine whether the case is a genuine one or not. In that time I could have planned a programme which would have helped thousands of refugees.'

[2] These are '1951 Convention Relating to the Status of Refugees' and the 'Protocol Relating to the Status of Refugees of 31 January 1967'. For Africa, there is also the OAU 'Convention Governing the Specific Aspects of Refugee Problems in Africa', 10 September 1969. Field staff are also advised to regard the *Collection of International Instruments Concerning Refugees* (1979), the *Handbook for Determining Refugee Status* (1979) and the *Conclusion on the International Protection of Refugees Adopted by the Executive Committee of the UNHCR Programme* as 'essential reading' (*ibid*. :8). The *Handbooks* also remind UNHCR field staff of a number of other international instruments which may help protect refugees. Among these is mentioned the special role of the International Committee of the Red Cross (ICRC) whose role in family tracing is immediately applicable to refugees. Its role in armed conflicts sometimes gives access to detainees, and this can 'complement' the work of UNHCR. The ICRC funded a family tracing service in southern Sudan.

recognized humanitarian principles not directly linked to the status of those in need. In short, when *in doubt, act*'. (1982:8.)[3]

The problem of the physical security of refugees is finally the responsibility of the host government. As Zia Rizvi has pointed out, the physical protection of the individual in a country of asylum is a *lacuna*. There are no adequate answers to the question of security and it is necessary, he said, 'to go into areas that are unexplored and that are not normally talked about. The real problem is that the individual...has to depend on the state for protection, the monster that we have created...which has further monsters at its disposal, like the notion of sovereignty and the question of national security - all the arguments you hear from a Minister of Interior, or a policeman, or a soldier.' If the notion of state sovereignty is not tackled, he warned, 'we are going to be a race of lemmings.' (Alternative Viewpoints 1984.) The role of UNHCR in protecting refugees in the country of asylum in relation to the state raises many difficult questions. Most are beyond the scope of a single study of one emergency response to an influx of refugees. Hopefully however the account of security problems in the southern Sudan which follows, illustrates the urgent need to pay more attention to these matters.

With the exception of the insecurity caused by UNLA incursions, this discussion aims to take a look at protection from a non-legalistic viewpoint - by examining some of the ways in which the failures of the assistance programme served to exacerbate the insecurity of refugees *and* their hosts. Insecurity, it is suggested, was increased as a result of weak policy, failure to consult, failure to report, inefficiency, the lethargy of individuals or the lack of sensitivity, courage, imagination, or commitment, insufficient resources, or, in some cases, what appears to be complicity with certain international and intra-national interests. These causes of physical insecurity could have been avoided and I try to suggest a number of ways this might have been done.[4] But a major cause of the insecurity, the political consequences of the impact of outside intervention and aid, mentioned again in Chapter Eight, cannot be avoided by such simple measures as I suggest.

The importance of going 'into areas unexplored and that are not normally talked about' is demonstrated by the fact that aside from the several thousand

[3] There are a number of analyses of the legal position of refugees, among the more recent are Goodwin-Gill (1983) and Avery (1983). Rwelamira (1983) has recently discussed some outstanding problems in the Convention of the Organization of African Unity (OAU). See Ayok Chol 1983; [for further discussion of legal issues relating to refugees in Africa, Eriksson *et al.* (eds.) 1981; Nobel 1982.] These works also contain extensive bibliographies on the subject.

[4] Although my recommendations go further, the UNHCR *Handbook* also points out that 'Often protection depends less on the fine print of a statute and more on swift appropriate action by UNHCR field staff.' (1983:206) In fact, had protection officers followed the spirit of the *Handbooks*, which place considerable emphasis on co-operating with government officials, prompt reporting, using the visits of delegations to stimulate more awareness of international protection agreements, informing local people about the rights of refugees, etc., many problems could have been avoided.

interviews conducted for this study, the greatest amount of paper I carried away from southern Sudan documented serious breaches of the human rights of refugees. These include cases involving the confiscation of property on entry into the Sudan or at roadblocks (official or unofficial), false imprisonment, discriminatory treatment by courts, beating, serious wounding, torture, forced movement and interference with the freedom of movement, unfair dismissal, outbreaks of violence between hosts and refugees, theft, illegal taxation, assault, loss of rights to agricultural land, forced labour, kidnap, rape and murder. These crimes were variously committed by ordinary civilians, and soldiers (Sudanese and Ugandan), security personnel, chiefs and policemen. For example, on 10 September 1982 a policeman went berserk, shot a Sudanese and threw a hand grenade into a refugee woman's hut. She narrowly escaped. Crimes were often committed by refugees against other refugees, as well as against Sudanese.

The actual cases collected involved perhaps 1,000 individuals. Yet, as one report of a three day protection[5] mission in August 1982 put it, 'The civilian population appears to accept the refugees without major problems, as most of them remember their own flight to Uganda some years ago....there seems to be no general problem of mistreatment of refugees apart from those rather isolated cases.'

Given that the population of Yei River District had grown from probably no more than 100,000 people living in widely scattered homesteads and villages to over 300,000 in only four years, perhaps it *is* remarkable that relations were no more antagonistic than they were. This is especially so when one considers that the influx radically altered the characteristics of the population as a whole in terms of such important social variables as religion, educational level, language, occupational skills, and ethnicity which greatly disturbed existing power relations in the district.

Even so, if the numbers of individuals who suffered loss of rights or who fell prey to arbitrary discrimination reflect tolerable levels, why should UNHCR or anyone else be concerned with the question of the physical security of refugees in a host country like the Sudan? Clearly they do not. Moreover, refugees are most unlikely to achieve economic independence in a climate of insecurity. A minimal requirement to allow both refugees and hosts to cope peacefully with such radical social and economic transformations is some consistency and predictability in the content, administration, and enforcement of the rules.

The insecurity of land tenure illustrates this problem. The assistance programme depended entirely on the capacity of refugees to earn their living through agriculture. In agreement with UNHCR, the *central* government in Khartoum had guaranteed them access to sufficient land. Yet no refugee in

---

[5] And the only one during my six month stay in southern Sudan in 1982. There was also only one official protection mission during the same period in 1983.

Yei River District had absolute security of his usufruct rights to land, even those which he had negotiated on an individual basis with a local farmer. It was very common for a refugee to be thrown off a piece of land after he had worked to clear it and had cultivated one crop. To provide refugees with security for subsistence agriculture as their means of livelihood requires local people to be convinced of the overall advantages to them in accommodating strangers.

The competition for available land, which encouraged local land-owners to reclaim land brought into production by refugee labour, could have been reduced had more thought been given to the problem. For example, had funds used for building the primary schools, which refugees had demonstrated that they could build themselves, been allocated to a programme to clear the tsetse fly from vast areas of otherwise arable land, competition for land would have been greatly reduced. And, if the insecurity of land tenure was more a function of overcrowding in some areas than it was of land shortage, then opening up these unused areas would have enabled the population to be spread out more evenly.

The failure to consider such dimensions of protection at the outset of the emergency, and to mobilize all possible resources to prevent insecurity, resulted in a gradual escalation of tensions between refugees and their hosts. Each protection report from Yei included longer and longer lists of violations of the rights of refugees and each concluded with an urgent request for a protection officer to be posted to the south. Take, for example, the 6 July 1983 report from just one settlement, Pakula Naima:

....a settler returning to his home.....was robbed of fish worth £S6.000. Several similar incidents took place between 19-24 June. Refugees have been stopped by native scouts at a road block, beaten and robbed of their possessions. One....has been hospitalized and another is reported....in very bad condition, unable to walk.

1. Mr. Omar Amini, 22nd June 1983, robbed of sugar, 4 kilos, cash, £S10; knife valued £S2.500;

2. Betty Lonjina, 19th June 1983, robbed of six kilos of beans, 2 parcels of milk, and 8 kilos of rice.

3. Yahiya Anne, 20th June 1983, robbed of 3 chickens, £S20. cash, one blanket and 2 kgs. of sugar.

4. Zaibuna Chandiru, 20th June 1983, £S10. cash, 5 litres of cooking oil, 3 packets of milk which she was taking to a funeral.

5. Paskwalina Suleiman, 19th June 1983, robbed of 10 kgs. beans, 15 kgs. rice, 2 tins of cooking oil, and 2 packets of milk.

6. Osnor Agina, 19th June 1983, robbed of 16 kg. rice, 1 kg. beans, 4 litres of cooking oil, one packet of milk and local medicines.

Each case involved beating, 'some more severe than others'. This report included details of similar thefts suffered by refugees near Limuru. Moreover, when police went to take statements at the hospital from some of the wounded, one of the victims was arrested. By this time relations had deteriorated so that one of the settlement officers had made a rule that a refugee could not send letters without his first reading them.[6]

As the programme officer put it, 'It is without any doubt that the arrival of big numbers of refugees has "upset" life in this area. What is happening here is in a way a "normal" reaction, however it needs close attention as refugees become easily victims [*sic*]. On the other hand discussions with local authorities would give us a better picture of their views and problems.'[7]

But the protection problems observed in southern Sudan were not simply the result of the enormous social dislocation caused by an increased population and the impact of an aid programme managed by outsiders, the situation must be viewed in the light of wider influences of both inter-state and global politics.

Refugees and the interests of the state

During their increasingly frequent forays across the Uganda-Sudan border, the UNLA looted, burned houses, and murdered refugees and Sudanese untold numbers of self-settled refugees were abducted and taken back to Uganda. Incursions into the Sudan by the UNLA posed great threat to the security of refugees *and* Sudanese. They were the very forces which led the Ugandans to their 'well- founded fear of being persecuted for reasons of race, religion, nationality, or political opinion...' (para. 6 & 7).[8]

The growing number of attacks on refugees across international borders by the armies which originally caused the exodus is alarming. There is a 'new mood' in Africa concerning refugees. On the one hand, host governments have increasingly demanded greater financial commitment from UNHCR; on the other, there is an ominous number of cases where state policy has manipulated sentiment in such a way as to endanger the security of refugees.

There are numerous examples of this new mood ... Since the dramatic expulsions from Nigeria in 1983 ... Refugees have been subjected to increasing pressure. In East

---

[6] The right of refugees to send and receive mail (noted in the UNHCR Handbook) was not made possible in southern Sudan. Local postal services were almost non-existent and usually one could not even buy stamps at the Yei Post Office. Expatriate officials were able to use the Kenyan postal services via their charter flights. Refugees, aside from a few employed by agencies, did not have such access.

[7] By mid-1984 a practice had developed whereby some local chiefs spread thin lines of ashes across roads. This was to mark a roadblock meant only for refugees. If one failed to stop (or perhaps even if he did stop) someone would leap out of the bush to beat and rob him. The programme officer equipped one courageous refugee with enough money to ride all over Yei River District to identify the location of these roadblocks so that co-operative local officials might have evidence to arrest those responsible.

[8] This definition of a refugee is taken from the 1951 UN Convention and the 1967 UN Protocol. For Africa, the Organization of African Unity (OAU) enacted a much more comprehensive and liberal convention in 1969. These laws appear in the *Collection of International Instruments Concerning Refugees*, UNHCR, (2nd Edition), 1979.

Africa, refugees have been 'swapped' between the governments of Tanzania and Kenya. Ugandan refugees in Kenya have been abducted, apparently with the connivance of local security services, and in Tanzania, the government is currently attempting to secure the removal of many Rwandan refugees from the Kagera area, victims of an earlier expulsion exercise [*sic*] implemented by Uganda. ...Lesotho, Mozambique and Swaziland have all been forced by the government in Pretoria to evacuate refugee members of the African National Congress, while Botswana has returned a number of Zimbabwean refugees to their country of origin. Since the beginning of 1984, several countries in East and Central Africa have been mounting joint security operations along their common borders. Ostensibly their objective is to root out bandits, smugglers and cattle rustlers, but such operations also serve the purpose of preventing other forms of cross-border movement which are unconnected with criminal activities. (Crisp 1984.)

The unwillingness of the UN to sanction its members who carry out such serious breaches of international law raises the question of whether any organization which directly depends on the support of these same member states is competent to carry out the protection functions with which it has been entrusted. (Guest 1983.) As the main financial support for UNHCR's budget comes from a minority of UN members, most of whom are western-orientated, conceivably this could at times limit its freedom to speak out against the actions of one of these nations? On at least one occasion, a member state tried to put pressure on UNHCR and the Sudan government to act in contravention of the Convention. When Ambassador Douglas, an adviser to President Reagan, visited the Sudan in 1983, he referred to the refugee influx in eastern Sudan as

...casual, rather than a response to persecution. He wondered whether UNHCR could not take steps (as they had done elsewhere) to discourage the wholesale flow, and suggested that the UN, US and Sudan government were not yet talking about the hard questions, e.g. how to limit new arrivals humanely. (Crisp 1984.)

And, as one protection officer put it in a discussion with the lawyer on my team, 'We should not make people feel that we are the advocates of the refugees. We should sacrifice some cases for the general good of the refugees, because if we push too much with cases of refugees it may endanger the work of the UN'.[9]

In Europe there are many human rights groups which take a special interest in the welfare of refugees, but in Africa UNHCR - and on a much more limited scale, the OAU - are the only organizations with offices established to undertake this responsibility. Amnesty is an independently-funded international humanitarian organization, but as far as refugees are concerned, its work is largely confined to cases where refugees are under

---

[9] The interview took place in the Yei office on 22 August 1983. This officer, like most protection officers I met in the field, had only recently graduated from law school. He had no previous experience in protection work. His remarks contradicted written policy (see, for example, UNHCR's *Handbook* 1982-3), but so did many other practices in the field.

threat of *refoulement* (forced repatriation). Even then its role is very limited, for when there was some outcry concerning the *refoulement* of refugees from Djibouti back to Ethiopia, Amnesty was far from prominent. Lack of funds may prevent Amnesty from maintaining a presence in areas of such special risk, but there is an *urgent* need for the continual monitoring of the protection services to refugees by some independent body.

As Rizvi maintained, the international community must be prepared to ensure the victim's protection regardless of whether he is fleeing from economic, ecological, or political disaster. Africa is a continent poised on the brink of self-destruction. He states clearly what is so often forgotten: that political and economic stability are inseparable.

The way things now stand, it is no more a question of hypotheses of catastrophe in a few years: the catastrophe is already there. It is there now....massive displacements of population...shake up the social fabric which is already weak, the economic structure which is also weak, and therefore the political structure which is....fragile. That is going to lead to violence, and violence is going to lead to repression and repression is going to lead to bad planning and poverty...and that is going to lead to displacement, and so on. The vicious circle will be complete in Africa. Perhaps it already is, and we are just closing our eyes. (Alternative Viewpoints 1984.)

Implementing protection

In the first instance, UNHCR is charged with the responsibility of promoting the granting of asylum and ensuring that no one is forcibly returned to the country from which they have fled. Determination of status, the process through which (normally) an individual refugee must first pass before he can expect the restoration of his or her other human rights, is not usually an issue when an African host country is receiving an influx of refugees. Asylum is usually granted *en masse*, although there are exceptions, where groups have been refused entry or detained and refouled. Only much later are questions likely to be raised concerning the status of particular individuals. But security within the country of asylum cannot simply be guaranteed by the granting of asylum. As Zia Rizvi put it, protection in these terms involves an international presence to encourage states to respect their obligations to give asylum: 'It more or less stops there. But for the individual refugee, the problems more or less *start* there, when the person is not *refouled* and is going to face a future of uncertainty.' (*ibid.*) His or her first task is to secure printed or written evidence of refugee status from the national and then the UN authorities.

Certainly a major threat to a refugee's security is the economic loss which accompanies uprooting. Quite rightly UNHCR has been given the role of co-ordinating material assistance to refugees. Without at least basic food and medical security, no individual or community can be expected to recover from the trauma of the loss and crisis which is associated with becoming a refugee. As UNHCR's *Handbook* properly emphasizes, its protection role can only be effectively implemented if its response to an influx is immediate, well-coordinated, and humane. In the absence of any of these characteristics, the delivery of an assistance programme may actually contribute to the insecurity of both refugee and host.

Refugees, according to the UNHCR *Handbook*, should be 'treated as persons whose tragic plight requires special understanding and sympathy; they should receive all necessary assistance and they should not be subject to cruel, inhumane or degrading treatment.' (1982:10.) UNHCR has the duty to ensure that the human rights of refugees are upheld in their country of asylum and that they are placed on the same footing as are the nationals of that country. The Convention stipulates these rights against illegal arrest, detention, and the like, as well as their economic and social rights which are also to be upheld.[10]

UNHCR also has the responsibility to promote the enactment of national legislation regarding the rights of refugees which are in accord with international laws. It must also promote a wider knowledge and understanding at all levels in the host society of these international principles for the treatment of refugees. Finally, UNHCR must undertake to work towards a situation when refugees may drop their special status either by returning to their country of origin or acquiring the right of permanent residence if not the nationality of their country of asylum.

Leaving aside the question of whether or not, or how, or the extent to which, member states of the UN (or that smaller group which contributes most to its budget) act to inhibit the UNHCR in the delivery of protection services, what resources does the High Commissioner have at hand to uphold the rights of refugees? Protection officers are always quick to point out that UNHCR has no army or access to coercive power to act on behalf of refugees. But in the Sudan, UNHCR's power to influence through discourse, diplomacy, or the use of the media has hardly been exploited. Nor has it apparently been recognized that the use of its economic power, the aid programme itself, has enormous potential for preventing many of the situations which give rise to breaches of the human rights of refugees.

In Sudan, despite the enormous political and economic constraints under which it worked, the office of the Commissioner for Refugees (COMREF) developed a remarkably humane policy for refugees. Its officers frequently argued against the policies of other sections of the government on behalf of refugees both as individuals and as a community. For example, there were several occasions when Nemeiry ordered the expulsion of refugees from Khartoum. As a result, COMREF negotiated a policy which resulted in a set

---

[10] The conclusions of the Expert Group on Temporary Refuge in Situations of Large-Scale Influx, 21-24 April 1981, restated these minimum basic human standards for the treatment of refugees. (UNHCR *Handbook* 1982:10-11.)

of guidelines, 'Regularization of Refugee Stay in Khartoum', but it lacked funds to make these widely available.

Sudanow, a government funded magazine, took a very enlightened approach to the question of refugees within the nation's borders. So did the national television services. UNHCR could similarly have made use of the potential of the media, for example, by offering its many films to local television, but only one was shown during my stay in the Sudan.[11] More seriously, only occasionally did the Khartoum UNHCR office have in its employ a protection officer who willingly and actively co-operated with COMREF by discussing cases or by supplying it with reports from the field. In fact, it appears that very few of the myriad of reports which left the Yei UNHCR office concerning protection issues were ever passed on to COMREF for action.

Apparently some protection officers see themselves only in terms of their role as international 'diplomats'. If the statements of one protection officer in the field are any guide, there appears to have been a dangerous development in UNHCR's understanding and interpretation of its role. For example, in the interview in Yei on 22 August 1983, one protection officer explained:

There has been a misunderstanding of international protection by many people and even by some staff members of the UN. The protection we give is only the protection that the embassy of a nation is expected to give to its nationals. If the refugee's life is at risk or if there is discrimination against him, then the protection officer can make arrangements to have him resettled in another country....We are not the lawyers of the refugees. We only give international protection. If you were not a refugee you could go to your embassy only for certain of your legal problems.

Again at a later point in this same interview, he said,

... the UN is not concerned with the physical protection of the refugee since this is the responsibility of the Sudanese government...although administrative measures could be taken to reduce the unfair treatment, the UN is not at all concerned with this.

Regarding a case involving the confiscation of a vehicle,

Criminal matters may have some aspects of protection, but although we may feel that one has been treated unfairly, we can't do anything between him and the advocate. It is their business. We can't pay for an advocate. If the...office has done so in this case and there is funds, I will not interfere. But in future they must not do it.

On hearing that UNHCR gave fuel for the refugee to take the lorry, the exhibition in the case, to Juba, and forgetting that this vehicle would have allowed this refugee to retain his independence, the protection officer said:

---

[11] The importance of public information concerning refugees was observed in the recommendations of the 1983 OAU meeting on voluntary agencies and refugees. (Nobel (ed.) 1983:19-21.)

This isn't proper. Assistance can be given you by the UN only for your basic essentials like food, shelter and clothing when you are in need. The truth is that UNHCR can do little about and should do little in your case.

He criticized the actions of a previous protection officer who had been concerned about this case and who encouraged the UNHCR to help the victim take it up in court. When he heard that the stolen lorry was now in Zaire, he suggested that the refugee should just 'forget about the lorry'. On the other hand, the protection files in the Yei office demonstrate a considerable degree of success by the programme officer and his Sudanese colleague, the project manager, in intervening in dozens of cases involving breaches of the rights of individual refugees. After reading the files, the protection officer remarked that he was surprised that the programme officer had not been asked to leave the Sudan. Infuriated, the programme officer requested in writing (29 August 1983) that this protection officer never be sent to his field office again.

The Sudan government long ago acceded to the international conventions concerning the rights of refugees. In 1974 it enacted its own legislation which acknowledged most of these internationally recognized rights[12]. But Sudan does not have the funds or other resources required to translate or disseminate the law, or to issue the identity cards which each refugee has both the right and the responsibility to carry. It is much less able to ensure a trained and equipped judiciary and police force in the area where hosts and refugees were expected to accommodate each other in a very short space of time. Even a copy of Sudan's Asylum Act (1974) was not available in Juba's UNHCR office until 1983 and none of the agencies working in the area were aware of its existence. The protection officer whom I have quoted had also not acquired a copy of the Sudan's laws; according to the programme officer, who had longer discussions with him, this protection officer had not even informed himself of such basic facts as the structure of local administration, or the hierarchy and powers of the courts in the southern region.

Seizing the opportunity

The implementation of an aid programme for refugees could be the opportunity for a host government to raise the standards of procedure at the local level through consultation, training programmes and through supplying copies of handbooks and guidelines. UNHCR could play an extremely positive role but funds must first be available for it to concentrate on this neglected area of development. It is not only the UNHCR which has failed to recognize the urgent need to upgrade the administrative and judicial capacities of poor countries. Many a development project fails because of the

---

[12] The 1974 Regulation of Asylum Act No. 45 of 1974, Sudan *Gazette*, No. 1162, (Leg. Suppli.) 183 (1974).

lack of a trained administrator.[13] The success of all programmes which aim to improve local conditions depends, in the final analysis, on these services.

Always, the most significant resource for the host government and the international community in coping with an influx of refugees, is the hospitality of the local people. Hospitality is a spontaneous response to human suffering which is not based on an understanding of international agreements or complicated standards of human rights which states have contracted to uphold. In southern Sudan it was the only resource upon which the refugees could rely. Especially in the early period of the influx and before international agencies arrived on the scene, many Sudanese acted at considerable personal cost on behalf of Ugandans. For example, in Kajo-Kaji a chief, Jafer Tongu, received hundreds of refugees on his own land. He bought food for them out of his own pocket and then rushed to Juba by motorcycle to demand that the government send lorries of food to keep the group alive. Much later, on 13 September 1983, when a group of Ugandan government and UPC party officials illegally entered the Sudan (one allegedly carrying a hand gun) and visited camps in his area, announcing they would be returning with lorries to take them back to Uganda, it was this same chief who alerted everyone concerned, even the President's office in Khartoum, to this breach of international law. Local officials, party to the illegal entry, successfully conspired to have him suspended from his position as chief, and a UNHCR officer dismissed the incident as unimportant, suggesting these 'visitors' were simply encouraging refugees to return to Uganda.

Nearly every refugee can relate stories of his or her first reception by local individuals who, in one way or another, attempted to give material expression to the sentence one so often hears on the lips of the Sudanese, 'Feel at home'. But in such a very poor country as Sudan, this genuine humanitarianism must be nurtured, developed and materially supported if it is not to be overwhelmed by the demands which will be placed upon it.

Since UNHCR protection officers are not involved in the work of administering aid programmes, they could involve themselves in promoting a sense of teamwork between refugees and members of the local community so that they share the responsibility for working out solutions. The onset of an emergency is the ideal time at which to establish such co-operation. It is crucial that the formal legal agreements into which the state has entered in order to qualify for external assistance for refugees should be explained

[13] Even when trained staff are available, they often work under impossible conditions. I believe that if a protection officer had even visited all the 'A' and 'B' courts in the district, acknowledging the extra workload imposed by the refugee influx by providing chiefs with a table, chair and perhaps even a stock of stationery, some chiefs might have been encouraged to improve on the standards of procedure. As it was, even the magistrate lacked most of such basics, and he had no vehicle to carry out his role of supervising the lower courts. For many months there was no magistrate in residence and the practice of endorsing sentences imposed by the other courts was not observed.

without delay to local people. The rights of refugees to protection of life, property, freedom of movement, employment, agricultural land, education and medical services as well as their responsibility to their hosts must be made clear to all concerned.

Refugees need to be informed by their hosts about local conditions, the availability of agricultural land, and local customs for obtaining rights to its use; they should be given an overview of the economic limits of the society they have entered. Very few Ugandan refugees had ever set foot outside their country before seeking asylum in the Sudan. Some elementary geographical and demographic information would have encouraged many of them to move further inland rather than congesting the border areas during the first two years. Once in the settlements, had refugees been given a realistic overview of the situation in southern Sudan, rather than allowing them to retain unrealistic expectations for the aid programme, they, like many self-settled refugees, might have been motivated to work more closely with the Sudanese for their mutual betterment.

Refugees need detailed information about where and how to apply for work permits, or for trading licences, and on their liability for taxation. Refugees urgently require information on the structure of local government, the role of the police, proper procedures of arrest and trial and rights of appeal. Even discussing such issues can encourage an improvement in procedures. It was found, for example, that there were no written rules concerning market taxes and when further research on the markets in Yei River District was conducted in 1984, the local council felt prompted to form a committee and to devise regulations. (McGregor in Wilson *et al.* 1985.)

Group meetings of refugees with local hosts are the ideal method for transmitting such information and refugees should be encouraged to ask questions which are, in themselves, an important source of information for assessing their needs. Most important, discussions which include members of the local community will help identify both the available resources which may be shared with refugees and the additional infrastructural development which will be required to cope with the increased population.

From the outset of an emergency, UNHCR and government officials could use such opportunities to explain to the refugees the political and security constraints under which the assistance programme will work, constraints which will limit their freedom of action. This has important implications both for the degree of participation of refugees which will be tolerated by the government, and for the kinds of self-organization which will be allowed. It is a sensitive subject, but it cannot be avoided. Refugees *must* be informed of their host's relations and policy towards their country of origin. If this reality is faced squarely and openly, refugees will be able to devise strategies for survival on the basis of a clear understanding of the possible dangers they may encounter should they decide to remain 'too near' the border or to engage in activities which are in opposition to their host's policy.

One Sudanese official in the south was particularly adept at dealing with this problem. In one meeting with Ugandan leaders, for example, he related how he had been asked by a refugee if they could collect money and food for fighters in the bush. He asked leaders to warn their people not to be so naive. He said he knew this activity would be going on - after all, the Sudanese had been 'in the bush' for seventeen years and civilians would naturally be helping those who were fighting on their behalf. 'But', he warned them, 'don't tell me about it. You never know. I might be transferred to the Security or the Police and I would be forced to arrest you.' At the same time, he encouraged them to organize self-help community groups. Sudan has taken the lead in recognizing refugee-based humanitarian groups. COMREF knows through experience that these organizations are far more efficient at delivering assistance to their community than international agencies.

Most refugee flows result from a political crisis and it is naive to believe that all refugees can be politically neutralized. (Given the kinds of regimes fro.n which they have fled, one might ask if it is even desirable to attempt to do so). Moreover, and despite the risks, it is essential that refugees be encouraged to reconstruct their community. As one perceptive refugee argues, there is a need for:

....collective responsibility on the part of the refugees....this may raise some resentment from the host people and government, but it is essential that refugees should be allowed a say in their own affairs, up to certain limits. Under present policies there is nothing that refugees resent more than authority. They are afraid of authority. They no longer have any faith in those who give authority, and have come to regard their advice as being given in bad faith. (Appe 1984.)

The idea of collective discussion at the outset of an emergency influx of refugees may be dismissed by policy-makers and agency personnel as too idealistic or naive, but this is the way the Sudanese project manager in Yei River District tried to deal with all matters which involved the local people and the refugees. Unfortunately he was not only limited by time, but by a vehicle which was frequently out of service.

Protection officers should not forget that even during the colonial period in Africa, an administrator who hoped to gain even a modicum of compliance from his subjects, however benign his project, was forced to recognize the importance of engaging the community in lengthy discussions. He was, furthermore, compelled to pay respect to local customs and to acknowledge the local point of view - unless, of course, he was prepared to attempt to force the people at the point of a gun. Should Africans today (either host or refugee) really be expected to accept a postion with less power than they enjoyed under colonial rule? And after so many years of administrative experience can UNHCR really expect its field staff to do the job with even less consultation?

The relative success of the self-settled refugees in working out a *modus vivendi* with the local people testifies to the importance of promoting grassroots consultation. In interviews conducted at Panyume in 1984, refugees reported having been 'well received', and it was 'through the efforts of the chiefs and security forces that their safety had been guaranteed relative to Uganda and Zaire.' (Wilson 1985.)

But these rights would seem to necessitate their [the refugees'] 'incorporation' into Sudanese society. To achieve this, refugees in self-settled areas have readily accepted the Sudanese chief and other authorities as the custodians of justice and place a great emphasis upon the establishment of individual patron relationships with Sudanese....refugees were allowed to appoint their own headman; in Panyume he was referred to as a sub-chief. These Ugandan leaders were responsible for dealing with disputes within their own group. What is notable is that they are not operating separately from the Sudanese social structure. In fact, they negotiate with, and forward cases to the Sudanese chief in a manner similar to the Sudanese themselves and this respect for the authority of the Sudanese has been reciprocated. (*ibid*).

In addition to providing information for refugees and locals, procedures for licensing vehicles, registering personal property, and issuing identification cards, should be introduced and implemented *immediately*. Rather than creating separate refugee offices which duplicate the functions of the local bureaucracy, would it not be more sensible to add specially trained staff to existing facilities so that the local government officers and the police could also acquire the skills and capacity to cope with the special problems that refugees present? If local officials were brought in as partners, the assistance programme could serve as an opportunity to increase general competence, to increase the sense of responsibility and of professionalism.

While medical care and food must be made available at the beginning of an assistance programme, it might be better if relief were given on the basis of individual needs which are expressed or identified by members of the local community. On many occasions during my fieldwork, Sudanese came to me to request help for particular refugees, and on more than one occasion chiefs acted as intermediaries on behalf of refugees who desperately needed food or medicine. Indigenous and refugee-based agencies are ideally placed to take a leading role in dispensing the necessary relief aid to those most in need, so long as their staff are closely connected to the population.

During the first years of the crisis in the south, the Sudan Council of Churches and the Catholic Church in Yei established an excellent record for assessing needs in co-operation with the Ugandans. SCC actually employed refugees in their programme from the start. Given adequate resources, they could have continued to develop a genuinely participatory programme which might have avoided some of the more serious problems which developed later on.

Unfortunately, much of the local initiative and genuine humanitarian feeling was discouraged by the arrival of the foreign 'experts' who took over the programme. By assuming the role of the superior 'advocate' for refugee interests, well-intentioned outsiders may quite unconsciously have nurtured the growing sense of alienation between the communities. As will be seen, by 1982-3, relations between local hosts and refugees in Yei River District had deteriorated to an extremely low and dangerous point.

Early problems

When refugees first began arriving in Yei River District there was no guidance as to their rights and responsibilities. Some refugees were subject to arbitrary treatment and much of the property which would have sustained them through their early period of adjustment to the Sudan economy was lost. The failure to uphold the Sudanese law against the confiscation of property not only caused suffering, but encouraged bitterness towards their hosts in a refugee community powerless to seek redress. For example, police confiscated two cars belonging to one refugee, and he has the dubious pleasure of seeing one of these, sold to a Sudanese, driving about Yei.

The failures of an aid programme can even contribute to the breakdown of law and order. For example, after the scandal regarding the diversion of food aid which took place in Juba in 1981, noted in Chapter Two, local officials were particularly keen to avoid any suggestion that they were involved in such practices. They attempted to prevent refugees from selling their rations. This was always a source of conflict because refugees were forced by circumstances to sell food in exchange for necessary items which were not provided such as salt, soap, etc. But when World Food Programme's (WFP) supplies failed, it was sometimes necessary to give refugees extra amounts of one or another item in the food basket, precisely so they *could* sell in order to survive. As has been noted, the policemen were then asked to turn a blind eye when these items appeared in the market.

The failure to organize and supervise procedures for bringing vehicles into the country, and the failure to encourage special customs consideration for refugees, resulted in many better-off Ugandans being forced to sell their cars at ridiculously low prices. So many of these vehicles ended up in Khartoum that the government instituted special procedures to force the Sudanese profiteers to pay duty. Furthermore, farm production in the district is discouraged by the lack of transport. Ugandans could have used their vehicles to maintain themselves and this would have also benefitted the economy of Yei River District.

Had identity cards been issued promptly, this would have reduced many problems for refugees. Official UNHCR policy (and the law of Sudan) stipulates that refugees *must* be provided with such identification. According to the Convention this is the government's duty but in the south, the repeated requests for this logistical help from UNHCR failed. Refugees did not have the 'tax receipt' all Sudanese men must carry for identification and the lack of a refugee identity card was the excuse for many incidents in which refugees were arrested, beaten or had their property confiscated. However, at the time

I was in the Sudan the head of the UNHCR Khartoum office put the argument to me that refugees would be more likely to move freely without interference and to 'integrate' themselves within the community more quickly, if they were *not* supplied with special identification.

Perhaps the most useful investment for the physical security of refugees would have been to have paid their poll tax immediately. This would have provided all men over 21 years of age with a document which would have allowed them to move freely and which carried with it the symbolic sense that they belonged to the area. Moreover, through receiving this tax, the local government would have also realized some immediate tangible benefit from the presence of refugees. How much money would have been involved in attempting such an experiment? Poll tax was set at £S6.000, or, at the then official exchange rate, US$ 4.58. If the percentages of men in settlements is a reliable guide to the overall proportions of those refugees who would have been liable to taxation, the total exercise would have cost no more than US$150,000 per annum.[14]

For some who know such areas in Africa, this suggestion will immediately raise the question, 'Who would benefit?' Petty corruption among officials is characteristic of all impoverished societies and humanitarians everywhere assume the burden of imposing equity and preventing dishonesty. But corruption and the diversion of funds are by no means inevitable.

Some local officials demonstrate admirable concern for improving conditions in their areas, but are hampered by lack of funds. For example at Kajo-Kaji a project was undertaken to build a road to connect the area directly with Juba thus cutting by half the existing journey to the great benefit of the sub-district. The work was being done by communal labour and with only hand tools.[15] The road connecting the town and Uganda border was also improved and one bridge was built near the town during my stay. In Yei, the town council could only afford to keep the electric power on for two hours each evening, but it was remarkably regular. The town had had a piped water system, but the pump was broken. The funds raised by collecting the poll tax from refugees in Yei town might have permitted them to replace the pump and to make clean water available to the entire community. As it was, even the hospital patients were forced to drink polluted water from Yei river.

But sceptics will continue to ask who would benefit from such an injection of capital into the district. In Yei River District, it appears that the balance of economic power is held by the northern Sudanese mercantile class while sub-

[14] Paying the poll tax for adult males would not only inject funds into the community, it would *save* money. Issuing an identity card involves more than its printing. (Printing costs for a durable card were estimated at £S1.) Refugees have to be interviewed, photographed (?), and methods have to be worked out to ensure duplicate cards are not issued. All of this requires time, staff, offices, transport, etc.

[15] Few refugees under the aid umbrella demonstrated a sense of communal responsibility. Those who were recruited to the project, failing to appreciate that this road might also benefit them, referred to it as 'forced labour'.

chiefs, chiefs, police, and local government officials are recruited from among the southern Sudanese; and the leaders of the Sudan Socialist Union (the political party) are also southerners. While the traders make a very important contribution to the area by bringing in manufactured goods and other commodities to the market, the prices they pay to farmers are low and to a large extent they prevent local penetration of the market (McGregor in Wilson *et al.* 1985.) It is the southerners, the officials, who collect the tax. Even presuming that all poll tax were pocketed by individuals, which it most certainly would not be, the injection of even this small amount of cash into the district might have contributed to encouraging more, rather than less, economic equality!

There is no way in which outsiders can impose economic democracy. In the final analysis, power relations are the responsibility of the people at the grassroots. Before simply dismissing this statement as heresy, it should be noted that a great number of security problems arose between refugees and just such local officials.

There was, as far as I could discover, only a 'gentleman's agreement' that refugees should not pay poll tax for the first 'two years' in the country. Among the self-settled refugees, of the 2,947 households who answered the question, 28.8 per cent had paid tax to collectors who had, in lieu of cash, sometimes confiscated property far in excess of the poll tax levy. At one time, all the shops within Kala settlement were closed by the local authority because the owners had no business licences. All the rules and procedures for the enforcement of taxes and fees need to be discussed and formalized. In YRD, rules were neither explicit nor explained; the resulting repercussions on relations between refugees and locals were serious, not to mention the interruptions to the economic pursuits of the refugees.

Conditions in prison

Even prisons are 'refugee affected' institutions. Laying aside the fact that visits to prisons should be on the regular agenda of any refugee protection officer, it would not be outside the UNHCR mandate for assistance to be given to improve prison conditions for both locals and refugees. From the time of my arrival in 1982 there was a lack of information concerning refugees who might be in prison. When Goli settlement was opened, a group of refugees broke into the store and later, fourteen were rather arbitrarily selected for arrest. All escaped except for one, who was very ill in hospital at the time. Perhaps it was the ease with which these men escaped that discouraged serious humanitarian interest in the prisons.

At one time when we were in Kaya, the programme officer asked me to interview five refugees who were being held in prison. Their cell was no more than 2 x 2 metres. It had no window. Although the prisoners were allowed out of the cell to be interviewed, even when standing outside the police station's doorway, the stench was overwhelming. Besides Kaya and Yei, there were two other prisons that I know of in the district. One of these was located in Kajo-Kaji, the other was near Morobo. These prisons were never visited. In addition, each 'A' and 'B' court had some kind of 'lock-up' attached to it.

When serious crimes were reported, there was a tendency for police to look for the nearest refugee to arrest. For example, in 1982 after a person was found murdered near Roronyo settlement, locals were all convinced that a refugee was responsible for the crime. In all, six refugees were arrested for this same crime. Appendix IV includes a statement written by a teacher from Limbe settlement who was unlucky enough to be riding to Roronyo after the murder. In it he describes his experiences and gives some other details about life in prison.[16]

It was not until 22 August 1983, that a protection officer finally visited the prison in Yei. He was accompanied by the programme officer and a medical doctor. Before the visit UNHCR was only aware of three cases there, but they *found* 62 refugees, or 27 per cent of the total number of 227 prisoners. The conditions in prison were poor for all, but refugees suffered greater disadvantages. For example, Sudanese prisoners could rely on relatives for food to supplement the little provided, but refugees did not usually have access to such help. The report described two refugees who had recently died in prison as having succumbed to a 'condition of severe malnourishment and disease.' Medical care was not available, and those referred to the hospital were expected to pay for medicines. Refugees had neither access to funds nor to the means to inform UNHCR of their plight. Most prisoners, both Sudanese and refugees, had no blankets and no one who was interviewed was aware of the right to appeal against his sentence.

Even more serious, of the 62 refugee prisoners, 30 men were either on remand, had been charged but not tried, or had been tried but not sentenced. One of these unattended cases had been in prison for three years, another for two and a half years. Twelve refugee prisoners were serving sentences of between four and six months on charges of 'idleness'.

The health condition of several of the refugee prisoners was so poor that permission was sought to allow the Ugandan doctor to visit the prison regularly. This service was soon interrupted, however. Following a theft of medical supplies from GMT's stores, Yei policemen demonstrated a remarkable lack of bias in arresting the suspects: both the Ugandan *and* the expatriate doctor were arrested! Before the guilty person was found, the refugee doctor had suffered intimidation, his houses in Yei and Kaya were searched, and his personal property was confiscated. He understandably feared returning to the prison to treat the men and women there (there were

---

[16] His statement also provides some insight into the relations which obtained between some refugees, especially when money was at stake. It is likely that the programme officer would have intervened in his case, had he been informed, but the headmaster kept the arrest a secret, apparently pocketing the salary of the absent teacher.

17 Sudanese women prisoners at the time). In September, 1983 two refugee prisoners were shot dead, both allegedly running away, but according to a medical report, one was shot in the chest.

Incursions

As has been noted, the major cause of the insecurity of both hosts and refugees in Yei River District was neither the absence of protection officers, nor the failure of UNHCR to carry out its mandate to promote knowledge of the rights of refugees but rather the fact that since the beginning of 1982, incursions by the Uganda National Liberation Army (UNLA) were a regular feature of life on the district's Sudan/Uganda border. Along this border of approximately 160 kilometres there were stationed, in 1982, only 224 Sudanese troops. At a base at Kajo-Kaji the Sudanese Army was represented by a major who commanded 100 troops; only three outposts, Kanjai, Litoba and Kerewa, were manned. On one occasion when an influx had been reported, I visited Kerewa. I found about 50 refugees - mainly women and children - guarded by three soldiers and I could only see one rifle. As Kerewa was inaccessible by road, the soldiers had either to walk or ride someone's bicycle back to Kajo-Kaji. The other army base at Kaya, was also headed by a major, who had 124 men under his command. He had soldiers posted at Lojulu and Morobo. When in October 1982, the commander of the army base at Yei finally decided to increase the numbers of soldiers stationed along the border, he had to *borrow* both lorries and fuel to transport his men to Kajo-Kaji.

There are no doubt many reasons why the Khartoum government lacked the will to protect this border. Sudan and Uganda enjoy friendly diplomatic relations. Protecting the border would have risked a confrontation which neither side would have welcomed. Other parts of the south of the Sudan were severely affected by guerrilla warfare fought by opposition forces based in Ethiopia. In 1982 Equatorians showed no interest in joining this opposition, hence there was less need there than elsewhere for men to maintain security.

UNHCR files contain reports of dozens of incursions by the UNLA, but a few examples from the report of the Kajo-Kaji project manager illustrate the point.

....Right from February 1983 the security along Sudan/Uganda was not good. During this period, there were several infiltrations of Uganda government troops....

1. Sera-Jali (near Litoba) - five miles: In early February, Uganda government troops secretly infiltrated into Sera-Jali in pursuit of a woman called Silvia Auwa ... On arrival they found some refugees and natives at a drinking party. They opened fire killing a native and wounding Silvia. They retreated safely to their base.
2. Andejo (Livolo area) - 12 miles: On 17th March Uganda government troops infiltrated into Andejo. Their motive was to capture Abubakar, an ex-chief of Midigo

County in Uganda. During this adventure, they killed two natives and a refugee. They also set over 300 houses including food stuffs on fire. They looted over 40 head of cattle. They too collected all members of Abubakar's family who were eventually mercilessly and cruelly mutilated to death.

3. Morewa (Sokae) Livolo area - 13 miles: On 12th March 1983, Uganda government troops again streamed into Morewa. During this incident five cattle farmers were taken captive. A fleet of cattle looted and food stuffs were gravely devastated.

4. Ajio (Livolo area) - 25 miles: On 28th March 1983, Uganda government troops undertook yet another infiltration into Ajio. In this incident, eleven people were cold bloodedly killed. Several others were taken captives. Cattle looted and food stuffs taken or destroyed.

These incidents have precipitated a state of insecurity along the border. The hooliganic acts executed by the Ugandan troops have not only caused fear both among the refugees and natives but have also ignited and inflicted starvation in the affected areas ... In order to stabilize the prevailing delicate state of insecurity at the border, the refugees should be moved ... These barbaric manoevres planted by the Ugandan army has sparked an exodus of both refugees and natives from the border. The most affected area is Livolo (Project Management, February and March Monthly Report, No. PRMA/WB/57-A-I/2)[17]

But so long as the opposition forces in Uganda had been able to hold the military positions, shown on the sketch map, as of July 1982 (Fig. 1:1, page 48) the refugees (and locals) who were inside the Sudan were relatively secure from the Ugandan army (although even before July there were incidents when UNLA soldiers entered the Sudan, killing, wounding, looting and burning houses). As the UNLA pressed the fight to the borders, from May 1982 onwards it was not only the *numbers* of the refugees, but their wretched physical condition which defined the influx as an emergency. Although thousands were forced to move to the settlements, others tried to remain in the already congested border areas. Recognizing now that the resistance inside Uganda had collapsed and the presence of these refugees on the border would attract even more incursions by the UNLA, the first reaction of the local government was to ask UNHCR to speed up the movement of refugees piling up at the reception centres. But the UNHCR office at Yei was woefully under-equipped for a task of this magnitude; by October only three of its small fleet of lorries still functioned. More serious, information that there *was* an emergency did not reach Geneva until mid-July (and then not through official channels), and the *first* protection mission, a three day visit, did not occur until late August 1982.

As the number of Sudanese suffering the results of incursions by the UNLA increased, the local officials became impatient with the slow response of UNHCR and in September 1982, issued refugees with an order to

---

[17] Recall the UNHCR's resistance, discussed in Chapter One, to undertake the removal of refugees from the border area in 1983 on the grounds that the donors would not be prepared to undertake the vast expense of establishing settlements.

quit the entire border area between the Kaya river and Kajo- Kaji. Many locals interpreted this order to mean that their Ugandan neighbours, even those who had been there for up to three years, must abandon their crops and personal property as well. Thousands more poured into the reception centre at Mondikolo. With their crops still in the ground near the border, many refugees attempted to slip back to their vacated farms to collect crops. The road between Kunsuk and Kajo-Kaji became unsafe as unauthorized individuals took the opportunity to assist officials in imposing the ruling to stay away from the border by robbing refugees and even raping women.

As a result of these disturbances, some two-thirds of the refugees registering for settlements from September to November were people who had formerly opted to remain on the border but who were now forced to relinquish their homesteads and move to the reception centres. Unlike the new arrivals from inside Uganda, these people were not suffering extreme levels of malnutrition and illness. This change in the composition of the new influx at reception centres had important consequences for the assistance programme.

The alarming condition of refugees who had been arriving in the settlement throughout the preceding months had prompted an increase in the numbers of medical workers from abroad. Normal delays in making such arrangements meant that medical officers arrived too late to have much effect upon the conditions of these people and some who arrived in September felt they had responded to a false alarm. In one case, the agency (OXFAM) began almost immediately to make arrangements to withdraw its emergency medical team. Fortunately, however, this arrangement was delayed, for a new crisis erupted in late December 1982.

Anticipating needs

If refugees are to be protected by the intervention of an emergency assistance programme, it is necessary to anticipate each new wave of arrivals. A great deal of money could be saved if long-range contingency plans were organized and supplies were ordered and shipped in advance. It might be thought that the nature of an emergency is such that it precludes anticipation, but this is not the case. Laying aside the predictability of the very first influx of Ugandans back in 1979, information was available which could have helped both the Sudan government and Geneva prepare for each group, and even to know the physical condition in which they were likely to arrive. It was unnecessary for UNCHR repeatedly to find itself unprepared for each new wave of refugees, but this occurred in March-April 1982, and again in May, September, and December. People continued to arrive in January 1983. In May-June of that same year thousands more registered for settlement. In 1984 thousands of the self- settled were disrupted and in December yet another influx from Uganda was reported. The information which would help ensure preparedness only requires someone - ideally the protection officer - to spend time along the border. For example, on September 2 1982, I walked along the border near Yumbe with a young UN volunteer attached to the UNICEF office in Juba. We met a group of people in frightful physical condition making their way towards the Kaya reception centre some 15 kilometres away. I talked about them with a Ugandan already settled there.

'Why did they come in this condition? Were they inside Uganda or have they been sitting here on the border?'
    'These people have come directly from Uganda.'
    'I heard, er, was there shooting this morning?'
    'Yes, this morning from over there.' (The man pointed towards the direction of the border.)
    'But when people come straight from Uganda, are they in this bad a condition?'
    'Yes, of course. They won't make it to Kaya in this condition.'

He had been a teacher at Ladonga Teachers Training College, destroyed by early battles. He had fled into the bush, but then had made his way to Kampala where he was employed until 1981. Later, however, in fear of his life, he had once again taken to the bush. How long? He replied, 'This time for roughly one year and three months.' Still believing that refugees were better off in settlements, I asked him where he had spent the last nine months since he had entered the Sudan here on the border.

'Well, I actually thought that the war would end soon so that I could go back to Uganda and serve my people there as a teacher. But seeing that conditions don't improve, I had to come here to this place and get settlement.'
    'What's happening inside Uganda now? What is the condition of the people?'
    'Well, Uganda is completely ruined, particularly the West Nile part.'
    'I am talking about the area that the guerrillas still control. What's going on inside there?'
    'There are these Acholi soldiers, actually they should be the national soldiers because they are the people who ... do the most havoc ... These people move from place to place, killing people, burning their huts, houses, and depriving them of their properties. At times when they see villagers, they shoot them in order to get certain things from them like money, cows, goods and so on.'
    'But are there still many people inside?'

We discussed the estimates I had heard of the numbers still trapped inside Uganda. He believed there were more than 100,000 still in this disputed area of approximately 5,500 kilometres. There were people, he pointed out, all along the bank of the Nile, but particularly large concentrations at Obongi, some 94 kilometres from the Sudan border. 'They are already moving this way, trying to get refuge here in the Sudan.'

This teacher helped me interview the family resting beside the path. They had been walking from their last hiding place for a week. I asked what they had eaten and they replied. 'Berries, pawpaws and lemons.' They had met guerillas on the way who had given them some groundnuts. As one theory was that these men tried to retain the civilians inside the country to provide them with food, I asked if the guerillas knew they were coming to the Sudan. They reported that the guerillas were *encouraging* the civilians to leave the area. They recalled the incident which had made them decide finally to move to the greater safety of the Sudan. The words are those of the teacher who translated the story.

He said around one week ago there were some women who went to Matuma to the market to collect their groundnuts from their fields. Then these soldiers of Obote went and surrounded these people and captured them. They took many of these women and killed some. Those people who were taken have not been returned. Up to now we don't know where they are. And those who were killed were left on the spot. It was a week ago in Matuma area. The things they collected - like groundnuts - were all collected in a place, grass was put on them and they were burned so that villagers could no longer feed on them. This was done by Obote's soldiers.

The UN volunteer and I had to leave the family. There was no bridge over the stream which separated us from our vehicle. But we paid two Ugandans to ride us out of the area on their bicycles and now writing this I cannot for the life of me remember why we did not similarly 'charter' transport for those four individuals who could walk no further. The local people (who by then were mainly Ugandan) were feeding them; perhaps I had remembered that all of the food stock for the reception centre at Kaya had run out. Even if they had made that journey to overcrowded Kaya town, they might have been worse off for food than where they were.

As a result of similar interviews with refugees who straggled over the border during the following weeks, in October it was possible to estimate that the Sudan would receive 80,000 new arrivals whenever the UNLA launched its attack. It was already known that a military build-up was taking place within Uganda; as soon as dry weather set in so that the grass in which people hid would burn, it was obvious the battle would begin.

Just before Christmas 1982, the UNLA launched simultaneous attacks all over the West Nile. They entered the market at Obongi and began firing on civilians. A church service was interrupted and most of the worshippers, including the clergy, were killed. From Christmas Eve, the routes from Moyo to Yumbe, Yumbe to Obongi and Kulikulia, Uwanga to Rhino Camp, were blocked by the UNLA. The details of the atrocities reported by refugees arriving at a Kimbe reception centre suggest there is some substance in the argument that the UNLA was intending to carry out genocide against the people of this area.

Before Christmas day, the two government officials arrested all trucks in Arua for the transportation of newly trained 'Your Militia' to Aringa County ... 20 people were killed at Kuru Sub-Chief's Headquarters and 10 others were murdered at the hospital area. Amongst these people there was a taxpayer called Silvano Onyayia who was murdered with his three children and their dead bodies were burnt by the roadside. The son and the wife have now fled to a new refugee camp on 3/1/83. In the same sub-county, the following persons were captured and ruthlessly murdered. A man known by the name of Maskini was burnt in his house on 28/12/84. On the same date, a man known by the name of Musa was burnt with his wife in a house. At a place known as Geyea, a church was destroyed on 28/12/82 - Sunday, with a *congregation*. Still in the same area of Odravu, seven babies were crushed into wooden pestles by the 'Militia' who call themselves Kitgum boys and left a written note in the site.[18] Their mothers too were killed and burnt. Three old men were captured and their heads crushed with heavy stones. This was done by 'Lira boys' who left a written note. Still in Odravu sub-county, 10 men were captured and their heads crushed also with a heavy stone. One of these men is brother of an old man known as Fadulul Bayiga, who has now joined refugee settlement at Goli Transit. In Rimbia parish of Odravu 15 elderly men were stabbed to death.

Generally, in Odravu sub-county, 365 houses or homesteads were burnt including food stuffs ... (Report from Kimba Transit, 4.1 1983.)

From the other end of the border, at Kajo-Kaji, the programme officer found the results of similar violence inside Uganda.

... Since 28/29 December 1982, all reception centres reported a *most alarming increase of arrivals* of whom *all* are direct arrivals from Uganda. Worse affected is the Kajo-Kaji area where an estimated number of 5-6000 refugees have crossed into Sudan since the end of December, and more are coming. These figures were confirmed by the local authorities in the affected border villages, and the commandant of the Kajo-Kaji Army Base who accompanied us on our border visit ... During our visit to the border hundreds of refugees could be seen walking towards Kajo- Kaji, or, since a shuttle service of lorries was introduced immediately, towards one of the four villages where refugees are being picked up. Groups of 50-80 Ugandans were seen resting under trees and in the fields as far as the eye could see. Most had been walking since Christmas Day from areas as far as Obongi or Rhino Camp on the Albert Nile.

Ironically, in view of the danger refugees represented to their security, in January 1983, local people along the border were *still* welcoming the new arrivals giving them land on which to build! It was no doubt the salvation of many, as UNHCR food stocks were by then depleted. During the last days of December 1982, reports indicate that 14,000 refugees registered for settlement at reception points along the border. Not only were there shortages of food, but also of medicines, tents, and blankets. The recently signed agreement with WFP was to supply food for only 36,000, so food had to be diverted away from the settlements to meet, at least partially, the demands of the new arrivals. OXFAM reported that in Mopoko settlement,

---

[18] There were repeated allegations that the UNLA used this method to kill infants. It was easy to dismiss them as hysterical exaggeration until I met one man in Wudabi. When asked about his hopes for the future, he replied, 'How can I go back after what I have seen.' He proceeded to describe how he had climbed a tree to escape the soldiers who entered his compound, and watched as they forced his wife to murder their baby by using a mortar and pestle. Then they shot her.

the weekly ration was one kilogram of unground dura and half a cup of fish powder (supplied and flown in by the Norwegian government). While, according to OXFAM, children under five need a very minimum of 1,000 Kcal daily for survival, in this settlement children were receiving only 533 Kcal. The crisis was exacerbated by the onset of the dry season. Wells dug earlier during the rains were now drying up. A drilling rig was flown into Juba during November, but it was a very long time before it began operating because of a dispute, already noted, over who had the right to use it and whether the needs of local Sudanese should take priority.

The distressing saga of unpreparedness continues. In the early months of 1983 the rains failed in the area near the border. The fact that the self-settled refugees (and the Sudanese) would therefore suffer severe food shortages was not anticipated by UNHCR. The influx at the reception centres mush-roomed. These included not only self- settled people whose food supplies had run out; thousands more entered from Zaire. Following a conspiracy between the UNLA and Zairois soldiers (about which information was available) people were given the choice either to return to Uganda or leave for the Sudan. And, of course, there was a constant trickle of new arrivals directly from Uganda. In June 1983, 11,000 registered for placement in settlements. Again, in 1984 and at the height of the farming season, when local food stocks were low, WFP supplies did not reach the area because of transport difficulties.

How did Ugandan refugees in these planned settlements survive the interruptions in the delivery of food? They had been transported to remote areas which were usually covered in forest or thick scrub bush and they were expected to build their houses quickly and begin farming.

The emergency programme not only failed to anticipate the arrival of new waves of refugees who would require extra assistance, but also each year WFP apparently forgot that rains would interfere with transporting food from Mombasa. During the height of the farming season in 1982, 1983, and again in 1984, all supplies from Mombasa were interrupted. As we shall see, the people were forced to sell everything they had, including their hoes, in exchange for food. As a result, most became dependent on *leja leja* - piecework for the locals - to maintain themselves.

WFP has no means of measuring the progress of refugees towards self-sufficiency; it simply bases its calculations on the time from which a settlement has been opened. The plan involves cutting rations by half after one season with subsequent reductions the following year. In Yei River District the policy was to cut off all food assistance after two years. I received a letter, dated 9 December 1982, from the Ugandan in charge of the agricultural programme and responsible for settlements achieving self-sufficiency. His letter conveys the dilemma in which he found himself and shows how interruptions in the supply of food to settlements forced refugees to neglect the very activity upon which they were expected to depend for self-sufficiency.

'I have been tied down preparing reports on Goli, Pakula, Kunsuk, Otogo, Mopoko, Roronyo, and Limuru, as WFP is hurrying to move the development ahead.' (All of these settlements were established in 1982.) 'Yet they had absolutely no time to approach food self- sufficiency.' Recall that when these people arrived in the new settlements, they first had to build their houses before they could begin clearing land for their farms. 'If my reports don't convince them, I will send you details of the progress, if any, on the above settlements.' Pakula settlement was opened on 29 June. His letter continues: 'I came from Pakula on 8 December 1982 and they had an absolutely empty food store for two weeks. The settlement is virtually empty as settlers are in search of food.

The agricultural officer concluded his letter with a sentence which reflects one of the effects of food insecurity on the refugees' ability to trust the agency which is primarily responsible for their protection: 'I hope a food weapon will not be used to eject back Ugandans.'

We have already seen how UNHCR handled the crisis in 1984 when the Sudan attempted to move the 40,000 refugees at risk in the Kajo- Kaji area. First, UNHCR opened only six new settlements. Then, according to the programme officer, in an attempt to stop forced removals of the self-settled, they systematically reduced assistance to those registering for settlement at the reception centre Mondikolo. Although, it had been planned to bring in contingency stocks for the numbers of people who might still be forced out of their homesteads, these supplies never arrived. In November 1984, when refugees were evicted from the Kaya area, again UNHCR was unable to cope with the crisis, having available stocks of food for less than 600 people for one month. Then in December 1984, despite all the interruptions in the delivery of food rations during all three of the previous growing seasons, fifteen settlements were deemed 'self-sufficient' and food aid was stopped.

The ring of insecurity

Some of the protection problems which arose in Kajo-Kaji suggest that the sudden flooding of an area with material assistance which was distributed without assessing the real needs of the refugees, contributed to many of the tensions which erupted. Individual personalities, of both refugees and locals, but perhaps especially officials and refugee leaders, are also a factor.

Up until August 1982 in the Kajo-Kaji sub-district there was only one settlement and it had been only irregularly assisted by UNHCR. Moreover, it was some 88 kilometres from the town. Local government officials had decided upon Mondikolo as the site for cattle owners, and Mogiri as the place for leprosy sufferers. Although earlier both had received some assistance, from 1981 the head of the Juba UNHCR office had refused to recognize these settlements; they were 'too close' to the border. Local people no doubt sympathized with those handicapped by leprosy as well as with their families, and the cattle-owners who had suffered such terrific cattle losses must have also been objects of pity. From time to time the programme officer at Yei had 'slipped' some material assistance to these settlements and SCC had taken the major responsibility for looking after the handicapped at Mogiri. But overall, the local people had no reason to be jealous of the refugees.

From mid-May 1982, as the numbers of new arrivals began to soar, those registering at the reception centres were given rations on a daily basis. The blankets issued, as was noted earlier, were whisked away from refugees as they were loaded onto lorries to leave the area. UNHCR had nothing else to distribute as all other supplies had also failed to arrive. But after the international media got hold of the story of the unattended emergency in Yei River District (which was immediately confirmed by the OXFAM field officer), Geneva sent a delegation to assess the scale of the problem. By mid-August an airlift had been mounted and supplies began to pour in. After that, the local Sudanese in the Kajo-Kaji area had the opportunity to observe a well-supplied assistance programme in full swing.

Following the September order for refugees settled along the border to move to settlements, the character of the population now registering in the Mondikolo reception centre changed. Earlier, the new arrivals comprised those who had remained in Uganda and who were in desperately poor physical condition.[19] By September, however, most of those registering for settlement (who were taken to the nearby Kunsuk settlement until it was 'full') were those people who had previously established themselves as self-settled refugees along the border. Their farms had been so productive as to have swamped the local market and earlier the local government official had urged UNHCR to buy food from his area so as to stimulate greater production and avoid a fall in price. As many arrived with vehicles or other assets which they could turn into cash to start up their lives in the Sudan, some of these self-settled refugees had no doubt already achieved a higher standard of living than many local Sudanese. Now the self-settled refugees were ordered to quit their homesteads. Many were forced to leave unharvested crops in the ground.

Of course, such people who had been once more uprooted needed some assistance: for example, a tent for shelter, while building another house in Kunsuk. But had the right to free movement been upheld and some transport been available, the majority could no doubt have subsisted on the produce from their own fields which were not, after all, so very far away at the border.

[19] In August 1982, Mark Malloch-Brown, then the deputy head of UNHCR's emergency office, was in the delegation which came to investigate the situation. Hardly an inexperienced member of staff, having managed a programme in Thailand, he told me that at Nyori reception centre he nearly fainted when he saw the condition of the children *and* adults. He found 30 per cent of the children were suffering severe malnourishment. It is very difficult to assess the nutritional status of adults, but the number of deaths which followed bear grim testimony to the level of suffering of that influx.

But the aid programme proceeded, following its standard plan of distribution, regardless of need.

Even refugees saw the dangers of their being singled out for assistance. At Kunsuk they suggested that UNHCR should give blankets to the locals who, having none, used fires in their houses to keep warm at night. An incident involving a conflict over the temporary use of a tractor owned by a local, Linus Kenny, illustrates the way in which the intervention of an outside agency with money and other resources can increase tensions.

The tractor, rented by UNHCR (no doubt at a higher price than could have been fetched locally), was placed in the hands of the Ugandan foreman of Mondikolo to transport building and other materials. Eye witness accounts detail the story.

The policeman had a problem. A car was broken down at Jalimo market and they asked the foreman of Mondikolo transit camp to lend the tractor. Francis Unzi, the foreman refused on the grounds that the tractor was now under contract to UNHCR. The police said that they had written to the owner asking his permission and they asked to see the contract. It was not available. The owner of the tractor was brought into the case and he confirmed that both the tractor and the fuel in its tank were now the responsibility of the foreman and UNHCR. The police wanted the case to be discussed with UNHCR officials, but Yei was another 160 kilometres away.

Francis Unzi, as an employee of UNHCR, said that if the policemen seized the tractor they would be responsible to that office. At this provocation, 'Sgt. James ordered the soldiers [*sic*: probably policemen, but they were armed] to throw Francis in the cell. The soldiers grabbed Francis, tied or held his arms behind his back, took his papers, his money out of his pocket, hit him on his face, kicked him in the back and [he] was then taken to the cell.'

Another refugee added to the hostilities by accusing the police of 'violating human rights on an international level' and started to walk out of the station. 'Hot words followed and they (the policemen) followed him and told him that they would also throw him in jail. He left shortly.'

Three days later the owner of the tractor bailed Francis out by signing a promissory note for £S50. The police, who had taken a total of £S456 returned about half of this money when Francis was released, but he was charged and directed to 'show up in front of Judge Jalingua's 'A' Court. A medical report claims damage done by severe beating. Capt. of Police - Daniel J. Ajal and all policemen were drunk.' (Arrest of Francis Unzi, 16 August 1982).

Once their patron was the UNHCR, not only Francis Unzi and his friend, Emanul Dumo, (who had pronounced on the human rights of refugees) but other refugees also gained a new confidence in their relations with local officials. Sabino Azzo, formerly in the Ugandan army who had been appointed an assistant district commissioner for Kampala by Amin, had, from 1980, managed to mobilize the people of Mondikolo settlement in a quite remarkable way. Although not assisted by UNHCR, the people had succeeded in getting a school started and had some self-help communal projects underway. Azzo had constructed the walls of a dry stone building for a clinic and an office. All it required for completion was some cement and roofing.

At one point all the members of the community had each contributed five piastres (1,000 piastres equal £S1) to finance a delegation from the settlement, led by Azzo, to walk through the bush (about 120 kilometres) to Juba to ask UNHCR for some assistance, mainly for medical supplies. On arrival they were promptly thrown out of both the UNHCR and the Sudan project management offices. Empty handed, they walked all the way back to Mondikolo.

Given his remarkable energy and demonstrated ability to organize people, when Kunsuk opened in August 1982, Sabino Azzo was asked to assume the job of foreman. His new status as a paid employee of UNHCR released even more of the creative energy of this unusual man, to the point where he also indulged in a few delusions concerning his position. At the first block leaders' meeting which I attended, his attitude had been transformed. He presented UNHCR with a list of demands which, to name only two, included a motorcycle for himself, and an ambulance for the settlement since there was no referral centre in the district and very little transport.

There was no evidence that he was dishonest, but he organized a new market and began collecting taxes from both refugees and locals for a welfare fund for the settlement. He even drew up a plan for a special bank for refugees, to be located in Geneva. He personally directed, from the first day he took up his position, the 'Kunsuk's Geneva Jazz Band'. He managed to get the people of Kunsuk to build three classrooms in a matter of only a couple of weeks. When a watchman was suspected of robbery, he organized a search party of Ugandans to recover the property from this Sudanese.

Charming and charismatic figure athough he was, not surprisingly, the chief and the local policemen up the road at Kajo-Kaji were incensed by his audacity. For example, he signed 'ADC Kampala' to one of his letters to the 'A' Commissioner, which was a complaint about the behaviour of the local people and their chief. Angered, the Commissioner demanded that UNHCR not only remove Azzo from his post as foreman, but that they transport him completely out of the sub-district. In the end, the programme officer was forced to comply.

It was decided to move Azzo to Tore settlement. He wrote a letter to UNHCR complaining about the injustice of it all.

... I am complaining of all the issues concerning my dismissal from the office of being foreman and abrupt transfer to another settlement. Which has a plan to lead me and my people into a position of misery, poverty, ignorance and disease which are common enemy of human being ... Were it to be one sort of punishment I feel I will accept. But this has been a deliberate plan of putting one's family, parents and other relatives in one pot and boil them up together because of one man's mistakes ...

After complaining about the arbitrary decision of the 'A' Commissioner in some detail, he pointed out how this abrupt transfer had forced him to 'uproot all the cassava and the other crops which I have planted early last year and early this year without compensation.' And he continues, 'Abrupt stoppage of my self-help projects ... Secret plans and plots of arrest on me' (19 October 1982). In another letter written three days later, Azzo asks for a transfer to another country.

... As I have earlier mentioned in my letter, I have settled half way in this two years period. And it is hard and waste of energy to start all over again from misery and poverty. One is always happy if his/her mistakes are shown to him/her and the punishment of it is awarded. In my case I feel my mistakes could not cost insecurity as it has been the case now ... The ring of insecurity surrounding me now personally in a country where I have taken refugee, [sic] throw my life in complete disarray bearing in mind to be a refugee I escaped death from my motherland ... I have not committed any offence against any Sudanese law since in 1980. I have been leading a peaceful life with the natives at Mondikolo ... Nor have I engaged myself in the politics of Sudan ... Sir, I have consider taken me to another country for protection of [the] innocent lives of my family members and relatives, but not into my mother land, or in any adjacent country with Uganda.

Azzo lists his dependents which include 23 individuals, 9 adults (2 over 65 years of age and the others, children under sixteen). Still in the process of moving this large family, on 20 November 1982, Azzo travelled in a UNHCR lorry to Yei. At the halfway point, Kala settlement, police manned a roadblock, the lorry was stopped. According to the report, two policemen emerged armed with a whip and a rifle. Everyone was ordered out of the lorry, and the corporal cocked his gun. One courageous refugee, Dario Eberu, a resident of Kala, later travelled to Yei to report the incident.

During daytime, lorry comes from Kajo-Kaji with refugees. I came to see the lorry. People climbed down ... Azzo with a sick person. Azzo refused to give policeman money and immediately police begins to beat, corporal threatening with gun. Two natives helped the police. Money bag removed from Azzo. Liwa [the UNHCR driver] counted the money. (I could not see how much it was.) Police took the money from Liwa, took Azzo's belt and watch. One of the policemen put on the watch and removed two handkerchiefs from Azzo's pocket and tyre sandals removed also. Azzo was beaten and pushed in cell.
Then they threw sandals and belt down. They took the money inside their fence. Everybody saw this. The policeman ordered people to leave the place. People went away. In the evening I went to look for cigarettes for my sick wife. When walking on the road I heard somebody shouting in the cell. I thought the police was killing Azzo. So I started to make alarm. [A 'whooing sound' used to warn, to summon people, and for mourning at funerals.] I remained on the road. People heard my alarm and many people answered it by making the same sound. Then the corporal was coming with his

gun towards the people to disperse them. People got scared and ran away. On my way back, I heard people saying that it was me who made the alarm. After that the police came at my home. The police ordered me to come out of my hut. Three of them ... They took me to police compound ... At the cell, the police who beat Azzo started to strike me. I was pushed in the cell. Around 11.00 pm at night, the corporal and the beater came again in the cell. They beat me again and Azzo and we had to go out. The policeman had a knife with him. I had to leave the place. I saw how they took Azzo out of the settlement in the direction of the river. I followed the policeman and Azzo. They did not see me because I was hiding myself. I heard how Azzo was mistreated again. The policeman came back and I went to the spot and found Azzo unconscious. I woke Azzo up and after a while helped him to sit. I tried to convince Azzo of going back home but Azzo did not want and said he wanted to go to Yei. I also went to Yei with him.'

Mr Azzo Sabino also gave a statement at the project manager's office in Yei.

'I went to Mondikolo with the approval of UNHCR office Yei and project manager west bank Yei ... The purpose of my visit was to see my ill child; to make preparations for the transfer of my family to Tore and to collect properties and relatives of Mr Unzi ... The assistant driver of the lorry was ill. He had stomachache. He went under a tree in Kala because he was too ill. I wanted to help him to go to the dispensary. Assistant driver wanted to go to Yei. While talking to assistant driver police had approached. I greeted the police, but corporal didn't want to greet me. Instead he pointed at my bag (waist belt bag). I said inside is the dictionary and another notebook plus two pens. In the bag was also £S125 ... I only told him that I had money without mentioning the amount. Corporal asked me to open the bag.

Azzo continues by describing the beating and how the refugees cried out to him in Madi simply to surrender the money. The beating continued but Azzo resisted handing over his money. Finally, after being seriously throttled, he 'gave in, was afraid to be killed and gave the bag.' After some hours in the cell, someone from the settlement brought him food. 'The policeman who had beaten me woke me up. I was tired and I was resting. The pain in my throat was too much and I had difficulties in eating. I took mainly water.' Sabino Azzo's description of the next events before Eberu raised the alarm include being threatened with a knife and beaten again. After having dispersed the crowd that gathered, the other refugee was thrown into the cell with Sabino, he too was beaten. Around '23.00 hours' Azzo was taken at gunpoint to the main road and walked to the end of the settlement. According to Azzo's statement, the policemen asked him, 'Why do you want people to kill us, you made a lot of noise. The people could have killed us. Now, you say to us, what you want.'

I could not answer because they started to kick me again. They threw me down and took my throat again. They kicked me also in the back. They left me lying on the road. Apparently Dario followed all the way, hiding himself. He then came to look for me and found me unconscious and made me sit. I could breathe again more or less normally. Dario wanted to go to Yei. I then saw the back of Dario [cut by the whip]. Then Dario wanted to go to Yei with me in order to get treatment and to report to the UNHCR office.

On 22 September a report was sent to the Juba UNHCR office detailing this case and that of Francis Unzi and it reminded the head of this office of two earlier cases. In August, Michael Otim, then employed as the family tracing officer for the International Committee of the Red Cross (ICRC), was injured. He was travelling with a convoy of lorries ferrying refugees from the Kaya reception centre. It began to rain and Otim had asked that two severely malnourished children be allowed to ride in the front of the lorry to protect them from the elements. A soldier, who had hitched a lift and was occupying a seat in the cab, objected to being asked to hold one of these children. He drew a knife and stabbed Otim just over his heart. The wound was 'superficial', only requiring stitches, but Otim was already traumatized. Some months earlier he had watched his parents being brutally murdered by knife at the hands of the UNLA. The report included another long-standing case involved Nasura Sultan, whose vehicle had been appropriated by a local businessman who refused to compensate him for its value.

... All these cases make me worried because they show very well that we have to react in order to protect the refugees. I have not the time and not the knowledge to do this effectively. As long as refugees obey the Sudanese laws we should be able to guarantee them safety and protection. I have the impression that many policemen and other government officials in the field are not at all well informed about UNHCR protection role, rights of refugees, etc. Moreover, I have the impression that nobody in our offices in Yei and Juba (perhaps you are the exception, I do not know) knows much about protection. We too need some briefing. It is also necessary that we show that we follow the cases reported to us, that we are really present and that UNHCR does more than giving out the food for WFP. Especially in emergency situations a protection officer is needed, should at least make an extensive mission and offer his/her services to refugees ... Perhaps you could think of a more permanent answer to our problem of missing a protection office in the south. (29.9.82)

Repatriation

Already in 1981, US$4.1 million had been made available for the reception and rehabilitation of Ugandan refugees returning home to the West Nile and the implementing partner, Lutheran World Service, had established its office in Arua. In 1983, the Yei office was instructed to distribute repatriation forms and the first group of 109 refugees were returned in mid-July. While no-one, certainly *no* Ugandan refugee, would ever argue that returning home in safety is not the best solution, the active mounting of the repatriation programme in Yei River District at a time when refugees were still pouring across the border and while battles continued within earshot of many settlements, served to introduce a new dimension of insecurity for refugees.

Pressure from within UNHCR to repatriate the Ugandans was also in fundamental contradiction to its policy to help them become self-sufficient within their own country of asylum. *At the centre of this contradiction is the belief that material assistance is the propelling force which moves people.* At a certain point, of course, the material conditions of life *are* determinants of people's decisions and it cannot be denied that many people did decide to accept repatriation because of the problems of survival in settlements. This is demonstrated in statements by people who joined the second official repatriation mission in September 1983.[20] The speaker is a boy of 21 years who was on his own in the Sudan.

I will not forget the hard times in the Sudan. I have gone hungry for a long time. In the settlements I have been labouring for food, now I feel it is unbearable. So I decided to repatriate. Quite many people had died and I fear I would also die since the medical services are not adequate.

An elderly man gave his reasons for returning:

I am 54 years and we are three here, but there are two children I have left behind ... who say they don't want to be killed. They protested and ran away, saying soldiers are still killing people in Uganda ... I have felt homesick and I known I am old now; if I die without seeing my birthplace, it will be a curse.

A young woman who was returning, unlike most others, had news of what she could expect back home:

In Uganda my home is in Terego Aripia village. An aunt died at Mopoko settlement. Our huts [in Uganda] were reportedly burnt and I hope to stay with my mother-in-law as she has already gone back home. Our cassava fields have been eaten up by rats I am told. My hardest experience in the Sudan was of food shortage and insufficient food rationed by the UNHCR which often is delivered very late. I have been labouring every day for food for the past three months. I don't want to work for somebody in the field like that. My reasons of repatriating are the death of my mother and food problems. Let people be careful because quite many may decide to follow us for the same reason. Particularly young men I am told are not safe there, so people must decide carefully. I don't know, I may be forced to come back. I have to see my relatives and make the funeral rites of my mother.

Repatriation: in whose interest?

The close of the period of anti-colonial wars was the occasion for UNHCR to achieve considerable success in repatriating large numbers of refugees back to their countries of origin. For example, after Algeria, refugees were

[20] Interviews were conducted with all returnees at the Yei transit camp by my assistants. The main reasons they gave for leaving the Sudan were food shortages, deficiencies in health services, the lack of education, and the belief that since death was imminent anyway, it was 'better to die at home'.

returned to Guinea-Bissau, Mozambique, Angola, and Zimbabwe. In 1972, southern Sudanese also began to return home after the cease fire. But at the very time refugees were being repatriated back to Uganda, following the overthrow of Idi Amin in 1979, thousands more were spilling out over its borders. Some would argue that it is still the aftermath of the colonial experience which lies at the root of mass exodus in Africa (el-Hassan 1984), but however one explains the causes, Africans have come to represent a very substantial proportion of the world's refugee population.

The expanding numbers of refugees in Africa are undoubtedly a major factor which has led some of the governments which fund UNHCR to promote repatriation as a 'solution', even where the government whose policies led to the exodus remains committed to them and where there is no reasonable guarantee that refugees may return in safety. Repatriation under these conditions began in Djibouti and became a test case for Africa. As Ambassador Douglas put it in his meeting with UNHCR staff in Khartoum in 1982, the office must look into the 'possibilities of encouraging *repatriation* after seeing the Djibouti experience.' [*sic*].

Repatriation represents a convergence of interests. Given the present levels of funding and the sheer pressure of numbers, host governments find it increasingly difficult to cope. For the countries of origin, the return of the refugees can serve to rehabilitate their tarnished international image. More to the point, the availability of funds for returnee programmes can help countries such as Uganda and Ethiopia 'stabilize' internal conditions. So long as funds are available to alleviate the economic causes of civil strife, no one should object. What is exceedingly objectionable is the charade which is being perpetrated by those who are involved in the so-called rehabilitation programmes for returnees. In Asmara, Ethiopia, for example, one Red Cross official told me that not one of the rehabilitation 'packages' were going to returnees. The only 'returnees' there had been back in Eritrea for five years. The aid which was being distributed under this programme was going to people on the basis of *need*. The reception centre at Asosa, built with funds from UNHCR for returnees from the Sudan, came to be used for Tigréy peoples by the Ethiopian government.

In order to attract funds to rehabilitate areas which have been de-populated, Uganda has also had to fabricate numbers (Crisp 1984.) It was claimed that by the end of June 1983, some 360,749 people had returned from Zaire and the Sudan. Although the UNHCR officer from Arua admitted to his colleague in Yei (as well as to my team which challenged the figures), that he was aware the figures were 'invented' by the Ugandan government, the statistics were printed on UNHCR stationery. Not only were the numbers of returnees invented, the statistics for the totals of the original population of each county from the 1980 census were also changed. On 3 September 1983, one refugee wrote the following letter to his fellow countryman, George Draduwe Madra, the District Commissioner, Moyo District.

Re: 1983 Spontaneous Returnees up till June and returnees repatriated by UNHCR from Zaire and Sudan.

I write you this nasty letter as a brother. I see you collaborating with the Ugandan government in denying the existence of the Ugandan people from Arua and Moyo in the Sudan. This is a costly mistake you are making which is eroding your morals and integrity as of all who do.

It is totally unacceptable to have a population of 64,109 in June 1983 in East Madi when the 1980 census says it was 48,789. How prolific have you become back home, to have this increase of 13,320? This is in fact a 27.3 per cent rise in only three years, to mention only the figures of East Madi alone. There are 13 settlements on the east bank where most from East Madi are settled. The population of your brothers in the east bank is 70,000 in settlements (camps) and about 10,000 self-settled. I know these people and have worked with them before.

The political motive of denying the presence of Ugandans here by having ghostly persons in your district to give high population figures of returnees is to accept the problem, but to jump to a unilateral solution without facing the facts. The fact that you submit such figures to UNHCR means that you receive material aid to that tune. That is trading on the sufferings of your own countrymen among whom you have blood relatives! This is another criminal offence, very degrading to humanity and integrity.

I believe the Ugandan problem is temporary if we all treat it with maturity. I am in the middle of human suffering caused by the actions of irresponsible political and military directives which will probably be ended before your professional administrative career; be well advised, therefore, brother, as all must live to face the consequences of their actions, be they Amin and Obote on a big scale, or you on your own small scale.'

The writer, obviously had some authority to speak to his colleague in Moyo. He had been agricultural officer for the district before the war and had also been responsible for the census in 1980.

Promoting certain repatriation programmes in Africa may be advantageous to some of the governments who fund UNHCR. For one thing, they have been accused of using aid as a means of promoting their own foreign interests *vis-à-vis* Ethiopia and Uganda (Crisp 1984.) But perhaps even more to the point, rehabilitation programmes for returnees are substantially less expensive than are assistance programmes and the period of foreseeable expenditure finite. In July 1983, the 109 returnees secured 44 hoes, 32 pangas, 94 blankets, 108 sets of plastic cups, bowls, plates and 30 plastic basins.[21] As WFP supplies had not yet reached Uganda, one month's supply of food for each was brought along from Yei.

The stated policy of the implementing partner was to give the returnees food rations for only three months. When it was criticized as too short a time, the UNHCR official at Arua pointed out in a letter that although 90 days was the standard UN/WFP/government agreement in such cases, the contract could be 'extended or transformed into a quick action project'. And in a letter

---

[21] This amount was described as 'more than usual' as this was a 'public relations exercise'.

on 22 August 1983, he admitted that 'Nobody can expect returnees to be self-sufficient within three months.' But only a month later when he visited settlements in Yei River District to explain the programme and refugees asked him to report on the well-being of those first returnees who arrived in Arua in July, he answered that since his office was in Arua, he did not know *where* the returnees lived. One wonders how this official would know when, or if, a 'quick action project' was required.

The report of a repatriation mission to Uganda in December 1981 (as well as another which took a few Zairois back across the border) make scarcely credible reading: The return of Acholi refugees from Sudan to Uganda: 1-4 December.

The original number of planned returnees was 104. However, on 30 November when UNHCR lorry went around Juba to the agreed points of collection, not a single refugee was waiting ready to be picked up. Even when UNHCR officials continued searching throughout the morning, there was no more success. Only after the self-styled 'chairman' of the group, Augustino Okello, was given sole charge of the lorry in the afternoon did the situation change. He returned with persons representing 68 refugees, and a number of children, the whole totalling more than the original 104. By the following morning, 1 December, the number dwindled to 40 as the transport reached Juba bridge, the last place where a change of mind could easily be effected. By arrival at Nimule the number 36. Two more of these were lost at Nimule and a further two at Atiak (Uganda), although three of these 34 found missing turned up the next morning at Gulu. Of these, 34 proved to be in no way related to the persons under whose names they were registered. Others, although genuine dependents, had earlier admitted to having a different identity from the 'named' party. It seems that only a dozen persons were still accepting the same identity in Gulu that they had claimed in Juba.

The report, written by a UNHCR official from Kampala, continued by noting the expense of the operation: each returnee costing US$130, but '... were one to count only genuine cases, the cost per head would increase to well over US$200. This figure, of course, does not include the UNHCR expenditure in Juba, or 'unseen' overheads.' He pointed to other questionable aspects of the exercise. It appeared that most of even the 34 who actually arrived in Uganda, had either used the opportunity to return home for a holiday or were more preoccupied with the festivities (all enjoyed a roaring party at Nimule the night before crossing the border), or with the 'hand-outs'. His cynicism was supported by the fact that most of the men who accompanied the mission had left their families in Sudan. Sadly, while doubting the sincerity of most, he noted there were women and children who 'did seem to be "serious" cases.' He strongly criticized the 'wisdom of large hand-outs of food and money, which effectively comprise almost an "inducement to return".'

Should UNHCR involve itself at all in repatriation in circumstances where there is no guarantee that refugees are secure? Do refugees need to be transported back to their homes? Already in 1982 some Ugandans were 'testing the water' by sending individuals, usually women, back home to investigate how safe it was for all to return. In 1983, when I accompanied the repatriation mission, I met a number of refugees whom I had known the year before in Goli settlement. Again, most were women and children.

Refugees already had their own scheme for returning to their homes as soon as it was safe, and for using the food they had grown in the Sudan to sustain a few numbers of their household while they re-established fields in Uganda. As one woman explained to me, she would be back to the Sudan shortly because she had left unharvested crops in the field. Certainly the returnees' 'rehabilitation' would have been facilitated by some assistance, and one would not have been bothered to see them using these items as capital to get started again at home. But the way in which LWF was implementing the aid programme for returnees in Uganda did not insure that aid would reach those in need. The materials were being sold, *apparently* by the chiefs who were made responsible for distribution. The 'allegation' that aid was being sold was *confirmed* in July 1983, when we visited Ariwara market in Zaire. There we found literally mountains of the particular items which were supposed to be distributed in Uganda and this was reported to UNHCR.

The problem for the Ugandans was not that they needed to be induced to return, or even provided with transport. They had walked out, most could walk back again. The problem was that it was still not safe for most of them to return and even women and children were often at risk.

The UNHCR programme officer who had accompanied this mission to Gulu understandably proceeded with considerably more caution when he was asked in 1983 to promote the repatriation of refugees for whom he was responsible. In June, he first went to see the situation in the West Nile for himself. Since it was unsafe (and it remained so through the end of 1984) to travel directly to Arua through Kaya and Oraba, he travelled through Zaire and this gave him an opportunity to report on conditions there as well.

He found further evidence of the movement from the Sudan into Zaire for medical treatment because services were so poor in the Sudan. His report expressed the hope that Médecins Sans Frontière's arrival in the Sudan would reduce the number of people forced to go to Zaire for more adequate care. Still anticipating renewed and sudden influxes of refugees, he urged UNHCR to establish the 'absolutely indispensible' radio link between Aru, Zaire, Arua and Yei. He found the security situation in Zaire much more serious than in the Sudan. Family tracing services, as in the Sudan, were completely ineffective. Even after successful tracing, 'ICRC has no funds to make arrangements for family reunion and has to hand over the case to UNHCR. As stated by ICRC Aru, there has not been one case where UNHCR has been successful in bringing about a family reunion ... Field officers of ICRC never visited Sudan refugee settlements.' The ICRC suffered similar problems in southern Sudan.

Concerning repatriation, from Zaire he was told 'about 200 refugees were repatriated under UNHCR auspices, some of those even came back because of difficulties to get enough food.' But he was informed that those who come from Terego, Maracha, and Arua town seem to enjoy 'fair' security conditions. Nevertheless at this time the Aru office had been instructed to freeze repatriation missions.

In Arua the programme officer met with the Archbishop (an Italian) who was convinced that all refugees should now return. He accused UNHCR and other agency personnel of keeping refugees in the Sudan and Zaire simply to retain their jobs. He argued that the situation in and around Arua was 'normal'. A similar discussion was held with the district commissioner who maintained that there were no problems in Terego and Maracha counties. Concerning the situation on the border where there was still active warfare, he said that 'the regional government is not willing to solve the problem.' Both the district commissioner and the Archbishop expressed concern that the refugees were not well looked after in the Sudan and that they did not have the right to free movement. The commissioner argued that it was the then Juba government, not Khartoum, which was against them. Ominously, concerning the problems which were to persist in southern Sudan, he said that *Uganda would try to prevent Sudanese from seeking refuge in Uganda.*

Discussions with another long-term resident expatriate in Arua suggested that while civilians might safely come back to 'lower' Terego, as far north as the village of Udupi, it should be remembered that it is not far from the first military post and that government troops disturb civilians when they are drunk. While he had no reports of killing, two girls had recently been 'taken' by soldiers.

The programme officer then left Arua and travelled north. He found the area of Yumbe and Koboko virtually empty, and that just south of Koboko town three civilians had been killed by soldiers. A priest reported to him that he could hear fighting every two or three days. Recent guerrilla attacks had succeeded in seizing a great deal of ammunition and weapons. At the Yumbe trading centre there were no civilians at all, everything had been destroyed. At the Yumbe hospital, he found about 350 civilians guarded by some 150 UNLA soldiers.[22]

Other discussions with teachers and students in Arua assured him that at least some Ugandans could safely return, but informants were described as 'categorical' on the point that neither ex-soldiers nor members of the Kakwa community should risk returning.

The conclusion which was reached as a result of this mission was that the 29 who had already personally approached the office in Yei would be repatriated. And while the programme officer was convinced then that

[22] Later, in July, when both the UNHCR and LWF representatives were asked about these people who were virtual prisoners at the hospital, we were told the people *liked* living in these abandoned buildings. They had never enjoyed such good housing.

refugees from Maracha, Terego and Arua as well as southwards from the town could safely go home, he advised that refugees from Aringa, Koboko, and Madi should be informed about the risks.

He went on to emphasize that the situation in West Nile was more confused than his report might indicate. Given the success of the opposition forces, during the rainy season the 'frontline' could move south to Maracha and Terego. 'Repatriation should keep very low profile until the end of wet season.' Only then a better assessment of the situation can be made. Moreover, the Ugandan government 'should give well defined guarantees for the security of the returnees. This is because an amnesty law seems impossible now that Uganda moves closer and closer to a widespread civil war.'

Underlining the fact that there were likely to be yet more people fleeing Uganda, the report ended with a recommendation that UNHCR offices both at Juba and at Yei should 'have budget provision for food in case of serious food shortage. This becomes inevitable now that influx is still very high.' The report was dated 10 June 1983, but all food supplies from Mombasa ceased from mid-July that year until the third week of October when, and yet again, an expensive emergency air lift had to be mounted.

Whose interest?

In whose interest are repatriation programmes under such conditions? It is insufficient to explain the persistence of some individuals in promoting them simply in terms of the interests of governments - host, country of origin, or even those governments which support UNHCR. It would appear that once an office has been established and has a budget, such programmes acquire a momentum of their own which overcomes all logic. The evidence suggests that there are those who have a professional stake in the success of a rehabilitation programme are quite prepared to overlook or even to deny hard evidence of the dangers refugees will face if they return home. Others who, like that programme officer in Yei, practise caution, are likely to come in for severe criticism. But is it sufficient to account for the enthusiasm of the young men at Arua for repatriation simply in terms of the inertia of individuals caught up in a bureaucratic swirl?

I travelled with a repatriation mission in July 1983. In the little time we had, the programme officer and I carried out extensive interviews with former returnees, people in markets, farmers in compounds far from the road (we even attended a funeral where about two hundred Ugandans were congregated), shop-keepers, and priests, both expatriate and Ugandan. The evidence we collected certainly did not encourage us to believe that everyone who returned would be absolutely secure. It began with an incident on the border with a drunken, heavily armed soldier who tried to force everyone out of the lorry for inspection. The persuasiveness of the young assistant district commissioner (ADC) for Arua allowed us to pass unmolested. En route to the place where the returnees would sleep that night, the car I was in stopped at the airfield where the same ADC warned the commander not to allow any soldiers to come near the refugees and to make sure his 'notorious' ones were kept inside. He emphasized in this conversation how damaging it would be to 'public relations' if they were disturbed that night. Instead, the soldiers 'disturbed' the drivers who were sleeping at the office of the Red Cross, badly frightening them.

We met a refugee who had returned a few weeks earlier with a letter from the UNHCR office. After having to pay bribes three times at roadblocks in Zaire, she reported her arrival to the DC's office in Arua. After three days she started receiving visits from members of the Youth Wing and from soldiers. She showed us how people in the area just outside Arua had to live, hiding all valuables under their wood piles or burying them many metres from their houses. She reported a number of cases in which soldiers had looted her neighbours at night. Shortly after our trip, she also returned to Sudan.

We found the trading centre at Omogu closed. One man had attempted to re-open his shop, but had been visited by soldiers who knifed him after looting the shop. Up the road and after having walked about 3 kilometres into the bush, we met a tobacco assistant, (it was he who took us to the funeral). We found, in terms of health and clothing, that the people were in about the same condition as the refugees who registered at reception centres in the Sudan. From the tobacco assistant we learned of the murder - later confirmed by priests - only two days before our arrival of a tobacco manager who lived just outside Arua. 'Soldiers', said this man, 'come every few days. If there is nothing to loot, you are likely to be killed.'

We met returnees who had expected to be given a place in school, but who were prevented because they had not joined the UPC. We were advised by leaders of the religious communities not to bring people back in small groups like this, as they would be unlikely to survive. Refugees should either remain in the Sudan or come all at once in a group. We found also that returnees were fleeing yet again to the Sudan. In one case a teacher went to a sub-chief for assistance but he was accused of having 'reported his maladministration to UNHCR Arua.' Fearing for his life, he had fled back to the Sudan.

The 109 returnees we had accompanied were 'welcomed' by a group of UPC officials dressed up in party colours. The photographs which were supplied to UNHCR to help in checking on the safety of refugees were instead handed over to the district commissioner's office. In his report, the programme officer, referred to the 'isolation' of both the UNHCR and LWF officials (who had both hotly denied any security risk to the returnees) 'from the realities of the situation', which:

is sharply contrasted with the understanding of the MSF team who informed me that every two or three days in Arua town there are incidents - from looting, harassing, to killing of civilians. Whenever there is fighting in the north, a wave of revenge against civilians takes place in the Arua area. Soldiers returning from the frontlines walk the small paths and attack civilians. Three women were accosted while washing clothes at River Orru by eight such men returning from the front, they were relieved of 2,000 shillings.

His report also pointed out that among the people interviewed 'there is no awareness of the presence of UNHCR. People think that such assistance as they do receive comes from the Red Cross.' He complained that all information available to UNHCR (and LWF) was filtered through government sources.

This report produced a series of angry protests from the Arua UNHCR official. In one of them he claimed that as far as the security situation in Uganda was concerned 'the rate of criminality prevailing [could] be compared with existing situations in other parts of the world.' In another he chided his colleague over the fact that his 'statement during the meeting gave me the impression that, for the time being, repatriation [*sic*] are made against your convictions, and *in opposition to UNHCR policy*.' (28 July 1983; emphasis added.) In mid-August he visited Yei and asked to be allowed to go to settlements to investigate for himself the attitudes of refugees towards repatriation. He declined to be accompanied by policemen, but later he must have regretted that decision. He was only narrowly saved by the quick thinking of John Issa, the foreman at Koya, from being stoned by angry refugees. Two reports written by refugee observers give some additional hints of the response of the refugees to his visit to Mopoko and Koya.

The UNHCR (ARUA) Representative's Visit to Mopoko on 14th August 1983
I am the UNHCR representative from Arua, Uganda. The rest of the West Nile region is safe, except Aringa and Koboko counties in the north. I have repatriated about 600 refugees from Zaire and the Sudan. UNHCR works jointly with the government of Uganda to ensure the safety of the returnees. When the repatriates reach Arua Town they are supplied with utensils, food and blankets.

If one wants to repatriate, one should fill repatriation forms and then one will be officially repatriated.

I have also come to try to find if the refugees can assist to bring peace between the guerrillas and the government forces.[23]

QUESTIONS
1. If I am repatriated from Mopoko to Arua, how shall I reach my home or place of birth?
Ans: UNHCR is responsible for taking people to their homes.
2. Why are Aringa and Koboko counties still battlefields?
Ans: The government troops seem to be weak but the guerrillas are strong. However, in the long run the government will control the situation.

[23] If this is a true and accurate account, it is a remarkable statement for a representative of a supposedly non-political humanitarian organization.

3. The war that drove us out of Uganda ignited from Aringa and Koboko counties. We still believe that the war might start again and drive out the repatriates, but why is Uganda government impatient to wait until there is complete peace in Aringa, Koboko and the rest of the country?

Ans: Could not answer. (Uproar from the audience: 'We are being led to the slaughterhouse').

4. I am from Aringa and my friend Leku is from Koboko. Do you want to take us to the frontline?

Ans: Let the people of Aringa and Koboko remain until the situation is controlled. (Audience: 'There is no point, we know your tricks.')

5. How safe should I be if repatriated?

Ans: The government will give cards to show that you are officially repatriated. (Audience: 'The bombs and bullets will not identify these cards.' Loud applause.)

6. I know of a man who was officially repatriated and he was then forced to join the government army. Why was that so?

Ans: Give me the name of that person and I will go and find out. (Name was not given.)

People's reactions during the meeting:

'This man is deceiving us and collaborates with Obote. Obote does not know that such people are harmful to his economy. Why are more transits opened? Transits for the Sudanese or Ugandans?' Everyone had a question to ask but time did not permit. There was an uproar and the representative was afraid. 'He has come to bother us,' shouted the audience. 'We were forced out and are being forced in again,' some shouted.

> P. Jama
> Uganda Refugee
> Agricultural Adviser
> MOPOKO

Brief Account of the UNHCR-Arua's Visit to Koya:

When the officer arrived on that day, he found the refugees already collecting their food ration for the week from the stores in the transit. When he introduced himself as the UNHCR-Arua, and stated he would like to know the opinion of the refugees about repatriation, I welcomed him to our local office and invited the block leaders and others around to hear from him what he would present to the refugees.

His first account of the situation in Uganda was that everything was improving and there were a lot of people in Arua town, as well as people of Maracha, Terego, Ayivu counties who were now going back to the villages. He had come to inform the refugees that they should now think of going back.

However, on the other hand, he did not recommend people from Koboko and Aringa counties to go back because the security situations in these areas were still bad. There were guerrillas there who had ambushed government forces and trucks. But then he said that the people who would like to be repatriated from these areas could be settled somewhere else instead of in Aringa and Koboko.

He expressed the hope that refugees would repatriate, because if they refused UNHCR would not know if the Ugandan government was violating the law which they had claimed is being followed. Therefore, UNHCR cannot come out to defend the refugees if they do not return and discover if Uganda is violating the law against repatriation.[24]

The majority of the refugees who were in attendance showed a negative attitude towards the UNHCR officer. They had several short questions in response to the explanation of the officer.

The first feeling was that every refugee very much wanted to return to Uganda if the following conditions could be met by the Ugandan government and perhaps UNHCR.

1. If Uganda/Obote accepted to negotiate with the guerrillas on a possible solution to Uganda's war problems, they would be ready to return immediately. For to them, the misunderstanding between the opposing forces remains a Ugandan problem. Therefore, they called for negotiation between Obote, Ojok (the Army Chief of Staff) and Paul Muwanga, to get together with leaders of guerrilla forces in a neutral country to discuss their differences.

2. UNHCR-Arua was asked if he could tell the refugees the conditions of their colleagues who had recently repatriated and what news they had sent through him.

Answering this question, he said that he did not know anything about their condition because no-one had reported to him about them.

He was then asked why he did not carry out this task himself because he knew that he would be paying a visit to Koya and he could convey messages that might convince the others of the situation.

To this he answered by saying that he stayed in Arua and he did not know exactly where the returnees lived.

3. On freedom of speech, he was asked what would happen to one who returned and perhaps stood in a crowd and said that Obote and his government are causing problems to people in Uganda.

He answered by saying he would advise no one to do that because there are a lot of people who work for UPC but live in uncertainty.

4. On the question of Ugandan refugees in Luwero District in Uganda, who were still fleeing from Uganda, he answered that there are no refugees in Luwero but only displaced people who had begun to resettle.

However, at first the officer indicated that he did not know anything about such cases. He accepted that details were heard over the radio that a total of about 200,000 Ugandan refugees were reported suffering in the areas of Luwero, Mukono and Mbarara because of security problems.

5. On the question of why he was sent to talk to us and Obote or Muwanga did not come and talk to the refugees, he answered that he would take this message back, but for his own case, he had come because he works for refugees even in Uganda.

As he was about to leave Koya for other settlements, the last point he made was that he would advise a team of refugee representatives to go and visit West Nile so that they could give a correct picture of the area. The refugees replied that this might be a plan to ambush the representatives and kill them.

[24] If this is indeed what was said at the meeting, it is unlikely too many refugees would offer themselves for such an experiment.

As the UNHCR official left, the atmosphere was tense with different exchanges of views about his visit. Many said that should there be attempts to repatriate refugees by force, they would prefer hiding in the bush and caring for themselves.
There was some abuse hurled at the UNHCR representative:

1. 'You are stupid enough to have come to represent Obote in a different colour!'
2. 'Do not be silly to pretend to explain to us that you think you know better than we do!'
3. 'Foolish white man has been bribed to come and engage us for his own work!'
4. 'If you think your stupid mother can care for us, take us to her rather than to Obote!'

> John Isse,
> Ugandan Refugee
> Koya Transit Camp, Sudan

In September 1983, another repatriation mission was organized for 144 people, mainly women and children. This time a protection officer was sent from Khartoum to accompany the group through Zaire to Arua. UNHCR Zaire was to send someone who would meet this group at Baze and escort them through the mazeway of police and military roadblocks in that country. (This arrangement was deemed necessary as in July on our return, heavily armed soldiers had tried to confiscate one of the three UNHCR lorries.) But there was another problem.

Yei was informed that the Ugandan government would not permit the refugees to be escorted across the border by any UNHCR officials. UNHCR suggested the Yei officer bring them as far as Aru and it would find some way to get them to Arua. The Sudanese project manager was asked to accompany the UNHCR protection officer, but he declined because as far as he knew, no official arrangements had been made with Kinshasa to guarantee safe passage through Zaire, to say nothing about the risk implied in leaving them before reaching Arua. He came to the residence where my team and I were working to explain what was happening. He said that unless his commissioner in Khartoum ordered him to go, he would refuse. 'UNHCR may be willing to play with people's lives. I am not.' The trip was put off but the refugees waiting in Yei transit camp were not officially informed why their return home was being delayed. When they did learn the reasons, 51 people changed their minds.[25]

On 26 January 1984, another regional meeting was convened by UNHCR at Juba to discuss the repatriation of refugees from Zaire and the Sudan. At this meeting Uganda's policy was described as one of reconciliation despite the fact that no amnesty had been offered. The Ugandan authorities questioned whether Zaire and the Sudan governments were 'doing everything possible to facilitate the return of the refugees.' In fact, it was

---

[25] Such people would have problems resuming life in Sudan. Many had 'sold' their houses and other property before joining a repatriation mission. Some who returned after being transported to Uganda in July were afraid to re-present themselves to UNHCR for assistance.

stated, the presence of the refugees may be an economic advantage to these governments leading them to prefer refugees to remain. While a very senior UNHCR official assured the Ugandans at the meeting that at least Sudan was not actively preventing refugees' repatriation, it was, he said, necessary to 'increase the protection function in the south, both in Yei and Juba, in order to monitor the situation more closely', but he had seen no evidence at any level of the Sudanese government wishing to keep refugees in the Sudan.

Again the discussions at this meeting centred around the belief that it is material assistance which determines where people want to live. Uganda complained that refugees were not returning because of the assistance they were receiving in asylum. UNHCR representatives noted that assistance was being phased out according to schedule, but conceded that there was a need for an improvement of the 'balance of assistance between Uganda and CA [country of asylum]'. It was also recommended that material assistance in Uganda should be increased and that 'Handouts in countries of asylum should be kept to a minimum ...' Although it took place on Sudan territory, the Sudan government was not represented at this meeting, neither were the refugees themselves.

Ever since the repatriation programme had been mounted in southern Sudan, refugees had been demanding that a fact-finding mission of refugees be allowed to travel to Uganda to report back to their fellows on what they found. There was frequently the request for Ugandan officials to visit them in settlements to discuss the problem of their return. At this meeting in Juba, the question was raised once again. According to the report:

... The role of representatives of HCR is to inform colleagues in the country of origin (CO) of the desire of refugees to see the situation for themselves. If ... agree[d], it is the responsibility of authorities of the country of asylum (CA) to see that CO authorities guarantee safety ... should returnees wish to return to the CA to explain to refugees how things are in the CO, they will be treated as foreigners and must follow the normal visa procedures existing between the two countries.[26]

Later on in 1984 when a group of people were sent on a fact-finding mission they included only those who had already signed forms indicating they were prepared to repatriate. Refugees were not convinced that they could report objectively and I received letters complaining about the bias built into UNHCR's response to their demand for an opportunity to make their own assessment of security.

Repatriation and the interests of the refugees

Is it really necessary for UNHCR to mount repatriation programmes? One of the resolutions arising from the International Symposium held in Oxford was

[26]The document reporting this meeting was 'leaked' at the International Symposium in March 1984. (See also *Africa Now* May 1984:9.)

that UNHCR should not make formal arrangements for repatriation without consulting refugees and unless there has been a major political change in the country of origin (see Appendix I: para 6.2.)

It is possible to consult refugees concerning repatriation under less hostile conditions than existed in the Sudan. If they had been informed about the possible provisions for their return at the beginning of their life in exile, the sudden interest of UNHCR in mounting the programme in 1983 would not have come as such an unsettling experience. As it was, UNHCR, the very agency responsible for their protection, came to be regarded by them as a source of fear. When I attempted to carry out interviews among the self-settled refugees at Panyume, some of my team were threatened with bows and arrows. Refugees had seen me, they said, leaving the Sudan in July taking their countrymen to their death.[27]

In the course of interviews in the settlements, the question was posed 'How do you see the future?', and if there was no response concerning their thoughts about Uganda, informants were prompted by the question 'Do you hope to return to Uganda in the near future?' Table 4.1 gives their responses as they were coded.

Assuming the answers reflected the attitudes of the entire household, in 1983 UNHCR could have expected a favourable response from nearly 4,000 people to their plans to repatriate Ugandans. Given the extreme feelings of at least a quarter of the people in the sample - those who do not intend to return until there is a change in government - it is obviously necessary to have an

TABLE. 4.1: 'Do you hope to return to Uganda in the near future?'

	%	No.
Plan to go to Uganda soon	3.3	67
Prefer to stay in Sudan	13.5	272
There is no security yet	20.2	408
'No idea'	18.2	367
'The war continues'	14.8	297
Not until there is a new government	24.6	496
All our relatives were killed	3.4	69
Feel insecure in the Sudan	.2	5
Will wait until others go	1.7	33
No reply	.1	3
Total	100	2,017

[27] In the discussion of methodology, Appendix II, there are other details about how the repatriation programme was a constant shadow over my research.

agency like UNHCR which can respond to those who do not share such strong feelings. For example, in one settlement a refugee slipped me a letter saying that as a supporter of the UPC, he wanted to return. He had been forced to flee simply because he was in the wrong place when war broke out. Had he made his views public, he was likely to have been regarded as a spy for Obote and a threat to the security of the others. He might even have lost his life at the hands of fellow Ugandans.

For those who anticipate no security in their own country, it is naive to believe that the non-availability of material aid on the other side of the border will *keep* refugees inside their own country. One government official who attended the International Symposium in Oxford called attention to this fallacy.

I came across some documents ... which indicated the number of Ugandans ... who had spontaneously and voluntarily returned [from Zaire]. The proof of their return was the number on relief assistance.

But I also made a careful calculation of the number of Ugandans who were moving ... to the Sudan side at the same time. It turned out that in fact the figures were almost exactly identical. What was the conclusion of this? ... refugees who were under pressure in Zaire ... did pass through the ... relief centres [in Uganda], did receive this assistance ... and used it to cross the border into southern Sudan (Alternative Viewpoints 1984.)

How many refugees actually need assistance to return to Uganda? Those who believe they face no dangers with officialdom and who know they will require material assistance, should have access to transport and help. That less than 300 people actually volunteered to return in 1983 suggests that only a few of those who intended to go back made use of the programme. It is not possible to know how many made their own way back home or how permanently they have established themselves in Uganda. Might it not be that refugees who self-repatriate have their own strategies for protecting themselves which might even be undermined by joining an official repatriation mission with all the publicity it would attract?

Addendum

In April 1985, the following report was received from Yei River District:

Since Jan., there have been repatriation missions. There is apparent famine in the 'new' settlements still under WFP rations, eg. just 2 weeks back, two children died in Affa settlement, from poisoning due to eating wild roots. The family had no food. These roots were eaten for food - causing the death of the children. These settlements are in areas scarcely populated with natives who themselves have barely enough for themselves. Therefore, the possibility of 'leja-leja'is nil. Some people walk over 12 miles to ... [find] 'leja-leja' and take three to four days before returning. In fact, all the settlers in the settlement were about to go on strike, if the settlement officer hadn't rushed to Yei to return with four lorries of food. Of late most priority seemed to be given to repatriation with the available UN lorries here. (26 April 1985.)

5
Food is the best medicine[1]

Introduction

One common explanation for the apparent failure of many refugees to look beyond their immediate survival needs and plans to reconstruct their future, is that they do not intend to remain permanently in exile. But in all poor societies, people are likely to have a more immediate sense of how fleeting is the temporal than are those who may take for granted an infrastructure which promotes good health and a stable food supply. The constant reminder of the immediacy of death may in part account for the greater emphasis which is placed upon interpersonal relations in most poor societies as well as for the elaboration of beliefs and practices concerning the spiritual.

It is widely recognized that without the provision of clean water, a stable food supply, basic sanitation and the elimination of such environmental risks as the mosquito or the tsetse fly, very little 'development', societal transformation or improvement in health care is likely to occur. The practice of curative medicine will not solve these problems. It could be argued that it is the lack of the basic requirements for environmental health which most sets the societies of the 'have nots' of this world apart from those of the 'haves'. Enthusiasm for the 'barefoot' doctor approach to the health problems of poor countries is a response to these realities. As one advocate put it:

The spectrum of diseases which we encounter in general in refugee camps ... is typical of the kinds of diseases we encounter in stable communities as well ... Where there has been a change in the last ten or fifteen years in the provision of health care [it] has been away from the idea that we can ever sort out these problems by putting white coats on people and give them a stethoscope and a syringe. (Dick 1984.)

There are several fundamental problems with the present emphasis upon primary or preventative health care as the solution for the health problems of poor countries when at the same time massive advances in health science and technology continue elsewhere. Early attempts to improve the health conditions in the southern Sudan illustrate this point. As part of the rehabilitation programme for the southern region after the cease-fire in 1972, international agency personnel drew up a health programme. The plan, the

[1] In 1981 while visiting the 'protection centres for weak children' organized by Sahrawi refugees in Algeria, a medical worker explained how they encouraged mothers to appreciate that it was food, not medicine, which would save the lives of their malnourished children.

Primary Health Care Programme for Southern Sudan 1977/8 - 1983/4, was published in 1976.

Even if this 'green book', as the plan is called, had been fully implemented during the eight years it was prescribed, it is unlikely that it would have brought about great improvement in the health of the people. Some of its weaknesses will be discussed shortly, but many simply reflect the fact that it was devised by outsiders and based upon inadequate knowledge of local environmental and social conditions. More to the point, however, it was based upon an assumption that *someone else* was going to ensure the other basic requirements of environmental health, an expectation that was not realized.

There is another fundamental problem with primary health programmes for the poor. Even if a health programme is drawn up in consultation with indigenous medical experts, it is unlikely that either the outsiders *or* the indigenous professionals (or anyone else with the resources) will ever be forced to subject themselves to the health care system they impose on others. During my fieldwork in southern Sudan two expatriate doctors were evacuated to Europe for treatment - one for a burn and the other for malaria. Funds are found in the Sudan for a surprising number of highly placed individuals to travel and to pay for curative treatment outside the country.[2] This is a general pattern in the so-called third world.

There seems to be an assumption that preventative and environmental health can be taught in a vacuum, outside the context of efforts to improve the totality of the lives of the poor and without the security of curative medicine, but this is not the case. A surprising number of the major health problems of the refugee settlements are the direct result of poverty and a significant number of illnesses are worsened by the failures of the aid programme. Everyone prefers to drink clean water and even if the specifics of the health hazards are not understood, most people regard human waste as polluting. I dare say that no one *prefers* walking barefoot in their fields, but even shoes cost money. If relatively small amounts of money were available to raise the general standard of living in the settlements and the surrounding region, much illness would simply not occur. The need is not so much for doctors but for a habitable environment, and a standard of living above the level of subsistence and debilitation.

'Everybody has to die once'

The great disparities of wealth and health services between the 'first' and

---

[2] It was regarded as an exceptional act of bravery on the part of the mothers that in 1984 two European babies were born in Yei. But they were delivered at home, not in Yei hospital. I suffered a shrapnel wound in Nairobi in the 1982 attempted coup. Although the wound simply required regular cleaning under sterile conditions, I was strongly advised not to return to the Sudan for even this minor treatment. But in 1983 one student who joined my team from Oxford University survived an emergency appendectomy in Yei hospital.

'third' worlds are so great that some doctors who work in poor countries have apparently reinterpreted the Hippocratic oath. In Africa it has become fashionable to speak of 'nature's way', although we all know that the real problem is lack of resources and that 'nature' is rarely permitted to take her own uninterrupted way where personal circumstances allow access to the fruits of modern scientific advance. As one nurse working for SCC put it, 'For 25 years I have been working to save lives in Tanzania. This is against the rules in southern Sudan.' Although most who believe that the first priority is to establish primary health care programmes would argue for a balance between curative and preventative approaches, balance was conspicuously lacking in the 'green book' programme for southern Sudan. Here the pendulum has made the full swing: curative medical facilities were sorely, if not completely, neglected.

The psychological response of agency personnel to a human disaster has received little attention. Viewers of a BBC film broadcast in early 1985 must have been shocked to hear expatriate medical personnel explaining the necessity to deny treatment (food or medicine) to those refugees from Tigréy who were unable to walk to the clinic, but humanitarians in the field are constantly faced with such decisions.[3] As de Waal (1985) provocatively puts it.

Most people who start working for relief agencies in Africa have not had previous experience of knowingly contributing to the suffering and death of large numbers of people. Relief agencies do not tend to attract people who have had this sort of experience, and they do not include it in their job descriptions when they are recruiting. Yet the disturbing activity of voluntarily being unpleasant to strangers is one of the most frequent experiences confronted by agency personnel in a relief situation.

Ken Wilson (Wilson *et al.* 1985), interviewed an elderly blind man who had walked 110 miles from Katigiri settlement to Kaya to trade tobacco, guided by his six-year-old son. 'The journey was so strenuous that it took him three months to recover, but enabled him to get some income to supplement and possibly justify the charity he received from a neighbour.' In a footnote, Wilson reports his own reactions to such suffering.

When I asked this man if he had anything to say to me, he said he was only crying with hunger and that's how I should know him. But I should know that he was not only crying for himself but for all the other vulnerables [i.e. handicapped] who, when times were hard, could not at least work for food or find new opportunities. He did not know how he could survive and that one could only trust in God. As his case unravelled, I started to cry quietly and there was silence. Then he told me not to worry, that I should just stop thinking. This is certainly the only comforting thing to do as a powerful westerner surrounded by the misery of disaster.

[3] 30 January 1985, Famine in Sudan: 'The Worst is yet to Come'

The situation for doctors working under such conditions is indeed difficult. It should not be surprising to discover that most individuals find it is necessary to manufacture mechanisms for coping with their fundamental powerlessness to alter the status quo.[4]

Denial is perhaps the most easy response to situations one is unable to change. As Chambers (1983) has observed, most experts, especially the foreign ones, never see the poor and can thus easily dismiss any report which challenges their opinions. For example, although a UNICEF study had identified sleeping sickness as the most dangerous disease prevalent in Eastern Equatoria and had singled out Yei and Torit as areas of high concentration (Kurup 1983), when the alarming number of reports of this disease began reaching the UNHCR office, especially from Kala settlement, the response from GMT was as follows:

... sleeping sickness is present in YRD, particularly on the Juba road in the Loka area and on the Kajo-Kaji road in the Limuro area. The cases are sporadic and have caused very few problems in terms of medical care. There is always the possibility that many cases are not being diagnosed because they do not come to the health units ... but again, I stress that it is not a major health concern. The disease can be diagnosed at any dispensary with a microscope, and [the] patient sent to Yei hospital for treatment. (12 June 1983.)

Not every medical doctor would agree that sleeping sickness is so easily diagnosed, since the symptoms patients first present are non-specific. A successful cure is dependent on early treatment. Moreover, only five out of the 25 settlements *had* a microscope and one of these was later stolen.

Another and all too common mechanism for dealing with scenes of death and misery is the convenient belief that 'Africans do not suffer as "we" do.' I cannot count how many times such reassurances were repeated by colleagues in the field. According to them, Africans do not suffer either physical or psychological pain in the same way as do 'white' people, 'They are *used* to death and suffering' and therefore no longer feel these things. There is perhaps no more dramatic way of expressing psychological distance or for denying a common humanity.

Another method of coping with the extraordinary differences in the standard of health care available in poor countries compared with those elsewhere is to deny the acceptability of better medical services to the poor. This belief has helped make more tolerable the vast differences in provision of health care even between refugee communities. For example, on one hand, OXFAM has severely criticized the health programme for Palestinians because medical staff make no house-to-house calls. (Coleridge 1982.) On the other hand, an OXFAM doctor described the programme in southern Sudan

---

[4] Facing my own powerlessness to stop suffering and death, the thought that everyone has to die once always flashed through my mind, but it gave little comfort.

which omitted far more than first house-calls, as 'adequate'. After pointing out this contradiction, I asked how he defined 'adequate' in this context. He was at first reluctant to answer, saying that if he did, I might think he was a racist. He eventually replied, 'We must just accept that Africans have culturally determined lower expectations for health.' It is not sufficient to categorize such views simply as 'racist' of course, but it is important to note the ways in which unexamined beliefs about non-western societies are important in shaping the actions of individuals in the field.

This doctor took his evidence from the fact that people resort to traditional healers or magical practices, sometimes in preference to available western medicine. This is a complicated topic, but the size of the queues at any clinic anywhere in Africa contradicts the notion that Africans are unconcerned about their health or resist 'western' therapy. That they may try every possible remedy does not set them apart from people in any society. In the case of many refugees it was the absence of other sources of medicines that led many to resort to herbs and leaves.

Evaluating an aid programme

Although no effective system of monitoring food production was being implemented in the southern Sudan, the objective of any assistance programme is to make refugees 'independent', 'independence' being minimally defined as independent of relief food. A more immediately available and a more empirical basis for assessing the effectiveness of an aid programme is to measure the health of the aid recipients. Refugees are expected to become independent through their own physical labour. The *UNHCR Handbook* elaborates in considerable detail the standards of medical assistance to refugees which should be applied. And it includes such requirements as keeping records of the births, deaths, and morbidity. Yet, as Kibreab (1983:1) has noted, 'There are no data that show what percentage of refugees who arrived alive in the country of asylum die in the circumstances that give rise to a refugee situation, or during actual flight and *during asylum phases*.'

The lack of these data should be a matter for serious concern. It is obviously in the interests of donors that the health and nutritional needs of refugees be well-attended, especially during the relief stage of the exercise. Yet in Yei River District both these basic needs were neglected. Refugees are expected to depend on their physical labour to remove themselves from relief rolls, yet are forced to divert other inputs; they are forced to sell their blankets and hoes to obtain food and medicines, for example, and they often had to eat the seed intended for planting. The evidence collected by the survey shows two things. First, that throughout 1982-4 some refugees continued to suffer from malnutrition; and second, in many cases, the health of refugees actually *deteriorated* under the aid umbrella. These facts are not officially acknowledged.[5]

The failure to supply the needs of the people who were the objects of the assistance programmes reflects all the standard problems which obtain in such an environment - the poverty and lack of infrastructure; bureaucratic bungling at the international level; inter-agency conflict and competition at the field level; a persistent shortage of qualified staff - especially to monitor the programme; the lack of authority to control the quality of the work of the voluntary agencies; the lack of consultation with qualified medical personnel among refugees; and insufficient supplies.[6]

But most importantly, there is no sound information on which to base aid policy. A general argument of this book is that assistance should be directed to the community as a whole on the basis of need and should not single out one group for special treatment. Ironically, the main problem with the programme in the Yei River District was that the German Medical Team (GMT), the agency given the responsibility for health, persisted in implementing an integrated programme despite indications that in this area, it would not work. The problems which developed with the health programme show how important it is that assistance programmes are both flexible and responsive to the immediate conditions in which they are implemented.

The Ugandan refugees arrived with high expectations for health services and they practised higher standards of sanitation than the Sudanese. They also demonstrated considerable knowledge about health and nutrition. As it

[5] In fact, in the interests of fund-raising, every effort is made to cover them up. In late 1982 Richard Greenfield, a scholar and reporter on the Horn of Africa, visited Goli, photographing some severely malnourished children he found while visiting households on the perimeters of the settlement. His reports over the BBC caused great consternation among agency staff in the Sudan as well as in London. One concerned charity even wrote to him to deny his statements but dropped the correspondence when confronted with photographic evidence. It would seem unfair to hold workers in the field responsible for protecting the image of a programme which is inadequate because of lack of funds from the donors, but messages informing Juba and Yei of the arrival of journalists always included warnings about their habit of looking only for evidence of failures. One agency official advised the programme officer in Yei to 'tell the truth, but not the whole truth.' On 1 October 1982, a message warned of a group of Dutch journalists who would be arriving in the middle of that month:

'...please take care with them in all senses. We had enormous problems with one of them ... He wrote some extremely nasty and unpleasant things about the HCR and the organization last year, which did nobody any good, and spoilt fund raising efforts in the Netherlands... Mr --- now tells me that his mission will be better... Nevertheless, I wanted you to be aware; also with regard to what --- [the programme officer] may tell him of past history, in an unguarded moment.'

[6] Refugee programmes are not funded on a *per capita* basis. Each emergency is separately funded. The Soviet bloc does not make direct contributions to UNHCR. Africa apart, refugees originating from countries supported by the Soviets always receive more press attention, more expatriate agencies get involved, and more funds are available. For example, in Thailand, as the then head of the UNHCR office in Bangkok described, at one point, so many expatriate doctors arrived there was no work for them. There were even funds to fly refugees to New York for emergency operations. (Barber 1982.)

was, Ugandans had a positive effect upon local practices. In Juba, for example, Ugandans are praised for having set the example of digging latrines which is now being followed by many Sudanese as well. Every self-settled refugee compound I visited in the Kaya area had at least one latrine. Many had attempted to protect a water source or to dig a shallow well. It would, for example, have been possible to have followed the model provided by Somalia. There, the standards of health care established in refugee camps were gradually extended to the local health programme and thus had the potential of promoting a long-term improvement in overall community health. And, unlike the situation among the refugees from the Ogaden, there were many qualified medical personnel among the Ugandans. They could have been used more effectively to upgrade the local programme.

Across the border, in Zaire, one case was reported in which Ugandans had established a separate health facility which was also open to the locals who previously had none. A Ugandan doctor had been put in charge of a settlement. He started a hospital with surgical facilities. Having escaped with his own vehicle, he was assigned the responsibility of supervising clinics in neighbouring settlements. As a result, local people found that the presence of refugees was an *advantage to them*, and Ugandans - rather than being totally dependent upon others - were taking responsibility for their own health.

Refugees outside the aid system in Yei River District attempted similar self-help schemes. With the permission of local chiefs, some opened clinics: later when this came to the attention of health authorities, the clinics were raided by police and their equipment was confiscated. Other refugees erected buildings in remote areas after GMT had assured them that if buildings were put up, staff and medicines would be supplied. In the years that followed, in only one case (a dressing station at Yundu) was this promise fulfilled.

Ugandans who got employment in the Sudanese primary health programme faced another type of problem. Better trained and more accustomed to discipline, their performance reflected on that of their Sudanese colleagues and this created tensions. Even coming to work on time was against the norm. Those who did not lose their jobs soon learnt the wisdom of simply acquiescing to entrenched practices. Clearly, another approach was needed in Yei River District. Had GMT been more flexible and responsive to local conditions, a satisfactory health scheme might have been devised. A health system run in the field by the Ugandans could have had a very positive effect upon the district.

The health programme in Uganda

Although I have little information on the actual functioning of the health programme in Uganda, its structure and objectives were described by Ugandan medical staff and other refugees. I describe it because it demonstrates the enormous gulf (at least at the ideological level) between the situation in the Sudan and the modest medical services which many in Uganda had come to consider normative. These services drastically declined in Uganda after 1979 and much equipment and many medicines were looted. Some appeared on the market in the Sudan.

Uganda had a primary health care system which emphasized prevention. There were four levels of health care, beginning with sub-dispensaries staffed by a dresser and a sweeper. Dispensaries, each employing a nurse, dresser, and a sweeper, served a maximum population of 5,000, and were supervised by the district nursing officer on a monthly basis. Health centres served a population of 10,000 and each was staffed by a medical assistant, two nurses, two midwives, a dresser, and a laboratory assistant. Both dispensaries and health centres provided curative care, and the availability of transport meant that emergency help was no more than two hours away from any unit. In the area north of Arua - an area of 4-5,000 square miles, where the bulk of the present refugee population came from - there were four hospitals, including a major hospital at Arua. These hospitals were reasonably well-equipped with good theatre services which were said to function round the clock; all bedding and meals were provided for in-patients. Medical services were free except at mission centres, where a subsidized fee was payable. Referral beyond the district level hospitals was possible when the need arose, and the referring hospitals provided transport.

The efficiency of these services was encouraged by a training programme which emphasized staff motivation and professional interest, and staff development was ensured by regular supervision and 'up- grading' courses. Negligence, it is said, was severely punished. Centres were stocked with the necessary equipment, a relatively constant supply of drugs, and regular payment of salaries and allowances for field staff. Moreover, Uganda enjoyed good public transport.

Perhaps one of the most fundamental differences between the programmes in the Sudan and Uganda, which the refugees remembered, was the requirement of a sound basic education for recruits to the medical profession. Nursing aides and dressers could only begin their two- year training after seven years of primary school: their training took place in hospitals under the supervision of nurses and doctors. An enrolled nurse had to have completed three years of secondary education before entering a two-year course leading to a certificate. All registered nurses and medical assistants had to complete their 'O' levels (but many had also finished their 'A' levels) before enrolling in the three-year training course. 'A' levels are a prerequisite for the laboratory technicians' four-year course.

Nor was preventative health care neglected in Uganda. Health centres were the focus for the educational work. Midwives organized mother-child health services. A team included health inspectors, assistants, health visitors, and their assistants. It conducted home visits and was responsible for the inspection of such public places as markets, abattoirs, and eating houses, as well as for the regular medical examination of the employees. There was an area-wide immunization programme. Special campaigns to control diseases like sleeping sickness, leprosy, and tuberculosis were run by the district medical officer with a team of well-trained auxiliaries. An annual national competition encouraged environmental health. The media (television, newspapers, and especially radio), were used to disseminate information. Schools were regularly visited and there were special radio broadcasts for school children. The Ministry of Health developed visual aids and other community teaching materials. Bore-holes were sunk in every sub-county, and maintained to ensure a reasonably clean water supply. Almost every home had a pit latrine.[7]

The health programme in Yei River District[8]

Following the 'green book', the primary health care programme in southern Sudan recognizes three levels of care, although there are a few dressing stations which are manned by persons with lower qualifications than those who staff the primary health care units (PHCUs). PHCUs are intended, according to the plan, to serve a radius of not more than ten miles. This is the distance presumed reasonable for transporting patients by foot. These PHCUs should serve a population of not more than 4000 people and are staffed by a community health worker who has been selected for training from among his own community. The long-term aim of the plan was to establish self-sustaining, self-financing units at every level. It was assumed that if the community health worker was nominated by his community, the people would accept his leadership and eventually pay both for his services and for the medicines they required. Predictably, this scheme failed.

Both local factionalism and national politics influence the choice of candidates. For example, the Kogwo PHCU, named for the local river, is in the village of Logo. The community health worker comes from a neighbouring village, Pisa, and the chief of Logo and his people assert that he was chosen against their wishes: a medical assistant from Yei selected him because he was a relative. Despite this, the Logo people might have accepted him if he had performed his duties properly. Many letters of complaint were addressed to GMT asking for his removal. At one point, when the Ugandan medical officer was present, the two communities nearly fought.[9]

---

[7] The concentration of the population relative to settlement patterns in the Sudan may have also been a factor in the widespread use of latrines in Uganda: 'Where else do you go where people won't see you?' was one Ugandan's response. 'There are no people around in Sudan. The place is all bush.'

[8] Or, 'this is Sudan', the sentence always repeated by expatriates when anything went wrong, but especially when Ugandans complained about the health programme. In West Africa, a comparable expression is Wawa, meaning West Africa Wins Again. These derogatory remarks are usually only uttered in the company of other Europeans.

[9] The readiness of local Sudanese to respond also to adequate health programmes is demonstrated by the positive response of these two communities to the immunization programme in 1983 when it was supervised by this Ugandan doctor.

Every community also had a representative of the Sudan Socialists' Union (SSU), the political party in power, and this representative often had as much or more influence within the community than did the local chief or other groups, such as religious organizations.

The plan requires nominees to be primary school leavers. In practice, some of those selected have not attained even this standard of education. More importantly, most workers never aspired to a career in community health, but lacked the money or the requisite grades to continue their education in another field, and had little choice. This undoubtedly affects motivation.

After nine (in some cases, only three) months' training, and despite their limited basic education, community health workers are assumed to be capable of dressing wounds, diagnosing and treating the most common basic diseases, and recognizing conditions that require referral - such as leprosy, tuberculosis, sleeping sickness, or meningitis. Responsible for drawing up his own work schedule, the PHCU worker is expected to spend three-quarters of it in 'field work', that is, teaching sanitation and nutrition, control of communicable diseases, and protection of the water supply. With the support of local leaders, he is ultimately expected to mobilize his people to build a store and to pay for his services. Given the basis for selection and the lack of training, it is not surprising that this level of mobilization has not been achieved and workers continue to depend on the government for salaries.[10]

A cluster of PHCUs are linked to a dispensary - the second level of health care - and these clusters are referred to as a 'complex'. Medical supplies for a complex are supposed to be sent from Juba at three-monthly intervals, but deliveries are highly irregular. For example, from January to June 1984, nothing was supplied to the district and the entire programme had to rely on medicines supplied by UNICEF for the refugee settlements. PHCUs were not supplied with stationery.

Most of the PHCUs *look* impressive: the buildings are prefabricated imports from Italy which, I was informed, cost $22,000 each.[11] Yet they are rarely open. I usually found the community health worker sitting in his home compound, not on duty.

A number of factors discourage these employees. Salaries are paid irregularly, and many have to go personally to Yei to collect their monthly pay. This may require a week's absence. The low salary (at present set at £S42)[12] encourages some to sell drugs. The moment the drug supply runs out, there is no longer any point in seeing patients. The demands of 'fieldwork' and the shortage of drugs are the most frequent excuses for being absent from the PHCU. But it is also discouraging to be expected to enlist local people to

---

[10] But my research suggests that there is *not* a shortage of cash in the district as such. It was found that many Sudanese now make the trip to Zaire where they pay for the superior health services available there since the arrival of the Ugandans.

[11] When I asked GMT's expatriate builder why the agency did not use local materials, his answer was that it would take too long. A building of the same size can be put up in three to four days. And no one can put a fist through mud walls, as so frequently happens to prefabs.

[12] At the time of this research, at the official rate one Sudanese pound equalled about £0.30.

carry out communal work when there are no funds for supplies (such as cement which is needed to protect water sources). Even if a community health worker is able to recognize illnesses requiring referral, there is no transport, and the experience in Yei River District suggests that most are *not* adequately trained to identify serious cases. For example, during 1983 and up to June 1984, not one PHCU worker had referred a case of leprosy or tuberculosis, although these are the main communicable diseases of public health concern.

Responsibility for supervising the work of the PHCU programme lies with the medical assistant, who is also in charge of a dispensary. Dispensaries (the second level of health care) are staffed by one medical assistant, two nurses, and a sweeper. In theory, this dispensary is the referral centre for five PHCUs serving a total of 24,000 people. A medical assistant should have completed secondary school before two years of training. Nurses receive their training on the job: after two years they receive a certificate. Dispensaries are supposed to be equipped with a microscope and to employ a laboratory assistant. In Yei River District, which according to the 1983 census has a population of around 350,000, there are only eight such complexes. Very few of the dispensaries have microscopes.

The medical assistant is responsible for seeing all cases referred to him from the PHCUs, referring to hospital those requiring surgery or treatment, supervising the work of each of the PHCUs within the complex, and ensuring the proper use of all drugs. He treats the patients who come to the dispensary and organizes and supervises the mother-child health clinics; he is also in charge of the immunization programme which in Yei River District only began during September 1982. Even if all PHCUs had been located 'not more than ten miles' from dispensaries, the distances would still have been too great for the medical assistant to supervise them adequately. In 1982, bicycles were sold to medical assistants at half price. Within a few months, most of them were 'off the road' because of lack of appropriate spare parts. Moreover, as a medical assistant has more training and usually a wider array of drugs than is available at PHCUs, the case load of the dispensary is too great for him to leave his post.

In addition to the dispensaries in the district, there are two health centres. One is at Tore and the other at Loka. In early 1983, Loka was closed when it was found to lack pit latrines. The Tore centre (a Sudan Council of Churches project), has a small in-patient ward, a midwife, two medical assistants, nurses, and a laboratory technician.

According to the 'green book', regular supervision of the complexes should be carried out by a medical doctor. Supervision is restricted to observation and, after the clinic closes, consultation with the health workers. To supervise one unit adequately, a doctor must leave Yei very early in order to arrive in time to observe the work. Distances are too great. Even before the refugees came, the one resident medical doctor and one nurse could not visit each unit even once a month. Supervision is thus limited to a hasty visit to deliver drugs and sometimes to transport a seriously ill person to Yei.

The attempt to cope with the medical needs of the emergency refugee influx in 1982 will be described below. Before then, the only increase in health services (outside the four refugee settlements) was a dressing station started in early 1982 at Yundu, a market near the border where thousands of unassisted refugees had settled. Despite the great rise in population, additional medicines were not available at the PHCUs or dispensaries. As noted, this put the refugees and the locals in direct competition for scarce resources, and encouraged the illegal selling of drugs.

There are no adequate referral centres in Yei River District. Two hospitals (in name only) are located at Yei and Kajo-Kaji. The expatriate doctor stationed at the Mandari Hospital, Kajo-Kaji, left early in 1983, and was not replaced. Neither hospital had a clean water supply and Mandari Hospital never pretended to have facilites for surgery. The conditions at Yei hospital are best described by the Sudanese Inspector of Health for the district in a memorandum presented to the Provincial Commissioner, dated 25 August 1982.

This noted that funds for the hospital had not been released for nearly two years, and the irregularly-paid staff had become 'disillusioned and dissatisfied'. At one point they went on strike. The hospital had no stationery, which meant there was no paper for keeping patients' records or even for admitting them. There was no fuel for sterilization of instruments and no towels for the operating theatre. At times there were no post-operative bandages, so scheduled surgery could not proceed normally.

The inadequate staff quarters were desperately in need of repair. The doctor himself lived in a house with huge holes in the ceiling - which allowed rats into the room as well as into the roof. The nurses' quarters, earlier destroyed by fire, had not been rebuilt. As a result, the medical assistant, theatre attendants, anaesthetic assistant, and nursing sisters, 'who, by the nature of their duties need to be accommodated near the hospital' had to live elsewhere. There was no X-ray machine, and no drugs for the treatment of tuberculosis - a disease prevalent amongst the local population as well as amongst refugees. Some latrines had been dug, but there were no funds for completing them. There was no source of uncontaminated water and staff and patients alike had to depend on the nearby river for bathing, washing, and drinking water. There was no money for feeding patients although the hospital had a kitchen. There was no place protected from rainfall for relatives to cook for patients, nor any place for them to sleep while staying there to care for them. At night the floors and verandah of the hospital were filled with sleeping relatives.

The hospital had *115* beds, but only *50* mattresses, and no sheets or blankets. The hospital vehicles (including the ambulance) had broken down and there was no money for spare parts to put them on the road again.

Supplies of all drugs were inadequate. There was no fuel for the emergency generator. Without fuel for his vehicle, the doctor was unable to meet his commitments of supervision or investigation of epidemics and in his memorandum he referred to a report from Kajo-Kaji of an epidemic of 'fatal dysentry' in that area to which he was unable to attend.

The response to the influx

The period from 1979 to 1982, when there were only five assisted settlements in Yei River District, would have been the ideal time to have established a co-ordinated health programme, to have strengthened the referral centres, and to increase the services available in remote areas where the population had risen so sharply. SCC had been meeting most of the exceptional health needs in four of these settlements and had built a medical centre at Tore which could have been developed into a hospital. There was ample time to have organized the emergency response well in advance of the waves of new arrivals.

During the early period, a large number of refugees with medical qualifications had arrived, and although most Ugandan doctors escaped to Kenya, a few fled to Zaire and the Sudan. Some even came from Kenya to the Sudan to offer their services, but on arrival were informed that the area had no need for additional doctors. Yet, in 1982, when the serious deficiencies of the programme attracted international attention, and the need for more doctors could no longer be denied, it was expatriate staff that were recruited. As one refugee rightly observed:

....there is something here which is absurd.... not [to] permit refugees to exercise their professions, including the medical profession. So you find highly-qualified medical people, specialists, going to other countries....If they had stayed in the country of asylum, they could have been in a position to work amongst their own people. It seems to me a bit absurd that because of such policies, refugees go seeking jobs elsewhere, and then you recruit expatriates to come and work where these people should have worked. (Alternative Viewpoints 1984.)[13]

Indeed, one of the doctors who tried to work in the Sudan is now employed by the World Health Organization (WHO) elsewhere in Africa. In 1982-3, other Ugandan doctors working in the prestigious Nairobi hospital expressed their willingness to come to the Sudan if employment could be guaranteed. Yet it was only in 1983, after two of the expatriate medical teams which responded to the emergency in 1982 had left the district, that GMT

[13] There is a general complaint that African medical personnel are unwilling to work in remote areas and this is the reason expatriates must be recruited. In March 1985, when I visited the Sudan, I was informed that some expatriate nurses were being paid $18,000 per annum. Sudanese doctors receive the equivalent of $2,000. I suspect that even if a Sudanese doctor's salary was only doubled, he also would be willing to go to the 'ends of the earth' to work.

finally agreed to employ the one Ugandan doctor who had remained in the area.

Given their availability, UNHCR could have involved qualified Ugandan doctors in planning, organizing, and implementing the health programme for the settlements from the first. This would have avoided many of the subsequent problems and would have allowed refugees to take responsibility for themselves in a critical area. This opportunity was missed and resulted in wasted resources.

The 1982 emergency began in April. By May the health programme was in chaos. Lines of responsibility had not been drawn. Some drugs came from the UNHCR store in Juba, others from SCC. As GMT was already responsible for the local health programme in the area, it seemed obvious that this agency should include refugees in its programme. Negotiations were going on between GMT and UNHCR, but the contract had not been signed. There were no emergency medical services at the reception centres on the border where thousands of critically ill refugees were congregated. Both adults and children were severely malnourished, yet there was no feeding programme at these centres.[14] The two Sudanese doctors stationed in Yei had no transport to move out of town. GMT's expatriate field staff for the whole district comprised two doctors, a nurse, and an unqualified assistant. The establishment of each new settlement caused even further chaos.

Ugandans were hastily recruited to man the clinics which should have been ready to meet the first arrivals (usually the most ill) at each new settlement. Recruitment was done mainly by the unqualified expatriate assistant. Penniless, all refugees are desperate for employment. With no Ugandan doctor to vet applications or positively identify those who turned up with certificates, the assistant had to rely on gossip and rumour, with the result that Ugandans without proper qualifications were often employed in responsible positions, while the highly-qualified were turned away. Thirty people interviewed in the survey were employed by GMT in the settlement health programme. Some of these may have been paid watchmen or sweepers, but it is worth noting that out of the 22 who answered the question regarding former employment, only five admitted to having worked in the medical field in Uganda. Of those who said they were dressers in Uganda, all had the requisite educational level required there, of between seven to fifteen years in school.

Among the 17 others, six said that in Uganda they had been 'only cultivators' (one of these had sixteen years of education); two had been students; two others had been primary teachers; one said he was a driver (but he had been to school for ten years); two were businessmen; one a labourer; one a catechist; and two were 'salaried non-professionals'. (Again these two

---

[14] Under pressure from a Geneva-based UNHCR official who visited in August, a feeding programme was started in Nyori, one reception centre. It only lasted a few weeks before supplies ran out.

individuals each had fourteen years of schooling.) Among the group were six who had never been to school. Some of those who had several years of post-primary education may have been soldiers with medical training who felt compelled to disguise their former occupation.

By the time I arrived in Yei in 1982, the town was flooded with refugees. Much of the time more than half the hospital beds were occupied by Ugandans. Few drugs were available in the hospital or the agency stores, so most prescriptions had to be purchased from the local chemist. Even when the drug supplies were placed completely under the supervision of GMT, there were still problems. Refugees could only get prescriptions between 7:00 and 8:00 a.m. After that time, the medical doctor left for field supervision and refused to allow any drugs to be released by the Ugandan attendant. Emergencies cannot wait, and so there was always the problem of finding funds for patients who required medicines outside this one opening hour. UNHCR had no budget for this extra expense so accounts had to be juggled or expatriates paid out of their own pocket.

Rations were issued only in settlements. With no provision for feeding patients in the hospital, patients relied on their relatives. Where were the refugee families going to live or cook? What was to become of those who had no family? From where were patients and their families in Yei going to get food? Even when a plan was devised for providing rations to patients referred from a settlement, it left unsolved the problem of providing special diets. People who are recovering from hepatitis or a hernia operation are unlikely to recover on a diet of beans, rice, oil and milk. Clothing was *never* available for the new-born and there was no budget for special formulae for infants of non-lactating mothers. And, with such a limited capacity to deal with emergencies, what about such luxuries as spectacles, crutches, or calipers for those refugees who had lost theirs in flight? There was no one to deal with the hundreds of such cases who presented their problems at the UNHCR compound in Yei.

Given the very serious health symptoms which refugees presented, adequate referral centres were urgently required. The population increase since 1980 would have justified the establishment of at least one (if not two) properly equipped and staffed hospitals in the district.

A primary health care system without such back-up services has a seriously demoralizing effect upon *all* personnel. It has yet to be demonstrated that preventive health education can be taught outside a context of confidence in curative medicine. Without proper curative facilities and transport to reach them, people are forced to consult traditional healers. These healers are able to give the patients and their families psychological reassurance and are willing to treat patients in their homes. Traditional healers do not 'work to rule' and are available after the 2:30 p.m. standard closing hours in the Sudan.

Ugandan medical workers said they were encouraged to observe strictly

Sudanese working hours. This was the frequent excuse for refusing to see emergency cases after 2:30 p.m. Even feeding programmes for the severely malnourished were closed at weekends, and some claimed that this was 'on instruction' from their employer.[15] The expatriate doctor responsible for supervising GMT's programme had no previous experience in Africa: she and the one German nurse, who left in mid-1982, were unable to cope with the amount of work assigned, and could not exercise authority over staff.

The Ugandan staff in the settlements quickly became demoralized: they lacked sufficient supplies to deal with the numbers and types of diseases they encountered, and had to watch people succumb to illnesses which could easily have been cured with adequate drugs. Having no referral centre, discouraged by low pay and inferior working conditions, and very soon aware that dereliction of duty would go unpunished, many resorted to alcohol, apathy, or corruption, or a combination of these. In one settlement, for example, the community alleged that the medical staff failed to open the clinic and were selling drugs, and a group of residents threatened to beat up the medical staff. The Ugandan administrator of the settlement called a meeting to iron out these differences, but the medical staff fled to the bush.

It could be argued that putting a team of Ugandan doctors in charge would not necessarily have prevented the decline in standards, but the improvement in discipline in those clinics supervised by the Ugandan doctor who began working in 1983 suggests otherwise. The example from Zaire lends credence to the argument that had Ugandans been supported in their initial efforts to develop a health programme which also served the locals, their work would also have contributed to good relations between the two communities.

Although the population of each settlement soon increased to over 3,000 people, the services provided differed according to the staff available or the location of the settlement in relation to the district's PHCUs and dispensaries, not in relation to population. Despite the large numbers of severely malnourished, none of the settlements had a therapeutic feeding programme for children or adults, except for a brief period in Goli, where a highly-qualified and committed Ugandan nurse took charge. The other settlements only offered supplementary feeds. In September at a co-ordination meeting, the OXFAM doctor reported that children in settlements were receiving only 70 Kcal in a supplementary meal which, as he pointed out, did not provide sufficient energy to justify the walk to the feeding centre.

Not only medicine but everything else was in short supply. For the

---

[15] In 1983, MSF workers took a different view of their professional responsibility but this caused tensions. On one occasion I needed transport and sent a messenger to ask their schedule of travel to settlements. After listing the locations to which they would be moving each day of the following week, the note ended with the warning 'Don't tell . . . of these weekend trips, as they are strictly clandestine and *verboten.*'

thousands of new arrivals from May through to July, there were no blankets, no tents, no clothing, no cooking utensils, no buckets, no milk, and hardly any cereal. The cold, rainy weather contributed to the heavy toll of human life. As noted earlier, the office in Yei - not by then recognized by Geneva - had been manned by a storeman. The emergency influx, which began in March, was dealt with by two temporary consultants who lived in Yei, and the programme officer, who commuted from Juba. A message from the programme officer underlines the situation: 'the new refugees are in immediate need of clothes. We see cases of women and men wearing leaves. The region is cold now and clothing is hardly a luxury. I emphasize the need for clothing for adults, particularly men, as previous experience has shown that most donated clothing is for children. We need clothing for everyone.' (19 July 1982.)[16]

To paraphrase the UNHCR policy, an assistance programme has the obligation to raise the condition of refugees to those of the local community, but if those standards are unacceptably low, it then has a duty to raise the standards for all.

Those responsible apparently did not accept the inadequacies of the programme and maintained that to treat Ugandans differently from locals would impede their integration. It proceeded on the *false* assumption that the health of the refugees was no worse than that of the locals. If no provision was already available, for example, for treating locals suffering from intestinal parasites, for immunizing them against contagious diseases, or for ensuring that rabies vaccine was available for emergencies, then the refugees should not enjoy these services. There were no drugs for asthma or yaws, and when rabies struck, two people died because no vaccines were available in the south. Similarly, in 1983 a meningitis epidemic among the self-settled refugees was reported by the Morobo medical assistant. The doctor decided to visit en route to Yei after a long, tiring, day of 'supervision' at Kaya. Four people had already died, and four others, exhibiting all the clinical signs of the disease, were shown to the doctor. Informed that there were many more similarly ill further up the road, the doctor simply instructed the medical assistant to administer sulphur as a prophylactic (some would be sent the next day) and to administer penicillin (also out of stock) to the ill. There was no attempt to determine the type of meningitis suffered. Returning to Yei, the doctor reported the incident to the Sudanese medical inspector who complained that he had no transport to follow up on this report. Apparently the epidemic was simply left to burn itself out in this remote area.

That in some cases refugees represented a serious health risk to the local population was not recognized either. In the case of bilharzia (*schistosomia-*

---

[16] Later that year at a meeting in London when I was asked what were some of the most critical needs, and I described the condition of the clothing in which so many refugees arrived, a doctor just returned from Sudan broke in with the comment 'I don't want this meeting to end on such an emotional note.'

sis) for example, the evidence suggests that the Ugandans brought the disease with them. Wright (in Wilson *et al*. 1985) found infective levels of *schistosoma mansoni* in Sudanese were significantly lower than among their self-settled refugee neighbours and lower than *all* settlement refugees studied. The likelihood of significant counter-infection to the locals was small, as self-settled refugees were fairly recent arrivals. This therefore provides a good reference level of *schistosomiasis* by which to assess the refugees. In addition, refugees sampled on the bases of home country origin showed similar levels of *schistosoma mansoni* infections to their home populations. The very long lifespan of the parasites in humans and the abundance of the intermediate host snail found in the rivers of the district makes the refugees potentially a serious health threat through their use of the rivers for drinking, bathing and toilet purposes. There were insufficient drugs for the treatment of bilharzia in Yei or Juba, although as was observed in an office note, 'the seriously long term risk of bilharzia is known and every patient will pass the point where the disease is curable. We are out of drugs for many months now.' (13 August 1983.)[17] In one area where the self-settled lived near Kaya, the population shot up from about 6,000 in 1979 to at least 40,000 by 1983. Thus the Sudanese and Ugandans were competing for the services of a single dispensary which could not possibly cope with the critical health conditions presented by refugees.

Criticisms of the health programme arising from any quarter were always countered with the response referred to earlier that 'this is Sudan'. UNHCR did attempt to put pressure on the agency to improve the quality of its services. But the agency succeeded in retaining its contract. Its performance in the field did not significantly improve.[18]

While Rome burned

As the British Broadcasting Corporation often warns its viewers, what follows may be disturbing. While anyone with field experience is aware of the problems of incompetence and inter-agency conflict and competition, even those agencies which try to avoid these problems believe it necessary to hide any dirt under the carpet, lest the public become disillusioned with *all* humanitarians. The problem is that this method of dealing with the situation does not solve it.

The problem of the effectiveness of humanitarian aid programmes is a

---

[17] Moreover, '*schistosoma—mansoni* consumes 79-97 per cent of its own weight of host carbohydrate per day which is the greatest for any human parasite, though damage to lipids and amino acids is minimal. Given the very high proportion of carbohydrates in the refugees' diets, it makes their contribution to malnutrition all the more serious.' (ibid.)

[18] It appears that in 1985, a change was made. The Germans withdrew from the district and the programme was thereafter funded through GTZ with AMREF supplying the technical personnel to maintain the primary health care programme.

complex one. Host governments are too dependent on the aid which agencies control to demand measures of competence. Donor governments, perhaps because of the compassionate nature of the aid programme, have not demonstrated concern either for results or for accountability. Perhaps the only way in which programmes will ever become more effective is for the humanitarian agencies to be made publicly accountable for the vast sums of money they at present distribute. But the only way in which public accountability could be approached would be through *independent* research which would monitor agency programmes: sound research, which would break the monopoly and control of information that the humanitarian agencies presently enjoy. While the logic of compassion suggests that to scrutinize the quality of the gift would be improper, the logic of economy suggests otherwise.

That UNHCR had itself assumed major responsibility for implementing the programme in Yei River District might have had the advantage of reducing the potential for agency conflict and competition. In general, the more agencies involved in a programme, the greater the problem of co-ordinating the work. The power struggles which occur between agencies in the field reflect a number of factors: the interests of donor governments who view agencies as their public face of humanitarianism; national and local host government interests; the objectives of the voluntary agencies; but perhaps most dangerous of all, the personal ambitions of individuals who believe they are doing good. Since UNHCR does not solicit independent evaluations of its programmes, success in getting or keeping contracts to implement programmes is seldom based on measures of competence or on any objective assessment of the actual work to be carried out. Rather, acquiring a contract depends on the ability to manipulate all the strings correctly at the same time. One Somalian WHO representative summed the problem up in this way: 'The longer they [expatriates] are in a country, the more clever they are at manipulating local politics. I wouldn't let an expatriate stay in *my* country more than two years.'

In some cases gifts, or even money, are dispensed to encourage approval of their programme or to ensure permission to enter or stay in a country. The ability to manipulate local politics through such means gives an advantage to those with greater funds and increases inter-agency jealousy and bickering in the field.

Foreign government representatives also try to manipulate agency/host government relations. In 1983, a new agency began working in health in eastern Sudan. The embassy of the agency's home government sent someone to call on the Deputy Commissioner for Refugees in Khartoum. He asked COMREF not to allow this agency to remain. The Deputy declined to follow the advice, suggesting that if something was wrong it should have been dealt with earlier, in the home country. Privately he told me that if this particular government did not like one of its own NGOs, it must mean the agency was a good one!¹⁹

It may be useful to describe the ensuing crisis in some detail, since it illustrates the tensions and even failures that can occur during times of serious crisis. One UNHCR official in the Juba office expressed the view that voluntary agencies were simply a recent manifestation of the 'scramble for Africa'. Understandably, given this perspective, OXFAM's offer of its services early in 1982 when the emergency began was declined. But even before May 1982, any impartial observer would have questioned the capacity of the agencies working in Yei River District to cope, especially with the health of yet another influx of refugees. But more refugees mean more funds. There is a temptation for some agencies to take on more responsibility than they can competently manage rather than to agree to inviting in others to assist. Apparently, the idea of utilizing appropriately skilled refugees or locals almost never crosses anyone's minds. The situation in the district was allowed to deteriorate.

Beginning in May and continuing through the first week of July, a series of radio messages and memos were sent from the field informing *both* the Juba and Khartoum UNHCR offices of the escalating numbers and of the lack of supplies. After several such messages,²⁰ one concluded with the warning: 'Inform Khartoum; if we are not careful this will become a public scandal'. An earlier message had included details of the scale of the influx:

'....on the Nyori road where we stopped, 35 people, two families, reported needing transport to come to settlement. When our lorry went, 92 boarded. Further down the road, there were at least 200 waiting and they were all too weak to walk....I had to hire one lorry at Kaya so we have three now moving from that end. This means at least 200 a day will be arriving here [Yei] and we do not know for how many days. Military [Ugandan] activities all along the border from Kajo-Kaji to Kaya. People on the border are leaving their crops. Attacks on the self-settled refugees include robberies, wounding (six are in the K-K hospital) and kidnap of some who have been taken back to Uganda....the concentration of refugees inside the border appears to have doubled....At any moment these people may all begin to move and it is clear that they are now health-wise in very bad condition. We must deal with present emergency and

---

¹⁹ In March 1985, when I visited the offices of the Commissioner, the deputy was in a dilemma. A California-based agency which only weeks earlier had been the subject of allegations of scandal in Ethiopia, had turned up in the Sudan. They said they had a lot of money to use in the Sudan. Should he let them work there?

²⁰ One read: 'On trips to border found alarming number desperately ill refugees for transport. 274 waiting Kaya, 300 Nyori road. Had to establish second transit centre on from Kajo-Kaji at Livolo. 80 new registrations per day in Kaya only. Sudanese authorities do not accept that our operation is hampered by lack of lorries, diesel, shelter in new settlements. Several cases of people dying near our Yei office and Yei hospital because of our delays, and number dying at border while waiting transport is shocking. Have requested Juba send extra landrover, drivers, diesel, and adequate amount of money to enable to relieve pressure. Must establish transit centre in Yei in view of lack of shelter in settlements.'

be prepared for more if it comes. Since I have been sending urgent radio messages almost daily, you can imagine that I find it very difficult to understand lack of substantial response from Juba.'

Emergency supplies ordered *before* May the previous year, for the March/April influx had not even arrived. Whatever were the reasons for withholding the information - that the south was facing an unparalleled crisis with which the programme could not cope - it was only when the British Refugee Council, OXFAM, and the international press got hold of the story that Geneva was informed.

When in Khartoum this leak was discovered, the head of one agency denied any emergency in the south. Perhaps, since he rarely left Juba, he was actually innocent of the real situation. But OXFAM immediately sent a field officer to confirm the facts and again offered an emergency medical team. Shortly afterwards, UNHCR flew in a delegation from Geneva to assess the situation. Their report, telexed to Geneva on 9 August 1982, demonstrates the seriousness of the neglected crisis.

Influx has been taking place since early in the year and amounted by June to over 30,000 refugees. Far from showing any signs of abating, there has been building in numbers in late June and July. Last week there has been a further dramatic increase. Influx has now reached over 900 a day. New arrivals are in poor condition....the organizational capacity to cope with this influx does not exist.
....conducted random sample of a hundred recent[ly] arrived refugee children aged between one and five. 20 per cent were suffering from severe marasmus type malnutrition [*sic*] (less than 70 percent weight for height) and further 10 percent had kwashiorkor (extreme swelling from malnutrition). The lives of this group are at immediate risk unless medical and therapeutic feeding programmes are established. At present these services are virtually non-existent....there are inadequate water supplies, etc. At the one settlement for which we could find good statistics, there was a death rate of 15 percent. For the West Bank, new arrivals as a whole calculated on an annual basis in an area where there is normally adequate food, these statistics of malnutrition are remarkable. Even with the provision of a general ration, nutritional deterioration will now continue unless special programmes are instituted.

Referring to GMT, the message underlined the fact that its capacities were 'over-estimated' and it had been agreed that further assistance was at least temporarily required. Confirming the urgent need for the OXFAM emergency medical team, in a later message it was stressed: 'No need for more OXFAM surveys, they should be ready to fill immediately gaps already identified....Their input needed at once to save lives.' As another message confirmed, the largest influx during 1982 was occurring on the west bank of the Nile, where 'the implementing capacity is weakest'.

But there was continued resistance to accepting the help of other agencies.

Two ministers in Juba were lobbied (unsuccessfully as it happened) to refuse to allow OXFAM to come in. The argument given was that more services were not only unnecessary for the refugees, but that this was just further evidence that UNHCR was solely concerned with refugees to the detriment of the Sudanese.

Now, under pressure from Geneva, GMT did organize a hasty trip to Zaire to recruit more Ugandan medical staff, and UNHCR mounted an airlift to bring in food and other supplies. This and later recruitment trips to Zaire resulted in further dissatisfaction with conditions in Yei River District. In Zaire the team found that:

...support for the refugees in this area is much better than in Yei area....They have over 30 lorries, three big stores with plenty of food. The medical staff (doctors) have UNHCR vehicles, the medical programme is paid for by UNHCR (at least salaries).... In Aru hospital, enough food is given to the refugees. They do not always get the same [diet] (they get even meat, eggs, vegetables, etc.). We are very much surprised about the differences in means employed at both sides of the border, while the refugee population appears to be the same (30 October 1982).

OXFAM's arrival was delayed (because of an attempted *coup* in Kenya during August 1982). To avoid further conflict, work was divided - OXFAM taking responsibility for the reception centres on the border. Led, not by a doctor, but a public health specialist, the OXFAM team was directed *not* to administer curative medicine unless UNHCR agreed to dig bore wells, as refugees there were dependent on polluted water. (UNHCR could not even supply settlements with enough wells and could not divert equipment to the border.) This decision pleased no one, least of all OXFAM's highly qualified and experienced nurses, who were limited to organizing a therapeutic feeding programme.

Now GMT decided to bring in its own expatriate emergency team. Despite advice from OXFAM, one of these (an administrator, not a doctor), was put in charge of co-ordinating the work of the agencies involved in health. Hearing of the crisis in southern Sudan, Médecins sans Frontières sent a mission to Yei River District to survey the situation. The following excerpts are from their published account.

In the heart of Africa....Francis Charhon and I made our exploratory mission in October. We wanted to evaluate the sanitary and nutritional conditions for the 70,000 Ugandans who are 'piling up' in camps along the....borders....We had not been able to collect any information from HCR about the situation of the Ugandan refugees in the Sudan....We only knew that these people were continuing to move from one country to another.... they came back [to Zaire] when in need of medical care or food, which could be provided more generously there than in the Sudan...

One afternoon [in Kaya Transit Centre] enlightened us more than the long reports on the situation of the newly-arrived refugees. The frequency of kwashiorkor in the children, and oedema in the adults is an indication of the extent of the interruption in normal eating habits. A rapid survey will confirm that 60% of children suffer from severe malnutrition. All these people lay there, resigned in their misery, waiting for UN trucks to be repaired to provide transport to other camps....As usual it is the children who need most attention, with their swollen bellies and faces which look old, their eyes too big. The women too, whose crinkled breasts don't produce enough milk to suckle their children. They are so malnourished themselves....

Around Yei we visited other transit camps which show us the same story, the same horrors, almost tedious in their repetitiveness. However, the organizations responsible for taking charge of refugee health, judge that the situation is not really serious. The German Medical Team present in the region for ten years, does not want to invest too big a part of their activities for benefiting refugees. Caritas has also been on location.... with three nurses and a doctor. Also OXFAM, which obstinately refuses to deal with anything except 'feeding programmes', leaving others the responsibility of caring for them.

....But how can one be satisfied with a health programme where dispensaries don't have enough anti-Paludins and no streptomycin for victims of tuberculosis, where the Ugandan nurses are left without supervision, and lepers deprived of Dapsone. Furthermore up to the present moment, no one has thought about prevention.... 'That's correct,' these people will tell us, 'but now there are enough of us to improve all that.' Let us wait and see.... In the meantime, Francis and I are tempted to think that MSF could have done something. Whatever the situation, they know that another 40,000 Ugandans are about to swell the ranks....in the case of an offensive (already announced) by the regular army against the guerrillas. It seems obvious to us that the burden will be too heavy (it's already enormous), for GMT and OXFAM....[21]

Some agencies make greater efforts than others to avoid public disclosure of competition and conflict. At the very time this report was published in France, agency staff were making valiant efforts to paper over the cracks and, whether intended or not, reduced international attention to the Ugandan refugee issue. Items had appeared in the British press reporting a 30 per cent rate of severe malnutrition among children, predicting a new wave of refugees, and implying that health conditions in settlements were in need of improvement.[22] One agency doctor who had been in Yei was said to have written a report in which he questioned that there even was an emergency in the south. A refugee working for this agency managed to read whatever he had written. Angered, he wrote to *The Guardian*. Excerpts from his (unpublished) letter, which he handed me in Wudabi in 1983, reveal the extreme frustration and bitterness felt by most refugees concerning the conduct of the health programme.

[21] (Translated by Rachel Ayling from *Médecins sans Frontières*, No. 15, Nov/Dec 1982).

[22] See 'Refugees Starving', *The Guardian*, 17 August 1982; 'Penalties of not running' (photograph captioned 'Orphaned by disease in a Sudan refugee camp'), *The Sunday Times*, 31 October 1982; and '80,000 may flee Uganda Purge', *The Observer*, 7 November 1982.

We have seen malnourished children being fed on a basic diet of milk or porridge. One multivite or iron tablet is given as the only additive until the recovery or death of such a child. Whether or not such a child vomits his feed every time, there is no examination of stool or blood for parasites, yet weights are recorded to check 'improvements'. Even a simple microscope is far from patients - about 50 miles away....A patient having a high fever is not even given an aspirin.... Anti-worming medicine is not given to patients who carry obvious physical symptoms. Most health centres run dry [of] drugs in a fortnight and nothing is replaced....we begin to doubt and question what happens to the donations given by UNICEF, WHO and many other organizations.... To....and its co-workers, this....seems to be unimportant. They care very little about the daily deaths of 3-4 persons. The graves are there for anyone to see....It is a deplorable state of affairs to see some white volunteers who come under the pretence of humanitarians playing a double game....While there are many who labour tirelessly....the majority....simply come to enrich themselves and even go to the extremes of the colour bar [*sic*]. Where blacks get low payment for the same jobs done by white expatriates, the whites get higher salaries. Although Dr ---- wants to hide the sufferings of Ugandan refugees, we know that the daily influx continues....It was not our wish to come into exile, to suffer, neither to live where we are now. Nor do we appreciate the least services to be rendered to what someone might call 'low class human beings'. We have different professionals in settlements, doctors, teachers, students, farmers, schoolboys, state registered nurses, widows, orphans, the disabled - and it was not our wish to come into exile. We suffer through no fault of our own.

It should not be assumed that only Ugandans and expatriates were dissatisfied with the quality of the health programme in Yei River District. The arrival of alternative agencies practising a higher standard of service gave many Sudanese the courage to speak openly about their long-standing grievances. Many unconfirmed stories were circulated. Those who took note of some allegations would not have been reassured by the following note:

We have received the following radio message from....in response to query about several boxes of medicine which arrived on two flights last week. 'Re. your R/261 seven boxes of medicines gift from ....The one box we opened contained expired injectible multivitamins. We have not checked the other boxes. There are eight boxes in our office...'

When funds did become available for rebuilding the hospital, GMT was chosen to implement them. The contract was awarded to a non-indigenous builder whose prices were so high that even UNHCR Geneva had forbidden the Yei office to use his services again.

At one point, when pressure on GMT had reached a very high pitch, it over-reacted to the chronic need for an ambulance for the Yei hospital. A note between two colleagues describes what happened:

....big battle over ambulances! Dr ---- went past all of us to convince Mr ---- [a Sudanese official] that he needed a fancy Mercedes ambulance. Remember during

Douglas' [US government representative] visit the patients' wheelbarrows at Goli dispensary? Mr. ---- asked me when he was in Juba and I told him that any hospital without a system of support, communication, etc. was useless. We agreed that if an ambulance had to be procured, it should be a modest type. [But] Dr ---- told Mr ---- that the Mercedes is available immediately, and it would take months to get a Landrover, etc., ho hum.

The luxurious ambulance was duly delivered to Yei hospital. Lacking fuel and radio contact, it was used throughout 1983 mainly to go to market during the week and to church on Sunday. On one occasion when there was an attempt to use it to transport a critically ill refugee, the doctor in charge demanded an excessive number of jerry-cans of fuel in exchange for its use; instead the patient was brought into Yei by OXFAM's Landrover.

Late in 1982, UNHCR made an attempt to co-ordinate the health programme. Three meetings were held during my fieldwork in 1982. Representatives from all agencies involved in health were invited. When the first meeting was called, only at the last moment was it remembered that the Sudanese Inspector for Health should be included. The tendency to ignore local institutions and officials when planning refugee programmes was, in fact, quite commonplace. At another meeting, certain plans were made which might have resolved the persistent quarrel over whether refugee health was worse or better than that of the Sudanese. OXFAM offered to carry out a health survey among the Sudanese. It also offered to set up therapeutic and supplementary feeding programmes in each of the settlements although by this time the need for this service in the reception centres had diminished. Later, however, agency conflict prevented the implementation of this plan and OXFAM eventually withdrew its team.

If agencies learn from such bitter experiences, then perhaps in some sense, the suffering they cause (or rather fail to prevent) would not be in vain. Unfortunately, however, the drama of unpreparedness was repeated in early 1983. UNLA attacks, which began on Christmas Day 1982, forced another wave of refugees to seek asylum in the Sudan. Again there was a need for more staff. More hurried trips were made to Zaire and, as noted, in 1983 GMT finally agreed to engage a Ugandan doctor. UNHCR also invited Médecins sans Frontières to assist at Yei hospital and to supply staff for certain settlements. But the attempt to maintain an integrated health programme based on the 'green book's' low standards for the whole population, persisted.

During 1983, the situation continued to reflect the absence of central competent co-ordination. Each agency felt free to do as it wished. Sudan Council of Churches which had always attempted to maintain a high standard of service, had a different drug list, and was better supplied, but was ignored in the agency scramble for contracts with UNHCR. After a bitter exchange between SCC and UNHCR, its only consolation was that it was given the contract to implement a programme for the vulnerable groups, that is, the physically handicapped, the elderly, and orphans.[23]

MSF and GMT supervisors gave contradictory instructions to field staff concerning the treatment of different illnesses. For example, one might advise a full three-day anti-malarial course for adults; another would say that a single dose was sufficient. (The latter eventually became the standard treatment.) There were no regular meetings to discuss common problems or to exchange information. Some agency staff were not even on speaking terms and UNHCR files are full of disparaging notes to the programme officer about the work of the others. For example:

Rumours abound concerning the arrival of a second MSF Team. Although you are aware of the conditions under which the initial request was made....Unless the MSF nurses can act independently they should not come here. It is not only pointless, but very embarrassing when expatriate nurses receive [i.e. require] greater supervision than local staff (as is the present situation), and this also creates more work for us.

Given the situation, this note concluded with the surprising advice: 'Also there is no need for another doctor in this area....(2 September 1983).

Monthly returns from various units were either irregular or did not appear at all. This was not surprising since report forms had been frequently changed, and the one in use at the time was too complicated for most field staff to complete. Proper statistics of births and deaths were never kept. There was little equipment and no stationery. Drug supplies were irregular and always inadequate. There was a chronic shortage of certain drugs, especially for treating intestinal parasites. In Limuru settlement (which *had* a microscope), 1,120 cases of various parasites were identified, but medicines supplied during the same period could only treat 150 patients. Early in 1984 a survey to establish causes of the widespread anaemia in one settlement (Katagiri) found 69.1 per cent of the sample to have hookworm infestation.[24]

Efforts to involve the community in public health projects failed completely, and little wonder, since neither Sudanese nor Ugandans appreciated or responded to the approach imposed by the expatriates. Their method of encouraging co-operation was to threaten to withdraw *all* health services, if a community failed to dig pit latrines for the clinic. The Sudanese project manager's inspection tour report (24 May 1983) illustrates a situation which was not atypical.

---

[23] Even then, after being excluded from all medical work, SCC's battles with GMT were not over. The Swedish nurse, responsible for assisting the vulnerables, was given a list of desperately needed medical supplies at Mogiri settlement. These included ointment and bandages for the sores of those who suffered leprosy. When the GMT doctor heard of this, he wrote an angry letter informing her that GMT was in charge and that if she took such supplies to Mogiri, he would be forced to remove them. It was at this point that the nurse made the comment that it was against the rules in southern Sudan to save lives, which was quoted at the beginning of this chapter.

[24] Personal communication, but see Wilson *et al.* (1985) for the results of another parasite survey.

Wudabi

Health Centre - The refugees have complained bitterly against nursing officer ------ for refusing to treat them. The health centre was closed from 15th to 16th of May 1983 on instructions of the SMO [senior medical officer] until the refugees responded to the call to dig 2 pit latrines at the Health Centre on a self-help basis.
Obituary: Between the 17th and 21st May '83, 16 refugees died. Of these, 8 died in the health centre....and 8 at the settlement. Causes of death are malnutrition, jaundice, diarrhoea, and vomiting....
Burial—cloth: No burial cloth was available in our stores for the 16 persons who died....
   I am writing to Wudabi, warning refugees to respond to the nursing officer's call to dig 2 pit latrines and to show better behaviour in future.

   I conducted a survey of this settlement from 5 June 1983. The clinic was still closed and no health services were available to Wudabi settlers, the nurse having been transferred elsewhere. Accusations that he was negligent in his duties, and an alcoholic, were later confirmed when he was put in charge of another settlement. A medical worker remaining in the settlement was waiting for transport to leave for Yei. She had broken her arm and the nurse had taken the box of medicines with him when he had been transferred. In the course of our interviews, among the seriously ill we found a woman lying helpless in her tent. Several days previously she had fallen from a tree, and had not even received first aid.
   Although from early 1982, Ugandans had been reporting that every refugee hut was infested with rats, no action was taken. In the settlements there is a bizarre form of entertainment for children: 'rat expeditions'. Adults dig under the wall of the house to allow rats to escape while someone inside beats on the walls. (Houses are dangerously weakened by this damage to walls.) Outside, the children (who have congregated with sticks) scream 'Rat running, rat running', as they charge about killing the rats which try to escape. On my first expedition, 'we' only got 32 rats: on the next, the total was 102. I was told I was unlucky. Some expeditions net over 200 carcasses of rats of all sizes. Like children everywhere, these had great fun carrying around the wriggling babies, and frightening the women who watched. After I reported back on my adventure, UNHCR decided to order 20,000 rat traps!
   Few Sudanese keep cats. It occurred to me that WFP might be advised to airlift cats to the area, since the rats were probably eating as much food as were the refugees! Moreover, people were bitten during the night: toes, fingers, and heels appeared to be particularly vulnerable to attack. It should not have been necessary for Dr Umar to point out in 1983 in his report to UNHCR that rats are 'reservoirs of infection for the following diseases: rat-bite fever, leptospirosis, plague, and salonelosis.'
   Towards the end of 1983, UNHCR finally did send a medical consultant to Yei River District. His intervention led to certain improvements. GMT

maintained responsibility for co-ordination, but regular meetings for supervisors - as well as inter-agency meetings - began. Exchange of information reportedly improved, and a common strategy for conducting the health programme was devised. Supervisors and field staff were given written instructions; a standard drug dosage plan was drawn up; seminars were organized for field staff as part of their in-service training; better records were being maintained; and stationery supplied. Two limited field surveys were carried out in early 1984; one, as noted, on bilharzia and anaemia, and the other on sleeping sickness.

Some months later, the situation had again altered. In 1984 MSF withdrew from the settlements and, with a reduced staff, only worked in Yei hospital. The settlement clinics were once again supervised only by GMT. Their staff position in June 1984 included two doctors, two medical assistants, one nurse, one midwife, one public health adviser, and one nutritional adviser. Although a considerably larger staff than at any earlier time, their numbers were still insufficient to supervise the 54 different health units in the district. The Kajo-Kaji sub-district was totally neglected. It was supposed to be supervised by an expatriate doctor, but he had not been in the country for most of 1983, and in 1984, due to the worsening military situation in the south, all GMT's expatriate medical staff were evacuated.

Death and its major causes

One obvious measure of the success of an assistance programme would be the assessment of the health of those who are its recipients. Arguments persisted among the agency personnel over whether the Ugandans' health was better or worse than that of the Sudanese, with GMT always asserting that the Ugandans' health was the better. In the absence of data, they claimed that the death rate among refugees was only 8-9 per thousand, compared with 20-25 per thousand among the Sudanese. Had proper statistics been collected, these differences would have been resolved. It is remarkable that *reports of the numbers dying are always used to collect money, but never to evaluate the consequences of the aid programme implemented with that money*. In March 1984, efforts were made to collect death statistics in the settlements. On the basis of records from one month, it was estimated that the death rate among Ugandans was 23 per thousand.

The conditions in refugee settlements are not conducive to record-keeping. Settlement offices often do not have a table or chair and stationery - a factor which cannot be overstressed since it is so often overlooked - is in very short supply. There were also other obstacles. Health workers reported directly to the agency which employed them, and were reluctant to co-operate with the settlement officer who was required to make comprehensive monthly reports to UNHCR. In Yei, the agency did not provide health records to either UNHCR or the Commissioner for Refugees' project management office.

The settlement officer was thus dependent on information supplied to him by the settlers.

There was little to motivate refugees to report deaths. Indeed, the aid programme is a disincentive to report them. Had funds been available to supply burial cloth, people would have been more likely to report, but usually a blanket had to be sacrificed to wrap the dead. For a time the programme officer supplied bales of burial cloth from his budget for 'food in transit'. Although cemeteries were established in each settlement, food rations for each household were based on numbers, and so in order to keep numbers up, most refugees reverted to the customary practice of burying in their own compounds.

In Roronyo, for example, where the settlement officer had the most extensive list of individuals who had died since the settlement opened (92), the survey indicated that a total of 180 (or 50 per thousand) had died during a period of thirteen months.

In addition to the constraints of the aid programme which encourage people to hide the death of a member of their household, there are also traditions which discourage the reporting of deaths. When someone dies, relatives have elaborate and expensive ceremonial responsibilities which are particularly burdensome in the conditions of life in exile. It is disgraceful to delay funeral ceremonies, but in certain circumstances it is tolerated. Thus people tended to keep quiet about a death, hoping their circumstances would change so they could afford the appropriate funeral. As will be discussed later, the psychological strain on refugees forced into this abnormal behaviour pattern is inevitably great.

In the survey, refugees were asked to state how many people from their household had been buried in the settlement. As settlements opened at different times, beginning in late 1979, and the arrival of refugees was spread over the entire period, the number of deaths reported could only be related to the time the first member of the household arrived in the settlement. The overall number of deaths for the period from the time the first settlement opened to the time of the interview was 0.41 per household. Although the year in which a death occurred was not recorded, observations in 1982-3 suggest that the highest number of deaths occur during the first few months of arrival in a settlement. This is dramatically confirmed by examining the number of deaths which occurred among the households arriving in 1983. Interviews were conducted from 28 May to 19 September 1983. Between 1 January 1983 and the time of the interview, the number of deaths was 89 per thousand among those households registering for settlement that year. In 1982, the first settlement opened in March and the number of deaths between then and the interview was 63 per thousand, a period of not more than 15 months.

The numbers of deaths differed by camps as well. See Table III.3 (Appendix III) for a comparison of all camps. The highest number dying per household occurred at Goli transit camp. It was opened in September 1982 and interviews were conducted exactly twelve months later. It first accommodated refugees who had had to be removed from a new site where the water supply had failed. It then began receiving part of the new wave of refugees entering the Sudan in early 1983. It was situated directly adjacent to Goli settlement. At times the population of Goli transit camp rose as high as 11,000. The opening of new settlements could not keep up with the demand. This meant that at times there were as many as 16,000 people living in one small area. There were never more than six functioning bore holes to supply water for both Goli and the transit camp. OXFAM attempted to dig three additional shallow wells, but the results were not satisfactory. People relied mainly on river water for both drinking and bathing. Overcrowding was compounded by a lack of pit latrines, food, drugs, and medical staff to deal with the critically ill at both locations. The clinic was located one kilometre from the settlement and two kilometres from the furthest household in the transit camp. Even at the times of the worst crises, health workers were not provided with bicycles. The overall average number of deaths per household among those who still remained in Goli transit camp at the time of the interview was 1.55. Based on a 10 per cent sample of only these households, a total of 1,660 people were reported to have died at Goli transit, suggesting a staggering death rate of 285 per thousand over a period of twelve months.

After Goli transit camp, Mopoko settlement which opened in May 1982 had the next highest overall number of dead per household - 0.68. Kunsuk was the third highest with an overall average of 0.56 deaths per household. Kunsuk opened in August 1982, and received a large number of the formerly self-settled refugees. Mondikolo - with an average number of 0.51 deaths per household - was the fourth highest among the settlements. Health services in the Kajo-Kaji sub-district are described in a report from project management. There were four settlements in this area: Mondikolo, Mogiri, Kunsuk, and Kala. The latter was located more than 40 miles from Kajo-Kaji.

All the settlements except Kala are not having proper and well-equipped medical centres. Three settlements, namely Kunsuk, Mogiri, and Mondikolo settlement and Mondikolo transit are only served with first aid boxes. These are not adequate to cater for the welfare of the refugees. The first aid boxes render services to refugees and the natives. The government hospital at Kajo-Kaji is far and is also short of medicines. It would be appreciated if one medical unit is established at Mogiri [the leprosy settlement] to cater for the settlements and the transit. Mogiri is centrally situate[d]....Most of the new arrivals are worn-out people and indeed destitute, as such, a proper medical administration to these desperate refugees is necessary. The transit is short of tents, consequently the new arrivals are usually exposed to cold....It is necessary that tents be provided....In March SCC donated clothes to the disabled refugees at Mondikolo settlement and the transit. It would be good if blankets are sent....to cater for new arrivals. (10 April 1983.)

Interviews in the Kajo-Kaji sub-district were conducted in late August 1983. The medical assistant at Kala had succumbed to such escapism as alcohol allowed him. There was no supervision of his work from Yei or Kajo-

Kaji. The 'first aid boxes' in the other three settlements were *totally* depleted. The dispensary at the Mandari hospital had also run out of drugs. The leprosy assistant at Mogiri was accused of selling Dapsone as a 'sleeping pill' to Sudanese. Certainly at the time of the survey he had none to supply to those whose disease had not been controlled. Formerly a Ugandan leprosy inspector, he had come to Mogiri with 50 of his patients, and he was probably unaware of the untreated lepers in Kunsuk and Kala.[25]

This man had great personal charm. Whenever the programme officer and I visited Mogiri, we were served a meal which included meat. Later, when I stayed in the settlement to conduct the survey, it became apparent that he kept the settlers literally in bondage. Respondents alleged that he charged them for used clothing provided by SCC, for the use of the grinder which had similarly been donated to the refugees, and for sending their children to kindergarten. Food for visitors, they reported was extracted from their rations and meat was paid for by taxing them. The day after we finished the survey, he reportedly complained that he was sure the people had divulged the 'secrets' of his regime. Again, the problem was lack of consultation with responsible members of the Ugandan community.

Death rates among the unassisted refugees were generally higher than in the settlements. Among those who settled during 1983 in the compound where the interview was conducted, the overall number of deaths was on average 0.70 per household, or 100 per thousand in a period of less than twelve months. The average size of these households is 6.35. The overall average number of persons buried in the compounds of the self-settled was 0.90 per household. See Figure III.4 and 5 for further analysis of deaths per unassisted households by year of settling.

On the basis of the March 1984 report the three major causes of death among refugees in settlements were identified. These, in order of frequency were, pneumonia and other respiratory tract infections; malnutrition; and diarrhoeal diseases. *All three of these causes of death reflect on the quality of the assistance programme.* Temperatures in the district may fall as low as 16°C during the rains. Throughout 1982 there were never enough blankets to issue one to each individual to say nothing of the lack of clothing. By late 1983, the UNHCR office believed it had distributed one blanket per refugee, but the

---

[25] It is impossible to present all the evidence collected on the inadequacies of the medical programme mounted in response to the influx of Ugandans. In July 1982, a Ugandan, employed by the Sudanese government as the leprosy inspector, reported that over 200 leprosy sufferers were trapped in the border areas without medicine. The OXFAM field officer was prepared to assist by supplying some of the medicines needed, but asked the head of the German Leprosy Agency in Juba to provide the Dapsone. She accused the Ugandan of lying and of being corrupt. Later, of course, his evidence was confirmed by the arrival of leprosy sufferers in considerable numbers, with their families. By then, rather than segregate them, it was policy to put them into other settlements. But medical workers were not trained to treat this disease and Dapsone was irregularly supplied. In 1984 the Oxford team found that Roronyo had just run out of this drug again for its 26 cases. (A. Pankhurst, in press.)

survey found that there were only enough blankets in settlements for 47 per cent of the population. Moreover, even blankets in use were not evenly distributed. We found individuals who owned several, while as many as thirteen people shared one. As noted, refugees had to sell blankets to buy food; they use them to bury the dead, and, as they were constantly in contact with the damp earth floor, the poor quality supplied meant that they quickly wore out.

Sleeping on the ground involves other health risks. Tumbu flies lay their eggs on the ground. At night the larvae penetrate the skin, and, if untreated, produce an abscess. During the emergency influx in 1982, UNHCR attempted to purchase local mats to supply one to each household, but in 1983 even this effort to improve sleeping conditions had to be abandoned. An objective assessment was made of sleeping conditions of the household in the survey. 'Adequate' was defined as a family sharing at least *one* straw mat, with a blanket for each individual. According to this definition, only 21.3 per cent of the households had 'adequate' sleeping conditions.[26]

Clothing was similarly in very short supply. The journey to the settlements had taken a long time and people often arrived without even one full set of clothes. A household was assessed as having 'adequate' clothing if each member had at least one item to cover the body. The findings are shown in Table 5:1.

TABLE 5.1 Interviewers' assessment of clothing provision
in refugee settlements

	%	Number
Adequate for all members of household	26.0	523
Adequate for adults but not children	24.8	501
Inadequate for all	49.1	991
Missing data	0.1	2
TOTAL	100	2,017

The lack of clothing interfered with school attendance. Of those who answered the question, 21.1 per cent of the households gave this as the reason for not sending children to school, but observing the schools in session suggested that the lack of clothes kept many more children than reported away from classes. Ugandan teachers themselves placed great emphasis

[26] Among the first purchases refugees made when they had sufficient income was a mattress and bed. An obvious income-generating industry would have been to set up a factory to produce them. Even locally made mattresses, bags stuffed with grass or sawdust, would have been preferable to sleeping on the bare ground.

upon being properly dressed (i.e. at least covered) for school, which put the poorest families at a disadvantage.

Nutrition in the settlements

In 1984 nutrition surveys were conducted in four settlements. (The method and full results are reported in Wilson *et al.* 1985.) In Limbe (one of the oldest settlements), Gumbari, Roronyo and Alero, the overall clinical rate of malnutrition was found to be 10.1 per cent among boys two and under, and 6.7 per cent among girls in this age group. Although the standard method of measurement in the age group is less reliable, the more surprising finding of these surveys was that among the six- to ten-year-old children, the rates of malnourishment were also elevated: 7.4 per cent among the boys and 2.4 per cent among the girls. These rates of malnutrition are high compared to those recorded elsewhere in Africa and were also considerably higher than those recorded by Médecins sans Frontières in a study they conducted eight months earlier in settlements in the same district. The point that WFP failed to supply food rations has already been belaboured, but in 1984, from July until at least mid- September when these studies were made, supplies of food were also interrupted. Moreover, the Oxford team's surveys were conducted during the rains, or the 'hungry' season, while the MSF survey was carried out during the food abundant season. Seasonal variations in nutritional levels are common in Africa. The differences between the male and female infants are difficult to explain, but those found among the older children 'may be the result of greater access to food (during preparation) by girls. The Lugbara have a saying that 'whoever distributes the food cannot go hungry!' (ibid.)

Why should refugees under the aid umbrella continue to suffer high levels of malnutrition? Malnourishment is not simply a function of the availability of food. And even the limited evidence collected in 1984 by the Oxford team suggests that there were fewer children in settlements who were clinically malnourished compared with the self- settled around Panyume. The issue of the complicated chain of factors which lead to the continued malnourishment of refugees (in and outside settlements) will be taken up in the next two chapters, but it is worth noting here that:

Refugees often have needs which they rate as high as food, for example, soap and clothing. ...the food given is one of the few assets which refugees have upon which to build a strategy for self-reliance in the future. Since it is distributed to all, it can play a role in alleviating the food problems of the very poorest sector of the society, though more success would be achieved through targeting assistance to the poorest. (ibid.)

The WFP food basket differs from country to country and from emergency to emergency within a country. Advice on food for refugees appears in Volume I of the *UNHCR Handbook* (1983:95-116), and quite correctly it warns 'WFP food aid does not provide all the components of a complete ration.' Fieldworkers are reminded that local foods are usually preferable to imports, that every effort should be made to provide familiar foodstuffs and to maintain traditional food habits, and that most refugee emergencies warrant the early appointment of a nutrition specialist. It does not, however, give guidance on how to sort out a myriad of practical problems relating to food distribution in the field. Rations arrive in bulk. Refugees rarely have appropriate-sized containers. Settlements have no scales and there are no calculators to work out the complicated mathematics involved in dividing shipments which arrive packaged in both pounds and kilograms. The problems with edible fat, for example, which is supplied in *both* solid and liquid forms, have already been discussed.

A full WFP basket prescribed for the Ugandans contains a daily ration of 2,000 Kcal, made up of 10 kg cereal; 0.9 kg beans; 1 kg milk powder; and 1 litre edible fat.[27] The diet is monotonous in the extreme and every visitor to a settlement met demands from refugees for 'a change in diet'. When rations were reaching the settlements, this complaint was viewed as further evidence of 'ingratitude'. But research suggests that the grumbling of refugees should be taken more seriously. (De Waal and Rolls, in press.) A phenomenon has been identified which is referred to as 'sensory specific satiety'. When people are repeatedly presented with the same foodstuff, this leads to substantially reduced appetite for it, even if it is potentially nourishing. Refugees are human beings and it is likely that they will trade their rations for novel, but less nourishing food.

Neither dura nor rice, the two cereals which were usually provided, are traditional foods for Ugandans. One group of Ugandans, most of whom had remained inside their country until January 1983, were fishermen. They and the other people who lived around the Nile or near other rivers in Uganda, were accustomed to eating fish daily and found the radical change in their diet difficult to accept. During one crisis of WFP supplies, the Norwegian government did airlift several tons of *powdered* fish, but this is *very* difficult to prepare in an acceptable manner.[28]

Even at the best of times, refugees rarely received all the ingredients of the ration at once. One month a settlement might receive its quota of cereal, with the milk and edible fat arriving with the next shipment. Often UNHCR was forced to purchase beans (the daily ration amounts to 75 kernels - a small handful) on the local market and this item was not always supplied. Salt was only occasionally purchased locally, but as the numbers of refugees increased, even this irregular supply ceased. No other source of vitamins or minerals was provided, not even spices. Sugar and tea were never included in the ration. Sometimes it was difficult for women to obtain a stone with which to grind the dura when that was the cereal supplied and on a few occasions when maize was the cereal, the problem of grinding was even more serious.

[27] In 1984 edible fat supplied was whale oil and refugees complained about its taste.
[28] A Swedish nurse wrote instructions which advised refugees on the few ways it could be made edible.

This may account for one of the other alarming findings of the Oxford study of parasites.

In faecal samples of one hundred refugees in Limbe settlement very large quantities of undigested food were found, which indicates that the already precarious food balance is even worse. Whilst the high prevalence of intestinal parasites and diarrhoea are no doubt partly responsible, inadequate cooking and chewing of food are also suggested. Many grains and beans were found whole or even hard in the faeces. The failure to cook adequately is probably mainly caused by lack of time, as women are so involved in wage labour. Rapid consumption without proper chewing may be an effect of hunger on communal eating. (in Wilson *et al.* 1985.)

As food aid was distributed on a per capita basis, households having more children than adults were able to manage better when rations were available.

Attempts to make up for the shortages in WFP supplies forced UNHCR to rely on donations from other agencies, particularly from the Sudan Council of Churches, and on other emergency donations from abroad. These included the fish powder from Norway and date-expired biscuits from bomb shelters in the Netherlands.[29] UNHCR also made sporadic purchases of food on the local market with the consequent effect of such sudden demand on prices.[30] Throughout 1982-3 there was rarely a month in which settlements received full quotas, and shortfalls were normally not made up. And in three consecutive years, the breakdown in WFP supplies coincided with the season of greatest food shortage in the district, which is also the busiest season in the agricultural cycle. This ensured that most people in settlements could not begin to attain self-sufficiency in food production in the period they were expected to do so. Instead, each year refugees were forced to depend for food on their earnings from piece work for local Sudanese and most subsisted on the cassava they received in lieu of cash payments. In 1983 and 1984 the cassava stock in some areas was sufficiently depleted for people to consume the young tubers which may even be dangerous.

The following notice sent to settlements by the Yei UNHCR field office illustrates the problem:

To: All Settlement officers/committee members.
This is to inform you about the transport problems with rice and milk powder from WFP. At the moment we have very serious delays in the arrival of rice and milk powder from Mombasa... Settlements like Kala, Morsak, Limbe, Mondikolo, Gumbari, Logobero, and Wudabi did not even get all the food they needed in July.

[29] Refugees complained that these biscuits were weevil-infested, but I was personally grateful to the Dutch because large numbers found their way to the market. Even if tasteless, my team and I found them a source of quick energy.

[30] If WFP had had cash, or if UNHCR could have planned its purchases of local food, it could have stimulated production rather than having irregular and negative effects upon prices. Self-settled refugees in Panyume and Kajo-Kaji produced surpluses which they could not get to market. In Juba there were often shortages of food. Could not WFP have sold its food in Juba and used the funds to purchase and transport local produce to refugees? Better yet, if refugees had their own funds, they would have organized their own distribution system.

UNHCR/PM and WFP are looking seriously into this matter. We are buying local food wherever we can. SCC has already given food to help out in this difficult situation. However, we will not be able to prevent further serious delay in the August distribution. We fully realize the consequences for you all. This letter is to assure you that the present problems do not mean that you are cut off from food supply. Neither does it mean that the settlement officer in your settlement has given wrong figures or does not defend your cause... (10 August 1983.)

Through local purchase and borrowing from other agencies, UNHCR supplied refugees with more than the prescribed amount of certain items which were available. A passerby might well have believed Koya had a thriving economy so long as he went no further than the market at the roadside. One Ugandan, formerly a medical student, wrote a tongue-in-cheek description of Koya, entitled, 'The Refugee Market in the Heart of Africa'.

Koya was a rather unlikely spot for an economic boom. Much of the bush had remained a Stone Age wilderness... But in the past 14 months, the distribution of food and other items to refugees by UNHCR has fuelled a dramatic - though not always welcome - transformation of the village. I recently visited the transit and file this report on the impact of trade.

Deep in the forest near Eastern Koya River, gongs and drums echo through a long tent, as wild-eyed children and bare-breasted women squat on rough biscuit tins, and a young man named Thomas Ayile energetically 'performs' an ancient war dance of the Aringa tribe. In this case, however, Ayile's dance signals that he is preparing to sell a full sack of rice to any passing 'mundukuru' [local term for northern Sudanese traders].... With 25 pounds he will [first] afford more than 10 bottles of 'waragi' [local alcohol]. [Then] the next night, Ayile explains, he will set off for the market at Ariwara in Zaire in hopes of finding gold. 'More than 100 of my friends have gone already'.

Ariwara is another famous African market in Zaire operating twice a week. It gathers nationals of Kenya, Sudan, Rwanda, Burundi, Uganda and a few Senegalese, who come to the country in search of minerals. [But] Koya - a gateway to Kenya, Uganda, Zaire, Egypt, Asia, Europe and America - stands a better chance of turning into an international market if the Arab businessmen pay attention. But, unfortunately, being a refugee transit camp, the only things sold at the moment are rice, blankets, oil, hoes, buckets, pangas, and salt. The Somali drivers from Mombasa, bringing food to the south, stop there for their tea and cigarettes.

A day does not pass without news of pickpockets and of thefts in the tents, whose owners are all in the markets waiting for passing trucks to stop. When one stops, the whole market population rushes towards it with different items in their hands. One day, a woman was trying to buy a bucket through a bus window, and had her 12 pounds snatched by another Koya parking boy. The boy who was selling the bucket tried to demand his money, but passengers in the bus thought he was just organizing a gang to rob the bus. So they turned and beat him up. He was pushed into the bus and brought to Yei police station.

The most profound effects of Koya trading business are being felt in the surrounding Kakwa and Pajulu [Sudanese] villages. They are abandoning their cassava and dura fields to depend on the Koya refugee rice which will in the future cause food shortage. Most of the local people cannot now afford some items because of price hike.

The refugees insist that Koya has no choice but to continue marketing. They are forging ahead... The boom will last, says one refugee representative from his tent office in Koya. After that, maybe we will have to think about trade promotion programmes to attract more business. Judging from recent experience, that can only mean more wrenching change for Koya. (Johnson, 10 September 1983.)

During the month of September, the 'wrenching' changes so cleverly satirized, continued - high numbers of deaths, desperate movements in and out of the transit, many returning to the borders. Only in late October was an emergency airlift finally mounted. Ironically, settlements which had been established for more than a year, and were presumed more able to support themselves, actually suffered most. The ration in Mopoko, for example, was one delivery of rice on 5 September which allowed each settler one plastic mug of rice. A second delivery on 15 September included powdered milk and oil. Each person received one and a half cups of powdered milk and three people shared two five pound tins of edible fat. Mopoko had received no cereal or locally purchased cassava flour in August.

Rains were a further threat to spreading the poverty evenly. Roads to some settlements could not carry the 30-ton lorries delivering supplies from Juba. The office desperately tried to direct scarce resources to the most critical cases. For example, Juba was reminded by the Yei UNHCR office that it should '...take into consideration that [such inaccessible] places like Katagiri, Adio and Dororolili [have] hardly any local population so [it is] very difficult for refugees to try to survive because of no labour possibilities.' (5 September 1983).

Not only did the food shortages during the last half of 1983 slow the progress of refugees towards self-sufficiency and cause unnecessary suffering and death, but the dependence of refugees on obtaining local food through their labour inevitably meant that the reserves of cassava for the Sudanese in Yei River District were also dangerously depleted.

If the settlement programme continues to be the policy for refugees in Africa, it becomes most urgent that their insecurity should not be increased by such a bureaucratic hiatus. Reforms are unlikely to be made in the present climate where agencies, even at the United Nations level, fail to co-operate in the field. What they do share is the concern that their public images should not be tarnished. Early in 1983, the local WFP office had been warned of the food requirements during the rains and UNHCR had suggested that supplies should be transported and stored in Juba to anticipate the need. Once the extent of the emergency was recognized, an airlift should have been immediately mounted. Understandably, the office in Juba was reluctant to saddle UNHCR with this extra expense. Everyone kept hoping that any day the lorries carrying WFP food from Mombasa would arrive. The long-term effects on the programme will be very difficult to overcome.

Leaving aside the question of whether or not the food basket (when full) constitutes an adequate source of nutrition for people whose health has deteriorated during long periods on a sub-nutritional diet, who are expected to build their homes, dig latrines, and start farming, the persistent shortages have other far-reaching social consequences.

The southern Sudan authorities, having already suffered public censure for one incident of food diversion, were anxious to avoid further similar accusations. Refugees were warned not to sell rations and the police were vigilant. But it was impossible to prepare an acceptable meal without bartering or selling some items for those missing or never supplied. The result was that many refugees *and* Sudanese were arrested. Then, at the height of the food crisis, when double rations of certain items were supplied, refugees were *expected* to sell. Now police were asked to relax the rules. This double standard further eroded law and order in the district and the refugees never knew when they could expect to be arrested or when they would be allowed to sell without fear. Rules aside, refugees were forced to sell any item at hand to buy the next meal. Blankets, cooking pots, plastic buckets and basins, hoes, and pangas made their way into the local market at extremely low prices.

A more serious social problem created by the irregularity of the supply of rations was the refugees' belief that the Sudanese were to blame for diverting food. The threat of violence against Sudanese officials was particularly acute in 1983, because the shortages of food coincided with the hand-over of settlements to their administration. Most of the newly appointed settlement officers were afraid to stay at their posts. While UNHCR had sent letters to each settlement explaining the cause of the delays and reassuring refugees that they were not permanently cut off from food, and that the settlement officer was not to blame, this did little to assuage tempers. In September 1983, at Wudabi, Ugandans took up pangas against their Sudanese administrator and only the quick action of the project manager prevented the army from moving in.

The problem was not limited to Wudabi, it was widespread. A note from the Sudanese project manager is illustrative.

I had been to Katagiri ... with Yei and Wonduruba policemen to investigate... On our arrival ... we found all persons involved in the affair had gone to dig [work] for the natives for food. I advised the settlers to be peaceful and promised to send some 'relief supply from UNHCR field office, Yei' in a day or two. On departure from Katagiri, the elders ... advised me to take back with me the settlement officer and his assistant for their security and return with the promised food (6 September 1983.)

What other sources of food were there for refugees living in settlements? Yei River District is rich in wild foods and there is still some game. Local people rely heavily on such food. But, even if refugees were familiar with wild edible plants, access was limited by rights of ownership held by locals. For example, a termite mound, a source of protein-rich food, was located within the confines of Gumbari. The owner demanded £S200 compensation. All trees which produced edible fruit or which were used for beehives, even the grass used for roofing, was claimed by someone![31] Hunting was strictly under the authority of a hereditary chief. It is possible to negotiate permission to use these resources, but one may not assume the right without serious penalty. A woman at Gumbari had walked 12 kilometres to cut 19 bundles of roofing grass. When she returned to collect them after they dried, she found the Sudanese owner had burned all but nine simply to remind her who owned the grass.

Some refugees arrived with livestock and poultry and this resource allowed many of the self-settled refugees to support themselves while getting established. Often it was the total depletion of this resource which led families finally to resort to moving to an assisted settlement. Table 5.2 shows the overall average number of livestock and poultry owned by refugees in the settlements compared with the households of self-settled who were interviewed.

TABLE 5.2: Average number of livestock and poultry per household

Type of livestock	Assisted refugees %	Unassisted refugees %
Cattle	0.03	0.44
Sheep	0.04	0.32
Goats	0.14	0.91
Poultry	1.63	2.98
No. of households	2,017	3,814

But obviously ownership was not evenly distributed, the majority of households in both groups having no animals or poultry. Table 5.3 shows the numbers and percentages of households having none.

As these data show, as far as ownership of livestock and poultry was concerned, the unassisted refugees were marginally better off than were

[31] A very serious case arose when children at Tore settlement ate mangoes from a tree. A child disappeared and reappeared some two weeks later ostensibly having been 'found' wandering in a game park inside the Zaire border. Refugees were convinced the owner of the tree had murdered the child. When she reappeared, her father was detained because this accusation was made openly, and sued in the local court. Finally to keep the peace, UNHCR had to pay several hundred pounds compensation. These quarrels over rights to the use of natural resources were a measure of the resentment local people felt towards refugees. On the other hand some refugees were allowed to join the dry season communal hunt. When I returned in 1983 refugees were full of stories of the particular methods and rules of these hunts.

TABLE 5.3: Number of households having no livestock or poultry

Type of livestock	Assisted refugees		Unassisted refugees	
	%	Number of households	%	Number of households
Cattle	99.3	2,003	91.3	3,481
Sheep	98.6	1,989	88.7	3,382
Goats	95.0	1,916	76.4	2,912
Poultry	72.0	1,452	51.9	1,981

refugees in settlements. When refugees first began arriving in large numbers in 1982, local chickens were very cheap and many refugees in settlements purchased them. Of the 28 per cent who owned poultry at the time of the interview, 19.5 per cent had acquired them or had added to their stock through local purchase. Later, however, in response to this demand, prices rose and it was no longer possible for most refugees to make such investments.

Some refugees arriving in settlements before 1983 had had time to grow crops and those who had received seed should at least have been able to grow vegetables. But when asked how they had used their last year's crop of vegetables (either having sold some or consumed all), 72.7 per cent of the households stated that seeds had not arrived in time, or they had not planted a garden for some other reason, or that their crop had been affected by drought. More alarming was the fact that 42.7 per cent of households in settlements claimed, at the time of interview, either not to have had access to agricultural land, to have lost it when locals resumed ownership, or not to have ploughed the land allocated to them because their time was taken up with building their house.

While the amounts were not quantified, we learned that some refugees in settlements did receive food from their self-settled relatives, but the main source of food for the settlements, besides WFP rations, was that which could be earned through labouring for local farmers. On entering the Sudan, most Ugandans were dependent on such piecework, or *leja-leja*, the vernacular term. Payment is either in cash or in kind - usually a quantity of cassava. The failure of the assistance programme to supply settlements adequately with rations meant a continued reliance on *leja-leja*, and is probably the main factor which has delayed agricultural self-sufficiency. The following report by one settlement officer describes the problems faced by refugees in 1983.

There has been nothing [to eat] apart from young cassava leaves which are very bitter ... the natives around the settlement have nothing to bring for sale as far as food is concerned ... those who have plots of cassava play about with refugees [*sic*]. You find an energetic man digging for four days to get a *kalaya* [basket] full of fresh cassava. This is nothing for a family of seven. It would be better if the man *with the only hoe in the family works, in his own plot*, but hunger has forced him out ... Worse still, there are old people who cannot go for the 8-20 miles [distances between this settlement and the nearest Sudanese farmers] and they have no one to bring them food. Actually when I come across such people they talk of it being better to have been killed than to suffer in starvation.

This report was not describing the situation in a *new* settlement, it was about Kala, one of the first agricultural settlements established after 1979 and one which should have been self-supporting.

The self-settled refugees who were interviewed were asked what other sources of income they had besides their own farms: 36.6 per cent answered '*leja-leja*'. In settlements, informants were asked how many days 'last week' they worked for locals. A cumulative figure for the household was recorded. Altogether, 6,059 days were reported as having been spent doing *leja-leja* in the week preceding the interview. In 55.6 per cent of the households, members worked for locals one or more days 'last week', or an overall average of three days per household. Refugees who worked for locals were expected to bring their own tools - a hoe or panga. Informants were also asked how many working days were lost 'last week' through illness and an overall average of 1.1 days per household was reported. These data suggest the average household lost 4.1 days per week to food production, at least during the week preceding the interview. One might have hoped the situation would have improved by 1984, but at Roronyo settlement, the Oxford team found that 'half the population went two, three or four days per week, with 11 per cent doing six days of *leja-leja* per week.' They also found that 'Some people ... may go off for several weeks at a stretch to do *leja-leja* in places where wage rates are better.' Ken Wilson reports having carried out a 'census' on the road outside Roronyo. Between 5.15 and 5.45 a.m. he counted '45 women, 15 men (2 on bicycles), 3 children and 2 babies! Some carried hoes and other implements, several had sacks or other containers to bring back the wages of cassava.' He learned that 30 men had used this route on bicycles even before he had reached the census point.

Some outsiders saw *leja-leja* as exploitative of the refugees, but my findings suggest that in many cases Sudanese were giving refugees the opportunity to work when their labour was not required. (Perhaps local peasants are aware of the importance of maintaining dignity and self-respect, but some refugees *have been* reduced to begging.) The Oxford team also found that:

At times the refugee demand for *leja-leja* becomes greater than the Sudanese ability to absorb it. This was particularly marked at Katigiri which was surrounded by a small ... population of Pajulu speakers... At the time of our visit a drought and WFP delivery failures had left most of the population at Katigiri dependent on eating leaves without any starch porridge: people were absolutely desperate. To obtain work required a 15 to 20 mile walk each way to Chief Gordon Sasa's area. (Wilson *et al.* 1985).

As both my own and the Oxford team's research were carried out during the busiest agricultural season, the significance of such interruptions to any progress towards economic self-sufficiency can not be over-estimated.

It was possible in the settlements to observe what people were eating and to confirm their frightening dependence on WFP rations and cassava earned through *leja-leja*. Unassisted refugees were asked what they had eaten the day before the interview. Their answers are shown in Table 5.4 below.

TABLE 5.4 'What did your family eat yesterday?' (unassisted)

Food eaten	%	Number of households
A carbohydrate (cassava, sweet potatoes) with a green vegetable or green beans	43.3	1,653
A carbohydrate with beans or groundnuts	26.7	1,019
Dura only	16.4	625
Meal included meat and one or more of the above	3.6	136
Fruit only	0.2	6
Did not eat at all	5.6	213
No reply	4.2	162
Totals	100	3,814

These data suggest that on the whole, unassisted refugees have a more nutritious diet than those living in settlements. Although a relatively small number ate meat, 46.7 per cent had a meal which did contain at least some protein. Interviews of the self-settled did not begin until July 1983, and continued to the end of September. Groundnuts were in season for part of this time. Many self-settled refugees had dura from the previous year's harvest.

In late August 1984, the Oxford team conducted a nutritional survey at Panyume (Wilson *et al.* 1985.) With the help of the local chief, all families in a radius of about two kilometres were invited to bring their children for examination: 414 refugee and 155 Sudanese children were measured. While one cannot assume the representativeness of either the 1983 interviews of self-settled households or this survey in 1984, nevertheless, the results are quite worrying. In the 1984 survey, bias was further encouraged by the fact that people were informed of the purpose of the survey and it was not conducted in their homes but in the chief's compound. Of the under- fives, 15.2 per cent of the Ugandans and 7.7 per cent of the Sudanese children were suffering clinical levels of malnourishment. Among the older children (6-10 years) 4.2 per cent of the 144 refugees measured and 13.7 per cent of the Sudanese measured were also found to be malnourished. Given the small numbers brought for examination, it is likely that healthy Sudanese children were engaged in agricultural activity.

Environmental health

Perhaps one of the most serious symptoms of the 'dependency syndrome' among refugees in settlements was their neglect of environmental health. All the compounds of the self-settled refugees I visited had latrines and, as noted earlier, many had attempted to protect their water supply or to dig shallow wells. My observations have been confirmed by others, notably Dr Allison Umar, the Ugandan doctor who lived among the refugees for three years before joining the health service. He expressed shock at the behaviour of the settlers. Among the unassisted refugees, he said it is normal practice first to construct a temporary shelter for sleeping, then to dig at least a hole for the latrine. The next essential building is the kitchen to protect the fire and food from the elements. Why have the standards of Ugandans under the aid umbrella declined?

Soap, during the time I was in Yei River District, cost 0.500 piastres (half a day's labour). Very few refugees could afford to buy it. The only source of oil to make soap - the nut from a tree locally known as the *lulu* - was unavailable to refugees as all such permanent crops were owned by the locals. It is not surprising that in many settlements scabies reached epidemic proportions. During 1982, UNHCR irregularly supplied soap to a few settlements, but most never received even one shipment.

Scabies is an affliction which requires time-consuming management to cure. Sufferers (which include adults as well as children), must be washed with soap, each spot must be broken open, and the body coated with medicine. This routine must be repeated daily. If a clean change of clothing is not available, the victim will become reinfected. Refugees seldom had more than one change of clothing.[32]

Access to clean water was a general problem throughout the district. In Kopera Chiefdom, for example, the *only* sources of clean water were the

---

[32] In Limuru where scabies had reached epidemic proportions, the nurse (who did have a supply of medicine) complained that most mothers either did not bring their children for diagnosis, or did not follow through with the treatment. I appointed a small child as his block's 'scabies officer' and he organized a meeting of the surprised mothers and children. The nurse demonstrated treatment, but it is unlikely that many of the mothers continued it after I left, since no one had soap or sufficient changes of clothing for the children.

bore-wells in the settlements.[33] The number of bores which UNHCR aimed to provide was four per settlement. Most of the time one or more of the pumps were broken. Sometimes women had to queue all night to get water, and life in the queue was often marked by quarrels, even fights, which broke out under the strain of waiting. A large proportion of the refugees, like the Sudanese, were forced to use polluted sources.[34]

As has been noted, all the settlements established from 1982 were laid out in rows of plots and refugees were instructed to place their house at one end of a plot with the latrines of four adjacent plots to be located together. A compound was complete when it had a house, kitchen, bath shelter, latrine, drying table (to keep kitchen utensils from contamination), and a rubbish dump. Contracts were given out to build houses for some of the first settlements, but this proved unsatisfactory. In Limbe, for example, Ugandan builders refused to allow fellow refugees to move into empty houses until payment was received. In Kala, people complained that their houses had been improperly built by Sudanese, and that they had had to rebuild. So, in 1982, it was decided to pay 'incentives' to refugees for building their own compounds. The buildings were made of mud. The amount to be paid was not fixed. Some of the budget had to be used to buy and transport grass and poles. Locals were encouraged to collect these items so that they could earn some money by selling to UNHCR.

There were many problems. Grass is seasonal and not available everywhere. Bamboo for poles had to be transported long distances from where it grew. UNHCR had insufficient transport to divert from transporting people (in October 1982, there were only three lorries still functioning) to hauling building materials to new settlements. As noted, when refugees cut their own grass or logs they risked conflict with the locals. Ugandans were able to build satisfactory houses from local wood, but there were always shortages of axes and pangas.

Of course, the unassisted refugees were forced to build their own houses without assistance. The Catholic Centre, Yei, through the assistance of Sudanaid, an indigenous Catholic agency, and the Sudan Council of Churches, did distribute some hoes and pangas to unassisted refugees.[35] Many refugees explained how this very inexpensive aid had enabled their families to survive. But there was a persistent shortage of pangas and tools throughout the district. One of the most effective forms of aid might have

[33] In theory, all resources provided for refugees were to be available for the locals. In practice, even where Sudanese lived close enough to a settlement to use such facilities as the wells, sharing was not possible. UNHCR did not have the resources to dig and maintain enough wells for the settlers.

[34] UNHCR, recognizing the seriousness of the problem, did send an additional staff member to Yei in 1983 to take over responsibility for water, and OXFAM provided a team which specialized in protecting springs and digging shallow wells.

[35] One priest had records of the names of heads of households and numbers in each, for several remote areas. It was his fieldwork which first led me to question the 'official' statistics on numbers of self-settled refugees, put at 20,000.

been simply to flood the area with such tools - perhaps until one found the metal being used for other purposes, for example, as tent pegs were used to make knives.

Only 3.9 per cent of all households in settlements had a 'complete' compound as defined. Length of residence in a settlement bore very little relationship to the completion of all items. Among those arriving in a settlement in 1979, no household had a completed compound; in 1980, only 6.6 per cent; in 1981, 11.8 per cent; and in 1982, 6.4 per cent. Of course, as people often pointed out, these structures wear out. Many indicated their bath shelter, blown down by the wind, or a broken drying table resting on the rubbish dump. Comparing the different settlements, the highest percentage of households having a complete compound was Old Tore with 27.8 per cent; next came Goli with 18.1 per cent; Roronyo 11.1 per cent; Limbe and Pakula with 9.9 and 9.2 per cent respectively.

So, although a few people finished their compounds in record time, most did not. Faced with the apparent failure of the 'incentives', UNHCR changed its policy. Hoping to encourage more communal attitudes, refugees were told that instead of paying individuals, the community should choose some project from which all could benefit. One settlement proposed that a bicycle should be purchased for each block. Once in the settlement, the bicycles were immediately sold and the money divided between each of the 24 households. Another settlement, Tore, decided to use its communal money for establishing a consumer shop. The committee in charge of the funds was corrupt.

Roronyo people were so furious with the policy change that they refused their 'incentive' monies altogether, insisting they be returned to UNHCR, and demanded a receipt to prove the money had reached Geneva. Not only did the switch in policy produce anger and frustration, it created serious individual hardship. People not physically able to build for themselves, had employed others, promising to repay when the incentive money arrived. It never did, and often such debts were paid by the surrender of blankets, tools, or rations. For example, at Pakula Naima, I received the following note from Mrs Hajat Mariamu:

I have got one question about the houses we built. As I myself have no power to do this work of building. At first they said they will pay ... up to now they do not pay ... what can I do now? I put somebody to build for me, but the person is now disturbing me because of money. On that very day I told him, if they pay the huts, I will come to pay him. Now he is annoyed because the thing has stayed so long.

The other one [problem] is that I want to open the hotel [tea shop] but the things like saucepans, bowls, cups and dishes plus plates are not here. What can I do now? The one which is affecting me terribly is the one of the hut. Because that person wants to accuse me. Please could you assist me as soon as possible? (5 September 1983.)

While one *can* dig a latrine with a panga and a basin, it is more difficult than with a spade. Very few spades were available in settlements. The standards of sanitation, practised more rigorously among the self-settled, declined. Within each block of 24 households, one plot - number 13 - was reserved for communal activites, that is, meetings, distribution of food, and a play area for children. In most settlements it was left uncleared and used as a public toilet.

By the time of the interview, only 30.1 per cent of all households had their own latrine. However, the interviews included all those still waiting in transit camps. Lacking tools, realizing they would eventually move to a settlement, and not being offered payment for the work, refugees in transit camps were not motivated to dig latrines. Comparing the oldest settlements, there are significant differences. Of the households in Old Tore, 72.2 per cent had a latrine; 16.2 per cent in Mondikolo; 46.2 per cent in Mogiri; 34.4 per cent in Kala; and 54.3 per cent in Limbe. One might be tempted to believe the incentive system worked. More households in the first four settlements established in early 1982 had latrines: Goli 75 per cent; Limuru 72.5 per cent; Roronyo 63.0 per cent; and Mopoko 73.2 per cent. But in Otogo, which was opened only two months after Mopoko (July 1982), only 29.8 per cent of the households there had dug a latrine by the time of the interviews. It is likely that the major factor influencing the success of the efforts to encourage sanitation is the availability of spades.

Again in late 1983 one agency, ACROSS, decided to introduce 'incentives' for digging pit latrines. Settlers were promised a bar of soap per household once each of the 24 families in a block had completed theirs. Dr Umar pointed out the weaknesses of this approach. ACROSS had not involved the medical staff in their campaign which should have been combined with a health education programme; and, as no proper inspection was carried out, it was easy for refugees to dig a hole one metre deep, cover it with walls and a roof, and say their latrine was complete - just to get the bar of soap.

The list of items required for a compound to be judged complete did not include a grain store. I have already mentioned the serious health risk - not to mention wastage - posed by the infestation of rats. The easiest way to avoid the problem would have been to store food in rat-proof granaries. Only 1.8 per cent of all the households had built one. There were many reasons why granaries were not a priority. Tools, building materials, and time were in short supply. Monthly rations were too small to justify the effort. It is likely, however, that the insecurity associated with the irregular supply of food rations was also a factor which caused refugees to be reluctant to build a granary before they had enough harvest to last through a season. In Limuru for instance, during my tour of the fields with the agricultural adviser, he told me that the settlers would now blame him if food deliveries were further delayed. They believed that once I had seen how well their sweet potatoes were growing, I would advise UNHCR to cut off rations! A granary might also give the impression that refugees were self-sufficient.

Health is no doubt also affected by the inadequacy of cooking utensils and water containers. An assortment of plastic basins and buckets arrived in Yei for distribution in the settlements. Of very low quality, they broke easily in transit or when dropped. Not surprisingly, very few refugees had arrived with their own water containers. Whatever the size of household in the survey, it was judged to have an 'adequate' supply if there were at least two, that is, one for bathing and laundry, and one for carrying and storing drinking water. By even this minimal definition, only 32.4 per cent had an adequate number of containers. Most families were forced to use one container for all these purposes and there were many who had not been included in the distribution at all and who borrowed or relied on empty oil tins or other containers which could be scavenged.

TABLE 5.5 Number of cooking pots owned by households in settlements

Number of pots	Households %	Number of households
none	19.4	391
1	34.9	703
2	38.8	782
3	6.0	122
4	0.8	16
5	0.1	3
Total	100	2,017

People were asked if they boiled water before drinking. Awareness of the importance of this precaution was often expressed by the angry retort: 'How can you boil water if you have only one pot to cook in?' Table 5.5 shows the number of cooking pots owned by households, including those brought with them and those distributed in the aid 'package'. Again, those households having none were using empty oil tins.

Ugandans are extremely resourceful and many know well how to make clay pots. In the course of the research, many such skilled women were identified, but the right kind of clay was not available everywhere, and there was no incentive to make more than one needed for one's own household.[36]

Food is the best medicine

The information presented here shows how complex health issues are. It also shows how a bad situation was certainly not improved by inter-agency fighting and administrative inadequacy. Because the issues are so complex

[36] An obvious income-generating activity would have been for UNHCR to purchase cooking and water pots and distribute them in those settlements where clay could not be found.

and because of the variation in needs, it must surely be evident that any aid programme must begin by looking at the world from the bottom up, by learning how to *see* how the recipients of aid perceive their opportunities, responsibilities, and constraints. Any programme which consistently ignores these factors is doomed at the outset.

Most of the failures of the health programme may be attributed to the unwillingness of the rich countries of the world to respond adequately to the crisis of mass exodus. The main source of food for refugees is from the World Food Programme, part of the UN Food and Agricultural Organization. UNHCR must negotiate with WFP to supply food for each emergency influx of refugees. Food for emergency relief is only a small part of the work of WFP; it is mainly concerned to provide food for development projects.

It is very easy to criticize WFP for its failures to supply appropriate food on time and in sufficient quantities, and for its bureaucratic problems which led to the failures to deliver food during the periods of greatest shortage. But it is not possible to justify a system of determining when rations should be cut off which is based on the number of planting seasons which have passed, and which does not take account of ecological differences in an area; or whether refugees have land, or tools, or seed; or whether, should all these be available and the rains have not failed, they are well enough to plant their fields. Some would argue the problems are more profound than these failures imply, that they cannot be simply corrected by changing practices, or replacing inefficient fieldworkers with those who are more professional.[37] But surely this would not make things worse.

Health workers may not be immediately reprehensible for the absence of drugs or the lack of adequate referral services. No doubt most humanitarians believe that it is better to do what they can under the circumstances than to refuse to make the compromises necessary to remain. Given the economic climate of industrialized countries and their high unemployment rates, it is likely that fewer rather than more people will be willing to act in ways which challenge the status quo. The grave danger of making such compromises, however, lies in the way in which it may lead individuals to develop beliefs about Africa in order to rationalize the inadequacies.

---

[37] That may be true, but the argument is like that of some in Britain who refuse to vote. As there is no difference between the two major parties, they will await the 'revolution' before trying to improve their society.

6
'Putting the last first'

Introduction

In the absence of community organizations among refugees which are empowered to identify and look after those most in need, agencies have relied on conventional definitions of the vulnerable, that is, the physically handicapped, the elderly, widows, and orphans. Statistical studies, just like programmes designed for 'the masses', cannot identify all those individuals and classes of people who are in serious need of special assistance. The best that this survey can do is to present data which demonstrates to policy-makers and refugee communities the extent and range of unmet needs. In addition, many case studies were collected.[2]

One of the underlying assumptions of refugee policy for Africa is that the basic unit of production is the normally constituted peasant family. (e.g. Land 1981.) At the same time, there is an appreciation among policy-makers that in the process of mass migration under conditions of extreme coercion, family structure has been adversely affected. The statement that the majority of refugees are women and children has become almost a cliché. Statistically this is true of nearly all populations, and the special significance of this fact for refugees is insufficiently understood.

Given the emphasis on pushing refugees towards economic independence, it is essential to discover just how refugee communities re-constitute themselves and what economic strategies they are capable of employing to survive without relief aid. The essential disabilities suffered by refugees could be grouped under three categories:

a. Their powerlessness *vis-à-vis* an alien social and economic environment which involves many factors which are beyond the powers of the assistance programme to alter;[3]
b. The physical and psychological toll on individuals which has immediate and long-term consequences for the capacity of the society to re-establish viable production units; and
c. The loss of assets, perhaps the most important characteristic of all refugees.

---

[1] I borrowed this title from Chambers (1983) who also borrowed it!

[2] In 1984 the Oxford team followed up on the survey and collected further in depth material. This discussion relies heavily on their work, especially on that of Alex de Waal, Alula Pankhurst, and Ken Wilson.

[3] That refugees in Africa may also need such basics as training in language or information concerning soil conditions, rainfall patterns, or crop suitability has been overlooked.

To be effective, an assistance programme must not only take account of how best to indemnify the victims for such loss of control over their lives, it must also be flexible enough to take account of the almost infinite variation in personal resources which individuals bring to their experience in exile. Policies which ignore individual differences, and which aim to give equal treatment to all, actually increase economic disparities, to the detriment of the most vulnerable.

The argument that assistance should be targeted to the poorest is unlikely to be controversial. The major question is: how can aid be differentially distributed to make sure that those most in need are given priority? However, not all refugees arrive in their country of asylum without assets. Wherever possible, refugees used the capital investments they brought with them to maintain their independence.

The lack of support in maintaining the assets with which they arrived has meant that from the beginning refugees were started on a downward economic spiral until many were finally forced to accept relief. Scattered throughout the district one may see tractors, generators, grinding machines, lorries and other vehicles which are not functioning for the want of a battery, tyres, or some other spare part. Even modest loans would have enabled some of these 'rich' refugees to maintain economic independence, not to mention the contribution to the local economy where such equipment is in short supply.

Assistance programmes are aimed at 'bringing the refugees to the level of the nationals'. It might be time to question what is meant by 'the level of the nationals'. In practice, it means bringing refugees to the level of the poorest in the society of the host. Humanitarians are extremely sensitive to the possibility of being criticized by the host government for creating islands of relative privilege in the sea of poverty which is characteristic of areas in which most refugees are found in Africa. Refugee communities in southern Sudan include a wide array of expensively educated, experienced skilled workers and professionals. Yet all who accept aid are expected to make their living through agriculture. The failure of policy to support entrepreneurial activity among refugees is a great loss to the economy of the host. While it has been well-established that economists' dream that the benefits from creating pockets of wealth would finally 'trickle down' to the poorest in society is an illusion, case studies of Ugandan households suggest that at least some of the refugees who have attained relative economic stability are supporting very large numbers of people. (Wilson *et al*. 1985.) Perhaps the perils of life in exile can also have the positive effect of increasing social responsibility as well as undermining it.[4]

[4] Mustafa Idrissi, the ex-vice president under Amin, who came to the Sudan with five Mercedes Benz cars, was supporting 30 people in his house near Yei. By 1983, however, poverty had forced him to send some of his dependents to a settlement. I visited the home of an Eritrean who had established a number of successful enterprises in Khartoum. There were, by count, 50 people living in his small compound in a very poor part of the city.

Defining and identifying the vulnerable

As the programme aimed to help refugees become economically self-sufficient in the shortest possible time through agricultural production, a first measure of vulnerability is the capacity of households to undertake farming as their means of livelihood. 'How many individuals know how to cultivate land?' might have been a first question. As noted earlier, although 80.1 per cent of the assisted refugees came from rural areas, only 20.1 per cent had previously earned their living through agriculture; among the unassisted refugees, 57.7 per cent said that in Uganda they had been cultivators or herdsmen.

On the face of it, agriculture as a means of livelihood was inappropriate for the majority of those in settlements and for slightly under half of the self-settled. This, in turn, may partly explain the failure of the settlements to achieve self-sufficiency and the greater agricultural productivity of the self-settled areas. It may also explain why so few hand tools remain in the settlements: over half the households (excluding the population of the three transit camps where tools were normally not issued) had only one hoe, 6 per cent had no hoe, and 15.3 per cent no panga. There is as yet no data to measure the extent to which lack of experience or interest in farming has affected production. But one might conclude that the imposition of such an inappropriate programme rendered the majority of refugees vulnerable.

There are other factors, however, which make the situation slightly less grim than these facts suggest. There is a strong tradition of food self-sufficiency in Uganda, and agriculture is included in the curricula of some secondary schools. Whatever the occupation of a father, a family having access to land will cultivate some of its own food. Children from around 10 years old are expected to do some cultivating when they are not occupied with school work.

Traditional practices, combined with economic changes since colonialism, have conspired to place most of the responsibility for food production on women. Among most West Nilers, with the exception perhaps of the Madi, those men who do farm concentrate most on producing cash crops such as tobacco and cotton. As noted, in some West Nile communities, the men are traders, others are employed as labourers, and many make their living through fishing. Many others joined the army. As women are the major producers of food crops, their greater numbers among the self-settled may also contribute to the apparently greater productivity of this community of refugees. Certainly one can conclude that the presence of more men in the settlements does not guarantee more agricultural production. Men are likely to prefer to concentrate their energies on other economic activities.[5]

---

[5] But opportunities are limited. The frustration this causes may partly account for why many men indulge in excessive drinking. Women often complained that their men will sell anything and everything, even the food rations, to purchase (locally-brewed) alcohol. Admittedly, women also drank, and one cannot be absolutely sure their drinking did not also lead them to sell essential items. However no man ever complained to me that women were guilty of such behaviour.

Formerly in Uganda the earnings of men and women were largely kept separate, each spouse having distinct financial obligations to the household. Women *controlled* the food they had produced, which was stored in their own granaries. In settlements, rations are issued to the head of the household and at least some men take these as their own personal expendable income, permitting the family to rely on what women can earn through piecework for locals, or *leja-leja*, to the great detriment of the family as a whole.

Formerly the West Nile was fairly self-sufficient in food production, with crops from different areas (and fish) circulating through trade from one part of the region to another. In the late 1970s people began selling produce to cities as far away as Kampala. In addition to cash crops such as coffee, tobacco, and cotton, some civil servants and others (forced to leave their jobs because of insecurity), returned to their rural homes and took up commercial farming. A few began to rear large herds of cattle.[6]

In fairness to men now living in settlements, it should be noted that one never heard a Ugandan, whatever his previous occupation, indicate that he was unwilling to *try* to grow his own food. About the strongest complaint I received was a note from one refugee, formerly a flight instructor, who first survived as a self-settled refugee with his wife and two children, and later moved to Otogo settlement.

... Madam I would be very grateful if you could try to find me some way to take up my career again in a civilian air industry. It is difficult for someone of my background to adjust himself to being a peasant farmer, although I have been seriously working to become self-sufficient in food production. I should point out that I am not alone. Many of my colleagues are also here in the Sudan wasting the investment made in their careers.

To name only a few, these careers included engineers, radar operators, a flight engineer, foresters, accountants (even an auditor for the former East African Community), railway engineers, expertise from all levels of the tobacco industry from growers to leaf managers, in addition to teachers, medical workers, and businessmen.

The data from the oldest settlements, together with observations, suggest that those who find the opportunity to escape the settlements do so - and at the earliest opportunity. As these are usually the able-bodied, their departure leaves behind those who are the more vulnerable and decreases the chances of the settlements becoming viable agricultural economies. The tendency, so often observed, of putting personal survival before social responsibility, means that any gainful employment is unlikely to benefit those who are left behind. The very presence of an assistance programme probably salves the consciences of those who desert their relatives in settlements.

Although no attempt was made to collect systematic data on the extent to which refugees employed outside settlements share earnings with settled

[6] One of these, Amin's ex-minister of finance, Moses Ali, retired to his home village to rear a large herd of cattle when he was dismissed from office. According to him, he had financed this venture from bank loans. In 1979 he was able to move all these cattle to Sudan by lorry. Although he moved to Pakistan, the herd has been used to support relatives he left behind.

relatives, I *heard* of only one case where this occurred. An elderly Nubi widow, living in Limbe, had a son who was a driver. As he plied the Juba/Yei road, it was convenient for him to stop en route to give his mother money from time to time. With the best of intentions, others would have had difficulty in getting transport to see relatives, as many of the settlements are so remote.

Another empirical basis for assessing the capacity of a family to make its living through agriculture is to count the numbers potentially able to cultivate, that is the people old enough and physically strong enough. The average size of households in settlements was 5.29; the overall average number per household who were able to cultivate was 2.75. The shortage of labour to farm interferes with education; 13.9 per cent of those giving reasons for children not attending school, said that it was because they were needed either to till the soil or to care for younger children while the mother went to the field. It is likely that the actual number is much higher. Parents were embarrassed to admit their children were not enrolled in school, and teachers reported that absenteeism, a constant problem, was always much higher when food supplies had run out in the settlements. This suggests that children are also involved in *leja-leja* or looking after the household in the absence of adults.

As noted, households range in size from one person to a family which had 26 members living on one plot. The smaller households (from one to three) had the highest percentages able to cultivate. Once the size of the family had reached six, the number of those able to cultivate dropped to an average of 50 per cent. Households having between seven and twelve members did not include any greater percentages of cultivators and in those households with thirteen and fourteen persons, the average dropped to 44 and 30 per cent. These data contradict the usual assumption that the larger the household, the more viable it is as a productive unit. In fact, once a household is larger than three persons, it was found that the ratio of people dependent on others to support them increased.

The vulnerability of all refugees in settlements is most starkly demonstrated by the lack of land upon which to farm. While the programme aimed to give each Ugandan household 10 acres of land for farming and this amount was expected to support five persons (Land 1981), the survey found - excluding the transit camps where land was not allocated - that *21 per cent of the population in settlements had no land*. Taking only the 78.5 per cent which had land, the average amount per household was 1.1 acre; only 0.2 per cent had as much as 5 acres; 80.2 per cent of the male-headed households and 85.7 per cent of those headed by women had 1 acre or less; 5.8 per cent of the male-headed and 2.9 per cent of the women-headed households had between 2 and 3 acres.

Table III.4 (Appendix III), shows the percentages of households having no land by settlement. One would have expected that these landless households would have been found in the newest settlements where there had been no time to allocate land, but in Kala settlement, 11.8 per cent had no land. In Limbe, another of the (older) settlements, 21 per cent could not farm for this reason, and by 1984, the Oxford team found that 37 per cent of the households in Limbe said they were not farming! (Wilson *et al.* 1985.)

The situation for the self-settled refugees was quite different. Data from 3,648 households shows that only 7.1 per cent had no land, 46.7 per cent had up to 1 acre, 43.6 per cent had between 1 and 5 acres, and the others all had more, ranging up to 7 of the households which had more than 15 acres under cultivation. One self-settled refugee family, not included in the interviews, had already cleared and cultivated 22 acres of forest. Another, Nasuru Okuti, reputedly a millionaire in Uganda, living near Morobo, is said to have a much larger farm. When these self-settled refugees were asked what was their main problem, only 4 per cent mentioned land, but 15 per cent cited the lack of tools and 0.19 per cent said that obtaining seeds was their main problem.

There was more than one way for assisted refugees to acquire land. In settlements the agricultural advisers were responsible for surveying and dividing the area which the local community, in theory, had agreed to hand over to the refugees. Earlier I alluded to the varying response of local communities to being asked to follow the central government's agreement to make such land available. The conflicts which arose were almost always settled to the disadvantage of the refugee. Often refugees cleared a piece of land and harvested a crop, only to be told that the owner was resuming control. Settlement land was often located too far from the settlement to permit women both to cultivate and to supervise the daily running of the household. Wild animals were a constant threat in many areas if crops were unsupervised. This is why, when rabies struck at Kala, it was so difficult to persuade the refugees to kill all dogs. Baboons were a particular problem in many settlements, and in Wunduruba, even wild buffalo roamed.[7] Some settlements were actually located within a game reserve and in other cases when the UNHCR office was surprised at the generosity of some chiefs in allocating sufficient land, it was discovered that it was infested by tsetse fly.

Many refugees in settlements, like the unassisted, acquired farm land through personal negotiation for each piece. The negotiation process and its political implications will be discussed later in this book, but suffice it to say here, from the point of view of those refugees with no assets, the process was extremely expensive. It often required the exchange of food rations or other material assistance. For example, one refugee in Mopoko gave his hoe for the use of one acre. By selling a bed he brought from Uganda, he paid others to

---

[7] In 1982 when Goli was first opened one young man escaped from an attack by a buffalo which then calved beneath the tree he climbed. He was stranded there - according to the reports - for three days.

dig for him, and used the rest of his money to start trading in cigarettes, salt, paraffin, and sugar.

Of the women-headed households who had land, 84.5 per cent had obtained theirs through allocations made by the settlement's agriculture adviser, 10.2 per cent through personal negotiations with locals, and 5.3 per cent had used both methods to acquire the land they were using. More of the men who were heads of households negotiated directly with locals for the land they used: 10.6 per cent reported they were only using land acquired in this way; 81 per cent got their land through the agriculture advisor; and 8.4 per cent used both methods to acquire land.

All self-settled refugees relied on personal negotiations to acquire land. They, too, reported the problem of some locals reclaiming lands after one harvest. However, as each piece had been individually agreed upon, there was less likelihood that a local could later use the argument that the refugee was farming on his ancestor's burial place. Moreover, in some cases at least, refugees could appeal to a local chief against a blatantly unfair local farmer. It may be, of course, that those least successful at personal negotiations with locals had already moved to settlements.

No one to cultivate

But a more serious problem is households having no one able to cultivate: 3.4 per cent were found to be in this situation. The size of these varied from 7 one-person households to one which had 14 members. Altogether these households represented 299 individuals. Assuming a representative sample, this means that there are nearly 3,000 people who live in family units where no one is able to cultivate at all. These households appear in our sample scattered over twenty different settlements. In 41.2 per cent of the cases, both spouses were present; women were heads of 30.9 per cent (over half of these, or 71 per cent, were widows); and the remaining households were headed by men with 11.8 per cent being under 21 years of age and 16.2 per cent adult men.

At the time of the interview 15 per cent of the members of the households where no one could cultivate were suffering from an acute illness. When asked why they had come to the settlement, 54.4 per cent cited illness, malnutrition, or 'death' as the reason; 23.5 per cent said they had been harrassed or pushed; and others came because they had no one to help them, their money had run out, or, as in 2.9 per cent of the cases, they had heard the settlements were 'better'.

The situation of these households supports the general observation that refugees used the settlements as places to send some of the most vulnerable. Although 58.8 per cent reported having relatives living outside settlements and 79.4 per cent had relatives in other settlements, the distances and lack of transport mitigate against their receiving help from them. The largest concentrations of the extremely vulnerable households were in Koya (14) and Otogo transit camps (6) and these were soon to be moved to settlements far beyond the reach of their relatives who were at the border or in other settlements. Four families who could not cultivate had already arrived at a newly-opened settlement - Morsak. At least in newer settlements people were still entitled to receive full rations: but two of the older settlements - Kala and Limbe - which WFP had already deemed to be self-sufficient, each had 4 such families, and the others were all in settlements where the rations had already been officially reduced. As these numbers appeared in the 10 per cent sample, the total numbers might even be greater. Agencies had no method of identifying families unable to cultivate, and even had they been able to, there was no programme for regularly supplying them with food.

The physically handicapped

As noted above, the more standard way of assessing the extent of vulnerability and of identifying those who qualify for special assistance is to count the numbers of orphans, lepers, and otherwise physically handicapped. Our survey did this. Based on the 10 per cent sample, 5,320 were physically handicapped or suffering from long-term (probably terminal) illness at the time of the interview, and 31.2 per cent of the households included one or more such persons. In 5.8 per cent of the households, one or more members of the family had leprosy; at least 1.3 per cent of the population had this disease. The same percentage of the population were crippled - 1.3 and 6.5 per cent of the households included at least one crippled person. Deafness affected 0.52 per cent of the population, with about half of these also unable to speak. And, according to the sample, there were 340 blind persons, or 0.32 per cent of the population.

Information collected from unassisted refugee households was less detailed. At the time of the interview, an average of 0.39 persons per household were judged to be ill or physically disabled. But these were found in 1,027 of the 3,814 households, in other words, just under one-third of the unassisted refugees had one or more members who were ill or disabled. Among those affected, the average number was 1.4 persons per household.

Orphans

Gathering an accurate count of the number of orphans is complicated. In most African societies a child is regarded as an orphan if *either* parent dies. However, we defined an orphan as being a child of 15 years or younger, *both* of whose parents were dead. According to the responses given in the interviews (and considerable effort was made to emphasize our definition of an orphan), 10.9 per cent of the population in settlements are orphans, or 19.1

per cent of all children 15 years and under. Presuming the responses are accurate, there are 11,630 orphans living in settlements.

To check further on the validity of these findings, the relationship of all children in this age group to the head of the household in which they were living was also analysed. It was found that only 60.7 per cent of the girls and 54.6 per cent of the boys 15 years and younger were living in households where the head of the family was either their mother or father. Even if all those chidren described as orphans had a parent living elsewhere, these data give yet a further indication of the extent to which families in settlements represent only segments of 'normal' families; they also indicate the great vulnerability of settlement populations.

In 1984 Alula Pankhurst (1985) undertook a study of orphans in Gumbari settlement. He interviewed 135 children under the age of 16 who had lost one or both parents. They lived in 53 households; about one-third had lost both parents. The parents of 41 per cent of these orphans had been killed since 1979; 9 children did not know what had happened to their parents as they had fled with other relatives; and 20 per cent of them had lost a parent in the Sudan after crossing the border. The main cause of these deaths was illness coupled with malnutrition as a result of inadequate diets during flight and after arrival. Other parents had been shot while returning to Uganda for food or being forcibly returned from Zaire, some had died in accidents while escaping, and one father was drowned by soldiers. One mother had died giving birth and another at a feeding centre. Nine other parents had died since arriving in Gumbari. According to Pankhurst (1985):

...the extended family network system seems to function efficiently in caring for orphans ... Over 90 per cent of the children in the sample had relatives in Gumbari itself, 70 per cent had relatives in the border areas and 67 per cent had relatives in other settlements.

In the few cases where there were no close relatives around, friends or neighbours brought up the orphans. In a couple of cases, salaried members of the settlement, such as the driver and the settlement chairman, were looking after several orphans. Only a handful of orphans lived alone. In these cases there was usually an older sibling who assumed the parental role.

It was often the death of a parent which triggered the movement to the settlement and this is why a number of orphans had come to Gumbari. Children are sent to settlements because of the availability of health care, education, and, according to Pankhurst's informants, especially because of food. When, as happened during the time of his interviews, there was no food in the settlement, some of the orphans normally resident there had been sent to live with relatives at the border. As he puts it, 'Population flows between settlement and border zones can be seen to respond to changes in the survival conditions. This could have considerable implications in terms of the decision to phase out relief.' (ibid.)

The Oxford team's nutritional survey revealed that about one-quarter of the malnourished were orphans.

In these cases we were not recording discrimination against orphans in healthy families but cases where the orphan was actually being looked after by someone who was already somewhat vulnerable. For example, in Roronyo there is a 3-year-old girl whose parents both died on the border. The girl's sister (now her guardian), who lives on her own with 6 other children (all of whom were underweight and one nearly clinically malnourished), rescued this little girl from a period of extreme starvation....The woman is suffering from a severe eye infection and is generally in a poor condition. As she put it, 'When the children cry from hunger all I can do is cry myself.' (Wilson in Wilson *et al.* 1985)

Without a more extensive study (such as differences in school attendance) which compared these children with those who have not been orphaned, it is not possible to know if they were in any way discriminated against within the household, but Pankhurst (1985) found many had 'devised resourceful ways to help their foster family.' These included trading either in agricultural produce or cigarettes, making and selling charcoal, making ropes, knives, hoe handles, skull caps, knitting, and mat-making in addition to helping in the house, on the farm, and doing *leja-leja* alongside the other members of the family.

The elderly

Given the degree to which family responsibility has been abandoned, life was also hazardous for the elderly in settlements. If one defines the elderly as those who were 45 years and older, there were 244 men and 276 women in this age group living in settlements. Given the important role which old people assume in family life in Uganda, it is not surprising to find it is difficult for them to adjust to the enormous social dislocation associated with life in exile.

Not only do the elderly have to adjust to normal processes of aging in an alien social environment, they have, for the most part, been stripped of the status associated with old age. Some do serve on the settlement dispute committees, but the other leaders are elected and refugee communities have not, for the most part, opted to reinstate traditional figures of authority. The idea of being buried away from their homeland has an even more profound significance and at least some of the elderly have opted to repatriate (even when their families have refused) in order to make sure they die in Uganda.

Many refugees reported that their elderly parents had refused to flee; others had got as far as inside the Sudan border and refused to move to a settlement, even when the rest of the family believed they had no option if they were to survive. Pankhurst (1985) interviewed an old and disabled man who had no relatives in the Sudan. He was totally dependent on WFP rations and would be reduced to begging when they were phased out. This was not unusual. Another, 'whose daughter died during their flight, virtually lost his

sight and speech overnight. He resented living surrounded by strangers ...
and refused to venture outside his hut despite his grandchildren's pleas.'
(ibid.)

Assisting the vulnerable

When UNHCR awarded the contract to SCC to implement a programme of
aid for the vulnerable, the budget for staff was based on the assumption that
only 10 per cent of the population would require special assistance. SCC had
already begun to distribute some material aid to lepers, cripples, orphans,
and the elderly and in some settlements they paid social workers; in others
there were volunteers. These workers were asked to identify the vulnerable
and to distribute such aid as used clothing or bars of soap. Deciding which
individuals require special assistance is difficult and unsatisfactory. First of
all, there is the matter of limited resources. When in one settlement the social
worker drew up a list of nearly 100 orphans, he was told that he must be 'more
strict' - SCC did not have the resources to help that *many* orphans. On what
basis was the social worker to decide which orphan was more in need than
another? Giving assistance to one member of a family introduces other
problems when all are as poor as the individual officially defined as
vulnerable. Sometimes the heads of such households understandably insisted
that the extra assistance be shared equally among all. Moreover, a cripple or
someone with leprosy living in a household where there were enough people
able to cultivate was less likely to go hungry than those members of a family
where no one could cultivate, or where the head of the family alone was
responsible for a number of young children. Certainly the physically
handicapped needed a special programme of assistance, but their long-term
problems would not be solved by the irregular distribution of bars of soap,
used clothing, or food.

Income-generating activities introduced into settlements largely excluded
the vulnerable. The policy of the agency responsible for implementing the
budget for such activities was only to support co-operatives. Settlers were
urged to include the handicapped in their co-operatives, but funds were
usually appropriated by the strong. In the survey, informants who were
physically handicapped were asked in what ways they might be able to earn a
living on the basis of previous experience or training in Uganda. A few had
skills which could have produced an income: these included handicrafts,
tailoring, cobbling, beer-brewing, petty trade, and carpentry.

Should assistance programmes for African refugees mount special
schemes for assisting the physically handicapped and orphans? In Gumbari
settlement, the handicapped started a tea shop and earned enough profit to
allow them to give free cups of tea to other vulnerable members of the
community. On the other hand, elsewhere, the Oxford team found a social
worker who was reluctant to encourage such activities, who repeated such

stereotypes about the handicapped as that they are 'dirty' and incompetent.

In many African societies such people are ostracized or, as in the case of orphans living with unrelated families, exploited. (One's position in society is always bound up with the presence of relatives who protect each other's interests, which is why family disruption is so serious.) Under normal circumstances, the mentally ill and physically handicapped will be fed by members of a community, but as they are unfit to contribute to the family economy, it would not be surprising if, under conditions of exile, this responsibility were neglected. During our interviews, no information was collected concerning traditional beliefs about the handicapped, but Orley (1970) found that, among the Baganda, leprosy and epilepsy were considered contagious. Mogiri was established for the first few leprosy sufferers that arrived. Later, however, most were sent to other settlements and there were many complaints that they were not given proper treatment by the medical staff, who either were not trained to deal with the disease or shunned such patients.

In 1983, it appeared that funds might become available for building a vocational school. Discussions were held with Ugandans, Sudanese, and agency officials to consider what were the appropriate subjects to be taught. Given the limited opportunity for employment in the district, would it not have been wise to use the limited funds for training the physically handicapped and to include Sudanese in such a programme from the outset?

Had funds been available for individuals, certain of the handicapped could have been helped to earn a living simply by providing the tools of their trade. In Otogo settlement, for example, I bought stools from a carpenter who was a polio victim. When war struck his area in Uganda, he had insisted his wife flee with the children, leaving him to face the soldiers in his own compound. But, as he said (with a smile) when the sound of gunfire came nearer, he decided he would prefer to be shot while escaping. He crawled the forty miles to the Sudan. Only once did he meet another human being, a woman who gave him some cassava. In Otogo, with only a panga, a hammer, and a saw, this man managed to make boards from logs he cut himself. With his wife's help, he had built their house and dug a latrine. Given his talent and energy, even a few more tools might have allowed him to support his family as he had done in Uganda.

Another man in Limbe, an amputee, was head of a family of 6 children; the eldest child was 15 and mentally retarded, the youngest was 2 months. Before the sudden death of his wife in mid-July 1982, she had supported the family through farming and *leja-leja*. It was said that she had simply worked herself to death. For some unexplained reason, associated (so the social worker vaguely claimed) with 'traditional beliefs', people in Limbe were unwilling to give this family any assistance. The man had been trained as a tailor and he asked me to buy a sewing machine so that he could support his household. ACROSS was the agency responsible for implementing the income generation programme, but it was against their policy to support individual projects. It was not until a year later that the UNHCR programme officer finally found money to buy a machine for him. The Oxford team found that he had stopped tailoring by 1985. He had been given some cloth and had sold the garments he made. He was unable to save enough to purchase more cloth. His main occupation in Uganda was as a blacksmith and in Limbe he had borrowed tools from a local Sudanese. The team actually purchased some of his products (arrows). But he was not interested in pursuing this occupation, pointing out how seasonal were the demands for his products. He wanted to return to tailoring.

Agricultural production and the more vulnerable

Observations in 1982 led us to the conclusion that the present methods of defining and assisting the vulnerable were inadequate. My team and I therefore decided that, in addition to counting the numbers classically defined as vulnerable, the survey would record those who were *most* vulnerable in relation to the demands of the assistance programme. We had observed that many people in settlements were unlikely *ever* to be able to grow enough food to support themselves.

Interviewers counted those people whose family circumstances and physical condition suggested that they would never be able to support themselves through farming and had no one else to help them. Each evening these cases were discussed and the interviewers were asked to explain both their subjective assessments and their objective criteria.

Two examples will help to clarify our method. For example, a half-Asian orphan who lived with an unrelated family was classified as vulnerable. The head of his household rejected the boy, beat him regularly, and refused him food. He had to beg from other households. On the other hand, when the head of a household was an aged widow, living with one or more young, healthy and apparently responsible sons, neither she nor her family were classified as vulnerable. Using this method of defining vulnerability, we concluded that 21.3 per cent of the settlement population would never be able to support themselves through agriculture. In other words, a total of 22,700 people are at serious risk and become more so as food rations are reduced, in line with UNHCR policy, and finally stopped altogether.

To further check on the validity of the criteria used to define the vulnerable, those cases where the household size equalled the number assessed as vulnerable were separately analysed. There were a total of 289 such families in this sub-sample, representing 14.3 per cent of all households. They account for 1,071 individuals, or 10 per cent of the total population of settlements. The analysis suggests my interviewers were remarkably objective in assessing vulnerability in these terms and lends credence to our conclusion that more than 20 per cent of the refugee population in settlements were totally dependent on aid.

TABLE 6.1: Type of family head of vulnerable households compared
with all households (assisted)

Type of family head	Vulnerable households		All households	
	%	No.	%	No.
Normal family, both spouses present	8.0	23	53.1	1,071
Male under 21 years	29.4	85	12.5	253
Female under 21 years	5.9	17	2.5	50
Adult female	20.0	58	9.0	181
Adult male	9.7	28	14.3	289
Widow (post-1979)	15.6	45	5.3	106
Widow (pre-1979)	11.4	33	3.3	67
TOTALS:	100.0	289	100.0	2,017

Table 6.1 shows the composition of these households according to the type
of family head and compares them with the overall distribution of family
heads. In only 8 per cent of the cases were both spouses present; 53 per cent of
families were headed by women; and in 35.3 per cent of cases the head of the
family, whether male or female, was under 21 years of age.

Compared with the population as a whole, the households which
interviewers assessed as totally vulnerable suffered a greater number of other
disadvantages. Against an overall average household size of 5.29, they had an
average of 3.71 persons per household. They ranged in size from 1 person to
16, but 47.4 per cent had more than 3 members. As demonstrated earlier, in a
family of more than 3 members, the overall ratio of those able to cultivate
begins to drop, making the larger households among this group also more
vulnerable: 10 per cent had no one able to cultivate.

The 289 families, where all members were identified as vulnerable,
suffered greater disabilities as compared with the overall average of assisted
refugees. They had fewer than average relatives in other settlements or in the
unassisted areas, and thus few people to call on for help. The distribution of
ages of this population also differed radically from that of the overall
population. (Figure 3:1 shows the overall age distribution.) Comparing these
289 families with the total population, there were 4.6 per cent more women,
and twice as many women over 45 years of age. There were more children
between 5 and 14 years and fewer under 5. The population as a whole had 4
times as many men between 20 and 44 years than did these 289 households.
There were more than twice the number of physically handicapped. And

there were 157 orphans and 120 individuals who were ill at the time of the interview. (This was slightly more than average for the whole population.)

A greater number (60 per cent compared with 55.1 per cent) had had no previous employment in Uganda, but had been dependents. When asked about their hopes of returning to Uganda, more than twice as many responded, 'All our relatives have been killed.' We found those who responded to the question in this way were also the ones who expressed the greatest sense of despair and hopelessness concerning the future. Such people often expressed their total resignation to the conditions in which they found themselves, and most of them believed that they would never be able, or live to see the day, when they could leave the Sudan.

We took a lot of trouble to find ways of defining and identifying such vulnerable households. Another of our methods for determining vulnerability was to draw up a list of 34 factors which - singly or together - would be likely to prevent people from being able to support themselves through farming. The factors included lack of tools or land, no other relatives in the Sudan, debts, a physically handicapped or ill person living in the household, etc. Since it was not possible to weigh the importance of each variable in determining vulnerability, the presence of each characteristic was given a score of 1. Using this method, all households proved to be to some extent vulnerable. Those having the highest score (the highest was 23), were households headed by widows, followed by adult females, and normal families. Those having the lowest scores were households headed by men under 21. Separate examination of some of these cases did not, however, confirm the validity of the method. Statistical methods will never be an adequate means for finding the truly vulnerable people who require special assistance. They can only be known by the members of their own community.

The vulnerable one year later

In 1984 the Oxford team followed up on households which had been interviewed in Roronyo settlement in 1983. Altogether 82 households were included in the survey and in 61 cases there were individuals who were either physically or socially handicapped, i.e. the elderly, widows, 'separated' wives, orphans, the blind, deaf, crippled, leprosy sufferers, or the household head was below the age of 21 years. In 1984, 54 of the 61 vulnerable households were still living at the same address. Of the seven 'missing' cases, two had repatriated, one had returned to the border, two were temporarily absent (at school or doing *leja-leja*), one had died, and one had exchanged plots to be nearer kinsmen. (Pankhurst 1985.) It was found that

...the condition of some vulnerable families has deteriorated... In approximately half the cases the number of household members has remained the same. However, of the remaining half, 60 per cent have fewer members. ... this could be attributed to families splitting in times of difficulty. For instance, a widow with five young children sent two of them to live with relatives in the border area and another to a brother living in a different settlement... In half the cases the households still had the same number [of hoes]. However, the majority of the remaining cases had fewer hoes than before. In several cases family members admitted having sold hoes to meet more pressing needs.

A more significant change is in the number of days spent on agricultural wage labour. The two surveys were carried out at the same time of year....A quarter of the cases did the same amount, over two-thirds did more, and less than one in ten did less. Wage labour is recognized by natives and refugees alike to be a last resort. (ibid.)

The Oxford team also found that 'vulnerability is a process in which a number of factors combine, it cannot be reduced to a single aspect or indeed to a prescribed set of limited factors.' (ibid.) There are, however, several characteristics which clearly distinguish the vulnerable. These include low physical mobility which affects agricultural production and ability to work for others, and the lack of even basic economic assets. The condition of the vulnerable is exacerbated by 'distress sales' of blankets, hoes, and cooking equipment to buy food when rations do not arrive, as well as by the absence of relatives near enough to offer support. One medical worker from Moyo hospital who had lost his left arm in a car accident was living alone at Limbe settlement. He had literally nothing but a burlap bag in his hut. To get food he had been forced to sell everything received from the assistance programme.

Among the 21 other households interviewed in the 1983 survey which did not include vulnerable individuals, 6 were not living at the same address in 1984. 'Although the reasons for changes in population could not be established, and the figures are small, this may indicate the greater mobility of those who were not classified as vulnerable... i.e. 6 out of 21 compared with 7 out of 61 households had moved somewhere else.' (ibid.) The Oxford team discovered that two of the households in the survey sample had *become* vulnerable during the year. In one case the house had burned down and in another, a woman died, leaving a 9-year-old orphan. In 1983 only 3.7 per cent of the household said they had no land but in 1984 10 per cent of the sample said they were not farming.

Consideration for the most vulnerable *families* is now not even a part of the assistance programme. The need for food rations is determined on the basis of overall numbers and the decision to cut them is based simply on the number of months a settlement has been occupied. At the same time, enormous amounts of money are spent on such facilities as school buildings in settlements which refugees are clearly capable of organizing and building for themselves. Near Kaya in an area of about 18 by 20 kilometres, on the Zaire/Uganda border, we found 12 self-help primary schools which, together with local Sudanese, the unassisted refugees had built out of local materials. In this area there were also many chapels and mosques which had been built on the community's own initiative. Would it not be more practical to redirect monies now spent on buildings to a welfare programme which first ensured that the most vulnerable families are supported?

Women: another vulnerable group?

Male domination is a feature of most societies, but given the general powerlessness of refugees, are women likely to be even more vulnerable? The question of whether or not women should be singled out as a vulnerable class must be answered in the light of both recent historical changes and the nature of the aid programme itself.

Some western observers believe the status of African women is even more inferior to men than in their own society. However, a number of studies have demonstrated that in the past the division of labour, the allocation of economic obligations within the household unit, and the elaborate protections built into the marriage system, gave African women more rights and protection than western feminists assume. (Hafkin and Bay 1976.) It has also been shown how the economic changes which occurred during the colonial period (and which have continued since independence) profoundly eroded women's position in society. (Smock 1975.) But despite the general deterioration of women's position, in most African societies women have retained certain rights and spheres of authority. An assistance programme could take account of these and actually encourage their maintenance.

In the West Nile, for example, and as in many African societies, womens' economic obligations to the household were supported by certain rights and privileges. While she was responsible for producing much of the food which the family eats each day, she also had access to her own land and her granaries were strictly under her own control. Men who farmed concentrated on cash crops. The food crops a man produced were usually kept in his own granary and he might use it for gifts to his family, particularly his sisters.[8]

While a wife is expected to prepare food for the husband's guests, if the guests are his relatives, he should not count on her being willing to draw from her own stock of food. A good-natured woman usually does so, but if there are tensions in the marriage, he can be sure that she will demand he provide the ingredients to feed his relatives. Among the self-settled refugees, such customary domestic arrangements could at least partially be maintained, but in the settlements, dependent as refugees were on rations and *leja-leja* and where there was not enough land, it is difficult for households to organize themselves along familiar lines.

The failure to recognize their pivotal position in the household economy, and the special needs and particular vulnerability of women in the refugee situation, has led not just to women being disadvantaged, although this is obviously the case, but to whole programmes going awry. Unfortunately, through ignorance and sometimes through personal prejudices, both policy-makers and fieldworkers often unknowingly contribute to the further weakening of women's position.

[8] This is a highly over-simplified comment on what is an elaborate and highly complex system of division of economic and social roles between men and women.

The male bias built into refugee programmes at the planning stage, conspires with the fact that African women do not normally expect to take on public roles. Ingrid Palmer (1982) observed that even where both spouses are present it would appear that the 'refugee women assume a lower social profile than usual, while patriarchy in the family intensifies... This is partly due to the new alien environment where men assume greater mobility and social visibility relative to women...' But, she continues, this is also due 'to the fact that *the dependent family is given attention by relief agencies through male representatives...*' That is to say, that the relief programme acts to bolster male status. In this regard the programme in Yei River District was no exception.[9]

Although few men in the settlement had formerly earned their livelihood through agriculture, the entire agricultural programme focused on men. Agricultural advisers were men; the 'productivity' committees in each settlement were composed entirely of men. Women who were not heads of households were not allocated their own land. The main cash crop introduced into a few settlements was tobacco and very few women participated even though some of them had extensive experience in handling this crop. Apparently the agency staff was unaware that when men grow cash crops, it cannot be assumed that the family will directly benefit; men have responsibility to their sisters and to other kin. If women want access to food or to cash crops, they must grow their own; it is not necessarily a male responsibility. Perhaps for this reason, we found as many women as men growing cash crops. Excluding the transit populations, when asked if the household grew cash crops (in addition to tobacco, vegetables are also sold), 21.5 per cent of those headed by men, and 20.9 per cent of the women-headed households, said 'yes'.

The responsibility for the time-consuming work of collecting water and preparing food for the family each day falls on women and children. One of the easiest ways to assist women is to ensure access to water near to the compound. It was the aim of the programme to provide settlements with a sufficient number of bore-holes, but the type of pumps provided required constant maintenance. Moreover, many of the wells were too shallow to supply water throughout the dry season. (It has already been noted that few households had adequate containers for collecting the day's supply.) Another time-consuming task is grinding grains to make them edible. The Sudan Council of Churches placed diesel-run grinders in Tore and Mogiri, but women were charged for the service. When hand grinders were placed in each block at Limuru settlement, this was done to help *men* generate income, yet grinding for the household had never been a male occupation.

Tables 6.2 and 6.3 compare some of the characteristics of households headed by men and women. According to these data women-headed households are in most cases slightly worse off than their male counterparts,

[9] But in 1985 UNHCR sent a woman to fill the post of head of the Juba office.

TABLE 6.2: Some characteristics of male- and female-headed households
(assisted)

Characteristic	Male-headed households		Female-headed households	
	Average no. per household	Number	Average no. per household	Number
Household size	5.50	8,252	4.70	2,423
Number able to cultivate	2.90	4,349	2.20	1,134
Days spent at *leja-leja*	3.26	4,889	2.26	1,170
Number born in settlement	0.14	217	0.12	64
Number of orphans	0.63	943	0.42	220
Number of widows	0.10	157	0.25	127
Number of married women separated from spouse	0.06	86	0.13	69
Number of lepers	0.06	93	0.09	45
Number of cripples	0.07	110	0.06	29
Number of deaf	0.03	45	0.03	13
Number of blind	0.01	20	0.03	14
Number of working days lost through illness	1.10	1,654	1.08	560
Number ill at time of interview	0.46	691	0.42	218
Number of blankets per person	0.47	3,841	0.48	1,173

although 7.1 per cent more of them were living in a completed house and 5.2 per cent more of these households had at least one hoe. But note in Table 6.3 the large difference in numbers judged by the interviewer on other criteria to be vulnerable. There were insufficient data to make a similar comparison for the unassisted refugee households.

The practice of issuing rations to the head of the family might also put the family at risk if the head were a man: 74.3 per cent of all families are headed by men. Among the 'normal' families (excluding those headed by a woman whose husband lived with her co-wife in the same settlement), 2.5 per cent of the registered heads of the household were women. Some women arrived first in the settlement and were registered as the head of the household. Later,

TABLE 6.3: Some (further) characteristics of male- and female-headed households (assisted)

Characteristic	Male-headed households %	Number	Female-headed households %	Number
Have relatives self-settled	76.4	1,145	69.5	360
Have relatives in other settlements	89.1	1,335	86.3	447
Have relatives in Zaire	46.3	694	36.7	190
% of household able to cultivate	52.7	4,349	46.8	1,134
% illiterate	16.3	1,342	16.8	407
Have no house	50.0	749	42.9	222
Have no latrine	69.0	1,034	72.6	376
Have inadequate number of water containers	67.1	1,006	68.9	357
Have inadequate sleeping conditions	21.7	326	20.1	104
Have inadequate clothing for all	47.6	712	53.9	276
Have no chickens	69.8	1,046	78.4	406
Have no hoes	33.6	503	28.4	147
Have no pangas	38.6	579	39.6	205
Have no goats	94.3	1,414	96.9	502
Have no sheep	98.4	1,475	99.2	514
In debt	33.2	498	26.1	135
Have no way of getting money	23.9	359	34.4	178
Counted as vulnerable	16.5	1,358	37.6	912

when their spouse joined them, 27 of these women, perhaps wisely, declined to surrender their designation as head of the family and were so able to retain control of the rations.

That rations were issued on the basis of numbers of individuals gave a few women some sense of independence. Men complained that this policy was eroding marriages, as some women were said to taunt their husbands, reminding them that they now had other sources of income. According to the men, marriages are now considerably less stable than they were in Uganda. Following a dispute, women often abandon their husbands, taking refuge in another household, carrying with them their 'share' of such items as buckets or cooking pots issued by UNHCR. The resulting disputes usually involve wife-beating. It would be understandable to find conditions of life in exile had indeed eroded marriage relationships, but given the lack of comparative information (to say nothing of the complications of any study of marriage stability), we did not look for such empirical evidence. Had rations been supplied to women only, marriages might have been further eroded, but there might have been a better chance that the rations would be used to feed the family.

Ugandan refugee women (as is doubtless the case elsewhere) arrived with some distinct disadvantages. Table 6.4 shows the amount of education of both men and women 15 years of age and over.

TABLE 6.4: The number of years of schooling of men and women over 14 years of age (assisted)

	Men		Women	
	%	Number	%	Number
No education	25.4	599	67.0	1,495
4 years or less	26.0	612	17.2	382
5-9 years	41.2	968	14.1	313
10 years or more	7.4	175	1.7	37
TOTAL	100	2,354	100	2,227

Communication was a great problem in the settlements. Women were the last to receive information which affected them. For instance, I found few women who knew of the Red Cross Tracing Service, which was responsible for trying to find lost relatives. Lists of names were simply posted in Yei and occasionally workers visited and posted them in settlements. Women (and many men) were even unaware of what the food ration was meant to include.

The inability to speak English was a major disadvantage. According to the sample, 37.2 per cent of the settlement population could speak at least some, but only about one-third of these were women. Nevertheless, in 1982, settlements were asked to elect only English-speakers as block leaders, obviously for the convenience of agency staff. However, the unfairness of this policy finally dawned on officials when, in Goli, the non-English speakers nearly staged a rebellion against the 'educated' class. After that, at every meeting which I attended, the proceedings were translated into the major language of the settlement.

The organization of settlements with elections of officers as devised by the UNHCR programme officer, aimed to encourage the widest possible participation of the community in directing its own affairs. Within each group of 24 households, making up a block, officers were elected. These included a block leader, an assistant, a secretary, and representatives to serve on the settlement's health, education, and agricultural committees. (In practice, only the latter were active.) The settlement chairman and other officers were elected from among the block leaders. Rules for running an election were circulated and refugees were reminded that women were eligible to stand for any office. But Ugandan women are unaccustomed to taking public roles. Unless called upon to do so, most women do not even speak at meetings where men are present. A total of 5.9 per cent held positions of responsibility in settlements of which only 14.8 per cent were women.

Eligible voters included everyone 16 years or older and those younger boys and girls who were heads of families. Voting demonstrates at least a minimum of interest in public matters. Excluding the transit camps (where proper elections were impossible) 51.5 per cent of the population over 15 voted and of those women who were eligible to vote, just less than half took part.

There were other opportunities for playing a part in community life. Each settlement had a dispute committee and some also had them in each block. There were religious organizations, co-operatives, Scout associations, branches of the Red Cross, and other *ad hoc* groups set up for particular projects. In all, 7.9 per cent of the population said that they belonged to one or other of such groups; of these 41.3 per cent were women. There were some salaried positions in each settlement. According to the sample, 1.1 per cent of the population is paid as a social worker, teacher, medical worker, etc. Of these only 21.1 per cent were women. Most of those employed to head women's organizations in the settlements were men. All expatriate agency personnel except the medical staff were men.[10]

One reason that agricultural programmes are unsuccessful is because they are not directed at women. Even when there was a special programme for women's cultivation, it was organized by *men*. While the sectoral policy, described in Chapter Two, was still operating, two competing agencies were involved in organizing women's groups. At that time, GMT, having failed to get the contract for implementing agriculture, started nutrition clubs for women and appointed an agricultural adviser to organize them. Thus each

[10] Apart from myself and an Oxford undergraduate who temporarily joined the research project, my team was also composed entirely of men though this was not for want of trying to employ women. Most women with the required educational standard had either married, or produced a child out of wedlock, or were in Juba. The problems of single women received altogether too little attention in this research.

settlement had, potentially, two (male) agricultural advisers; one for the settlement and one for the women's nutrition club.

For women the attraction of the nutrition club was that tools and seed were provided. After it was discovered that women tended to drop out of the club (to work in their own fields) once they had a hoe, it became the policy to lock up the club's hoes after each meeting. All members were supposed to work on the communal plot at the same time. This approach to assisting women had a very mixed success. Women quarrelled over which of them had worked more and thus had a right to more of the harvest. Aside from such problems (and the question of whether settlements really needed two trained agriculturalists), the nutrition clubs probably brought more tangible benefit than did the income-generating projects organized for women by ACROSS.

Again, the failures of these projects resulted from a combination of agency bias and the tendency for men to seize opportunity to the disadvantage of women. SCC had placed sewing machines in some settlements, but I found they had all been taken over by men, and women did not even get a chance to use them. Tailoring co-operatives organized by ACROSS also ran into similar difficulties. Men did not allow women access to the machines.

Selling cooked food and tea was a popular way of earning cash. But again, funds were not provided to individuals and co-operatives always tended to be taken over by males. Women often asked for personal loans, as did many men, to establish some income-generating project, but apparently they were not regarded as good credit risks.

There are many reasons why refugees find themselves in debt. The need to employ someone to build a house, as mentioned earlier, is a common reason why women and the handicapped fall into debt. Among the sample, 31.4 per cent of the households reported having borrowed money since arrival and not yet having repaid it. Of these, 21.3 per cent were headed by women. That fewer women were still in debt may have been less a function of need than of the difficulty of getting credit.

The budget for women's projects was always *far* below that allocated for men's. Some had as little as £S30 start-up money, while a project like a butchery co-operative could receive several hundred pounds. Projects for women tended to be limited to handicrafts and embroidery, the profits on an item (equivalent to about 25 pence) did not justify the many hours required to complete it. Moreover, there was a limited market since refugees could not usually afford to buy table-cloths or crochet work. Raw materials for most mats and baskets had to be purchased elsewhere and there were never sufficient funds to supply all who could have made them. Such shortages led to friction.

GMT had programmes for Sudanese women and had opened a handicraft shop in Yei. But the limited and poor quality of materials used to produce handicrafts and the lack of a clientèle to buy, quickly discouraged the women trying to earn income in this way.

There was apparently no tradition in the West Nile of women organizing themselves outside the family unit, unlike the situation in West Africa where women have a long history of powerful societies. The solidarity of these groups has played an important role in lessening the effects of men's tendency to oppress them. (Ardener, S. 1975: 29-51.) Efforts to organize women's groups to generate income ran into a host of problems. Female solidarity is a rare commodity in any society and it may be even more difficult to get women to work towards common goals in a community which has suffered the experiences of refugees and in which extreme scarcity of resources encourages competition. In addition, the demands of domestic work under the conditions of life in the settlements make it difficult for the very women who most need to generate income to participate.

The lack of solidarity among women was exacerbated by agency competition and conflict. Where more than one agency was involved in organizing women, those under one agency's umbrella were often unwilling to co-operate with those under another. The more educated women were sometimes reluctant to join in with their illiterate sisters. The result was that more of the non-literate women were in the nutrition clubs, while the income-generating organizations usually included those women of the educated class who were members of 'normal' families. Women who had spouses, especially those who were employed as teachers, medical workers, and the like were notably unsympathetic to the plight of those who were surviving on their own with young children. The most important institutional protection of women against unfair treatment, the wider family, was sadly disrupted by the death and displacement of relatives in the course of their flight. The case of Florence is not untypical.

Florence, married with two children, had worked as a secretary in Kampala. Her husband was killed in 1981. On arrival in the settlement, a single woman with young children to support, she had agreed to marry again. The new husband did not regularize the marriage because Florence had no family to whom he had to answer. Subsequently, he took another wife and paid the dowry her parents demanded. This put Florence and her children at a disadvantage in the household in which they lived together with his parents. Respect for a woman's position is very much bound up with the presence of relatives and a 'proper' marriage. In addition to farming, of which she had no previous experience, she brewed beer to earn cash.

Florence was selected for a two-week leadership training course in Yei. Having been appointed as the nutrition club's treasurer, she was responsible for its £S50. As no provision had been made in Yei for food or accommodation, and Florence had to send food to her children left behind in the settlement, she spent the money, hoping to be able to replace it from beer sales. On her return she confessed her debt to the other women. To make enough beer required endless days of *leja-leja* to acquire the cassava. Florence did not have the strength.

She tried to join the sewing co-operative to earn cash, but the other women refused. She was already under one 'umbrella'. Even when I paid Florence's debt (which was the second excuse the women gave for excluding her), they would not allow her to join. The chairman of this co-operative was married to the man employed by ACROSS to organize women's groups. He appeared unconcerned over the unforgiving attitude of his wife. Apparently almost everyone in the community looked down on Florence.

In Otogo, however, and without any help from an agency, women began making baskets and other household items from sorghum straw. Since most women made their own, at first these generated no income. I was able to put them in touch with a tourist shop in Khartoum. The latest report is that they had earned enough to buy three sewing machines. However, they still depend on the willingness of UNHCR staff to carry the baskets from Yei to Khartoum when travelling by charter plane.

Where it exists, an assistance programme for refugees ought to take account of male resistance to women's organizations. Many Ugandan men objected to their wives participating in women's organizations. In all the settlements (except those under SSRAP) the women's income-generating projects were led by men.

When I met the women in settlements without their male 'leader' present, I was accused of inciting women to rebellion. In one settlement, Wondurubu, where the group actually had a woman as their leader, this problem was frankly discussed. They reported that some husbands beat their wives, on principle, if they attended one of the meetings. Their tea co-operative had failed because some husbands refused to allow their wives to take their turn running the shop. Only those women with more 'progressive' husbands had continued to participate.[11] In the absence of a sufficient number of enlightened Ugandans who could devote themselves to this entrenched social problem, agencies would be better advised to help individual women with projects which they could carry out in their own compounds. There were ways in which women could have used their 'non- controversial' agricultural skills to generate cash. Growing onions is highly lucrative and the crop can be stored for long periods. Yei River District is laced with rivers and it would have been possible to develop irrigated perimeters for women to grow onions and other vegetable crops. A number of simple technologies have been developed for lifting water. Although some women had the highly specialized skills required for growing tobacco, this labour intensive crop also requires the labour of men and they are unlikely to encourage women's participation. Bee-keeping, using improved hives, could also have been promoted. An

[11] I did not recommend militancy as a way of overcoming this problem. In fact I suggested that after each meeting, wives should take more trouble over the preparation of a meal to encourage their husbands to believe that the women's meeting could contribute to the welfare of the family rather than to its breakdown. But my words tasted sour in my own mouth, when I remembered that, at best, the ingredients available for cooking were limited to cereal, oil, milk and beans.

indigenous Kenyan company offered to supply the technical and administrative services and the industry would have given work to tailors and carpenters. The company sent a proposal to the Commissioner in Khartoum, but for whatever reason the idea was not picked up by the agencies which are in charge of income-generation. The most common income-generating activity among women was brewing beer from cassava or sorghum, and for this product there seemed to be an unlimited market.

Responsibility without authority

The failure of the assistance programme to meet those most in need who remained outside the settlements, placed an inordinate burden on many women which forced many of them to take decisions which were disruptive to their family life. In case after case we found that it was a woman who was finally the one who took the decision to go to a settlement, acting against her husband's wishes. One of my team describes such a case.

Fatuma Achipa lived with her husband in the Kuru area of northern Arua. In 1979 because of disturbances, they moved to Obongi, some 40 or more miles eastwards along the bank of the Nile where her parents lived. Meanwhile the rest of her co-wives shifted to the Sudan. During the 1982 operations, she was forced to come to the Sudan where the husband had settled. This was early in 1983. At the border things were not that right, with starvation and sicknesses very rampant. This made her seek the boss's [i.e. her husband's] opinion on coming to the camp. He refused. She wasn't satisfied, she made another request. This time she was very affected by jaundice and children very seriously suffering from malnutrition. When he turned down the request, she packed up and headed for the nearest reception centre which directed her to Koya.

She has lost over seven people, most of whom died due to the effects of malnutrition... Long before this, four were shot, two of whom were soldiers and the other two civilians. She has two orphans living with her, these are nephews of the husband. There's also a half orphan, a daughter of her co-wife who died early this year. [Concerning how many are ill] There's no one very ill, but she still suffers from the effect of the jaundice... Children suffer from scabies. One of the very malnourished kids is now recovering from its sickness. She said, 'As my husband tends to care very little about me and the children, even his own late sister's orphans, I feel I can just subsist here on what I'm given by the UNHCR.'

The penalties of acting against a husband's wishes can be severe. Certainly he will feel relieved of all responsibility for his wife and children and such actions normally lead to divorce. With no relatives of her own to fall back on, such separated women are extremely vulnerable. Another such woman, also married to a polygamous husband, in 1983 found they had nothing on which to subsist. Her husband refused to agree to come to a settlement, and 'She tolerated the situation for a bit until it was aggravated by the death of her child who died due to improper feeding. This compelled her to disobey her husband and she made her way to the camp. ...She now remains with her one child and her sisters.'

Women's lack of experience in taking independent decisions often led them into great difficulty when they found themselves alone and responsible for children. One day in Limuru a woman and three children appeared, having walked several miles from their compound in the bush. The visit of a sister with a message from her father had prompted her to venture to the settlement to get medical treatment for the children. I asked one of my assistants to interview her. This is her story as he recorded it:

Zaida Bako - self-settled widow. 'My name is Zaida Bako and I am a self-settled refugee two miles away from the Limoro Settlement. I have a quarter of an acre of groundnuts, two quarters of sorghum. I also have a maize field of peas. My husband died in the middle of June this year. He was a soldier by profession and he has left me with a daughter of about five years. My mother too has died, and naturally, I have six little sisters who are now with me. I am now caring for seven children who are all malnourished...

'From the day my husband died, my brother-in-law says he cannot stay happily any longer in our house in Sudan. He is unmarried and has gone away from home. His whereabouts are not known to me. I have no income except what I [earn] from the locals to find some food for us at home.

'My sister has come to visit me. The purpose of her visit is to see and report on our health conditions to my father. My father lives along the border. His message to me was that if the children were in appalling condition, I was to move to the settlement. I have come to enquire about going to the settlement. I have no agricultural tools except a hoe which I had brought from Uganda.' Now the hoe is so little [that is, worn down], that I think it will be no use up to the end of the year. I have eight chickens which I had brought from Uganda. She wept as she answered my question: 'What most upset you and what is your deepest problem?' 'My husband is dead: I can't get over worrying about that for long. But the children who are in very poor health make me feel upset. Nobody helps me at all. I can't help weeping.'

Question: 'Why didn't you move earlier?'

'I had nobody to give me the courage and besides I can't carry all the children with me at such a long distance to the transit. I am prepared ... except the problem of transport.'

Atima, my assistant, concluded his report with a description of the three children who had accompanied Zaida.

1. One of the children has swollen cheeks. Her gums are eaten up and teeth are painful. The child is 3 years old.

2. The other is a girl of 4 years old. She has dysentery which has been for three weeks already. The woman brought her for treatment but was told that drugs were out of stock.

3. The third child is a boy of two years who has dysentery. His hair has turned silvery brown, he has scabies, and is weak.

Women and malnourished children

Feeding programmes were usually organized when a settlement first opened and when the health of the population was at its most critical stage. It has already been noted that the aid programme did not consistently provide adequate feeding programmes for the malnourished children in settlements, but even when these services were available there was still the perennial problem of a low initial response rate and a high number of drop-outs. I often observed a marasmus child sucking at a dry breast, the mother seemingly unaware that her child was dying through lack of food. Most expatriate observers as well as the Ugandan medical staff viewed such behaviour as irrational or as an indication of the ignorance of women. The behaviour of women at Mopoko did little to encourage anyone to look further for reasons why mothers were failing to co-operate with efforts to save the lives of their children. There, it was reported, women were demanding to be *paid*, not only for cutting the firewood to cook the special meals, but for feeding their own children.

I began looking for an explanation for such behaviour which appeared so irrational to observers. (See my own report of this situation in Chapter Two, and page 283.) I found a number of reasons for the high rate of non-compliance with feeding programmes for malnourished children. For one thing, treating a severely malnourished child is a full-time occupation since the child must be fed several times a day. The location of the feeding centres usually meant that a mother (or other caretaker) had to spend the entire day away from the household. In itself, this fact alone is sufficient to account for many of the women's demands. But in addition, women have other lives dependent on them. Most of them needed time to spend on other pressing household duties including cooking and carrying water, not to mention the fact that when settlements opened people were occupied in building and mudding houses, digging latrines, planting seeds when they had them, etc. When WFP supplies failed, women were forced to do *leja-leja* to feed the *other* members of the family. In retrospect, it would seem quite reasonable to compensate women for their time in the feeding centre so they could supply the household with food. But there were other reasons which encouraged women to stop coming to the feeding centres.

While aware that it was the lack of food which caused their child's illness, the food children were given was totally unfamiliar. Mixing oil with milk is completely foreign, and women say that the gruel tastes 'disgusting'. No sugar was added and there was no attempt to offer a variety of food to stimulate a child's appetite as a mother would normally have done at home.

Children are normally fed on demand. The idea of force-feeding an infant, on schedule, is unheard of and the experience of trying to impose such a régime is highly unpleasant for the mother. Mothers would comply so long as a nurse was watching, but when unobserved would usually respond to the protests (usually screams) of the infant. The medical staff often behave as though the mother is personally to blame for the child's illness and many are often roundly scolded for not co-operating. It is likely that Ugandan women, as in most African societies, are held responsible for the well-being of their children. In Sierra Leone, for example, a child's illness is taken as evidence that the mother has broken some taboo. (Harrell-Bond 1975;1975*b*.)

Efforts to rehydrate a malnourished child tend to increase diarrhoeal symptoms. Many women are aware that their youngster is suffering from other illnesses which require treatment and the feeding programmes did not include medical examination or any other treatment. Women often told me it was useless to go to the feeding centre if medical treatment was not also given. This is not an irrational view, and given the circumstances in the settlements, a women may well be forced *not* to accept the aid offered.

The Oxford team collected 97 case histories of malnourished children in settlements, among both refugees and Sudanese living near Panyume. In their analysis they attempted to distinguish a 'main' cause of malnourishment. In about half the cases, the 'main' cause was extreme vulnerability. Extreme vulnerability was defined as including some debilitating factor together with a set of social circumstances which led the child to receive inadequate support. About one-third of the children came from female-headed households and in many of these cases the woman was herself ill or incapacitated. About one-quarter of the children were orphans and again, many of these had joined already vulnerable families. In other cases one or both parents were either mentally or physically disabled or incapacitated by illness or torture. In two cases the child was disabled; one had been beaten over the head and body by the rifle butts of Ugandan soldiers and showed signs of complete mental/physical retardation, and the other was incapable of standing and appeared to have some kind of cretinism. The mother of this latter child appeared mentally retarded and the father was described by the

TABLE 6.5: Mental health and malnourishment

Psychological state of child's guardian	Child's health	
	Not malnourished %	Clinically malnourished %
Acutely anxious and severely depressed	0	4
Acutely anxious	0	4
Severely depressed	0	27
Mildly anxious and/or depressed	41	54
Good mental health	59	12
Number	29	26

interviewer as psychotic. Child disablement is not necessarily a cause of neglect leading to malnourishment, as other disabled children were observed who were not suffering malnutrition.

Poor mental health may be an additional complicating factor leading to the neglect of children. The Oxford team administered an adapted form of a mental health instrument designed to diagnose clinical levels of anxiety and depression. The numbers tested were extremely small, and the results must be regarded as both preliminary and experimental. However, the correlation between the psychological states elicited by this scale and the incidence of malnourishment is too striking not to suggest that the problem requires more serious attention if assistance programmes are to deal adequately with the problem of malnutrition.

The Sahrawi refugees, who manage their own health programme, have established centres for such sick children and their mothers. (Harrell-Bond 1981.) A neighbourhood committee in the settlement takes care of her household during the mother's absence. These 'protection centres', as they are called, are small camps located away from the main community. A very strict régime has been instituted which includes the daily examination of each child and its mother, and training in how to care for the child. As one responsible noted, by daily weighing of the child, the mother learns that it is food, not medicine which will cure her child. Apparently also aware of the psychological needs of these mothers, there is not only a strict regime, but regular social and musical evenings are organized in these protection centres.

Family planning services and the problems of women

The UNHCR Handbook notes that contraceptives should always be made available to refugees, but this instruction was ignored. Family planning was not part of the health programme for Yei River District. While in Khartoum, I had been informed that refugee women in eastern Sudan were practising 'back-street' abortions and that there was a high rate of mortality. I was asked to include a question in the survey about the acceptability of contraceptives among Ugandans in order to provide data which would encourage GMT to provide these services. On the basis of my previous experience in Africa, I did not believe there would be interest in contraceptives and did not follow this advice. It was not until we had been interviewing for over a month that I realized how very wrong were my initial assumptions.

In Limbe settlement, a group of men presented me with a petition demanding that these services be incorporated into the health programme. Family planning had been a part of the health programme in Uganda. They pointed out that many women were dying in childbirth as a result of the lack of medical facilities and the other problems they were facing in exile. (Hepatitis during pregnancy had already resulted in a large number of deaths in this and other settlements.) As these men pointed out, as refugees, they had to limit the number of children to support. While many suffered low fertility, others found the threat of pregnancy disruptive to conjugal relations. Later, I was presented with a memorandum from a group of women; the demand for family planning was top of the list. Further discussions suggest that this need was quite widely felt. A few individuals had received 'the pill' from the GMT doctor when they had personally requested it. One Ugandan declared he absolutely never wanted any more children and - perhaps because his request was so unusual - underwent a vasectomy operation in Juba.

As there was more than one registered nurse with extensive experience in family planning, it would have been possible for the Ugandans to have organized their own services - at least for the settlements. Contraceptives are freely available in Khartoum and those who promote the extension of such programmes throughout Africa will immediately see the value of such an example for the Sudanese in the south.

Gender blindness

On the face of it it might be concluded that women do not suffer any greater disabilities in exile than do men. Moreover, one might argue, they are unlikely to suffer as severely from being uprooted since they may resume their normal domestic life once they have settled in their country of asylum. Even though many formerly had careers outside the household or were students, it might be easier for them to adapt to domestic roles. But the very nature of customary female roles in this cultural setting means that ultimately women have to take the major responsibility for managing the home. (Christensen 1982.) It is the women who must ultimately find the food to feed the children, carry the water, cut the firewood, and nurse the ill. The insecurity of poverty ultimately falls most heavily on her. The assistance programme did not aim to discriminate against women. Rather it was the ignorance or indifference of those who ran the assistance programme combined with the undue emphasis upon equality. As with GMT's health programme, this could only lead to failure simply because the recipient population was so variegated. Women may be poor or illiterate, but they do have a good grasp of their needs. However in relation to the men who determined aid policy they were indeed a 'muted' group (Ardener, E. in Ardener, S. 1975) and aid policy tended to reinforce their 'muting' within settlement society. Women were thus at a double disadvantage. Even though I was a woman, it still required special attention to inspire women with sufficient confidence to discuss their particular problems with me. It was almost impossible to meet with the women alone - men were always hanging about to listen. One tactic to get rid of them was to raise a topic which is taboo for men to discuss.[12]

---

[12] Given the problems of lack of soap, private bathing facilities, and even cloth, I could not imagine how refugee women dealt with menstrual flow. Once this was the topic of our discussion; to the amusement of the women, the men fled.

I must admit that at times I did attempt to incite women to rebellion. I related stories from West Africa of mass demonstrations by women which I had witnessed. In Tore, where a man kept the womens' sewing machine buzzing from early morning until dark, I recommended the women take over the community centre where he worked. In Kala, where no rations were distributed as the settlement was deemed by WFP to be self-sufficient, I suggested one woman take her three starving children to Yei and hand them over to agency staff. In the same settlement, where a woman was still bleeding heavily months after having given birth to premature twins, and where, refugees complained, the doctor only delivered drugs late in the afternoon, refusing to see the critically ill, I recommended refugees surround the car with all such patients. But few Ugandan refugees, much less the women, were aware they had *any* rights. The fundamental reality - that no one gives power, and that it must be taken - was not part of the thinking of these desperate and starving people. Certainly Ugandan women must decide for themselves if their interests will be better served through collective action. Until they do, it is unlikely that the present agency programmes (organized and implemented by men) will benefit women who are indeed a specially vulnerable category. Nor will aid officials be able to identify and serve the needs of those vulnerable women who are now least able to care for themselves.

Women may be 'muted', but this should not be interpreted to mean that they are either ignorant of their needs or unable to express them if the situation is right for them. In Limbe, one of several settlements where women put their complaints on paper, I was given the following petition. It gives poignant expression to just some of the burdens women bear.

These are the problems facing us women of Limbe Settlement

1. Family planning should be introduced in the settlement.

2. If possible fund[s] should be given to the women's club so that when a woman is in trouble she goes and borrows it after which she will bring it back in a short while.

3. There are a good number of orphans ... what aid can we get to support them with if the UNHCR stops giving us aid? They mostly suffer from hunger and [lack of] clothing.

4. We have expectant mothers who mostly suffer from change of diet. Can you please help to send us a few hens to introduce poultry especially for the women's club? So that whenever a woman is expecting, she will be provided with eggs and even the chickens.

5. In Sudan here we have found out that there is a kind of sickness called eppetites [*sic*: hepatitis]. And when a woman is expecting and she happens to be attacked by it, she is most likely to die. Can you find us a way of sending medicine so that when a woman is pregnant she should be given the medicine to save both the mother and the child's life?

6. The number of bore-holes are not enough, so please can you increase the number so that we don't drink the dirty water from the stream which sometimes give us worms like bilharzia?

7. Widows are suffering a great deal, especially in the field work, getting clothes and foodstuffs as well. So whenever there is help, it should be given to these women so that we take care of our properties ourselves to give us a good service.

8. The names of widows and orphans were listed and so far nothing has been done ... we would like you to tell us something about it.

9. In the settlement men have work for earning their living, so can we also be given the privilege also? This possibly can be done by making our own hotels [tea shops] on our own.

10. The present grinding mill we have cannot grind maize and so what can we do with the maize provided by UNHCR? If possible provide us with one grinding mill.

11. Some of our women were sent for courses [leadership courses] ... and after the course they [the agency] do not remember us. If at all you know something about it, can you tell us why they did not do it, because we wasted a lot of time for nothing?[13]

12. Can you please help get us some few sacks of cement for cementing the tops [of graves] of our sons, daughters, brothers and husbands who have passed away?[14]

Do women refugees suffer more or less than men?[15] While the results of the psychological test administered by the Oxford team cannot be regarded as conclusive, it found as many men suffered psychiatric morbidity. (de Waal in Wilson *et al.* 1985.)[16] Loss of status may be a more severe problem for men since so few of them are able to resume former occupations, while women's roles remained the same. Superficial observations and case histories suggest, however, that men are more likely than are women to express their frustration in ways which are socially disruptive.

For example, excessive drinking has already been mentioned, but marital problems (including wife-beating) are also quite common. Such behaviours place even greater burdens on women. This, together with bearing the major responsibility for providing for the household under these conditions, would seem overwhelming. Problems for women worsen and programmes of assistance fail, precisely because policy-makers and field officers are gender blind. But gender blindness does not, as we have seen, lead to gender neutrality.

[13] The agency responsible for health had organized these leadership training courses. Such training had been available in a women's centre in Juba for years, and many capable Sudanese graduates of the course were unemployed. Before coming to the Sudan, a consultant for women's development programmes in Khartoum had lived for many years in Uganda. When her contract was completed, she had travelled to Juba to offer to work in the refugee programme. It was not taken up. She is now working in Kenya. If expatriates are required to administer programmes for women, would it not be wiser to employ women who have such relevant experience in Arica?

[14] Herein lies a tale. I could not believe these women could seriously be asking for cement for grave markers when the programme was not even providing them with soap or salt, but apparently it was a matter of 'keeping up with the Jones' and of social responsibilities to the dead. I visited the Limbe cemetery, and the mystery of an earlier disappearance of building materials was solved. There I found several graves neatly covered with squares of smooth cement, carefully marked with the names of and appropriate farewells to the deceased. Obviously someone on the building site had capitalized on some refugees' need to give such respect to the dead.

[15] Spring (1982) found that among the refugees living in Zambia, the women, through marriage, were able to more easily 'assimilate' than the men.

[16] But, it should be noted, Orley and Wing (1979) also reported a much smaller sex difference in Uganda.

7

The 'over-socialized concept of man'

Explaining the inexplicable

I did not set out to collect data to demonstrate that African refugees present symptoms of mental illness, and actually resisted facing the possibility that African refugees might share such problems with other refugees about whom I had read. I had an unrealistic and naive faith in the power of the family system to buffer individuals undergoing stress. What I had failed to anticipate was both the extent to which the demands of individual survival undermined social values, and the time that it takes for new supportive social units to establish themselves in the absence of kinsfolk.

The real and apparent lack of support for each other, the refusal to co-operate under circumstances where co-operation appears advantageous, and the prevalence of destructive and anti-social behaviour puzzles and frustrates aid workers and researchers alike. These behaviour characteristics are often referred to as the 'dependency syndrome', a blanket term used for all the undesireable social behaviour found in the settlements. However, like all blanket terms, it can hide more than it reveals, and in the case of the Sudan, this way of categorizing refugee behaviour leads to wrong diagnoses of its cause and thus inevitably, wrongly aimed aid projects.

Two brief examples may clarify what I mean by the behaviour which is too easily characterized as irresponsible or dependent by observers. Both incidents were ones which I found difficult to accept, let alone explain. However explanations must be found if aid programmes are to be effective and, later in the chapter, I shall detail some of the basic economic and political characteristics of the refugee experience which produce and encourage these behaviours.

The first example occurred in 1982 at a late-night meeting of block leaders in Limbe. They reported the death of a woman who had recently given birth, and told the programme officer that *he* must find an orphanage for this infant. Weary from the long and hectic day, we did not spare their feelings. We reminded them that even had there been an orphanage, which there was not, this baby was the Ugandans' responsibility, not ours. They were the ones who had to find a substitute mother for the baby.

A second incident occurred in Kala settlement. The chairman pointed towards a house where a woman had given birth only a few hours earlier that morning. I asked to visit her and I found the mother attempting to chop firewood. The morning was bitterly cold. Inside the house the newborn baby lay uncovered on the damp earth; crouching beside it were two other shivering, half-naked children, staring up at me through the uncovered doorway. I was furious. 'Why,' I asked, 'is this woman chopping her own firewood?' The chairman explained that she had no relatives. 'Who gives a—?' I asked, 'where are the *neighbours*?' By this time the neighbours were in evidence, curious to know what had upset me. No one moved, so I took the axe in my own hands. The new mother immediately retired to her hut to lie down. To my humiliation, I was not strong enough to cut the wood with the dull axe! Finally a member of the committee took the axe from me and chopped the wood. As it turned out, *he was one of the neighbours*!

In this case, the chairman tried to cool my rage by explaining that 'In Uganda it is one's kinsmen who help, not one's neighbours. 'But,' I said, 'this is NOT Uganda! You *must* re-define social responsibility.' But both the programme officer and I had the impression that all such admonitions usually fell on deaf ears.[1] Why is it then, that refugees behave in this way? To begin to answer this question, we need to pay more attention to the psychological state of the refugees.

Does the mind matter?

Recently Ron Baker (1984) observed that in his research on the psychological needs of African refugees, he could find 'neither systematic analysis nor acknowledgement of psychosocial issues', either at the theoretical or practical level. He found most documents concerned with African refugees dominated by the 'demographic and practical'. He asks 'Why? Do refugees in Africa not have intense emotional reactions to being uprooted? How is mental illness perceived and dealt with among African refugee populations?' And he asks whether 'policy makers, planners, managers, researchers, and writers [are] so steeped in a developmental social engineering approach ... that they are in the grip of an over-socialized concept of man...?' By an 'over-socialized' concept of man, Baker refers to the way in which some social scientists consider human behaviour to be the result of social and cultural processes, to such a degree that individual psychology and individual responses are greatly under-valued. In the refugee situation, the individual and the individual's needs are submerged in the rush to deal with the multitude. I have already referred to situations in which the failure of aid policies to deal with specific, local, individual, situations led not only to the failure of programmes to meet refugee needs, but also to the creation of new problems and difficulties. In this chapter, I describe the ways in which the

---

[1] It appears that the programme officer has also come to accept the futility of outsiders trying to impose social responsibility. As he puts it in a letter, 'Perhaps it is good *not* to design very fixed social structures for refugees in settlements and to accept that they make their own - also unjust - society. UNHCR, a government or a volag [voluntary agency] will never be able to influence continuously and profoundly a refugee community and perhaps I should say *should* not want to do this. I believe more in a functioning "disorder" than a hypocritical "order"'.

failure of the aid programme to recognize individual psychological needs, and the failure to acknowledge the likely effect of the stresses of the refugee situation on individuals, leads directly to increasing numbers of psychologically disturbed individuals and may trigger psychosis.

But the 'over-socialized' view of man may also be applied to views of group processes. In group situations, the 'over-socialized view of man' assumes that once people are together, man's 'social nature' will quickly develop a social structure which will ensure the equitable and acceptable distribution of resources, no matter how limited those resources may be. And it also implicitly assumes that people will continue to be able to create social support systems, establish norms and act as responsible, autonomous individuals, unaffected by circumstances, no matter how destructive and debilitating those circumstances may be. Both assumptions may be unreasonable.

Humanitarian aid programmes, as Baker observed, do not take account of the need for psychological services for African refugees. In Khartoum UNHCR supported a counselling centre for urban refugees. It employed seven social workers and one highly qualified Sudanese psychiatric social worker, and in 1981-1984, the UNHCR staff member in charge of the centre was a qualified clinical psychologist. But it was most concerned with helping refugees with immediate practical problems of living in Khartoum and in organizing income-generating projects. Moreover, as this centre was thought to focus too narrowly on individual cases, in 1985 its phasing-out began. In southern Sudan there was no provision for IC, the UNHCR code for individual cases, beyond a counsellor in Juba who was not trained or expected to deal with psychological problems.

As Baker rightly observed, the emphasis was on programmes. This was not for lack of evidence of individual cases of the psychologically disturbed. No one could deny there were individuals who were clearly psychotic; perhaps because agency personnel had little or no previous experience in Africa, there was a tendency for them to view the bizarre behaviour of some Ugandans as simply a manifestation of the cultural trappings which all of them carried into the Sudan, along with their school certificates. Although there is a growing body of literature on the psychology of African societies, still,

For many, particularly in Europe and America ... Africa is an interesting, rather exotic place where anthropologists occasionally collect fascinating data on 'primitive' peoples ... there is a general acceptance of Africa's need for medical services ... When, however, one talks about mental illness in Africa and indicates that there are acute problems in this field, eyebrows begin to be raised and polite incredulity is frequently encountered. (German in Orley 1970.)

The first School of Psychiatry in East Africa was established at Makerere University. Professor German, who headed this school at the time, described a 'queue of mentally sick folk whose numbers might astonish the armchair theorists descended from Rousseau. Psychiatric problems in Uganda are not over the hill of 50 years hence, but are standing now at the clinic gate.' (ibid.)

When this was written Uganda was still relatively prosperous and reasonably stable; how much longer might that queue be today? In southern Sudan one was faced with evidence which suggests that few refugees escape the psychological scars of flight and exile. Even some of the most apparently stable will confide that they regularly dream of war, violence, and death.

I persist in looking for the most economical explanations for the abnormal social behaviour which I observed and resist the notion that the solution, except for the minority of cases, lies in psychiatric medicine or counselling therapy. However, the data that I collected, and the further exploratory and preliminary work done by the Oxford team, suggest that serious attention to these matters is long overdue.

Indirect evidence for psychological stress

In Limbe, one child (a budding artist) presented me with a picture of his house in the settlement. Later in Limuru, I found children drawing lorries and figures in the dirt, part of their kindergarten assignment under the trees. Always on the look out for new ways to collect expressions of culture, I sponsored a drawing contest. Teachers were asked only to instruct children to draw impressions of 'refugee life'. Prizes were set at £S15, £S10, £S5, with 20 £S1 'honourable mentions'. Although not all settlements responded in time, before I left I had collected over 200 drawings. Refugee life, as interpreted by the vast majority of these young artists is not as I had expected - lorries delivering food, compounds and houses cheek by jowl, schools under trees. They saw 'refugee life' in terms of violence. Some representative examples of their work appear in Appendix VI. The children drew pictures of soldiers shooting their mothers, infants lying bleeding to death, houses burning. They drew pictures of men tied to trees, decapitations, dogs eating human corpses. They drew groups of children and adults, crouching in the forest, ribs jutting or bellies swollen with starvation. The word 'refugee' itself seems to be associated in the minds of children with their experiences of violence, death, and starvation.

I was concerned that the content of these pictures might have been influenced by the teachers who announced the instructions for the contest. To test the validity of the initial results, in 1984 I asked the Oxford team to supervise the collection of more drawings, and to ensure the delivery of a 'neutral' introduction to the competition. Even though one year had passed since the earlier drawings and one might have assumed that time would erase the memory of some of these experiences, the team found that the children continued to draw 'disturbing and realistic pictures of massacres, lootings and gunfights, almost always based on first-hand experience, so that the characters (dead or alive) could be named.' (de Waal 1985, in Wilson *et al.* 1985.)

Perhaps more disturbing than the pictures were my interviews with very young children who all too frequently responded to questions about their future aspirations with statements about how they would return to Uganda to kill 'the Acholi'.[2]

Another source of data on individuals' feelings about their situation, one unfortunately I did not tap systematically, was the songs composed in exile. The themes of those translated for me during performances showed a preoccupation with death, suffering, hunger, and violent revenge. Those which were sung with greatest enthusiasm promised Obote and his 'Acholi' the justice they deserved.[3] Many songs are dirges. According to my assistants, these songs are now performed as part of social events much more frequently than they were in Uganda.

Indirect evidence of clinical levels of depression and anxiety

Prompted by indirect indications that refugees were suffering psychological stress, and by observations made during the research, it was decided that one of the members of the Oxford team should attempt to do further work on this topic. He decided to use a cross-culturally validated test (Wing *et al.* 1974) which had also been used in Uganda. (Orley and Wing 1979.) It was administered to a random sample of adults in one settlement and to a number of self-settled refugees and Sudanese at Panyume. The instrument used in the interview, the Present State Examination, was modified to examine neuroses, primarily depression and anxiety. The scale was administered in 1984 by Alex de Waal and Alula Pankhurst together with three Ugandan colleagues. Given the inexperience of the interviewers and the very limited number of cases, one must entertain serious reservations regarding the validity of the results. (Eyton and Neuwirth 1984.) There is, however, a strong justification for presenting these results in order to stimulate further work.

The results of 57 interviews were independently diagnosed by clinical psychologists in Oxford. Only 13 were found to have no psychiatric problems. Seven were diagnosed as suffering anxiety, 6 suffered anxiety together with

---

[2] It is disturbing to consider that a generation of children have not only endured the traumas represented in their art, but are growing up in conditions of continued economic and social insecurity.

[3] For example,
I am dead
If this boy dies I will jump into the bush
If an Acholi comes
I will shoot him twice
And escape into the jungle

Ah! Nimeri Oyite Ojok
has brought Saba Saba artillery to kill us
You shoot us with B 10
The Acholis have no brothers
In fact we don't live with you.

depressive features, 19 suffered depression and 11 suffered depression with anxiety features. Three-quarters of this very small sample suffered an 'appreciable psychiatric disorder'. In Uganda, Orley and Wing (1979) found that only 25 per cent of the population of two villages had such 'disorders "above threshold level", including 5 per cent with "definite" disorders'.

The criteria used for diagnosing clinical depression consisted of the presence of depressed mood combined with at least four of the following symptoms: loss of weight through lack of appetite; loss of interest in activities; self-deprecation; social withdrawal; feelings of hopelessness; suicidal ideas; early waking; impaired concentration; neglect due to brooding and anergia. (de Waal op. cit.)

It is believed that any person who met these criteria would be seriously affected by depression. The depressives in the Limbe sample presented primarily somatic symptoms in contrast to the conventional symptoms of the typical European depressive, who is more likely to display feelings of guilt and depression. In Limbe, people complained of headaches, bodies which ached even when they did no work, constant exhaustion, anergia and retardation, sleeplessness, loss of appetite, and loss of libido.

Typically, an interviewee would answer the question, 'What has been troubling you most in the last month?' with a description of aches and pains... Weakness every day. Pain in the head, on the top and round the back of the neck. Pain round the waist and in the back and shoulders. Fire in the head; it feels like the skin is coming off.... (de Waal op.cit.)

Three people in the sample were contemplating suicide and one had seriously attempted it.

Marital status - where spouses were present - appeared to be related to mental health: 'Only 17 out of 39 married people were depressed.' Similarly the absence of members of an individual's close relatives other than the spouse, seemed to distinguish cases suffering depression: 'Of the 28 with family members in the settlement, only 11 were primarily depressed.' (ibid.)

Commonsense, as well as a body of psychological literature (e.g. Golan 1978), support de Waal's statements that

...adverse life events are a cause of depression, though there are complex factors which make some people more vulnerable than others to it. Everybody in the Limbe study had lost a country and at least one close relative. Many had lost many close relatives and witnessed horrifying incidents such as massacres. Therefore, the normal link between an adverse life event and depression has in general been swamped by the number and magnitude of adverse life events. (de Waal op.cit.)

A close link was found between depression and the scale of an individual's losses,

...crudely measured by the number of people in one's immediate family who had died since the outbreak of the war - and depression. Three of the four suicidal cases had lost all the members of their immediate families. Of 16 people who had lost five or more members of their close family, 13 were depressed, one anxious with depressive features, one psychotic and only one without any evident psychiatric problems (yet). (ibid.)

Twenty-four persons in the sample suffered clinical levels of anxiety (i.e. they were unable to function normally) and 34 suffered panic attacks at least once a month. These attacks involve the sudden onset of disabling fear accompanied by trembling, sweating, heart beating fast, dizziness, palpitations, dry- mouth, choking etc. which may last for a few minutes or up to an hour or more.

In fact, the statistics here are misleading. Though 19 people suffered from depression without accompanying clinical levels of anxiety, not a single one of these people was completely free of anxiety symptoms. Indeed, the very diagnosis of 'agitated depression' suggests the presence of symptoms that could have been interpreted as anxiety. In Limbe, the dividing line between 'depression' and 'anxiety' is fairly arbitrary. (ibid.)

In conclusion, then, with even the limited amount of evidence available, it is likely that the incidence of psychiatric illness among refugees is relatively high. These data suggest the need for further research, and they also establish the need for humanitarian aid programmes to consider the mental health of refugees in Africa. In western societies, it is accepted that the levels of depression and anxiety suggested by our interviews would be 'seriously disabling'. If aid programmes could identify and alleviate some of the causes of anxiety and depression, then both the health and effectiveness of the refugees would improve. While the death and destruction that impelled the refugees' flight cannot be removed by the aid agencies, some of the other important causes of anxiety can be mitigated. The important factor that has not previously been recognized as significant, and one which has caused much distress in the settlements, is bereavement, and it is this that I now want to turn to.

Bereavement

Some psychological studies of refugees from other countries have drawn on theories developed out of studies of reactions to bereavement. Among Chilean refugees, Munoz (1984) found that:

The bereavement experience may be interpreted as a result of loss of roots, the geography, the emotional support, the cognitive world, and the status which they had enjoyed prior to exile ... the parallel between exile and bereavement is presented here as a symbolic key which unlocks the psychological world of the exile. I believe that by making this parallel between exiles and bereavement, we might eventually be able to interpret consistently the exile experience.

That it *is* possible to generalize the experience of being uprooted is supported by studies of the illnesses of students studying abroad. (Zwingmann 1983.)

The US government takes seriously the possibility that even the temporary loss of one's country and exposure to an alien culture can have adverse psychological effects upon members of its foreign service. The symptoms which diplomats are warned they may suffer include stress, 'common to any anxiety-producing situation, [which] may be severe or mild, may last several months, or appear only fleetingly.' Several associated physical and emotional symptoms are listed: sleepiness, apathy, depression, compulsive eating or drinking, homesickness, and exaggerated yearning for all things and friends 'American', insecurity of professional judgement, negative stereotyping of host nationals, fear of being cheated, decline in efficiency, recurrent minor illnesses, and obsession with cleanliness. Children may not escape such symptoms as regression in toilet training or social behaviour, interrupted sleep, skin eruptions, stomach disorders. Older children may manifest culture shock by finding it difficult to maintain academic competence, working out their anxiety in disruptive behaviour and sometimes even 'experimenting' with drugs, alcohol, sex.[4]

It is usually argued that the culture and landscape of the countries in which most African refugees find asylum is more familiar to them than is the case for refugees elsewhere. However, for most Ugandans, the Sudan represents a wrenching change from the familiar. Only a minority in Yei River District shared a common mother-tongue with local Sudanese, and very few had crossed the border into the Sudan before 1979 - even those who lived just on the other side of the Kaya River. That many local Sudanese had also been refugees and some had lived in Uganda was a mixed blessing. Depending on their own experiences in exile in Uganda, they were more or less sympathetic with the new arrivals.

The refugees in southern Sudan had not only lost home and country. As we have seen, those who suffered psychiatric disabilities (as measured by the PSE scale) had all lost immediate relatives. The Oxford team found evidence in their case studies of some of the 'components' of grief identified in studies of bereavement. (Parkes 1972.) These components of grief include:

1. Process of realization. A shift from avoidance and denial to acceptance. It was common at the beginning of the interview for a person to deny that he or she had lost any relatives, and later for them to admit that certain family members had died. One man began by saying his brother lived nearby and the rest of his family were in Uganda. Later, we discovered that *all* his family, with the exception of his wife, had been killed in Uganda, and his wife had also recently died in Limbe.

---

[4] *Foreign Service Assignment Notebook*, (October 1978). This handbook includes an essay entitled 'Exploring New Cultures' which suggests, as preventative therapy, a list of questions which people arriving at a new posting may use as a guide to learn about the new culture. This list might be a useful guide for refugees!

2. Alarm reaction. Symptoms of fear and panic were frequent, many people were restless and irritable, sometimes even violent.

3. The urge to search for the deceased. This component is complicated by the fact that many people do not know of the fate of relatives. One manifestation of the urge is general anxiety and restlessness. Another is actual searching behaviour. Several of the returnees interviewed [prior to their repatriation] ...said they were going back to Uganda to rejoin relatives or to look for relatives. In some cases, I later discovered that some of these relatives were either suspected or even known to be dead.

4. Anger and Guilt. Feelings of guilt were uncommon...but anger, either suppressed or openly expressed was common.

5. Feelings of internal loss or self-mutilation. This usually took the form of psychosomatic complaints, hypochondriasis or suspicions of poisoning. Some people complained of depersonalization, one said he felt like a stranger everywhere, others said that for a long time they had felt numb.

6. Identification phenomena. ...Amongst the Ugandans in Limbe it was common for respondents not only to idealize the past...but to identify strongly with Uganda....Ugandan refugees were intensely patriotic. (de Waal op.cit.)

A symptom which did not fit into these categories was the number of people (twenty) who expressed 'simple ideas of reference; they believed that other people were watching them, laughing at them or even trying to harm them. The most extreme example of this was a young man, N.A., who was suicidal, who thought that his neighbours were trying to kill him with axes.' (ibid.)

It is clear then, that bereavement, especially when occurring so frequently, can itself cause temporary psychological dislocation and great distress. The situation is made more painful, however, by the way the refugee experience interacts with the mourning and burial rites that should be carried out. In normal situations, mourning rites are a crucial part of the process by which individuals accommodate bereavement.

Mourning

Earlier in the book I referred to the general belief often expressed by outsiders that Africans do not suffer the same emotional feelings after bereavement as 'we' do. According to Baker (1984), an apparently stoic response to intense suffering may be an appropriate, though costly, initial defence system.

The inability to mourn when and where it is appropriate is felt [to be] or is at stake. To show intense emotions at these high points of threat may lead to discovery, scapegoating, brutalization, or even death. The feelings of loss must be contained, but at what price? (Baker 1984.)

Later, in a camp, refugees are still in a highly vulnerable psychological state.

To allow oneself to enter into a mourning process at this time is likely to be anticipated as leading to even greater feelings of insecurity. Particularly when such reactions are hardly acknowledged in the policies, structures and practices of such holding centres. So what happens to these dammed-up feelings? Commonsense and Western clinical experience suggest that they do not simply disappear, but continue to exert a profound and dynamic influence on a person's behaviour, thoughts and interpersonal relations. And this may continue for the rest of life if not satisfactorily resolved. (ibid.)

Refugees in Africa have not only experienced the loss of roots, geography, emotional support, and the culture and status they enjoyed before flight; the scale of death from military violence, illness, and malnutrition may actually be far greater than that experienced by most refugees who have been the subjects of psychological research.

Earlier, I discussed the tendency of refugees to conceal the death of a relative. The inability to finance the ceremonies (and usually travel) that are associated with proper mourning may in part account for the severity of the panic attacks which were described to the interviewers in Limbe.

Parkes (1972) in his section of *atypical grief*, discusses delayed grief reactions, and remarks that panic attacks are frequently associated with this form of grief. As de Waal observed, delayed grief reaction certainly seems an appropriate explanation for many of the cases of panic. During the civil war or flight, when often it was not even possible to bury the dead, the bereaved do not express normal grief, but an unhealthy numbness. Later, some relatively minor event acts as a trigger to release the pent-up mourning, which sometimes takes the form of frequent panic attacks. In all but two of the 34 cases reported to suffer panic attacks, it was possible to establish that some significantly adverse life event had occurred in the few days before the onset. These included the death of a relative, the day a person left Uganda during a military bombardment, when a relative was repatriated, when property was looted, and following the 'loss' of a relative through marriage.

In the short term, the failure to observe mourning practices may be a necessary adaptive response; for instance during a battle or while fleeing one does not have time to mourn. But in the long term it is likely to be pathogenic. All societies recognize the need for mourning, if possible by the graveside. In instances where there is no grave, some societies have developed alternatives, such as war memorials, the tomb of the unknown soldier, etc. (de Waal op.cit.).[5]

In this section, the significance of bereavement, and the importance of mourning rituals have been shown. It is a limitation of the over-socialized view of human nature that informs so many aid policies. Aid is not applied to maintaining social institutions. Refugees are expected to cope by being appropriately 'social', but they are denied the resources to re-establish the

---

[5] Recall the request of the women at Limbe - for cement to mark graves.

real bases of social life, the exchanges and rites which make a truly sociable and co-operative life possible. In fact aid workers often feel able to denigrate and devalue the 'customs' which might help people to survive with more dignity.

The statistical data collected during our survey indicated the widespread disruption of family life that occurred among refugee populations. There are indications of marriage breakdowns, separation of partners inflight, loss of children and so on. The significance of these situations for personal well-being cannot be overestimated. There is, then, a case for suggesting that aid programmes should accommodate the need to re-establish as many as possible of the pre-existing social institutions of the refugees.

Maintaining customs

Certainly one factor contributing to the insecurity of refugees is the impossibility of observing mandatory traditional customs - in other words, normal social responsibilities. I have already mentioned that poverty usually prevents the transfer of an adequate amount of wealth to a bride's family to legalize the marriage contract. Except for some of the young men who were constantly appealing to UNHCR for funds to pay their dowries, the suggestion that perhaps the custom had outlived its usefulness did not strike a responsive chord. For fathers, the marriage of a daughter was one incontestable potential source of money. No refugee could afford to turn his back on the possibility of getting cash, even if he had to pursue his son-in-law from Yei to Aru (Zaire) and back. The worst things that can befall a young man who breaks the customary rules of marriage is to have to face his in-laws in court, or to have his wife reclaimed by her family.

While the legal tangles following breaches of marriage rules are expensive and lengthy, at least those involved are only required to deal with *the living*. This is not the case when someone dies. The failure to perform burial rites according to custom is subject to supernatural sanctions. A proper burial is the most important act of respect which can be paid to the deceased. There is probably no greater disgrace to a family than to have failed to observe funeral customs. Many refugees are haunted with the memories of those relatives they left unburied in the bush while fleeing for their own lives. Some risked personal safety to return to dig graves, and one field commander told me that even after battle they bury the bodies of the enemies, as he put it, 'out of respect'. Even the children's drawings portrayed painful memories of the unburied dead. One child drew a picture of a dog feeding on a body and wrote the caption: 'We could not even bury our dead. Dogs ate the bodies of our family.'

It is not enough simply to dig a hole and cover the corpse: it must be properly wrapped. Families would be willing to go to sleep hungry to find the money to buy cloth. As noted, the lack of funds for burial cloth explains the fate of so many UNHCR-supplied blankets. Refugees often painfully recalled how, when they were hiding in Uganda, they had to resort to banana leaves to wrap the dead. In settlements, the incentive to hide the fact that a relative has died (lest his name be struck off the ration list) only adds to the sense of guilt and betrayal.

A decent burial is only the beginning. Deaths must be announced to all the family and this involved refugees in a considerable amount of movement between settlements and to the areas where their self-settled kinsfolk live. One announces the death of a spouse to one's in-laws with a gift - usually a goat. There are many other mandatory payments. One refugee told me why he was so deeply in debt. He had lost all but one son, when another relative died in his settlement household. He had to inform his in-laws. Believing as they all do that the failure to observe proper funeral procedures will cause further misfortune, illness and death in the family, and unwilling to risk his remaining son's life, he borrowed £S40 to buy a goat and travel to the border.

Funerals involve the expense of feeding the family which gathers for the occasion. These ceremonies should be elaborate, involving drinking, special funeral dances, and plenty of food for visitors. When the settlement foremen were Ugandans, some held back sacks of grain in the store saying these were a supply upon which to draw for food for funerals. Always prone to impute the worst motives for any activity which deviated from the equal distribution of rations to all, these men were suspected of holding back food to sell for personal gain. Perhaps they were corrupt, but the need in settlements for such a reserve seems, on reflection, quite reasonable. For those deaths which are not reported, such gatherings are usually held away from the settlement in the compounds of self-settled relatives. One way of avoiding the misfortunes associated with the failure to bury properly those killed in Uganda is to observe such ceremonies later on. If a refugee manages to get any money, he is likely to use it first to fulfil these traditional obligations.

A hive of mourners

Perhaps the best way to portray the force of customs and the crises which arise for refugees under conditions of extreme poverty is to reproduce excerpts from a description of Aluma Ponziano's wife's death in childbirth and her burial. Ponziano was a student at Moyo Senior Secondary School when the war broke out. He met and married Irine not long after they had settled in Kala. Shortly after marrying, Aluma was converted and he and his wife 'started to seek God and read the Bible.'

A year later, on 18 December, Irine began her labour. He first called a grandmother who had experience as a traditional midwife. She was not home. 'The next nearest woman was Mrs Vuni so I moved to her. ... she promised to come immediately.'

Traditional methods used at delivery make things harder for the expecting mothers. Experience and beliefs controlled all things. It was believed that earlier misconduct such as marital unfaithfulness, theft, disobedience to mothers-in-law, grudges, oaths taken in anger, calling God to kill... done before or during pregnancy would surely cause complications...

Aluma details many of the other taboos observed by pregnant women. Sitting outside the hut, he listens to the women interrogating his wife as her labour becomes seriously prolonged. Very late in the process, the midwife and medical assistant are called to help.

Mrs Selle was the first to arrive. She gave Irine some tablets ... She also enlarged her vulva with a pair of scissors. When the time for deliverance was come, blood issued out through the nostrils as well as the vagina. Amid long ... agony and cries of pain, the baby came out... [It] neither cried nor moved. ... The baby was dead. It was a boy.

From Aluma's graphic description of his wife's death, which quickly followed, we may deduce this young woman simply haemorrhaged to death.

Already informed of the fate of the baby, a crowd had gathered outside the hut. It fell to Aluma to inform them that:

'Irine too is dead.' Unbelief and horror gripped them. Those outside rushed in... Almost immediately the air was filled with ullulations and wailings which drew a thick crowd to my compound. If one entered a beehive, I believe one would understand what it felt like to be amongst these mourners. The noise of wailing and ullulations added up to make my home a hive for mourners. The women cried and jumped about, their sleeping breasts slapped against their chests. Others crossed their hands on their heads and forgot the tears and mucus which got mixed up and rolled across the wide open mouth. They were too miserable to bother about wiping it off. The men folded their hands across their chests and bowed their heads in grief.

Early the next morning Aluma was visited by another 'devout Christian' living in the settlement. He warned Aluma, 'These heathen relatives of yours will put you to hard testing by demanding that you conform to superstitions which they call the traditions of our ancestors. But be courageous and stand up for Jesus.'

Grinding stones around their necks

Aluma describes some of the customary funeral practices. It should be noted that nearly *all* involve compensating ritual specialists and making other expenditures.

... Traditional funeral ceremonies were full of rituals which varied according to sex, age, marital status and the types of deaths in some cases. Women who died while pregnant also went through specific rites. The details and meanings of these rites were now fast fading from the minds of this present generation which hangs between two conflicting civilizations. Not even all the elders today were accustomed to them; some were also ignorant of certain rituals for certain occasions.

Could it be that under the conditions of exile, these refugees are more anxious to revive customs which were, as Aluma suggests, already forgotten by most people? In voluntary re-settlement situations, the concern of communities with maintaining cultural institutions has been widely observed. Migrant Greeks in Australia, for example, are so 'conservative' that young women who return to their village of origin report feeling 'liberated'! (Bottomley 1984.) The need to re-establish some symbols of 'normal' community life in refugee situations is likely to be much greater. When certain cultural practices are associated with payments, and when poverty and starvation are widespread, it is hardly surprising that mourning rites take on such importance.[6]

Aluma, describing rituals associated with the burial of males and females, points out that 'Rites at funerals amongst the Madi were numerous indeed and if one wrote them all down it would make a very thick book. Some of these, which the people were now insisting he follow, were not only expensive, but offensive to his new-found faith as well. But when he attempted to stop the women from treating his wife in the prescribed manner, his father's brother pointed out that Aluma had failed to consider one significant fact: Aluma had not paid his in-laws' the bride price. If they wanted to, they could demand he pay now before allowing Irine's body to be buried!

The reactions of the community which Aluma described, suggest it would not be a wholly unreasonable idea to set up a loan scheme which allowed people to borrow in such emergencies.

In the meantime the news of my refusal was spreading outside amongst the mourners. Murmurs of disapproval swept all round the crowd. My in-laws sent for me. When I stepped outside to them I was met by many troubled gaze on the faces everybody present. I looked down and slowly and carefully made my way to where my in-laws sat in a group on one side and my relatives on the other side. Among them I saw my mother who would not raise her eyes up. I know she was worried beyond words and must have been at great pains at my refusal. Agavuru, an elderly man with one leg amputated, was the first to address me.

'You said you will not conform to our customs because your religion does not allow that. But you must remember that you have not paid anything, not even a single cent, on our daughter. I am her paternal uncle but her real father will come. When he comes are you ready to settle everything as he demands? If you agree to this well and good. We shall not accept from you anything just now. You look for your people to bury her,' he said, and another of my in-laws took the floor.

'This means he did not consider our daughter as a wife otherwise why should he prefer to have her buried in so shameful a way - without paying her the usual age long respect accorded to all women in honour of their womanhood? Ever since I started to breathe decades and decades ago I have never seen, leave along hearing, a thing like this,' he finished.

[6] See page 312, for Cheik Ante Diop's explanation for certain entrenched practices in Africa.

The women also joined the chorus of protest, one pointing out that the failure to observe custom now would endanger all women who might be pregnant in the future. Ultimately, despite his arguments, Aluma was defeated and the rituals were performed.

Digging the grave produced a similar financial and social crisis. Money was needed for various relatives and Aluma, as husband of the deceased, was expected to undergo ceremonies and to spend time in seclusion. Aluma refused and 'people were thrown into a tumult. They came to me begging me not to refuse if all I hoped to be free from similar misfortunes. Convinced that I would never be safe without having to undergo all that tradition demanded, each of my relatives came to me pleading earnestly that I relent.'

Among them was his maternal uncle, thought to have mystical power over nephews. The idea of refusing to follow *his* authority was unthinkable. As one relative put it, 'If he ignores an uncle I will know for certain that the many books he has read have made him lose his head.' One Christian pointed out that if Aluma thought he was committing a sin by following the rituals, he could always confess later. But another relative suggested that Aluma might be among those who pretend to be holy, but 'might be the very one to go to hell in the end.'

Although they gave in grudgingly, the family decided it was time to get on with the more immediate matter of burying the corpse. Before any burial could take place my people and my in-laws sat down to settle certain matters first. These included the payment of certain sums of money to my in- laws.

These included a fee for 'asking permission to bury the baby' and also it was necessary for Aluma to give some money towards the cost of his marriage. 'Under normal circumstances, i.e. had we not been destitute refugees, my in-laws would demand that I pay all the bride-price on my wife first before she could be buried.' As it was they settled for £S35 so long as Aluma agreed that he was now in debt and that he would pay his debt, once 'his economic situation improved'. He recalled that at an earlier funeral in Kala, when the husband could not pay these costs, the husband had gone for the police to force the in-laws to allow the burial to proceed. Aluma was saved by the generous contribution which the mourners made on this day. 'Some of the cost was met by "Vurra Funeral Association" which we had formed on realizing the need for such an association in our refugee settlement. I had to borrow money to add to what the mourners and the Association contributed. By around 5 p.m. Sudan local time the needed amount was paid and my wife and her son went into their graves.'

Aluma's bed, which was made of bamboo, was used as the stretcher to carry the body to the grave. Normally this stretcher would have been thrown away, but Aluma could not afford to lose his bed and he further offended the community by retrieving it. Despite the ritual danger in which he is thought to place himself in by doing so, he says he still 'sleep[s] on it and breath[es].'

About a month later his wife's father came to visit Kala from a settlement on the east bank of the Nile, Kit 4. When he was ready to return, he asked Aluma for money for transport. Aluma was advised it was against custom 'to escort a mourner on his return journey or give...him any transport or transport money.'

I could not help violating this merciless, unconsoling tradition. This man had lost his dear daughter. He.had walked more than a hundred miles to pay his last respects at her grave site. Sorrowful, he wanted now to return to his settlement where he would continue to be tormented by the memories of his dear daughter's death.

Aluma broke with yet another tradition and gave him £S7. It would be encouraging if all refugees were as amenable to change as Aluma appears to be.

From then on I started to question the necessity and the implications of every action I see people take in my society around me. The strictness and importance attached to traditions in most aspects in my society are simple grinding stones tied around their necks. It makes me wonder the more when I see how determined they are to continue to carry this load despite its unfairness to humanity.[7]

Crisis and loss

The significance of social custom in situations of stress should now be clear. But there are other factors which are important in determining a refugee's reaction to his situation. 'Crisis theory' explains the response of individuals to stress by focusing on the crisis situation which causes distress. A psychological crisis occurs when a person faces an obstacle to important goals, and one which cannot, for a time, be overcome by his customary methods of problem-solving. Stress, notes Baker (1984), should be differentiated from crisis, although both occur when normal coping methods do not lead to mastery of a particular problem.

One may link crisis theory to refugee experience in the following way. Stress is an inevitable consequence of being uprooted. If the refugees' coping skills are good and if an environment (services, resources, etc.) is provided that ensures basic survival needs are met, [if] there is a real hope for a better future, the stress remains manageable. The person can plan with some optimism to build a new life and cope with culture shock, alienation, losses of varying kinds, loneliness, etc. If neither of these conditions exist, then the stress level can rise rapidly and the person shifts into a state of unrelieved crisis. (ibid.)

[7] It may be that the insecurity and poverty of refugee life re-validate the knowledge of the old men, knowledge which was formerly challenged and devalued. If this is so, it may be that a gerontocracy is beginning to emerge, but one which is relatively free of the checks and balances found in more settled situations. The restriction of refugee education programmes to the primary level will reduce the challenge to other forms of knowledge and the emphasis on the subsistence agriculture minimizes the economic independence of younger men. Aluma's conversion to Christianity may be part of a broader struggle in which power relationships are being fought out along religious lines. The rigidity of the aid programme may contribute to greater conservatism.

The symptoms associated with unrelieved crisis or stress include explosive, violent behaviour, profound depression, loss of personal identity, depersonalization, psychosomatic symptoms, and sometimes psychotic withdrawal. All these types of behaviour were observed among Ugandan refugees.

People are said to experience crisis in three characteristic ways: as a threat, as a loss, or as a challenge. Each of these characteristic responses have different associated emotional components: threat leads to a heightened state of anxiety; loss is accompanied by feelings of sadness, depression, grief, and worthlessness; and challenge results in feelings of hope and the expectation that new situations have the potential for improving the person's life.

In terms of assisting refugees, the way refugee workers and host communities respond to these different affective components may be crucial to the way the refugee deals with his or her emotional responses. Thus, if our reception and ... policies and programmes neither acknowledge nor appropriately respond to the threat and loss which refugees experience, it is likely that we add to the individual's psychological trauma. Further, if we have nothing practical or concrete to offer other than years of camp experience and long term unemployment, then the refugee has no opportunity to react positively to the challenge of his or her situation. Loss and threat will dominate the individual's world, and become entrenched. (ibid)

Baker draws three important conclusions which may help to suggest ways an assistance programme could give appropriate support to refugees.

1. A crisis should not be viewed as an illness or a pathological experience.
2. A person can remain in an active crisis state - a state of maximum disequilibrium - for four to six weeks. While in this state, an individual may be more amenable to help than at any other time in the process. Thus it is crucial that intervention should occur while the person is in this active crisis state.
3. In the last phase of the process - that of re-integration - adaptive and coping methods may become strengthened, which will enable individuals to consolidate and deal with future problems constructively. Alternatively, maladaptive methods of adjustment may become entrenched, making a person even less able than before to master his present life situation or future problems.

What emerges is the importance of experiences in the early period of exile; interventions, if they are to have a positive effect, should occur in the first few weeks. In these terms alone, assistance programmes in Africa always arrive too late. Moreover, since most African refugees resist aid for as long as possible, the populations of settlements probably include many who have already passed the optimum period for recovery.[8]

[8] Perhaps the relatively small amount of assistance that came from local people, the few hoes, medicines, and the small amount of used clothing distributed by SCC and Sudanaid in those early days of the influx, was the key to the psychological health of many refugees. Many recall with overwhelming gratitude the small acts of charity they experienced during the first days after arrival.

Settlements versus independence

From his experience, James Appe (1984), a Ugandan refugee, made many similar observations.

After the long and fearful journey across the border, only gradually should a refugee be made to feel that he has 'arrived'. He must be kept somehow 'on the run'. He should be assisted on a very small scale so that he can see himself creating his new home. He could feel then that it belongs to him and would care for it. This would help him rediscover himself. 'After such a trial, I'm able to achieve this. Perhaps I had not really died. No I'm still my old self.' This alone will enable the refugee to set up a sound basis for his assistance, by his own efforts.

But, he admonishes, a programme should be:

designed only after on-the-spot interviews with refugees and careful assessment of their particular problems as individuals and as a group ... the solution is to give the refugees greater responsibility for assisting themselves - they must be assisted marginally in order to assist themselves totally...

...What happens when a refugee is put into a situation where he is made to depend entirely on aid agencies to tell him what and how much to eat, and when and where to sleep? In the end he will let agencies 'think' for him. This means that he has no personality that he can respect.

...Personal responsibility must be followed by collective responsibility... Refugees should, and could be given maximum freedom to identify their own problems.

His analysis of the relationship between aid and the refugees is full of insight and concludes:

...The one fundamental problem: the reason why it is so often difficult to assist refugees, is that they are not recognized as having any responsibility for their affairs at the beginning - and this affects the whole subsequent programme and will last as long as the refugees remain where they are. Refugees must not be settled, but must be allowed to try to settle themselves. (ibid.)

As was discussed in the Introduction, for many Ugandans it was being forced to accept assistance by going to a settlement which marked the beginning of their status, refugee. And, as we have seen, most of them came to the settlement because of illness or hunger; the move involves acquiring a stigma: one can no longer look after oneself. Some people refer to it as 'giving up'. (de Waal op. cit.) But who is taking over? Almost everyone now appreciates that in principle food aid is a 'bad' thing. You should only give it when people are dying for want of food then you should stop, or, if you continue, make them work for it. There is the implicit assumption that one can only know when to stop if the people one is helping are under one's control or one is deciding on how they earn the food. Giving assistance *on demand* does not allow such control of distribution; SCC and the Catholics' manner of helping refugees was much more economical.

While no empirical evidence was collected to support the hypothesis that unassisted refugees demonstrated fewer symptoms of psychological ill-health than did those in settlements, there was no doubt that they were at least spared the adverse effects of the near total loss of autonomy suffered by assisted refugees. My visits to the compounds of the self-settled often gave me the impression that some of these people even enjoyed a sense of well-being. Many expressed pride that despite everything they had managed to survive. I rarely came away with such an impression from a visit to settlements.

My team of interviewers included unassisted refugees. The relative merits of life outside and inside the settlements were constantly and heatedly debated. The evidence, especially from the comparative study of schools, was disturbing to those who argued for settlements. In settlements there was no system of regular inspection such as teachers had been accustomed to in Uganda. Conduct and discipline had broken down to an alarming degree. The team member responsible for this study found:

Drinking during working hours - especially at break time. I have met teachers who are smelling [of] alcohol in the class and one teacher who was exercising her muscles (i.e. flogging) on school children after a dose of 'waragi' [local brew]. ...One parent said [this] was a habit for her. I even learnt of a case where, after getting boozed up, a teacher decided to march out of his class for a parade in the football ground at 12.00 noon. (Dramundru 1982.)

At the same time, the 'self-help and integrated schools were found to be maintaining a superior standard of teaching and there is better discipline among both staff and pupils.' Although the teachers outside settlements received little or no pay, they were 'more conscious of their responsibility to society ... although most of them are not trained, they are more dedicated.' (ibid.)[9]

The failures of teachers, medical or agricultural workers to maintain professional standards would appear to be less than excusable, since under the circumstances their skills were vitally needed by the community and most were able to continue their careers, even if under very difficult conditions. But the Ugandan community contained a wide range of professional skills which were, for the most part, unemployable in southern Sudan. One might be able to calculate the economic loss to Africa of the years of investment in the education of the many professionals who are now expected to farm for their livelihood, but one cannot calculate the psychological costs of the loss of status to the individuals concerned. As de Waal observed:

Everyone, whether a soldier, a blacksmith, a judge or an olympic athlete, (to give four examples from our sample), is given a hoe and told to dig.'

[9] Their requests for assistance made during the course of this research were also realistic. They asked for textbooks, stationery for children, etc; rarely did anyone mention the lack of a salary. Responding to such initiatives would not only be less expensive, it would allow refugees to set their own priorities and perhaps to maintain their own self-respect.

He describes this process as being 'almost like a ritual humiliation.'

People dream about and brood on their past occupations. One man, a herbalist, was obsessed (in the lay sense) with his bicycle that had been looted in Uganda. A young man was longing for a sewing machine to start up a small business. But when he was given the chance of joining a co-operative of tailors, he refused; he did not trust any of the other members. Later, he had the opportunity to apply for one from the social worker, but he did not take the initiative. 'I can never regain what I had in Uganda,' he said, 'So what is the use of trying?' (1985.)

It is certainly possible that not only the loss of professional status, but the loss of power and autonomy in the settlement programme may 'slow down or even reverse the process of gradual psychological recovery from the massive trauma of war'. (ibid). The failure to consult refugees concerning the kinds of assistance which they see as most beneficial accounts for many of the problems one observed.

Making the victims the villains

Assistance programmes for African refugees aim to cater for the needs of the majority. The queues of people whose particular need has not been caught in that net are the bane of any agency office. Field staff are overworked and they are not trained to cope with most of the individual problems which present themselves. Budgets for feeding and housing individual cases, or ICs, are limited (or, as in Yei in 1982, non-existent). Sometimes, even if staff wish to help, they realize that to do so will require them to pay money out of their own pocket. Since there was no objective means for distinguishing genuine cases from charlatans, there was an unfortunate tendency for many field officers to approach *all* refugees as though they were in this latter category. The frustration of the fieldworkers, which arises from a general sense of inadequacy, may account for the hostility which one so frequently observed in their relations with refugees. Even to be seen by a field officer, refugees must wait for extremely long periods. In Yei I observed one young man who had to wait literally seven days outside the office for an appointment. To hear his problem took exactly ten minutes.

Some refugees decide to get attention by dramatizing their frustrations. In one notorious case, a refugee threatened to hang himself if not immediately allowed to talk about his problem with someone. The overworked official on duty, preoccupied with his accounts, advised him to 'proceed'. He did, and it was only at the very last moment, as he was about to step off his makeshift gallows before a spellbound audience of other waiting refugees, that the weary expatriate surrendered to this psychological pressure. Sometimes, almost ruefully, fieldworkers joke about their way of dealing with individual cases. One tells the story of the time he shouted at a minister to get out of his office. He always left his office door open for ventilation. Whenever he felt the shadow of a refugee trying to get his attention about a problem, without raising his head from his papers, he would shout, 'GET OUT'. One day the shadow was the minister. The assistance programme itself encourages refugees to develop manipulative techniques to draw attention to their legitimate problems.

But the individual cases which turn up at agency offices often represent the needs and problems of a large number of people, not to mention their personal trauma which require specialized treatment. For example, Moses Dafala, 34 years old, a victim of torture, was the head of a family of 14 living in Gumbari settlement. In the 1970s he had joined the air force. In 1979 he found himself at the front line. Disgusted by the undisciplined behaviour of the officers who, by this time, were mainly Sudanese (he saw them looting property and deserting the battlefield), he buried his own uniform and weapons, donned civilian clothes and was one of the first to present himself for surrender in Kampala. Sent to Tanzania as a prisoner-of-war, he was released during Binaisa's brief period in office. Re-arrested, he was sent to Luzira prison. He arrived in the Sudan as a refugee in late 1982 and began reporting for medical attention.

On 23 November 1982, he was referred to Juba by the medical inspector at Yei hospital. The referral note describes his symptoms as '...suffering from chronic headache for 3 years, and he cannot hear well.' On 22 December 1982 Mr Dafala was seen at the Juba hospital where it was recommended he be referred to Khartoum for further tests. This advice was not followed, and he was ordered to return immediately to his settlement. He appealed to the UNHCR office in Juba.

I have the honour to inform you that I am a Ugandan refugee from Gumbari refugee camp. I was referred to Juba for medical treatment since 22/12/82... While in Uganda I became a prisoner of war and was badly beaten. A bullet passed through my groin [Following my] release from Luzira prison ... I was admitted to Burabika Hospital for mental [treatment] due to the beatings. Sir, my immediate and crucial complaint is that the GMT doctor, Juba Branch, seems to disagree with my Doctor in Juba Hospital's advice, referring me to Khartoum for further treatment and is instead asking me to return to the Camp as shown on my Refugee Medical Referral Card attached. But sincerely my health is deteriorating and I feel it necessary to follow my Doctor's advice for the better [sic] of my life... (25 February 1983.)

Nevertheless he was sent back to Gumbari. He was seen in August 1983 by the Ugandan doctor who by then had joined the health service in Yei and who wrote:

...The above named [Dafala] is a Ugandan refugee. He has been complaining of chest pain (retrosternal), associated with cough and sputum; pain down the vertebral column; severe headaches and general body aches and weakness ... the pain is made worse by any manual labour. Previously there were streaks of blood in the sputum which have ceased after antibiotic treatment. But still other complaints continue. No history of weight loss (significant) and nocturnal fevers or sweats.

Social history

He was a prisoner of war for 3 years, during which period he underwent all forms of physical torture. He attributes his present symptoms to this. He also has severe family responsibilities. Having lost his father earlier and a brother too, he is the eldest living son. By custom and tradition, the responsibility of looking after a mother who is ailing, the orphans left by the brother and the other siblings - a total of thirteen (13) or so - rests squarely on him. With no source of income and the present state [of his health] that cannot warrant any manual or physical labour, he is really [a] tormented soul... He has already been treated with PPF, ampicillin, and analgesics, but apparently without any remarkable change.

Physical examination is unrevealing - the present symptomatology seems more psychiatric in nature, *though full physical investigations haven't been done due to lack of facility.*

He is therefore referred to your end *for further physical examinations of*

1) CXR ⟨ PA
          (R) Lateral

2) Sputum for AAFBs and Culture (if possible)

3) Blood for Hb, ESR, WBC ⟨ T
                               D

4) Others deemed necessary before instituting any measures... (3 August 1983: emphasis added)

Despite the lack of medical confirmation, the UNHCR Yei office simply referred him to Juba as a 'psychiatric case'. This time in Juba he found an even less enthusiastic welcome. After an interview at the GMT office, he reported the results to the UNHCR counsellor (a Sudanese) in a letter.

... I was surprised to see the doctor of GMT very angry and in a mood almost ready to fight me as if I had offended him previously. He tore the letter of the doctor of the regional hospital to pieces and asked me to leave immediately. I didn't know what to do except to report to the counsellor's office. --- [name of counsellor] had sent me back to GMT to obtain a written letter to this effect. When I went they promised to have no more dealings with me. I am now left with no alternative but to appeal to you to help me in this critical condition in which my health really needs attention. Your response to this matter is highly awaited.

For the counsellor to override the decision of GMT required the authority of a more senior official in the sub-office. That his colleague in Yei had described Dafala's problem as 'psychiatric' (which for many expatriates equals 'nuisance'), may have influenced his reaction. Refusing to refer Dafala to Khartoum, he ordered him to return to Gumbari settlement.

Dafala argued that he could not continue to face his economic responsibilities in a settlement where food rations were soon to be cut. His constant illness would not allow him to cultivate. He asked for a loan to start a tea shop, pointing out that he preferred to support his own family rather than depend on hand-outs. Reluctantly the UNHCR official agreed, provided Dafala would undertake *in writing, never* to return to the office again. With the signed document in his hand, he radioed Yei authorizing the programme officer to make the loan.

Mr Dafala did start a tea shop, just outside the Yei UNHCR office; this being one of the busiest places in town, he began to make a profit. But his business caught the attention of the Sudanese authorities who threatened to close it down because he had no licence. The project manager, who believed that refugees should have at least two years without taxation, intervened on his behalf.

Then the business was interrupted by the death of an unassisted relative. Dafala had to organize the funeral and travel to the border to collect yet more dependents. He returned to Yei to find that another refugee, who already had a job in the UNHCR office, had started another tea shop on his pitch. Given the attitude of the expatriate staff towards his case, it is not surprising that he concluded that there was a conspiracy between the other Ugandan and the programme officer to displace him. In 1984 Dafala was back in Gumbari. He had married, but this was no doubt a mixed blessing as the woman's family had turned up to demand an extortionate dowry. They threatened to take her away with them if he did not pay. Some people were said to have urged the family to consider his health and the general poverty associated with life in exile and it is not known whether or not they relented.

It is unproductive to blame fieldworkers for their inhumane way of dealing with such individual cases. They are not trained. Within the agency bureaucracy they are not rewarded for involving themselves with individuals. In fact, fieldworkers are often warned against 'getting involved'. But it is alarming to observe that assistance programmes are dominated by an ethos in which the victims of mass exodus are treated as the villains.

Not a statue or a picture

One of the highest priorities of the Ugandan refugees was education. This was demonstrated by the efforts they put into building schools in the self-settled areas, but building secondary schools without assistance was beyond their capacity.[10] The assistance programme for the settlements only aimed to provide primary education although the 'right' to an education is enshrined in the 1951 Convention. (Ramaga 1985.)

According to our survey, 21.9 per cent of the settlement population was between the ages of 15 and 24, and 57.6 per cent of the men in this group, or 6,420, had been enrolled in school in Uganda before the war began in 1979. At that time in the West Nile alone there were at least 8,000 young people enrolled in post-primary educational institutions. Many of the refugees in Sudan had been studying elsewhere in Uganda, some at Makerere University as well as at other institutions of higher learning throughout the country. Almost the first question these young people asked on reaching a settlement was, 'Where is the school?' UNHCR was prepared to pay the fees of those who found places in Sudanese schools, but the south does not have enough places for its own young people. In addition, the failure to provide identity cards meant that even if funds to travel were available, it was difficult for refugees to 'find' those schools which might offer them a place.

Some young Ugandans who had completed their 'O' or 'A' levels took up teaching. Unfortunately too many of these 'stranded students' formed the groups of listless, apathetic, angry, and sometimes even violent young people who were always so visible in settlements, and who hung about the UNHCR offices in Yei and Juba, and even in Khartoum. Every settlement had at least one psychotic and most of these were young men whose education had been abruptly terminated and who had been unable to cope with having had all their aspirations for the future so completely dashed.

One such young psychiatric casualty was Jaago. Among his other literary accomplishments was a meticulously kept record of the names and places where people had died in Uganda and Sudan as a result of atrocities committed by the Ugandan army. He had already appealed for help to the UNHCR office and at some point it had at least been inferred to him that he was 'mad'. At that, he had insisted on being diagnosed and had caused sufficient trouble in the UNHCR office to be sent to the Yei hospital for examination. The doctor, in writing, declared him sane. With this evidence he went straight to the police, hoping to open a case against the programme

[10] But in 1983, out of desperation, one of my team, Tom Dradria Andima, got the idea that refugees *could* build their own secondary school. Thirteen months later the Lutaya Senior Secondary School opened for 180 students and already the building of four new classrooms is underway. This was not accomplished without a lot of help from the Sudanese (the Catholic mission gave twenty acres and church members supplied some food); the project manager (who helped in many ways, but especially with transport of building materials from settlements, advice, and moral support); the agencies (who were first reluctant, but later gave materials and UNHCR agreed to pay scholarship costs); the full-time commitment of Tom and Adile Sakio Bornfree who lived on the site for one year cajoling, motivating and administering the building programme, for which labour was supplied almost entirely by them and other interrupted students; and a Jesuit priest, Victor Mathias, who was the intermediary between all of the interested (and disinterested) parties. Money and a lot of moral support was given by Oxford University students.

officer and his Ugandan assistant. As he pointed out in his subsequent note to the project manager:

...metals have their melting points and liquids their boiling points as well. HUMAN BEINGS HAVE THEIR BREAKING POINTS.... But all human beings do not have the same BREAKING POINTS. ... others have low breaking points and others high breaking points. The officials are fortunate because me in particular has a very very very very HIGH BREAKING POINT. Otherwise with the trouble that [is] being faced by me, I would have already reached my breaking point and done something bad.[11]

When I first met him, Jaago had just delivered a note to Nehemiah Iyega, the Yei project manager. He had given as a return address, 'Nowhere student, But Humanitarian in Nature, P.O. Box 100% Under God's Protection.'

Ref: *Accusation of two UNHCR officials due to their Bad Act.*[12]
Dear Sir, With much pleasure and gratitude, I would be very grateful if you would allow or give me the chance to accuse Sjoerd van Schooneveld, the Assistant Programme Officer and Salome who works under UNHCR Field Office, Yei, of their inhumane, uncultured, unreasonable, maltreatment on me since 4th April 1983, instead of solving my problems I had come for. I'm accusing both of them in front of you of torture, corruption, oppression, suffering, starvation, madness, kleptomania, illiteracy, mendacity, suicide, homicide, sororicide, fratricide, patricide, matricide, parricide, egotism, favouritism, separatism, plagarism, misanthropism, sophism, colonialism, neo- colonialism, imperialism, and what have you. The two also believe undiplomatically that I'm mad, stupid, silly, illiterate, ugly, inhumane, unsmart, hypocrite, polytheist, atheist, mountebank, agnostic, spouse, proselyte. Why they have believed me so I cannot tell, even they cannot explain. But they will have to tell or explain me the why, in front of you, so you may take my case into consideration. The following are eye-witness to prove that I'm not what they have believed. But I'm normal, I repeat, but I'm normal. Except that due to continuous suffering, and disappointment from my fellow human beings, I have become uneasy, disappointed, and rather halfway frustrated.

Jaago then lists about 30 people whom he wishes the project manager to bring to Yei to affirm his sanity. He continues:

Thus, when I'm approved to be normal. For the suffering I have faced from these two since I dropped into their office on 4th April, 1983, the following will have to be punishment on them for my suffering.

Jaago lists his demands and, not surprisingly, the first on the list of the 'punishments' due to the UNHCR office is:

[11] Jaago remembered and adapted these lines from one of the books set for his 'O' level literature course, a play by Imbuga (1979).
[12] I apologise to Jaago if his extremely small handwriting, or my lack of vocabulary, have led me to make errors in reproducing his thoughts.

1. They will have to educate me abroad while I complete my education, particularly in Britain.

He continues by listing a new bicycle, a radio, food, 'five hundred pounds for my financial loss since 18th March 1983', and clothing. The list of clothing includes trousers, shirts, boots, slippers, spectacles, and two neckties. The reason he gives for his needing such finery is that:

With all these I will be sure to appear like a man and a living man. Not a statue or a picture. Hoping that all will be taken into consideration, I will be delighted. Because without your help, I won't stay comfortable in this poor world.

When Jaago entered my office, he was able to converse normally. I gave him pen and paper and asked him to write his recent experiences. He wrote a sensible account of the events which brought him to the Sudan from his 'A' level course in Uganda. Many refugees appeared to get psychological relief from writing, but there was always a shortage of pens and papers. Once it was known, however, that I was a willing reader and would supply stationery, I received many useful documents including personal histories and analyses of the recent conflict in Uganda. These added greatly to my knowledge of events.

The need for psychiatric treatment is not always so dramatically evidenced, but the lack of opportunity for continuing education appeared to be a very common trigger for individual breakdown. I briefly employed one refugee who had been interrupted in his training as an air traffic controller. On 11 September, after a few days of work, he wrote the following note, asking to resign.

I hereby wish to inform you about my health conditions since I crossed into the Sudan. When I crossed to take refuge in Sudan, I immediately started to worry about the shape of my future. One has to shape his/her future from a young age, that is through academic education, institutional training, and take an active part in building up a society. I have so many close friends scattered in many countries, where it is difficult to meet them. Most of the people of my age are in exile either in Zaire or here in Sudan. They have no hope of proper education. Their education is mostly limited to an elementary stage whereby they will not grow into adults ... taking [an] active part, and so be constructive in building up a good society that will help improve living conditions back in our homeland, Uganda. Summing up all these have killed my moral[e]. I am mentally depressed. To overcome all these worries, I took to alcohol so heavily. But the more alcohol I took, the more I thought about the whole situation I am in. In November 1982, I had a mental case which lasted two days. So I resigned from alcohol and cigarettes. But again, in February this year, I again had a mental case which lasted five days and a mental depression of two weeks. The last case was June this year which was so severe that my relatives lost hope of my ever recovering.

I very much appreciate your efforts to make the world understand the African refugee situation... Those of us who understand your aims and the assistance you are rendering us really don't have enough words of thanks...[13] Unfortunately you are soon leaving. I thank you very much for registering me to work for you, but I regret to inform you that I am so depressed and have a terrible headache that I have tried to ignore but in vain. The c/quine tablets have not helped either. I suspect that I am soon having another mental case. Please could you relieve me of my duties before it gets worse? Very sorry but I feel so much pain in my head. If you need to talk to me in person, I am available. (September 1983.)

No doubt it would be unrealistic to expect an assistance programme to finance the thousands of African refugees whose education has been interrupted by war. But the monies that are available for refugee education are 'discriminatory', that is, directed by the political interests of the donors. For example, there are funds for some refugees from South Africa and Namibia (Gerhardt 1984); Scandinavian countries and other sources fund scholarships for Eritrean refugees, but there were *no* special programmes to ensure the most able Ugandan refugees were able to continue their studies.

Poisoner

It would have been instructive for those who still believe that the psychosocial needs of African refugees can be ignored to have been present during one dramatic event at the Yei office during July 1982. I was alone in the office when it began. Josiah Matovu, the foreman from Roronyo, arrived by lorry with an entourage. I saw him helping an old woman out, her clothes soaked with blood, and with fresh blood seeping down her face from a deep skull wound.

Josiah was exhausted. The night before, the old woman had been accused of being a poisoner and, to save her from certain death, he had locked her in the store. Her attackers (about 400) congregated in the office compound. Some even pelted rocks at him as he faced them, his back firmly against the door to discourage their breaking it down. He had stayed in that position all night. For Roronyo this was not the first such case of assault on innocent women. After treatment, this old woman slowly recovered in a tent pitched, for her safety, outside our bedroom door.

Josiah had barely finished relating these events when another lorry ground its way through the muddy entrance. The programme officer leaped out, chasing after the agency doctor who had, by chance, also just driven in. In this lorry lay a 23 year old Omuganda woman who, having given birth only nine days earlier, had tried to commit suicide by swallowing glass. She was taken to Yei hospital where she gradually recovered.

---

[13] Some refugees did *not* understand my aims. One, living in Europe, wrote a letter to certain refugees in southern Sudan informing them that I was a British spy supporting Obote. I am not quite sure of the logic, but he sent a copy to the Secretary of State, Whitehall, London as well as to the High Commissioner for Refugees, Geneva.

According to Orley (1970), suicide among the Baganda is very rare, and is so shameful that bodies are not even buried with other relatives. In this young woman's case, it might have been predicted that she would make such an attempt. Born into a wealthy family, her husband's high position in Uganda had maintained the protected life she had been accustomed to. She was an unwilling refugee, but as her husband came from the West Nile, they found it necessary to seek asylum. They went first to Zaire, but when their house was looted and burned by Zaireois soldiers, they fled to the Sudan and were sent to Goli.

Accustomed to visiting Nairobi for any medical care, she insisted her baby be delivered in the hospital rather than in the settlement. Facilities in Yei hospital hardly met her expectations. Women in the maternity ward must usually share a bed and there is no linen. As her husband had to remain behind to care for their other child, she had no one to bring her food. The day she left the hospital, I observed her quietly waiting all day outside the office for the lorry to return her to Goli. It was not surprising to hear later that she was suffering from post-natal depression.

One of the most serious and widespread symptoms of the psychosocial state of the Ugandan refugees was the frequency of assaults on, and even murders of, individuals who, in the atmosphere of sickness and sudden death, had been identified as 'poisoners'. Untold numbers of scapegoats, often whole families, were driven out of settlements. Others were murdered. In July 1982 the situation in Roronyo had become so serious that two policemen had to be sent to keep order. A note was sent round from the Yei UNHCR office to all the settlements informing Ugandans that the Sudan law did not tolerate such accusations. Those found guilty would be taken to the High Court for trial. Those who assaulted the accused would be charged with intent to kill.[14]

Several very unpleasant cases have come to our attention from Roronyo and Mopoko. Let everyone take notice that the settlement foremen, having warned the entire community, are henceforth authorized to take into immediate custody anyone who accuses anyone of poisoning or witchcraft and that person will be taken directly to ... Juba for trial. Anyone who does physical violence to anyone accused will be tried under the criminal code of the Sudan.

It is understandable that when people are very weak from hunger and ill, some inevitably die. This is not, however, an occasion for hysteria. We strongly advise educated refugees to behave responsibly. A continuation of events such as those which have raged in Mopoko and Roronyo will not be tolerated. (7 July 1982.)

But, on 21 September 1982, the foreman of Otogo (a settlement opened in late July) addressed the following message to the agency responsible for health, copy to UNHCR.

---

[14] In the Sudan and also in Uganda, as in most former British territories, witchcraft accusations were made illegal. (Harrell-Bond 1975.)

Ref: Investigation into Causes of Sudden Death
This is to bring to the attention of your office that we have been experiencing certain cases of sudden death for the last one and a half weeks... In our last month's report ... we had a death toll of over thirty people of whom most were women and children. Now since [the settlement opened] the death toll has reached over 55 people. In our report we stated that most of these deaths were caused by prolonged malnutrition and certain diseases originating from the borders. And indeed it is true that most of these people brought to the settlement in bad condition had hardly any chance of survival...

The whole cause of writing to your office is something extraordinary. [In the first] half of this year, we have ... seen several deaths of suddenness. One of these deaths was witnessed by Dr Catherine when she came with the vaccination team. A boy of about ten or twelve years complained of pains in his joints and backbone, which was followed by a headache. The boy ... was treated for malaria. This boy came and collapsed nearby the office. He was helped by the Askari [guard] to the shade...

The most confusing issue came in. The mother of the child rushed to the scene and stated her child might have been poisoned. She ... carried the child away into the blocks for local traditional treatment... The results of which was the death of the child after a few hours of that same day... Later in the following week, a young woman died in a sudden manner. Again a man took two of his children, a boy and a girl, to the dispensary suffering from pains... The boy was treated with some PPF injection and he is still alive but in bad condition ... the girl of this same man wasn't treated in the same manner *due to the shortage of the PPF drug.* Later that day, the girl died. We have about four of these cases.

Now we are in a confused state of mind. For we Africans - sorry to state so - have still a very strong belief in traditional poisons...

The foreman goes on to relate how he had tried to control the situation but, as he put it, 'The settlers still insisted on the presence of poisoners.' He explained that among his community were people of certain tribes who are known in Uganda for being poisoners (old stereotypes) and that some of these had already been driven from other settlements on this charge. But, as he explained, he was personally unconvinced of the competence of the dispensary personnel.

... on the scientific side, we think there must be some disease which is causing such sudden deaths... I personally think that something in connection to meningitis or tetanus or other diseases could be the cause of these sudden deaths.

He again reminds the agency that he has already watched 58 people being buried in his settlement and that many others are lying ill with similar symptoms. He asks them to send someone to investigate and to ensure that the clinic is properly supplied with medicines.

In 1983, with the problem still raging in Otogo, the foreman asked the local chief to take an accused man into custody for his own protection. The Ugandan was mentally retarded and completely incapable of answering any charges. Two days later, children found his body; he had been murdered and left lying in a field.

In some societies, death and illness, except when they strike the elderly, are not regarded as normal events, but are explained as resulting from interpersonal malevolence. Methods to discover the guilty and their punishment and the cures which have been devised for the afflicted vary from society to society. There is a considerable body of evidence which supports the view that the frequency of accusations of sorcery or witchcraft increases when a society is undergoing an accelerated rate of change, or when its people are suffering extreme economic deprivation. (Harrell-Bond 1978.) There is also evidence that people rely more heavily on supernatural explanations when they believe their community to be under the threat of physical or cultural extinction. (Harrell-Bond and Machin 1971.) In fact, one scholar, Cheikh Ante Diop of Senegal, suggests that the experience of imperialism in Africa had the effect of crystallizing and institutionalizing practices like witchcraft, sorcery, and cannibalism as a defence against the annihilation of the indigenous social systems.[15]

Some social effects of settlement composition

There were many factors which contributed to the extreme insecurity of refugees in settlements and which were so frequently expressed in the cry 'poisoner'. Some of the factors which led to accusations of poisoning were the direct result of the assistance programme. It is for this reason that we can say that at least some of these problems were actually imposed by the programme of assistance.

Ugandan refugees saw the Obote government's continued attacks against the civilians of the West Nile as the implementation of his alleged genocidal threat to turn the area into a game park. The continued economic insecurity of life in the Sudan enhanced the Ugandans' fear of physical extinction. The high death rate resulting from the failure of the assistance programme to supply rations regularly to the settlements, together with the absence of an adequate medical service, ensured that these fears were perpetuated.

The composition of the settlement communities forced people to live in social conditions radically different from those to which they were accustomed. Unassisted refugees could choose their neighbours, at least to some extent, as well as the distances between compounds. In settlements, however, each household was assigned a plot 25 metres (later 50 metres) square and told *where* to build their house, *where* to dig the latrine. As noted earlier, few had the opportunity to choose their neighbours: plots were assigned in the order people arrived at the settlement.[16]

[15] Personal communication. It was his view that rising standards of living in Europe have led to the general dissipation of witchcraft beliefs and the practice of so-called black magic. Clinging to these beliefs and even institutionalizing them, according to him, served as a psychological mechanism which preserved Africans' identity. Unrelieved poverty has contributed to their continued influence and fossilization.

[16] The overall ethnic composition of the settlement as compared with the unassisted households interviewed was shown in Table 1.1, p.50 (Chapter One) [see Figure III.I (Appendix III) for the ethnic composition of each settlement].

Most of the settlement populations were dominated either by the Madi or the Lugbara, but some, as Figure III.1 in Appendix III shows, were equally divided between the two groups. The 'others' included fourteen different ethnic groups originating from all over Uganda. Some of these were members of groups now believed to be loyal to Obote's government. As one of my team pointed out, living in a settlement was like living in Kampala in the sense of being forced to adjust to people of different backgrounds. It is possible that this forced 'urbanization' of the West Nilers might, in the long run, have a positive effect. As one professional pointed out, 'It is the first time we have had the opportunity to get to know about each other, to learn how different groups behave and think.' In the short term, however, it has led to considerable conflict and exacerbated refugees' paranoia.

Religious affiliation has long been a basis for political divisions within Ugandan society. Obote is a Protestant. Although the majority of Ugandans are probably Catholic, in certain regions Islam is the dominant religion and is associated with the Nubi community and those Lugbara-speakers who live in Aringa County. As noted earlier, during the Amin regime, there were advantages in converting to Islam. Father Peter, the resident Catholic priest in Yei who had been a refugee in Uganda, told me with some amusement the dates and places of the Catholic baptisms of certain prominent Ugandans who are now Muslims. Mustapha Idrissi, the ex-vice president, was one of these. On the other hand, it should be recalled that many Muslim families who allowed their children to go to school found that conversion to Catholicism was part of the syllabus.[17]

The assistance programme did not provide support for religious organizations. However, the willingness of refugees to build churches and mosques demonstrated the priority of re-establishing those familiar institutions. Although most Sudanese were Protestant, it was the local Catholic church which was most involved in supporting the efforts of the refugees to re-establish their religious life. Only 2 per cent of the assisted refugees said they worshipped with the locals in their own churches, and most of these were Catholic. I often suggested that, instead of building another chapel in the settlement, it would be wiser to plan a permanent building that could also be used by the locals, who usually worshipped under grass roofs.

With only a small amount of encouragement and support, religious leaders could play an enormously important role in bringing stability to refugee communities. I recorded sermons in chapels in the unassisted areas: many

---

[17] All settlements contained both Christians and Muslims, with either Catholics or Muslims forming the majority. Figure III.2, Appendix III, shows the religious composition of each settlement. The overall representation of the three religions among the assisted population was: 48.8 per cent Muslim; 46.7 per cent Catholic; and 3.8 per cent Protestant. Among the unassisted households interviewed, there were slightly more Protestants - 6.8 per cent; while 31.4 per cent were Catholic and 36.5 per cent were Muslim. But the data were missing for 966 interviews, or 25.3 per cent and at least one refugee explicitly expressed disapproval of including this question in the interview.

preachers spoke about the breakdown of social values and the need to live peacefully together. Some lay preachers ran active training programmes for the young. In many settlements, the Muslims had started a *madrassa* (a Koranic school). Had some of these religious leaders been consulted on priorities for the assistance programme and had they been encouraged to exercise their accepted authority within the community, many social problems might have been alleviated.

It was not unusual for the Sudan to receive defectors from the Ugandan National Liberation Army. Sending these men to settlements inevitably created problems, as the other refugees were convinced they were spies sent to watch them. When three Alur soliders defected with the intention of moving through Kenya to join Museveni's guerrilla fighters, they first had to be protected from the other refugees, and when they left, it was taken as evidence that they had returned to the UNLA and the worst fears of the refugees were realized. There were refugees who had been members of the UPC, the present ruling party; their present loyalties, motives for being in the Sudan, and intentions for the future were always doubted by the others.[18]

That as many as three different groups were sometimes waging guerrilla warfare in Uganda further contributed to the social unrest in settlements. While most refugees were totally disillusioned with *all* of them, the differing loyalties of those who still believed that the armed forces would resolve the trouble in Uganda contributed to factionalism. Some guerrilla fighters were as undisciplined as the present UNLA and civilians had suffered greatly at their hands; a few of these men were living in the settlements, having opted out of the struggle. It is not surprising that social relations in settlements were marked by extreme distrust, suspicion, and fear, and that violence on a massive scale could so easily be triggered off. Tensions were running particularly high in Koya transit camp in July 1983. Most of its residents were unwilling recipients of aid, having been either driven from the self-settled areas struck by the drought, or forced out of Zaire, where they had been taking care of themselves. Long delays in finding sites for more settlements left thousands of people with little more to do than wait. Trouble-makers had a field day in Koya, as one of my team - Johnson Oreyama - discovered when he decided to inspect the situation.

Test of Wills - Koya Goes Wild

Ever since the Tanzanian tanks first rumbled across the border ... Uganda has been an isolated land of mystery and misery ... thousand[s] of Ugandans... are in exile, most of them in the Sudan. But little is known of the conditions they left behind. While in

---

[18] I received a note in one settlement from a refugee who was a UPC supporter, explaining that he had been caught up by the war and unwillingly driven out. He was enquiring about repatriation and had set the date (after the harvest) when he would return. Also it would be interesting to know just how he would return, and just how many of those who have been officially repatriated were those who had no objection to Obote's rule. The number of those officially repatriated (to the end of 1984) was less than 1,000 in all.

Kampala the conditions are uncertain, in Koya, a refugee transit camp [of] about 9,000 people ... launched a bitter protest against what was called 'poisoners'.

An acrid haze drifted through the pathways of Koya Block 17 last week as demonstrators burned makeshift barricades and fought pitched battles with the relatives of the so-called poisoners. I spent 24 hours in the strife-ridden camp.

My report: Along the bustling commercial pathway of Block 17, middle-class women darkened their tents and stood on their balconies to stage a one-hour *cacerolozo* [sic] a rhythmic thumping of pots and pans. In Block 16, the Teregos, a Lugbara group from Arura, blew their horns and demonstrators hurled wild fruits into a gigantic block jam [of people] that extended for some three blocks. The poisoners, outnumbered, retaliated with bows and arrows.

Similar scenes occurred throughout Koya about three months ago, when a peaceful day suddenly turned ugly. Tens of thousands of refugees took to the camp office to express their unhappiness with the regime of the former foreman. The camp foreman cracked down amid scenes of violence that were to be the worst in almost 12 months. When it was over, one poisoner was dead.

The protest was not the first of its kind. In May, Koyans engaged in a similar demonstration that left two people badly beaten. But last week's outbreak was far bigger and confirmed a growing, broad-based impatience with poisoners.

The demonstrators demanded an end to deaths by poisoning. Spearheaded by Abdul, a member of Block 17, who claims that a certain woman in the next block poisoned his child, the protest movement has attracted support from a broad range of Koyan opinions: Block leaders, secretaries, and *mukungu* [block chiefs]. Its leading figure is Augustino Amolu, a 29 year old ex-cashier with the Ugandan Army. Said he, 'We are pacifists in attitude and active in behaviour. If they poison us, we shall endure for a while, BUT!!!...'

A police team sent from Yei ... denounced the demonstration as a selfish plot and vowed not to tolerate further claims and accusations. As a first push and clean up, Abdul, the father of the dead child, was arrested and jailed for jeopardizing camp security. Settlers threatened to stage another strike to protest Abdul's arrest. The whole story is that within the camps there are certain groups of people who are believed to be wizards poisoning fellow settlers. This is a fact hard to deny or accept. A woman accused of killing the child, confessed at the time of beating that she had in the past killed two people using traditional poison made out of roasted snakes and frogs. In my next investigation I will try to find out how they go about this. While settlers have vowed to continue beating such people, the woman is now living on the UNHCR compound in Yei, southern Sudan, because of fear [and] shows no signs of giving up her malpractices. So the contest of wills in Koya is far from over. (Johnson, reporting from Koya this morning, 8.30 a.m. 8/7/83.)

Attempts to cope with the problem

Appeals to Sudan law, even posting police in settlements, had little effect on the frequency of accusations of poisoning. At every settlement meeting the subject was brought up. Ugandans strongly resented the government's attempt to move the legal definition of the crime from accused to accuser. There were few who did not share the belief that people were actually being poisoned. My anthropological explanations only amused them. How could I know anything about this? 'You are not an African.' They knew these people from back in Uganda. A report, dated 10 August 1982, arrived on the UNHCR desk from Limuru:

Subject: Ruzeta Yeivo

The above mentioned woman is a refugee... She has been brought in front of me for the case of poisoning a certain pupil... She was caught pulling both the fingers and toes of the corpse (traditionally strictly prohibited)...

(i) She sat on the front part of the corpse which is traditionally a place for the relatives - that was also a sign.

(ii) She covered the mouth of the corpse with her palm. This was also a sign. There have been different stories about the acts of this woman right from Uganda and all these statements were agreed by her [as] true... I also believe that she might have done this thing... However, with the help of the Block Leader we have tried to prevent the community from beating her.

The foreman referred to the bulletin sent to the settlements instructing them how to deal with such accusations. Since he was convinced of her guilt, he had asked the woman to sign a confession. Most important, as he emphasized in his letter, the refugees would no longer allow her to live in the settlement.

Shortly after this message was delivered, the foreman, his officers, the accused (now accompanied by her 9 year old grand-daughter), and one of her accusers, arrived in Yei. I interviewed the woman to discover her side of the story. It was decided that an Eritrean, and temporarily a consultant for UNHCR, Berhane Woldemichael, and myself, should accompany them back to Limuru. We asked the foreman to precede us to call a meeting of the entire settlement.

Not having experienced mass hysteria before, we drove cheerfully to Limuru. It took two hours and threats that the next month's food would be withheld, to get most of the 3,000 plus people to congregate. We sat in the middle, facing the adults, the children were sitting on the ground behind us. I had given the woman a dress, and sitting together with her granddaughter in the row with the settlement officers, she looked clean and respectable. The woman who had accused her and one young man who had assaulted her sat in front of us on the ground. The consultant and I both knew how cases are 'talked' in Africa. We took turns.

Berhane began by citing the laws of Sudan and informing the settlers what was about to happen to the two before us. When it was my turn, I dramatized the sad story which had led to the violence.

A child had died of malaria at the clinic. The mother tied the body on her back and returned to her block. Everyone was wailing. Ruzeta Yeivo, the accused, a friend of the bereaved mother, helped her untie the dead child and began to prepare it for burial. Rigor mortis had set in; the legs had to be pushed together, the hands placed under the head as a pillow. As she was about to begin to wrap the body for the grave, this wicked woman [the accuser] sitting before us, came on to the scene and began screaming 'poisoner, poisoner'. Suddenly, the crowd forgot they were mourning and began to beat this poor old woman.

The people listened in hushed silence to my story being slowly translated sentence by sentence. My performance finished, believing that I had won their hearts, I asked 'Now, is there anyone in Limuru who would still call this woman a poisoner?' To our astonishment, the whole crowd went wild, fists in the air, screaming 'poisoner, poisoner, poisoner'. Before I thought of the obvious danger in which we had placed ourselves - to say nothing of the poor woman and her granddaughter - I was making a quick calculation of just how many lorries we would need to make good the threat of taking all 3,000 accusers to court!

It was Berhane's turn. We still disagree on the exact words he used and my tape recorder had temporarily failed, but we both remember how he berated them. Such ignorance, such stupidity was beyond imagination. 'No wonder Africans have never made it to the moon!' They quietened down. He asked if now, having had time to think, was there any wise person among them who has something to say? But, one by one, men and women stood up, only to point their fingers at Mrs Yeivo and asking such pointed questions as 'Where is your husband?' - intended to let us know that even her husband refused to live with her because she was a poisoner.

The headmaster of the primary school joined these '*unwise*' speakers and we learned how the granddaughter had been implicated. A few days after the first incident, two youngsters had had an argument and slapped each other. The headmaster identified one as the 'poisoner's granddaughter'. Another riot had broken out and the little child needed to be rescued. Mrs Yeivo had a grown-up daughter living in another block in the settlement. People had been throwing stones at their house and the husband was threatening to divorce his wife because of this family association with an alleged poisoner.

Things had clearly gone too far for Berhane: hearing the headmaster confess to having flogged the small girl, he sacked him on the spot.[19] As he pointed out to the mob, 'No one who believes in poisoners should be allowed to teach children.'

The mood changed: if someone's means of livelihood could be taken away just like that, we were obviously serious. A deep bass voice spoke from the back of the crowd, it trembled as the man spoke.

We came here because of fear. We ran from Uganda because of fear. We came here so we would not have to be afraid. But now there are people who want us to remain in fear. Now it arises that there are certain elements, there are a number of people in the

---

[19] The headmaster was an excellent teacher; in order to regain his job, he was asked to write an essay entitled 'Anyone who believes in poisoning, poisons the minds of children.' Hopefully this had a therapuetic effect and he gave much service in the camps. It should also be noted that hysteria is not a permanent state of mind.

camp who are trying to make other people feel unsafe. Example number one. There are some people who undress themselves naked at night and then go and dance at your door and throw certain objects which cause fright. For instance, certain grains are thrown over the roof. You try to come out: they run so fast. If I organized a hunt within my block and if we arrested such a person naked and we brought him in - on what shall we accuse him?... In a few cases ... those people were hunted, but because they come at the wrong time of night, it is difficult. What would we do in case we arrest such a person?

Berhane encouraged the man: 'Yes, such a person should be arrested. But why can't you catch them?' He then reminded him of dreams and explained hallucinations and their possible causes. Miraculously, the message got through; the man understood.

Then another 'wise' man called for a compromise. We sent the crowd away - or at least we tried to. They had been so reluctant to congregate, but now we could hardly get them to leave. Hundreds of them walked slowly past the woman, shouting abuse at her and waving their arms threateningly.

Alone with the block leaders, the discussion continued. Although the teachers among them were frightened, they insisted on arguing that poisoning exists.[20] Suddenly, however, the accuser confessed to having been wrong all along. The boy who had beaten the old woman apologized. He admitted he had been too upset to think properly - it was his relative who had died. I asked them to beg the woman's forgiveness.[21] I handed over the money to buy a goat, and instructed the accuser to cook a meal for the accused and other members of both families. 'Since you are so good at gossiping in this settlement, now let the block leaders gossip to all that these two families eat together.'[22]

With more than a few qualms concerning the safety of the woman and the child, we returned to Yei. I continued to check to see what was happening in Limuru. More than a year later the woman was still living peacefully in the settlement. She said a few people refused to greet her, but otherwise life was as it had been before. I know of only one other case where a victim accused of poisoning, having survived the initial attack, is still living in the same settlement. This was a woman who lived in the office compound with her small son, under the constant protection of the settlement officer. She had no

[20] Willis (1978) argues that 'It is obvious that, alone in the whole body of sorcery beliefs, "poison" corresponds to an idea in current and accepted western belief since it has a putatively empirical basis. This fact, it may be suggested, gives it a heightened validity under the pressure of western influences and accounts for its vogue among the Fipa, especially those in closest contact with the centres of modernization.' But, see also Harrell-Bond (1978) for a discussion of the functions of such beliefs among the elite in Sierra Leone.

[21] To 'beg', in West Africa at least, is to put oneself literally at the feet of the person to whom a request is being made and denotes total humility and inferior status. There, it is irresistible, and requests made must be granted. I had hoped that Ugandans would react similarly.

[22] Eating together in Africa symbolizes many things, but most important, mutual trust. See Harrell-Bond (1978.)

family anywhere, was afraid to stay in her own house in the block, was unable to cultivate, and was ostracized by all.

While Berhane's and my intervention at Limuru might be judged successful, this solution could obviously not be generally recommended. It is doubtful whether either of us would knowingly have undertaken such a risk again. In the long term, it is only an assistance programme which is flexible, which allows people to retain their sense of autonomy, and which provides basic food and medical security which can alleviate some of the conditions of insecurity which give rise to these events.

Poisoning and profiteering

Unfortunately, there is no evidence that the frequency of accusations of poisoning has abated. Why? I discovered that beliefs in poisoning were being actively encouraged by some herbalists who made their living out of diagnosing and treating the ill. While there is a growing appreciation in medical circles of the value of traditional folk medicine, little attention has been paid to the social roles of herbalists in modern Africa.

Ugandan communities, like people everywhere in the world, have developed their own explanations and treatments for illness. There are only a few modern African states which have, as a policy, sought to incorporate these folk systems into their modern medical services. Uganda was *not* among these few. In those African countries which have officially rejected traditional medicine, herbalists are often unable to practise openly without fear of arrest. There is no doubt that many do provide psychological comfort and that some of the medicines they prescribe contain therapeutic chemicals. The problem is that, in addition to prescribing herbs, these practitioners also involve themselves in divining (which, at times, may also have psychological value), administering oaths, and often indulging in black magic as well. As Professor German put it:

Witchdoctors and bewitchments, the occult and the sadistic, are not the peculiar heritage of the African. They are rather the unsurprising accompaniment of poor social conditions, of fear, of ignorance and despair, and as such they are found, even today, in every civilization on earth. The witchdoctor is certainly an integral part of African cultures: he stands between man and spirits; he offers, and sometimes provides peace of mind to the distraught and anxious; he is regarded as an expert in matters cultural and spiritual and sometimes in health; sometimes he is sincere, often a quack. He may be unhygienic, unskilled and avaricious - so is the back street abortionist... If we could be less Europe-centred ... attention to such comparisons might well be a rewarded line of research ... more valuable perhaps than the heuristically sterile exercise so frequently indulged in of exclaiming at the witchdoctor ... as if such individuals comprise a separate, shabbily colourful dead end in human social evolution. (in Orley 1970.)

While hiding in the bush inside Uganda or living as self-settled inside the

Sudan, most refugees were forced to survive without adequate medical services. By the end of 1983, the situation in settlements had only marginally improved. In desperation, people turned to anyone claiming to know how to cure diseases, and thus provided a ready market for the services of herbalists and encouraged the expansion of the profession. Among the unassisted refugees interviewed, 57 per cent said they relied upon local herbs when they were ill. Under these conditions, herbalists had gained enormous prominence.

It is difficult to interview herbalists or 'witchdoctors' as Professor German terms them.[23] They guard their knowledge, usually passing it on to only one apprentice. Their dubious position *vis-à-vis* the law and modern medicine makes them particularly reticent about discussing their practices. As their treatments involve as much contact with the supernatural as it does the use of different herbs, they are loath to subject their beliefs to logical analysis.

In 1982, settlement foremen were asked to collect lists of the names of herbalists and the diseases they believed they could treat. In one settlement alone there were 93 such practitioners! It is especially important to note that it is believed that if someone can cure you of poisoning, he will also know the secret of *making poison*. This is generally the case in Africa, but see Orley (1970) for evidence from Uganda. The availability of even the limited medical services in settlements poses a threat to their own income, and for probably all of these reasons herbalists among the Ugandans were reluctant to be interviewed.[24]

The Oxford team found 14 practising herbalists in Limbe, 12 of whom were Lugbara (the minority group in Limbe). Five of the herbalists were interviewed, four of them had been trained and the range of diseases they treated included jaundice, gonorrhea, swelling, headaches, childbirth difficulties and mental disorders. One had discovered that a certain tree bark cured his leg swelling and now only used this in his practice. All of the herbalists said they prayed before working, but only one claimed to having spiritual 'power'. The team purchased 22 different herbs, most of which were allegedly cures for poisoning.

The cure

I began to explore this problem by learning about the 'cure' for those who had

---

[23] Because of the importance of the role of herbalists working as diviners and administering oaths in courts, I have interviewed dozens of them in several West African countries. It is always difficult to gain their confidence. My strategy was to consult them about real personal problems. I often paid for medicines to ensure my children passed their exams, and once my small son was used as the 'voice' of a friend living in Britain. One I consulted in Sierra Leone was a ventriloquist, his stone 'spoke'. He only saw people before full daylight or in the evening so his secret was not revealed.

[24] I must admit that after learning about their practices, I did not make a great effort to interview them. Once I stumbled on a man making his 'medicines' and asked him what he could cure. He assured me he had nothing to do with poison.

been 'poisoned'. In Uganda, I was told, herbalists applied used motor oil! The patient is 'washed' in the open air, a powdered root is mixed with the oil, and the herbalist rubs the entire body until the herb produces a foam, 'evidence' that the poison is 'coming out'.

We discovered we could predict that a settlement would suffer a spate of poisoning events when the WFP food allocation included solid, not liquid, edible fat. The solid vegetable oil was used in place of old motor oil. Apparently herbalists could not pull off the same effect with liquid vegetable oil. Victims are warned that their treatment does not 'mix' with 'western' medicines, thus discouraging the exposure of the herbalists' malpractices, or further competition from the trained medical workers. Their patients thus often died of untreated malaria or pneumonia.

Herbalists actively seek out patients. In Limbe, I found the midwife lying ill, having been treated for poisoning. I took her aside and asked how she, a trained person, could subject herself to such treatment which included small incisions in the neck, made with an unsterilized blade? She admitted that, as a Christian in Uganda, she had never consulted such people, but in the bush they had been forced to rely on herbs. Recently she fell ill and, thinking it was a malaria attack, she had taken medicine. She continued working but became worse. Three herbalists from the nearby Koya transit camp came (uninvited) to offer their services. Her mother was frightened because each of them said her daughter had been poisoned. The midwife was finally persuaded to subject herself to their treatment. She admitted that any improvement was more likely due to the bed rest than to the treatment.

People pay heavily for the herbalist's treatment, both financially and in the number of lives which are unnecessarily lost. I came across one such 'washing' in Otogo. The herbalist had heard that morning that a man was ill and had rushed to tell him he had been poisoned in his sleep; some malevolent person had entered the compound and thrown the poison at the house. The victim had a high fever and pulse rate, and was shivering in the cold wind. I stopped the entire performance and forced the family to take him to the clinic. I warned the herbalist that if he was ever caught washing another patient, he would be arrested, and then suggested he warn his colleagues that the same fate would befall them.

The difficulty was that neither I nor anyone else had authority to back up such threats. Such charlatans diagnose *any* and *every* illness as 'poisoning'. People dying from pneumonia are stripped naked for the 'washing' whatever the weather. And, of course, usually those guilty of the malevolent act must be 'found' and punished, whether or not the victim dies of the poison.

A colleague anthropologist, Dr Jeanne Brown, informed me that one agency had employed a 'chief' herbalist for their settlements. Her colleague had given this herbalist a test in African curative herbs and found he lacked even a basic knowledge of standard medicinal plants.

When our survey was conducted in Wundurubu, this 'chief herbalist' declined to attend the medical meeting. But his 'colleagues' from the clinic informed me that not only was he being paid a salary, he also charged everyone he treated. Worse still, they had to compete with his new status, accorded by the expatriates, with many patients now preferring his services to theirs. The situation was compounded by their own lack of medical supplies and the fact that the most senior member of staff at the clinic was a Sudanese who had less training than the Ugandan staff. This made it easier for the herbalist to compare the 'western' treatment negatively with his own. They complained that residents in the settlement were unwilling to co-operate with the preventive programme, as the herbalist had other solutions for their complaints.

Recent reports from the field indicate that the herbalist's practice is thriving under the blessing of the agency.[25] A report submitted to UNHCR was apparently accepted without a murmur.

A native 'medicine man' has been formally [employed] in Wunduruba settlement. His major treatments are for hepatitis, dysentery, and poisonings. He is working under the direction of the medical assistant [untrue] in the area... I took the decision to place him in Wundurubu (soon in Dororolili also) because of the constant movement of settlers (suffering from assorted diseases) to find one elsewhere. The results appear satisfactory. More precise recordings are being taken to give a more accurate picture of this activity. (30 June 1983.)

The numbers game

Since the beginning of 1984, some herbalists have devised a new method of exploiting the poor and insecure Ugandan refugees. According to reports, it began in the Kaya area, this time among the unassisted refugees. The order for their removal to settlements, noted earlier, had, no doubt, made them more insecure. A herbalist divined that a particular member of one clan - now living in Zaire - had entered into a contract with another herbalist to make himself rich. To get rich, according to this method, one must write down a long list of the names of relatives and assign each one a number. Over an unspecified period of time, the herbalist arranges for each of these members of the family to die. Just before death, the victim will *see* his 'number' appearing somewhere on his body, usually the back. When all the relatives have died, the person who has paid heavily for these services will simply wake up rich.

The Kaya herbalist supported his allegations with a convincing story describing one of the clan members; this information had been unwittingly divulged to him in the first consultation with one member of this family. He then rattled off a long list of the potential victims, citing names so common

---

[25] At one time there was talk of setting up a laboratory for the study of traditional herbs, apparently without understanding the enormous expense of such an undertaking and the scientific expertise such pharmaceutical studies require.

that he could be sure that some at least would be among the group. People became hysterical. The herbalist reassured them: if they paid enough, he could arrange a ritual which would protect them. The price, however, was high: some two hundred Sudanese pounds, cloth, meat, sugar, soap, etc. - all the things which every refugee lacks. Almost overnight the frightened family managed to get these things together and all met in the herbalist's compound for the protective ritual. People were relieved but they left the compound cursing the relative in Zaire, saying that he must certainly die for the crime he attempted to commit against them.

Now all over Yei River District people began seeing numbers appearing on their bodies. In Wudabi settlement, the Ugandan doctor was asked to examine a woman who was ill; her husband reported having seen a number. As the hysteria has spread, the prices for protection have risen.

The problem of witchcraft and sorcery in association with refugee populations may be more general in Africa. In a recent report, Richard Hall discusses the efforts of the Zambian government to halt a wave of ritual murders. The area affected is Kalabo where 'Life ... has been disturbed by refugees fleeing across the border from the civil war in Angola. The influence of refugees is blamed for the resurgence of traditional beliefs.' (*Observer*, 26 August 1984.)

Meeting the psychosocial needs of African refugees

Very early on, when Ugandans began arriving in the Sudan, a psychiatrist from Juba hospital visited the UNHCR offices to point out that the refugees would be likely to present special problems. But his offer to survey the situation was declined. There is a need for general recognition that African refugees, like those elsewhere, are often psychologically disturbed by their experiences. No doubt special services should be provided, ideally from within the community itself. Psychiatric medicine should be available for those who need it. At present, the usual approach is to prescribe Valium indiscriminately.

Policy-makers cannot afford to be ignorant of the traditions and customs of the refugee communities for whom they are planning programmes of assistance. If expatriate personnel continue to dominate implementation of assistance, then they must be adequately instructed. As we have seen, naivety concerning traditional African society has led at least one agency to raise the status of the herbalists who are cleverly exploiting and exacerbating the insecurity of refugee communities. This mistake could have been prevented by consultation with the Sudanese themselves.

The settlement officer now in charge of Wudabi discovered the scandalous activities of herbalists in his own settlement. He told me he watched one man move from market to market with his bag of medicines, supplying herbs and potions to practitioners in settlements. He hoped to organize the arrest of this supplier. The World Food Programme might even have been asked to supply liquid oil in the rations since only the solid fat was used to 'cure' the poisoned. But none of these 'solutions' actually tackle the root problems which give rise to both individual psychoses and to the general insecurity of the whole population which results even in mass hysteria. The data have revealed problems which could quite clearly be alleviated by a different approach to assistance.

The most fundamental change required is to permit the community as a whole to determine its own priorities. For Ugandans, one of the first priorities was to start up schools and places of worship. Supporting the development of these two institutions with which people are familiar and which bring the reassurance associated with order and discipline might have reduced the feeling of insecurity, and, perhaps, given rise to some hope for the future. The need for an adequate health service is obvious.

The effects of sub-nutritional diet on mental health

However, there is perhaps a more fundamental cause of the psychological disturbances and anti-social behaviour observed among the Ugandans to which neither anthropologists nor psychologists have given sufficient attention, namely the growing body of evidence linking certain behavioural patterns with sub-nutritional diets. The problems of food supply for the refugees in southern Sudan have already been discussed in some detail. It has also been shown that the standard of health for many refugees actually declined after entering the aid system. The lack of a balanced diet may, in fact, lie at the root of many of the psychosocial problems which we observed. Some evidence from another Ugandan community deserves to be considered in this context.

In 1972, Colin Turnbull published a study of the Ik, a community of hunters and gatherers living in the mountains bordering Kenya, Uganda, and the Sudan. It should be emphasized that there are no historical ties between the Ik and the Ugandan refugees now in southern Sudan to explain the parallels in their behaviours.

Turnbull is most famous for his studies of the Mbuti pygmies, the 'forest people', and if any criticism could be made of his earlier work, it would perhaps be that he over-romanticized this African society. His study of the 'mountain people' (Turnbull 1972) shocked the anthropological world.

Communities which live by hunting and gathering require huge areas of land. The Ik had depended for their living, to some extent at least, on hunting and gathering. (Heine 1985). During the colonial period they had lost access to a great deal of their territory and those whom Turnbull studied were subsisting through agriculture. There was then a drought which gradually led to the famine conditions in the Karamoja. When Turnbull first arrived, he did not fully appreciate that an entire community was beginning literally to starve to death before his eyes. He warns his readers in the preface:

In what follows there will be much to shock, and the reader will be tempted to say 'how primitive ... how savage ... how disgusting' and above all, 'how inhuman'. In living the experience I said all those things over and over again. The first judgements are typical of the ethno- and ego-centricism from which we can never quite escape, however much we try, and are little more than reaffirmation of standards that are different in circumstances that are different. But the latter judgement, 'how inhuman', is of a different order, and supposes that there are certain standards common to all humanity itself, from which the people described in this book seem to depart in a most drastic manner. In living the experience, however, and perhaps in reading it, one finds that it is oneself one is looking at and questioning; it is a voyage in quest of the basic human and a discovery of his potential for inhumanity, *a potential that lies within us all*. Many of us are unlikely to admit readily that we can sink as low as the Ik, but many of us do, and with far less cause. (Turnbull 1972.)

Among the Ik the family was the first institution to collapse. While they still insisted on living in villages.

... the villages have nothing that could be called a truly social structure, for they encompass no social life, and despite the fact that members of a village mistrust and fear each other more than any others, in direct proportion to their proximity and completely without regard to family and kinship. The mistrust begins even within the compound, between a man and his wife, and between each of them and their children. (ibid.)

The publication of Turnbull's book created a storm, as the subsequent debate in *Current Anthropology* showed.[26]

His indignant colleagues accused him of irresponsibility, falsifying his data, unbridled subjectivity, exaggeration, excess emotionalism, incompetence, and even lying. But the guns fell strangely silent when James Knight's 'On the Ik and Anthropology: A Further Note' appeared in the same journal. In quiet academic language, he pointed out a simple truth:

The discussants appear to minimize or disregard, however, the specific role of starvation in generating the behaviour and conditions observed among the Ik. A knowledge of the effects of hunger is essential if the Ik and the issues their society has raised are to be understood and placed in perspective. Both Turnbull and his reviewers appear to recognize that starvation was the primary stress under which Icien society was transformed ... but they seem to consider starvation or famine as a generalized, simply disruptive stress. Instead, its effects are highly specific... (1976).

He went on to explain that human starvation is actually most often 'semi-starvation' as food intake is usually reduced rather than completely stopped. He cites the 'standard reference' for the study of the effects of starvation

---

[26] Vol 15, No 1, March through to Vol 17, No 4, Nov - Dec 1976. The storm continues until 1985. See Heine (1985).

which was 'assembled over a quarter of a century ago by Keys *et al.*' (1950).[27]
These authors exhaustively examined the psychological and physiological
effects of 'natural semi- starvation'; and they reported the results of the
'Minnesota Experiment', a well-controlled experiment undertaken during
World War Two (significantly) *in order to obtain data in anticipation of the need
to plan relief operations in Europe.* The effects observed in both natural and
experimental situations were similar. But as Knight goes on to say,

The effects of natural starvation generally tended to be more severe and widely
variable, however, since the experimental group was subjected to calorie reduction
alone, while exacerbating factors such as dietary deficiencies and societal disruptions
are generally present in a natural family [as they are in refugee situations]. (op.cit.)

The characteristic set of behavioural changes which were observed in both
the natural and experimental conditions included: depression; irritability;
nervousness; obliteration of sex drive; loss of concentration; apathy;
vindictiveness; reduction of humour to sarcasm; neglect of personal hygiene;
'loss of concern with the niceties'; and an overriding concern with food and
eating.

Behaviour habits acquired during periods of food deprivation are abandoned or
modified with notable reluctance. Again, these changes are induced solely by dietary
restriction in an otherwise undisrupted and unremarkable environment. 'The
behavioural changes ... were universal among the [experimental] subjects; hence they
may be considered as "normal" reactions under the given circumstances although
they deviated markedly from the preservation pattern of behaviour...' The differences
between Turnbull's earlier description of the Ik ... and that in *The Mountain People*
seem to be a clear function of these characteristic human reactions to prolonged semi-
starvation. (ibid.)

Ramgasami (1985) describes the *process* of famine which, from her
research and reading of other studies, she says can be broken up into three
phases, each with its own distinct pattern of social behaviour. Famine, as she
points out, has been known over the ages as a period of violation of normal
human ties, during which cannibalism, necrophagia, and such other
practices have been reported. Famine studies have concentrated on the social
behaviour of a community in its 'death throes' and have ignored the 'long
march, the anxiety and the distress' that precedes it. To ignore the earlier
phases of famine is to 'ignore famine itself'.

Earlier, Turnbull had referred to the Ik as 'fun-loving people' who 'thrive
on work' and 'love to help one another' and 'are a great family people'. Their
transformation into a people

...as unfriendly, uncharitable, inhospitable, and generally mean as any people can
be...indifferent to their own plight and that of others, so preoccupied with food that it

---

[27] And see Dirk (1980), for an overview of studies of behavioural responses to famine.

became their very word for 'goodness' was clearly a highly predictable result of famine. In view of the frequency of patterns of flight and societal collapse documented by Keys *et al.* and the more recent disruptions generated by famine observed in West Africa, the most remarkable aspect of the Ik may well be the cohesiveness of their social network under such stress...the Ik are clearly not the enigma Turnbull considers them. (ibid.)

The decline in standards of sanitation in the settlements as compared with the self-settled has been noted. I am reminded of a talk with Dr Allison Umar, when he visted Yei in 1982. We walked the 5 kilometres from Yei to the transit centre to see 300 fresh arrivals sitting there amidst filth and rubble. The foreman reported that several dangerous snakes had come into the clearing. I advised him to hand out pangas and get the people to clear away the bush from the perimeters. No one moved. I shrugged and said something to the effect that it would not be my funeral.

As we walked back towards the town, I asked Dr Umar how he explained such incredible apathy. 'They have,' he quietly replied, 'been living for so long, hiding in the bush inside Uganda in terror of being found by the soldiers. They have only had cassava to eat over the past two years. They have seen the most inhuman atrocities committed before their eyes. They have watched their relatives die from diseases never known before. This has become normal. They cannot even remember another way.' And, as James Knight explained to his colleagues: 'Significantly, in the present context of the debate over the Ik, these behaviours do not quickly disappear after relief from food deprivation, but perisist for several months even if an unlimited good diet is available.' (ibid.)

The stark fact is that refugees in Yei River District did not have access to an adequate diet, even under the assistance programme. The aid programme has not alleviated hunger. While policy-makers search for clever techniques to engage the co-operation of refugees in a process which will lead them towards economic independence through agriculture, they have failed to recognize that these efforts can never be successful until the basic food problem is solved. The shortage of nutritious food may itself be the basis for many of the psychosocial problems, and the behaviours associated with the so-called 'dependency syndrome'.

During my fieldwork in 1984 I asked refugees to describe how they behaved when they had been deprived of food for a prolonged time, and some wrote essays on this topic.

As you know, food is the most vital fundamental factor of life. Without food we behave strangely. You can easily grow angry. You do not have any interest to converse with your friends. You think only of food. You can easily become a thief. You always look sick and gloomy. You always hate people talking to you. You can easily sell all your property and begin to beg from others. You always stay sick, fainting, and as well die. (Akuti Simon, Limuru, 7 September 1983.)

Anything when asked from anybody...made another annoyed, brutal and [one] would [be] unable to answer a question. [In the settlement] when lacking food again [we] become rude automatically. That is how me and my fellows behaved when deprived of food for a long period...all of us would lose their proper behaviour. (Amedou Pauline, Limuru, 8 May, 1983.)

Another writer, who remains unidentified, first describes how he was driven to steal in the market. Then, without a place to sleep and extremely hungry, he '...went to one of the watchmen of the hospital. When I reached to him, I was very hungry again. I introduced myself to him in such a polite way and well-disciplined. One of the easiest tricks which I spoke out to him was, I introduced myself as the son of a famous man. As he was an old man, he simply accepted my word. After which I was given a great deal of food to eat.'

Another essay - unsigned - reports:

One evening, uncle's wife prepared us a meal. The amount was not sufficient. Having noticed that, I grew annoyed. The hunger was so terrible that I could not bear....Small children were my enemy when I had nothing in my stomach. I put some scratches on their heads, so I was feared by them. The constant starvation led to theft, which I thought by that time was a good activity, but it is not. Anyway, it saved me during that time.

As this writer explains, it was his having been beaten after being caught stealing cassava in the field of a local Sudanese which 'made me flee to the camp'.

Maku Olokoko describes his reactions to conditions which finally forced him out of Uganda.

We started to suffer from hunger exactly on 11 October. It was Saturday evening when we ran to the bush for fear of killings....It was rainy season, every night it rained, yet we used to uproot our cassava from our fields at night while raining. We slept in caves turn by turn for three months until things in the fields finished. Then I and my fellows took refuge in the nearest country, the Sudan.... It was January 1981 during dry season. We had no food and no way of getting money. We started to exchange our properties...with foodstuff. This...took one month and then [food was] over. Still it was dry season, we did not know what to do. Everyone of us became so rough that any slight mistake done by me or my fellows, I or anyone, was beaten for. Mere greetings were considered to be insults. Somebody big in stomach was hated for disturbance. Quarrels were picked always. We all became cruel. We later decided to sell our small sisters and brothers, even wives, to the natives, but [they] had no market [money] for them. Then we turned to looking for fruits....We even ate grass. This happened in the month of February up to the middle of April (two and a half months).

Maku goes on to say that later, when rains began and they could work for the locals, 'It was [also] high time for girls and women to go for prostitution which helped a lot in feeding us (of course, those who had sisters...). We very well knew it was wrong, but it was beyond human control.' It is interesting to note that this writer credits a local Sudanese official for having stopped the prostitution by taking the girls and women to Kala settlement.

It is unfortunate that instead of recognizing that the inadequacies of the assistance programme contribute to the anti-social behaviour with which they are often confronted, fieldworkers are prone to blame the victims. So often, one sees refugees being treated like erring children. Alula Pankhurst discussed the mechanisms used by fieldworkers to insulate themselves from the suffering around them which, in turn, leads them to stereotype refugees as 'either sheep (dependent, unthinking) needing a *shepherd*, or wolves (greedy, lying, calculating, mercenary) needing a *hunter*.' (Personal communication.) Much energy is devoted to working out the latest techniques that the refugees might have invented to cheat and manipulate 'our' systems. Presumably it is believed to be in the interest of the donors that surprise censuses (one was even done in the night), are carried out in settlements to prove just how many people really are there. Then, because of inefficiency or the failure to plan, as so frequently happened in Yei River District, when there is no food at all to distribute, instead of spreading the alarm, fieldworkers feel obliged to conspire within the hierarchy of the agency community to protect its humanitarian image. A UNHCR official from Geneva told me, that once when no food was getting through to refugees in Zaire because of the war in Uganda, he learned about it not from his own field officer, but from the *International Herald Tribune*.

8
A case of understanding

Refugees: problem or opportunity?

Having followed this narration of the problems of delivering assistance to the refugees in Yei River District thus far, the reader must be asking just how refugees *were* surviving there. This question cannot be satisfactorily answered by research which focuses only on refugees.

In the absence of independent research concerning refugee issues, policy-makers, as we have seen, have been forced to rely more on beliefs than on empirical data. The debate about whether or not all refugees 'deserved' assistance in planned settlements is a case in point. Chambers (1979) argued in favour of the settlement policy, but Hansen (1979;1982) found that refugees valued the relative autonomy of living among the local community, even when they suffered greater economic deprivation than did those who were in settlements. More recently Chambers (1985) has raised another series of questions which can be answered only by research. He asks whether or not, and under what particular conditions, assistance which is targeted to refugees might serve to further impoverish sections of the host community.

There also are questions which cannot be properly answered by refugee-centric research. As Chambers points out, 'refugee-related research and writing almost always start and end with refugees, with hosts either not considered or treated as secondary or incidental' (ibid.) He goes on to explain that this concentration of research and planning on refugees - on their numbers, on their desperate plight, and on the daunting difficulties in achieving 'durable' solutions for them, presents problems; for no matter how much is done, it never seems to be enough really to help. Chambers (1985) aims to alert his readers to the bias that characterizes not only assistance programmes, but also the embryonic field called refugee studies. This bias results from focusing on refugees in isolation from their social field and it leads directly to the neglect of studies of the impact of refugees on their new

---

[1] Taken from a comment made by one of my team at our last meeting together. His exact words: 'I think that UNHCR has a big task to tell the refugees what it is they are doing. Because if they give them what they have and the refugees do not know, do not understand their system, it is worse than none at all. So I think that the problem between the refugees and the agencies that assist them, is a case of understanding.' Another, speaking on the same topic, said, 'What I think the research did was to inform the refugees about their obligations to UNHCR ... what they could and could not expect. Refugees do not know who is the cause of their suffering. Refugees are in a confused situation. What they need is a consciousness about their situation.'

environment, and particularly their impact on the poorer members of the host community.

My research was also undertaken from a refugee-centric perspective, but it very quickly became apparent that to answer the question of how refugees survive, it was necessary to examine their relationships with their hosts. As is stressed in the discussion of methodology (Appendix II), one learns more about refugees from studies which are not so narrowly defined. One of the unexpected findings of this study and one which resulted from adopting a wider perspective, was that the refugees were making a very positive contribution to the local economy.

What the data suggest is that host governments would be well-advised to view an influx of refugees as an opportunity, rather than as a problem. The change in perspective that is required goes much further than simply recommending that assistance in an area should be targeted on those most in need, and much further than insisting that aid should be available for developing the infrastructure - roads, medical, water, and education services - of the refugee-affected area. The new perspective calls for aid which is 'fine-pointed' so that it can respond to the creative energy which is released as people are forced to struggle for survival under new conditions and through new relationships. Assistance should be available to fill in the gaps which arise in the wake of such enormous population movements and to respond to the many new opportunities and problems which arise in a situation which is so dynamic and fluid. This kind of assistance cannot be planned 'in Geneva'.

A review of the results of the research programme leads inevitably, I think, to the conclusion that current approaches to humanitarian assistance must be reviewed. There are three major critical points which emerge from the research project in Yei River District. The first is that assistance programmes cannot be implemented effectively by agencies which are hierarchical and bureaucratic. Second, assistance plans cannot be managed by officials, whether outsiders or hosts, who are unwilling to engage in discourse with the people whom they aim to assist. And the third critical point which emerges quite clearly, is that while assistance plans, projects, and programmes cannot be 'rule-bound', because they *must* be flexible; that nevertheless, *rule-making* will be an important aspect of the assistance process. This latter is an important point and one which I will illustrate shortly.

The evidence from YRD suggests that the arrival of refugees in an area could be the opportunity for the positive transformation of the political economy, a transformation which would assist refugees and host alike. The factors which lead to the loss of this opportunity will be evident from earlier discussion of the specific problems caused by the imposition of aid in the district. I now want to specify some of the projects which might have been, but which never were. The objectives of assisting refugees through community development might have been better achieved through such projects. As with all interventions these would also affect the 'political economy' of this area, but they would be interventions in response to grassroots statements of need.

I have already mentioned the local efforts to build a road by hand labour from Kajo-Kaji to Juba. The purpose of this road was to allow the agricultural surplus of one region to be redistributed to an area of food shortage, through Juba market. Investment in bridges, a few lorries, and storage facilities would have had many consequences for both the local host *and* refugee communities. Improved transport facilities might have permitted returnee Sudanese businessmen and refugee agricultural producers to have had a dynamic effect on the system of control of the Juba market. The market now appears to be dominated by one section of the community, but had the road been built, then some *modus vivendi* between the entrenched traders and the newcomers would have had to have been achieved. Recall how in the Kajo-Kaji area the solidarity of Ugandan and southern Sudanese broke the monopoly of northerners and forced them out. But because of the near impossibility of gaining access to the Juba market because there was no direct road, all the energy and commercial enterprise of these people were trapped in the Kajo-Kaji 'corner' and led to the illegal opening of the Uganda border. This had at least two effects. The first was that the economic benefits of the production of the region spilled over into Uganda and was lost to the Sudan. The second was that, given the continued instability in Uganda, the insecurity of many refugees was increased.

New industries could have been established. The growing demand and escalation of prices for bicycles, for example, suggest that southern Sudan could have sustained the output of an 'assembly plant'. The price of a bicycle rose from £S90 to £S380; in September 1984 it was £S240. All that is required to assemble bicycles is a few tools and the organization of imported components. The number of Ugandans who made their living through bicycle repair suggests there was no lack of expertise to assemble them. Both the road and a bicycle factory would have benefited refugees and hosts alike.

One of the industries which the ODA team recommended should be encouraged in Yei River District was bee-keeping. A marketing system was already established, with northern traders plying the roads in their *arabia* [lorries] to buy honey at collection points. The Sudanese use traditional hives and throw away the wax. The ODA team held the view that Sudanese were not ready to adopt improved hives. But many Ugandans already had the requisite experience. Ignoring the value of the beeswax, the use of improved hives involves at least two other industries - carpentry and tailoring. The refugee population included many skilled carpenters and tailors which the local market could not absorb (McGregor in Wilson *et al.* 1985.) I have already noted that a Kenyan company was ready to invest its own small resources in such a project and there was no lack of open land for hives. This industry would have been of particular benefit to the vulnerable groups since women, many of the handicapped, and even children can be taught to manage bees. There may also be considerable ecological benefits from increasing the number of bees.[2] Given the evidence, to be discussed shortly, of the ways in which the Sudanese were quick to adopt some of the practices of the Ugandans, it is unlikely that they would have failed to see the value of using improved hives themselves.

I now want to discuss another case where effective assistance would have also required some of the rule-making that I mentioned earlier. Cattle in the district had been wiped out long ago by disease. The Ugandans brought thousands of cattle into the Sudan. Assistance which was flexible enough to respond to opportunity, could have permitted the development of a cattle industry in the district. When the need was known, emergency veterinary services should have been flown in at once. Cattle owners could have been assisted, so that they could retain their herds, instead of being forced to sell them to survive. For once they were gone, these cattle owners had to join the other destitute who left for settlements. Defining pastoral land would have required rule-making, governmental intervention, in co-operation with local leaders. Probably such deliberations would have given rise to another demand: a programme to control tsetse fly in affected parts of the district. Had this been provided, land which had been in use when such programmes were in motion, could have been brought back into production not just for cattle, but also for cultivation.

There were always shortages of fish in the market in Yei. Fish came, as was noted, from Uganda, either directly through guerrilla- protected corridors or through Zaire. In 1984 'Dinka' fish, i.e. fish brought in by Dinka, were on sale in Yei, but prices were high and beyond the reach of most refugees and their 'poorer hosts'. Yei River District is laced with rivers but refugees came into conflict with locals when they tried to fish them. The Ugandan population included thousands of people who had been fishermen. Their strong dietary preferences might have been sufficient to motivate them to develop fish-farming skills and the rivers and streams could have fed the ponds.

The potential for ecological damage caused by such a dramatic rise in

---

[2] The cost to start up a unit of 500 hives together with all the necessary auxiliary materials required was estimated by Muhoria and Associates, a private Kenyan company, to be $US14,285. and would pay for itself in less than two years. As this company reported in a letter to the Commissioner for Refugees, Khartoum, it had been doing research on the potential of the African wild bee 'as an instrument against desertification together with its other income-earning products' in Tanzania, Kenya, Sudan and Uganda. It observed that not only was bee-keeping a source of income, but that its pollination aspect would produce value over and above the income from its products. (30 December 1983). The International Bee Research Association, Buckinghamshire, UK, has recently reported that in Rumania, in 1977, it was found that 'the annual value of honey yielded per hectare of robinia forest was half as great as that of timber yield produced. The indirect benefits of apiculture to fruit and seed production through pollination is often much greater than the value of honey produced. (*The European Timber Trends and Prospects*, No.IV (in press).)

population was already obvious in 1982. There was not only the heavy demand for fuel and building materials, the agency building programme required bricks which were burnt with wood. Re-forestation projects could have been started immediately, as the refugee population included senior foresters. By 1984 tobacco farmers at Mopoko settlement had reason to fear they could not continue growing this cash crop because the trees in that area had all been cut down.

Tree-planting might have contributed in no small measure to preventing disputes between locals and refugees. The Sudanese depended to a considerable extent on the wild for game and various foods. The Oxford team found that 'Around many settlements Sudanese have repeatedly requested restrictions on charcoal, brick and rope production as these are denuding the environment. Frequently, these grievances were expressed in supernatural terms...the spirits of trees (especially large ones of certain species), are being disturbed.' (Wilson in Wilson *et al.* 1985.)

Had nurseries been established in various parts of the districts, they could have provided a 'non-controversial' means for women to have earned an income. Citrus trees, had they been planted even in 1982, could have been bearing fruit by 1985. Although bananas would grow in many parts of the country, there were *very* few places where they were available. The value of fruit for the diet of the malnourished is obvious. Even if there had been funds to buy fruit for the feeding programmes, it was not available.

The agricultural potential of the district has not been fully exploited. Even modest technological changes would result in greater production. Wisely, agriculturalists among the refugees had rejected a proposal for a tractor project proposed by an aid agency. Instead, they recommended animal traction. I have mentioned the great amount of surface water available. In Torit, the Boy Scouts produced a water-powered irrigation pump which would have been suitable for use along some rivers for irrigation. Onions are an extremely profitable crop; since they can be stored they do not represent the marketing problems posed by such vegetables as tomatoes and aubergines, for which seeds were provided. There were never enough onion seeds. According to McGregor, one of the Oxford team, northern traders controlled the sale of all locally produced onions. The others she found on sale were much smaller and came from Zaire. (Wilson et al. 1985.)

All the good arguments against expanding tobacco industries in the world aside, it should be noted that Sudan uses its scarce foreign exchange resources to import 80 per cent of its *domestic* requirements. Sudan used to rely heavily on 'border tobacco', that is, the commodity was smuggled over the border from the West Nile. The National Tobacco Company (NTC) has been encouraging the development of this industry in Yei River District, but the crop is labour intensive and requires experience and training to grow it.

Among the refugee populations there are hundreds of highly experienced tobacco growers, not to mention all the other skills required to manage this industry. In fact, many of the senior staff of NTC today *are* Ugandans. But because the Asylum Act, stating the rules governing their right to work, had not been disseminated, some of them at least posed as Sudanese. Unfortunately, even though NTC is a private company, it could not respond to the potential growth offered by the arrival of the refugees. It could not afford to import flues, thermometers, fertilizers, pesticides, and additional transport.[3]

What was the main restraining factor which prevented the local community from undertaking such projects for improving their economy? From the government's point of view, the problem is always the lack of foreign exchange. But *capital, foreign exchange, is the most valuable resource which humanitarian organizations bring to such a refugee emergency*.

'Exploitative' hosts?

Refugee-centrism gives rise to many misunderstandings. The myopia of outsiders leads to experiences which reinforce their views of the hosts as exploiters of refugees. Unfortunately, agency staff only meet host government officials in situations of tension and potential conflict, and they learn about the locals through the complaints of the refugees. Information concerning what is actually going on between hosts and refugees is unavailable to most outsiders.

Early in 1982, when refugees were registering at reception centres along the border and were in the state of health which led to the high number of deaths reported in Chapter Five, many of the local chiefs were reluctant to allow refugees to leave the border areas. As was noted, at Nyori there were even arrests and detentions aimed, we thought, to discourage any refugee migration to settlements. These local people were in Chambers' words, the 'poorer of their hosts'.

Given our refugee-centric perspective, the programme officer and I both dismissed such behaviour as evidence that the hosts were malicious, and that they were exploiting the poor refugees' cheap labour in return for the paltry amounts of cassava upon which the Ugandans were forced to subsist. But on reflection, perhaps the chiefs were being selective in who they insisted remain. The refugees who were detained were not the ill and the starving, but those who had been cultivating there for some time. Many refugees who went to settlements retained their land rights on the border. Only *detailed* studies of such relationships would uncover what was really going on, but it now seems to me that our initial judgement was too hasty.

For some time the Project Development Unit at Yei has been encouraging coffee growing. Near Wudabi there is a tea plantation. The value of these cash crops has not escaped the attention of wealthy Sudanese from Juba, and

---

[3] The government has thus far neglected to impose the rule, and NTC does not include tree planting in its programme for expanding tobacco.

some 'absentee landlords' had already established farms in the district. The land near the border is particularly suitable for coffee. Local people do not welcome this intrusion and do not regard the government as having the right to allocate their land. Allowing refugees even temporary rights over land on the border was one means of clearing and bringing unused land under cultivation, making it more difficult for outsiders to assume control. Recall that local people as well as Yei officials resisted the efforts of one Sudanese to force the refugees at Mopoko to be moved from the area which allegedly was for land for his coffee plantation. One unconfirmed story has it that another of these prospective coffee growers from outside the district had built himself a house somewhere in the bush between Morobo and Kaya, and that Ugandans and Sudanese had co-operated in producing certain effects which led him to fear the area was haunted. This example, if it is true, together with information collected by the Oxford team about relations with some Sudanese chiefs, suggest that 'the poorer hosts' may be politically strengthened by the arrival of the even poorer refugees. They welcomed refugees as allies in local conflicts.

Already in 1982 certain types of exchanges were taking place between refugees in settlements and Sudanese who lived in the vicinity. As part of the aid programme refugees were supplied with vegetable seeds not locally available. I learned from Ugandans that the Sudanese were asking to 'borrow' seedlings from their nurseries. And, since many plants were unfamiliar to them, they not only had to learn how to cultivate them, but Ugandans were asked for advice on how to cook them. In 1983 the programme officer required that each settlement donate 15 per cent of its vegetable seed to locals.[4]

When the survey was being conducted at Limuru, I invited the Chief of Kopera Chiefdom to share a meal with the team. He arrived with his sub-chiefs several hours too early, and in the midst of a meeting with the agricultural advisor and the productivity committees from the blocks. They were discussing their problems which included disputes over land and a fight between locals in the market. The proceedings of the meeting were translated for the benefit of the chief.

According to him this was the *first* time he had been consulted about the presence of refugees in his chiefdom, the agency staff had dealt with the sub-chief residing nearby. He recommended that those refugees with land

---

[4] Doubtless such inputs had the effect of improving the diets of the Sudanese who cultivated the vegetables. Moreover, Sudanese who were interviewed by the Oxford team at Panyume reported that they began eating breakfasts because they had seen the Ugandans taking this early meal. Ugandans were also influencing the farming practices of the Sudanese through *leja-leja*. Ugandans plough deeper and often told me the Sudanese were lazy because they 'only scratched the surface of the soil'. Defending the Sudanese, I explained that it was their pattern of shifting agriculture, of only using the most fertile areas, which allowed them to farm in this way. Digging deeper may not, in fact, be the best way to handle all the soils in the district, but many Sudanese are apparently now following this practice because it saves time weeding.

problems should consult him individually, and he would try to resolve their problems. He promised he would sort out the problem of the market which had resulted in violence. He was *most* interested to know what had happened to the vegetable seed; it turned out that the sub-chief, present at the meeting, had appropriated it for himself.

The chief, who had so attentively listened to the reports of the settlements' agricultural progress, requested that the agricultural advisor visit *his* farmers in the area. He commented on the poor quality of the district's extension services and said he was sure that the Sudanese farmers would also welcome the kind of supervision the refugees were receiving. Fortunately, this Ugandan agricultural advisor responded positively, saying that as he had a bicycle, transport would be no problem.[5]

Outsiders who will take the time can not only facilitate such encounters between hosts and refugees, but can use them to pinpoint needs. Research is the best way. This chief pointed out that there was no shortage of land as such, but that large areas in his chiefdom were unusable because of tsetse fly. He was old enough to remember that the British had made efforts to control this pest and that formerly the land was in use. He also explained another source of jealousy between his people and the refugees. Between Limbe settlement and all the way to Kala, there was not *one* source of uncontaminated water outside the settlements.[6]

A borehole was planned for the nearby intermediate school because refugees had been permitted to attend it. I spent some time with the chief and the principal of that school writing up a project which they then submitted to OXFAM. It promised free local labour for a scheme of shallow wells and protected springs, and requested that the programme be financed and implemented by this agency. If research were institutionalized, as part of the programme of assistance, it would be possible for a researcher to return to learn the results of this encounter. Through consultative relations between agency staff and government officials, it would be possible for the aid programme to capitalize on such opportunities to encourage amicable relations.

That the arrival of refugees and outside agencies was having an enormous impact on the economy could be seen by even the most superficial observation. The market in Yei grew dramatically for example. Initially I dismissed its expansion as simply a response to the artificial and temporary demand created by the agency-financed projects. Items seldom available in Yei in 1982 had appeared by 1983. These included bicycles, mattresses,

[5] I say 'fortunately' because in the course of ODA's study of their area, the Sudanese near Limuru had complained of the arrogance of the Ugandan clinic staff which discouraged many of them taking advantage of these new services.

[6] In theory, boreholes in settlements were supposed to be available for local use as well. This was quite unrealistic. Locals usually lived too far away to make use of them. If they lived near a settlement and tried to use one of the wells, they would find a long queue most hours of the day *and* night. Refugees viewed the wells as their own property.

batteries, torches, stationery, film, and certain imported foods. But the sudden expansion of Baze, a town on the Zaire border, and Kaya, which nestled between the Zaire and Ugandan borders, could not be explained solely in these terms.

It was in Otogo settlement, in 1983, that I became most aware of the scale of the economic impact of refugees on Yei River District. As has been described, refugees were asked to report how many days they had spent doing *leja-leja* during the preceding seven days, and a cumulative number of working days for each household was recorded. The numbers were so high I became alarmed. I sent a note to the ODA team's anthropologist, asking her just how she would interpret these findings? Were refugees taking jobs away from the Sudanese, and creating poorer hosts? Were Sudanese simply sitting back and allowing this cheap labour to do their work? Or were the Sudanese opening up more agricultural land?

The two main impediments to economic development in the district identified by the ODA survey were the lack of agricultural labour and the lack of markets. Even in 1983 in some parts of the district Sudanese had no place to buy such basic items as matches, salt, sugar, or tea. Given the refugee-centric focus of my research, I realized that I would not be able to study the changing agricultural practices of the Sudanese in response to the influx of refugees. It was obvious, however, that this explosion in available labour and the evidence that it was being so extensively used, must result in greater production by the Sudanese farmers.[7] Indirect evidence of their greater productivity was the growing demand for such consumer items as bicycles.

Markets

I asked one member of my team, Atima Ayoub, to study the settlement markets and to extend his investigation to include some of those in self-settled areas. His survey was carried out between June and mid- September. In 1984, further data were collected concerning refugee livelihood, and one member of the Oxford team studied the Yei market in considerable detail, collecting further information on the progress of their markets and the income-generating projects funded through the assistance programme from 11 settlements. (McGregor in Wilson *et al.* 1985.) Both studies of markets are limited by being carried out during the rains and just before harvest began.

Given the failures in the settlement agricultural programme which have already been detailed, it is not surprising to find that many refugees have had to innovate and to develop modes of livelihood which have little or nothing to do with the objectives of those who came to assist them. How *were* refugees surviving? As one of the Oxford team puts it,

[7] And indeed when a more detailed study was conducted at Panyume, evidence that locals were expanding acreage under cultivation emerged. (Wilson in Wilson *et al.* 1985.)

...with initiative, stamina, and foresight to an extent which completely overshadows the aid programme's contribution. Indeed some of the problems refugees are tackling are apparently unperceived by those planning the assistance programme. It is ironic that some survival strategies are disapproved of, or even defined as illegal. (Wilson in Wilson *et al.*)

The major contribution of the assistance programme for refugees in Yei River District was the indirect injection of capital into the region. How refugees and others used that capital has produced quite a different result than was intended. A major failure of the programme was that it did not take account of the great economic variation which obtained within the district.

Instead it appears that policy-makers believed the planned agricultural settlements of only 3,000+ people should be able to develop self-sufficient economies; the importance of such matters as supply and demand within them or beyond the boundaries of the immediate environment of each settlement had not been considered. Lacking tools, seeds and secure access to a sufficient quantity of agricultural land, many refugees were thrown onto trading while others were forced to rely on wage labour.

There were many disadvantages for those who found themselves depending on the market for their survival. They had insufficient capital and thus depended on the aid package to start trading. Their freedom of movement was threatened by the lack of identification cards or tax receipts, and this problem was compounded by the growing attitude among locals that 'refugees belong in camps.' (Ramaga 1984.) But perhaps most important, they were a highly visible threat to those who controlled the commercial sector.

Every refugee settlement had a market either within its perimeters or just outside. As had already been mentioned, during the survey of the unassisted refugees more than one hundred locations were identified where a market is open at least once a week. The growth of markets in the district was so rapid that still in 1984 despite their interest in collecting taxes, the Yei Rural Council was only aware of 12 markets in the Yei sub-district.

It was noted that the results of both studies of markets in 1983-4 were affected by the season in which they were conducted, it being the leanest time of the year. Moreover, Ayoub found great differences within the district, depending on the extent to which local people were already involved in trading, the time when a settlement had opened, 'i.e. the new ones are still far behind the business world', and the distances between settlements and Yei or Kajo-Kaji.

The plan for each settlement included a 'business' district, and one of the first developments one could observe was the establishment of a market. In 1983 Ayoub made a list of all items on sale in each and the prices which were charged. The number of items on sale ranged from 30 to 75. In addition he found a variety of 'private businesses including: beer clubs, shoe and bicycle repairers' groups, carpenters, hairdressers, blacksmiths, tailors, hotels, etc.'

(Ayoub 1983b.) The wider economy of this region aside, the success of the settlement markets was affected by the proximity of another or by its location in relation to established Sudanese markets. As Ayoub put in his report:

... some markets have adverse effects on others. This specially occurs between settlements which are less than five miles away from each other....people tend to be more attracted to the markets of the other....an example...is what is happening between Limbe and Koya, or Roronyo and Logobero, or Mopoko and Gumbari ...although Koya is a mere transit centre, the active business interests of the people has drawn the attention of settlers in Limbe....trading activity in Roronyo is more lively than it is in Logobero. Similarly Mopoko attracts more people than Gumbari. Another factor that influences the prosperity of markets is the trading interests of the local population....e.g. Mogiri and Mondikolo. In this case, both are attracted by Kajo- Kaji market of Wudu....Morsak is likely to suffer another blow [in addition to its proximity to Otogo market] because Ombasi, [a Sudanese market] just four miles away, has a very developed market. (1983a).

The planners failed to appreciate that where there *was* a Sudanese market, locals would be enraged at having to compete with another one established *inside* a settlement. Repeatedly the location of markets was a source of controversy between refugees and locals.

Limuru has this problem. Refugees have set up a public market in their business area right inside the camp, and they view this as an advantageous position for their already set up boutiques and hotels. [But]...the authorities prefer to transfer the site to another area some two miles away from the camp. They argued that their choice was more central, a place which both natives and refugees would benefit from. So the settlement officer will have to cope with the disputes; but it should be remembered that [at] the peak of the controversy [there] was a rampant fight at the market place between the conflicting parties....many local authorities are now....trying to gain control of refugee markets. In some cases market dues are collected, and hawkers and traders are taxed. The tax on hawkers and traders is fixed (£S1) per month. As for traders in beer clubs and public markets, amounts ranging from 5pt - 25pt are collected. This money sometimes compensates those who sweep the markets. But the tax from hawkers goes to the government. In Goli, the job of the cleaning of the marketplace is held by a Sudanese and a Ugandan.

Later on, after the survey in Limuru, the decision was taken to situate the market 300 metres from the settlement. In 1984 when McGregor visited this settlement she found that troubles had erupted once again and one man was killed.[8]

Whether located within the settlement or at the site preferred by the locals, the latter were quick to take advantage of the presence of the refugees. Refugees, lacking funds, relied on their few possessions, their rations or other

[8] '...the refugees seized this opportunity to demand the transfer of the market back to a central location (using the argument that the disabled could not otherwise participate in trading)....Tensions continue. Refugees claim that locals move with knives in the market-place and that there have been unofficial arrests.' (McGregor op. cit.)

items distributed by the assistance programme, to exchange for such essentials as salt, soap, sugar, tea, and matches.[9] Ayoub found that:

Generally goods sold are of small quantities. The local population brings cassava (raw and flour), ...They also bring wild food like honey, termites, white ants, and mushrooms. Venisons [*sic*] are also sold stealthily by them, mostly in camps distant from police or game rangers, e.g. Dororolili, Kala, etc. Few [of the] locals deal in hawkery business in which most Ugandan boys [are] specialists. Refugees, on the other hand, deal in both UNHCR plus WFP items or manufactured goods (got from Yei shops). Refugees sales are influenced by season and aids [i.e. assistance] given. One finds that most 'ACROSS-provided' vegetables [i.e. grown from seeds provided by the assistance programme] are not seen in markets until late July or August.

Already few in number, the sheer scale of the settlement populations with their markets led to the collapse of most of the Sudanese rural markets. In 1983 in only two areas did Ayoub find that the Sudanese markets were having a 'greater impact' on settlement markets, and these did not operate daily. These were Ewatoka, located near Wudabi, and Kajo-Kaji; the three settlements nearby, Kunsuk, Mogiri, and Mondikolo, found their markets 'superseded'. (ibid.)

In such areas, as Ayoub said, where there were locals who 'were enlightened long ago', the refugees have simply 'added to [the] commercial advantages reaped by these traders.' Since 'no refugee has capital large enough to compete with these more developed enterprises, it is likely that aspiring businessmen in these areas [will] have to resort to another kind of trade.' On the basis of his data, he recommended that people turn to hotel catering businesses as a means of 'challeng[ing] the native domination of business' or, given individuals' lack of capital, that they should form co-operative businesses. Sadly, Ugandans appear to lack the necessary solidarity to work together in the way that allows some migrant communities to establish an economic foothold.

Ayoub had a great deal to say in his report about one source of income generation and expenditure in the district - alcohol consumption. He attributed the importance of this means of earning cash to the fact that 'beer is [the] refugees' last resort after all his frustrations.' But in camps where he found drinking to be the 'highest' there were no beer clubs. 'All settlements east of Yei - with the exception of Roronyo - fall under this category.'[10] He also found another 'contradiction'. This was that '...in places where drinking rates are highest, one would expect the brewers to get a lot of money. But once again that is not always true.' Why? Because 'drinking on credit is also highest in such settlements.'

[9] This may account for the few items owned by the households where Ayoub made complete inventories of all material possessions.

[10] Only further research could explain *this* phenomenon! However, the programme officer strongly opposed the sale of alcohol in settlements.

In those settlements where the clubs exist, they are either located near the original public markets or ... some distance off, depending on the community development worker's plans. In settlements like Goli, Mopoko, Roronyo, Logobero, Tore, and Otogo, beer clubs exist. In others, beer clubs are apparently non-existent, though drinking is going on heavily. As for drinks like *maruwa* that need a lot of attention, they are usually drunk from homes so as to cater for its requirements. For those unfamiliar I should explain that *maruwa* requires constant boiling water to replenish the bowls and clean the tubes from which it is sipped. (ibid.)

Kala, he found, suffered from being a great distance from a town and this causes prices to be much higher. Tea was twice as high and clothing on average cost £S1.500 more per garment. On the other hand, Kala, like Pakula Naima, benefited from the proximity of large concentrations of unassisted refugees whose 'crops are nearly always amongst the first harvested. This has resulted in their crops reaching the market before the assisted settlers' own produce.' In Pakula, for example, at the time of the survey, he found the market 'full of free settlers' produce, e.g. groundnuts, maize, etc. sold very cheaply'.

Ayoub found other industries already underway. For example in those settlements which had plenty of wood available - Dororolili, Pakula and Wudabi - settlers were making doors and other furniture. In Dororolili chairs and tables were sold for £S5, but were cheaper at Wudabi. These items were made and purchased by refugees.

Already in 1983 the problem of transporting vegetables to market was, in Ayoub's view, discouraging the growing of food surpluses which are 'so needed in Juba - even Khartoum'. But it was not just vegetables, 'All production is affected. Right now over 100 bags of charcoal are awaiting transport to market to Yei. ... over five sacks of cabbages were stranded in Dororolili. This can discourage interest.' He concluded his report by noting that settlement markets were not altogether an unmixed blessing.

For on the one hand, markets have been welcomed with joy by the locals. They are pleased with the new life brought to their areas. In some areas, the locals even boast of refugees as belonging to them. [But] it should also be remembered, however, that many refugee markets have been scenes of clashes between the people taking part in them - refugees and refugees, natives and natives, or refugees and natives. Often consumption of alcohol is more responsible though.

'Free' settlement markets

The 'political economy' of the Kajo-Kaji sub-district was radically altered by the arrival of the refugees and Sudanese returnees who had been in business in Uganda. I have already mentioned that through a boycott, the northern businessmen had been successfully excluded from participating in the economy of Kajo-Kaji. An apparent *modus vivendi* has been worked out there between refugees and returnee businessmen, at least as far as the division of areas in which they each operated. Just outside the town were two separate market areas, one entirely controlled by the returnees, the other by refugees who had arrived with capital. There may even have been some specialization, but Ayoub did not study these markets.[11]

He went to Jalimo, a market further inland along the Uganda border where according to the local chief, there were 8,000 people, three-fifths of these being refugees. The refugee population was made up of Kakwa, Lugbara, and Madi speakers. In Jalimo he found a wide range of economic activities which included: shoe and bicycle repairers, butcheries, brewers, hotels, shops, market stalls, hawkers, and tailors. Commodities on sale included produce (mainly food) which was both locally grown and imported from Uganda. Manufactured goods also came from Uganda. Through his description of this market we can glimpse the different economic roles taken by refugees and locals. The latter appear to have retained the upper hand; refugees have specialized in providing services, or are employed by Sudanese.

There were 34 buildings in which businesses could be accommodated. At the time of his study, only 21 were 'operational on a full-scale private basis'. Four of the shops were *managed* by refugees, but owned by returnees from Wudu (the market near Kajo-Kaji).

Licence is compulsory and this ranges from at least £S40 upwards... regulated [on] the amount of assets in stock. Some of the shops have almost all types of goods found in the most well-stocked shops in Wudu, Kajo-Kaji, or even Yei. There are many goods which have been brought in from Uganda. Products like cigarettes...paraffin, tea leaves, fish, air cured tobacco, and some cloth bear the marks of Uganda, entering through Moyo. Hawker businesses are mainly found in the hands of refugees. The licences for these businesses are fixed at £S7.500. Prices vary little from elsewhere in Yei District except...cloth and fish are more expensive. (ibid.)

Ayoub found nine hotels (i.e. restaurants) which were open on the three market days, with 'fewer than five operational throughout the week.' Three of the hotels were operated by locals, but most of the hotel business was in refugees' hands in buildings rented from locals.

At the moment hotel business[es] are suffering a state of recession. This is because there is not much movement of people within and along the roads. However, there is also enough to eat at the moment as it is the right season for [the] harvest of maize, groundnuts, greens, etc. Necessary commodities like flour, meat, or liquid capital [*sic*] are also factors which influence hotels in Jalimo. Tea is scarce, but the price is just the same, i.e. 5 pt or 10 pt. A meal of meat ranges from 50 pt to 65 pt a plate. Also other

[11] That there was *some* specialization was evidenced by the fact that the whisky on sale at Kajo-Kaji was only available from the returnee's shops. It came from Uganda and obviously the returnees were more likely to be able to deal with the UNLA which was selling the commodity, than were refugees! Returnees maintained at least one brothel in this market, the women - refugees.

things, e.g. steamed maize, steamed potatoes, cassava, or cakes are sold at prices ranging from 5 pt to 10pt. (ibid.)

Beer clubs, apparently doing a thriving business, specialized in four types of locally-brewed alcoholic drink. Licences were mainly in the hands of Sudanese, with refugees managing the clubs and supplying the brews. Clients included both 'natives and refugees who mix freely'. The butchery was owned by a local, but he employed two Muslim refugees. Shortages of cattle in the area meant that meat was scarce. To have an animal slaughtered, hawkers had to pay £S3.000 to £S3.500.

The market place, set aside from the shops, was fenced and guarded by local police 'probably to maintain civil obedience and ensure collection of dues'. Market dues ranged from 5 pt to 75 pt depending on the quantity for sale. 'A sack of groundnuts or cassava flour is charged a fee of £S1 - £S2, depending on the market situation.' Some items, he mentions pots, do not accrue fees until they are sold since the likelihood of a sale is more remote.

The Yei market

In 1984, 116 interviews were conducted in the Yei market representing 'a 22 per cent sample of a trader population averaging 500 on a full day'. (McGregor in Wilson *et al.* 1985.) Those who have not seen an African market may find her description useful.

Men and women, young and old, are involved in trading. The market opens at 8 a.m. at which time traders queue outside the market entrance. They pass the tax office in turn, collect a receipt for their payment of market dues. Traders take up their accepted position in the market place, and although there is no formal layout as such, each commodity has its own area and regular traders always return to the same pitch. Stalls are available only for the sale of tobacco or fish....Otherwise sales take place on the ground, vegetables and other goods being laid out on sacks. Scales are not used for measurement...except in the shops of the northern traders (outside the food market); measurement is by means of small tins or glasses. (ibid.)

According to McGregor's survey and her other observations, about 40 per cent of the traders in the market are refugees. In addition to the lingua franca, Juba Arabic, she found 16 other languages spoken in the market.

Although the majority of traders...are Sudanese, the refugees tend on the whole to deal in larger quantities than the Sudanese (especially in the vegetable sector). The role of the Ugandans may therefore be greater than that suggested by their numbers.

The two populations specialize in the types of vegetables they sell and are also segregated within the market. Significantly, McGregor found that 'over the past two years...refugees have moved away from the sale of their own produce or rations to the sale of tomatoes, cabbages, onions and other vegetables imported from Zaire. Such refugees have found their own place in the marketing system and the role they play is often distinct from that of the local Sudanese.' (ibid.)

The source of all goods found in the market revealed that an unexpectedly low percentage of traders relied on produce grown in the locality. McGregor speculates that the lack of locally grown produce in the Yei market may be the result of the farm-gate purchases made by the northerners who transfer it directly to the Juba market. Since the sale of subsistence surplus is limited to an area of not more than two miles in radius, she concluded that Yei does not represent a market demand which would be sufficient to absorb an increased output from the rural areas. Thus, 'The potential for refugees to sell future agricultural surplus in Yei (once 'self-sufficiency' is attained) would therefore seem low.' Of course, her survey was conducted just before harvest begins, so 'the seasonal factor must again be borne in mind - in the dry season the volume of traffic increases considerably and the profitability of marketing ventures consequently changed [prices fall]. Future marketing will also be affected by the withdrawal of food aid.' (ibid.)

Other evidence that growing numbers of refugees are being forced into trading to survive as rations are withdrawn is also suggested by the fact that McGregor found that 54 per cent of the refugees she interviewed had been trading in the Yei market for less than one year. She also found transport to be the major constraining factor on market development.

For refugees to penetrate the Juba market will require official intervention, *rule making*, at a very high level. McGregor gives an example:

A group-farming project in Limbe settlement tried to sell their own sweet potatoes in Juba. Transport costs were covered by an agency. The northerners in control of the Juba market effectively blocked the sale of these 100 sacks by refusing to offer a fair price. Lack of storage facilities meant that on the third day the refugees were forced to sell at an absurdly low price. (ibid.)

The case of the northerners' control over the sale of onions in Yei has already been mentioned, but they also engage in 'speculative buying, such that entire supplies of maize flour can disappear from the market place. When there is a shortage, these stocks will be sold off at high prices from the northerners' shops.' (ibid.) Obviously one urgently needed intervention, which could be financed by outside aid, is not only a subsidized transport system to the Juba market, but storage facilities for local farmers to enable them to compete with these traders.

Apart from the market, there were other commercial activities in Yei town, but 'unlike marketing where the refugees have acted to transform the system radically, sectors such as carpentry and metal work have not been penetrated by refugees.' (ibid.) This was not, as we shall see, for want of skilled workers. Of the total of 26 tea shops found in central Yei, six were owned by refugees and capital is one of the major constraints for business. (ibid.) McGregor asked refugees how they had overcome this problem. Each tells a story of a struggle for survival and moving on a downward economic spiral.

The Ugandan tea shop owners had all either brought money with them, or had some other form of assistance in establishing their businesses. One had used the profit from a private medical clinic in Yei (in Uganda he had been engaged in medical research), as well as money brought with him. Another had brought a lorry... which he used to generate income by hiring it out and later selling it. One brought money with him, and increased his capital by agricultural wage labour....In Uganda he had owned a shop and had been a landlord of nine rented houses... and also owned a farm.... Another shop owner was a woman whose husband had given her money which she supplemented with income from handicrafts. Another was an ex-army general and unwilling to give further information. ... none of the shop owners had managed to accumulate sufficient capital from sources entirely within southern Sudan.

Tea shops are not the most secure way to make a living. With no water system, delivery from the river must be paid for and 'owners may spend up to £S10 per day on this cost alone'. (ibid.) And food supplies are also a major problem; some owners may be forced to travel to Kaya to purchase maize flour or rice. Rents paid by these refugees range from £S40 to £S70 per month and licence fees from £S15 to £S100 per annum. In addition they had to pay 'health' taxes. Seasonal fluctuations in demand made it difficult to survive. During the rains most people could neither afford the time nor the money to eat at a tea shop. Some also complained that Sudanese resented them; one because he occupied one of the best sites for business. Others claimed to have been harassed or forced to make payments not due.

Unlike other skilled occupations, bicycle repairing in Yei is monopolized by refugees. They have been able to engage in this business because of its informal nature....little is needed besides skill and a spanner to start a business. The majority...set up under a tree and have no overhead costs. Thus the constraints of capital are overcome. (ibid.)

Income generation in settlements

The assistance programme included a budget for income-generating activities in settlements. The programme as it was being implemented during 1982-3 was built around co-operatives. In 1982, and before ACROSS could find a suitable employee to take over the implementation of this budget, SCC's employee, John Yebuga, a Ugandan, had set out guidelines for co-operatives. According to the rules, funds would be given as a loan, and a percentage of profits paid back into what aimed to become a perpetually revolving credit scheme. Refugees responded to this idea, and had begun to plan their commercial activities along these lines. But after John Yebuga's detention, described earlier, ACROSS took over this responsibility.

Its approach to stimulating economic activities was to advise refugees to form co-operatives around particular skills. After proving their seriousness by putting up a building with a lockable door, they were to be provided with funds and/or equipment. I have already pointed out some of the pitfalls of this approach. For many complicated reasons refugees were not motivated to work in co-operatives. For example, time was of a premium to people who were having to do *leja-leja* or their own farm work for a living. Some businesses (like cobblers) did not need buildings, and refugees resented being asked to build them simply to prove their good faith. Women and the handicapped were largely excluded by this requirement.

ACROSS abandoned Yebuga's loan system in favour of simply giving money or equipment to those co-operatives which qualified. This meant that once a settlement's budget was used up, there were no funds for new ventures. The most able bodied were the first to lay claim to the CD (community development) budget. A loan system has its own inherent discipline and could have been managed by a settlement committee which was answerable to the community as a whole.[12]

Consumer shops were the most popular; some of these co-operatives had more than twenty members. Since the profits earned by a shop were unlikely to support more than one household, it was not worth anyone's time to build the shop or attend the meetings held to keep a group 'co-operating'. In 1984 such a shop at Mopoko earned for its membership of ten a monthly profit of £S40. (McGregor op. cit.)

But among the fundamental flaws in plans for income generation in the settlements was that 'the structure of projects and guidelines for assistance were drawn up with scant knowledge of the economic realities of the environment in which they would operate.' (ibid.) For example, as McGregor discovered, Yei had only five carpentry workshops, each with a maximum of four trained employees. Yet they already were supplying the local demand. In one settlement alone, a co-operative having 12 highly skilled carpenters was funded. They depended on ACROSS and other agencies to buy their total output of desks, chairs, etc. Similarly, Yei already supplied all its own tailoring requirements. As McGregor noted, 'Sale of settlement-produced garments by redistribution to the vulnerables can only continue with long-term agency support. When agencies discontinue buying, workshops will be left to function on their own.' (op. cit.) Settlement businesses could be viable *only* if they had transport and could break into the

---

[12] The programme officer 'found' some money in his own budget for CD and he and I experimented with a loan system as a way of stimulating income-generation. I was instructed not to mention the availability of the money, but to identify possible good credit risks. For example, one man who together with his brothers in Uganda had owned a transport company which plied the Arua-Kampala road, asked me how he could get money for a bicycle so that he could start trading. I sent him to the programme officer who loaned him the necessary money. He signed a contract to repay within six months. Within two, he was able to pay back the loan. I sent many others. One was a Bunyoro living at Wudabi. He had managed a saw mill in Uganda and said that if he had some simple hand equipment, he could produce boards from the enormous quantities of wood near that settlement. Timber for building was always in short supply. A widow from Limbe asked for a loan to set up a tea shop on the Yei-Juba road.

Yei market with competitive quality and prices, or if they could manage to penetrate the Juba market with all that this entails. Yet agencies positively discouraged the movement of skilled craftsmen away from settlements.[13]

Another fundamental problem was the failure of the refugee agencies to co-ordinate their community development with local programmes. In Yei the government had an office established to promote co-operatives in the district. Headed at the time by Vigil Jima, a Sudanese who demonstrated considerable awareness of local problems and who had a team of trained workers, his office was not consulted until much later. Nevertheless, refugees were instructed they should incorporate locals into *their* CD projects. In fact, reports to UNHCR asked for information on how many Sudanese were participating in co-operation and on the school management committees. In Chapter Two I noted how Mr Jima lost some of his staff to the assistance programme when it was recruiting settlement officers, and, in Chapter Six, I mentioned that Sudanese women, (like the refugees) who were 'under' GMT's community development programme, also quarrelled with other women who were in government-sponsored programmes.

By the time ACROSS staff did consult Mr Jima on the legal position of co-operatives established in settlements, he was so angry that he simply told them it was illegal for refugees to form co-operatives, so ACROSS changed the name of their projects to 'community development'. Had a different approach been taken, and since it was *not* illegal for refugees to belong to co-operatives, injecting funds and encouraging their participation in *his* (i.e. the government's) programme might have better served the interests of integration.

In 1984, McGregor visited 11 settlements to check on the progress of the income-generating projects funded by the programme. She found some community development projects had collapsed because of leadership problems, but this alone did not explain all their failures. She thought it more likely that because profits were so low, people were compelled to spend their time 'farming or doing casual labour instead of being free to commit their time and effort to CD projects.' In her view, these projects would never be successful unless the profits made them into viable full-time propositions for their members.

[13] In 1982, when Goli carpenters wanted to begin production, ACROSS was reluctant to supply them with tools at that time, lest they abandon agriculture and set up business in Yei. By 1983 the head of this co-operative had managed to escape and find work in Juba. Field staff often resented refugees who they thought were unwilling to conform to the programme's expectation that all make their living *primarily* from agriculture. But such highly skilled people can make a more positive contribution to the economy through the use of their training. One of my assistants for example, an economist who could speak French, was not *allowed* to go to Juba to look for work. Later when I intervened and took him myself, a French company asked him why he had not come months earlier when they were recruiting. He was also offered a job teaching at a secondary school in Juba. However because relationships between this refugee and agency staff were so fraught, and because Ugandans thought he was a spy, his future in the Sudan was insecure. Eventually the Canadians resettled him. What is ironic is that he *wanted* to remain in Africa to study the economic impact of refugees on their hosts.

In one settlement the CD advisor described the carpentry co-operative as in 'chaos', and people were refusing to co-operate as 'they struggle for profits'. She found the blacksmiths had never built their building so they never qualified for aid. She met one skilled and disabled blacksmith who had set up on his own, but he had 'virtually no tools. Agency protocol prevents aid from being supplied as he is an individual without a structure [i.e. building].' She found that:

...the skilled or dedicated members become disillusioned and leave to set up their own projects. It is notable that much viable economic activity in the settlements has been started without agency support and that such initiatives, if supported, may produce a higher investment return than new projects brought in from outside. For example...individually owned tea shops and consumer shops, functioning without aid are often on a sounder economic footing than agency supported co-operatives...one blacksmith in Mopoko never joined the agency-supported co-operative scheme, but when it collapsed, he set up on his own (i.e. took over the trade) with two hammers, two pliers, and one file brought from Uganda. (op. cit.)

It is not surprising that McGregor questioned the 'long-term developmental potential' of CD!

There has been no attempt to assess the direction refugees themselves take in their efforts to generate income using their own initiative. Instead of identifying such initiatives and assessing the problems faced and channelling aid into these areas, agencies tend to impose their own ideals on the community, supporting projects of their own choice, which are implemented according to rules laid down by the agency. This makes a mockery of the concept of community development. Instead of facilitating development as the community itself deems appropriate and instead of supporting indigenous efforts, the nature of desirable development of the community is determined by the aid donor - by definition a body not belonging to the community in question.

Agency policy towards income generation in the settlements instead of reducing dependency and helping refugees on the path to self-sufficiency, rather increases their dependency. This waste of resources will continue until projects are planned taking into account the economic structure of the district. A more efficient use of resources would be to direct funds into the development of a transport network; this would benefit both refugees and Sudanese alike. (ibid.)

Taxation

From the time refugees began entering the Sudan there was an urgent need to regularize the payment of customs, poll tax, business licences and market fees as they were applied to the Ugandans. Although there was an informal agreement that refugees should not pay taxes for the first two years, or until they had reached 'self-sufficiency', among the unassisted refugees interviewed it was found that 22.3 per cent had paid poll tax (867 or 22.7 per cent did not answer the question). There were no exemptions from market dues or business licences outside the settlements. The problem of importing vehicles has already been discussed in Chapter Four.

When McGregor began her research in Yei market in 1984, she found 'no written material...and much contradictory information was given by different members of the Rural Council' concerning their system of taxation in markets. The arrival in 1984 of a young woman interested in studying markets caused quite a stir in Yei. Security personnel stopped and questioned her 15 times during the first day of interviews! The Rural Council began holding meetings to which she was invited and showed great interest in the results of her research. But she found that:

Despite informal understanding that refugees should not be taxed, there was no interim period of tax exemption... Markets at present unlevied, remain so purely as a result of inefficient administration. The Rural Council was apparently unaware of the existence of many markets. Their figure of 12 markets is a gross underestimation... Markets situated within refugee settlements themselves are defined as illegal, although some such 'illegal' markets were being taxed. (ibid.)

Officially, tax collecters are paid £S75 per month, but she found in practice, once the tax book was full, they were paid 25 per cent of what they had collected. This worked out at about £S45 per month, thus there was an incentive to overcharge. Tax monies were not used to develop the market facilities - building more stalls, public pit latrines, fencing and rubbish pits - these improvements were supposed to be done by the traders on a self-help basis.

Considerable conflict had arisen over arbitrary taxation in rural markets. In some places only the Sudanese paid taxes, in others only the refugees, in yet others, *everyone* had to pay up. Not all tax collectors had enough education to keep accounts and assess the tax.

Understandably McGregor was reluctant to release her findings, fearing they would further such irregular practices. But the reaction to her report was quite the opposite to what she expected. Some months later, after a meeting, a circular was sent round, (with copies sent) to the commissioner for the province, the director of the regional Ministry of Regional Affairs and Administration, the resident magistrate, the executive officer of Yei Rural Council, the chief of police, all chiefs and sub-chiefs, and all settlement officers.[14] It laid down the ground rules for market taxes and business licences as they applied to refugees and informed everyone that *until a decree* was issued by the Regional Ministry of Regional Affairs and Administration, Juba, indicating otherwise, refugees who were living in settlements, are 'exempted from social service tax and other related taxes'. (No:WAC/Y/25 A.1 XR/47.A.1, 19 January 1985.) The notice required all traders to hold a

---

[14] The notice also included strong warnings to 'game scouts and youth associations' and chiefs were asked to warn their people that the 'practice of charging travellers both refugees and nationals will not be tolerated...' (ibid.)

licence, but if refugees only intended to sell *within* settlements, it would be issued free of charge. Refugees selling their produce in markets *inside* settlements were also exempted from market dues.

Rule-making in response to changing conditions and circumstances must be an on-going process. These new rules (or the regularizing of old ones) obviously favour refugees in settlements to the disadvantage of the unassisted and give them an edge in their competition with Sudanese traders. Without identification cards, which would indicate their time of arrival in the Sudan, and with no means of assessing their economic status, these new rules are likely to have some important consequences for the self-settled. Certainly one may predict that markets *within* settlements will gain more prominence. Their registered populations may even grow.

There could be further implications of a far-reaching and more sinister type. There are signs, which greatly contradict the spirit of ICARA II (not to mention the OAU Charter), that UNHCR would prefer to limit its protection responsibility only to those refugees under the aid 'umbrella'. The arbitrary definition of those refugees living in Djiboutiville in 1983-4 as 'economic migrants' rather than refugees is a case in point. (Crisp 1984; Harrell-Bond 1985.) It is said that a deal has been struck with the Mexican government whereby only those people living in UNHCR-assisted settlements will be granted refugee status. We have seen, in Chapter Four, how the unassisted refugees, subjected to harassment and murder during the disturbances near Kaya in late 1984, were said to be outside the protective arm of UNHCR. Even when deposited in Goli transit, they were not assisted. In Port Sudan in 1984, only a fixed number of identity cards were issued although it was known that the numbers of refugees were far greater. As Freire (1970) put it, 'Once named, the world in turn reappears to the namers as a problem and requires of them a new naming.'

How *were* refugees surviving?

In 1984 the Oxford team carried out a livelihood study of a 10 per cent sample of households in four refugee settlements and interviewed 36 households near Panyume. Some of their findings concerning the further impoverishment of the families identified in 1983 as vulnerable have already been discussed in Chapter Six. All but one of the settlements they visited were on the list to be cut off from food aid in December 1984 and, as has been tediously repeated throughout this book, the WFP rations were not getting through once again at the height of the 1984 agricultural season.

They found that refugees in the three older settlements not only still suffered shortage of land, but were actually doing less cultivation than the previous year. Vegetable and groundnut production had been severely affected by drought. The most successful households

...had cleared the little land allocated and then sought further land from relatives and neighbours....about one in ten households...also negotiated privately with local Sudanese for small additional plots, normally only about an acre....These fields are apparently all (cultivated) on a share cropping basis - two fifths of the harvest to the patron was a common figure, but rarely were payments strictly agreed and other gifts of WFP food, tobacco and so on may also be requested. (Wilson 1985a.)

The Oxford team's full report discusses the relative success in obtaining land in terms of the indigenous socio-political structure (which varies widely throughout the district) and the success of refugees to be incorporated into that system. Their findings also support my observation that the intervention of the agency programme severely interferes with the development of the patron-client relations which facilitated that process. However, at Limbe the settlement 'chief' has been remarkably successful in beginning to overcome these problems and it was the view of the Oxford team that refugees in settlements are becoming 'wiser' about their position *vis-à-vis* locals in the face of the withdrawal of aid.

An important point which their report also confirmed was the willingness of refugees to cultivate if they could get control over land. In each of the households having an adult male they said they 'could manage and indeed required at least two more acres.' However, some added that 'only if food is provided to the settlement to relieve them from agricultural wage labour...will they be able to clear these fields.' The problem of losing land rights to locals has continued around the settlements, but this problem was not encountered in the self-settled areas in 1984.

TABLE 8.1: Settlement livelihood*

	Settlements		
Modes of livelihood	Limbe %	Gumbari %	Roronyo %
Farming	63	83	90
Leja leja	68	69	79
Mugati (bread-cakes)	8	13	7
Alcohol production	33	18	23
Charcoal manufacture	8	7	2
Other trades and crafts	9	26	25
Salaried employment	8	9	6
Number of households sampled	80	77	82

* from Wilson et al. 1985

Agency staff are often impatient with complaints that refugees have to travel great distances to cultivate land allocated to them. However, in 1984 the Oxford team found that it was not only the other constraints - lack of tools, seeds, the demands of domestic work - which caused agricultural failure; the problem of wild animals continued. 'Being far from the settlement in a strange land was often ...frightening, and this [fear] was confirmed...by the killing of a refugee woman by a lion near Mambe settlement.' (Wilson 1985*a*.)

Refugees' survival strategies include, as was demonstrated in Chapter Three, the deployment of members of a household group in both settlements and self-settled areas. As with my own research, the livelihood survey conducted by the Oxford team in the settlements did not take account of possible reciprocal relations between relatives beyond the settlement. The Oxford team did find however that, since 1983, refugees within settlements had begun to develop co-operative relationships which included share-cropping, land-sharing, work parties, and labour employment. Employed refugees were also paying other refugees to do *leja-leja* for them.

The Oxford team found that most of the households have diversified their approach to survival by working to earn income from several different sources. The results of the survey of three of the settlements are shown in Table 8.1[15]

Leja-Leja continues to be as, or more, important than cultivation. At times the refugee demand for *leja-leja* becomes greater than the Sudanese ability to provide it. This was particularly marked at Katigiri which was surrounded by a small and relatively uncommercialized group of Pojulu speakers...who rely on hunting and gathering for a large part of their income. At the time of our visit to Katigiri a drought and WFP delivery failures had created a level of destitution whereby most of the population was dependent on eating leaves without any starch porridge. To obtain work required a 15 mile walk each way to the area of Wonduruba. Most of the refugees could not manage this and the atmosphere suggested that the settlement was about to disperse.[16]

While generally refugees work 'for different employers each time', one virtue of *leja-leja* which the Oxford team suggests, is the emergence of regular patronage relations. 'In Alero, one-fifth of those doing *leja-leja* told us that they were fed by their employer and seven per cent were lent a hoe.' (Wilson 1985*a*.) In the self-settled area studied, they found that *leja-leja* was becoming

[15] I do not include the results from Alero where all the sample was not interviewed, but it is interesting to note that far fewer, 39 per cent, earned income from *leja leja* and more, 11 per cent, hold salaried employment. This settlement was one of the newer ones, established in late 1983, and was close to Yei: 26 per cent were taking advantage of the Yei market to sell charcoal. The other settlements were farther away and lacked transport (and perhaps by this time, trees!). Alero residents had been allocated one acre of land: 63 per cent had cleared and planted it, 11 per cent had only cleared it, 11 per cent said they had 'started', and 16 per cent had not made significant attempts.

[16] See the description of Katirigi's earlier problems in 1983 on pages 383 and 386, of Appendix II.

less 'exploitative' as refugees were becoming increasingly self-sufficient. (Wilson *et al.* 1985.)

Activities which have been combined in Table 8.1 as 'crafts and trades' include some done mainly by women: making *mugati*, a small deep fried cake from flour, milk powder, and sometimes sugar (obviously relying for supplies on WFP rations), alcoholic drinks, pottery, and mat-making. Refugees also earned from such skilled trades as mending bicycles and shoes, and a number of children earn money by crocheting skull caps, especially popular among the Muslims. Both men and women were involved in petty trading:

One small boy brings paraffin from Yei to Alero market (about seven miles) earning £S5 (£1.50) per week; a female household-head brings cassava from Morobo to Alero market (about 30 miles) twice a week earning £S10 (£3), and another cuts and sells grass locally for building.

One clear observation about all these income-generating activities is that they greatly diversify the household economy. In the Alero sample, only 34 per cent did not have any cash income in addition to agriculture and *leja-leja*, and 40 per cent had one activity....At times multiple activities were performed by the same person...almost every conceivable economic niche has been exploited. Obtaining capital...was an obvious constraint and to overcome this the selling of aid...and WFP food has been particularly important. (ibid.)

What is most significant about their findings is that except for salaried employment, these income-generating activities were almost without exception organized and the capital raised (diverted from aid) by the refugees themselves. Only a negligible number reported earning income from aid-sponsored projects.

The provision of aid in goods is probably based on the assumption that the programme knows best what aid is needed. When aid is sold in this way, it is often suggested that therefore aid was not needed. On the contrary it would seem likely that aid in cash was what was needed, so that people could meet their needs as defined by them. (ibid.)

The Oxford team found that even during the time of their study, the withdrawal of food aid was having the effect of 'putting people out of business'.

We were told that demand had declined and that they had eventually had to 'eat' the little capital which they had raised with such a struggle. The much lower proportions of people found trading in the self-settled area supports the view that most of these activities ...can exist only because refugees in settlements are subsidized. Indeed much economic activity is really just a way of using otherwise unproductive time to provide a small income...many...[have] given up due to the poor returns. In Roronyo, for example, someone tried to take tomatoes the 15 miles to Yei on foot (along the roadway refugees had cleared themselves), but he 'got tired and sold them cheaply on the way'. Someone else tried to run a small store from this same distance, but found it too arduous to transport supplies. People were also found to have given up mat-making because of the difficulty in obtaining materials. (ibid.)

As Ken Wilson also points out in the discussion of patterns of refugee livelihood, it is a mistake to believe that their degree of involvement in the trading and service economy indicates financial success. It is the *visibility* of such activities which probably accounts for the misconception. In fact '*the involvement of Ugandans in petty trading and crafts in the district as a whole* (whilst the indigenous Sudanese concentrate on agriculture), is *probably caused as much by the marginalizing of refugees from agriculture as by their supposed entrepreneurial abilities.*' (1985a, emphasis added.)

The Oxford team also conducted a nutritional survey in four settlements (836 children were measured), as well as at Panyume. As noted the latter survey included 270 refugee and 104 Sudanese children. Malnutrition among the refugees in Panyume was higher than in settlements, but in the settlements the rates had doubled since the March 1984 Médecins Sans Frontières' survey which the Oxford team replicated. The increase in malnutrition was probably due both to the absence of food rations, and to the fact that the survey was conducted during the rains, the time of the greatest shortage. Detailed interviews were conducted with the parents or guardians of the malnourished children identified by the surveys.

Just over half the malnourished came from obviously 'vulnerable' households (that is, where one or both parents was physically or mentally disabled, the household female-headed, the child an orphan without adequate support and such like). The others generally came from very poor but not totally destitute households where a variety of factors were identified including maternal lactational failure, serious diseases and, in some instances, parental neglect....The fact that malnutrition rates were higher in the self-settled population seems to reflect that...aid does somewhat alleviate the circumstances of the poorest. (Wilson 1985a.)

The data from one self-settled area is not sufficient to make general statements about the comparative well-being of self-settled refugees either vis-à-vis those in settlements or the Sudanese. However, the team believes that at least for Panyume, their findings 'exploded the myth that self-settled refugees were somehow better off than the Sudanese (they were actually markedly poorer).' (ibid.)

The data from Panyume also revealed how it is overly simplistic to conclude that self-settled refugees are either better off than those in settlements or that they are worse off, 'living in abject misery and somehow too ignorant to come to settlement'. (ibid.) In fact, their circumstances, as was found in the settlements, varied from household to household. However, the team concluded from all of these sources of data, that when aid is withdrawn, those refugees who are now living in assisted settlements could well be much poorer than those who have remained outside them unassisted. They go so far as to predict that the settlements will 'collapse'.

Dodging the issues

The idea that people will abandon settlements when the aid is withdrawn implies that a great deal of effort and expense may have been invested for little return. The Oxford team believes that the

...main reason for this failure [of settlements] to meet the programme's objectives is that the administration of the aid programme is locked into a set of concepts and manner of functioning which renders it...[unable] to identify and respond to the differing needs of the various categories of refugees. Lack of information and understanding concerning what the refugees were experiencing and the social and economic responses of individuals and groups under such stress, meant that it could not be predicted how providing aid would affect their livelihood. Furthermore, under intense time (and other) pressure, officials generally remained in the office and made only formal visits to the 'field'; thus *they did not realize how unaware they were of the indigenous economic and political processes occurring* and so failed to obtain advice from Sudanese and refugees, let alone devolve sufficient and appropriate authority. Perhaps the overwhelming sense that they were 'doing good' enabled them to dodge questions of their actual impact. The underlying basic assumptions of refugee programmes (and the aid business generally) mean that headquarters' attitudes and inherent agency structure often determine both the level and type of aid provided, and the form of relationship to exist between donor and recipient. This mitigates against true participation, since it tends to involve attempts to 'structure' the recipients so that aid can be imposed. (ibid. emphasis added.)

Even such limited information on the political consequences of the intervention of outsiders on this district, which already was bearing the burden of the sudden influx of thousands of people, reveals how very dangerous is the ignorance of the contradiction between the stated 'non-political' objectives of humanitarian assistance and the actual political impact of their interventions. All societies under 'normal' conditions are characterized by tension, competition, and conflict. These are usually managed through intricate processes of the exercise of power, influence, and authority. (Adelman 1976.) The extent to which coercion, force, and violence were being exercised in Yei River District revealed how badly out of control the situation was. In a letter from the programme officer about this book, he urged me to remember sympathetically these terrible political constraints under which the humanitarians were operating. But to a very great extent both the failure to understand the political implications of interventions, was *contributing to the very problems with which they had to contend*. How Yei River District would have adjusted to the transforming impact of the population increase without the outsiders' help will never be known. One of the problems for most Africans is that they are rarely 'allowed' the opportunity to find their own political solutions.

More may be needed than conventional prescriptions

In 1979 Robert Chambers wrote a paper which attempted to examine why, in their studies of the failures of pastoral development schemes, social scientists had neglected the role of the administrator. He points out how powerful is the influence of the administrator on the type of interventions made, interventions 'which so frequently fail or lead to unintended results'. Administrators, he emphasizes, are the ones who implement, or fail to implement programmes or policies, and when things go wrong, they blame the pastoralists 'for being ignorant'. The social scientists, he says, then busy themselves to prove just how 'rational' pastoralists are, and how their actions constitute an appropriate adaptation to a hostile environment. But, he points out, 'administrators' behaviour might also be rational, it might be a similarly "rational" adaptation to a different sort of hostile environment.' The 'physical and cognitive' alienation of administrators from the reality of the pastoralists causes them to be particularly vulnerable to belief systems composed largely of myths. The outcome is the co-existence of two belief systems about the same reality. His prescription is training for the administrators to help them overcome their 'anti-nomad' ideologies.

The problem with Chamber's prescription is that the 'hostile reality' to which the administrator has so ably adapted is not simply a myth which can be exploded by training. The ideological and physical alienation are a direct outcome of a development official's own position within a global structure of economic and political inequality.

In the years which have passed since the publication of the Brandt report there are *fewer* people who would argue against the school of thought which sees the underdevelopment of the poor countries as a dynamic structural process which has its roots 'in the exploitation of one class by another and one state by another'. (Clark 1984.)[17]

Nearly everyone understands how poor countries are further impoverished by the worsening terms of trade, the control of manufacturing by industrialized nations, the massive expenditure on armaments and increasing militarization. It is becoming obvious even to casual observers that it is the concentration of control over resources (including even information)[18] which is depriving people who are in the greatest need, and which also leads to the necessity to tighten control on their liberty and self-expression.

---

[17] Adrian Clark conducted a study for Euro-Action Accord (EAA), an independent development organization, on the question of Africanization of their staff. He included a discussion paper in his report which represents his personal views and not necessarily those of EAA. I have drawn heavily upon this paper. I thank EAA for permission to quote (and paraphrase) this internal document. That such discussions go on *within* agencies is a positive sign that many are prepared to question the premises from which they work. That they are not publically debated reflects the financial insecurity which all voluntary agencies suffer. Approaches to aid will only change when there is also an *independent-minded public* prepared to support them.

[18] Humanitarians are usually more interested in literacy programmes than they are, for example, in teaching English or French. I was asked to address a group of students planning to go to 'do development' in the 'third world'. Some were very critical of those who respond to advertisements for English teachers, since only the 'elite will benefit'. One Ugandan whom I had invited along asked them how Africa could ever advance if it did not have access to the information available only in European languages.

Underdevelopment, in sum, is not simply a problem of a lack of certain material goods and services by certain people; rather it is a problem of structural imbalances in the world political and economic order. It is not a problem that can be overcome by simply providing people with the means to satisfy their immediate material requirements. Even in those cases where such material assistance succeeds in providing some respite, there is no guarantee that this will lead to an ongoing dynamic process of development while an overall distribution of power remains the same. (ibid.)

While development initiatives have their roots in the charitable concerns of people from industrialized countries, it is no secret that official aid is largely concerned with the economies of the donor countries, that strings are attached to its use, and that aid is used to exert pressure on the internal politics of beneficiary countries. Independent development organizations and humanitarians *believe* they 'cannot be accused of the same type of motivation; they are not generally linked to political vested interests and do not seek any economic return on their aid.' (ibid., but see Harrell-Bond 1985.) However, as Clark points out, there are several features of these organizations which, as he puts it, require critical analysis:

1. Few have sufficient understanding of the process of underdevelopment or have any desire to combat the northern-based entities which contribute to this process;
2. Most confine their assistance to material, technical, and educational inputs and emphasise the role of community self-help in the belief that this is sufficient to promote a process of real development;
3. Few provide the political recognition and solidarity desperately required by genuinely popular third world movements and governments;
4. Nearly all are responding not solely to the plight of underprivileged and oppressed peoples but to a need by relatively privileged people...to donate money etc. to 'good causes'. In that people generally expect some sort of emotional feed-back...or require emotional contact from the outset...organizations publicize their work and establish direct sponsorship schemes in such a way that risks reinforcing stilted views about people in the third world and about the best ways of helping them;
5. As with all organizations, NGOs...develop bureaucratic vested interests with regard to jobs, decision-making roles etc. Few...manage to maintain the flexibility to radically transform their ways of operation or even to call them into question;
6. ...few...have been prepared to admit any substantive control within the organization [to]...the people they are endeavouring to assist - although such a transfer of responsibility is one of the main objectives at the project level. (1984:116-8.)

None of these points, however, need to be regarded as negative criticism if one *believes* that everyone has a right to become involved in tackling the problem of development, regardless of their expertise or awareness; or if one believes that people have a right to steer clear of political issues and remain neutral; that people are right to expect emotional gratification from their charitable involvements; and that it is natural to want to conserve one's own job, even where one accepts that others could do it more effectively; or that it is entirely logical to retain the decision-making power in the hands of the donor (or its representative, the fieldworker), rather than in those of the receiver society.

On the other hand, there is another *belief* system about the same reality. If one accepts that outside meddling in the affairs of 'third world' countries is a major reason for their under-development; that there are already too many unqualified people setting themselves up as development experts; that projects often build up unrealizable expectations; that political neutrality - unless positive - effectively lends support to the status quo; that it allows privileged people to take comfort in their charity, rather than encouraging them to question that privilege; that nobody has the right to make a living from other people's underdevelopment; and if you believe that the use of money is best decided by the user rather than by the giver - then there is room for asking whether the other system of *belief* is perhaps the real obstacle to development, rather than being the motivating force for good that humanitarians like to believe.

Is 'no strings' better?

I have already referred to the recent publication by Turton and Turton (1984) in which the successful adaptation of a community of pastoralicts to a famine situation has been described. They found that the Mursi had 'shown themselves to be both resilient and inventive in the way they have responded, in the *absence of systematic outside intervention* in their affairs, to the last ten years of drought and hunger.' In fact, the only help they received was the rather accidental distribution of some *free food aid* which was received at a collecting point by *representatives* of their starving community and *transported* by them *back to their own people*. The lessons which they draw may 'be fairly obvious', but the practical problem these researchers face is how to use their case study to influence relief agency policy. 'We have in mind both the practical problem of information gathering, and "ideological" resistance from the relief agencies themselves.' (ibid. emphasis added.)

In order to achieve by design what was, in this case achieved by accident, one would need information about local conditions which was detailed enough both to give a reliable 'early warning' of need and to make a sensible decision about when to cease the emergency food distribution. Information of this sort is, of course, rarely, if ever available, and assuming that there are no insoluble logistical problems, there is likely to be a second obstacle, coming from within the relief agencies themselves, to the rapid organization of 'free relief'.

As they say, there is wide recognition of the evils of famine camps but 'this very recognition seems to have led to a growing resistance to the concept of relief "with no strings attached".'

This is seen in the rush of agencies to get out of relief and into 'rehabilitation' and in attempts to link relief, when it is given, to development projects, usually through food-for-work programmes. In the case of the Mursi it can be categorically stated that a food-for-work programme would have been counter-productive. They do not need to be persuaded to do the work necessary to provide for themselves...a food-for-work programme would have produced precisely the situation it was intended to avoid.

The Turtons call the resistance to free relief ideological because it is 'at least partly, based on cultural prejudice: the *belief* that people such as the Mursi lack motivation and resourcefulness to work out new solutions to the problem of their own economic self- sufficiency.' They go on to call attention to the dangers of the use of the word, 'rehabilitation'. It is

...dangerous because it contains the implicit assumption that the people to be 'rehabilitated' can only be made to stand on their own feet with the help of outside direction. This is a dangerous assumption, if only because the literature on agricultural development is littered with examples of projects which did not achieve their objectives because of a failure to appreciate both the subtlety of local knowledge and expertise and the ability of people to adapt their indigenous social institutions to new circumstances. It is of course, convenient for the development worker to *believe* that the reason why people are hungry is that they are ignorant and technically unsophisticated, since this makes the task of proposing "solutions", based on supposed superior modern technology, that much easier. (*ibid*. emphasis added.)

But the problem is not simply imposing solutions based upon superior modern technology. Very few voluntary agencies or even government-sponsored development programmes are today promoting advanced technological development in the so-called third world. *Quite the opposite*, appropriate technology, informal education, preventative health - these are the buzz words today. Humanitarians may have never thought about how their enthusiasm for 'appropriate' technology for the poor countries of the world may be supporting those very interests they believe themselves to be undermining, the interests which resist and obstruct the transfer of technology to poor countries. Certainly Schumacher did not promote the idea that there were two sorts of 'appropriateness', one for the rich and one for the poor. As McRobie writes in a preface to the posthumous publication of a collection of Schumacher's lectures:

Taken as a whole *Good Work* rounds off and makes explicit Schumacher's case that the choice to technology is one of the most critical choices now confronting any country, rich or poor. The poor countries must secure technologies appropriate to their needs and resources - intermediate technologies - if the rural masses are to be given a chance to work themselves out of poverty; but the rich countries probably stand even more in need of a new technology, smaller, capital-saving, less rapacious in its demands on raw materials, and environmentally non-violent. The people of the poor countries must be helped to raise themselves to a decent standard of living. We ourselves must also work for a more modest, non-violent, sustainable life-style. That is surely the way toward greater equality between and within nations. (1980: x-xi.)

The micro-chip, for example, has had a revolutionary impact on the societies and economies of the rich countries of the world. Why can not poor countries have access to this (after all, very inexpensive) technology? Lack of a secure power supply may be one answer. Does anyone go on to ask why, in the 1980s, poor African countries *still* do not have access to secure power supplies? This is an especially relevant question for southern Sudan.

A hydro-electric project at Fula Rapids has been on the books for years. It was even included as one of the submissions for funding to ICARA II. At present all of the southern region's electricity supply depends on diesel which is transported 1,800 kilometres from Mombasa, a three week one-way lorry trip. Sudan requested $7m to begin this project to supply the demand for electricity in Juba and on the east bank of the Nile. The report pointed out 'The Fula Rapids project would meet 100 per cent of the electricity demands of Eastern Equatoria at a full-stage development cost of only 21.8 per cent of the diesel-electric costs per kilowat hour, assuming a price of $0.70 per litre of diesel oil.' (para 848.)[19] The report goes on to point out that 'Low cost hydropower would permit industrial development in Equatoria, facilitate irrigation, allow hospitals and schools to be electrified and permit the establishment of elementary telecommunications in the Provinces.' (para 950.)

Development agencies have been working in southern Sudan since 1972. One cannot help asking how far the salaries and travel costs alone of all the employees who have come and gone would have contributed towards the supply of the capital costs for this project.[20] Moreover, even the application of intermediate technology could have long ago harnessed the vast amount of now wasted water power in Yei River District. Water power is not the only energy which is being wasted in Yei River District, and waste of energy is not limited to the district.

Energies

Barring any further cataclysm attracting media attention to southern Sudan, by the time this book is published it is likely that most of the assistance programmes will have been withdrawn, the humanitarians will have moved on, and refugees will be working out their own salvation as best they can, without outsiders and without aid. After reading an earlier version of this data, one colleague wrote from Khartoum, 'Though this may really frighten

[19] Recall that development agencies are almost the only source of diesel in the south. Sudan's foreign exchange crisis is so severe that normally it cannot afford to supply it.

[20] Lachenmann and Otzen point out that there is no problem of funds for relief, in fact there is sometimes too much money available and that agencies try to hold over some of these funds for longer term needs. The failure to educate the public on the long-term needs of people in poor countries keeps agencies dependent on the 'starving child' appeal, and makes it more difficult for the funds which clearly are available to be transferred to projects which have lasting value. These authors also criticize the authoritarian nature of aid programmes which nips 'self-help...in the bud'. They refer to the process as the 'helper mak[ing] a vassal of the person he is trying to help.' (1981:81.)

you, the YRD programme is one of the best examples we have of all your recommendations and preferences, especially refugee participation and integration with local communities.' From what I observed in eastern Sudan, this comment is likely to be very true.

Although we have seen the failures of the emergency programme in great detail, we have also seen that while aid was not used in the way it was intended, refugees nevertheless made use of the assistance provided to survive. No doubt many more would have died without it, although we have insufficient data to test even that assumption. We have seen that in at least four settlements the malnutrition rates in 1984 were lower than among children living in the small community at Panyume. Compared to elsewhere in the Sudan, humanitarian agencies *are* likely to view the operation in southern Sudan as a success.

The very grave danger in writing a book about the failures of humanitarian relief agencies is that it will be taken as a ready-made excuse by those who support them to stop giving their money. Given the present situation in Africa where millions are threatened with death by starvation and where even the most careful predictions suggest that the worst is yet to come, such a reaction would sign the death warrant of untold millions. *Africa needs more, not less assistance.*

Monsters of concern

Were it not for the fact, that in the foreseeable future the media will continue to bombard the public of rich countries with hard images of human suffering, and that more and more humanitarian energy will necessarily be focused on Africa, it would not be so necessary to carry out such research or to report findings which are so disturbing.

In their study of the Mursi, the Turtons ponder the question of the relative value of aid to people who were victims of famine in south-western Ethiopia. They admit that 'Systematically distributed relief would certainly have saved many lives, especially, one must assume, those of young children.' (1984.) But, they go on to point out, if that aid had been distributed in emergency feeding stations which required people to congregate around them to receive their daily 'hand-outs', the Mursi would have been turned into 'permanent refugees in their own country'. Moreover, that kind of assistance would 'have saved lives at the cost of destroying a way of life - a complex mode of adaptation for which there exists no viable short-term alternatives.' (ibid.) For a very long time, outsiders have been 'helping' Africa destroy their old modes of adaptation. There is not too much evidence to nourish the belief that outside intervention has produced a positive synthesis of the old and the new which makes better use of the energies of both the helpers and the helped.

Even had it been the aim, which it was not, one book is not going to turn off the energy of those whom O'Neill calls the "monsters of concern." They can be called monsters because their doing good, their wanting to save, is done in the interests of experienc[ing] themselves as above or outside the lives of those for whom they care. Their efforts are infected with a kind of superfluity, with doubts concerning truth and reality that have no counterparts in the lives of those for whom they intend to help.' (1975:64.)[21] What sociology can do is to 'secularize' what O'Neill refers to as the essentially 'redemptive tasks of humanity'. For, as he goes on to say, caring is the very essence of our humanity: 'Care...is the domicile of our being together.' (ibid.: 64.) The fault lies with the ideology of compassion, the unconscious paternalism, superiority, and monopoly of moral virtue which is built into it.

The Mursi *did* receive assistance, *the difference was how it was given.* In 1979, and again in 1980, the Relief and Rehabilitation Commission (RRC) of the Ethiopian Government set up temporary distribution points on the east bank of the Mago River.

Once the food had arrived by lorry at the distribution point, it was divided into individual loads and given out to all comers, who then carried it back to their home settlements. This procedure was, presumably, adopted out of sheer necessity, there being insufficient staff and equipment available to set up elaborate distribution centres of the 'soup kitchen' variety, but its benefits were obvious (Turton and Turton 1984.)

The Turtons go on to list the benefits of this approach to assistance. First, the food reached the famine victims with maximum speed. Humanitarian agencies are always far too late. In a discussion of the *process* of famine, Ramgasami (1985) calls upon her own research and that of a number of other studies to show that the 'studies we have today are not of famine at all, but only its terminal phase'; instead accounts begin 'with the moment of state intervention.' She points out how the Famine Code of India (1893), as well as the contemporary 'Scarcity Manuals' used in her country, list among the *premonitory* signs of famine the 'unusual movement of herds and people', and their 'aimless wandering'. But these symptoms she demonstrates are the symptoms of the *final phases of a famine.* 'The state, as well as the do-gooders, the voluntary agencies, do not enter the arena *until the process is resolved against the victims.*' (emphases added.)

Fortunately for the Mursi, the RRC was prepared to respond in a manner which most humanitarians would regard as haphazard, providing food aid to

---

[21] I recall a recent meeting of church-based agencies on the problems of hunger. In a panel discussion concerning approaches to aid I was asked if I believed in an 'interventionist God or....' Since my theology failed me on the first part of the question I cannot remember the other type I might have believed in and I was too intimidated to remind the audience that the question would have little immediate relevance to the hungry they wanted to help either.

'all comers' who were the very ones still having sufficient energy to carry the food back to their home communities. Humanitarians are obsessed with concern over counting heads and bags of food to make sure none 'has fallen off the back of the lorry', i.e. fallen into some opportunistic hands.[22] This refusal to *trust* means that those who are most in need of food, unlike the Mursi, *are forced* to make the 'long and potentially fatal journey to distribution points.' (Turton and Turton 1984.) They, unlike the Mursi, *are forced* to remain away from home for long periods just to receive their daily 'handouts' from a feeding station. And, again unlike the Mursi who were allowed to remain at home to use their energies on essential subsistence activities, people at feeding stations *are* often *required* to divert their fading energies into food-for-work projects designed by outsiders to 'rehabilitate' them.

As the Turtons point out, had the Mursi been 'rehabilitated' by humanitarian agencies the process would have risked destroying 'precisely those qualities of resilience, technical sophistication, inventiveness and sheer human determination to survive that must be tapped, rather than ignored, if outside intervention in their affairs is to be anything but counter-productive.' Indeed, if humanitarians do not begin to understand that effective aid cannot be imposed, *it may well be worse than none at all.*[23]

Becoming a 'facilitator'[24]

Is there any role at all which outsiders, can play in refugee assistance or any other kind of 'development' enterprise which is anything *but* iatrogenic?[25] The quotation from O'Neill, which appears on the frontispiece of this book, points to one of the very great dangers of sociological work. This is that although it has hardly begun to fathom the depths of human injury, it will service ideologies which have come far too soon to conclusions. However sympathetic one might be with reactions of so many from poor countries who in their most vulnerable moments express the wish that all outsiders should simply go home (Erb and Kallab 1975), it would be unfortunate if this were the conclusion drawn from this study.

In March, 1984, at the symposium, Alternative Viewpoints, where many of the participants were African, there was *no* talk about there being *no role for outsiders, or no need for aid.* To the contrary, but the resolutions and

[22] Those who saw a recent BBC film concerning the relief operation in western Sudan may recall one aid worker using this phrase to describe the shortfall of one or two bags of grain between the time the lorry left Khartoum and arrived at a feeding station. The commentator felt obliged to tell the viewers that the missing food had actually turned up the following day.

[23] Research such as that reported by the Turtons could actually be extended to test the question of whether imposed aid is worse than none at all. Although they assumed the Mursi suffered great loss of life, at least among the children, they did not test this assumption.

[24] American, from 'to facilitate'.

[25] '(Of disease) caused by process of medical examination or treatment'. *The Concise Oxford Dictionary*, Seventh Edition (1982).

recommendations of that meeting, which appear in Appendix I, call for quite a different approach. That they were passed by consensus by a group of refugees, government officials, and humanitarian workers reveals just how much *can* be accomplished by discourse. One might sum up the lesson of that meeting by saying there need to be *more* opportunities for outsiders to crawl out of their Mercedes and down off their pedestals to listen. (Chambers 1983; Moan 1984.) The appeal of such a reversal in approach to those who fund refugee assistance, will be how much further the money will go. Some of the ways money could be spent to better effect have been noted throughout the book. But more money *is* needed.

In presenting the findings of this research I opted for the case-study method because it seemed the best way to open a field which has heretofore not been exposed to the hard light of empirical scrutiny from an independent, participatory stance. Every chapter in this book, every topic which was treated (and the very many more which were left out, forgotten, or gone unnoticed to be discovered by the perceptive reader) cries out for 'further research'. The study of forced migration involves economic, social, political, psychological, ecological legal, and even technological issues of such theoretical importance that it is a wonder that scholars have neglected this field for so long. (Baker 1983:vii.) A great deal of the existing literature on refugees is not based on research and many theoretical discussions rely only on official, in-house reports. Much of it is filled with jargon, terminology borrowed from policy-makers, but not re-examined. A first task is to clear these away. Some researchers have almost by chance, as in my own case, seen the relevance of the study of refugees to their other theoretical interests, or have included refugees because they happened to appear within the populations they were already researching. Others' fieldwork, limited by lack of funds, is all too brief to allow them to make the contribution to the field which is so urgently needed.[26] Excellent studies have been conducted by scholars who worked as agency consultants and so were unable to publish their findings. There are those who have begun to apply their research skills to this field of study and to test the power of theories derived from various disciplines, but there remain so many questions - conceptual, theoretical, and methodological - that the most appropriate reaction at the end of a research project is that of Portnoy's doctor, 'Now ve may perhaps to begin.' (Roth 1969.)

While the work of the student of society is to 'instruct the world in the very thing [it] learned from the world', O'Neill goes on to caution us about our relationship to that world which we attempt to 'instruct'.

---

[26] One notable exception is the anthropological study of a locality in Athens-Piraeus where between 1922-24 Asia Minor Greeks were settled.(Hirschon 1976.) This case deserves attention as it presents an opportunity to examine sixty years of settlement experience, the effects of policy, and other long-term issues.

Sociological care is not paternalism. It does not righteously diminish the responsible growth and variety of opinion that it will surely meet. It is not parasitic. Yet it is nurtured only in belonging to others. It seeks community without wanting to dominate the community. Sociological care is mutual; it remains active only in giving and being given life. Sociological care is not simpering. It is not exercised from empty need, or from loneliness. It is a musical response to a dance. Sociological care is not burdened. It does not work from obligation. Nor from guilt or any self-abasement. Wild sociology sings the world. Yet it always has a particular task, a local need, a definite work to do, not wasted in vain generality or empty intentions. Wild sociology never ceases to learn from what it believes it knows. (ibid.:71)

These 'beatitudes' might also be applied to the humanitarians' work.

Earlier in this chapter, I quoted one of my assistants who observed that refugees do not know who [or what] is the cause of their suffering. Refugees, he said, are in a confused situation. Like refugees, what we all need, researchers and humanitarians alike, is consciousness of our situation.

I do not choose to conclude this book with another list of prescriptions to be applied - the errors of imposing aid and the reversals necessary to alter the situation have already been too clearly articulated in the voices and painful experiences of the refugees - except to underline the fundamental prescription which is implied by the title of this book. *Imposing aid can never be successful.* And if this course is pursued further, humanitarians will only continue to contribute to the breakdown of societies which in turn will call for greater and more terrifying methods of controlling them.

I have argued in the introduction that it is the moral loading of issues which has prevented humanitarians from scrutinizing their work. The researcher's role is to 'secularize' that virtue, to expose the fallacies and wrong premises upon which it has been operating in relation to refugees and other victims of forced migrations.

Specific prescriptions, actions, can only be determined when humanitarians are convinced through the logic of morality of becoming *facilitators*, to use their resources, money, skills, influence, and energy, to facilitate those changes in the circumstances of the poor which the poor themselves have determined as the next best thing for them to do. In the final analysis, it is those whom we wish to help to whom we must be finally accountable. Researchers can be facilitators too, by lending their skills to the poor and powerless, to work out together just what may be the next best step. It was Andrew Pearse who first helped me to understand that this was a proper role for research. But none of this good work can be done in an atmosphere of distrust, it cannot be, as O'Neill puts it, 'a *solo*'. Our work cannot be properly alive in us unless it begins in the deepest trust towards others to understand, and to reciprocate the care which we intend.

Alternative viewpoints: resolutions and recommendations

A Message to the Second International Conference on
Assistance to Refugees in Africa (ICARA II)

The Symposium, 'Assistance to Refugees in Africa: Alternative Viewpoints', held in Oxford, England, 27-31 March 1984, and comprising 150 participants, including representatives of refugees, governments, national and international bodies, refugee workers and academics, welcomes the fact that ICARA II has been convened. The Symposium recognizes that ICARA II is just the beginning of a process of infrastructural development in refugee-affected areas. The Symposium hopes that following the financial pledges made at the Conference, the implementation of projects will entail the full participation of refugees and refugee organizations as well as host governments. A primary concern of the Symposium is to ensure that any material assistance to refugees is linked to the protection of those refugees within the host country. This protection, which includes both physical and economic security, is the responsibility not only of the host country, but also of the international community. The Symposium emphasizes the necessity for refugee involvement in all aspects of protection, voluntary repatriation, and material assistance. The Symposium also strongly believes that a durable solution to the refugee problem in Africa can best be achieved by tackling the root causes that generate refugees.

Resolutions of the Symposium

1. The Symposium calls upon the international community to address itself urgently and seriously to the root causes of refugee exoduses; to take the measures necessary to obviate further refugee exoduses, and facilitate the return of refugees to their country of origin if and when they wish to do so. The Symposium calls upon the international community to examine the pressures that can be brought to bear on governments that provoke refugee exoduses. The members of the Symposium express their commitment to the cause of refugees and oppressed peoples, and call on all other individuals to work towards the goal of a world without refugees.

2. The Symposium welcomes the commitment of African governments to instruments such as the United Nations Universal Declaration of Human Rights and OAU Convention on Refugees, and welcomes the decision of the

Organization of African Unity to establish an African Commission on Human and Peoples' Rights. The Symposium calls on all African governments to remove the conditions which create refugees and to protect existing refugees by observing the provisions of these instruments, above all by observing the principle of non-refoulement. The Symposium also calls on all African governments to make every effort to resolve national conflicts and protect minorities.

3. The Symposium recognizes the important financial contribution of those countries which give assistance to refugees in Africa, urges those countries to increase their contributions, and calls on all countries currently not making such contributions to do so. The Symposium calls on all countries to desist from the pursuit of any political, economic, or military policy that creates or perpetuates the conditions that provoke refugee exoduses in Africa and elsewhere.

4. The Symposium calls on the UNHCR, host governments, donor governments and NGOs urgently to promote the participation of refugees in all decision-making structures and procedures affecting their conditions of life.

(i) At the local level, this would involve an obligation on the part of the UNHCR, host governments, donor governments and NGOs to develop appropriate fora and procedures for refugee participation in decision-making and in the monitoring of local expenditures on refugees. This obligation should be reflected in the text of implementing agreements.

(ii) At the national level, existing refugee organizations should be recognized and involved in policy-making procedures on relevant issues. This would include the vetting of implementing partners, and monitoring the extent to which money raised in the name of refugees is spent on refugees. Where refugee organizations do not exist or where they are not fully representative, other forms of refugee participation should be facilitated.

(iii) At the international level, efforts should be made to find ways to allow refugee participation in relevant structures and procedures, without compromising the humanitarian, non-political status of host countries.

(iv) The Symposium urges the UNHCR, NGOs and host governments to employ refugees.

(v) Above all, refugees must participate in any decisions concerning voluntary repatriation.

Recommendations of the Symposium

1. Economic Development
The Symposium recommends:
1.1 That refugees and refugee communities be enabled to become economically self-reliant as quickly as possible. The Symposium therefore

welcomes the UNHCR's report on Refugee Aid and Development, and calls on the international community to provide the resources that would enable its recommendations to be implemented.

1.2 That relevant bodies place greater emphasis on allowing refugees and refugee organizations to administer development funds and projects.

1.3 That where integrated development plans are introduced, equal access to the available resources is guaranteed for refugees.

1.4 That where refugees are leaving a country in which a civil war or liberation struggle is taking place, development funds be made available for areas not under the control of the central government in order to prevent or reduce the outflow of refugees from that area.

2. Education and Training

The Symposium recommends:

2.1 That educational programmes for refugees, including vocational training, be prepared with regard to the fact that refugees come from diverse backgrounds and into different situations. They cannot, therefore, be treated as a single unit.

2.2 That relevant organizations aim to provide a balance in educational provisions for refugees, allocating scarce resources between non-formal, primary, secondary, vocational and further education sectors in accordance with the specific needs of each situation.

2.3 That in the light of the above recommendations, educational liaison committees be established in each host country, bringing together refugee representatives, relevant NGOs, UNHCR staff and Education Ministry officials, to formulate appropriate educational policies and practices.

2.4 That information on all aspects of education be urgently made available to all refugees through the development of refugee educational counselling services, manned by professionally qualified staff with appropriate information relevant to all levels of education.

2.5 That a system of examination, assessment and certification be devised for implementation by the UNHCR and local Ministries of Education, which will be equivalent in standard across countries, which will be recognized by governments and academic institutions, and which will provide better access to education to refugees without certificates and documents.

2.6 That the UNHCR, relevant NGOs and host governments give much greater emphasis to non-formal modes of education in view of the fact that it affects the largest number of refugees, including the majority of refugee women.

2.7 That within the area of non-formal education, special attention be paid to the development of projects organized by refugees, and to the training and proper payment of non-formal educators. Non-formal education (distance teaching, radio broadcasts, village class, home and community teaching) must also be used to teach refugees in areas such as health, agriculture, child-care, nutrition, hygiene, and practical skills such as sewing, weaving and pottery.

2.8 That vocational training programmes for refugees be devised only after a careful study of job opportunities in both host and home countries.

2.9 That vocational training be linked to productive work, and that agencies sponsoring such training assist refugees to find their first job through the provision of equipment, advice, introductions and temporary material support.

2.10 That the search for a larger number of appropriate educational opportunities and bursaries for refugees at post-secondary level be intensified, and that students and placements be selected by professionally qualified panels and with regard to future employment opportunities.

2.11 That refugee education policy always be developed with regard to the host country's educational policy, in order to optimize the use of resources for the good of both refugees and the host community.

2.12 That as refugee education is preferably integrated into the national education system of the host country, instruction will be in the language of the host country. If this is the case, however, refugees require two special provisions: first, that extra language training be provided; and second, that additional classes to maintain the refugees' own language and background also be given.

3. Health

The main health problems in refugee settlement areas are brought about by failures in public health. The Symposium therefore recommends:

3.1 That a strong emphasis be placed on preventative health care without removing refugees' rights to receive adequate curative care.

3.2 That primary health care be implemented in refugee settlements in line with the host government's policy, and that health facilities be provided where they do not exist for both refugees and the host community.

3.3 That the UNHCR mandate be re-examined so that it is able to provide health and other forms of assistance to internally displaced people.

3.4 That the host governments and implementing partners increase their efforts to employ suitably qualified refugees in their refugee health programmes, and that refugees be trained in the prevention and treatment of common diseases.

3.5 That the UNHCR co-ordinate and support programmes in the areas of countries that are likely to host a refugee influx, and train personnel and prepare contingency plans so as to effect a rapid response to refugee emergencies.

3.6 That greater co-ordination be achieved in the health programmes of different agencies operational in the same area. That the drugs used are only those recommended by the UNHCR and World Health Organization. That greater efforts be made to monitor the standards and success of such programmes.

3.7 That greater access to relevant research be provided to refugee health workers. That further research be conducted into the provision of health care to urban refugees and into health care generally.

4. The Media

The refugee situation is regrettably one of the most dramatic in Africa today. The Symposium recommends:

4.1 That the media make a much greater effort to understand this situation, of which the traditional image of starving children is but a caricature.

4.2 That all those involved in refugee situations recognize the importance of a partnership with the media. Equally, the media must recognize its responsibility to publicize the plight of refugees. This is often essential to their security. NGOs must actively seek to inform the media in their home countries on the refugee issue.

4.3 That the media are encouraged to understand the political and economic contexts of refugee situations, and the ability of refugees to play a substantial part in the management of their affairs. Refugee self-help is a better story than the usual one of helpless dependency.

4.4 That refugees be encouraged to gain experience in dealing with the media, and to supply the media with more and better information.

4.5 That the right of refugees to information and communication services be formally recognized in the international instruments governing the status and conditions of refugees.

4.6 That within refugee settlement areas, efforts be made to ensure that no single group of refugees has control of these information and communication services.

4.7 That host governments be encouraged to give journalists free access to refugee communities within their countries.

4.8 That the local media in host countries be encouraged to give coverage to refugee issues and to allow the refugees' voices to be heard.

5. Protection

The Symposium recommends:

5.1 That all countries which have not yet acceded to the relevant international legal instruments on the subject of refugee protection be urged to do so at an early date.

5.2 That countries which have acceded to the relevant instruments re-examine any reservations which they may have made at the date of accession or subsequently, with a view to the lifting of such reservations, and to review any relevant national legislation for the same purpose.

5.3 That the UNHCR be actively involved in the monitoring of the protection offered to refugees by host governments and insist of the granting of refugee status to all those eligible.

5.4 That identity cards and other necessary documents be issued as a matter of course to all refugees at an early date following their arrival in the country of asylum. That funding be made available for such documents, and that all information obtained in the registration process remain confidential and not divulged to the country of origin. That in no circumstances should refugees incur expenses in connection with the registration and documentation process.

5.5 That the rights and duties contained in any relevant legislation be made known to all persons affected, including refugees, members of the host community, and officials of the host government - particularly those in the police and immigration services.

5.6 That consideration be given by the responsible parties to the development of appropriate methods of encouraging the absorption of the concept and context of refugee rights into the ethics of the host community.

5.7 That all UNHCR staff members be adequately trained and equipped to handle protection issues.

5.8 That the international community strongly condemn the recent occurrence (in flagrant violation of international law and human morality) of the refoulement of refugees in East Africa, involving Kenya, Tanzania and Uganda. That the international community give urgent attention to the present position of these refugees, addressing itself to every means of alleviating their plight. That the international community consider appropriate methods of strengthening the machinery for the international protection of refugees, in particular, methods aimed at the prevention of such incidents and the possibility of imposing sanctions following contraventions of the fundamental legal principle of non-refoulement.

5.9 That all countries adopt a more liberal policy in connection with the granting of asylum, in particular, those European countries which have introduced legal or administrative barriers to the granting of asylum.

5.10 That NGOs and the UNHCR strengthen their co-operation in every aspect of refugee protection.

5.11 That host governments be helped by the international community to resist military incursions designed to weaken or violate the protection of refugees.

6. Repatriation

The Symposium recommends:

6.1 That voluntary repatriation be a decision taken by the refugee alone. The role of UNHCR is to provide information which will help the refugee arrive at that decision. Fact-finding missions undertaken by refugee leaders are an important part of this information-gathering process.

6.2 That only when the decision to repatriate is taken should be UNHCR and governments concerned effect arrangements for the return. In particular, the UNHCR should not make formal arrangements whithout consulting refugees and where there has been no major political change in the country of origin.

6.3 That neutral observers from bodies concerned with human rights be involved in the assessment of the situation in a country of origin and that these observers monitor the whole process of voluntary repatriation.

6.4 That the UNHCR introduce appropriate methods of verifying the safety and protection of refugees who have voluntarily returned to their countries of origin.

6.5 That in the light of these recommendations, the UNHCR refrain from entering into further tripartite arrangements such as those governing the process of repatriation from Djibouti to Ethiopia, and that the UNHCR urgently explore ways in which refugees and refugee organizations can be directly involved in the planning, implementation and monitoring of future voluntary repatriation programmes.

7. Resettlement

Africa prefers to solve refugee problems within the African context. However, it is recognized that there are special cases where resettlement is the most suitable durable solution. The symposium recommends:

7.1 That refugee resettlement be the subject of a special study, which examines the opportunities for the resettlement of African refugees in areas other than North America and Western Europe.

7.2 That when this study is completed, the UNHCR, NGOs, relevant governments and refugee representatives meet to discuss its recommendations, make proposals for action, and implement these proposals.

7.3 That in view of the fact that resettlement often deprives refugee communities of their most skilled and talented members, relevant organizations and refugee representatives consider methods of reducing the demand for resettlement where it is not essential to the health and safety of the refugees concerned.

7.4 That resettlement countries examine their current selection procedures and consider granting priority to

(i) vulnerable refugees, especially the handicapped.

(ii) refugees who have failed to gain recognition from the host government.

(iii) refugees who have been granted mandated status.

(iv) refugees with or without the recognition of the host government and whose protection cannot be guaranteed in the host country.

(v) refugees whose skills are not required in the country of first asylum and whose prospects of returning to their country of origin are remote.

7.5 That selection for resettlement always be determined on the basis of real need, and not on the basis of special connections or any other form of discrimination, and that, except on special protection cases, the host government also be involved in ensuring fair selection according to the priorities cited above.

7.6 That, where possible, resettlement be carried out on a family basis.

8. UNHCR/Host Government/NGO Relations

The Symposium recommends:

8.1 That all refugees be provided with full and accurate information regarding their own rights and the obligations of the host government, the UNHCR and relevant NGOs.

8.2 That all refugees be provided with full and accurate information regarding the roles of and the relationship between the host government, the UNHCR and relevant NGOs.

8.3 That the UNHCR consider expanding the brief of its Public Information Officers to include information for refugees, and provide funding for the publication of that information.

8.4 That the UNHCR finance the production of "Blue Books" by refugees for refugees.

8.5 That the UNHCR guarantee all refugees access to a regular postal service.

8.6 That refugees be provided with regular, full and accurate information regarding any events in their settlement area, in the host country generally, in their country of origin or elsewhere that is relevant to their situation.

8.7 That refugee representatives, however chosen, receive orientation and training that will enable them to perform their duties in an effective and efficient manner.

8.8 That, in drawing up projects for UNHCR funding, governmental and non-governmental agencies include information on the nature of refugee participation in the planning, implementation, monitoring and evaluation of the project, and that funding be withheld from proposed projects which fail to include such information.

8.9 That refugee organizations engaged in humanitarian work be given NGO status in the country or countries in which they are operational.

8.10 That NGOs refrain from withdrawing from projects before their planned completion dates, and that NGOs work through and with local staff, refugees and refugee organizations, thereby allowing projects to continue after the withdrawal of the NGO.

8.11 That independent research into refugee issues be encouraged by the UNHCR, NGOs and host governments, and that funding and other forms of support be provided for the establishment of specialized centres dedicated to refugee research and the training of refugee workers.

Notes on methods and statistical data

Introduction

Researchers deserve a full discussion of the theoretical and conceptual issues involved in devising a methodology for studying refugees, but given the wider audience to whom this book is directed, I will simply discuss how the statistical data were collected and point out a few of the pitfalls which await other researchers. Many of the problems are similar to those faced by earlier researchers who depended on a colonial administration for access to the subjects of their study. The imagery of refugees as a subject people could be pushed much further. (Asad 1973.)

This study was directed towards assessing the quality and effectiveness of an emergency assistance programme, but in general, such a focus is too narrow. Researchers would be advised *not* to introduce unnecessary problems by focusing their studies on 'refugees' to the exclusion of other people living in an area - even when the object of their study is some aspect of the refugee problem. To focus on the issue of refugee status in such an explicit way is to introduce additional incentives for respondents to withhold information. This is particularly the case when studying refugees who are assisted. Moreover, to include everyone living in a particular area in a study will generate more information on the relationships which obtain between refugees and their hosts. As a result, one will be able to more accurately assess the relative economic positions of both populations. This issue, who was the poorer, was always debated among the agency staff. As is the case with research which seeks to analyse race relations, one learns much more about social relations in a plural community by *not* studying race but by studying the economic, political and social relations between the various groups. (Harrell-Bond 1967.) Hosts and refugees hold stereotyped views about each other's communities, but people nevertheless relate to each other as individuals. A more authentic description of a complex social reality is obtained by observing actual relationships rather than by asking about ideas.

Although UNHCR is expected to monitor the quality of the assistance programmes implemented through the agencies it funds, it has devised no systematic method for achieving this. I did not set out to collect quantitative data, but monitoring aside, during 1982 I observed there was a continual and urgent need for empirical data upon which to *plan* the programme of assistance. Decisions were being made and budgets allocated on the basis of individual impressions or educated guesses. For example, the project to assist the specially vulnerable was planned on the assumption that no more than 10 per cent would need special assistance when food aid was withdrawn. The survey showed the numbers to be much higher. While not a perfect method, a survey designed to generate specific information, is likely to produce a more reliable basis for planning than guesses and impressions.

I also hoped to demonstrate that it is possible to organize a system to monitor assistance programmes which is cheap, rapid, and which could be replicated by every emergency programme simply by employing one permanent staff member having the appropriate research skills and experience. But quantitative data always raises more questions than it answers, so research must necessarily rely heavily on qualitative data, the sort of information which is generated by anthropological methods. Research which is an institutionalized part of an assistance programme would have the advantage of being able to develop and change methods of aid delivery, and of being able to constantly refer questions back to the informants for explanation.

If approaches to assistance were more flexible, if they responded to need, a different research approach to planning and monitoring would be required. For example, if food aid was needed to make up local deficits, one might need only to monitor market prices so that when prices paid to local producers started to fall below acceptable levels, the food aid could be withdrawn.[1] Providing credit schemes (or even giving money away) might have the desired effect (Harden 1985), and would call for yet a different method of evaluating the results. Instead of counting blankets issued per head, a study of fertility, morbidity, and mortality rates might be the most objective basis for assessing the effectiveness of assistance programmes. Rather than depending only on outsiders to conduct such research, it might be better organized through a local university, reducing another of the effects of the 'colonial-like' situation which refugee studies encounter.

One of the values of independent research which is consultative and participatory in approach, is its power to begin to bridge the chasm which now exists between hosts, refugees, and agency workers. I hoped that the participation of refugees in assessing themselves and the programme would not only help change their consciousness, but would also encourage a change in fieldworkers' attitudes towards refugees and stimulate more dialogue. The need for this was demonstrated by the response of one fieldworker to the presentation of the team's report to the inter-agency meeting held in Kala settlement in September 1983. (Appendix V.) Enroute back to Yei, he was overheard to ask, 'Who gave that refugee the right to speak to us like that?'

---

[1] For example, in Yei River District certain areas produced surpluses, but farmers had no means of getting produce to the market in Juba where scarcity kept prices inordinately high. Yet food aid was transported from Kenya, through Juba to the district where prices were already depressed. With careful monitoring would it not have been possible to have sold the food aid in Juba and have given refugees money to buy local food? Such an approach would require a different methodology.

The survey

Settlements were laid out in blocks of 24 family or household plots and these were all numbered. A systematic random sample was drawn on the basis of a random starting number and a fixed interval. The questionnaire was devised in consultation with refugees, and the UNHCR programme officer. Its design drew heavily on my research findings from 1982 but it would still would have benefited from more detailed knowledge of the customary practices of both communities, of refugees and hosts. For example, insufficient attention was paid to how rights over land were allocated *within* households. While in retrospect I suspect that the practice of allocating land to male heads of households and the more general male bias of the programme had the effect of disenfranchising women, I cannot be sure that households did not make their own adjustments, giving women their own portion of the limited land available.

The questionnaire was translated into Madi, Lugbara, and Swahili and was tested and adapted in Otogo settlement in households other than those included in the sample.

Depending on the size of household, the interview took from 45 minutes to more than one hour. There are debates about the use of a long questionnaire and this book has not exploited all the data collected. Questions like, 'What are your main problems here?' may be the most useful in opening discussions which lead the investigator into unexplored territory. One of the values of our long questionnaire was the manner in which it threw up interesting discrepancies which would not have been revealed through other approaches. A rather superficial example is the data concerning occupational background compared to numbers of years in school and other non-African languages spoken which revealed the numbers of ex-military personnel who were living in the settlements. But in general one may say that a long questionnaire is evidence that insufficient anthropological work has been done to determine first what differences require counting.

The team of interviewers included students whose education had been interrupted at 'A' level as well as university students, a qualified lawyer, and an economist. Most of the team had had previous experience as interviewers for the 1980 census in Uganda. The method they had learned for ascertaining ages of the elderly - relating age to historical events - was followed in the survey. Some might fear that using refugees as interviewers would inject a particular bias into the results; I cannot guarantee that at one time or other an interviewer did not collude with an informant to withhold information. However, I found my team as curious as I to learn about their community. Their ability to see the problems from a number of perspectives is demonstrated in the report they wrote for the inter-agency meeting, Appendix II. The survey began in Otogo settlement on 28 May and was completed on 19 September 1983. At first, using the Ugandans as translators,

I conducted all the interviews. When confident that the first three could conduct interviews alone, I began to train more assistants.

A comparison of the results of a 5 per cent sample and the 10 per cent sample interviewed at Otogo suggested that a 5 per cent sample was sufficiently reliable. In Wudabi, Logobero, and Gumbari only 5 per cent of the households were interviewed. But once I had a sufficient number of trained interviewers, we reverted to the larger, 10 per cent sample.[2] I interviewed the larger sample not only because the smaller the sample, the greater is the chance that certain characteristics which occur infrequently will not be discovered at all, but because one of the objectives of the research was to involve refugees in assessing themselves in relation to the programme. The more people included in such discussions the more likely this objective would be achieved.

The possibility that a population might be 'over-researched' is often debated, but in fact, I found that once it had been agreed that the survey could be conducted in a settlement, people who were not included in the sample often expressed disappointment. Perhaps powerless people everywhere appreciate the personal attention given them in an interview. For refugees there were few possibilities to discuss and reflect on recent experiences in quite the way the interview permitted. Most of the women included in Oakley's (1984) study found value in the experience of being interviewed.

By September 1983 there were 22 settlements and 3 transit camps under the Yei office. As each new settlement opened, people were moved to it from transit camps. This mobility might easily have resulted in our counting the same people twice. The problem was avoided by the fact that we surveyed the new settlements and transit camps last; during September the transport system entirely collapsed, so no refugees were re-located at the time of these interviews.

Altogether there were 20,170 households in 25 locations and the average household size was 5.29, but varied between settlements and these data are shown in Table 3.4.

Introducing the survey

One of the most serious methodological issues facing a researcher studying refugees is the pervasive distrust which hangs like a cloud over *all* relationships. While still recommending that research should be an integral part of an assistance programme, a major problem for me was my close association with UNHCR. (This was complicated by the belief some held that I was a 'spy' either for the British, Obote, or both!) I worked to overcome these handicaps by the manner in which I presented myself and the research

[2] The results from the three settlements have been weighted to correspond to the data from other settlements.

to refugees in settlements and whenever possible acted as a source of information, an advocate, or an intermediary for individuals who had problems. (Oakley 1981.)

On arrival at a settlement, the team and I held a meeting with the block leaders (and anyone else interested). I explained the purposes of the research, and that I was an independent researcher, paid by a university, and not an agency.

I attempted to demystify the research methods, by explaining why it was necessary to interview a sample of households. The questionnaire was explained and some questions read out. Everyone was offered the opportunity to read it (or have it read to them). I carried a pocket computer with which I demonstrated how the answers are reduced to numbers for analysis. One of those present was asked to draw the random starting number from a hat, and the entire sample was drawn in their presence. A rough schedule for interviews was drawn up at this meeting and block leaders were asked to inform their plot members, and later to accompany the interviewers to these households.

I pointed out that as a researcher, I was a student and had come to them to be taught. If I were to portray their situation accurately, I would have to rely on their willingness to instruct me. I made it clear that no one *had* to co-operate and that if the entire settlement decided against participation, we would leave with the next transport. I emphasized that even if a household agreed to be interviewed, they could refuse to answer specific questions and I explained why a 'no reply' was preferable to a false response.

Acknowledging their frequent complaint - that refugees have no voice - I promised to represent them and their situation as honestly as my skills and the information they gave permitted.[3] I emphasized that the results were unlikely to have any immediate impact upon their situation: I hoped for no more than that the study would contribute to the improvement of future assistance programmes for refugees elsewhere in Africa. I did promise to forward specific complaints and requests to the programme officer when I returned to Yei. Refugees are said by some to be 'overly demanding', but this stereotype was not confirmed by my personal experience, but then I usually said no even when asked for a cigarette.[4]

---

[3] This is a very casual statement about the profoundly disturbing role of the student of human society. John O'Neill has observed: 'A good part of what we call social science is the study of individuals who are miserable enough to be the object of sociological inquiry. The wealthy, for the most part, escape sociological investigation...But the poor...do not write memoirs. Their lives have to be documented, which means that their lives are the subject of ethnographies, questionnaires, and films. Thus the practice of sociology is entirely dependent upon the different forms of access to other individuals' lives, at the same time that sociology pretends to be a remedy for such inequality.' (1975:62.)

[4] Given my own smoking habit I could not have afforded to supply the thousands of other deprived addicts! My shameful answer to them was usually that I was afraid to give them tobacco knowing how Lugbara dealt with poisoners.

To illustrate the possible value of the research to other refugees, I explained how most policies are presently formulated by outsiders who have little information to guide them. This was demonstrated by asking how many had made their living through farming in Uganda and explaining that it was mainly through lack of knowledge that policy-makers had hit on agricultural settlements as the standard way of helping African refugees become economically independent. Perhaps many other refugee communities were like so many of the Ugandans who had many other skills which could be utilized, but had not actually been farmers.

The introductory meetings were never hurried. People were encouraged to discuss any topic or raise any question. I found that they knew scarcely anything about the organization and funding of aid programmes, and very little concerning their rights or responsibilities.[5]

The role of the Sudanese government was discussed. Refugees were annoyed at the replacement of their own settlement foreman by a Sudanese. I explained the structure of refugee aid programmes and asked them to recall how similar programmes had been organized in Uganda when the Sudanese were their guests. Questions about the Sudanese economy were discussed, the causes of its poverty, and I pointed out the fact that the Sudan was actually paying out the greatest costs of hosting refugees. I tried to help them understand why officials became so annoyed when the refugees sang songs in praise of 'Geneva', and reminded them how arrogance and insensitivity would jeopardize their aim to live peacefully in the Sudan. In each settlement, separate meetings were held with teachers, religious leaders, agricultural advisers and their productivity committees, women, medical staff, members of co-operatives, and former students.[6] The lawyer on the team met with the dispute committees and he also visited courts outside settlements. Once most of the interviews were being conducted by the Ugandan team, I spent my time learning from informal discussions with individuals. I let everyone know that I was available during all waking hours for discussions and they were encouraged to listen in and comment when going over interview results with the team.

Administering the interviews

A day in a settlement began with a team meeting at 7.15 a.m. to plan the schedule of interviews. Except for a lunch-break, work continued until

---

[5] Two Oxford university students joined the team for one month in 1983 and Ugandans were shocked to discover these two young people had only recently become aware there were refugees in southern Sudan. They could not believe their situation did not receive wide publicity in Britain.

[6] The latter were asked to write essays and it was through this means that I identified some of those whom I added to my team of interviewers.

evening. After dinner, the day's interviews were discussed and I read over the notes and verbatim statements recorded. One member of the team was responsible for cross-checking the coding of each interview.

Interviews were conducted in the household plot and every member was asked to be present. In order to increase the accuracy of answers concerning material resources owned by each household, interviewers were encouraged to position themselves so that they could look into the house. Assuming that the presence of one familiar person who also had some authority would be useful, the block leader was asked to be present at the interview. The value of this technique to encourage greater 'honesty' is dubious, but one consequence was that it gave the block leader an opportunity to become more intimately acquainted with his 'community' of 24 households. Each interviewer conducted no more than six interviews during a day.

The questionnaire was designed with the aim that refugees should regard their participation as a means of assessing their situation somewhat apart from the aid programme, to reflect on their experiences of flight and on how they survived outside settlements. But the problems of collecting reliable data from survey methods are increased by the refugees' general awareness that aid is distributed on a per capita basis. One means of overcoming this problem and one which could have been exploited much further, was to try to discuss how they were personally coping with shortages. Questions did allow refugees to describe their experiences of flight. When asked about material possessions, items not part of the aid package were also included. For example, when refugees said that they had no knives because none had been distributed, they were challenged with a question as to how they peeled cassava. (Those who had no knife either borrowed from a neighbour or used a panga, but we found many who had fashioned knives from the tent pegs supplied by UNHCR!) Other items such as cooking pots, buckets and blankets were actually counted by the interviewer and interviewee together, and since the plots afforded no privacy, it was difficult for informants to conceal any item.

Despite efforts to ensure that every member of the household was present for the interview, this was obviously not always possible. The period of the interviews - May to end September - coincided with the planting and weeding seasons. Not everyone was prepared to give up a day's work in the fields to be interviewed. A more serious obstacle was shortage of food. Rations were never complete, but WFP supplies from Mombasa stopped altogether from mid-July and this forced all the able-bodied to seek work from locals in exchange for food. Often people had to walk for many miles to find work and sometimes had to be away from the settlement overnight. Nevertheless we asked people *not* to go out to work, but to remain in their households the one day we were interviewing in their part of the settlement. In Wudabi we were asked to compensate people for giving up a day of *leja-leja*, and at the time this did not seem unfair. In this settlement, and in Logobero we gave each household 50 piastas after the interview was completed. Later, however, we dropped this practice and it did not seem to affect attendance.

Altogether, 78 per cent of household members were present at the interviews or just over one in five was absent.[7] Block leaders were asked to confirm that they were acquainted with any absent member. In only 22 cases did a block leader deny knowing an individual who was claimed to be a member of the household. Reasons given for absences of those present in the settlement included: attending the clinic for medical treatment; working in the fields; doing piece-work for locals; attending school; visiting the market; fetching water (which usually involved waiting hours in a queue at a borehole or travelling some distance to a river); and hunting. Others had travelled and were said to be visiting relatives in other settlements, harvesting crops on the border, travelling to Juba, Yei, or Kaya for one reason or another, or attending a funeral outside the settlement. Altogether 2,353 individuals were recorded as members of households but absent at the time of the interview.

In Chapter Five I have explored the problem of absentees in some detail. Obviously the survey missed an opportunity to collect data which would be more interesting than simply confirming or disproving UNHCR population estimates. We could have explored the details of relationships between refugees in settlements and those living outside them. And it would have been better to concentrate on modes of livelihood by examining what each member contributed to the household, what he was doing and, for those who were absent, where he was doing it. It would be better to begin a study from the assumption that refugees use the aid programme as only one part of their strategy for survival. My failure to understand this more fully from the outset unnecessarily limited the amount of such important information collected.

Another argument for surveying the total population in a refugee-affected area is that it would have produced more information concerning the use of refugee-labour. This study, biased as it was towards refugees, did not render enough information to comment, in more than a speculative fashion, on relationships between hosts and refugees. This is unfortunate since the aim of the assistance programme was to 'integrate' refugees with hosts, and thus this topic should have been included in the evaluation.

The response to the survey in settlements

It was possible to do some quick statistical analysis in the field, and at a final session with members of the settlement we told them something of what we had found. I soon learned that my team was not only able to present the purposes of the research at initial meetings but were much better than I in discussing the results with the leaders of the community after the survey was completed. At one of the last settlements surveyed, Morsak, I relieved them

---

[7] In some settlements interviewers found an empty plot in their sample, these, and the few refusals, were replaced by taking the plot directly adjacent.

of the necessity of translating every sentence into English for my benefit and they took complete charge of the final meeting. In September we still had three new settlements and the three transit camps to survey. Given the few households in these settlements, we decided to split up, with smaller teams interviewing in Adio, Katigiri and Wundurubu.

The reactions of settlers at Adio, reported by Emmanuel Agala Olikare, were fairly typical of what we encountered in most settlements

...news was passed round the blocks for the meeting - we needed all the block leaders. It also happened to be the day when their food items in the store (cassava flour, beans, oil and biscuits) were to be distributed. The first rumour went that Barbara's children, who convince people for repatriation, have come for a meeting to meet only block leaders.

The meeting took place, about two hours. We drew the sample for the blocks to be interviewed. There were 35 plots altogether. In the meeting we told them that through such a research their voices will be heard in the outside world. They said that at least each family should be interviewed because their problems are varied....They then asked us to read the questions all through before they could depart for their food distribution.

We could not begin the interviews before noon because all the block leaders and family heads are in the office premises [receiving rations]. On our way to Block 1 we got some people under a mango tree....they said we are Barbara's people who are military men from Uganda. Then one reasonable one came and greeted us and escorted us to block one. We later on came to find him to be the husband of the first person to be interviewed. (20 September 1983.)

However, the team that went to Katigiri met with considerably more resistance than normally had to be overcome. Ferdinand Vuciri Lali reports.

First of all I explained to them that the research team had come to compile an objective report on the experience of the refugees from entry into Sudan to their life in the settlements, their opinion, and impressions of the settlement programme. The research, we told them, would help to evaluate the implementation of the refugee programme.

...the settlers did not show any appreciation. They just waited and questioned us, especially on what we would do with death records.... of all the questions in our questionnaire, they appreciated the section on food which was the only problem they had in Katigiri, and their settlement officer was well-informed about that....They also argued that our sampling identified a few households....therefore, it was a voting or election system and they demanded to know for which government this was being done. That of Uganda or of Sudan? It took us about a full hour explaining to them the sampling and why we had to interview a restricted percentage...

(a) *No compromise*
They finally accepted that they could be interviewed but only in teams of blocks or a general meeting...I finally declared to them, when all our efforts to explain seemed fruitless, that Katigiri was one the last settlements we had come to, and we couldn't afford to alter the procedures of the research;

Suggesting that they would leave if this was the settlement's final answer, the team promised

...for the sake of Katigiri hold a general meeting to elicit their general views and give them an outline of our findings there. [And, as an aside in the report] their proposals implied to me that the society was much more tuned to mob reaction.

Continuing his report, Lali lists some other objections.

(b) *Fear of espionage*

Some of the men further alleged that we were on a spying mission....They demanded the leader of our research team and said she was a woman whom they had known since Uganda.[8]

She had come around again to undo them. They feared that our immediate objective was to hoodwink the people into getting repatriated...

The meeting continued on, apparently for hours, until finally

...when it was already dark, without a lamp...the critics' tempers cooled and their words were less hard....They said they would not harm us or do anything to us;....The meeting was adjourned informally because many people...slipped off silently.

The problem for the team was they could *not* leave, as there was no transport back to Yei. The next morning:

...it took us some time to decide whether we should venture to visit the homes or not. The memory of the threats remained fresh in our minds....We later plucked up our courage and went out. The first few interviews we conducted were slow, because the household heads were reluctant to answer the questions, but not courageous enough to boldly expel us....Eventually we gained momentum...people became increasingly encouraged to be interviewed as we visited more households.

In the end they were able to interview all of the households, having to replace only two in the sample because of refusals. The team also met with the different groups. At the meeting with the students:

...I talked with the students about the possibilities and necessity of forming a society that would be academically benefiting...I also gave them a talk about the progress at the Lutaya site....They were encouraged to hear about it [for the] first time, and promised to mobilize a team to participate in the exercise...my research colleague...talked to them about students as an instrument of consciousness in the society, a necessity in the settlements. (17 September 1983.)

The population in transit camps was very large. At the first meeting in Otogo transit camp those who attended were very hostile and even the Ugandan foreman was unco-operative. It was decided I should allow the team to get on with the interviews in transit camps on their own. Again the major problem was my identification with UNHCR, which refugees believed was encouraging repatriation. Moreover, many of these disgruntled

[8] See page, 22.

people had been driven unwillingly by the drought on the borders, to register for settlements, and had then been forced to remain in crowded conditions for months with insufficient food.

The response to the survey at Goli represents the other extreme of attitudes we encountered. Charles Male reports:

...of the three transits the refugees term their co-ordinator - 'The right man in the right place'. For a transit camp such a person like Mr Yusuf Atuma is needed because in transits people are usually very stubborn, prepared to do anything....

After comparing the administration with others he had seen, Male goes on to point out the problem of accommodation which he described as

...really very acute, there are three to four family heads per tent and the average number of persons per tent is nine. At the meeting of the block leaders, the people expressed their thanks and gratitude to us for having turned up to see what is happening in Goli transit and report exactly whatever we see. I had to explain to them the importance of our mission....What we have already done and the few achievements, i.e. the abrupt changes and modifications in the agencies implementing UNHCR policies in the settlements.

After the survey, at another general meeting and the following message was sent back to me.

Thanks for all what you have told us, you have just hit the nail on the head, particularly by choosing our own brothers to assist her in the whole programme. Since our escape to Sudan, we never had such ideas and all what we thought of was our daily ration of rice which at times does not come. We were ignorant about the assistance...and all those involved in it...generally we are sorry for all the conspiracy about all what is happening on the Ugandan refugees now in the Sudan. Particularly we are sad to tell you about what happened here recently. On the 8th August, 1983 a visitor from Holland arrived...he uttered the following: 'We in Europe have heard that you refugees in southern Sudan are Amin's people and all of you are Muslims.' This statement really made us feel depressed and annoyed [*sic*]...this same man deceived us that his name was Peter with no title, but in the visitor's book, he signed 'van Kricken'....We refugees should have a newspaper so that we can present our problems to the outside world...despite all problems you might encounter, we still pray that your report will be effective. (20 September 1983.)

'Good' and 'bad' settlements

The extent to which the reliability of data relating to population totals varied between settlements and the varying responses to the survey, raise interesting questions concerning the social relations within every settlement and the attitudes that refugees developed towards the aid programme and the expatriate 'interveners'. Some settlements gained a reputation for being more 'troublesome' than others; there was a tendency among agency personnel to explain this by using negative stereotypes. That is to say, that certain ethnic groups who predominated in the 'problem' settlements, particularly the Lugbara from Aringa County were considered to be troublemakers.

I do not have sufficient data to support my own theory of why it might be that some settlements were more difficult to manage than others, but I suspect that there is a direct relationship between the logistical failures of the aid programme and the response of the refugees as a community. Adio settlement was established at a time of great shortages of food, tools, and transport to supply building materials which were not available on site. Refugees were being transported to Adio at a time when there were only four Sudanese households in the vicinity on whom they would have to depend for *leja leja*. One could expect Adio people to become disillusioned in a very short time. The report from Katigiri, where my team received such a cool reception and where there had already been a riot over food, provides another illustration of the relationship between logistics and community 'trouble'.

As Lali reports:

... Since the settlement is only in its third month of existence, the settlers rely entirely on food rations. Distribution of such rations has been variably spaced ... Distribution on 13 September was recorded as one bag of beans per block, two of milk and 24 tins of oil. On 8 July - 6 August and 13 August about four bags of rice were distributed to each block; an emergency food reserve was distributed a fortnight after.

The food crisis continued until the settlers came to the administration freely demanding food. There was no food ... and they demanded the blankets [reserved for the next arrivals] in store so that they could sell them to buy food. This commotion went on and sent the settlement officer hurrying to Yei for aid. He arrived back with 50 bags of cassava but the campaign for selling the blankets was already accomplished.

A good number ... still go for *leja leja* for their daily food, but cases of failure to find work are frequent; the factors being long distance ... (minimum 2 miles), few people to work for, and language problems ... Up to now some advertise their blankets and other household utensils in market ... and buy food with the money.

The whole of Katigiri is grown with so much bush that allocation of plots has become impossible and labourers ... have not been paid for the last two months. Among the implements distributed, one type of hoe and the axes could not be used. The former was too weak and the latter blunt. Spades were given for every two families and a pick axe for every four ... Hoes are not enough. Some of the new arrivals have no hoes at all. Some of the hoes distributed are hopeless [SSRAP imported US garden-type hoes.] They are too weak for use ... There were 300 good hoes brought; this consignment was distributed up to a fraction of block 12, the rest ... received none. The weak hoes we could see were thrown about in the compounds of the settlement, unuseable ... Only 50 pangas have been brought. These were distributed to eleven blocks and people share them. The axes are blunt and could be better used for crushing stones. All these could be seen in the compounds; nobody uses them. [Nor, apparently, could they even sell them.] The sickles were distributed to all families ...

but because new arrivals have no hoes, they have been using the sickles for slashing and clearing their plots. Many are broken at the handles and long bamboo handles are improvised. There are also [only] five spades per block ... the settlers had to plant some seeds, i.e. groundnuts, 16 bags of 20 kg each. This is insufficient and there were bitter complaints. Millet, 1 bag, is insufficient; dura, 1 bag, insufficient; maize, sufficient; beans, sufficient; cabbage and vegetables, sufficient.

... there is no feeding programme in Katigiri (17 September 1983).

The study of the self-settled, unassisted refugees

As explained in the Introduction, I did not initially intend to include unassisted refugees in the research. According to UNHCR (which provided the Sudan government with its population estimates) there were only 20,000 unassisted refugees living in the Yei River District.[9] It was soon apparent that this was a considerable underestimate. The programme officer had drawn up a short questionnaire which was administered to about 120 households in late 1982. When the importance of the relationship between settlements and unassisted refugees became clear, I decided to extend the research to include both groups. Not expecting to be able to extend this research very far, I began by using the team of trained interviewers and administered the same interview schedule, despite its obvious limitations.

These interviews began near Kaya, an area densely populated with refugees. Before 1979 there had been fewer than 6,000 people living there; now every inch of land, over the hillsides and stretching up to the rocks, was cultivated. It was possible to train some of the many educated refugees living in the area to continue the interviews under the supervision of John Avrudia, formerly a student at a teachers' training college in Uganda. The enthusiasm of these people at Kaya persuaded me to collect more data, but it was impractical at this point to revise the questionnaire.

When, however, we moved on to Panyume we met with serious resistance. The refugees there claimed to have seen me at Baze on the first repatriation mission in 1983, with the UNHCR lorries transporting 6,000 Ugandans (there were actually only 105) back to Arua 'to their death'. They assumed our study was a ruse organized by UNHCR to identify them in order to repatriate them forcibly to Uganda. In one compound my team met several men armed with bows and arrows who informed them that should they take a step nearer, it would be their last!

---

[9] This may not be the case for all African host governments, but the Sudan has no means of assessing the numbers of refugees who live outside of settlements. All 'official' figures are determined by agency officials. Again this is an important function which local university researchers should undertake. When I reported that rather than hosting only 20,000 unassisted refugees in Yei River District, the number was at least 100,000, the UNHCR representative asked why it was that Sudan under-estimated the burden it was shouldering when 'all over Africa' other governments were 'exaggerating' theirs.

In Panyume, the refugees and Sudanese had jointly organized a number of projects and the local Sudanese chief recognized a 'refugee chief'. I discussed my problem with these chiefs, and the leaders of the SSU. It was decided that under the supervision of Asiku Romano, a Ugandan, formerly principal of the farm training school, Arua, the interviews would be conducted by refugee students living in the area. In the Kajo-Kaji area, two members of my team, together with the Sudanese principal of a primary school very near the Ugandan border, trained a team of local teachers and students to conduct interviews.

At the same time as these interviews were being conducted, one of my team, Gabriel Dramundru, collected data for his comparative study of schools in the self-settled areas and in settlements. Another member of my team, Atima Ayoub, responsible for the study of markets in the area, conducted some interviews of the self-settled south of Limuru settlement. Other assistants were employed to administer interviews in other areas where they lived. Father Peter Dada of the Catholic Centre held regular meetings of lay catechists who worked in the self-settled areas. At one of these I recruited some of these people to conduct interviews in the areas served by their chapels.

Altogether 3,814 interviews were conducted in the five areas shown on Map 3. Households were identified by their location in relation to a market. The interviewers identified 118 such market centres, most of them having been established since the 1979 influx of Ugandan refugees. The population of unassisted refugees accounted for by these interviews was 27,281, with an average household size of 7.15. Table III.2 shows the numbers of households interviewed in each of the five areas, the year the households first settled at the place interviewed, and the mother tongue of the residents. The results show a tendency for ethnic groups to cluster together.

Many areas known to be inhabited by self-settled Ugandan refugees were not included in the study, even in the border areas. Some are so remote that they are even difficult to reach by bicycle. Only a handful of the Yei interviews were conducted in the town; most of those interviewed from this area were living on the outskirts where there was agricultural land. It is possible that up to two-thirds of Yei town's population of 23,478 were refugees. While refugees were concentrated in the border areas and in Yei, households were also scattered throughout the district. For example, a cluster of self-settled - mainly Nubi refugees - lived near Limbe settlement on the Juba road, having moved there in 1979.

Population of the district

It is not possible to estimate the total population of unassisted refugees in the district from the interviews alone, but some census data were available. In 1981 a Social Monitor Study put the total population of the district at

149,824. From the survey of settlements and interviews from the self-settled areas, we know that at least 43,901 of the refugees were already living in the district by the end of 1980.

In March 1983, the official government census put the population of the district at 355,688. Given the numbers of Ugandans who had already entered the district by the end of 1980, one might assume that there are no more than 100,000 Sudanese in the population and that the number of refugees in YRD *could* be as high as 250,000. It is also worth noting that among the thousands registering for settlements in June 1983, some were coming directly from Zaire and Uganda (and there was a major influx as late as December 1984).

Census data are never wholly reliable, and this is especially the case with those collected under the conditions which obtain in this part of the world. According to the 1983 census, the population of the region had doubled from around 700,000 in 1980/81 to 1.4 million in 1983. In a recent note, the economic advisor to the Ministry of Agriculture could not find 'any rational explanation' for this enormous increase. (Wade-Brown, December 1984.) She 'guestimated' that the number of self-settled refugees in the region was about 200,000 and asserted that the national census did *not* include those refugees who were living in camps. At the time of the census there were, according to UNHCR, 48,627 refugees in settlements in Yei River District. But Wade-Brown's statement *contradicts* information obtained by the head of the Juba UNHCR office in September 1983 when it was affirmed that the census *did* include settlements.

In September 1983 there were, according to UNHCR, 70,000 Ugandans living in camps on the east bank of the Nile and no one knows how many are self-settled there or in Juba town itself. It would not be unreasonable to guess that there are as many as 350,000 Ugandans living in southern Sudan.[10]

The reactions of the team

Participatory team research has its own built-in hazards and rewards. To describe our team's relationships as intensive, or the work demanding, is to understate the dynamics of our relationships or the schedule that we maintained. We had two tents. I slept in one and the young men spilled out of the other. We travelled between settlements in lorries and on one occasion, we walked. We carried bicycles, food, and equipment, including stools to sit on. We worked from early till late at night. We argued, discussed, got angry, told jokes, sang, and we certainly laughed together a great deal.

A considerable amount of social levelling took place. One who first arrived

[10] Accepting this figure does not, of course, resolve Wade-Brown's problem of accounting for the entire 700,000 additional people counted in 1983 as compared with the census in 1981. One must agree with her when she concludes that 'In the absence of any rational explanation of the difference between these two sets of statistics and of any other reliable and up-to-date population estimates, both of these sources should initially be considered suspect.' (ibid.)

for work in his coat and tie was immediately asked to cook and temporarily given the title 'minister of food'. If I failed to take a daily bath, I was given no peace, even though I argued that the wind was bitter cold. We ate better than refugees, at least we ate more - the ingredients were usually the same. Occasionally we bought dried fish and chicken, and we drank tea with sugar. They gained weight; I lost 20 pounds. On our last night together in Yei we sat down to reflect on the experience of the past few months. The excerpts from that conversation which follow suggest that refugees are capable of examining themselves as well as criticizing the programme.

...

When I joined Barbara's team, I hadn't thought I would become a better lawyer, but more of an anthropologist. After learning that Dr Barbara had done a lot of research on the sociology of law, it made me think a lot about doing such research and I hope that I will get the chance ... I hope that my professional bias as a lawyer will one time come to an end and I will try to use my profession to the benefit of society ... My short time of work has helped me a lot to know about the outside world and I think will also assist the outside world in also learning about the conditions among our community ... conditions which have been neglected by the develop-- the so-called developed world.

...

As one of us has said, this research has made feel that once again we are in school ... Now among our brothers we saw a lot of things. I found I was able to write some few reports about my fellow refugees. I have seen how people behave in various places ... there is fear in most of the refugees.

...

This research has touched us all, but me particularly ... I have seen the dangers of sitting waiting instead of assisting ourselves ... I have seen how our people are divided up, each group following his own ideas. This research has helped to draw our attention away from our own sufferings and most of these experiences we have shared together and I am thankful for being made more aware of these things.

...

I want to talk about my technical experience. [This person did not work in the settlements, but coded the interviews of the self-settled households.] Self-settlers are living under terrible conditions. There are no schools, no dispensaries ... as they are refugees, under UNHCR protection, it's my opinion that they must begin to assist them as well as those who are in settlements. As they have expressed their problems - their problems in fact are not many ... medicines, problems of food, problems of land.

Concerning the social side [of our team], it was positive. Because before coming here I was isolated ... how can I say, I was in an intellectual coma, so my brain was not functioning. But when I came here, I could work ... I found a very amicable social climate. I could work. My concentration is improving, it increased. The way of communication, it is very important to me.

...

As we moved from settlement to settlement, we have found out that UNHCR has failed to assist us in almost all areas ... the whole thing according to me has been a waste. If [only] there could be a new foundation laid to try to improve the settlements so that everything could go on in order ...

...

In one way or another we have been labelled as spies, the refugees think we are spies, the agencies think we are spies too ... I am taking this opportunity to say to each one of us that as we go back to our people we must represent ourselves as people who are ready to assist and not to spy on them ... to realize that our whole attitude is to unite and serve them, despite all conditions and ... to show our good qualities. Now we are aware, we have tried our best, knowing that we have one aim - to achieve progress one day.

...

We should go to the organization nearest us before going up to Geneva. We must ask OAU what *it* is doing about refugees in Africa.

...

As one of the older [i.e. first employed] members of the team, at first I looked on the research as passing time, but later I learned the usefulness of the whole thing. One of the first things was meeting people I never thought of meeting again, but because of the research work, I got to meet them. Secondly, I also learned how to make a questionnaire. I got help to transform it into Lugbara and into Madi. I learned a lot from that. Thirdly, the research ... educated me on what was happening all around the world.

I missed school since October 21st 1980. I didn't go to class after that. I came to Zaire. I left Zaire, came to Sudan, still was stranded without any purpose. I came to the Sudan, got myself employed, I left after a year and a half, and after staying for that six months ... I met Dr Barbara Harrell-Bond and of course, once again I was in class ... I got some little salary ...

When I went to the self-settled area, I thought about myself, what my own people thought of me, that I was representing them ... some day when they go through the files, they will find my name as somebody who was trying to assist fellow refugees, fellow people, not somebody who was a stranded student. [Referring to a report he wrote which was sent to Geneva] I felt I was responsible for my people, me with all my problems. At least some of us know what happened at that time and the assistance that we provided. I also was given some administrative skills. If I am not mistaken a third of the settlements were administered by me. As concerns the general research, I met a lot of people who were really suffering, others weren't suffering so much. I didn't meet these people before and I really know the problems of being a refugee. I thought of myself, but now I feel I am not one of the worst. I think anything small I should share with a brother or give to a brother who is really suffering...I've learnt of the administrations of the various settlements, about local government, I've been made to know that refugees have a voice ... I learned to actually think of other people or of other cases which are more serious ... I learned to judge what is good and what is bad through the settlements and through the self-settlers. I think all of here would say we have become better persons.

...

The Ugandan youth must become responsible, we have been misled, we must take over from the old ... it is high time we take responsiblity for ourselves, we can't expect someone to come and do it for us. We must do it for ourselves and all this I learned through this research...

...

Summary

A number of points emerge from our experience of designing and implementing a major social survey among refugees in Sudan. Perhaps the most important general point is that qualitative data is absolutely essential if efforts to collect useful quantitative data are to succeed. By this I mean that general anthropological data will provide the information that will indicate what sorts of specific statistical data will be most useful; and it will also provide the context against which statistical data can more satisfactorily be interpreted.

A second more general point which emerged, is that the survey work provided the possibility of collaboration between groups who generally lived and worked in splendid and uninformed isolation. By this I mean not only the various religious and ethnic groups, but also the three major segments of the aid programme - the refugees, the local Sudanese and the aid agencies.

And a third general point to emerge is that social surveys and evaluative work can be done locally, provided that a person and funds are allocated for such work. Both expertise and initiative are available locally and there is no need to import yet another team of expatriate 'experts'.

There are of course, specific methodological problems that emerged during our research. The two major problems were dishonesty and fear. Both are related and either could have seriously distorted our results. However, once the causes of fear and dishonesty are understood, they can be more readily taken into account in research design. It is here that the value of qualitative data cannot be under-estimated. I have pointed to the factors which encouraged the inflation of population numbers and the suppression of the death rate and to the factors which encouraged non-cooperation, as they entered into the narrative of the book. I have also discussed the statistical checks and repeat surveys that were used to validate our findings, and I have indicated the limitations of our findings. By including anecdotal and descriptive material, and by including documents written by the refugees themselves, I have tried to present a richer picture than that provided by the statistics alone. For all that, the statistical picture that emerges from the survey data, tells its own story. That story is that the aid programme is not working. The other data suggest why.

QUESTIONNAIRE 1983

A: *Questionnaire administered to households in settlements*

1. Name of settlement
2. Address

Questions describing household

3. How many people normally live in this household?
4. Number in household now present?
5. Where are the absentees?
6. Block Leader; do you know these absentees?
7. Who first came to this household?
8. When did you come?
9. In which year were you first disturbed by soldiers, whereby [*sic*] you were not settled in your household in Uganda?
10. Did you first run to Zaire?
11. Can you remember when you first entered the Sudan?
12. After entering the Sudan, where did you go next?
13. How long were you self-settled?
14. Why did you come to the settlement?
15. Many people have died both from natural causes and the war since the liberators (Tanzanians) came to Uganda. How many of your relatives have died?
16. How many have you buried in ————————————————— (settlement)?
17. How many babies have been born here in the household?
18. How many axes do you have?
19. How many hoes?
20. How many spades?
21. How many hammers?
22. How many knives?
23. How many saws?
24. How many sickles?
25. How many members of your household are capable of cultivating?
26. How many cattle did you bring to ————————————————— (settlement)?

27. How many cattle have you now?
28. What happened to the missing ones?
29. Do you keep cattle for consumption, for bridewealth or for cash?
30. How many sheep do you own now?
31. How many goats do you own now?
32. Did you have sheep or goats when you arrived in ——————————
   ——————————(settlement)?
33. What happened to them?
34. How many chickens do you own now?
35. Did you acquire them in ——————————————————(settlement) or did you bring them with you?
36. What do you use the poultry for?
37. How many children of school age are living in your household?
38. How many attend school?
39. How many children of school age are not enrolled?
40. Why don't these children go to school?
41. Who is the head of the household?
42. How many children in this household have no mother or father living?
43. How many have leprosy?
44. How many are widows?
45. How many are crippled?
46. How many are deaf?
47. How many are dumb?
48. How many are blind?
49. How many women are married whose husbands do not live in this settlement?
50. Clothing siutation (objective assessment by interviewer)
51. Is your house complete?
52. Do you have a bath shelter?
53. Do you have a rubbish dump?
54. Do you have a latrine?
55. Do you have a grain store?
56. Do you have a drying table?
57. Do you have a kitchen?
58. Do you have a resting shelter?
59. Do you boil water before drinking?
60. How many containers for water do you have?
61. What do you sleep on?
62. How many blankets do you have?
63. How many cooking pots do you have?
64. How many stools/chairs do you have?
65. Did you grow vegetables last year?
66. What did you do with them?
67. How does your household get money?

68. How many of you worked for locals last week?
69. How many days altogether?
70. How many working days were lost last week because of illness?
71. How much land have you acquired for cultivation?
72. How did you acquire this land?
73. How do you see the future?(prompt) Do you hope to return to Uganda in the near future?
74. Does your household grow cash crops?
75. How many members of your household are ill now?
76. How many huts are used by your household?
77. Do you read and write in your language?
78. How many bicycles does your household own?
79. Has anyone in your household got married since you came to —————— ——————————————————(settlement)?
80. (If yes) What has been done to make the marriage acceptable?
81. Has your household borrowed money since you arrived in —————— ——————————————(settlement)?
82. Are any members of your household living as refugees in Zaire?
83. Do you have relatives living as refugees in Zaire?
84. Do you have self-settled relatives in the Sudan?
85. Do you have relatives who have recently returned to Uganda?
86. Do you have relatives living outside the continent of Africa?
87. Do you think it is better to live on your own outside a settlement or in a settlement?
88. Does your household have any relatives living in other settlements in the Sudan?

Questions directed to each individual in the household

89. What is your relationship to the head of this household?
90. When did you arrive in ——————————————————— (settlement)?
91. What is your age?
92. Are you a member of any co-operative society in ——————————— ——— (settlement)?
93. Where did you live in Uganda?
94. In which county did you make your home?
95. What is your mother tongue?
96. Do you speak Swahili?
97. Do you speak English?
98. Do you speak other foreign languages?
99. How many years did you attend school?
100. What standard did you reach?
101. What was your occupation in Uganda?

102. What is your religion?
103. Do you attend religious services in the settlement or with the Sudanese?
104. Do you hold any official position in the settlement?
105. Did you vote in the last settlement elections?
106. Do you hold a salaried position in the settlement?
107. What can you do to earn money?
108. How did you earn money in Uganda?
109. Are you presently attending school?
110. When did you stop going to school in Uganda?

B: Questionnaire administered to households of self-settled refugees

1. Where is the location of your household?
2. When did you leave your home in Uganda?
3. When did you settle here?
4. Where did you settle before?
5. How many people live in this compound?
6. How many adult males?
7. How many adult females?
8. How many males aged 0-5 years?
9. How many females aged 0-5 years?
10. How many males aged 6-16 years?
11. How many females aged 6-16 years?
12. How many acres do you cultivate?
13. Is the cultivated land in the same area or broken up?
14. Where did you get your seeds?
15. What other sources of income have you?
16. What did your family eat yesterday?
17. Do your children go to school?
18. Which school do they attend?
19. When you are ill, which dispensary do you visit?
20. If none available, how do you treat illnesses?
21. How many people in your household have died since settling here?
22. How many people in your household have died since 1979?
23. How many children have been born in your household since settling here?
24. What are your main problems here?
25. Why don't you register to go to an assisted settlement?
26. Are other members of your household now living in assisted settlements?
27. What is your mother tongue?
28. How were you taking care of yourself in Uganda?
29. How many cattle do you have?
30. How many goats do you have?
31. How many sheep do you have?

32. How many chickens do you have?
33. Who is the head of the household?
34. How many are ill or disabled?
35. Have you paid poll tax?
36. What is your religion?

Additional statistical data

TABLE III.1: Distribution of relatives by camp (assisted)

Having relatives:	recently returned to Uganda	in other settlements	outside settlements in Sudan	living in Zaire as refugees
Old Tore	5.6	77.8	61.1	70.6
Kala	10.9	92.5	75.3	10.0
Mogiri	0.0	92.3	46.2	15.4
Mondikolo	5.4	94.4	73.0	13.5
Limbe	28.4	97.5	74.1	43.0
Goli	40.3	95.8	72.2	72.2
Limuru	11.8	92.5	64.9	14.5
Mopoko	33.7	89.0	82.9	71.6
Roronyo	24.7	88.9	71.6	42.3
Otogo	24.1	95.2	77.4	48.8
Kunsuk	7.1	88.9	72.2	12.3
Pakula	27.8	91.9	78.7	55.7
Wudabi	15.4	95.1	92.3	59.0
Gumbari	17.1	100	88.9	61.1
Logobero	31.0	93.0	71.4	32.5
New Tore	29.9	86.1	72.1	62.3
Wonduruba	18.3	84.7	60.6	43.7
Dororolili	11.8	69.0	60.3	43.1
Dokuni	8.8	85.9	83.1	18.6
Morsak	11.1	95.3	81.5	35.0
Katigiri	27.8	86.1	66.7	52.8
Adio	11.4	91.4	91.4	68.6
Goli Transit	5.6	71.0	58.9	34.6
Koya Transit	12.6	81.2	80.7	48.7
Otogo Transit	13.9	94.3	83.3	62.9

TABLE III.2: Numbers of self-settled households interviewed in each area by year first settled 'here' and mother tongue*

Mother tongue	Area 1: Kimbe 'When did you settle here?'					
	1979	*1980*	*1981*	*1982*	*1983*	
Kakwa	57.3	50.3	49.2	45.7	52.0	
Nubi	0.6	0	1.7	0	1.0	
Lugbara	38.3	47.0	47.4	51.3	47.0	
Madi	0.6	0.7	1.7	1.6	0	
Others	3.2	2.0	0	1.4	0	
Number households interviewed	535	149	116	374	102	1,276

Mother tongue	Area 2: Panyume 'When did you settle here?'					
	1979	*1980*	*1981*	*1982*	*1983*	
Kakwa	60	39.1	37.2	9.7	7.4	
Nubi	0	0	0	0	0	
Lugbara	36.8	54.7	61.6	89.7	91.5	
Madi	1.6	6.2	1.2	0.6	1.1	
Others	1.6	0	0	0	0	
Number households interviewed	125	64	86	680	282	1,237

TABLE III.2: (*continued*)

Mother tongue	Area 3: Kopera 'When did you settle here?'					
	1979	1980	1981	1982	1983	
Kakwa	0	0	25.0	0	0	
Nubi	0	0	12.5	0	0	
Lugbara	100	100	62.5	100	100	
Madi	0	0	0	0	0	
Others	0	0	0	0	0	
Number households interviewed	6	2	8	51	63	130

Mother tongue	Area 4: Yei 'When did you settle here?'					
	1979	1980	1981	1982	1983	
Kakwa	9.9	5.6	16.7	15.0	5.2	
Nubi	57.7	52.8	29.2	5.0	5.3	
Lugbara	18.3	27.8	33.3	75.0	84.2	
Madi	1.4	5.6	12.5	0	5.3	
Others	12.7	8.2	8.3	5.0	0	
Number households interviewed	71	36	24	20	19	170

Mother tongue	Area 5: Kajo-Kaji 'When did you settle here?'					
	1979	1980	1981	1982	1983	
Kakwa	51.8	12.2	9.3	13.3	12.3	
Nubi	0	0	0	0	0.4	
Lugbara	28.9	18.9	20.6	55.2	70.6	
Madi	18.1	61.1	67.0	29.5	15.9	
Others	1.2	7.8	3.1	2.0	0.8	
Number households interviewed	83	90	97	293	245	808

* Here and elsewhere the number does not always equal total number of interviews because some questions were not answered or recorded.

TABLE III.3: Average number buried 'here' (in settlement) per household since first member arrived

Settlement	Average number buried in settlement per household	Number of months between camp opening and interview
Old Tore	0.50	48
Kala	0.46	34
Mogiri	0.38	34
Mondikolo	0.51	34
Limbe	0.21	24
Goli	0.38	15
Limuru	0.29	15
Mopoko	0.68	13
Roronyo	0.22	13
Otogo	0.19	11
Kunsuk	0.56	12
Pakula	0.28	12
Wudabi	0.41	9
Gumbari	0.33	9
Logobero	0.19	8
New Tore	0.31	10
Wonduruba	0.31	7
Dororolili	0.42	6
Dokuni	0.27	4
Morsak	0.11	3
Katigiri	0.08	4
Adio	0.00	1
Goli Transit	1.55	11
Koya Transit	0.40	11
Otogo Transit	0.46	5

TABLE III.4: Percentage of households with no land by settlement

Settlement	
Old Tore	16.7
Kala	11.8
Mogiri	7.7
Mondikolo	13.5
Limbe	21.0
Goli	1.4
Limuru	11.2
Mopoko	1.2
Roronyo	3.7
Otogo	8.3
Kansuk	1.4
Pakula	1.3
Wudabi	24.4
Gumbari	2.8
Logobero	2.3
New Tore	16.7
Wonduruba	29.2
Dororolili	38.9
Dokuni	84.5
Morsak	90.9
Katigiri	52.8
Adio	94.3
Goli Transit	89.7
Koya Transit	98.4
Otogo Transit	100

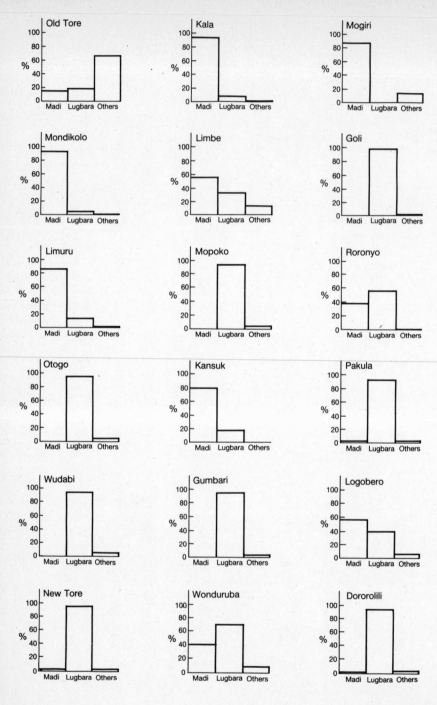

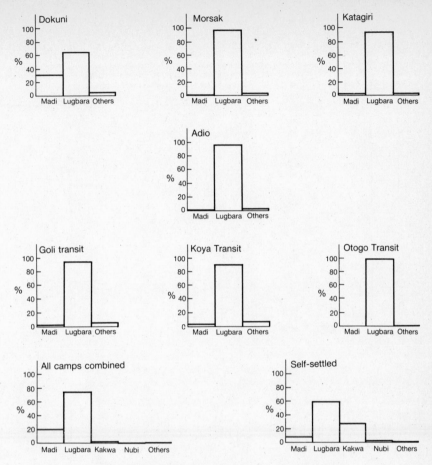

Fig. III.1. Ethnic distribution of each settlement.

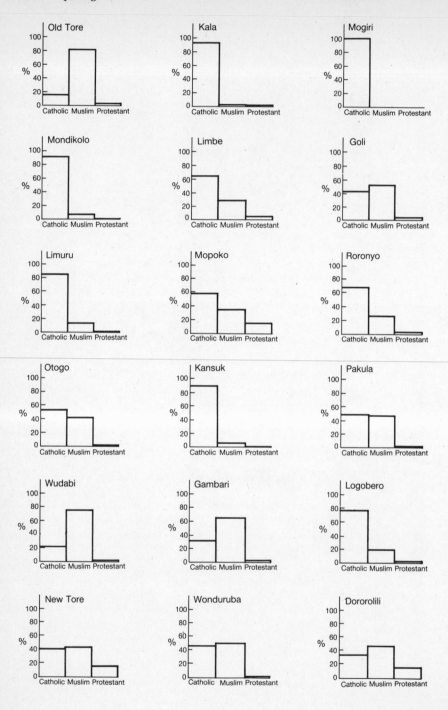

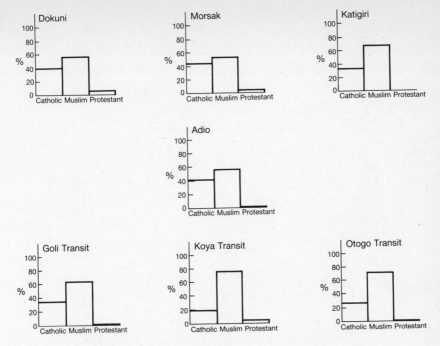

Fig. III.2. Religious distribution of each settlement.

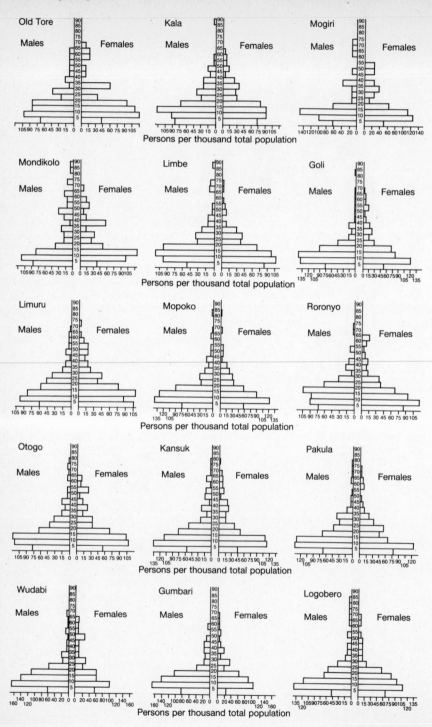

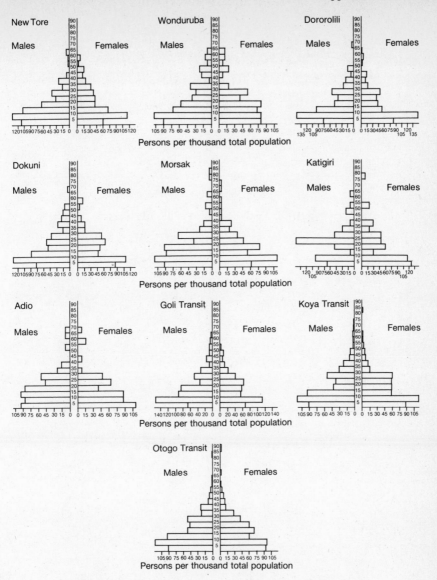

Fig. III.3. Age distribution of each assisted settlement.

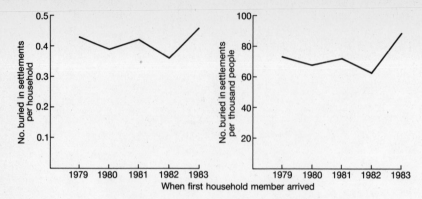

Fig. III.4. Analysis of deaths in settlements.

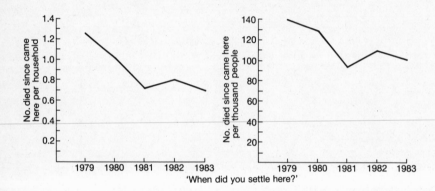

Fig. III.5. Analysis of deaths for self-settled.

Conditions in prison

Reference: Report Pertaining to the Problems Caused During Remand in Yei Prison from 9th November 1982 to 5 March 1983.

Introduction: It is obvious fact that every individual has an obligation to himself/herself and most important, to his country. Just as a refugee, I too, like a citizen of this country, am charged with the divine duty of fostering and implementing government policies and objectives.

It follows that if any institution like the legal authority summons anybody from any society, so as to give evidence on an incident which affects the community, one has to respond without hesitation. If it is a case of murder, the rights of the deceased has to be defended and causes of his/her death must be uncovered for appropriate action. And so it happened that nature had arranged for me also to face such a trial. On November 8th of 1982, I took a cousin to his parents at Roronyo Settlement after some treatment for hookworms. On my return the following day I was arrested by the police who told me that a case was opened in Yei central Police Station and I was supposed to go and give my own evidence.

At first I was not alarmed because I knew I was innocent of any crime that could lead to convicting me and so I accepted the custody without suspicion. The following day I was escorted at gunpoint by a policeman to Yei Police Station with an attachment note that quoted code number 251. I did not know that I was already condemned of murdering somebody I did not know or saw.

On reaching Yei Police Station I was aggressively greeted by the news that I was responsible for having killed somebody at Roronyo. This information shocked me into a temporary coma.

Steps taken to Obtain Information From Me:

a) A piece of iron rod - the size of six inches nail - was put in between my fingers and nylon thread was interwoven between my fingers and the nail, then ends of the thread were pulled so much so that the opposite pairs of my fingers pressed the hardest against the iron rod.

b) Meanwhile heavy beating rained all over my body - even much more on the head. The number of beats I could remember before I lost consciousness was fifty strokes of whip. Perhaps that policeman stopped when his hand got fatigued, me I did not know. The only answer I could give was a wild cry for the humiliations inflicted on me. Maybe prophets can only give evidence on a situation without bearing witness. Thereafter two days I found myself in Yei Prison, too disabled to realize why I was there.

It was there when I found four other fellow victims of circumstances arrested for the same case: the fifth, I was told got discharged after a tip of £S65 to the investigator of the case. Then I was the sixth killer of the same person whom I killed maybe through imagination. After consoling myself for a week with sleepless nights over the crime I did not commit, an investigator came around and told me probing into my case could take even two years. I simply deduced that my fate was completely sealed.

Conditions in the Prison

1. Everybody in the prison was expected to bear the burdens of work, whether on remand or a convict, young or aged. Perhaps the convicts have benefits such as limited freedom sometimes is allowed. But one remanded of murder case does not deserve any relaxed guard.
2. Nature of labour could be fetching water in drums whose capacity is equivalent to four jerrycans of water; strictly carried in pairs. Much of the period I was there, I was one of those trained for bricklaying, 200 per head whether you are quick or slow, young or old, a little healthy or sick, you have to languish up to the last moment.
3. Feeding is only adequate to keep on going. With percentages of say 1% composition for a balanced diet because I am not sure of the test of a balanced diet for potato leaves cooked with leaves of beans and other vegetations believed to be edible when there was no repulsion after eating. Unless one arranged for private feeding, life in prison is at stake, as far as food is concerned. The bread made out of dura was good for a desperate person.
4. Dormitories have cemented floors but provision for sleeping on and covering from cold is the duty of each prisoner. The houses are occupied by bed bugs, lice, and worms.
5. The fact that people have to queue in the toilets, every prisoner is exposed to the infection of one contagious disease or other. And so unless you stay there one day, you can't leave the prisons without some infections.
6. Medical facilities are practically unavailable. The hope is wild (herbs) drugs when prisoners are taken out to work.
You are expected to account [pay] for your treatment. On the other hand when money is found during searches, the penalty is several strokes on the buttocks.

Moral Support from Fellow/Refugees/Settlers - NIL

1. The settlement authority by then claimed to have reached the UNHCR office - Yei and the boss in the office was Mr Nehemiah who had promised to

them, he would follow up my case. This fact was disproved by lack of action taken.

2. My Headmaster expected to be the proper figure head in putting pressure on higher authority as far as the affairs of his staff member is concerned, decided to shut his mind, lips and ears about my awkward situation.

3. My Deputy Headmaster whose bicycle I had used for the journey to Roronyo Settlement was the first defendant. He refused to report to the police until a letter of arrest was sent to the settlement authority, in case of further protest against my defending my rights.

In the course of time, the other three co-detainees who were from the same family fished their way out at the charge of £S55 per head. Then I realized now two of us remaining would in long run face the court. On getting the information that it is a way of life to squeeze some money out of a prisoner, here. And that if I wanted really to be discharged, I should accept the usual ransom as imposed.

Consequential losses incurred

1. The members of my family had to accept to starve as a prize for my release. The records of ACROSS seed buyers will confirm that my brothers sold four bags of rice at £S156. The negotiated amount with my investigator dropped from £S200. to £150. and had only a balance of £S6.

2. During the four months detention period about £S100 was spent to cater for my additional feeding and medical care.

3. You will find from the H/m's [Headmaster's] files on pay sheet my incentives for January and Feb. 83 was not paid - £S100. The local concerned persons; comprising of the Headmaster and his subordinate and about two to three members of our School Management Committee vetoed that the policy of UNHCR is to pay those teachers who worked. Just as if I chose to go to prison, they decided to take the amount as lost. And yet technical persons like the Headmaster could help in civilizing those misinformed, about the fate of somebody on remand.

4. Due to the injuries sustained in prison up to now I feel my capability compared to a normal person for certain heavy work is yet just half of what I used to be.

Request for assistance

1. It was my intention to buy a sewing machine with the proceeds from the sale of rice under perfect market conditions. Then my accrued incentives could purchase a bicycle for the household. But now nature imposed the already explained predicament which resulted a heavy loss of personal revenues, and sustaining of severe injuries thus reduced me not far from disabled. It follows that I would permanently remain the same as the little

salary I get has even to pay for the little job I could do. Affording now goods like a bicycle for the rest of my future remains the furtherest at the horizons of my mind.

2. I am not saying you must consider this case, but from the humanitarian background, as a responsible fellow for research into human problems like mine, I am only grateful because the facts I have uncovered is reflected to many other refugees suffering in the no man's house and it has reached the access of the proper person so that the world's concerned moralists may know about it. ...(10 August, 1983).

Thank you with regards
Sincerely yours,

In another letter written in response to my request for more information on prison conditions,——wrote the following:

In one of the prisons in my country of asylum - Yei prison, similar treatment is accorded to both citizens and aliens in regards to accommodation, feeding, work, etc. But differences appear for the common belief that a refugee on remand convicted of any offence is stubborn, guerrilla and unpredictable and so, a guard with the strictest discipline is ensured during working hours. Just even in the prison premises the refugees are suspected for manuplaiting (*sic*) ways and means of escape.

Report to the inter-agency meeting at Kala settlement

This report was written by my team of interviewers after completing the survey. Its presentation on 24 September 1983 was at the invitation of the Sudanese general project manager, Mr Alexander Najib. Different members of the team drafted sections on the topics for which they had greater responsibility, and Charles Male was selected as their representative to read it out to the meeting. He 'practised' his presentation several times before the others. I was not present at the meeting, but I was told that the expatriates and Sudanese officials did take the recommended tour of Kala.

. . .

Our report is based on a study of the West Bank settlement, transits and field study of three areas among spontaneously settled refugees. A total of 3,814 interviews were conducted among them and 10 per cent sample of families among the assisted refugees were interviewed. Specialized studies were made on protection, markets and education. Basically, we were a team of six and I am here to represent them. This report has been written by several of us.

Since this is a meeting of agencies and time is limited, we have confined ourselves to pointing out problems which can be remedied by those responsible and to making suggestions which we believe are practicable. Some people may not like our report because we point out failure and weaknesses, but we believe that unless we are honest, no improvements can be made. We Ugandans see our society declining in every way and our research team is alarmed about our future as a community.

Distribution

Many things have gone wrong with the idea that relief aid should be distributed equally. Equally often means per family head, but not per capita, and all families are not the same size. Some items are distributed once only and those who arrive late never receive them. Although Sjoerd [the UNHCR programme officer, Yei] tells us that everyone should now have a blanket, we found, for one example, a tent of 13 people with only one.

There are many reasons why this inequality exists. The repeated crises caused by WFP (World Food Programme) necessitates selling of items. Relief items are often the only assets owned by refugees and we found disciplinary committees illegally fining wrongdoers and confiscating (and selling) these goods to pay fines. There are not enough hoes in some families for all of those capable of cultivating land. Distribution is not carried out on the basis of need. There are very many who cannot ever feed themselves and they receive no extra attention.

We found committees and block leaders paying themselves in food and although UNHCR has been clear about the illegality of this practice, the keeping of rations for 'funerals' and for 'visitors' is too common. Whenever we were offered food for our team by a 'generous' committee, we knew something was wrong. The unwillingness of the Ugandan community to care for its weakest members but to demand so-called equal treatment, finds the plot of a severely crippled man in Morsak at least 3 km from the centre: he is forced to cross a shaky log bridge on crutches.

The sub-nutritional standard of present rations provided by WFP together with their haphazard distribution has forced tens of thousands of refugees to daily *leja leja* (piecework). We believe that the crisis over this past two months has set 'self-reliance' back at least one year, but still WFP continues to implement its schedule of reducing food supplies further, preventing refugees from working for themselves. We believe that UNHCR and the government should make serious protests against WFP policy. I do not have to mention the many recent cases of civil disorder. The coincidence of food shortages, the handover to the PM [project management], and the attempts to convince refugees to repatriate have increased insecurity. There are far too many accusations that the Sudan government is responsible. We of the team know better, and we tried to educate our brothers, but it is highly unfair to our host government to bear the brunt of the blame and the hostile reactions of the refugees. The new settlement officers suffer many handicaps and this present crisis has only added to their burdens.

Administration

The most serious problem here is that of leadership. No one is seen to have the final authority in the settlement and this is, to a great extent, caused by the agency competition which the settlers have been too quick to adopt. Someone said that money is the root of all evil, but whether that is true or not, it is certainly power. The [Sudan] government is always the weakest partner because everyone knows where the money comes from. If the SO [settlement officer] or chairman corrects the social worker, he is told his boss is SCC [Sudan Council of Churches]. Similarly, with health staff and all other employed refugees. We have witnessed a dramatic decline in professional standards among those trained in Uganda to do their job, and among the unskilled who have suddenly been employed, there is little incentive to do their work properly. Agencies simply accept reports without checking.

SOs are mostly untrained and inexperienced and lack of confidence to face their task. Some of them are so insecure as to have become defensive and the 'open' files, 'open' stores, 'open' government policies laid down are not being followed in many settlements. This breeds insecurity and tension, and leads to even more authoritarian leadership. Some SOs were even afraid to have settlers participate in our drawing and essay contest - presumably they thought the aim was to allow refugees to criticize them, when the real aim was to get refugees to look at themselves. Every day more letters of accusation and defence circulate through the offices of the PM (project manager) and agencies.

Elections are not democratically organized in many places and in Mondikilo the secretary told us that they did not *need* elections, although in our interviews we learned of much discontent. Settlement meetings - where the community could be drawn closer together - are too rarely held and people remain uninformed about policy and programmes. We of the team blame our brothers because under the foreman system (which so many resented being changed) we had a chance to do something better than was done. Systems of communication in the settlements - at the best - stop with block leaders who utterly fail in most cases to transmit information. For example, Sjoerd's rat control letter was not disseminated, but in most cases, like our publicity about the Lutaya school project, remained locked in the SO's or chairman's file until we came to undertake interviews. Short courses should be organized immediately and literature made available to SOs and committee members to help them develop the skills they need for their job. Agencies should include SOs and chairman in their different meetings to familiarize them with programmes and encourage refugees to respect them.

Health

There is hardly any point in mentioning health problems. We know only too well what the answer is. However, while we were in Kala, a child fractured its right arm. There was nothing available to set it properly so this child will carry evidence of neglect of health throughout its life. Doctors are said to come unannounced and only deliver drugs. Rarely, we are told, do they see patients.

We invite you to make a little tour of Kala. In B1.2/16 there were, a few weeks ago, twins [born] whose mother did not have enough milk. There was none in the dispensary. There are eight TB cases here and insufficient drugs. One man in B1./1 - responsible for two living skeletons among his many dependents - is coughing blood. Our Ugandan health workers everywhere are loath to refer patients for a variety of reasons, but one woman here in Kala delivered prematurely in January, and one can of milk was supplied - despite the promise of more. Her infant has survived but she continues to bleed: sometimes so much she is faint. Yet she has not yet been examined by a doctor or referred.

There is a woman at Mondikolo whose foetal movement stopped eight months ago. She looks hugely pregnant and her skin is blotchy showing she is ill. She has not been seen [by a doctor]. In block 13 you may visit Justin Anyanzo who arrived healthy, but today he is crawling on one leg. Whatever disease attacked him has *never* been diagnosed. In B33/7 lives a blind woman, her old mother and a sister and four small children, one at the breast. They receive no regular extra ration other than the occasional help from SCC. While you are walking around you could also stop at B15/4; 13/12; 23/12; 9/18; 16/23 and 20; 6/15; 21/23; 23/18; 25/24 and 27/6. These tragic cases were found with only a 10 per cent sample.[1]

Death rates in settlements are shocking, but the reality is never recorded because of failure to report to the office of GMT [German Medical Team]. In Roronyo 190 people have died but the records show only 92 [deaths]. We found graves in plots were common.

Supplies of medicine for leprosy cases ran out in Mogiri and we found four cases never served at Kunsuk. While at Mondikolo, waiting for transport, we had reports from Mandari hospital each day for four days. A Sudanese woman was in labour - [only] the baby's hand was out all that time. We were told we should take her to Yei when the transport came. Perhaps you can understand why refugees get furious when they hear the usual excuse for poor medical facilities: 'this is Sudan'.

Community Development

No one seems to have defined the term community development. We think this money was intended by the donors to help the weakest, but it is presently being mainly used to help the able-bodied. Women are systematically excluded except for small amounts of money for what appears to be leisure time activities rather than income generation. The profits on a table-cloth are £S1.000.

There is apparently no feeling that there should be accountability for CD [community development] expenditures to the community as a whole, either by the agency responsible or the CD worker and his committee in the settlement. Father Victor has pointed out to us that when people say 'Geneva is our boss' that is wrong. He says 'Refugees are our boss, as we are spending their money', but we found no CD worker who even knew the budget for his settlement in order for him to constructively plan for the community.

There is not enough money to undertake projects which would really raise incomes, and then refugees are being GIVEN what there is, not loaned it, which is what we thought was supposed to happen last year. Hence there is no opportunity to instil discipline which a loan would involve. People are told the obvious: if fewer people are involved the profits will be greater, and co-

---

[1] [Not quite true, the chairman had taken us on a special guided tour.]

operatives are finding ways of crossing names off their lists. In Mopoko and elsewhere, women must attend a meeting three times a week or their names are removed. In Limuru, the consumer's shop association holds 'secret' meetings and those not included in the small group are not informed that they have missed a meeting until afterwards. Co-operatives don't work here in Kala either. Only three tailors are benefiting from the two machines and when we were there, the members all confessed that they had been cheating the society for 10 months. This was never reported to SCC by the social worker. The SCC machine in Tore - given for men *and* women - is used by two men exclusively. The requirement to build before getting equipment sounds OK but the problems of getting materials, the inability of women to build, the long delay in supplies of capital, discourage people.

Once again, CD is the scene of agency conflict. Women under GMT can't join the development clubs under ACROSS in some settlements. We found no evidence that women have yet profited from the nutritional clubs and wonder why there needs to be a separate advisor for women - given the shortage of agricultural staff. In one settlement the agricultural advisor refused to allocate land to the women as their club was under GMT. Bicycles can't be loaned to colleagues because one is ACROSS and another is GMT and so on. Things were much better when UNHCR followed the 'sectoral' approach and we recommend its being re-instituted. If helping everyone equally is sincerely the aim, it would be better to spend more on women and handicapped and the truly vulnerable groups. Here in Kala there are 270 women-headed families. Most can never be self-sufficient through agriculture. UNHCR, however, estimates that only 10 per cent of the population is vulnerable.

CD projects are supposed to include Sudanese, yet we found in Yei the government also has a similar programme. According to its head no effort has ever been made to co-ordinate refugee/Sudanese CD with Sudanese CD. He complained that GMT's women groups among his Sudanese women competed with his own programme and like in our settlements, women under different 'umbrellas' were quarrelling. He also noted that his staff in the field had no transport while agency staff in settlements were all provided with bicycles. More serious for his programme has been the loss of staff to the better paid positions in the agency programmes which are temporary. 'Why,' he asked, 'couldn't the Sudan government, agencies and UNHCR just sit down and plan together to use scarce resources?'.

Education

Reports on schools in self-settled areas and integrated schools as well as those in settlements will soon be available. We have observed self-help and integrated schools are maintaining a superior standard of teaching and there is better discipline among both staff and pupils, compared with settlement schools. The teachers in these schools outside settlements who receive meagre pay or none at all are more conscious of their responsibility to society and in my (i.e. my colleagues') view, although most of them are not trained, they are more dedicated. A lot still needs to be done in settlement schools. The headteachers and staff are faced with the task of adjusting themselves and pupils to the challenges of a new society. Maintenance of discipline, proper administration, and professional ethics is a major issue to be handled in settlement schools. Most of us are aware of the need to improve performance from these schools and we recommend the following:

1. Monthly meetings for head-teachers to discuss problems and find viable solutions.
2. In-service courses, workshops, seminars for the untrained cadre in the teaching profession.
3. Armchair inspections by education officers should be discouraged.
They should pay regular and even surprise visits to these schools to acquaint themselves with the problems of each.
4. Consider the idea of inter-settlement transfers to ensure discipline and a more equal distribution of qualified teachers; for example, at present the Dakoni settlement has only one Grade II teacher.

According to our findings, about 35 per cent of school-aged children are *not* enrolled in settlement schools because of no clothing, food problems, the requirement to do domestic work or *leja leja*. Attendance of those enrolled - where we could find operating registers - is irregular, and we believe this is the result of food shortages and undisciplined communities which allow children to dance all night on school nights. Drinking and smoking among children is too common and no one seems offended by the loss of our Ugandan standards.

The protection of refugees and law and order in settlements

The effect of the standard of administration of justice and the refugees, ignorance concerning the legal implications of their life - their rights and duties - has led to adverse results. Little attention has been paid to make refugees aware of their rights. The refugees' situation among the community of nationals is that of a people who have lost their human right to defence before the law. There have been cases of false imprisonment with little response from UNHCR.

The lack of an office delegated with the full-time duty of protecting refugees has rendered them susceptible to the procedural defects in the performance of the police and courts. The PM has been most co-operative and active in taking measures against unfair treatment of refugees. However, due to its immense administrative commitments, it cannot be expected to do all that a separate office created for the purpose could achieve.

Refugees, too, are culpable. Their brothers may be falsely imprisoned for long periods and they do not inform PM or UNHCR; for example, the Limbe teacher whose colleagues kept quiet and 'ate' two months of his salary while he remained four months in Yei prison uncharged and untried. Some disciplinary committees also practise irregular procedures. In Pakula, our team found an alleged 'thief' being beaten to extract a confession. While some committees have achieved remarkable co-operation with local chiefs in their administration, others have not. Those responsible should organize some seminars where all these committees could meet and learn from each other's mistakes and successes and be trained by a qualified Sudanese on law and proper procedure as well as their rights.

Agriculture

Although we found settlers determined to become self-sufficient, there are many impediments. Some have already been noted in the discussion on food. Nowhere could we find people who had the sufficient tools for whatever reason. Seeds were often late or not enough or non- viable. Land problems are acute in many settlements. In Limuru the land allocated is not only far away but is infested by tsetse fly and we are made to understand that sleeping sickness has recently struck Kala, in addition to their rabies problem and unvaccinated dogs. Cattle are dying in Morsak and have mostly already died in Mondikolo yet veterinary service is not available. Again, it is the problem of agency co-ordination. One such trained person is in a settlement, Limbe, with hardly any animals. Why can't such a person travel among settlements regularly? Here in Kala, chickens have nearly all died both this and last year for lack of treatment. Poultry farming is one of the projects supposedly encouraged by the agencies. Eggs have been delivered - imported from Kenya - for bringing improved breeds to the Sudan. They were distributed in 50s and 60s - many were broken, others were eaten just because the recipients did not have hens willing to set. Why not encourage a local breed? Many Ugandans brought improved poultry with them. Why not use them instead of relying on imported exotic chickens? Wild animals are a continuing problem to farmers and that is why, here at Kala, people resisted killing their dogs. At Dororolili the problem of even lions, hyenas and buffalo is so serious that people fear to walk out of their houses at night. We learned that buffalo have walked through the settlement at night.

Self-settled

We know now that in YRD [Yei River District] there are more Ugandans outside settlements than in assisted settlements. These people are apparently better off in terms of integrating with Sudanese although there are problems. They have taken the initiative to build many schools, chapels, mosques and we even found two dispensaries which they had built. One, at Renu, is complete with staff houses, but GMT promises to send a staff person and supplies have never been kept. As far as we could find out, no extra medicines have been supplied to these areas despite an incredible rise in population and recently three or four private clinics run by refugees have been closed and two microscopes confiscated. These 100,000 plus people would be the cheapest to assist. Their requests are more reasonable than ours in settlements. Tools, textbooks, blackboards, medicine, clean water, seeds, were most often mentioned. Agencies who helped them would at least know they were helping Sudanese at the same time.

Markets

One of the little sung success stories in the refugee programme is the market system which has been established with literally no aid or programme. YRD's big problem has been the lack of markets in the rural areas and now they are there, thriving, and benefiting natives and refugees alike. Serious attention should be paid to the need for transport to carry produce from settlements to Yei and later Juba and now to help shopkeepers carry commodities needed to sell from Yei to the settlements. This is most urgent in the settlements which are far away from main centres. Six sacks of cabbage lay in Dororolili and two hundred sacks of charcoal in Wudabi. There is no way for either to reach the market, yet agency vehicles ply all these roads and we say we want to help income generation.

This need for transport is even greater among the self-settled as some of them are producing surpluses in significant quantities already and next year there will be even more. If, as Mr Asiko says, it will be the self-settled who will be feeding the settlements, the agencies should take another look at the transport developmental needs of the areas. A positive way to start would be to fund some privately-owned lorries owned by refugees and put them on a regular route which would pass all settlements and border points weekly. This would assist the Sudanese farmer too, who now depends on the vehicles and buyers originating from the north and who pay very low prices to the producers. An investment in such a system would require only a bit of initiative on the part of someone to organize it and it would pay for itself very quickly.

Retail traders in the self-settled areas pay extremely high licensing fees. Yet in settlements people pay nothing although there have been attempts to collect fees. It would be good to standardize policy in this field as in the case of the collection of poll tax which happens among some self-settled and not among others.

Repatriation

Although it was not a direct part of our research, we found everywhere that refugees believed Barbara had come to register them for repatriation. After the UNHCR man came from Arua, we were almost unable to continue our interviews and at Panyume some of our team were threatened with bows and arrows as one had seen her travelling with Sjoerd at Baze, and was sure she was helping take people back to be killed. UNHCR should use refugees to explain about repatriation and their rights because, as one put it, 'When a white man brings the forms, people believe that the white man has seen the situation and it is OK.' We think that there should be the proposed fact-finding mission before any more repatriation and we find it funny to be told that parts of Uganda are OK but don't go back to other parts. Our people in the settlement are in deep confusion and the incident last week at Mogiri and Mondikilo where Ugandans were allowed to visit settlements straight from Moyo makes us all wonder if there is anything like protection of refugees.

Conclusions

Our report has been very critical and it may appear that we Ugandans are not grateful for what is being attempted on our behalf. That is not the case. We are most grateful to Sudan. Many of us experienced a different welcome in Zaire and we know who is really our benefactor. As we have moved about the settlements we have tried to educate our brothers and we feel that perhaps this is one of the important side effects of our research. We feel that if expatriate agency staff had the opportunity we have had, to do intensive fieldwork, they would appreciate that we have only touched on a few of the problems which need improvement and we have confidence that if you take the tour I suggested earlier, you will find it more difficult than we (who have now seen so much suffering over the past four months) to simply accept the status quo. From what we have learned about refugee programmes elsewhere, we believe that what we have in YRD is probably better than most anywhere. On one hand, that is a frightening thought. On the other, let us all, Sudanese, refugees and expatriates together, strive to make it much better.

Children's conception of 'refugee life'

OTOGO REFUGEES SETTLEMENT

BLOCK 24. PLOT A. By: Gordon J BUGAT

TRANSIT GOODS

TRANSIT GOODS

THIS IS LIFE IN SETTLEMENT

Food been brought for Refugees. Stores fruitfilled with rice. No troubles,

PICTURE 1

THIS IS NUTRITION CLUB MEMBERS FOR THEIR LESSONS IN OTOGO SETTLEMENT?

By Gordon J. Bugg .T.

(HOW WE STAY IN THE BUSH WHEN WE'RE CHASED AWAY BY THE SOLDERS
(TIME OF OBOTE)

By OPIKU PHILLIP AMYIRAE!
KALO PRIMARY SIX PUPIL)

References

Adams, A. (1979). An open letter to a young researcher. *African Affairs*, 78, No. 313, 451-79.

Adelman, H. (1976). Authority, influence, and power: a discussion. *Philosophy of the Social Sciences*, 335-51.

Africa Confidential (1983). Uganda: northern quagmire, Vol. 24, No. 22, November 2.

Aga Khan, Prince Sadruddin (1981). *Study on human rights and massive exoduses.* UN Economic and Social Council, Commission on Human Rights, 31 December.

Al-Bashir, A. (1978). Problems of settlement of immigrants and refugees in Sudanese society. Unpublished D.Phil. thesis, University of Oxford.

Alternative Viewpoints (1984). The proceedings of the International Symposium, 'Assistance to refugees: Alternative Viewpoints', held in Oxford, March 1984. Full transcription is available at the Refugee Studies Programme, Queen Elizabeth House, Oxford University.

Appe, J. (1984). Obstacles to assisting refugees. Special report on the Oxford Refugee Conference. *Disasters*, April.

—— (1983). Flight, *Okike*, No. 24, June.

Ardener, E. (1975). The 'problem' revisited. In *Perceiving Women* (ed. S. Ardener), J. M. Dent, London.

Ardener, S. (1975). Sexual assault and female militancy. In *Perceiving Women* (ed. S. Ardener), J. M. Dent, London.

—— (ed.) (1975). *Perceiving Women*. J. M. Dent, London.

Asad, T. (ed) (1973). *Anthropology and the colonial encounter*, Ithaca Press, London.

Asiku, R. (1984). My experiences as a refugee in the Sudan or why I remained self-settled! Paper presented at the International Symposium: Assistance to refugees: Alternative Viewpoints, Oxford, March.

Avery, C. L. (1983). Refugee status decision-making: systems of ten countries. *Stanford Journal of International Law*, Vol. 19, Issue 2.

Ayok Chol, A. (1983). Refugee rights and obligations in Tanzania: A case study of Mpanda District. A Research Report for the UNHCR, Geneva, University of Dar es Salaam, May.

—— (1983a). The refugee law and practice in Africa with emphasis on the Tanzanain experience'. Unpublished thesis for the Master of Laws, University of Dar es Salaam.

Ayoub, A. (1983a). Market activities in refugee settlements. September. Unpublished.

—— (1983b). Market research - Jalimo sub-county free settlement area. Unpublished September.

Baker, R. (1984). Is loss and crisis theory relevant to understanding refugees in Africa? Unpublished paper presented to a meeting on the psychosocial needs of refugees, 22 June, Refugee Studies Programme, Queen Elizabeth House, Oxford

—— (ed.) (1983). *The psychosocial problems of refugees*. The British Refugee Council, London.

Barber, M. (1982). The relief operation for Kampucheans in Thailand. Unpublished Paper presented to the seminar, The Crisis of Mass Exodus, Queen Elizabeth House, Michaelmas Term, 1982.

Beidelman, T. O. (1973). Review of Colin M. Turnbull, *The Mountain People. Africa*, Vol. 43 No. 2, 170-1.

Bell, W.L. (1984). Overseas aid: the man and the mission. *The Round Table* pp. 291-8.

Betts, T. (1974). *The southern Sudan: the ceasefire and after.* The Africa Publications Trust, London.

Bottomley, G. (1984). Women on the move: migration and feminism. In *Ethnicity class and gender in Australia*, eds.G. Bottomley and M. de Lepervanche M. George Allen and Unwin, Sydney.

Chambers, R (1979a). Rural refugees in Africa: what the eye does not see. *Disasters*, 3, No.4, 381-92

—— (1979b). Administrators: a neglected factor in pastoral development in East Africa. *Journal of Administration Overseas*, Vol. 18, No. 2, April, 84-91.

—— (1983). *Rural development: putting the last first.* Longman, New York.

—— (1985a). Memorandum to the House of Commons Foreign Affairs Committee. Institute of Development Studies, University of Sussex, 21 January.

—— Hidden losers? The impact of rural refugees in refugee programmes on the poor of their hosts. *International Migration Review*, Special issue on refugee issues: Current status and directions for the future, (in press).

Christensen, H. (1982). Survival strategies for and by camp refugees. United Nations Research Institute (UNRISD), Geneva.

Clark, A. (1984). Some wider perspectives of Africanization - discussion paper. In *Report on Africanization*, Euro-Action Accord, July.

Clark, D. L. and Stein, B. (1984). Documentary note: the relationship between ICARA II and refugee aid and development. Refugee Policy Group, Washington DC, 16 November.

Coleridge, P. (1982). Predicaments of Palestinian civilians in Lebanon. Paper presented to the seminar The Crisis of Mass Exodus, Queen Elizabeth House, Refugee Studies Programme, Oxford, Michaelmas Term.

Conclusions on the international protection of refugees adopted by the executive committee of the UNHCR programme, (1984). UNHCR, Geneva.

Conventions and protocol relating to the status of refugees (1981). HCR/INF/29/Rev.4, UNHCR, Geneva.

Crisp, J. (1984). Voluntary repatriation programmes for African refugees: a critical examination. *Refugee Issues*, Vol. I, No. 2, December.

—— (1984a). Finding funding and then the returnees. *African Business*, November.

Day-Thompson, M. (1984). Some comments on the refugee population in southern Sudan on the west bank of the Nile. Paper presented to the International Symposium, Assistance to refugees: Alternative Viewpoints. Oxford, March.

de Waal, A. (1985). After the carnage. In Wilson *et al. Occasional Papers of the Refugee Studies Programme*, Oxford.

—— (1985). The sanity factor. unpublished ms, Refugee Studies Programme.

Dick, B. (1984). Address on refugee health. Paper presented to the International Symposium, Assistance to refugees: Alternative Viewpoints, Oxford, March.

Dickie, A. (1983). Yei smallholders survey, Part I and II. Planning Department, Ministry of Agriculture and Natural Resources, Southern Region, Juba.

Dirks, R. (1980). Social responses during severe food shortages and famine. *Current Anthropology*, Vol.21, No.1, February.

Documentation for the June 20-23 Conference (1980). Background and project summaries, Vol.1, Economics and Project Implementation, Vol.2 National Committee for Aid to Refugees, Khartoum.

Dramundru, D. G. (1982). The trials of refugees' education in southern Sudan. A survey report with particular reference to Ugandan refugees in settlement schools in Yei River District. Refugees Studies Programme, September. Unpublished.

El Hassan, A. (1984). Address opening the International Symposium. Special report on the Oxford Refugee Conference. *Disasters*, April.

Erb, G. F. and Kallab, V. (eds.) (1975). *Beyond dependency: the developing world speaks out*, Overseas Development Council, London.

Eriksson, L-J., Melander, G. and Noble, P. (eds.) (1981). *An analysing account of a conference on the African refugee problem, Arusha, May 1979*, Scandinavian Institute of African Studies, Uppsala.

Eyton, J. and Neuwirth, G. (1984). Cross-cultural validity: ethnocentrism in health. studies with special reference to the Vietnamese. *Social Science and Medicine*, Vol.18, No. 5, 447-53.

Fanon, F. (1964). *The wretched of the earth*. Grove Press, New York.

—— (1967). *Black skin, white masks*. Grove Press, New York.

Farah, Abdulrahim A. (1984). Follow up to ICARA II. A letter from the United Nations Under-Secretary General for Special Political Questions to the Refugee Policy Group, Washington, D.C., 6 September.

Foreign Service Assignment Notebook. (1978). 28 October.

Freire, P. (1970). *Pedagogy of the oppressed*, (trans. M. B. Ramos), New York, Herder and Herder.

Gellar, S. (1983). The Ratched-McMurphy model: a critique of participatory development models, strategies and projects. Paper presented to the African Studies Association Annual Meeting, Boston.

Gerhardt, G. (1984). Educational assistance to refugees from South Africa and Namibia. *Refugee Issues*, Vol.1, No.1, July.

German, G. A. (1970). Introduction to *Culture and mental illness: a study from Uganda*, J. Orley.

Golan, N. (1978). *Treatment in crisis situations*. The Free Press, London.

Goodwin-Gill, G. S. (1983). *The refugee in international law*, Clarendon Press, Oxford.

Gorman, R. (1984). Refugee repatriation in Africa. Paper presented to the International Symposium, Assistance to Refugees: Alternative Viewpoints, March.

Goundrey, K. G. (1984). The problem of asylum for refugees - a suggested approach. Derap Working papers, Bergen, March.

Greenfield, R. (1979). Africa's leaking frontiers. *West Africa*, 4 June.

—— (1979a). Sudan's leaking frontiers. *New African*, August.

—— (1980). Refugees in North-Eastern Africa: the Situation in 1979. *The Round Table*, No. 277.

—— (1984). The OAU and Africa's refugees. In *The OAU After Twenty Years*, eds. El-Ayouty and I William Zartman), Praeger, John Hopkins; International Studies Series.

Guest, I. (1983). Blow to hopes of defending refugees. *Guardian*, 20 October.

Hafkin, N. J. and Bay, E. G. (eds) (1976). *Women in Africa: studies in social & economic Change*. Stanford University Press, Stanford.

Hansen, A. (1979). Once the running stops: assimilation of Angolan refugees into Zambian border villages. *Disasters* 3-4, 369-74.

—— (1982). Self-settled rural refugees in Africa: the case of Angolans and Zambian villagers. In *Involuntary migration resettlement: the problems and responses of dislocated people*, eds A. Hansen, and A. Oliver-Smith. Westview Press, Boulder, Colorado.

Handbook for Determining Refugee Status, (1979). UNHCR Geneva.

Hansen, A. and Oliver-Smith, A. (eds.) (1982). *Involuntary migration resettlement: the problems and responses of dislocated people.* Westview Press, Boulder, Colorado.

Harden, B. (1985). Why Hickenlooper is Ethiopia's Catch-22. *Guardian*, Third World Review, 4 January.

Harrell-Bond, B. E. (1967). Blackbird Leys: a pilot study of an urban housing estate. Unpublished M.Litt. thesis (Oxon).

—— (1975). *Modern marriage in Sierra Leone: A study of the professional group.* Mouton, The Hague.

—— (1975a). Legitimacy and the politics of status. *Africa Law Studies*, No.12.

—— (1975b). An adultery dispute with no legal remedy. *Kronik van Afrika*, N.S.

—— (1977). The influence of the family caseworker on the structure of the family: the Sierra Leone case. *Social Research*, Vol. 44, No. 2.

—— (1979). Local languages and literacy in West Africa. *UFSI Reports*, Vol.17, No.1.

—— (1978). The fear of poisoning and the management of urban social relations among the professional group in Sierra Leone. *Urban Anthropology*, Vol. 7, No. 3.

—— (1979). The unofficial urban courts in Freetown, *UFSI Reports*, 4-part series, Nos. 37-40.

—— (1981). The struggle for the Western Sahara. *UFSI Reports*, 3-part series, Nos. 38,39,40.

—— (1982). Ugandan refugees in the Sudan. *UFSI Reports*, 3-part series, Nos. 48,49,50.

—— (1983). Alarming, arrogant analysis. In 'As I see it', *SUDANOW*, August.

—— (1985). Humanitarianism in a straitjacket. *African Affairs*, Vol.84, No. 1, January.

Harrell-Bond, B. E. and Fraker, A. (1980). Women and the 1979 Ghana Revolution. *UFSI Reports*, No.4.

Harrell-Bond, B. E. Howard, A. and Skinner, D. (1978). *Community leadership and the transformation of Freetown 1801-1976.* Mouton, The Hague.

Harrell-Bond, B. E. and Karadawi, A. (1984). But will it be just another ripple in the pool? *Disasters*, April.

Harrell-Bond, B. E. with Machin, B. (1971). A note in response to 'human sacrifices in Benin history'. *Archiv Orientalni*, April.

Harrell-Bond, B. E. and Rijnsdorp, U. (1975). *Family law in Sierra Leone*, Afrika Studiecentrum Leiden, Holland.

—— (1977). The emergency of the 'stranger permit marriage' and other new forms of conjugal union in rural Sierra Leone. In *Law and the Family in Africa*, (ed. S. Roberts), Mouton, The Hague.

Harrell-Bond, B. E. van Schooneveld, S. and Waldemichael, B. (1982). Towards self-sufficiency in settlements. Paper presented to the Khartoum Conference on Refugees, September.

Hatch, J. (1983). Peasants who write a textbook on subsistence farming: report on the Bolivian traditional practices project. *Rural Development Participation Review* 2,2, Rural Development Committee, Cornell University, Ithaca, New York, Winter, 17-20, as quoted by Chambers, 1983.

Heine, B. (1985). The mountain people: some notes on the Ik of north-eastern Uganda', *Africa*. 55(1).

Hirschon, R. B. (1976). The social institutions of an urban locality of refugee origin in Piraeus, Greece. Unpublished D.Phil thesis, Oxford University.

Hoorweg, J. C. and Marais, H. C. (1969). *Psychology in Africa: a bibliography*, Afrika-Studiecentrum, Leiden.

Imbuga, F. D. (1979) *Betrayal in the city*. East African Publishers House, Nairobi.

ICARA Report of the Secretary General, (1984). Southern Region's Project 7. A/Conv. 125/2, 23 March.

International Instruments Concerning Refugees, (1979). UNHCR Geneva.

Income-generating Activities for Refugees in the Sudan, (1982). International Labour Organization.

Karadawi, A. A. (1977). Political refugees: a case study from the Sudan 1964-72. Unpublished M.Phil.thesis, University of Reading.

—— (1982). Relationship between government and non- government organizations in refugee work in the Sudan. Paper presented at the Khartoum Conference on Refugees, September.

—— (1983). Constraints on assistance to refugees: some observations from the Sudan. *World Development*, Vol. 11, No. 6, pp. 537-47.

Kesey, K. (1962). One Flew Over the Cuckoo's Nest, Methuen, London.

Keys, A. Borzek, J. Henschel, A. Michelson, D. and Taylor, H. (1950).*The biology of human starvation* (2 vols). University of Minnesota Press, Minneapolis.

Kibreab, G. (1983). *Reflections of the African refugee problem: a critical analysis of some basic assumptions*. Research report No.67, Scandanavian Institute of African Studies, Uppsala.

Kline, D. (1984). How politics stand in the way of humanitarian agencies' aid to refugees and the hungry. *Christian Science Monitor*, 25-31 August.

Knight, J. (1976). On the IK and Anthropology: a further note. *Current Anthropology*, Vol.17, No.4, December.

Kurup, K. B. (1983). *An appraisal of nutrition and other related survey activities in the southern Sudan*. UNICEF Sudan Country Office, Khartoum, April.

Lachemann, G. and Otzen, U. (1981). The world refugee problem - a challenge to development policy. German Development Institute, Berlin.

Land, A. C. (1981). A report on some refugee situations in the Sudan and a proposal for the involvement of ACROSS in four Ugandan refugee camps in Yei River District, Eastern Equatoria, southern Sudan. ACROSS, July 1981.

Laslett, B. and Rapoport, R. (1975). Collaborative interviewing and interactive Research. *Journal of Marriage and the Family* November, 1975.

Li-Liyong, T. (1984). How to maintain refugees in your midst for the love of humanity whilst the United Nations High Commissioner for Refugees looks over Khyber Pass and doles out goodies to Afghan and Vietnamese expatriates: a spirited diatribe. Paper presented to the International Symposium, Assistance to refugees: Alternative Viewpoints, Oxford, March.

Lissner, J. (1977). *The politics of altruism: a study of the political behaviour of development agencies*. Lutheran World Federation, Geneva.

Lock, S. (1984). Observations concerning the voluntary repatriation programme for Ethiopian refugees wishing to return to Ethiopia from Djibouti - made during a visit to Ethiopia and Djibouti February 1984. *World University Service Report*, April.

McGregor, J. (1985). Marketing in Yei River District'. In Wilson *et al*.

McRobie, G. (1980). Preface in E. F. Schumacher, *Good work*, Abacus Press, London.

Malloch-Brown, M. (1984). Introductory address to the International Symposium, Assistance to refugees: Alternative Viewpoints, March, Oxford.

Malwal, B. (1985). *The Sudan: a second challenge to nationhood*. Thornton Books, New York.

Melander, G. and Noble, P (eds.) (1978). *African refugees and the law*. Scandinavian Institute of African Studies, Uppsala.

Middleton, J. (1965). *The Lugbara of Uganda*. Holt, Reinhardt and Winston, New York.

Moan, F. (1984). African safari. *The mustard seed*, Newsletter of the Jesuit Refugee Service. August.

Morss, E. (1984). Institutional destruction resulting from donor and project proliferation in the sub-Saharan countries. *World Development*, Vol. 12. No.4, 465-70.

Munoz, L. (1984). Exile as bereavement: socio-psychological manifestations of Chilean refugees in Great Britain. *British Journal of Analytical Psychology*, 53:22-32, as quoted by Ron Baker.

Myers, M. (1985). Secondary education self-help and integration; some observations. In Wilson *et al*.

Newspaper Articles (1982) *The Guardian*, 17 August.

(1982) *The Observer*, 7 November.

(1982) *The Sunday Times*, 31 October.

(1984) *The Guardian*, 5 October.

Nichols, B. (1984). Church and state abroad: squaring off? *World View*, Vol. 27, No. 3 March.

Nobel, P. (1982). *Refugee law in the Sudan*. Research Report No. 64, Institute of African Studies, Uppsala.

—— (ed.) (1983).*Meeting of the OAU-secretariat and voluntary agencies on African refugees, Arusha*, March. Scandinavian Institute of African Studies, Uppsala.

North-South: A Programme for Survival (1980). Report of the Independent Commission on International Development Issues under the chairmanship of Willi Brandt. Pan Books, London.

Oakley, A. (1981). Interviewing women: a contradiction in terms. In *Doing Feminist Research*, (ed. H. Roberts). Routledge and Kegan Paul London.

ODEC News (1984). Oxford Development Education Centre, 72 Cowley road, Oxford, March.

O'Neill, J. (1975). *Making sense together: an introduction to wild sociology*. Heinemann, London.

Orley, J. (1970). *Culture and mental illness: a study from Uganda*. East Africa Publishing House, Nairobi.

Orley, J. and Wing, J. K. (1979). Psychiatric disorders in two African villages. *Archives of general psychiatry*.

Osman, A. Kurssany, M. and Kurssany, I. (1984). *The impact of refugees on social services on refugee-affected areas in the Sudan*. Report from the Commission for Refugees, Khartoum, September.

Palmer, I. (1982). Women refugees in urban and rural settlements. Paper presented at the Khartoum Conference on Refugees, September to UNHCR.

Pankhurst, A. (1985). A perspective on vulnerable categories. In Wilson *et al*.

Parfitt, T. (1985). *Operation Moses*, Weidenfeld and Nicolson.

Parkes, C. M. (1972). Bereavement: studies of grief in adult life. Penguin Books, Harmondsworth, London.

Pearse, A. and Stiefel, M. (1979). Inquiry into participation - a research approach. UNRISD/79/C.14 Geneva, May.

Pile, S. (1984). Suddenly the silent ones get a word in. *The Sunday Times*, 1 April.

Powers, C. (1983). Southern Sudan: sinkhole for foreign aid. *Los Angeles Times*, 22 April.

Primary healthcare programme in Southern Sudan 1977/8-1983/4. (1976).

Ramgasami, A. (1985). "Failure of exchange entitlements" theory: a response. Paper presented to the International Workshop: Women's role in food self-sufficiency and food strategies. Paris, 14-19 January.

Ramaga, P. (1984). The limits of refugee protection policy in the Sudan: with particular reference to Yei River District, west bank, Eastern Equatoria. Paper presented to the Refugee Studies Programme seminar, Oxford, Michaelmas Term.

Report on the conference on the situation of refugees in Africa, Arusha, Tanzania, (1979). UNHCR (REF/AR/CONF/RPT.I) 1979

Report to the military commission by a team on a fact-finding tour of the war affected districts of Nebbi, Arua and Moyo from 25th October to 26th November 1980. Available from the Refugee Studies Programme, Queen Elizabeth House, Oxford.

Ressler, M.E. (1978). Accountability as a programme philosophy. Paper presented at a conference: Disasters and the small dwelling, Oxford Polytechnic, Oxford, April 19-21.

Rizvi, Z. (1984). The protection of refugees. Paper presented to the International Symposium, Assistance to refugees: Alternative Viewpoints, Oxford, March.

Rolls, E. T. Rolls, B. J. and Rowe, E. A. (1983). Sensory-specific and motivation-specific satiety for the sight and taste of food and water in man. *Psychology and behaviour,* 30 185-92.

Rolls, E. T. and de Waal, A. (1985). Long-term sensory-specific satiety evidence from an Ethiopian refugee camp. *Psychology and Behaviour*.

Roth, P. (1969). *Portnoy's Complaint*. Jonathan Cape, London.

Rwelamira, Medard, R. K. (1983). Some reflections on the OAU Convention on Refugees: some pending issues. *The Comparative International Law Journal of Southern Africa*, July.

Schumacher, E. F. (1980). *Good Work*. Abacus, London.

—— (1978). *Small is Beautiful*. Abacus, London.

Shawcross, W. (1984). *The Quality of Mercy*. Andre Deutsch, London.

Smock, A. C. and D. R. (1975). The politics of pluralism, a comparative study of Lebanon and Ghana. Elsevier, New York.

Spring, A. (1982). Women and men as refugees: differential assimilation of Angolan refugees in Zambia. In *Involuntary Migration*, ed. A. Hansen and A. Oliver-Smith.

Stein, B. N. and Sylvano, M. T. (eds.) (1981). *Refugees Today, International Migration Review*, Vol. 15, Spring-Summer 1981.

Turnbull, C. (1972). *The mountain people*. Touchstone Books, New York.

Turton, D. and Turton, P. (1984). Spontaneous resettlement after drought: an Ethiopian example. *Disasters*, March.

UNHCR (1982). Special support unit: Mishamo, rural settlements for Burundi refugees, Rukwa Region, Tanzania. Mid term review. Unpublished.

UNHCR (1982, 1983). *Handbook for emergencies*, Part One: Field operations; Part Two: Management, administration and procedures. UNHCR, Geneva.

Wade-Brown, E. (1984).A note on population data, Equatoria Region (working draft). Directorate of Planning, Equatoria Region Ministry of Agriculture, 29 December.

Willis, R. G. (1985). Changes in mystical concepts and practices among the Fipa. *Ethnology*, Vol. 7, No. 2: 139-157.

Wilson, K. B. (1985). Refugee livelihood. In Wilson *et al.*

—— (1985). The ecology of nutrition. In Wilson *et al.*

—— (1985). The refugee impact and the development of Sudanese agriculture. In Wilson *et al.*

—— (1985a).Some aspects of aid and livelihood among Ugandan refugees in south Sudan. *International Migration Review.*

Wilson K. B., McGregor, J. Wright, J. Myers, M., de Waal, A. andPankhurst, A. The Lutaya expedition: report on research in Yei River District. Refugee Studies Programme Occasional Paper No. 1 (in press).

Wing, J. K., Cooper, J. E. and Sartorius, N. (1974). *Measurement and classification of psychiatric symptoms*. Cambridge University Press.

Wright, J. (1985). Intestinal helminths report. In Wilson, *et al.*

Zwingmann, A. A. (1983). *Uprooting & health: psycho-social problems of students from abroad*, W.H.O. Geneva.

Index